FROMMERS

COMPREHENSIVE TRAVEL GUIDE

PORTUGAL 12TH EDITION

May 23 - June 3, 1993

by Darwin Porter
Assisted by Danforth Prince

PRENTICE HALL TRAVEL

NEW YORK • LONDON • TORONTO • SYDNEY • TOKYO • SINGAPORE

Thou 23 - June 3, 1993

FROMMER BOOKS

Published by Prentice Hall General Reference
A division of Simon & Schuster Inc.
15 Columbus Circle
New York, NY 10023

ISBN 0-13-333501-1
ISSN 1044-2278

Manufactured in the United States of America

CONTENTS

MAPS

A Disclaimer

Although every effort was made to ensure the accuracy of the prices and travel information appearing in this book, readers are advised that prices fluctuate in the course of time and travel information changes under the impact of the varied and volatile factors that affect the travel industry. The authors and publisher cannot be held responsible for the experiences of the reader while traveling. Readers are invited to write the publisher with ideas, comments, and suggestions for future editions.

Readers should also note that the establishments described under Reader's Selections or Suggestions have not in all cases been inspected by the authors and that opinions expressed there are those of the individual reader(s) only and do not in any way represent the opinions of the publisher or author of this guide.

When a $ Is Not a $

Portugal is one of the most inexpensive countries in which to travel in Europe. But first-time U.S. visitors often panic at price quotations, because Portugal uses the same $ sign to designate its currency. The **escudo** is written as 1$00. The dollar sign is written between the escudo and the **centavo,** of which there are 100 to the escudo, thus 1$50 is 1 escudo, 50 centavos.

There is no fixed rate of exchange between the escudo and the dollar. At press time, 1 escudo was worth approximately $.0067 (a little more than half a penny) in U.S. coinage, meaning you could buy 150 escudos with 1 dollar. There is no way to predict what the escudo will be worth when you arrive—so check with a banker, at home or in Portugal, for the latest information.

INTRODUCING FROMMER'S PORTUGAL, MADEIRA & THE AZORES

1. THE REASON WHY
2. USING THIS GUIDE

At the dawn of the Age of Exploration, mariners believed that two-headed, fork-tongued monsters as big as houses lurked across the Sea of Darkness, waiting to gulp ships down their fire-lined throats. It was even feared that white men would turn black if they ventured near the equator.

In spite of these formidable problems, Portugal—in what has been called its "épopée of yesteryears"—launched legendary caravels on missions that became historic: Vasco da Gama to India, Ferdinand Magellan to circumnavigate the globe, Bartholomeu Dias to round the Cape of Good Hope. In time, Portuguese navigators explored two-thirds of the earth.

1. The Reason Why

Although the Iberian country was in the vanguard of world exploration, it has never been as successful in attracting visitors to its own shores. Outside of Greater Lisbon, the Algarve, and Madeira, in the past Portugal was unknown to the main-line tourist, although it offers sandy beaches, art treasures, a respectable cuisine, unique Manueline architecture, inexpensive handcrafts, a mild climate, moderate hotel tariffs, and friendly people. The country may be small—roughly about the size of Maine—but like Mighty Mouse, it packs a powerful punch. Portugal measures only 136 miles at its widest point, and 350 miles at its longest span.

I have set myself the formidable task of seeking out the finest in Portugal, but the premise of this book is that the best need not necessarily be the most expensive. Hence my aim is not only to familiarize you with the offerings of Portugal, but also to stretch your dollar power, to show you that you need not always pay high prices for charm, top-grade comfort, and first-rate food.

In this guide I'll devote a great deal of attention to those old meccas—Lisbon, Estoril, Cascais, Sintra—focusing on both their obvious and hidden treasures. But important as they are, they do not fully reflect the diversity and complexity of Portugal. To discover that, you must venture deep into the provinces.

Unlike many nations in Europe, Portugal defies a coherent plan of sightseeing. It is a patchwork of treasures, with many of the choicest items tucked away in remote corners. To sample the best of Portugal, especially some of its most intriguing accommodations, you'll have to seek out a faraway country estate deep in the heartland, or perhaps a 14th-century monastery now converted into a *pousada* (tourist inn) in the old Roman city of Évora in Alentejo, or even an 18th-century palace in Seteais, where Lord Byron worked on *Childe Harold* in the front garden. Living outside of Lisbon whenever possible will, of course, give you a chance to get acquainted with the Portuguese, a more difficult task in most capital city hotels.

THE PEOPLE

The Portuguese have developed a character decidedly different from that of the people of Spain, their neighbor nation on the Iberian Peninsula. Those who travel among and mingle with the Portuguese usually return home filled with a special warmth for the people. They are easily approachable and helpful, and you may find after you've left that you have made several lifetime friends and correspondents.

In Portugal, the family as an institution remains firmly entrenched, even in the aftermath of revolution and upheaval. Many of its people have no close friends outside the family unit. The Catholic church still enjoys strong influence over many segments of society. It is rare to meet a Portuguese Protestant or other non-Catholic.

Although people in the cities have become increasingly sophisticated, their counterparts down the economic and social scale, especially in the countryside, tend to retain traditional social roles. Some Portuguese women still work in the fields with their men, sowing seed, guiding oxen, carrying milk jugs, and harvesting. Children often labor in the fields alongside their parents. The wife of a fisherman may help repair nets and then sell the catch in the streets, returning in the evening to her cottage to do all the housework, cooking, and mending.

In Lisbon the people dress well, particularly in the business district. In the country you still see traditional garb; some older women still wear black shawls draped around their shoulders and carry baskets of produce balanced on their heads.

The Portuguese are a proud people. Life is more formal in the industrial north of Portugal, while in the south, in the Algarve, the approach to life seems more casual, and the people's attitude more relaxed and friendly.

WHY CHOOSE PORTUGAL?

It may be presumptuous to give you reasons to go to Portugal. Dozens may have already occurred to you. If you're of Portuguese ancestry, you may want to trace your ancestors or relatives. I'll merely add a few that you may not have thought about.

To Learn the Meaning of *Saudade*

The word is hard to translate, evoking a mood of melancholy, a sense of sadness expressed most dramatically in Portuguese music. One scholar called it "the nostalgic memory of past greatness, the myth of a golden century, the deep sense of loss which has been called Atlantic melancholy." You'll want to listen to *saudade*'s most heart-wrenching and poignant expression, *fado*—Portugal's most authentic and absorbing art form. Classically beautiful singers will entertain you. Clutching a traditional black shawl around herself, the *fadista* raises her sensitive voice in a dimly lit tavern near the Alfama and the docks, singing the plaintive and poetic songs of her people. It doesn't matter whether you understand the words. The power and the dynamic quality of the lament transcend language, forming their own vocabulary, finding their own reality.

To See Something Majestic

Atop the highest turret of the seemingly impregnable fortress of St. George in Lisbon, the sounds of the quays and streets are only a distant hum. A great eagle encaged within the fortress bewails its captivity. And whenever all sounds seem to have faded, the unnerving scream of one of the castle's white peacocks shatters the tranquillity. Then you understand why the ancients trembled at the harsh, discordant shrieks of this bird—supposedly ill-omened harbingers of war, blood, and death.

Below, oceangoing vessels trudge out of the custard-brown harbor toward the Atlantic. There before you are ancient facades; teeming, narrow city streets and rolling hills; major religious monuments; and steel-and-glass testimonies to technology. You can sit straddled upon a giant cannon that once protected the wealthiest of maritime empires and which trembled through many an earthquake. In a glance you can view Roman occupation, Visigothic walls, Moorish remains, the conflict with Spain, the cradle of the Portuguese empire, and the modern world.

To Wander Back into the Middle Ages

Involve yourself in rural life, the very soul of Portugal. To sample a way of life fast disappearing, go to, say, Entroncamento, in the bull-breeding province of Ribatejo. This village, like so many others in Portugal, exudes the simple rusticity and warmth of a people still connected spiritually to the land.

From any street, you can see the outskirts of vineyards, in which cork trees are interspersed. Streams flow swiftly through the vineyards on their way to the nearby Tagus. You can follow one up into the foothills; and if you have a string and hook, chances are that you'll be having fish for supper.

The men come in from the fields at dusk, heading directly for the taverns for carafes of deep-purple wine topped with an inch of froth. An entire family—including the mother, father, and children, even friends—works behind the serving tables, drawing glasses from the damp, cool casks. Once you're inside one of these bustling taverns, someone will motion you toward a serving table, give a quick jerk on his earlobe, a wink of the eye from under a dark beret, and a repeated flip of his thumb toward his lips—the lever on the cask creaks.

To Build Bridges to Other People

Crusty and tough, yet as warm as life ought to be, the people of Portugal are the greatest experience in this still provincial country. Their bridges of giving are strong and sturdy. Those travelers accustomed to a smile or friendly gesture used to cover an ulterior motive may find themselves clumsy in dealing with the Portuguese. But once you let yourself go, venturing into the countryside and exposing yourself to the Portuguese way of life, you'll feel the kindness of a remarkable people.

For example, you might stop a white-bearded farmer in Alentejo and innocently inquire about directions. Don't be surprised if he invites you inside his family compound, where all the activity really takes place. Here he grows the produce that feeds his large family, barters with his neighbors, and generally carries on the business of living. He'll ask you to warm yourself at a hearthside fire, while he takes out a large loaf of bread, slicing it and spreading it with home-churned butter, then coating it with farm-grown honey kept in a large crock. Wine made from his own grapes will be offered in ceramic mugs.

When you leave, again don't be surprised if he tells you with conviction that the next time you pass through, you're to bed down as a guest of his family.

To Feel the Impact of the Sea

While the Portuguese fishermen are the challengers of the sea, the women are the guardians and sentinels. At Nazaré, Portugal's most colorful fishing village (north of Lisbon), the ritual of launching and bringing in those brightly painted Phoenician-inspired boats is as regular as the tidal rhythm of the sea. The bearded fishermen, in their long, tasseled stocking caps and plaid shirts, push out to the sea, paddling continuously, riding through the fury of the first breaker. When at sea, they search for the best fish-producing waters, letting down their nets and depositing their catch at the bottom of the boat. Perhaps they will return to shore early with smiles of victory; but too often their return is delayed. Tragically, an occasional storm may rise suddenly to strike them down.

As the sun sinks, the women of Nazaré, immobile as statues, wait on the beach for the return of their men. They have spent the first part of the day gossiping and repairing nets; but when it's time for the homecoming of the fleet, they gather quietly at the water's edge. Standing there in lonely vigil, they say not a word, a silent understanding among them. While the young girls wear seven bright petticoats, the older women are nearly always draped in black. There is no one who has not lost a father, a brother, or a son. Tightening their woolen black shawls around themselves, they gaze out to the now-darkening sea, squinting their eyes, searching for the first signs of the high-bowed seeing-eye boats. When the fleet appears, the women cross themselves many times in gratitude to their protector saint, then rush out to do their part in unloading the boats.

The sea gives life and takes it away.

2. Using This Guide

In brief, this is a guidebook giving specific details (including prices) about Portuguese hotels, restaurants, bars, sightseeing attractions, nightlife, and tours. Establishments in *all* price ranges have been documented and described.

About 10% of the recommendations include the luxury hotels, such as the Palácio at Estoril, while 35% suggest inexpensive accommodations: budget hotels, guesthouses, or country inns, offering provincial-style bedrooms with private bath. The greatest number, 55%, fall in the middle price range.

In all cases, establishments have been judged by a strict yardstick of value. If they measured up, they were included, regardless of price classification. The uniqueness of this book, I think, lies in the fact that it can be used either by society types ("We always stay at the Ritz in Lisbon") or by escudo-lean collegians ("There's this little restaurant in Lisbon where a prato do dia will cost about $6").

But the major focus of this book is centered on the average, middle-income traveler who'd like to patronize the almost wholly undiscovered establishments in Portugal—that is, the first- and second-class hotels or some of the better, but less heralded, restaurants, where you can often get a superb dinner.

In Portugal, of course, a first-time visitor is often bewildered as to what to see. The country suffers from lack of publicity. People know of Lisbon, Estoril, Sintra, and the Algarve, and that's about it.

However, I've penetrated deep into remote villages, such as baroque Lamego in the provinces. Naturally, all the big-time attractions are explored as well, ranging from Byron's glorious Eden at Sintra, to the sunny beaches of the Algarve, to the coastal villages of the north.

SOME DISCLAIMERS

No restaurant, inn, hotel, *pensão,* shop, or nightclub paid to be mentioned in this book. What you read are entirely personal recommendations—in many cases the proprietors never knew their establishments were being visited or investigated for inclusion in a travel guide.

A word of warning: Unfortunately, costs change, and they rarely go downward. The government virtually imposes rent control on its hotels, and many establishments have gone 2 or 3 years before changing their tariffs. Owing to sudden improvements or upgrading, prices in other places have skyrocketed.

Always, when checking into a hotel, inquire about the tariff. This policy can save much embarrassment and disappointment when the time comes to settle your bill. Unfortunately, you cannot ever insist on being charged the precise prices quoted in this book, although every effort has been made to secure the accurate tariffs as much as they were foreseeable.

AN INVITATION TO READERS

Frommer's Portugal, Madeira & the Azores hopes to maintain a continuing dialogue between its writer and its readers. All of us share a common aim—to travel as widely and as well as possible, at the best value for our money—and in achieving that aim, your comments and suggestions can be of aid to others. Therefore, if you come across an appealing hotel, restaurant, nightclub, or even sightseeing attraction, please don't keep it to yourself. Your letters need not only apply to new establishments, but to hotels and restaurants already recommended in this guide. The fact that a listing appears in this edition doesn't give it squatter's rights in future publications. If its services have deteriorated, its chef grown stale, its prices risen unfairly, whatever, these failings need to be known. Even if you enjoyed every place and found every description accurate, a letter letting me know that, too, can cheer a gray day. Send your comments to Darwin Porter, c/o Prentice Hall Travel, 15 Columbus Circle, New York, NY 10023.

GETTING TO KNOW PORTUGAL

In an increasingly mechanized age, there is still Portugal.

It is a land of gardens and natural produce, of abundant flowers, a place that still values the artful homemade touch. The wine you drink may be from your host's own casks, the tablecloth made by his wife, the bread fresh from the oven and baked by a daughter-in-law.

A long line of expatriates, including exiled royalty, knows what has long been called "the last foreign country of Europe." That the society has been termed "feudal" forms part of its medieval charm for many. But change is in the air. Even so, visitors are still rare in the more remote parts of Portugal. One Canadian couple were themselves the subjects of sightseeing interest as they made their way through a village en route to a 14th-century church.

You can divide your Portuguese holiday into four parts, spending the first part of your trip in **Lisbon** and at the Costa do Sol resorts of **Estoril** and **Cascais.** Perhaps you'll allow time for a series of day-trips from the capital, going to **Sintra, Nazaré, Tomar, Fátima, Óbidos,** as well as the scenic spots south of the **Tagus.**

The second phase can be devoted to one of the hotels on the **Algarve** in the south, studded with sandy beaches. En route to the Algarve, you can detour through the **Alentejo** district, stopping at the old Roman city of **Évora.**

Before leaving continental Portugal, you should experience the relatively unknown north. Go there to see towns and monuments—**Coimbra, Porto** (home of port wine), **Viana do Castelo**—and some of the country's finest scenery. Before beginning your homeward trek, you can wind down in the islands, either **Madeira** or in the more remote **Azores.**

On your Portuguese holiday you should allow for recuperative days in the sun and at the sea, all of which will fortify you to drink in Lisbon's charms: listening to fado songs, seeing its museums, attending a bullfight or an opera, dining in a palace, browsing through numerous handcraft shops.

When traveling through the countryside, it's best to plot your trips so that you'll stop over at the government-owned pousadas (tourist inns), ranging from restored castles on the Atlantic coast to mountain chalets.

1. Geography & History

GEOGRAPHY

Forming part of the Iberian peninsula with Spain, Portugal has a coastline about 500 miles long. It is bounded on the west by the Atlantic Ocean, on the north by the Spanish provinces of León, Extremadura, Galicia, and in the south by Andalusia. Continental Portugal totals 34,139 square miles, but its Atlantic islands, including Madeira and the Azores, extend the size of the country for another 1,201 square miles. The Azores, however, lie some 700 miles west of Lisbon.

Portugal has four major rivers, including the Minho in the north, which separates the country from Galicia, its northern Spanish neighbor. Other rivers include the Douro of port wine fame, the Tagus which flows into Lisbon, and the Guadiana. Part of the Guadiana forms an eastern frontier with Spain.

Northern Portugal, composed of the mountainous province of Trás-os-Montes and Alto Douro, plus the provinces of Minho and Douro Litoral, is the land of *vinho verde* (green wine). The upper Douro Valley is known for its port wine production.

The coastal strip of Beira Litoral is south of the Douro, which is known for its pinewoods and cereal production. Further inland and to the east, Beira Alta and parts of the northern rim of Beira Baixa jointly share the Serra da Estrêla, the highest mountain range in the country.

The valley of the Tagus cuts through the province of Ribatejo with its flat and fertile fields. Alto Alentejo lies southwest of Ribatejo, and is known for its cork oaks and olive trees. Much of Portugal's wheat comes from the Beja district in Baixo Alentejo.

The south of Portugal is called the Algarve, whose terrain is most often compared to that of either Andalusia to the east in Spain or to North Africa to the south.

The Regions in Brief

COSTA DO SOL (not to be confused with Spain's Costa del Sol) The glittering beachfront strip outside Lisbon is a world unto itself, centering at the chic resorts of Estoril and Cascais. On the northern banks of the mouth of the River Tagus, this is the Portuguese Riviera, long a home to exiled European royalty.

ESTREMADURA Here the first seeds of the Portuguese empire were planted. A land of contrasts, Estremadura has always looked to the sea for conquest and food. Its chief centers—at least for the visitor—are Óbidos, Nazaré, and Fátima.

THE ALGARVE The southern terrain of Portugal attracts the beach lover, and the region overflows with foreign visitors in July and August. This is a Riviera of far greater magnitude than the Costa do Sol, centering around such resorts as Praia da Rocha, Silves, Albufeira, Vilamoura, Faro, and Monte Gordo, among dozens of others. Sagres, part of the Algarve, is the extreme southwestern corner of Europe.

ALENTEJO AND RIBATEJO These adjoining provinces form the heartland of Portugal. Ribatejo is known for its bull-breeding pastures. The Tagus, coming from Spain, flows through the territory. Alentejo, called a "plain of fire and ice," is filled with cork-producing plains.

COIMBRA AND THE BEIRAS These three provinces of central Portugal take in the university city of Coimbra. The provinces include Beira Litoral (coastal), Beira Baixa (low), and Beira Alta (high). Portugal's highest landmass, the Serra da Estrêla, is included in the area.

PORTO AND THE DOURO Portugal's second city, Porto, is the home of port wine. The Douro, from Rio do Ouro, or river of gold, flows through some of the world's richest vineyards. Porto is surrounded by several popular resorts, once former fishing villages. These include Póvoa do Varzim.

THE MINHO DISTRICT The northwestern corner of Portugal is almost a land unto itself, with the district beginning some 25 miles north of Porto. Its major centers are Viana do Castelo, Giumarães, and Braga.

TRÁS-OS-MONTES The far northeastern province of Portugal—and the least visited —this is a wild, rugged land whose name means "beyond the mountains." It extends south of the Upper Douro at Lamego and stretches north to Spain. Vila Real is its capital.

MADEIRA This island lies 530 miles southwest of Portugal, and is a mountain peak of a volcanic mass, now turned into one of the world's most famous tourist islands. The wintering English gentry first discovered its charms. Today it is an autonomous archipelago of Portugal, only 35 miles in length and about 13 miles in breadth at its widest point.

THE AZORES This archipelago spans more than 500 miles from the southeastern tip of Santa Maria to the northwestern extremity of Corvo. The main island is São Miguel, about 760 miles west of Portugal and 2,110 miles east of New York. The chain of the Azores is one of the most isolated in the entire Atlantic Ocean.

HISTORY

Early Civilization

From about 8,000 to 7,000 B.C., tribes occupied the valley of the Tagus, stretching into Estremadura and Alentejo. Pottery and various artifacts attest to their presence. Neolithic people built hilltop forts which greeted the arrival of the Celtic people around 700–600 B.C. Excavations have revealed important settlements in the north of Portugal from this time.

It is believed that those early traders, the Phoenicians, established some sort of trading outpost at Lisbon around 900 B.C. The Carthaginians, in time, recruited Celtic tribesmen to fight the growing might of Rome.

The Arrival of the Romans

From 210 B.C. on, the Romans colonized most of Iberia, although they met great resistance from the Celtiberian tribes of the interior. Viriatus looms large in Portuguese history as a freedom fighter who held up the Roman advance. But by the time of Julius Caesar, Portugal had been integrated into the Roman empire. His colonies included Olisipo (now called Lisbon).

Christianity arrived near the end of the 1st century. By the 3rd century bishoprics had been established at Lisbon, Braga, and elsewhere. With the decline of the Roman Empire, barbarian invaders crossed the Pyrénées into Spain in 409 and eventually made their way to Portugal. The Visigothic empire dominated the peninsula for some two centuries.

Moors and the Christian Reconquest

In 711 a force of Moorish warriors arrived in Iberia, and their advance quickly spread to Portugal. They preferred to erect settlements in the south instead of the north. The Christian Reconquest—called the *Reconquista*—is said to have begun in 718.

In the 11th century much of northern Portugal was taken from the Moors by

Ferdinand the Great, king of León and Castile. Before his death in 1065, Ferdinand set about to reorganize the western territories into Portucale (now Portugal).

The Birth of a Nation

Ferdinand handed over the country of Portugal to his illegitimate daughter, Teresa. (The land south of the Tagus was at that time still held by the Moors.) Unknowingly, the king had launched a course of events that was to lead to the birth of another nation.

Teresa, although born out of wedlock, was firmly bound in marriage to Henry, a count of Burgundy. Count Henry accepted his father-in-law's gift of Portugal as his wife's dowry, but upon the king's death, he coveted the territories in Spain as well. His own demise cut short further aggrandizement of territory.

Teresa now ruled in Portugal, casting a disdainful eye on and an interfering nose into her legitimate sister's kingdom in Spain. Teresa lost no time mourning poor Henry, but took as a lover a Galician count, Fernão Peres. Teresa's refusal to guard her own affair with Peres and stay out of everyone else's affairs led to open strife with León.

Her son, Afonso Henriques, was incensed by his mother's actions. Their armies met at São Mamede in 1128. Teresa lost and was banished along with her lover.

Ungrateful son or not, Afonso Henriques was to become the George Washington of Portugal. In 1143 he was proclaimed king, and official recognition eventually came from the Vatican in 1178. His enemies in Spain temporarily quieted, Afonso turned his eye toward the Moorish territory in the south of Portugal. Supported by the armed might of Crusaders from the north, the Portuguese conquered Santarém and Lisbon in 1147. Upon his death in 1185, Afonso was succeeded by his son, Sancho I, who continued his father's work of consolidating the newly emerged nation. Sancho's heir, Afonso II, ruled for 12 years, beginning in 1211. Like his father and grandfather, he carried on the war against the Moors.

Sancho II was an adolescent when he ascended the throne. Extremely devout, he returned to the clergy much that had been confiscated during his father's reign. However, he still couldn't pacify the clergy and was eventually excommunicated. His brother, Afonso III, was named king, ruling from 1248 to 1279. During the latter's reign, the Algarve, the southern district of Portugal, was finally taken from the Moors, and the capital was moved from Coimbra to Lisbon.

Dinis, the son of a bigamous marriage, ruled Portugal from 1279 to 1325. He is sometimes known as the poet king or the farmer king, and he founded the country's first university, in Lisbon, in 1290. Dinis married an Aragonese princess, Isabella, who was later canonized, although evidence indicates that the vigorous young king would have preferred a less saintly wife. Isabella was especially interested in the poor. Legend has it that once she was smuggling bread out of the palace to feed them when her husband spotted her and asked what she was concealing. When she showed him, the bread had miraculously turned into roses.

The son of these two famous monarchs, Afonso IV is remembered today for having his son's mistress, the legendary Inês de Castro, murdered. Early in life Afonso's son, who would later rule as Pedro I, was betrothed to a Spanish princess, but fell in love with her beautiful lady-in-waiting. Inês was deeply attracted to him, and their affair blossomed. Eventually Inês was banished from the country, although she returned upon the death of the Spanish princess to live openly with Pedro. Jealous sycophants in court persuaded Afonso IV to sanction her murder. Pedro never recovered from the shock of seeing his dead mistress. Patiently he waited until his father died and then he set out to seek revenge. Tracking two of the assassins to Spain, he had them returned by force to Portugal, where he had their hearts torn out. The king announced that he had been secretly married to Inês, and according to the story, he had her body exhumed, crowned queen, and seated on the throne, summoning the members of the court to pay her homage and kiss her hand. Inês and, later, Pedro were buried at Alcobaça, where their tombs are frequently visited today.

During Pedro's reign (1357–67), the influential representative body, the Cortes (an assembly of clergy, nobility, and commoners), began to gain ascendancy, while the majority of the clergy, greedy for power, fought the sovereign's reform measures, thus allying the people more strongly with the crown. Pedro's son, Ferdinand I (1367–73), saw Portugal invaded by Castilian forces, Lisbon besieged, and his dynasty face demise.

In 1383, rather than submit to Spanish rule, the Portuguese people chose the illegitimate son of Pedro as regent. The house of Avís was thereby established. João de Avís (1383–1433) secured Portuguese independence by defeating Castilian forces at Aljubarrota in 1385. His union with Philippa, granddaughter of Edward III of England, produced a son who oversaw the emergence of Portugal as an empire —Prince Henry the Navigator.

The Coming of a Maritime Empire

Henry's demand for geographical accuracy and his hunger for the East's legendary gold, ivory, slaves, and spices drove him to exploration, along with his desire to promote Christianity by joining with the fabled Christian kingdom of Prester John and driving the Muslims out of North Africa. Facing him was a Sea of Darkness, where ships supposedly melted in the equatorial regions, sea serpents flourished, and strange beasts sought to destroy any interloper.

Henry established a community of scholars at Sagres on the south coast of Portugal to develop navigational and cartographical techniques. He infused the court with his zeal and brought his nation to face a destiny imminent from the time of their earliest contacts with Phoenician and Greek mariners. Henry was responsible for the discovery of Madeira, the Azores, Cape Verde, Senegal, and Sierra Leone, and he established the blueprint for continued exploration during the rest of the century. In 1482 Portuguese ships explored the mouth of the Congo; in 1488 Bartolomeu Dias rounded the Cape of Good Hope; and in 1497, Vasco da Gama reached Calicut (Kozhikode) on India's west coast, clearing the way for trade in spices, porcelain, silks, ivory, and slaves.

The Treaty of Tordesillas, negotiated by João II in 1494 for as yet undiscovered lands in the Western Hemisphere, ensured Portugal's possession of Brazil, not discovered until 1500. Utilizing the wealth of the whole empire, Manuel I (the Fortunate, 1495–1521) imprinted his imagination and name upon great monuments of art and architecture. His reign inspired Portugal's Golden Age. By 1521 the country had begun to tap the natural resources of Brazil and had broken the spice-trade monopoly formerly held by the Venetians. Portugal dominated all access to the Indian Ocean, as the first of the great maritime world empires.

João III (1527–57) ushered in the Jesuits and the Inquisition. When his son Sebastião disappeared in battle in Morocco in 1578, leaving Portugal without an heir, the way was opened for Spanish control. Philip II of Spain claimed the Portuguese throne and began 60 years of Spanish domination. In the East, Portugal's strength had been undermined by Dutch and English traders.

The House of Bragança

A nationalist revolution in 1640 brought a descendant of João I to the throne as João IV. This began the house of Bragança, which lasted into the 20th century, as well as a long series of revolutions and intrigues. João IV arranged an English alliance, wedding his daughter to Charles II. For her dowry he "threw in" Bombay and Tangier. In 1668 the Treaty of Lisbon with Spain gave Portugal recognized independence.

All Saints' Day, 1755. The great earthquake destroyed virtually all of Lisbon. In 6 minutes 15,000 people were killed, thousands while attending morning masses. The Marquês de Pombal, adviser to King José (1750–77), met the emergency and later reconstructed Lisbon as a safer and more beautiful city. Yet he was an exponent of absolutism, and his expulsion of the Jesuits in 1759 earned him powerful enemies throughout Europe. His virtual dictatorship had its beneficial side, however; he curbed the power of the Inquisition and reorganized and expanded industry, agriculture, education, and the military. On the death of his patron, King José, he was exiled from court.

In 1793, Portugal joined a coalition with England and Spain against Napoléon.

An insane queen, Maria I (1777–1816), plus an exiled royal family, made overthrow by a military junta easy. The Cortes was summoned, a constitution was drawn up, and Maria's son, João VI, accepted the position of constitutional monarch in 1821. João's son, Pedro, declared independence for Brazil in 1822 and became a champion of liberalism in Portugal.

From Republic to Dictatorship

The years 1853–1908 felt the rumble of republican movements that assaulted the very existence of the monarchists. In 1908 Carlos I, "the painter king," and the crown prince were assassinated at Praça do Comércio in Lisbon. His successor was overthrown in an outright revolution on October 5, 1910, which ended the Portuguese monarchy and made Portugal a republic.

Instability was the watchword of the newly proclaimed republic, with revolutions and uprisings occurring two or three times a year. An attempt to remain neutral in World War I failed when, influenced by its old ally, England, Portugal commandeered German ships in the Lisbon harbor, which promptly brought a declaration of war from Germany.

The precarious foundations of the republic collapsed in 1926 when a military revolt established a dictatorship, with Gomes da Costa as its head. He was followed by Fragoso da Carmona, who remained president until 1951, but only as a figurehead. António Salazar became his finance minister in 1928, rescuing the country from a morass of financial difficulties. He went on to become the first minister, acting as (but never officially becoming) head of state. In World War II, he asserted his country's neutrality, although he allowed British and American troops to establish bases in the Azores in 1943.

In 1955 Portugal joined the United Nations. Salazar suffered a stroke in 1968 and died in 1970.

Modern Portugal

The old dictatorship was overthrown on April 25, 1974, in a coup dubbed "the flower revolution" because the soldiers wore red carnations instead of carrying guns. Change swept across the land, and Portugal drifted into near anarchy. Finally, after several years of turmoil, plus frequent failures of provisional governments (there were 16 from 1976 to 1983), a revised constitution is in force. Defining Portugal as a republic engaged in the formation of a classless society, the constitution calls for presidents to be elected by popular vote for 5-year terms. The prime minister is appointed by the president, who also names other members of the government. A unicameral Legislative Assembly is made up of representatives elected by the people to 4-year terms.

Of its once extensive territorial possessions, only the Madeira group and the Azores in the Atlantic, and Macau on the south China coast, are still under the flag of Portugal. The year 1976 marked great change for the country in the realm of rulership. In that year, the Azores and Madeira were granted partial autonomy. Macau received broad autonomy, and all the colonial territories in Africa became independent countries—Angola, the Cape Verde Islands, Portuguese Guinea, Mozambique, and São Tomé and Príncipe (islands in the Gulf of Guinea). The Portuguese colony of East Timor in the Indonesian archipelago was released by Portugal but immediately seized by Indonesia.

Portugal joined the European Common Market in 1986, but unemployment remains a serious problem. The country had to resettle some 700,000 refugees from its former colonies in Africa, including Angola. Emergency steps to improve agriculture and industry have been called "wrenching."

After a long slump in the 1970s and 1980s, tourism has been on the upswing in mainland Portugal, with visitors coming in by the thousands in the 1990s. Portugal is considered one of the safest countries of all Europe in which to travel.

THE PEOPLE

The Portuguese have a mixture of ethnic ancestry. The blood of the first Ibero-Celtic tribes (later called *Lusitani* by the Romans), Phoenicians, Carthaginians, Romans, Germans, Visigoths, Moors, Jews, Arabs, and Berbers flows in the veins of the Portuguese of today, making a description of the people as being of homogeneous Mediterranean stock perhaps the most accurate assessment. A small African minority has appeared in the country as a result of decolonization of Portugal's African territories. The provinces of the country present a diverse set of social structures; some are classless but impoverished, others have well-defined hierarchical parameters. Despite the declaration in the constitution that the republic is "engaged in the formation of a classless society," the nature of humankind makes social and economic divisions inevitable, especially when they are based on land ownership, urban or rural environment, and regional variation, to name only a few variables.

LANGUAGE

Portuguese is a Romance language, evolved mainly from a dialect spoken when Portugal was a province of the Spanish kingdom of León and Castile. Portuguese has developed separately from other Romance dialects, such as those that evolved into the Spanish language. After Portugal became an independent country in the 11th century, its borders were pushed southward to the sea, taking in areas previously governed by Muslim Moors. The language called *Mozarabic,* spoken by the Christians living as Moorish subjects, was integrated into the Portuguese dialect, and the language of Portugal came into being. The basic language of today, both oral and written, was solidified and perfected in Lisbon, the capital, and Coimbra, the ancient university city. Of course, there are regional variations and pronunciations.

One writer suggested that Portuguese has "the hiss and rush of surf crashing against the bleak rocks of Sagres." If you don't speak it, you'll find French, Spanish, and English commonly spoken in Lisbon, along the Costa do Sol, and in Porto, as well as many parts of the Algarve. In small villages and towns, hotel staffs and guides usually speak English. The native tongue is difficult, but the Portuguese people are helpful and patient. Gestures often suffice.

---

2. Architecture, Arts & Crafts

ARCHITECTURE

Little ancient architecture has survived in Portugal, with mere traces of Roman, Byzantine, Visigothic, and Moorish building remaining. Castles dating from the 12th century can be seen, however, the Bragança citadel being the most outstanding. Fortifications dating from the 14th century are at Lisbon and Amieira, their architecture borrowed respectively from the city fortresses of Italy and the crusader castles of Syria.

Cathedrals and churches were built in styles ranging from Romanesque to Cistercian (a blend of Romanesque and Gothic), to true Gothic. An example of the latter type is the monastery at Batalha, which bears the stamp of the English stonemasons imported to build it. Most of the ecclesiastical structures today are a mixture of architecture and decoration, having been changed through the centuries to memorialize successive monarchs. Changes in ornamentation have therefore resulted in decoration in Manueline, Palladian, and baroque design, of both interiors and facades.

The style known as **Manueline** (named for Manuel I, 1495–1521) was a design unique to Portugal. It was mainly used as decorative architecture to change old structures rather than for new buildings (except for the Tower of Belém and the Jerónimos Monastery, also at Belém). It was used to construct portals, porches, and interiors. This architectural invention, sometimes called Atlantic Gothic, was flamboyant and exuberant, an expression of Portugal in the age when its seaborne empire flourished.

Since that time, Portuguese architecture has been mostly imitative, following such foreign styles as Renaissance, Palladian, Italianate, baroque, rococo, and Spanish. The use of new or original design has not been encouraged. True, azulejos (see "Arts & Crafts," below) have been used to some extent for embellishment even in modern times, giving a Portuguese flavor to borrowed architectural design. Examples of this can be seen at the João de Deus and Infanto Santo housing projects and the Gulbenkian Foundation complex and Exhibition Hall in Lisbon.

ARTS & CRAFTS

Two Portuguese artists who gained recognition outside their own country are **Nuno Gonçalves** and **Domingos António de Sequeira**. Gonçalves (1482–1552) was court painter to King Afonso V. He is especially known for the retable of St. Vincent, a six-paneled altarpiece representing 15th-century society and showing Lisbon's patron saint being given homage by the court and people of Portugal. Sequeira (1768–1837), also subsidized by the court, went from academic neoclassic painting to a later technique similar to Goya's. The charcoal drawings done late in his career are his finest works.

All the artistic trends have been tried in Portugal, but through the years of restlessness and oppression in this century, many promising painters left the country and have become more closely linked with foreign art.

Sculpture has not been an outstanding art form in Portugal, although there are a few noteworthy works in ecclesiastical and tomb ornamentation done in the Middle Ages. Except for the impressive work of sculptors and stonecarvers during the Manueline period in the early 16th century, the major departure from the ordinary was in the 18th century: **Machado de Castro** produced the equestrian statue of King José I in Praçá do Comércio in Lisbon, plus statuary at Mafra where he lived and taught.

Later sculptures of merit are the *saudade* in stone done by **Soares dos Reis** and portrait busts of children by **Teixeira Lopes**. Considered the top 20th-century Portuguese sculptor is **Francisco Franco** (*not* the Spanish dictator). Not attributed to any individual stone sculptor are two well-known works: the huge *Christ in Majesty* stela overlooking the estuary of the Tagus River, and the *Padrão dos Descobrimentos* (Monument to the Discoveries) beside the Tagus commemorating the 500th anniversary of the death of Prince Henry the Navigator in 1460.

The Portuguese preferred working in wood rather than in stone, with some beautiful examples from the late Middle Ages. Fine, often exotic, wood from the East, Madeira, and Brazil were used to carve altarpieces, wall coverings, and ceilings of cathedrals and palaces. The 16th-century **Coelho family retables** are outstanding examples of wood-carving skill. Fine wood furniture was also turned out by skilled craftsmen.

A distinctive and important Portuguese craft is the making of ceramics called **azulejos**. Because of the decorative design of these tiles, a 15th-century import from Andalusia, they were adopted by the builders in Portugal. Change in fashion has taken this ceramic art from the Moorish polychromatic design to Dutch Delft blue and white (to compete with Dutch imports) back to muted colors. They were mass-produced to meet postearthquake rebuilding needs in the 18th century and can be seen in the design of public structures, churches, and private houses put up under the direction of the Marquês de Pombal.

Another craft from early days still followed in Portugal is the weaving of **Arraiolos rugs**. In the 16th century, Moorish women in the Alentejo district produced the rugs, and they are still woven in Persian-inspired patterns.

3. Literature & Music

LITERATURE

Manuscripts of song lyrics from the 12th century are the oldest written Portuguese literature. Many of them came from the oral poetry recited by the people of Iberia in ancient times. The oral lyrics were adopted and adapted by court troubadors, public entertainers, and even clerics and aristocrats. The *cantigas* (lyric songs) were mainly songs of the court. After the rule of King Dinis, the *romanceiro*, or Castilian ballad, replaced the lyric songs. Portuguese was used from the 14th century for telling historic tales in poetic form. The lyric tradition of the court troubadors continued off and on until the mid-16th century.

Meanwhile, Portuguese prose began to appear in the chronicles of court life, many with literary merit, like the work of **Fernão Lopes** in the 15th century. By the 16th century, chroniclers changed their focus to the global discoveries and Portugal's oceanic empire. The nation's India ventures led also to the writing of travel books. One of the most popular of these was the work of **Fernão Mendes Pinto,** known as "the Father of All Lies." His *Peregrinaçam (Pilgrimage)* and other writings were based more on his colorful imagination than on fact, but they read well.

High on the list of literary figures of Portugal is **Gil Vicente,** father of Portuguese theater. He lived in the late 15th and early 16th centuries and was acclaimed for his *autos* (religious dramas) and farces. His satirical, often ribald, wit might have signaled the birth of theatrical greatness in the country, but he fell out of favor with the court, and soon after his death his work was drastically censored and some of it destroyed by the Inquisition, which banned secular theater.

Luís Vaz de Camões (1524–80) is Portugal's most famous poet and a national hero. Also an explorer in an age when that was the honored vocation, he was a kinsman of Vasco da Gama, who discovered the sea route to India in 1497–98. Da Gama's exploits were the subject of *Os Lusíadas,* an epic poem by Camões.

Many Portuguese writers preferred to use the Castilian language for their work during the Habsburg sovereignty over both their country and Spain from 1580 to 1640. However, the most widely circulated work attributed to a 17th-century Portuguese writer was the one that became the prototype of 18th-century epistolary novels. Published in French, *Lettres portugaises (Portuguese Letters)* contained five letters purportedly written by a nun from Beja, **Sister Mariana Alcoforado,** to her lover, the French Chevalier de Chamilly. The letters describe their passionate love affair with lyric clarity.

The Age of the Discoveries was a time of glory for Portugal, and since that time the people have tended always to look backward to that glory in their literature and their lives. Although some realism can be seen in more recent literary efforts, lyric poetry is still predominant. Romanticism was the only European intellectual movement whose effect is visible in Portuguese literature, as it fit the people's innate mood and their belief in Portuguese nationalism. This belief, blended with an uncertainty caused by growing unrest early in this century, resulted in a provincialism on the part of Portugal in general and its literature. Lyric poetry and historical novels and novellas are expressions of *saudade,* a nostalgia based on a fatalistic melancholy. One writer around the turn of the century described *saudade* as "the key to understanding the Portuguese soul" and concluded that "progress was not possible for a people whose past will always be more attractive than their futures."

A poet and dramatist who escaped this pall of *saudade* and broadened the scope of Portuguese literature was **Fernando Pessoa** (1888–1935), who has been called the country's greatest poet after Camões. Some writers who disagreed with Pessoa's metaphysical focus have turned to neorealism, but they are little known outside their own country.

An interesting Portuguese work that has achieved notoriety in recent years, probably only exceeded by that accorded the 17th-century *Portuguese Letters,* is *Nova Cartas Portuguesas (New Portuguese Letters).* It is the work of the **"Three Marias,"** Maria Isabel Bareno, Maria Teresa Horta, and Maria Fátima Velho da Costa. This women's lib volume has been widely circulated in Portugal.

MUSIC

Folk songs from ancient times and sacred and secular music from the church and courts have played their part in Portugal. Musical plays and choral pieces evolved eventually into opera, which is still the country's most popular form of classical music. A student of Franz Liszt, **Alfredo Keil** was successful as a composer of Romantic opera. Today he is remembered for his patriotic hymn, *A Portuguesa,* Portugal's national anthem. Lisbon's opera houses still draw devotees of serious music, although the fare offered is mainly of foreign origin.

The Lisbon Philharmonic, the National Radio System's Symphony Orchestra, and the Gulbenkian Orchestra and Chorus give frequent performances, especially in the capital.

The *saudade* that has influenced the country's literature is most clearly present in the fado songs, traditional expressions of the sad, romantic, nostalgic mood of Portugal.

Unless you have experienced the nostalgic sounds of fado, the songs of sorrow, you do not know Portugal. Certainly not its soul. The fado is Portugal's most vivid art form; and no visit to the country should be planned without at least one night spent in a local tavern, where this traditional folk music is heard.

A rough translation of *fado* is fate, from the Latin *fatum,* meaning prophecy. Fado usually tells of unrequited love, jealousy, a longing for days gone by. As one expert put it, it speaks of "life commanded by the Oracle, which nothing can change."

Fado found its earliest fame in the 19th century when Maria Severa, the beautiful daughter of a gypsy, took Lisbon by storm, singing her way into the hearts of the people, and especially the heart of the Count of Vimioso, an outstanding bullfighter of his day. Legend has it that she is honored by present-day *fadistas* who wear a black-fringed shawl in her memory.

In this century the most famous exponent of fado has been Amália Rodrigues, introduced to American audiences in the 1950s at the New York club La Vie en Rose. She was discovered while walking barefoot and selling flowers on the Lisbon docks, near the Alfama. Fado is also sung by men, who are called fadistas as well.

Clutching black shawls around themselves, the female fadistas pour out their emotions, from the tenderest whisper of hope to a wailing lament of life's tragedies. As they sing, accompanied by a guitar and a viola, they seem to lose all contact with the surrounding world, standing against a black gas street lamp, without benefit of backdrops or makeup—just standing there. They seemingly outdo the Rhine's Lorelei in drawing you into their world of tenderness and fire. Though much enjoyment can be derived from understanding the poetic imagery, a knowledge of Portuguese is not essential. The lyric power, the warmth of the voices, and the personality of the singer communicate a great deal.

4. Food & Drink

Portuguese food was summed up well by Mary Jean Kempner in her *Invitation to Portugal:* "The best Portuguese food is provincial, indigenous, eccentric, and proud—a reflection of the chauvinism of this complex people. It takes no sides, assumes no airs, makes no concessions or bows to Brillat-Savarin—and usually tastes wonderful."

The basis of much Portuguese cooking is olive oil. Garlic is used extensively and forms the basis of many dishes. However, if you select anything prepared to order you can request that it be *sem alho* (without garlic).

It's customary in most establishments to order soup (invariably a big bowl filled to the brim), then a fish and a meat course. Potatoes and/or rice are likely to accompany both the meat and fish platters.

In many restaurants, the chef features a *prato do dia*—that is, a plate of the day, which is actually several listings. These dishes are prepared fresh that day, and often are cheaper than the regular offerings.

Dining hours in Portugal are much earlier than they are in Spain. The best time for lunch is between 1 and 2:30pm; for dinner from 7:30 to 9pm.

REGIONAL SPECIALTIES

Many Portuguese begin their meals with *percébes,* roughly translated as goose barnacles. These little devils are the subject of much controversy. One local newspaper in Lisbon suggested to tourists that if they "can bear their repulsive appearance," they'll find "an incomparable morsel of delicious seafood" within. Others claim that all they taste from barnacles is brackish seawater.

There will be no controversy among those who begin with their meal with **camarãoes** (shrimps). Most restaurants serve a heaping, delectable platter full.

Of course, another way of beginning your repast is to select from the offerings of trays of *acepipes variados,* Portuguese hors d'oeuvres, which might include everything from a sea creature known as "knife" to the inevitable olives and tuna fish.

From the soup kitchen, the most popular broth is *caldo verde,* literally green broth. Made from cabbage, sausage, potatoes, and olive oil, it is commonly encountered in the north. Another ubiquitous soup is *sopa alentejana,* simmered with garlic and bread among other ingredients. The Portuguese housewife is canny, knowing how to gain every last morsel of nutrition from her fish, meat, and vegetables. The fishwives make a *sopa de mariscos* by boiling the shells from fish, then richly flavoring the stock and lacing it with white wine.

The first main dish you're likely to encounter on any menu is **bacalhau** (salted codfish), the *o fiel amigo* (faithful friend) to the Portuguese. As you drive through fishing villages in the north, you'll see racks and racks of the fish drying in the sun. Bacalhau has literally saved the lives of thousands from starvation, and the Portuguese not only are grateful to it, they like it as well.

Foreigners may not wax as rhapsodical about bacalhau, although it's prepared in imaginative ways, reportedly one for every day of the year. Common ways of serving it include *bacalhau cozido* (boiled with vegetables such as carrots, cabbage, and spinach, then baked together); *bacalhau à Bras* (fried in olive oil with onions and potatoes and flavored with garlic); *bacalhau à Gomes de Sá* (codfish that has been stewed with black olives, potatoes, onions, then baked and topped with a sliced boiled egg); and, finally, *bacalhau no churrasco* (barbecued).

Aside from codfish, the classic national dish is **caldeirada,** once described as the Portuguese version of a savory Mediterranean bouillabaisse. Prepared at home, it is a simple kettle of fish, with bits and pieces of the latest catch. From the kitchen of a competent chef, it is a pungent stew with choice bits and pieces of fruits of the sea.

Next on the platter is the Portuguese sardine, which many gastronomes have called elegant. This unassuming fish goes by the pompous Latin name of *Clupea pilchardus,* and is found off the Atlantic coasts of Iberia as well as France. Many of the sardines come from Setúbal, a city south of the Tagus, which is most often visited on a day trip from Lisbon. As you stroll through the alleys of the Alfama, or pass along the main streets of small villages throughout Portugal, you'll sometimes see women kneeling in front of braziers on their front doorsteps, grilling these large sardines left behind for domestic consumption. To have them grilled, order *sardinhas assadas.*

Shellfish is one of the great delicacies of the Portuguese table. Its scarcity and the demand of foreign markets have led to astronomical price tags. However, tourists devour them, many lamenting later when the bill is presented. The price of lobsters or crabs changes every day, depending on market quotations. Therefore the tariff doesn't appear on the menu. Rather, you'll see the abbreviation, "Preco V.," meaning variable price. When the waiter brings one of these crustaceans to your table, ask the price. That way you'll avoid shock when your sin is tallied up.

If you do decide to splurge, make sure you get fresh shellfish. Many of these creatures from the deep, such as king-size crabs, are cooked, then displayed in restaurant windows. If they don't sell that day, I suspect the chef places them there tomorrow.

When fresh, *santola* (crab) is a delicacy. It's often served stuffed (*santola recheada*), although this specialty may be too pungent for unaccustomed Western palates. *Amêijoas,* the baby clams, are a reliable item of the Portuguese kitchen. *Lagosta* is translated as lobster; in fact, it's really a crayfish, best when served without adornment. If you see the words "piri-piri" on the menu following lobster, rush for the nearest exit. This is a sauce made of hot pepper from Angola. Jennings Parrott once wrote: "After tasting it you will understand why Angola wanted to get it out of the country." However, in fairness, many foreigners accustomed to hot, peppery food like this dish.

A wide variety of good-tasting and inexpensive fish dishes is also available: *salmonette* (red mullet) from Setúbal; *robalo* (bass); *lenguado* (sole); and the sweet-tasting *pescada* (hake). Perhaps less appealing to the average diner, but preferred by many discriminating palates, are *eirós* (eels), *polvo* (octopus), and *lampreias* (lampreys), the latter a seasonal feature in the northern Minho district.

Porto residents are known as "tripe eaters." The specialty is *dobrada,* tripe with beans, a favorite of the workers. The *cozido à portuguesa,* is another dish much in demand: a stew often employing both beef and pork, along with fresh vegetables and sausages. The chief offering of the beer tavern is *bife na frigideira,* beef in a mustard sauce, usually served with a fried egg on top, all piping hot in a brown ceramic dish. Thinly sliced *iscas* (calves' livers) are usually well-prepared and sautéed with onion.

Meat, especially beef and veal, is less satisfying. The best meat in Portugal is *porco* (pork), which is usually tender and juicy. In particular, order *porco alentejano,* fried pork in a succulent sauce with baby clams, often cooked with herb-flavored onions and tomatoes. In the same province, *cabrito* (roast kid) is another treat, flavored with herbs and garlic. Chicken tends to be hit-or-miss, and is perhaps best when spit-roasted a golden brown (*frango no espeto*). In season, game is good, especially *perdiz* (partridge) and *codorniz estufada* (pan-roasted quail).

Cheese (*queijo*) is usually eaten separately and not with fruit, as in France. The most common varieties of Portuguese cheese are made from sheep or goat's milk. A popular variety is *queijo da serra* (literally, cheese from the hills). Another much-in-demand cheese is *queijo do Alentejo,* plus *queijo de Azeitão.* Many prefer *queijo Flamengo* (similar to the Dutch Gouda cheese).

Desserts

Locked away in isolated and remote convents and monasteries, nuns and monks created original sweet-tooth concoctions. Many of these dessert specialties have been handed down over the years and are nowadays sold in little pastry shops throughout Portugal. In Lisbon or Porto, and a few other Portuguese cities, you can visit a *salão de chá* (tea salon) at four o'clock in the afternoon where you can sample these delicacies. Regrettably, too few restaurants feature regional desserts, many relying on caramel custard or fresh fruit.

Portugal doesn't offer many egg dishes, except for the omelet. However, eggs are used extensively in many of the sweets. Although egg yolks cooked in sugar may not appeal to you, you may want to try some of the more original offerings. Perhaps the best known are *ovos moles* (soft eggs sold in colorful barrels) that originate in Aveiro. From the same district capital comes *ovos de fio* (string eggs).

The most typical dessert is *arroz doce,* rice pudding flavored with cinnamon. As mentioned, flan, or caramel custard, appears on all menus. If you're in Portugal in summer, ask for a peach from Alcobaça. One of these juicy, succulent yellow fruits will spoil all other peaches for you forever. In first-class restaurants, the waiters go through an elaborate ritual of peeling it in front of you. Sintra is known for its strawberries, Setúbal for its orange groves, the Algarve for its almonds and figs, Elvas for its plums, the Azores for their pineapples, and Madeira for its passionfruit. Some people believe that if you eat too much of the latter, you'll be driven insane.

THE WINES OF PORTUGAL

One of the joys of dining in Portugal is to discover its regional wines. With the exception of port and Madeira, they remain little known to most of the world.

Among the table wines, my personal favorites are from the mountainous wine district known as **Dão.** Its red wines are ruby-colored, their taste often described as velvety, whereas the white wines are light and delicate enough to make a fit accompaniment to Portuguese shellfish. From the sandy dunes of the **Colares** wine district, near Sintra, emerges a full-bodied wine made from Ramisco grapes (this wine is served at the Palácio de Seteais hotel). Of Colares wine, a Portuguese writer once noted that it has "a feminine complexion, but a virile energy."

The *vinhos verdes* (green wines) have many adherents. These light wines, low in alcoholic content, come from the northwestern corner of Portugal, the **Minho** district. The wine is gaseous, as it's made from grapes not fully matured. Near Estoril, the **Carcavelos** district produces an esoteric wine, commonly served as an apéritif or with dessert. As it mellows, its bouquet is more powerful. The Bucelas district, near Lisbon, makes a wine from the Arinto grape, among others. Its best-known wine is white, with a bit of an acid taste.

Port wine is produced in a region on the arid slopes of the Douro. Only vineyards within this area are recognized as yielding genuine port wine. The wine is shipped from Portugal's second-largest city, Porto, which the English have dubbed Oporto. Drunk in tulip-shaped glasses, it comes in many different colors and flavors. The pale dry port makes an ideal apéritif, and you can request it at a time when you might normally order dry sherry. The ruby or tawny port is sweet or medium dry, usually drunk as a liqueur after dinner. The most valuable port is either vintage or crusted wine. Crusted port does not mean vintage—rather, it takes its name from the decanting of its crust. Vintage port is the very best wine. In a period of a decade, only three years may be declared vintage.

Port is blended to assure a consistency of taste. Cyril Ray called it "one of the heartiest and handsomest of wines." Matured in wooden casks, the wood ports are either white, tawny, or ruby red. At first the wine is a deep ruby color, turning more like the color of straw as it ages.

Port wine had "perpetuated and glorified the fame of Porto," as one citizen put it. The first foreigners to be won over by it were the English in the 17th century. In more recent times, however, the French import more of the wine than the British. The grapes are still crushed by barefoot men; but this shouldn't alarm you as the wine is purified before it's bottled.

Its greatest chic was in times gone by, but **Madeira** wine remains popular. It was highly favored by the early American colonists. Made with grapes grown in volcanic soil, it is fortified with brandy before it's shipped out.

The major types of Madeira are Sercial (a dry wine, drunk as an apéritif, once a favorite with characters in Galsworthy novels); Malmsey (the dessert wine that the Duke of Clarence allegedly asked to drown in to escape torture at the hands of his brother); and Boal (a heady wine used on many different occasions, from a banquet following a hunt to a private tête-à-tête). Perhaps one of the finest statements ever made about Madeira wine is the following: "It gives vivacity to a social gathering, profundity to a solitary meditation, helps a man to think well of his friends and to forgive his enemies. . . ."

WATER & BEER

Drinking water is safe in Lisbon, along the Costa do Sol (Estoril and Cascais), and in Porto. In less-visited towns and villages, you may want to order bottled water. You can ask for it to be with or without "gas."

Beer (*cerveja*) is gaining new followers yearly. One of the best of the home brews is sold under the name of Sagres, honoring the town in the Algarve that enjoyed associations with Henry the Navigator.

PLANNING A TRIP TO PORTUGAL

This chapter is devoted to the where, when, and how of your trip to Portugal—all those issues required to get your trip together and take it on the road.

In this chapter I concentrate on what you need to do *before* you go, plus getting to and around Portugal. In addition to helping you decide when to take your vacation, I answer questions you might have about what to take, where to gather information, and what documents you need. I also cover various alternative and specialty travel options, such as educational travel, and include tips for special travelers.

1. Information, Entry Requirements & Money

SOURCES OF INFORMATION
Before you go, get in touch with one of the overseas offices of the **Portuguese National Tourist Office.** The main one is at 590 Fifth Ave., New York, NY 10036-4704 (tel. 212/354-4403). In Canada, offices are at 500 Sherbrooke St. W., Suite 930, Montréal, QB H3A 3C6 (tel. 514/843-9328), and at 4120 Yonge St., Suite 414, Willowdale, ON M2P 2B8 (tel. 416/250-7580).

Other useful sources of information are newspapers and magazines. To find the latest articles that have been published on your destination, go to your library, ask for the *Guide to Periodical Literature,* and look under the city/country for listings.

You may also want to contact the State Department for their background bulletins. Write to the Superintendent of Documents, U.S. Government Printing Office, Washington, DC 20402 (tel. 202/783-3238).

A good travel agent can also be a valuable source of information. If you use one, make sure he or she is a member of the **American Society of Travel Agents (ASTA)**. If you get poor service from a travel agent, write to ASTA's Consumer Affairs Department, P.O. Box 23922, Washington, D.C. 20006.

And finally, we come to the best source of all—friends and other travelers who have just returned from your destination.

ENTRY REQUIREMENTS

U.S., Canadian, British, Australian, New Zealand, and Irish citizens with a valid passport do not need a visa to enter Portugal if they do not expect to stay more than 90 days and do not expect to work there. Those who, after entering Portugal, find that they would like to stay more than 90 days, can apply for a permit for an additional stay of 90 days, which as a rule is granted immediately.

MONEY

There are no restrictions on how much foreign currency you can bring into Portugal, although visitors should declare the amount brought in. This proves to the Portuguese Customs Office that the currency came from outside the country and therefore the same amount or less can be taken out.

The basic unit of Portuguese currency is the escudo (plural: escudos). Because of fluctuations in relative values of world currencies, I suggest that you get in touch with any bank for the latest official exchange rate before going to Portugal.

Portugal is one of the most reasonably priced countries in which to travel in Europe. But first-time American visitors often panic at price quotations. The Portuguese **escudo** is written as 1$00—the dollar sign between the escudo and the **centavo**. Bank notes are issued for 20, 30, 50, 100, 500, 1,000, 5,000, and 10,000 escudos. In coins of silver and copper, the denominations are 1, 2.50, 5, 10, 20, 50, and 100 escudos.

The Escudo & the Dollar

As of this writing $1 U.S. dollar equaled approximately 150 escudos, and this was the rate of exchange used to calculate the dollar values given in this guide (rounded to the nearest nickel). This rate fluctuates from day to day and may not be the same when you travel to Portugal. Therefore *the following table should be used only as a general guideline.* Always check last-minute quotations.

Escudos	U.S.$	Escudos	U.S.$
2$	.02	100$	.67
5	.03	150	1.00
6	.04	200	1.35
10	.07	300	2.00
15	.10	400	2.70
20	.14	500	3.35
25	.17	600	4.00
30	.20	700	4.70
35	.24	800	5.35
40	.27	900	6.05
45	.30	1,000	6.70
50	.34	2,000	13.40
60	.40	3,000	20.00
75	.50	4,000	26.80

Traveler's Checks

Traveler's checks are the safest way to carry cash while traveling. Most banks will give you a better rate on traveler's checks than for cash. The following are the major issuers of traveler's checks.

American Express (tel. toll free 800/221-7282 in the U.S. and Canada) charges a 1% commission. Checks are free to members of the American Automobile Association.

Bank of America (tel. toll free 800/227-3460 in the U.S., or 415/624-5400, collect, in Canada) issues checks in U.S. dollars for a 1% commission everywhere but California.

Citicorp (tel. toll free 800/645-6556 in the U.S., or 813/623-1709, collect, in Canada) issues checks in U.S. dollars, pounds, or German marks.

MasterCard International (tel. toll free 800/223-9920 in the U.S., or 212/974-5696, collect, in Canada) issues checks in about a dozen currencies.

Barclays Bank (tel. toll free 800/221-2426 in the U.S. and Canada) issues checks in both U.S. and Canadian dollars and British pounds.

Thomas Cook (tel. toll free in the U.S. 800/223-7373, or 212/974-5696, collect, in Canada) issues checks in U.S. or Canadian dollars or British pounds. It's affiliated with MasterCard.

Each of these agencies will refund your checks if they are lost or stolen, upon sufficient documentation or their serial numbers. When purchasing checks ask about refund hotlines; American Express and Bank of America have the greatest number of offices around the world.

Currency Exchange

Many hotels in Portugal will simply not accept a dollar-denominated check, and if they do, they'll certainly charge for the conversion. In some cases they'll accept countersigned traveler's checks, or a credit card, but if you're prepaying a deposit on hotel reservations, it's cheaper and easier to pay with a check drawn upon a Portuguese bank.

This can be arranged by a large commercial bank or by a specialist like **Ruesch International,** 1350 Eye St., Washington, DC 20005 (tel. 202/408-1200, or toll free 800/424-2923), which performs a wide variety of conversion-related tasks, usually for only $2 U.S. per transaction.

If you need a check payable in escudos, call Ruesch's toll-free number, describe what you need, and note the transaction number given to you. Mail your dollar-denominated personal check (payable to Ruesch International) to their office in Washington, D.C. Upon receipt, the company will mail a check denominated in escudos for the financial equivalent, minus the $2 charge. The company also sells traveler's checks dominated in escudos, and can help you with many different kinds of wire transfers and conversion of VAT refund checks. They'll mail brochures and information packets upon request.

---

2. When to Go—Climate & Holidays

CLIMATE

"We didn't know we had an April," one Lisbon resident said, "until *that* song came out." "April in Portugal" is famous, both the song and the season. Summer may be the most popular season, but for the traveler who can chart his or her own course, spring and autumn are the delectable seasons.

For North Americans, the climate of Portugal most closely parallels that of California. The Portuguese consider their climate one of the most ideal in Europe, and it is. There are only slight fluctuations in temperature between summer and winter, the overall mean ranging from 77° Fahrenheit in summer to about 58° Fahrenheit in winter. However, the rainy season begins in November, usually lasting through January. The proximity of the Gulf Stream allows Portugal's northernmost province, the **Minho,** to enjoy mild, albeit very rainy, winters, even though it's at approximately the same latitude as New York.

Snow brings many skiing enthusiasts to the **Serra de Estrêla** in north-central Portugal; but, for the most part, winter entails only some rain and lower temperatures in the other provinces.

The **Algarve** and especially **Madeira** are the exceptions: They enjoy warm and temperate winters. Madeira, in fact, basks in its high season in winter. The Algarve, too, is somewhat of a winter Riviera, attracting sun worshippers from both North America and Europe. Summers in both tend to be long and hot, crystal clear and dry.

Lisbon and **Estoril** enjoy 46° to 65° Fahrenheit temperatures in winter, rising to between 60° and 82° Fahrenheit in summer.

Travelers have dubbed Portugal a "country for all seasons."

Lisbon's Average Daytime Temperature and Rainfall

	Jan	Feb	Mar	Apr	May	June	July	Aug	Sept	Oct	Nov	Dec
Temp. (°F)	57	59	63	67	71	77	81	82	79	72	63	58
Rainfall "	4.3	3.0	4.2	2.1	1.7	0.6	0.1	0.2	1.3	2.4	3.7	4.1

HOLIDAYS & FESTIVALS

Watch those holidays and adjust your banking needs accordingly. Holidays include January 1 (New Year's Day and also Universal Brotherhood Day); February 7 (Carnival); Good Friday in April (dates vary); April 25 (Anniversary of the Revolution); May 1 (Labor Day); May 25 (Corpus Christi); June 10 (National Day); August 15 (Assumption); October 5 (Republic Day); November 1 (All Saints' Day); December 1 (Restoration of Independence); December 8 (Immaculate Conception); and Christmas Day.

---

3. Health & Insurance

HEALTH

Portugal does not offer free medical treatment to visitors except for citizens of certain countries, such as Great Britain, that have reciprocal health agreements. Nationals from such countries as Canada and the United States have to pay for medical services rendered.

You will encounter few health problems traveling in Portugal. The tap water is generally safe to drink, the milk is pasteurized, and health services are good. Occasionally the change in diet may cause some minor diarrhea so you may want to take some anti-diarrhea medicine along.

Carry all your vital medicine in your carry-on luggage and bring enough prescribed medicines to sustain you during your stay. Bring along copies of your prescriptions that are written in the generic—not brand-name—form. If you need a doctor, your hotel can recommend one or you can contact the American embassy or consulate. You can also obtain a list of English-speaking doctors before you leave from the **International Association for Medical Assistance to Travelers** (IAMAT) in the United States at 417 Center St., Lewiston, NY 14092 (tel. 716/754-4883); in Canada at 40 Regal Rd., Guelph, ON N1K 1B5 (tel. 519/836-0102).

If you suffer from a chronic illness, talk to your doctor before taking the trip. For such conditions as epilepsy, diabetes, or a heart condition, wear a Medic Alert Identification Tag, which will immediately alert any doctor to your condition and provide the number of Medic Alert's 24-hour hotline so that a foreign doctor can obtain medical records for you. For a lifetime membership, the cost is $30. Contact the **Medic Alert Foundation,** P.O. Box 1009, Turlock, CA 95381-1009 (tel. toll free 800/432-5378).

INSURANCE

Before purchasing any additional insurance check your homeowner's, automobile, and medical insurance policies as well as the insurance provided by credit-card companies and auto and travel clubs. You may have adequate off-premises theft coverage or your credit-card company may even provide cancellation coverage if the ticket is paid for with a credit card.

Remember that Medicare only covers U.S. citizens traveling in Mexico and Canada.

Also note that to submit any claim you must always have thorough documentation, including all receipts, police reports, medical records, etc.

If you are prepaying for your vacation or are taking a charter or any other flight that has cancellation penalties, look into cancellation insurance.

The following companies will provide further information:

Travel Guard International, 1145 Clark St., Stevens Point, WI 54481 (tel. toll free 800/826-1300), offers a comprehensive 7-day policy that covers basically everything, including lost luggage. It costs $52, including emergency assistance, accidental death, trip cancellation and interruption, medical coverage abroad, and lost luggage. There are restrictions, however, which you should understand before you accept the coverage.

Travel Insurance Pak, Travelers Insurance Co., 1 Tower Sq. 15 NB, Hartford, CT 06183-5040 (tel. toll free 800/243-3174, or 203/277-2318), offers illness and accident coverage, costing from $10 for 6 to 10 days. For lost or damaged luggage, $500 worth of coverage costs $20 for 6 to 10 days. You can also get trip cancellation insurance for $5.50.

Mutual of Omaha (Tele-Trip), 3201 Farnam St., Omaha, NB 68131 (tel. toll free 800/228-9792, or 402/345-2400), charges $3 a day (with a 10-day minimum) for foreign medical coverage up to $50,000 which features global assistance and maintains a 24-hour "hotline." The company also offers trip cancellation insurance, lost or stolen luggage coverage, the standard accident coverage, and other policies.

HealthCare Abroad (MEDEX), 243 Church St. NW, Suite 100D, Vienna, VA 22180 (tel. toll free 800/237-6615, or 703/255-9800), offers a policy, good for 10 to 90 days, costing $3 a day, including accident and sickness coverage up to the tune of $100,000. Medical evacuation is also included, along with a $25,000 accidental death or dismemberment compensation. Trip cancellation and lost or stolen luggage can also be written into this policy at a nominal cost.

WorldCare Travel Assistance Association, 605 Market St., Suite 1300, San Francisco, CA 94105 (tel. toll free 800/666-4993, or 415/541-4991), features a 9- to 15-day policy, costing $105, including trip cancellation, lost or stolen luggage, legal assistance, and medical coverage and evacuation.

Access America, 600 Third Ave., P.O. Box 807, New York, NY 10163-0807 (tel. toll free 800/955-4002, or 212/949-5960), has a 24-hour "hotline" in case of an emergency, and offers medical coverage for 9 to 15 days costing $49 for $10,000. If you want medical plus trip cancellation, the charge is $89 for 9 to 15 days. A comprehensive package for $111 grants 9- to 15-day blanket coverage, including $50,000 worth of death benefits.

---

4. What to Pack

Always pack light. Sometimes it's hard to get a porter or a baggage cart in rail and air terminals. Also, airlines are increasingly strict about how much luggage you can bring, both carry-on and checked items. Checked baggage should not be more than 62 inches (width, plus length, plus height), or weigh more than 70 pounds. Carry-on luggage shouldn't be more than 45 inches (width, plus length, plus height) and must fit under your seat or in the bin above.

Note also that conservative middle-age Portuguese people tend to dress up rather than down and that they dress very well indeed, particularly at theaters and concerts. Nobody will bar you for arriving in sports clothes, but you may feel awkward so include at least one smart suit or dress in your luggage.

Better-class restaurants usually demand that men wear ties and that women not wear shorts or jogging clothing, but those are the only clothing rules enforced.

Pack clothes that "travel well" because you can't always get pressing done at hotels. Be prepared to wash your underwear, etc., in your bathroom and hang it up to dry overnight.

The general rule of packing is to bring four of everything. For men, that means four pairs of socks, four pairs of slacks, four shirts, and four sets of underwear. At least two of these will always be either dirty or in the process of drying. Often you'll have to wrap semiwet clothes in a plastic bag as you head for your next destination. Women can follow the same rule.

Take at least one outfit for chilly weather and one outfit for warm weather. Even in the summer, you may experience suddenly chilly weather in the Portuguese mountains or along the seacoasts, especially in the north of Portugal. Always take two pairs of walking shoes in case you get your shoes soaked and need that extra pair.

---

5. Tips for the Disabled, Seniors, Singles, Families & Students

---

FOR THE DISABLED

Before you go, many agencies can provide advance-planning information.

For example, contact **Travel Information Service**, Moss Rehabilitation Hospital, 1200 W. Tabor Rd., Philadelphia, PA 19141-3099 (tel. 215/456-9900). It charges $5 per package for its data, which will contain names and addresses of accessible hotels, restaurants, and attractions often based on firsthand reports of travelers who have been there.

You may also want to subscribe to *The Itinerary*, P.O. Box 2012, Bayonne, NJ 07002-2012 (tel. 201/858-3400), for $10 a year. This travel magazine, published bimonthly, is filled with news about travel aids for the handicapped, special tours, information on accessibility, and other matters.

You can also obtain a copy of *Air Transportation of Handicapped Persons*, published by the U.S. Department of Transportation. It's free if you write to Free Advisory Circular No. ACI 2032, Distribution Unit, U.S. Department of Transportation, Publications Division, M-4332, Washington, DC 20590.

You may also want to consider joining a tour for disabled visitors. Names and addresses of such tour operators can be obtained by writing to the **Society for the Advancement of Travel for the Handicapped**, 347 Fifth Ave., New York, NY 10016 (tel. 212/447-7284). Yearly membership dues in this society are $40 or $25 for senior citizens and students. Send a self-addressed stamped envelope.

The **Federation of the Handicapped**, 211 W. 14th St., New York, NY 10011 (tel. 212/206-4200), also operates summer tours for members, who pay a yearly fee of $4 (U.S.).

For the blind, the best information source is the **American Foundation for the Blind**, 15 W. 16th St., New York, NY 10011 (tel. toll free 800/232-5463).

FOR SENIORS

Many senior discounts are available but note that some may require membership in a particular association.

For information before you go, write to *Travel Tips for Senior Citizens* (publication no. 8970), distributed for $1 by the Superintendent of Documents, U.S. Government Printing Office, Washington, DC 20402 (tel. 202/783-5238). Another booklet—and this one is distributed free—is called *101 Tips for the Mature Traveler*, available from Grand Circle Travel, 347 Congress St., Suite 3A, Boston, MA 02210 (tel. 617/350-7500, or toll free 800/221-2610).

SAGA International Holidays runs all-inclusive tours for seniors, preferably for those 60 years old or older. Insurance is included in the net price of their tours. Contact SAGA International Holidays, 120 Boylston St., Boston, MA 02116 (tel. toll free 800/343-0273). Membership is $5 a year.

In the United States, the best organization to join is the **American Association of Retired Persons,** 1909 K St. NW, Washington, DC 20049 (tel. 202/872-4700), which offers members discounts on car rentals, hotels, and airfares. AARP travel arrangements, featuring senior citizen discounts, are handled by American Express. Call toll free 800/927-0111 for land arrangements, 800/745-4567 for cruises. Flights to and from various destinations are handled by both numbers. The mailing address is The AARP Travel Experience from American Express, 400 Pinnacle Way, Suite 450, Norcross, GA 30071.

Information is also available from the **National Council of Senior Citizens,** 1331 F St. NW, Washington, DC 20004 (tel. 202/347-8800), which charges $12 per person to join (couples pay $16), for which you receive a monthly newsletter, part of which is devoted to travel tips. Discounts on hotels and auto rentals are available.

Elderhostel, 75 Federal St., Boston, MA 02110 (tel. 617/426-7788), offers an array of university-based summer educational programs for senior citizens throughout the world, including Portugal. Most courses last around 3 weeks and are remarkable values, considering that airfare, accommodations in student dormitories or modest inns, all meals, and tuition are included. Courses include field trips, involve no homework, are ungraded, and emphasize liberal arts.

Participants must be over 60, but each may take an under-60 companion. Meals consist of solid, no-frills fare typical of educational institutions worldwide. The program provides a safe and congenial environment for older single women, who make up some 67% of the enrollment.

FOR SINGLE TRAVELERS

Unfortunately for the 85 million single Americans, the travel industry is geared to couples. Singles often wind up paying the penalty. It pays to travel with someone, and one company that resolves this problem is **Travel Companion,** which matches single travelers with like-minded companions and is headed by Jens Jurgen, who charges between $36 and $66 for a 6-month listing in his well-publicized records. People seeking travel companions fill out forms stating their preferences and needs and receive a mini-listing of potential travel partners. Companions of the same or opposite sex can be requested. For an application and more information, contact Jens Jurgen, Travel Companion, P.O. Box P-833, Amityville, NY 11701 (tel. 516/454-0880).

Singleworld, 401 Theodore Fremd Ave., Rye, NY 10580 (tel. 914/967-3334, or toll free 800/223-6490), is a travel agency that operates tours for solo travelers. Some, but not all, are for people under 35. Annual dues are $25.

FOR FAMILIES

Advance planning is the key to a successful overseas family vacation. If you have very small children you should discuss your vacation plans with your family doctor and take along such standard supplies as children's aspirin, a thermometer, Band-Aids, and the like.

On airlines, a special menu for children must be requested at least 24 hours in advance, but if baby food is required, bring your own and ask a flight attendant to warm it to the right temperature. Take along a "security blanket" for your child—a pacifier, a favorite toy or book, or, for older children, something to make them feel at home in different surroundings—a baseball cap, a favorite T-shirt, or some good luck charm.

Make advance arrangements for cribs, bottle warmers, and car seats if you're driving anywhere.

Ask the hotel if it stocks baby food, and, if not, take some with you and plan to buy the rest in local supermarkets.

Draw up guidelines on bedtime, eating, keeping tidy, being in the sun, even shopping and spending—they'll make the vacation more enjoyable.

Baby-sitters can be found for you at most hotels, but you should always insist, if possible, that you secure a baby-sitter with at least a rudimentary knowledge of English.

Family Travel Times is a newsletter about traveling with children. Subscribers to the newsletter, which costs $35 for 10 issues, can also call in with travel questions, but Monday through Friday only from 10am to noon eastern standard time. Contact **TWYCH**, which stands for Travel With Your Children, 80 Eighth Ave., New York, NY 10011 (tel. 212/206-0688).

The Portuguese adore children, especially their own, but they are most tolerant of other people's youngsters. Even on shopping expeditions, store owners are fond of giving children candy while parents make their purchases. So definitely take your children along to Portugal, providing you warn them repeatedly to stay out of the way of cars, as Portugal has one of the highest car accident rates per capita of any country on the continent.

FOR STUDENTS

The largest travel service for students is **CIEE** (Council on International Educational Exchange), 205 E. 42nd St., New York, NY 10017 (tel. 212/661-1414), providing details about budget travel, study abroad, working permits, and insurance. It also sells a number of helpful publications, including the *Student Travel Catalogue* ($1) and issues International Student Identity Cards to bona fide students for $10.

For real budget travelers it's worth joining **IYHF** (International Youth Hostel Federation). For information write AYH (American Youth Hostels), P.O. Box 37613, Washington, DC 20013-7613 (tel. 202/783-6161). Membership costs $25 annually except for under 18s, who pay $10.

---

6. Alternative/Adventure Travel

Mass tourism of the kind that has transported vast numbers of North Americans to the most obscure corners of the map has been a by-product of late-20th-century affluence, technology, and democratization.

With the advent of the 1990s, and the changes they are bringing, some of America's most respected travel visionaries have perceived a change in the needs of many of the world's most experienced (and sometimes jaded) travelers. There has emerged a demand for specialized travel experiences whose goals and objectives are clearly defined well in advance of an actual departure. There is also an increased demand for organizations that can provide like-minded companions to share and participate in increasingly esoteric travel plans.

Caveat: Under no circumstances is the inclusion of an organization in this section to be interpreted as a guarantee either of its credit worthiness or of its competency. Information about the organizations coming up is presented only as a preliminary preview, to be followed by your own investigation should you be interested.

INTERNATIONAL UNDERSTANDING

About the only thing the following organizations have in common is reflected in that heading. They not only promote trips to increase international understanding, but they also often encourage and advocate what might be called "intelligent travel."

The Friendship Force, 575 South Tower, 1 CNN Center, Atlanta, GA 30303 (tel. 404/522-9490), is a nonprofit organization existing for the sole purpose of fostering and encouraging friendship among disparate people around the world. Dozens of branch offices lie throughout North America and arrange for en masse visits, usually once a year. Because of group bookings, the price of air transportation to the host country is usually less than what volunteers would pay if they bought an APEX ticket individually. Each participant is required to spend 2 weeks in the host country (host countries are in Europe and also throughout the world). One stringent requirement is that a participant must spend 1 full week in the home of a family as a guest. Most volunteers spend the second week traveling in the host country.

Servas (translated from the Esperanto, it means "to serve"), 11 John St., Room 407, New York, NY 10038 (tel. 212/267-0252), is a nonprofit, nongovernment, international, interfaith network of travelers and hosts whose goal is to help build world peace, goodwill, and understanding. They do this by providing opportunities for deeper, more personal contacts among people of diverse cultural and political backgrounds. Servas travelers are invited to share living space with members of communities worldwide, normally staying without charge for visits lasting a maximum of 2 days. Visitors pay a $45 annual fee, plus pay a $15 deposit for access to lists of international hosts, fill out an application, and are interviewed for suitability by one of more than 200 Servas interviewers throughout the country. They then receive a Servas directory listing the names and addresses of Servas hosts who will allow (and encourage) visitors within their homes.

SENIOR-CITIZEN VACATIONS

One of the most dynamic organizations of postretirement studies for senior citizens is **Elderhostel,** 75 Federal St., Boston, MA 02110 (tel. 617/427-7788), established in 1975. Elderhostel maintains an array of programs throughout Europe, including Portugal. Most courses last for around 3 weeks and represent good value, considering that airfare, hotel accommodations in student dormitories or modest inns, all meals, and tuition are included. Courses involve no homework, are ungraded, and are especially focused in liberal arts. This is not a luxury vacation, but rather an academic fulfillment of a type never possible for senior citizens until several years ago. Participants must be at least 60 years of age. However, if two members go as a couple, only one needs to be 60. Anyone interested in participating in one of Elderhostel's programs should write for the free catalog and a list of upcoming courses and destinations.

One company that has a reputation based exclusively on its quality tours for senior citizens is **SAGA International Holidays,** 120 Boylston St., Boston, MA 02116 (tel. toll free 800/343-0273). Established in the 1950s as a sensitive and highly appealing outlet for aged (mature) tour participants, they prefer that joiners be at least 60 years of age or older. Insurance and airfare are included in the net price of any of their tours, all of which encompass dozens of locations in Europe and usually last for an average of 17 nights.

HOME EXCHANGES

For home exchanges, which can be fun and can save you money, contact the following:

World Wide Exchange, 1344 Pacific Ave., Suite 103, Santa Cruz, CA 95060 (tel. 408/425-0531), will list your home and also send you three booklets of listings.

Vacation Exchange Club, 12006 111th Ave., Suite 12, Youngstown, AZ 85363 (tel. 602/972-2186), has many Portuguese listings and charges $24.70 to list your home in their spring and winter listings. Subscribers pay $16 for the listings only.

International Home Exchange Service, Box 190070, San Francisco, CA 94119 (tel. 415/435-3497), charges $35 for three directories annually. The fee includes a listing in one of them. Seniors get 20% off.

7. Getting There

BY PLANE

Although Lisbon is a major gateway city to Europe, in bygone days travelers went to France or England first and then began their Grand Tour, perhaps (but most likely not) stopping over in Portugal.

Air transportation has changed this habit, and more and more sun-seeking travelers are beginning their European adventure in Lisbon. Portugal is, in fact, one of the European countries closest to North America, and it costs less to fly from New York to Lisbon than from New York to Paris, Amsterdam, or Frankfurt.

In the paragraphs that follow I'll describe the basic structure of airfares, exploring various methods of cutting your air transportation costs, and then I'll deal with methods of traveling within Portugal once you arrive.

Since deregulation, the airlines have competed fiercely with one another for traffic. To many destinations, an airline now proposes a fare structure; another airline then files a competing and perhaps different fare structure. The competition may or may not result in a uniform price structure for all airlines flying to that particular country.

It all adds up to chaos—but often *beneficial* chaos for the alert traveler willing to study and consider all the fares available. The key to bargain air fares is to shop around.

In what follows I'll point out the current options available for flying directly to Portugal—only two airlines do so and they are **TAP** (the Portuguese international airline) and **TWA**. If you don't want to fly directly to Portugal, then remember to check all the airlines to find the most inexpensive transatlantic fare that coincides with your itinerary and travel plans.

TAP to Lisbon

When it was established in 1946, TAP only flew between Lisbon and the then-Portuguese colonies of Angola and Mozambique. Over the years the number of destinations has increased and the technical skill of the airline has improved. Today TAP flies to more than 50 destinations and has earned the respect of the travel industry for its selection in 1987 by Federal Express to provide maintenance for that carrier's fleet.

Like the early Portuguese explorers, the airline goes to four continents, touching down in the New York City area at both JFK and Newark, New Jersey; at Boston, Toronto, and Montréal; plus nine destinations within Portugal. Among the most popular of these are Lisbon, Porto, Faro, Funchal (Madeira), and Terceira (the Azores).

TAP's modern fleet, which includes L-1011s, A-310s, B737s, and B727s, benefits from an impressive record of punctuality, safety, and comfort. TAP flies frequently on much-used routes originating in most of the major cities of western Europe. Its routes to Lisbon from London are especially value-conscious, sometimes priced so attractively that a reader might combine a sojourn in England with an inexpensive side excursion to Portugal. What better way to celebrate the "Old Alliance" between the two countries than with an investigation of them both during the same itinerary?

STOPOVER OPTIONS Although both TAP and TWA fly between North America and Lisbon, TAP gives passengers the option of stopping midway across the Atlantic in the Azores, and also makes baggage transfers and seat reservations on connecting flights within Portugal much easier.

TICKET OPTIONS Several ticket options exist for transatlantic passengers eager to experience both Portugal and its national carrier. At press time, TAP offered a winter senior citizen fare from New York or Boston to Portugal. The round-trip fare was as low as $605. The definition of a senior citizen is a traveler 60 years of age or older. An interesting feature in TAP's senior citizen fare is that an accompanying traveler pays the same fare as the senior citizen but doesn't have to be in that age category. The maximum stay abroad with this type of ticket is 3 months. Tickets must be purchased at least 14 days before departure. This fare is of special interest to retirees who wish to escape winter, because spring arrives very early in Portugal. The almond trees are in full bloom in the Algarve in the last weeks of January, and in Lisbon the spring flowers are in bloom in early February.

Most passengers prefer to travel in Portugal in the spring, summer, and autumn. One of TAP's most popular tickets is called a midweek **APEX fare.** The cost differs with the season, but is competitive with similar fares carrying similar restrictions on other airlines. Its price varies, depending on the day of the week and the season of the year, from $659 to $982. Tickets may be purchased 14 days before departure. In some cases, a $100 penalty is imposed for any changes made after payment on either leg of a passenger's itinerary. Nevertheless, if your plans are flexible enough, and if you're aware of your date of return, this might be the ticket option for you. For families, one strong attraction is the fact that children under 12 traveling with a parent pay between 50% and 75% of the adult fare.

For the purpose of APEX tickets, TAP divides its calendar year into three seasons: basic, shoulder, and peak. The cheapest season stretches between November 1 and December 12 and from December 26 until March 31. The most expensive season, when passengers tend to book most transatlantic flights solidly, stretches between June 1 and August 31.

Clients who prefer not to specify when they will return home, or who can't purchase their tickets within 14 days prior to takeoff, usually opt for an **excursion fare.** Costing more than either of the APEX options, it requires that passengers stay from 7 to 180 days before jetting back to North America. On this ticket, peak season lasts from June 1 to August 31.

None of these options takes into account any promotional fares TAP or its competitors might have initiated by the time you schedule your trip. These seem particularly attractive during low (midwinter) season. At press time, a low-season APEX ticket from New York or Boston to either the Azores or Lisbon sold for only $498 round-trip. It required a 7-day minimum and a 30-day maximum stay abroad. It was completely nonrefundable in the event of any necessary changes, and carried many other restrictions and penalties. Despite these inconveniences, many passengers considered its bargain price well worth the restrictions.

The most exclusive, and the most expensive, class of service available on TAP is named after the seafaring pioneers who spread Portugal's empire throughout the world. **Navigator Class** passengers benefit from better service, food, and drink. Navigator Class is TAP's name for business class and is comparable to first class on other major carriers.

For exact departure dates and up-to-the-minute tariffs, you can phone a reservations clerk at TAP. In the continental U.S., dial toll free 800/221-7370.

TWA to Lisbon

A more limited air service is offered by Trans World Airlines. It flies only to Lisbon from North America, and does so only from JFK Airport in New York. Nonstop flights depart 5 days a week in winter, and 6 days a week in summer. On days when no nonstop flight is available, TWA usually offers flights from New York to Madrid, Spain, with continuing connections on another airline (usually Iberia) to Lisbon.

The least expensive high-season tickets on TWA between New York and Lisbon, as of this writing, cost $932 for departures and returns between Monday and Thursday, and $982 for flights on any Friday, Saturday, and Sunday. Taxes and security fees (which usually form a combined total of around $30) are extra. This ticket required a 14-day advance purchase, and a delay of between 7 days and 2 months before activating the return portion of your ticket. The price quoted above, as stated, is for high-season transit. Shoulder-season fares for the same kind of ticket were reduced by between $100 and $200, and low-season fares by between $200 and $300, respectively.

Connections can be made from most major points throughout North America on TWA's network, but if you live anywhere outside of New York, you must prepare yourself for an airline transfer at Kennedy.

Be alert to special price promotions within TWA's fare structure, some of which match similar offers at TAP almost dollar for dollar. At press time, a low-season APEX ticket from New York to Lisbon cost $498 round-trip, required a 7-day minimum and a 30-day maximum stay abroad, and carried many restrictions and penalties. Though this probably won't be in effect by the time you actually plan your trip, similar offerings will probably appear. Keep checking with the airlines, and keep your available flight dates as flexible as possible.

Subject to change, TWA offers a one-way youth fare of between $300 and $391, depending on the season, between New York and Lisbon. Tickets of this type can only be purchased at the last minute, since they are booked *only* within 72 hours of departure. This is available only to travelers age 25 or under, if space is available. They cannot be mailed, and must be purchased in person at any TWA ticket counter.

Other Good-Value Choices

BUCKET SHOPS   The name originated in the 1960s in Britain, where mainstream airlines gave that (then pejorative) name to resalers of blocks of unsold tickets consigned to them by major transatlantic carriers. "Bucket shop" has stuck as a label, but it might be more polite to refer to them as "consolidators." They exist in many shapes and forms. In its purest sense, a bucket shop acts as a clearinghouse for blocks of tickets that airlines discount and consign during normally slow periods of air travel.

Charter operators (see below) and bucket shops used to perform separate functions, but their offerings in many cases have been blurred in recent times. Many outfits perform both functions.

Tickets are sometimes—but not always—priced at up to 35% less than the full fare. Perhaps your reduced fare will be no more than 20% off the regular fare. Terms of payment can vary—say, anywhere from 45 days prior to departure to last-minute sales offered in a final attempt by an airline to fill a disturbingly empty craft.

Bucket shops abound from coast to coast, but to get you started, here are some recommendations:

Maharaja Travel, 393 Fifth Ave., 3rd floor, New York, NY 10016 (tel. 212/213-2020, or toll free 800/223-6862), has been around for some 20 years, offering tickets to 400 destinations worldwide.

Access International, 101 W. 31st St., Suite 1104, New York, NY 10001 (tel. 212/465-0707, or toll free 800/825-3633), may be the country's biggest consolidator. It specializes in thousands of discounted tickets to the capitals of Europe. Flights are usually on regularly scheduled U.S.-based airlines.

Out West, you can try **Sunline Express Holidays, Inc.,** 607 Market St., San Francisco, CA 94105 (tel. 415/541-7800, or toll free 800/877-2111), or **Euro-Asia, Inc.,** 4203 E. Indian School Rd., Suite 210, Phoenix, AZ 85018 (tel. 602/955-2742, or toll free 800/525-3876).

Since dealing with unknown bucket shops might be a little risky, it's wise to call the Better Business Bureau in your area to see if complaints have been filed against the company from which you plan to purchase a fare.

Travel Avenue, 180 N. Des Plaines, Chicago, IL 60661 (tel. toll free 800/333-3335), is a national agency whose headquarters are in Chicago. Its tickets are often cheaper than most shops in that it charges the customer only a $25 fee on international tickets, rather than taking the usual 10% commission from an airline. Travel Avenue rebates most of that back to the customer—hence, the lower fares.

CHARTER FLIGHTS Strictly for reasons of economy (and never for convenience), some travelers are willing to accept the possible uncertainties of taking a charter flight to Portugal.

In a strict sense, a charter flight occurs on an aircraft reserved months in advance for a one-time-only transit to some predetermined point. Before paying for a charter, check the restrictions on your ticket or contract. You may be asked to purchase a tour package and pay far in advance. You'll pay a stiff penalty (or forfeit the ticket entirely) if you cancel. Charters are sometimes canceled when the plane doesn't fill up. In some cases, the charter-ticket seller will offer you an insurance policy for your own legitimate cancellation (hospital certificate, death in the family, whatever).

There is no way to predict whether a proposed flight to Lisbon will cost less on a charter or less in a bucket shop. You'll have to investigate at the time of your trip. (And remember that some charter companies have proved unreliable in the past.)

Among charter flight operators is a name possibly remembered from one's younger days, the **Council on International Educational Exchange** (Council Charters), 205 E. 42nd St., New York, NY 10017 (tel. 212/661-0311, or toll free 800/800-8222). This outfit can arrange "charter seats on regularly scheduled aircraft."

One of the biggest New York charter operators is **Travac,** 989 Sixth Ave., New York, NY 10018 (tel. 212/563-3303), which operates charters from New York to continental destinations.

REBATORS To confuse the situation even more, rebators also compete in the low-cost airfare market. These outfits pass along to the passenger part of their commission, although many of them assess a fee for their services. Most rebators offer discounts that range from 10% to 25% (but this could vary from place to place), plus a $20 handling charge. They are not the same as travel agents, although they sometimes offer similar services, including discounted land arrangements and car rentals.

Rebators include: **Travel Avenue,** 180 N. Des Plaines, Chicago, IL 60661 (tel. 312/876-1116, or toll free 800/333-3335); **The Smart Traveller,** 3111 SW 27th Ave., Miami, FL 33133 (tel. 305/448-3338, or toll free 800/226-3338 in Florida and Georgia); and **Blitz Travel,** 8918 Manchester Rd., St. Louis, MO 63144 (tel. 314/961-2700).

STANDBYS A favorite of spontaneous travelers with absolutely no scheduled demands on their time, standby fares leave your departure to the whims of fortune, and the hopes that a last-minute seat will become available. Most airlines don't offer standbys, although some seats are available to London and to Vienna from which you will have to go by train, plane, or other means to Portugal. These fares are generally offered from April to November only.

Virgin Atlantic Airways (tel. toll free 800/862-8621) features both a day-of-departure and a day-prior-to-departure standby fare from New York to London. **Tarom Romanian Airlines** (tel. 212/687-6013 in New York) offers a year-round standby from New York to Vienna.

GOING AS A COURIER This cost-cutting technique may not be for everybody. You travel as a passenger and courier and for this service you'll secure a greatly discounted airfare or sometimes even a free ticket.

You're allowed one piece of carry-on luggage only; your baggage allowance is used by the courier firm to transport its cargo (which, by the way, is perfectly legal).

As a courier, you don't actually handle the merchandise you're "transporting" to Europe, you just carry a manifest to present to Customs.

Upon arrival, an employee of the courier service will reclaim the company's cargo. Incidentally, you fly alone, so don't plan to travel with anybody. (A friend may be able to arrange a flight as a courier on a consecutive day.) Most courier services operate from Los Angeles or New York, but some operate out of other cities, such as Chicago or Miami.

Courier services are often listed in the yellow pages or in advertisements in travel sections or newspapers.

For a start, check **Halbert Express,** 147-05 176th St., Jamaica, NY 11434 (tel. 718/656-8189 from 10am to 3pm daily); or **Now Voyager,** 74 Varick St., Suite 307, New York, NY 10013 (tel. 212/431-1616). Call daily from 11:30am to 6pm (at other times you'll get a recorded message announcing last-minute special round-trip fares).

BY TRAIN

Thomas Cook's European Railroad Timetable

If you plan to travel heavily on the European railroads, you will do well to secure the latest copy of the Thomas Cook European Timetable of Railroads. This comprehensive, 500-plus-page timetable documents all of Europe's main-line passenger rail services with detail and accuracy. It is available exclusively in North America from **Forsyth Travel Library,** P.O. Box 2975, Shawnee Mission, KS 66201 (tel. toll free 800/FORSYTH), at a cost of $21.95 plus $4 postage priority airmail to the U.S. and $5 (U.S.) for shipments to Canada.

Routes to Lisbon

If you're in England, you can spend 2 or maybe 2½ days reaching Lisbon by train. You must go via Paris, departing from London's Victoria Station, taking the rail/Hovercraft/rail/service over the English Channel and arriving in such French ports as Calais and Dieppe, where you continue the rest of the way by train.

Once in Paris, the most luxurious way to reach Portugal is by the overnight Paris/Madrid *TALGO* express train, leaving from Gare d'Austerlitz and arriving in Madrid's Chamartín Station, where you have to transfer to the *Lisboa Express,* with departures from Madrid's Atocha Station.

One train leaves from Madrid daily at 1:50pm, arriving in Lisbon without changes. The trip takes 9 hours. Another train departs Madrid at 11pm daily, arriving in Lisbon at 8:45am. Passengers must change trains at Entroncamento. Trip time: 10 hours. For more complete information about rail connections, contact **Caminhos de Ferro Portuguêses,** Calçada do Duque 20 (tel. 01/34-63-181 in Lisbon).

Another train, the *Sud Express,* departs from Gare d'Austerlitz in Paris and goes through to Lisbon and Porto without a change of trains in Spain. Bookings are made through the Portuguese National Railroad from one of its representatives (see "Getting Around, By Train," below).

BY CAR

Driving to Portugal is not often a viable option unless you are in neighboring Spain, and even then distances across hot, dusty terrain can be staggering.

Motorists from England can cross the English Channel from one of the Channel ports, such as Dover, and arrive in Calais, France, but then they face a road distance of 1,320 miles across all of France and Spain to reach Portugal. If you're in Britain, it would be better to take one of the Brittany Ferries (see below) which will take you from Plymouth to Santander on the north coast of Spain in 24 hours.

Motorists wanting to avoid the long drive might consider the Motorail service operated from Gare d'Austerlitz in Paris to Lisbon. It operates daily in summer, carrying passengers and their automobiles separately. Passengers take the *Sud Express* arriving the next morning. Cars are sent on a separate train which arrives the following day. This ticket can be purchased from the French National Railroads list of offices under "Getting Around, By Train" below.

BY FERRY

Brittany Ferries operates a ferry service twice a week from Plymouth (England) to Santander on Spain's northern coast, taking 24 hours and carrying cars and their passengers. Bookings are possible from Brittany Ferries, Millbay Docks, Plymouth, PL1 3EW, England (tel. 0752/221321 for ferry reservations). From Santander you can drive west to Spain's Galicia, then head south toward Portugal, entering through the Minho district.

BY BUS

There is no particularly good bus service from the Continent to Portugal. Flying, driving, or going by rail are the preferred methods.

Eurolines operates two coaches a week—on Saturday and Tuesday—leaving from London to Lisbon. Two coaches a week (Wednesday and Saturday) go to the southern coast of the Algarve, depositing passengers at either Faro or Lagos in Portugal. Departures are from London's Victoria Coach Station. Details are available from **The Coach Travel Centre,** 13 Regent St., London, SW1Y 4LR (tel. 071/730-0202).

---

8. Getting Around

BY PLANE

Portugal is a small country, and flying from one place to another is relatively easy—that is, where airports exist. The train is the usual method of public transportation. Nevertheless, **TAP Air Portugal** flies four times a day to Faro, the capital of the Algarve, and Porto, the capital of the north. Services to Faro are likely to be increased in the peak summer months of July and August. There are also four flights a day to Funchal, capital of Madeira, plus limited service to the Azores. Service is usually on 727s.

For ticket sales, flight reservations, information about the city and the country, you can get in touch with the polite personnel of TAP Air Portugal at 3A Praça Marquês de Pombal (tel. 01/57-50-20, the airline's reservation number), in Lisbon.

BY TRAIN

The Portuguese railway system seems underdeveloped when compared to those of the more industrialized nations of Western Europe. Still, the connections between the capital and more than 20 major towns are mainly electric and diesel. Express trains run between Lisbon and Coimbra (the university city), as well as Porto. Leaving from Lisbon's waterfront, electric trains travel along the Costa do Sol (Estoril and Cascais) and on to Queluz and Sintra.

In Lisbon at the **Apolónia Station,** connections can be made for international services and the Northern and Eastern Lines. **Rossio** serves Sintra and the Western Lines; and at the **Cais do Sodré** connections are made for the Costa do Sol resorts of Estoril and Cascais. Finally, trains leave from the **Sul e Sueste** for the Alentejo and the Algarve. In addition, express trains connect Lisbon to all the major capitals of Western Europe, and there is a direct link with Seville.

Daily express trains in summer depart Lisbon for the Algarve (except on Sunday). These leave from the Barreiro Station (across the Tagus—take one of the ferries departing frequently). Off-season service is reduced to four times weekly.

MILEAGE BETWEEN TOWNS AND CITIES
Distance in Miles

	Aveiro	Beja	Braga	Bragança	Castelo Branco	Coimbra	Évora	Faro	Fátima	Guarda	Leiria	LISBON	Porto	Santarém	Setúbal	Valença do Minho	Vila Real	Vila Real de St. António	Viseu
Aveiro		236	75	199	135	36	187	311	86	112	71	151	42	115	182	121	114	313	59
Beja	236		311	365	174	206	48	94	159	240	164	119	278	121	88	358	377	77	293
Braga	75	311		143	204	105	263	287	161	163	150	227	33	190	258	50	66	388	115
Bragança	199	365	143		191	193	317	449	249	125	235	315	157	278	346	199	85	442	147
Castelo Branco	135	174	204	191		99	126	258	97	104	104	160	171	108	164	251	163	251	118
Coimbra	36	206	105	193	99		158	242	56	116	42	122	73	85	153	153	128	283	60
Évora	187	48	263	317	126	158		132	110	192	93	230	230	64	154	310	289	125	238
Faro	311	94	287	449	258	242	132		223	324	185	354	354	230	154	434	422	32	376
Fátima	86	159	161	249	97	56	110	223		171	14	86	128	38	150	208	184	236	115
Guarda	112	240	163	125	104	116	192	324	171		146	226	135	174	230	215	97	317	53
Leiria	71	164	150	235	104	42	93	185	14	146		80	114	43	111	194	169	241	101
LISBON	151	119	227	315	160	122	230	354	86	226	80		194	48	31	274	301	196	181
Portalegre	184	130	254	241	50	81	93	185	128	80	104	194	221	96	120	277	207	168	112
Porto	42	278	33	157	171	73	230	354	128	135	43	194		158	225	77	72	355	83
Quintanilha	218	384	161	19	210	232	335	468	38	254	111	334	176	297	365	217	104	448	166
Santarém	115	121	190	278	108	85	64	230	38	174	43	48	158		75	238	213	165	145
Setúbal	182	88	258	346	164	153	154	154	150	230	111	31	225	75		305	280	162	212
Valença do Minho	121	358	50	199	251	153	310	434	208	215	194	274	77	238	305		122	435	162
Vila Real	114	377	66	85	163	128	289	422	184	97	169	301	72	213	280	122		414	68
Vila Real de St. António	313	77	388	442	251	283	125	32	236	317	241	196	355	165	162	435	414		370
Viseu	59	293	115	147	118	60	238	376	115	53	101	181	83	145	212	162	68	370	

For **information** about rail travel in Portugal, phone 01/87-60-25 in Lisbon.

Railway information and tickets on the **Portuguese National Railroad** may be obtained in North America from its representatives, Rail Europe (the French National Railways), 230 Westchester Ave., White Plains, NY 10604 (tel. toll free 800/345-1990). This organization's main office (see above) can handle requests for information and ticketing for clients from around North America. If you want, however, to drop in on one of the organization's branch offices, these are maintained at 360 Post St., San Francisco, CA 94108 (tel. 415/982-1993; 11 E. Adams St., Chicago, IL 60603 (tel. 312/427-8691); 100 Wilshire Blvd., Santa Monica, CA 90401 (tel. 213/451-5150); 800 Corporate Dr., Fort Lauderdale, FL 33334 (tel. 305/776-2729); or 1500 Stanley St., Montréal, Québec (tel. 514/288-8255).

If you're visiting the environs of Lisbon, such places as Cascais or Sintra, refer to "Getting Around," in Chapter 4, under "By Electric Train."

Senior Discounts

Those 65 years or older benefit from the 50% discount policy of the Portuguese Railway Company. These tickets are good all year.

Rail Passes

EURAILPASS Many travelers to Europe have for years been taking advantage of one of its greatest travel bargains, the **Eurailpass,** which permits unlimited first-class rail travel in any country in Western Europe except the British Isles, and also includes Hungary in Eastern Europe. Passes are purchased for periods as short as 15 days or as long as 3 months.

Here's how it works: The pass is sold only in North America. Vacationers in Europe for 15 days can purchase a Eurailpass for $390; and a pass for 21 days costs $498; a 1-month pass costs $616; 2 months, $840; and 3 months, $1,042. Children under 4 travel free providing they don't occupy a seat (otherwise, they must pay half fare). Children under 12 pay half fare. If you're under 26, you can purchase a **Eurail Youthpass,** which entitles you to unlimited second-class travel for 1 or 2 months, costing $425 or $560, respectively.

The advantages are tempting. No tickets, no supplements—simply show the pass to the ticket collector, then settle back to enjoy the scenery. Seat reservations are required on some trains. Many of the trains have couchettes (sleeping cars), for which an additional fee is charged. Obviously, the 2- or 3-month traveler gets the greatest economic advantages; the Eurailpass is ideal for such extensive trips. Passholders can visit all of Portugal's major sights, then end their vacation in Norway, for example.

Fourteen-day or 1-month voyagers have to estimate rail distance before determining if such a pass is to their benefit. To obtain full advantage of the ticket for 15 days or 1 month, you'd have to spend a great deal of time on the train.

Travel agents in all towns, and railway agents in such major cities as New York, Montréal, or Los Angeles, sell all these tickets. A Eurailpass is available at the North American offices of CIT Travel Service, the French National Railroads, the German Federal Railroads, and the Swiss Federal Railways.

Eurail Saverpass is a money-saving ticket that offers discounted 15-day travel, but only if groups of three people travel constantly and continuously together between April and September, or if two people travel constantly and continuously together between October and March. The price of a Saverpass, valid all over Europe, good for first class only, is $298 for the 15 days.

Eurail Flexipass allows passengers to visit Europe with more flexibility. It is valid in first class and offers the same privileges as the Eurailpass. However, it provides a number of individual travel days which can be used over a much longer period of consecutive days. That makes it possible to stay in one city and yet not lose a single day of travel. There are three passes: 5 days within 15 days for $230; 9 days within 21 days for $398; and 14 days within 1 month for $498.

With many of the same qualifications and restrictions as the previously de-

PORTUGAL RAIL SYSTEM

Atlantic Ocean

S P A I N

To Tuy & Vigo
Caminha
Valença do Minho
Viana do Castelo
Barcelos
Braga
Chaves
Bragança
Póvoa de Varzim
Guimarães
Mirandela
Porto
Baulhe
Vila Real
Armarante
Espinho
Regua
Pocinho
Sernada
Viseu
Guarda
Vila Formoso
Aveiro
Nelas
To Salamanca & Paris
Cantanede
Sta. Comba Dão
Pampilhosa
Covilhã
Figueira da Foz
Coimbra
Fundão
Pombal
Castelo Branco
Leiria
Tomar
Abrantes
Caldas da Rainha
Castelo de Vide
To Madrid
Santarém
Setil
Portalegre
Elvas
Mora
Estremoz
Badajoz
To Sevilla
Sintra
Vila Viçosa
Cascais
LISBON
Casa Branca
Évora
Setúbal
Alcácer do Sal
Reguengos
Moura
Sines
Beja

Tãmega Line ❶
Corgo Line ❷
Tua Line ❸
Douro Line ❹
Vouga Line ❺

Silves
To Huelva & Sevilla
Lagos
Tunes
Sagres
Tavira
Vila Real
de Santo António
Faro

scribed Flexipass is a **Youth Flexipass.** Sold only to travelers under age 26, it allows 15 days of travel within 3 months for $340, or 30 days of travel within 3 months for $540.

BY CAR

So many of the scenic parts of Portugal are so isolated from a train or bus station that it's almost indispensable to have a private car if you plan to do much serious touring. That way, you're your own free agent, unhindered by the somewhat fickle timetables of trains and buses, which often limit your excursions to places close to the beaten track.

There are few superhighways in Portugal, and the few that exist are often interrupted by lengthy stretches of traffic-clogged single-lane thoroughfares. The roads, however, provide access to hard-to-reach gems, undiscovered villages, mountain passes with panoramic views and waterfalls, rustic country inns, hidden beaches and sandy coves, all the charms of rural Iberia.

Car Rentals

Most visitors opt for an auto-rental plan providing weekly rentals with unlimited kilometers included in the overall price. Three of North America's major car-rental companies maintain dozens of branches at each of Portugal's most popular commercial and tourist centers, at rates that are usually competitive.

Budget Rent-a-Car (tel. toll free 800/472-3325) maintains offices in more than a dozen locations within Portugal. The most central—and most used—of these include Lisbon, Faro (the heart of the Algarve), Porto, Praia da Rocha (also a popular Algarve destination), and Madeira. If you're searching for their rock-bottom rates, their least expensive car is a four-door Renault 4, which costs about 21,900$ ($146.75) per week with unlimited mileage, plus 17% tax. This price requires a 48-hour advance notice before your departure from the U.S. The Renault 4 has manual transmission and no air conditioning. Collision damage waivers cost an optional 1,140$ ($7.65) per day. If you decline this option, you are responsible for the first 200,000$ ($1,340) worth of damage to the vehicle if you have an accident. On more expensive car rentals at Budget, the insurance costs rise to 1,900$ ($12.75) per day, and renters without it are responsible for the first 500,000$ ($3,350) worth of damage. Because Portugal has one of the highest accident rates in Europe, it is an excellent idea to buy this extra insurance.

Note carefully that some North American credit-card issuers, especially American Express, sometimes agree to pay any financial obligations incurred after an accident involving a client's rented car, but only if the imprint of their card is on the original rental contract. Because of this agreement, some clients opt to decline the extra insurance coverage. To be sure, you must check with your individual credit-card issuer. Know in advance that even though the card's issuer may eventually reimburse you, you'll still have to fill out some complicated paperwork, and usually advance either cash or a credit-card deposit to cover the cost of the repairs.

Budget's least expensive car with automatic transmission is a midsize vehicle, costing around 65,000$ ($435.50) per week, with unlimited mileage, again without air conditioning. A car with air conditioning is a Ford Scorpio at around 110,000$ ($737) per week. Many renters, when faced with the increased cost for a car with automatic transmission and air conditioning, simply opt instead to drive around Portugal's roads with a stick shift and the windows open.

Hertz (tel. toll free 800/654-3001) has about 22 locations within Portugal, and requires a 2-day advance booking for its least expensive tariffs. A Ford Fiesta (or a similar car) with manual transmission and no air conditioning costs around 23,000$ ($154) a week, with unlimited mileage, plus 17% tax. Its collision damage waivers range from 1,500$ ($10.05) to 1,700$ ($11.40) per day, depending on the value of the car, and are optional. Without them you're responsible for anywhere from 35,000$ ($234.50) worth of damages.

Avis (tel. toll free 800/331-2112) maintains offices in both downtown Lisbon and at the airport, as well as at around 17 other places throughout Portugal. The main office is at Avenida Praia da Vitória in Lisbon (tel. 01/56-11-77). Tariffs range from 18,000$ ($120.60) to 24,000$ ($160.80) per week depending on the season, for their cheapest car, an Opel Corsa. At the opposite end of the spectrum, a Mercedes 190, Mercedes 200, or Mercedes 300 goes for a year-round rental rate of around 347,000$ ($2,325) per week, with unlimited mileage. At Avis, the collision damage waiver, depending on the value of the car, goes for between 1,200$ ($8.05) and 2,550$ ($17.10) per day.

Driving Rules

Continental driving rules apply in Portugal, and international road symbols and signs are used. It is now compulsory to wear safety belts. Speed limits are 55 m.p.h., but only 37 m.p.h. in heavily populated or built-up sections. On the limited number of express highways, the speed limit is increased to 75 m.p.h. Off the beaten track, gasoline stations are few and far between.

ORGANIZED TOURS

Many people never see anything of the Iberian Peninsula except perhaps Spain. You may have wondered about Portugal—whether it's worth a visit, what there is to see and do, how to get around. One way to get a look at the country and dip briefly into its culture is to take an organized tour. Consult a travel agent for the best ones currently offered.

Remember: The advantages of such tours are many. You need not be afraid of traveling alone or perhaps with timid companions. Everything is arranged for you —transportation in the countries visited, hotels, service, sightseeing trips, excursions, luggage handling, tips, taxes, and many of your meals. You're even given time to go shopping or to nose around on your own to find interesting attractions. And you may find that some members of your group have interests that are similar to your own, so you can chat and compare notes. Take a copy of this guide along with you, and you'll recognize many places to which you will probably want to return on your own someday.

American Express Vacations, P.O. Box 5014, Atlanta, GA 30302 (tel. toll free 800/637-6200 in Georgia, 800/241-1700 outside Georgia), offers some of the most comprehensive programs available. If the company doesn't have what you want, you can ask the staff to package a tour especially designed for you.

Trafalgar Tours, 21 E. 26th St., New York, NY 10010 (tel. 212/689-8977, or toll free 800/854-0103), has an exceptional schedule of moderately priced 14- to 32-day tours to Spain and Portugal. (Two go to Morocco as well.) Ask about the CostSaver tours, which book you in tourist-class hotels to keep costs trimmed.

HITCHHIKING

There's no law against it, but it isn't commonly practiced. If you decide to hitchhike, do so with discretion. Usually, Portuguese auto insurance doesn't cover hitchhikers.

---

9. Suggested Itineraries

The cities and towns below are not ranked in order of importance.

1. Lisbon
2. Estoril
3. Cascais
4. Sintra
5. Óbidos
6. Nazaré
7. Fátima
8. Sagres
9. Faro
10. Évora

11. Tomar
12. Coimbra
13. Porto
14. Guimarães
15. Braga
16. Valença do Minho
17. Funchal (Madeira)

If You Have 1 Week

DAYS 1–3 Everybody heads for Lisbon, the gateway to Portugal. Count on losing the first day for rest time. On the second day, see the highlights of Lisbon, including St. George's Castle and the major attractions of Belém, such as Jerónimos Monastery. On the third day, while still based in Lisbon, I suggest that you explore the environs, heading first to Quelez Palace, 9½ miles from Lisbon, then going on to Sintra, 18 miles from Lisbon.

DAYS 4–5 Anchor into one of the resorts along the Costa do Sol, principally Cascais and Estoril. This sun coast, also called the "coast of kings," is easily reached from Lisbon. You can relax in the sun or continue to take a number of excursions. The most interesting sights are at Guincho, near the westernmost point in continental Europe, and Mafra, which is Portugal's El Escorial.

DAY 6 On your sixth day, head south from Lisbon across the Tagus (see Chapter 11) to such intriguing destinations as Setúbal, 31 miles from Lisbon. After exploring the area and visiting Palmela Castle, you can continue south toward the Algarve. However, if it is running late, seek accommodations in and around Setúbal. Except for a pousada or two, the accommodations on the somewhat barren route between Lisbon and the Algarve are sparse.

DAY 7 On your seventh day, you will have reached Sagres, the extreme southwestern corner of Europe, 183 miles south from Lisbon. For a description of what to see and where to stay in the Algarve, refer to Chapter 13.

If You Have 2 Weeks

Spend the first week as outlined above.

DAYS 8–10 Once you've reached the Algarve, settle into your favorite village, town, or resort, and explore the full length of the coast. Allow a minimum of 3 days and nights. For example, if you stay at Faro, you will be roughly in the center of the Algarve and can branch out in either direction, east or west. The coastline stretches a distance of 100 miles, but it will be slow moving, regardless of which direction you select.

DAY 11 On the 11th day, if you must leave, I recommend that you return to Lisbon via a different route, heading first for Beja, the capital of Baixo Alentejo, 96 miles north from Faro. After a stopover there, you might continue north to Évora, 90 miles to the east of Lisbon, where you may want to spend the night. After exploring Évora the next morning, you can drive west to Lisbon.

DAYS 12–14 From Lisbon, fly to Madeira for a minimum of 3 days, spending time in the sun but also a full day exploring this island, one of the most beautiful in the world.

By now you may have run out of time. If not, the treasures in the north of Portugal beckon to you.

If You Have 3 Weeks

Spend your first two weeks as outlined above.

DAY 15 Heading north from Lisbon, stop over at Óbidos, 59 miles away. After a visit, the next recommended stopover is at Alcobaça, 67 miles from Lisbon. This former Cistercian monastery was once the richest and most prestigious in Europe. Since accommodations in both these places are extremely limited, your target for the first night should be the well-known fishing village of Nazaré, 77 miles from Lisbon. (*Warning:* Hotel space is extremely tight in summer.)

DAY 16 Head for Batalha, the spectacular "Battle Abbey" of Portugal, built in a Gothic-Manueline style and located 73 miles north of Lisbon. From Batalha, drive east to Fátima, the world-famous pilgrimage site, which is 36 miles east of Nazaré and about 88 miles north of Lisbon.

DAY 17 Head to Tomar, lying in the east, 85 miles from Lisbon.

DAY 18 Drive north to Coimbra, whose university is among the oldest in the world. The town, 124 miles north of Lisbon, is rich in attractions and makes a suitable overnight stopover.

DAY 19 Drive north to Porto, some 175 miles from Lisbon. This is Portugal's second city, home of port wine.

DAY 20 I recommend that you at least "dip a toe" into the folkloric Minho district in the far-northern reaches of Portugal; visit Guimarães, called the "cradle" of Portugal, 31 miles from Porto; and Viana do Castelo, Portugal's northern city of folklore, lying 43 miles north of Porto. Overnight in Viana do Castelo.

DAY 21 After that, it's back to Lisbon if you wish, a trip that will absorb most of your final day.

---

10. Where to Stay

The government-sponsored **pousadas,** similar to Spain's paradores, were originally created for Portuguese holiday-seekers in remote sections of the country. The Portuguese government has fashioned these inns in historic buildings, such as convents, palaces, and castles. Often they stand in beautiful physical settings. Generally (but not always) the pousadas are in regions that do not have too many suitable hotels: everywhere from Henry the Navigator's Sagres to a feudal castle in the walled city of Óbidos. The tariffs are moderate, but a guest can't stay more than 5 days, as there is usually a waiting line of other visitors. Special terms are granted to honeymoon couples.

Travel agents can make reservations at pousadas, or else you can contact **Enatur —Pousadas of Portugal,** Avenida Sta. Joana Princesa 10, 1700 Lisboa, Portugal (tel. 01/848-1221).

A more recent addition to the accommodations scene in Portugal are the **solares,** mostly spacious country manor houses of the Portuguese aristocracy that are now being restored and opened as guesthouses. Many date from the days of the Discoveries, when navigators brought riches back from all over the world and established lavish homes that have passed down to their heirs. Most of these are along the Costa Verde, between Ponte de Lima and Viana do Castelo, although they are found all over the country, from the coastal area that was the seat of shipbuilding and sailing power to the Alentejo plains.

Information on the solares program is available from the **Portuguese National Tourist Office,** 590 Fifth Ave., New York, NY 10036 (tel. 212/354-4403). For a tour of the solares or to make reservations, get in touch with **Direcção Geral do Turismo,** Divisão do Turismo no Espaço Rural, 86 Avenida António de Aguiar, 1099 Lisboa Codex (tel. 01/57-50-15). If you prefer to stay on the Costa Verde, you can receive information and assistance from Central Reservations for the Houses (manor houses) of **Delegação de Turismo** de Ponte de Lima, Praça da República, 4990 Ponte de Lima (tel. 058/94-23-35). You can arrange to go from one solar to the next through this office.

One of the best associations for arranging for stays in private homes is the **Associação das Casas em Turismo,** Torre D2-8A, Alto da Pampilheira, 2750 Cascais (tel. 01/284-44-64). It has both manor houses and country homes where accommodations can be arranged in all the major tourist districts of the country.

ADVANCE RESERVATIONS

Advance reservations for peak-season summer travel in Portugal are essential, especially since many of the country's hotels are filled to the seams with vacationing Europeans. Unless you're incurably spontaneous, you'll probably be better off in Portugal, even in low season, with some idea of where you'll spend each night.

11. Fast Facts: Portugal

The concierge in your hotel is usually a reliable dispenser of information, including the location of the nearest pharmacy or advice on transportation problems, as well as bullfight tickets. However, should you desire more immediate or more detailed answers to your questions, the following brief summary of some of Portugal's fast facts may prove helpful.

For more specific data about Lisbon, see "Fast Facts: Lisbon" in Chapter 4, "Getting to Know Lisbon."

BABY-SITTERS: Check with the staff of your hotel for arrangements. Most first-class hotels can provide competent baby-sitters from lists that the concierge keeps. At smaller establishments, the baby-sitter is likely to be the daughter of the proprietor. Rates are low. Remember to request a baby-sitter no later than in the morning if you're going out that evening.

BUSINESS HOURS: Most shops are open Monday through Friday from 9am to 1pm and 3 to 7pm, Saturday from 9am to 1pm. Business offices are generally open Monday through Friday from 9am to 1pm and 3 to 5:30pm (sometimes 6pm). The majority of banks are open Monday to Friday from 8:30am to 3:30pm.

CAMPING AND CARAVANS: Portugal provides parks for campers and house trailers (caravans) near beaches and in wooded areas all over the country. Some have swimming pools, athletic fields, markets, and restaurants among other facilities, while many are simply convenient sites with water and toilets away from the hustle and bustle of cities and towns. For a guide to such parks, their classification, equipment, and capacity, get in touch with **Federação Portuguesa de Campismo e Caravanismo,** 5 de Outubro 15, 1000 Lisboa (tel. 01/52-33-08), or ask your travel agent.

CIGARETTES: The price of American-brand cigarettes (which varies) is always lethal. Bring in at least 200 cigarettes as allowed by Customs. If you're saving money, try one of the Portuguese brands as an adventure. Many smokers have found Portuguese tobacco excellent.

CLIMATE: See "When to Go" in this chapter for information and a temperature chart.

CURRENCY: See "Information, Entry Requirements, and Money" in this chapter.

CUSTOMS: You may be asked how much tobacco you're bringing in; the limit is 200 cigarettes or 50 cigars. One still camera with five unexposed rolls of film is allowed duty free; also a small movie camera with two reels, a portable tape recorder, a portable record player, a portable musical instrument, and a bicycle (not motor bikes). Campers and sporting types are allowed to bring in one tent and camping accessories (including a kayak not exceeding 18 feet), a pair of skis, two tennis rackets, a tackle set, and a small firearm (for hunting only) with 50 bullets. A normal-size bottle of wine and a half pint of hard alcohol are permitted, as are a "small quantity" of perfume and a half pint of toilet water.

Upon leaving Portugal, citizens of the United States who have been outside the U.S. for 48 hours or more are allowed to bring in $400 worth of merchandise duty free—that is, if they have claimed no similar exemption within the past 30 days. Beyond this free allowance, the next $1,000 worth of merchandise is assessed at a flat rate of 10% duty. If you make purchases in Portugal, it's important to keep your receipts. On gifts, the duty-free limit is $50.

DRUGSTORES: The Portuguese government requires selected pharmacies (*farmácias*) to stay open at all times of the day and night. This is effected by means of a rotation system. Check with your concierge for locations and hours of the nearest drugstores, called *farmácias de serviço*. In general, pharmacies in Portugal are open Monday to Friday from 9am to 1pm and 3 to 7pm, Saturday from 9am to 1pm; closed Sunday.

ELECTRICITY: Many North Americans find that their plugs will not fit into sockets in Portugal or Spain, where the voltage is 200 volts AC, 50 cycles. In the unlikely event that you managed to force the plug of your appliance into the outlet, you would destroy your appliance, upset the hotel management, and possibly cause a fire. Don't try. Many hardware stores in North America sell the appropriate converters, and the concierge desks of most hotels will either lend you a converter and adapter or tell you where you can buy one nearby. If you have any doubt about whether you have the appropriate converter, ask questions at your hotel desk before you try to plug anything in.

EMBASSIES AND CONSULATES: If you lose your passport or have some other pressing problem, you'll need to get in touch with the **U.S. Embassy,** on the Avenida das Forças Armadas (Sete Rios), 1600 Lisboa (tel. 01/726-66-00). Hours are 8:30am to 12:30pm and 1:30 to 5:30pm Monday to Friday. If you've lost a passport, a photographer will be recommended who can provide the proper size photos for American passports.

The **Canadian Embassy** is at Avenida da Liberdade 144 and 156, 1200 Lisboa (tel. 01/347-48-92), and is open Monday to Friday from 8:30am to 12:15pm and 1:30 to 5pm.

The **British Embassy,** 37 Rua São Domingos a Lapa, 1200 Lisboa (tel. 01/396-1122), is open Monday to Friday from 9:30am to 12:30pm and 3 to 5pm.

The **Embassy of the Republic of Ireland,** Rua de Imprensa A. Estrela s/n, 1200 Lisboa (tel. 01/396-1569), is open Monday to Friday from 9:30am to noon and 2:30 to 4:30pm.

The **Australian Embassy,** Avenida da Liberdade 244 (second floor), 1200 Lisboa (tel. 01/52-33-50), is open Monday to Friday from 9am to noon.

New Zealand does not maintain an embassy in Portugal.

EMERGENCIES: For the police (or for an ambulance) in Lisbon, telephone 115. In case of fire, call 32-22-22 or 60-60-60. The Portuguese Red Cross can be reached at 61-77-77. The national emergency number in Portugal is 115.

ETIQUETTE: In general, Portugal is considered a polite country. Women often kiss each other once on both cheeks when they meet. Men extend a hand when introduced; if they are good friends, they will often embrace. All services require a visitor to say thank you—*obrigado* for a man and *obrigada* for a woman. "Please" is *por favor.* It's customary to greet people with a *bom dia* in the morning, a *boa tarde* in the afternoon, and a *boa noite* in the evening. Always bring flowers—not wine—if you're invited to someone's home. Stretching—either at the dining table or on the street—for some reason is considered extremely impolite.

FILM: This is so expensive that I suggest you bring in all that Customs will allow. There are no special restrictions on taking photographs, except in certain museums.

HOLIDAYS: See "When to Go" in this chapter.

INFORMATION: See "Information, Entry Requirements, and Money," in this chapter, as well as individual city chapters for local information offices.

LANGUAGE: See "Language" in this chapter.

LAUNDRY: Most hotels in this guide provide laundry services, but if you want your garment returned on the same day, you'll often be charged from 20% to 40% more. Simply present your maid or valet with your laundry or dry cleaning (usually lists are provided). *Note:* Materials needing special treatment (such as certain synthetics) should be called to the attention of the person handling your laundry. Some establishments I've dealt with in the past treated every fabric as if it were cotton.

LIQUOR LAWS: You have to be 18 years of age to drink. Liquor is sold in most markets, as opposed to the package stores in most of the United States. In Lisbon you can drink until dawn. There's always some bar or fado club open serving alcoholic beverages.

MAIL: While in Portugal you may have your mail directed to your hotel (or hotels), to the American Express representative, or to General Delivery *(Poste Restante)* in Lisbon. Your passport must be presented for mail pickups. The general post office in Lisbon is at Praça do Comércio (tel. 01/34-752-41 or 01/37-20-07).

MAPS: If you'd like a map before your trip to plan your itinerary, you can obtain one from Rand McNally, Michelin, or the AAA. These are sold at bookstores all over America. **Rand McNally** has retail stores at 150 E. 52nd St., New York, NY 10022 (tel. 212/758-7488); at 23 E. Madison St., Chicago, IL 60602 (tel. 312/332-4627); and at 595 Market St., San Francisco, CA 94105 (tel. 415/777-3131). The U.S. headquarters of **Michelin** is at P.O. Box 3305, Spartanburg, SC 29304 (tel. 803/599-0850, or toll free 800/423-0485).

NEWSPAPERS/MAGAZINES: The *International Herald Tribune* is sold at most newsstands in Lisbon and in most big cities and resorts, either in major hotels or along the street. If you read Portuguese, the most popular centrist newspaper is the influential *Diário de Notícias.* To the right of center is *O Dia,* to the left of center is *O'Dario*. The European editions of *Time* and *Newsweek* are sold at most major newsstands.

PASSPORTS: See "Information, Entry Requirements, and Money" in this chapter.

PETS: Pets brought into Portugal must have the OK of the local veterinarian and a health certificate from the home country.

RADIO/TV: In Lisbon there are two major TV channels—**Channel 1 (VHF)** and **Channel 11 (UHF)**. Many foreign films are shown, often in English with Portuguese subtitles.

RELIGIOUS SERVICES: Portugal is a Catholic country, and there are places of worship in every city, town, and village.

REST ROOMS: All major terminals (airports and railways) have such facilities, and Lisbon has several public ones. However, you can often use the rest room at a café or tavern, as there is one on practically every block. It is considered polite to purchase something, however—perhaps a small glass of wine or whatever.

SAFETY: Whenever you're traveling in an unfamiliar city or country, stay alert. Be aware of your immediate surroundings. Wear a moneybelt and don't sling your camera or purse over your shoulder. This will minimize the possibility of your becoming a victim of crime. Every society has its criminals. It's your responsibility to be aware and be alert even in the most heavily touristed areas.

TAXES: Since Portugal and neighboring Spain simultaneously joined the European Economic Community (EEC), or Common Market, on January 1, 1986, Portugal has imposed a value-added tax on most purchases made within its borders. Known in Portugal as the **IVA**, its amount is almost always written into the bottom line of the bill for any purchase a foreign visitor might make. Hotel bills are taxed at 8%. Car rentals automatically include an additional 17% tax (less than in some other European countries). Such deluxe goods as jewelry, furs, and expensive imported liquors include a 30% built-in tax. Because a scotch and soda in a Portuguese bar carries this high tax, many imbibers have changed their choice of alcohol from scotch to Portuguese brandy and soda, or, more prosaically, beer.

To get a refund of the IVA tax on those purchases that qualify (ask the shopkeeper), present your passport to the salesperson and ask for the special, stamped form. Present the form with your purchases at the booth marked for IVA tax refunds at the airport. You will get your money refunded right there at the booth.

TELEGRAMS/TELEX/FAX: At most hotels, the receptionist will help you send one of these messages. Otherwise, go to the nearest post office in Portugal for assistance.

TELEPHONES: Calling from **pay-phone booths** in Portugal, providing you have the right change, will allow you to avoid high hotel surcharges. Most booths take 2$5, 5$, and 25$ coins. Put the coins in a slot at the top of the box while you hold the receiver, then dial your number after you hear the dial tone. Once a connection is made, the necessary coins will automatically drop. If enough coins are not available, your connection will be broken. A warning tone will sound and a light over the dial will go on in case more coins are needed. For **long-distance** (trunk) calls within the country, dial the right trunk code, followed by the number you want.

Telephone calls can also be made at all post offices, which will also send telegrams. Calls to Europe are made by dialing 00, followed by the country code, the area code (not prefaced by 0), then the phone number. The country code for the United States and Canada is 1.

TIME: Portugal is 6 hours ahead of the United States (eastern standard time). For the local time in Lisbon, phone 15.

TIPPING: Portugal has now caught up with the rest of Western Europe. Most service personnel expect a good tip rather than a small one, as in former times.

The hotels add a service charge (known as *serviço*), which is divided among the entire staff. But individual tipping is also the rule of the day: 50$ (35¢) to the bellhop for errands run, 50$ (35¢) to the doorman who calls you a cab, 100$ (65¢) to 200$ ($1.35) to the porter for each piece of luggage carried, 500$ ($3.35) to the wine steward if you've dined often at your hotel, and 300$ ($2) to the chambermaid.

In first-class or deluxe hotels the concierge will present you with a separate bill, outlining your little or big extras, such as charges for bullfight tickets, etc. A gratuity is expected in addition to the charge, the amount depending entirely on the number of requests you've put to him or her.

For a normal haircut, you should leave 100$ (65¢) behind as a tip to the barber. But if your hair is cut at the Ritz, don't dare leave less than 200$ ($1.35). Beauticians get 150$ ($1); a manicurist, around 150$ ($1) also.

Figure on tipping about 20% of your taxi fare for short runs. For longer treks—for example, from the airport to Cascais—15% is adequate.

Restaurants and nightclubs include a service charge and government taxes. As in hotels, this service is distributed among the entire staff, including the waiter's mistress and the owner's grandfather—so extra tipping is customary. Add about 5% to the bill in a moderately priced restaurant, up to 10% in a deluxe or first-class establishment.

For hatcheck in fado houses, restaurants, and nightclubs, tip at least 100$ (65¢). Washroom attendants usually get no more than 25$ (15¢). The shoeshine attendants of Portugal get 100$ (65¢) per shine.

GETTING TO KNOW LISBON

1. ORIENTATION
2. GETTING AROUND
3. FAST FACTS: LISBON
4. NETWORKS & RESOURCES

In its golden age it was called the eighth wonder of the world. Travelers returning from a trip to Lisbon reported that its riches rivaled those of Venice.

As one of the greatest maritime centers in history, the Portuguese capital has enjoyed exotic riches from the far-flung corners of its empire. Aside from the wealth of cultural influences, Lisbon stockpiled goods, beginning with its earliest contacts with the Calicut and Malabar coasts. Treasures from Asia brought in on Chinese junks to Indian seaports eventually found their way back to Lisbon: porcelain, luxurious silks, rubies, pearls, and other rare gems. The abundance and variety of spices from the East—tea, indigo, turmeric, ginger, pepper, coconut, cumin, betel—were to rival even Keats's vision of "silken Samarkand."

From the wilds of the Americas came red dye-wood (brazilwood), coffee, gold (discovered in 1698), diamonds (unearthed in 1729), and gemstones. All this extensive contact signaled a new era in world trade, with Lisbon sitting at the center of a great maritime empire, the hub of commerce between Europe, Africa, and Asia.

HISTORY IN BRIEF

Many Lisboans claim unabashedly that Ulysses founded their city. Others, more scholarly, maintain that the Phoenicians or the Carthaginians were the original settlers. The body of the country's patron saint, Vincent, is said to have arrived in Portugal on an abandoned boat, with only two ravens to guide it. It is further alleged that the birds lived in the cathedral tower until as late as the 19th century.

The Romans settled in Lisbon in the 1st century B.C., building a fortification on what is now St. George's Castle. The city was captured by the Visigoths in the 5th century A.D., a conquest later followed by long centuries of Moorish domination beginning in A.D. 714. The first king of Portugal, Afonso Henriques, captured Lisbon in 1147. But it wasn't until 1256 that King Afonso III moved the capital there, deserting Coimbra, the major university city of Portugal.

The Great Earthquake

"From Scotland to Asia Minor, people ran out of doors and looked at the sky, and fearfully waited. It was, of course, an earthquake," as once chronicled a *Holiday* article. Tidal waves, 50 feet high, swept over Algeciras, Spain. The capitals of Europe shook.

It was 9:40 on the morning of All Saints' Day, November 1, 1755. The churches were packed to overflowing; smoky tapers and incense burned upon the altars. After the initial shock, 22 spasms followed. Roofs caved in; hospitals (with more than 1,000 patients), prisons, public buildings, royal palaces, aristocratic town houses, fishermen's cottages, churches, and houses of prostitution—all were toppled. Overturned candles helped ignite a fire that would consume the once-proud capital in six days, leaving it a gutted, charred shambles. Voltaire described the destruction in *Candide:* "The sea boiled up in the harbor and smashed the vessels lying at anchor. Whirlwinds of flame and ashes covered the streets and squares, houses collapsed, roofs were thrown onto foundations and the foundations crumbled." All told, 30,000 inhabitants were crushed beneath the tumbling debris.

When the survivors of the initial shocks ran from their burning homes toward the mighty Tagus, they were met with walls of water 40 feet high. Estimates vary, but the final tally of all who died in drownings and the 6-day holocaust that followed is put at around 60,000.

Voltaire cynically commented on the aftermath of the disaster, particularly the *auto-da-fé* that followed: "It was decided by the University of Coimbra that the sight of several people being slowly burned with great ceremony was an infallible means of preventing the earth from quaking."

After the ashes had settled, the Marquês de Pombal, the prime minister, ordered that the dead be buried, the city rebuilt at once. To accomplish that ambitious plan, the king gave him the power of a virtual dictator.

What Pombal ordered constructed was a city of wide, symmetrical boulevards leading into handsome squares dominated by fountains and statuary. Bordering these wide avenues would be black-and-white mosaic sidewalks, the most celebrated in Europe.

LISBON TODAY

The mixture of the old (pre-earthquake) and the new (post-earthquake) was done so harmoniously that travelers today consider Lisbon one of the most beautiful cities on earth. Under a stark blue sky, the city's medley of pastel-washed houses dazzles, like a city in North Africa. The Tagus, the river flowing through Lisbon, has been called the city's "eternal lover."

Sea gulls take flight from its harbor, where trawlers from Africa unload their freight. Pigeons sweep down on Praça do Comércio, also known as Black Horse Square. From the Bairro Alto (upper city), cable cars carry Lisbon's denizens down to the waterfront. The sidewalks are characteristic black-and-white mosaics forming arabesques. Streets bear colorful names or designations, such as the Rua do Açúcar (Street of Sugar). Fountains abound: One, the Samaritan, dates from the 16th century. Wide, symmetrical boulevards split through the city to new high-rise apartment houses, while in other quarters laundry hanging from 18th-century houses laps the wind.

It is a city that gives nicknames to everything from its districts (the Chiado, named after a poet) to its kings. Fernando, who built one of the most characteristic walls around Lisbon, was honored with the appellation "The Beautiful."

Many who have never actually been to Lisbon know it well from watching World War II spy movies on late-night television. It would be only natural, you'd assume, to see Hedy Lamarr slinking around the corner any moment. During World War II, Lisbon, officially neutral, was a hot-bed of intrigue and espionage. It was also a haven for thousands of refugees. Many of those—such as deposed royalty—remained, settling into villas in Estoril and Sintra.

1. Orientation

ARRIVING

By Plane

Both foreign and domestic flights land at Lisbon's **Portela Airport,** which lies about 4 miles from the heart of the city. For all airport information, telephone 01/80-20-60. A Green Line bus, known as the *Linha Verde,* carries passengers into the city for 200$ ($1.35) for one zone. The bus goes as far as the Santa Apolónia Rail Station. Service is daily every 15 minutes from 7am to 9:20pm. There is no charge for luggage. You can also go by taxi. Passengers queue up, British style, in a usually well-organized line at the sidewalk in front of the airport. The average taxi fare from the airport to central Lisbon is 1,200$ ($8.05), including a surcharge for your suitcases and a tip.

For ticket sales, flight reservations, information about the city and the country, you can get in touch with the polite personnel of TAP Air Portugal at Praça Marquês de Pombal 3A (tel. 01/57-50-20, the airline's reservation number), in Lisbon.

By Train

Most international rail passengers from Madrid and Paris arrive at the **Santa Apolónia Station,** the major terminal of Lisbon, lying by the Tagus near the Alfama district. Two daily trains make the 10-hour run from Madrid to Lisbon. Rail lines from northern and eastern Portugal also arrive at this station. Other rail terminals include **Rossio,** where you can get trains to Sintra, and the **Cais do Sodré,** with trains to Cascais and Estoril on the Costa do Sol. At a final station, **Sul e Sueste,** you can board trains to the Algarve. For all rail information, at any of the terminals above, call 01/87-60-25.

By Bus

Buses from all over Portugal, including the Algarve, arrive at the **Rodoviária Nacional,** Avenida Casal Ribeiro 18 (tel. 01/53-77-15), which lies near Praça Salhanha, about a 30-minute walk from the Praça dos Restauradores. Buses no. 1, 21, and 32 will deliver you to the Rossio, and bus no. 1 goes on to the Cais do Sodré, if you're checked into a hotel at Estoril or Cascais. At least three buses a day leave from Faro, capital on the Algarve, and two *expressos* (express buses) head north every day to Porto. There are 14 daily buses leaving from here to Coimbra, the university city in the north.

Daily buses run between Madrid and Lisbon (trip time: 10 hours). For more information contact **Rodoviária Nacional,** Avenida Columbano Bordalo Pinheiro 86 (tel. 01/72-67-123 in Lisbon).

By Car

International motorists must arrive through Spain, the only nation connected to Portugal via road links. You'll have to cross Spanish border points, usually of no great difficulty. Roads are moderately well maintained. From Madrid, if you head west, the main road (N620) from Tordesillas goes southwest by way of Salamanca and Ciudad Rodrigo to reach the Portuguese frontier at Fuentes de Ónoro.

If you have a rented car, make sure that your insurance covers Portugal. Driving is on the right side of the road, and international signs and symbols are used in Portugal. There are 15 border crossings, and most of them are open daily from 7am to midnight.

CITY LAYOUT

Now in its seventh century as the center of the Portuguese nation, Lisbon is the westernmost capital of continental Europe. Part of its legend is that it spreads across seven hills, like Rome. If that statement were ever true, it has long since become historical, as Lisbon now sprawls across more hills than that. Most of it lies on the right bank of the Tagus.

No one ever claimed that getting around Lisbon was easy. Streets rise and fall across the legendary seven hills, at times dwindling into mere alleyways. But exploring it is well worth the effort.

Lisbon is best approached through its gateway, the **Praça do Comércio,** bordering the Tagus. Like a formal parlor, it is one of the most perfectly planned squares in Europe, rivaled perhaps only by the Piazza dell'Unità d'Italia in Trieste, Italy. Before the earthquake of 1755, Commerce Square was known as Terreiro do Paço, the palace grounds, as the king and his court lived in now-destroyed buildings on that site. To further confuse matters, English-speaking residents often refer to it as Black Horse Square, so named because of its statue (actually a bronze green) of King José I.

Today the square houses the Stock Exchange and various ministries of government. Its center is used as a parking lot, which destroys some of the harmonious effect of its praça. In 1908 its most monumental event occurred, the reverberations of which were heard around the world. King Carlos I and his elder son, Luís Filipe, were fatally shot by an assassin. It would hold on for another 2 years under the rule of a younger prince, but the House of Bragança came to an end that day on Black Horse Square.

Directly west of the square stands the City Hall, fronting the **Praça do Município.** The building was erected in the latter 19th century by the architect Domingos Parente.

Heading north from Black Horse or Commerce Square, you enter the hustle-bustle of the Praça Dom Pedro IV, popularly known as the **Rossio.** The "drunken" undulation of the sidewalks, with their arabesques of black and white, have led to the appellation, used mainly by tourists, of "the dizzy praça." Here you can sit, sipping strong unblended coffee from the former Portuguese provinces in Africa, while a boy gives you one of the cheapest and slickest shoeshines in Europe. The statue on the square is that of the emperor of Brazil, Pedro IV, himself a Portuguese.

Opening onto the Rossio is the **Teatro Nacional Dona Maria II,** a freestanding building whose facade has been preserved. In 1967–70, workmen gutted the interior to rebuild it completely. If you arrive by train, you'll enter the **Estação do Rossio,** whose Manueline architectural exuberance is a worthy sight.

Separating the Rossio from the Avenida da Liberdade is the **Praça dos Restauradores,** named in honor of the restoration—that is, when the Portuguese chose their own king and freed themselves from 60 years of rule by Spain. That event is marked by an obelisk.

The main avenue of Lisbon is the **Avenida da Liberdade,** a handsomely laid-out street dating from 1880, and once called the antechamber of Lisbon. The Avenue of Liberty is like a mile-long park, with shade trees, gardens, and center walks for the promenading crowds. Flanking it are some of the finest shops, headquarters for many major airlines, travel agents, coffeehouses with sidewalk tables, and such important hotels as the Tivoli. The comparable street in Paris would be the Champs Élysées; in Rome, the Via Veneto.

At the top of the avenue is the **Praça Marquês de Pombal,** with a statue erected in honor of Pombal, the 18th-century prime minister credited with the reconstruction of Lisbon in the aftermath of the earthquake.

Proceeding north, you'll enter the splendid **Parque Eduardo VII,** named to honor the son of Queen Victoria, who paid a state visit to Lisbon. In the park is the **Estufa Fria,** a greenhouse that is well worth a visit.

Neighborhoods in Brief

BAIXA The business district of Lisbon is called Baixa, its architecture characterized as Pombaline, referring to the 18th-century prime minister again. Many of the major Portuguese banks have their headquarters here. Running south, the main street of Baixa separates the Praça do Comércio from the Rossio. In fact, a triumphal arch leads from the square to the **Rua Augusta,** where there are many clothing stores. The two most important streets of Baixa are the Street of Silver (Rua da Prata) and the Street of Gold (Rua do Ouro), now called Rua Aurea, both taking their names from the silver- and goldsmiths whose shops were (and still are) found there.

CHIADO If you head west from Baixa, you'll enter a shopping district known as the Chiado. From its perch on a hill, it is traversed by the **Rua Garrett,** honoring the Portuguese poet and dandy of the 19th century. Many of the finest shops in the city, such as the Vista Alegre, a china and porcelain house, are here. One coffeehouse in particular, A Brasileira, has been a traditional gathering spot for the Portuguese literati.

BAIRRO ALTO Continuing your ascent, you arrive at the Bairro Alto (the upper city). This sector, reached by trolley car, occupies one of the legendary seven hills of Lisbon. Many of its buildings were left fairly intact by the 1755 earthquake. Containing much of the charm and color of the Alfama, it is of interest mainly because it is the center of some of the finest fado cafés in Lisbon, including A Severa and Lisboa a Noite. In addition, some of the best restaurants in the city are found here, as well as unpretentious taverns featuring hearty Portuguese cuisine.

ALFAMA East of the Praça do Comércio lies the oldest district of Lisbon, the Alfama. For a more detailed description of this section, refer to Chapter 7. Saved only in part from the devastation of the earthquake, the Alfama was the Moorish sector of the capital. Centuries later, before the earthquake struck, it was the residential district of aristocrats. Nowadays it is occupied mainly by stevedores, plus fishermen and their barefoot *varinas* (fishwives).

Overlooking the Alfama is **St. George's Castle,** once a Visigothic fortification, and later used by the Romans. Destroyed and rebuilt so many times that its history is a jumble, the present castle dates from the 12th century.

On the way to the Alfama, on the Rua dos Bacalheiros, stands the **Casa dos Bicos** (the House of the Pointed Stones). This early 16th-century town house, not open to the public, is graced with a facade studded with diamond-shaped stones. And while it was partially demolished by the earthquake, it remains an impressive sight.

BELÉM In the west, on the coastal road to Estoril, is the suburb of Belém (Bethlehem). It contains some of the finest monuments in Portugal, a few of which were built during the Age of Discovery, near the point where the caravels set out to conquer new worlds (at Belém, the Tagus reaches the sea). At one time, before the earthquake, Belém was an aristocratic sector filled with elegant town houses.

Two of the principal attractions in all of Portugal stand here: the **Jerónimos Monastery,** erected in the 16th century in the Manueline style, and the **National Coach Museum,** the finest of its kind in the world. Actually, Belém is Lisbon's museumland, containing the **Museum of Popular Art,** the **Ethnological Museum,** and the galley-stuffed **Naval Museum.**

CACILHAS On the south side of the Tagus, where puce-colored smoke billows out from the factories, is the left-bank settlement of Cacilhas. It is inhabited mainly by the working class, yet visited by right-bank denizens for its seafood restaurants, such as the Floresta (see Chapter 6). You can reach the settlement by way of a bridge or by taking a ferryboat across, leaving from Praça do Comércio.

Of course the most dramatic way to cross the Tagus is on the **Ponte 25 de Abril,** the longest and most expensive suspension bridge ever erected in Europe, the total outlay exceeding $75 million. The bridge opened up that sector of Portugal lying south of the Tagus. Its towers peaking at 625 feet, the bridge is 7,473 feet long. Standing guard on the left bank is a monumental statue of Christ with his arms outstretched.

Street Maps

Arm yourself with a good map before setting out. The best one is published by **Falk,** and it's available at most newsstands and kiosks in Lisbon. Those given away free by tourist offices and hotels aren't adequate, as they don't list the maze of little streets.

Finding an Address

Finding an address in the old quarters of Lisbon is difficult, as street numbering at times follows no predictable pattern. Therefore, when trying to locate some obscure address, always ask for the nearest cross street before setting out. That will save you much time and frustration.

Addresses consist of a street name followed by a number. Sometimes the floor of the building is given as well: Avenida Casal Ribeiro 18-3°. That means that the building is at number 18, but the particular address is on the third floor. However, in Lisbon the ground floor is not called the first floor as in the United States. So, for Americans the third floor is actually the fourth floor. "ESP" after a floor number indicates that you should go left, and "DIR" means head for the right of any floor.

---

2. Getting Around

Public transport is inexpensive but inadequate at times. Yet considering the hilly terrain of the city and the fact that many of the streets were designed for donkey carts, the Portuguese manage very well. However, even the most skilled chauffeurs have been known to scrape the fenders of their clients' rented limousines while maneuvering through the narrow alleyways.

A lot of the city can be walked, especially by those adept at hill climbing. However, to get from one point to the other—say, from the Alfama to the suburb of Belém—you'll need public transport or your own car.

Evamarie Doering of Belmont, California, writes: "In the 15 years since my last visit there, Lisbon has become one of the noisiest cities I've ever visited. Traffic is outrageous; driving is difficult because of the speed and the tendency of the natives to ride six inches from your rear bumper. The buses, of which there are a great many, are *very* noisy, and produce volumes of smoke. Honking of car horns seems to be a national pastime."

BY ELECTRIC TRAIN

Lisbon is connected with all the towns and villages along the Portuguese Riviera by a smooth-running electric train system. You can board the train at the waterfront **Cais do Sodré** station in Lisbon, heading up the coast all the way to Cascais.

Only one class of seat is offered, and the rides are cheap. Sintra, that third major destination in the environs, is not reached by the electric train. You must go to the **Estação do Rossio** station, opening onto the Praça Dom Pedro IV or the Rossio, where frequent connections can be made. The one-way fare is one class only. On the Lisbon-Cascais, Lisbon-Estoril, or Lisbon-Sintra run, the one-way fare is 135$ (90¢) per person.

BY SUBWAY

Lisbon's Metro stations are designated by large M signs, and the system blankets 24 stations. A single ticket costs 55$ (35¢) per ride if you purchase it from a vending machine, 45$ (30¢) if purchased from a toll booth. You can purchase 10 tickets at one time at a toll booth, each ticket costing 42$50 (30¢). Ten tickets purchased at a vending machine will sell for only 40$ (25¢) each. One of the most popular trips, and likely to be jam-packed on *corrida* (bullfight) days, is from the Avenida da Liberdade to the Campo Pequeno, the brick building away from the center of the city. Service is daily from 6:30am to 1am.

BY TRAM & BUS

These are among the cheapest in Europe. The trolley cars, such as those that make the steep run up to the Bairro Alto, are usually painted a rich Roman gold. The double-decker buses, on the other hand, come from London and look as if they need

Big Ben in the background to complete the picture. If you're trying to stand on the platform at the back of a jammed bus, by the way, you'll need both hands free to hold on.

At the foot of the Santa Justa elevator, lying on the Rua Aurea, a stand will give you a schedule pinpointing the zigzagging route of these trams and buses. Your hotel concierge should be of help to you also.

You will pay a flat fare of 125$ (85¢) on a bus if you buy the ticket from the driver. The transportation system within the city limits is divided into zones ranging from one to five. The price of your fare depends upon how many zones you traverse. You can purchase a book of 10 tickets called *módulos*. If so, depending on the number of zones traveled, your fare will range from 28$ (20¢) to 84$ (55¢).

On a streetcar a ticket purchased from a driver costs 105$ (70¢). However, prepurchased *módulos* mean rides ranging from 28$ (20¢) to 56$ (40¢), depending on the number of zones traveled.

BY TAXI

Taxis in Lisbon tend to be inexpensive and are a popular means of transport for all but the most economy-minded of tourists. The taxis usually are diesel-engined Mercedes, charging a basic fare of 130$ (85¢) for the first 480 yards. After that, you'll be assessed another 6$ (5¢) for each additional 117 yards, with 20% additional for night fare from 10pm to 6am. The driver is allowed by law to tack on another 50% to your bill if your luggage weighs more than 66 pounds. If you travel outside Lisbon, the driver is allowed to charge you 43$ (30¢) per kilometer. Most Portuguese tip about 20% of an already-modest fare.

Many visitors stay at one of the Costa do Sol resort hotels, such as the Palácio in Estoril and the Cidadela in Cascais. If that is your situation, then you'll probably find taxi connections from Lisbon prohibitively expensive. Far preferable for Costa do Sol visitors is the electric train system (see above).

BY ELEVATOR CAR & FUNICULAR

The **Santa Justa Elevator,** just south of Rossio Square, is one of the most convenient methods of transportation in the city, as it links Rua do Ouro with Praça do Carmo, otherwise a steep climb. A one-way fare is 25$ (15¢). Lisbon also has a trio of funiculars, including the Glória, going from Praça dos Restauradores to Rua São Pedro de Alcantara; the Bica, from the Calçada do Combro to Rua do Boavista; and the Lavra, going from the eastern side of the Avenida da Liberdade to Campo Mártires da Pátria. A one-way ticket costs 25$ (15¢).

BY FERRYBOAT

Long before the Ponte 25 de Abril (see below) was built, reliable ferryboats chugged across the Tagus, connecting the left bank with the right. They still do, and are as popular as ever, as many Portuguese find the bridge too expensive to cross with their automobiles. Therefore they leave their cars at home and take the ferryboat to work.

Most of the boats leave from the Praça do Comércio, heading for Barreiro and Cacilhas. On the Lisbon-Cacilhas ferryboat, the single fare is 75$ (50¢) one-way. However, if you purchase your ticket from a vending machine, the cost is reduced to 70$ (45¢). If you plan to make several trips back and forth across the river, you can buy a block of 20 módulos. If you use two módulos on each trip, the cost of the fare is reduced to 56$ (40¢) per one-way passage.

BY PONTE 25 DE ABRIL

As mentioned, this suspension bridge, the largest ever built in Europe, connects Lisbon with its left bank and the district south of the Tagus. For a small car, the toll charge is 45$ (30¢), increasing to 100$ (65¢) for a larger automobile. Not only can you take the bridge to reach Cacilhas, but you can use it for such cities as Setúbal in the south, and Évora, the old Roman city in the east.

SPECIAL TOURIST PASSES

Tickets valid for 4 to 7 days of travel on all the city's trams, the Metro, buses, funicular, and the Santa Justa Elevator costs 1,000$ ($6.70) or 1,400$ ($9.40), respectively. These discount passes may be purchased daily at the Santa Justa Elevator, just south of Rossio Square.

BY FOOT

Central Lisbon is relatively compact and because of heavy traffic is best explored by foot. That is virtually the only way to see such districts as the Alfama. However, when you venture farther afield, such as to Belém, you'll need to depend on some of the public transportation outlined.

BY CAR

Driving is extremely difficult in congested Lisbon and potentially dangerous, as the city has an alarmingly high accident rate. It always feels like rush hour in Lisbon (theoretically, hours are from 8am to 10am, 1 to 2pm, and 4 to 6pm Monday through Saturday). Parking is seemingly impossible. Save your car rentals for making excursions from the capital. If you drive into Lisbon from another town or city, call ahead and ask at your hotel for the nearest garage or parking possibility. Leave your vehicle there until you're ready to depart Lisbon.

Car Rentals

The major international car-rental companies are represented in Lisbon, charging a base minimum rate of 4,200$ ($28.15) per day, although this charge varies widely. Car-rental kiosks are found at the airport or else you can rent from one of the offices in the center.

These include **Avis,** Avenida Praia da Vitória 12 (tel. 01/56-11-77), open daily from 8am to 7pm, and **Hertz,** Rua Tomás Ribeiro 50 (tel. 01/53-98-16), open Monday through Friday from 9am to 6:30pm. **Europcar,** Avenida António Augusto de Aguiar 24 (tel. 01/53-51-15), is open Monday through Saturday from 8am to 8pm and Sunday from 2 to 6:30pm.

Gasoline

Lisbon is well stocked with garages and gasoline pumps; some are open around the clock.

---

3. Fast Facts: Lisbon

The concierge in your hotel is a usually reliable dispenser of information, bullfight tickets, and general advice. However, should your hotel not be staffed with an English-speaking person, or should you desire more detailed answers to your questions, the following brief summary of basic information about Lisbon may prove helpful.

AMERICAN EXPRESS: Star is the representative of American Express in Portugal, and it will hold or forward mail for you, providing you are a client. There, too, you can buy tickets for tours, exchange currency, and, of course, cash American Express traveler's checks. Its offices are at Avenida Sidónio Pais 4A (tel. 051/53-98-71). It's open Monday to Friday from 9am to 12:30pm and 2 to 6pm. The main office is near Pombal Square and easily reached by bus.

AREA CODE: The area code for Lisbon, Sintra, Estoril, and Cascais is 01.

BABY-SITTERS: Most first-class hotels can provide competent baby-sitters from lists that the concierge keeps. At small establishments, the sitter is likely to be a relative of the proprietor. Rates are low. Remember to request a baby-sitter early—no later than the morning if you're planning on going out that evening. If you get a sitter fluent in English, count yourself lucky.

BANKS: What bank to use? Check with your home bank before your departure as many banks in Canada and the United States have affiliates in Lisbon. The majority of the banks open at 8:30am, closing at 3pm Monday to Friday. Three major banks include **Banco Português do Atlântico,** Rua Aurea 112 (tel. 01/34-61-321); the **Banco Expírito Santo e Comercial de Lisboa,** Avenida da Liberdade 195 (tel. 01/54-12-18); and at the airport a branch of **Banco Totta & Açores** (tel. 01/34-26-222), which is open at all hours of the day and night, including holidays. More banks in Lisbon offer night service. For example, the **Banco Borges & Irmão,** Avenida da Liberdade 9A (tel. 01/34-21-068), is open Monday to Friday from 6 to 11pm, and the **Banco Pinto & Sotto Mayor,** Praça dos Restauradores (tel. 01/34-26-222), is open Monday to Friday from 3 to 7:30pm.

CLIMATE: See "When to Go" in Chapter 3.

CRIME: See "Safety," below.

CURRENCY EXCHANGE: See "American Express" and "Banks," above. There is also a currency exchange booth at Santa Apolónia station and at the airport—both open 24 hours a day. The post office (see below) will also exchange money.

DENTIST: If it's dental attention you need, place a call to Centro de Medicina Dentaria, Calçada Bento da Rocha Cabral (tel. 01/68-41-91). Some of the dentists there speak English.

DOCUMENTS FOR ENTRY: See "Information, Entry Requirements, and Money" in Chapter 3.

DRUGSTORES: A central and well-stocked one is **Farmácia Azevedo,** Rossio 31 (tel. 01/34-27-478). Pharmacies that are closed post a notice indicating the nearest one that's open.

ELECTRIC CURRENT: See "Fast Facts: Portugal" in Chapter 3.

EMBASSIES AND CONSULATES: See "Fast Facts: Portugal" in Chapter 3.

EMERGENCIES: To call the **police** (or for an **ambulance**) in Lisbon, telephone 115. In case of **fire,** call 01/32-22-22. The **Portuguese Red Cross** is reached at 01/30-17-777.

HAIRDRESSERS/BARBERS: Men can go to any of the big **barbershops** in the deluxe hotels, such as the Ritz in Lisbon. For women, three **hairdressers** in Lisbon are particularly recommended: Cabeleireiro Martins, 31-1° Avenida Defensores de Chaves (tel. 01/54-89-33); Cabeleireiro Isabel Queiroz do Vale, 35-1° Avenida

Fontes Pereira de Melo (tel. 01/54-82-38); and Lúcia Piloto, Avenida da Liberdade 12 (tel. 01/34-20-535).

HOSPITALS: In case of a medical emergency, ask at your hotel or call your embassy and ask the staff there to recommend a physician who speaks English; or try the **British Hospital,** Rua Savaiva Carvalho 49 (tel. 01/60-20-20), where the telephone operator, staff, and doctors all speak English, of course.

INFORMATION: The **Portuguese National Tourist Board** is at Avenida António Augusto de Aguiar 86 in Lisbon (tel. 01/31-55-091). The **Instituto de Promoção Turística** (Portuguese Council for Tourist Promotion), Rua Alexandre Herculano 51 (tel. 01/68-11-74), is another good source of information. For information about Portugal before heading there, you can make contact with the **Portuguese National Tourist Office,** 590 Fifth Ave., New York, NY 10036 (tel. 212/354-4403).

LAUNDRY: Keeping your clothes clean can be a problem if you're not staying long in Lisbon. Do-it-yourselfers may want to take their clothes to a self-service laundry, **Lavimpa,** Avenida de Paris 22A (tel. 01/89-03-88) (Metro: Alvalade). It's part of a chain that has three other branches in Lisbon, one at Estoril, and one at Cascais.

LIBRARIES: If you're looking for a library for research or whatever, the **Biblioteca Nacional (Lisboa),** Campo Grande 83 (tel. 01/79-50-130), near University City, contains more than two million volumes (books, periodicals, nonbook material) and is open from 9:45am to 5:30pm Monday to Friday mid-July to mid-September, from 9:45am to 7:30pm Monday to Saturday in winter. In addition, the **American Cultural Center** at Avenida Duque de Loulé 22B (tel. 01/57-01-02) has a library of some 8,000 volumes and 132 periodicals. It's open from 2 to 6pm Tuesday, Wednesday, and Friday, 2 to 7pm Monday and Thursday.

LIQUOR LAWS: See "Fast Facts: Portugal" in Chapter 3.

LOST PROPERTY: Go in person (don't call) to the municipal **Governo Civil,** which is next to the San Carlos Opera House. Hours are Monday through Saturday from 9am to noon and 2 to 6pm. For items lost on public transportation, inquire at the **Carris** office at the top of the Santa Justa Elevator (tel. 01/36-61-41), which is open Monday through Saturday from 3 to 7pm.

LUGGAGE STORAGE/LOCKERS: These can be found at the Santa Apolónia station, located by the river near the Alfama.

NEWSPAPERS/MAGAZINES: See "Fast Facts: Portugal" in Chapter 3.

PHOTOGRAPHIC NEEDS: One of the best places to go for your film needs, including the processing, is **Fotosport,** Terminal de Rossio, Loja 120 (tel. 01/32-78-70), which is open daily from 8am to 10pm.

POLICE: Call 346-61-41.

POST OFFICE: While in Portugal you may have your mail directed to your hotel (or hotels), to the American Express representative, or to General Delivery (*Poste Restante*) in Lisbon. Your passport must be presented for mail pickups. The general post office in Lisbon is at Praça dos Restauradores 58 (tel. 01/34-70-05), and hours are daily from 8am to 10pm.

RADIO/TV: See "Fast Facts: Portugal" in Chapter 3.

RELIGIOUS SERVICES: Roman Catholicism is the leading religion in Portugal, and you find churches everywhere. If you're a Protestant, a Baptist evangelical church exists in Lisbon. It's the **Igreja Evangélica Baptista de Lisboa,** Rua Filipe Folque 36B (tel. 01/53-53-62), with Sunday services in Portuguese at 11am and 7:30pm (also at 7:30pm on Wednesday). For Jewish readers, services are held at the **Shaare Tikua Synagogue,** Rua Alexandre Herculano 59 (tel. 01/68-15-92). From April to October, service is at 8pm Friday. However, in other months, the service is at 10:30am Saturday.

REST ROOMS: All major terminals (airports and railways) have such facilities, and Lisbon has several public ones. However, you can often use one at a café or tavern, as one of these establishments exists practically within every block. It is considered polite to purchase something, however—perhaps a small glass of mineral water.

SAFETY: Whenever you're traveling in an unfamiliar city or country, stay alert. Be aware of your immediate surroundings. Wear a moneybelt and don't sling your camera or purse over your shoulder. This will minimize the possibility of your becoming a victim of crime. Every society has its criminals. It's your responsibility to be aware and alert even in the most heavily touristed areas. Don't leave anything, especially your luggage, in an unguarded car. In recent years, there have been a lot of break-ins.

SHOE REPAIR: Your needs can be answered at **Silva e Neves Lopes,** Rua Rodrigo da Fonseca 182B (tel. 01/68-70-55), in the vicinity of the Ritz Hotel. Hours are Monday through Friday 7am to 8:30pm and Saturday from 7am to 1pm.

TAXES: See "Fast Facts: Portugal" in Chapter 3.

TAXIS: See "Getting Around" in this chapter.

TELEGRAMS/TELEX/FAX: At most hotels the receptionist will help you send a telegram. If not, there is a cable dispatch service open 24 hours a day, at **Marconi** (the Portuguese Radio Communications Office), Rua S. Julião 131. To send telegrams from any telephone to points outside of Portugal, dial 182 to reach Marconi. To send telegrams within Portugal (and your language skills had better be good to handle this one), dial 113 from any telephone. Most foreign visitors leave the logistics of this to the concierge of their hotel, assuming that the hotel offers this service. Telexes and faxes can be sent from most hotels or else you can go to the post office (see above).

TELEPHONE: The area code for Lisbon and environs is 01. To make a local call in Lisbon, you can use one of the many telephone booths, but you'll need some coins. You can talk for 3 minutes for 15$ (10¢). For most long-distance telephoning, particularly transatlantic calls, go to the central post office in Lisbon at the Praça dos Restauradores 58 (tel. 01/34-70-05). Give an assistant there the number you wish, and he or she will make the call for you, billing you at the end. Some phones are equipped for using calling cards, including American Express and VISA. You can also purchase phones card from the post office in denominations of 500$ ($3.35).

TIME: See "Fast Facts: Portugal" in Chapter 3.

TIPPING: See "Fast Facts: Portugal" in Chapter 3.

TRANSIT INFO: **TAP Air Portugal,** Praça Marquês de Pombal 3A, can be reached at 01/57-50-20. For **airport information,** call 01/80-20-60, and for **train information,** dial 01/87-60-25.

WEATHER: To find out about the weather, if you don't speak Portuguese, ask someone at your hotel desk to translate one of the weather reports that appear daily in the leading newspapers of Lisbon.

4. Networks & Resources

FOR STUDENTS

Contact **Tagus,** Praça de Londres 9B (tel. 01/88-49-57), which provides data on low-cost travel not only in Portugal, but in Europe. Always check their discounts against those of other airlines to see just how much of a reduction you are getting.

FOR GAY MEN & LESBIANS

Before you go to Portugal, you can order *Spartacus,* the international gay guide ($27.95) from Giovanni's Room, 1145 Pine St., Philadelphia, PA 19107 (tel. 215/923-2960, or toll free 800/222-6996 outside Pennsylvania).

Lesbians traveling abroad may want to order a copy of *Gaia's Guide International,* although this book is primarily concerned with the United States. It, too, can be ordered from Giovanni's Room.

Gays and lesbians socialize mainly in public bars, restaurants, and clubs, as there is no major social center for them. The many public parks of Lisbon are extremely dangerous after dark. The scene is liveliest in the Bairro Alto, especially along Rua de São Marçel.

FOR WOMEN

A good meeting place is the **Editora das Mulheres** bookstore, Rua da Conceição 17, or the IDM (Informação e Documentação das Mulheres), Rua Filipe de Mata 115A. The latter is a center for women with a small library, plus a café patronized only by women. It's run by a women's collective. Foreign visitors are welcomed in English. Neither meeting point has a phone.

FOR SENIOR CITIZENS

Mature Outlook maintains *Travel Alert,* providing documentation to its members about discounted prices on tours and vacation packages, featuring Iberia. Discounts can range from hotels to car rentals. To become a member, you must be 50 years of age or older. The $9.95 fee covers a magazine and newsletter with data on package tours. For more information, contact Customer Service Center, 6001 N. Clark St., Chicago, IL 60660 (tel. toll free 800/336-6330 in the U.S.).

Before you go, refer to "Tips for Seniors" in Chapter 3, "Planning a Trip to Portugal."

LISBON ACCOMMODATIONS

When you check into a hotel, you'll see the official tariffs posted in the main lobby as well as somewhere in your room, perhaps at the bottom of the closet. These rates are dictated by the Directorate of Tourism and are strictly regulated. They are really a form of rent control. They include the 13.1% service charge, a 16% Value Added Tax, and a tourist tax.

Most hotels will allow you to keep your room or deposit your luggage there until noon. From that point on, the manager can add the cost of an additional full day's rent to your bill.

When checking into a hotel, clear up the all-important question of how many meals, if any, you plan to take in the dining room. Full pension (board) means a room and three meals a day; half board means a room, breakfast, and at least one other meal. It is proper for the hotel clerk to ask which of those main meals, either lunch or dinner, you'll be taking. Those on the half- or full-board plans must pay for a meal even if they miss it. It saves you money to take full or half board, as you are granted a reduction in the overall rate, as opposed to staying at a hotel and taking your meals there on an à la carte basis. But the manager is not obliged to grant you a discount on a pension plan unless you are staying at his establishment 2 full days and nights.

Should an infraction such as overcharging occur, you may demand to be given the Official Complaints Book. In this tome you can write your allegations. The hotel manager is then obligated to turn your comments over to the Directorate of Tourism, where they are reviewed by a staff to see if any punitive action should be taken against the establishment.

Hotels in Portugal are rated from five stars to one star. The difference between a five-star hotel and a four-star hotel will not always be apparent to the casual visitor. Often the distinction is based on square footage of bathrooms and other technical differences.

When you go below this level, you enter the realm of the second-class hotel and the third-class, the latter comprising the most raw-boned and least-recommended hotels in Portugal. However, some can be good.

Tourist inns, not government run, are known as **estalagems.** Often these offer some of the finest accommodations in Portugal, many decorated in the native or *típico* style and representing top-notch bargains.

The **residências** are a form of boardinghouse, except without board. Only a room and breakfast are offered at these establishments. The **pensão** is a Portuguese boardinghouse that charges the lowest tariffs in the country. The deluxe pensão is a misnomer. The term simply means that the pensão enjoys the highest rating in its category. The accommodation is decidedly not luxurious. A luxury pensão is generally the equivalent of a second-class hotel. The boardinghouses are finds for the budget hunter. Many of them prepare a good local cuisine with generous helpings. For bottom-of-the-barrel type of living, there are both first-class and second-class boardinghouses.

Coastal hotels, especially those in the Algarve (see Chapter 13), are required to grant off-season (November to February) visitors a 15% reduction on the regular tariff. To attract more off-season business, a number of establishments extend this, starting the reduced rates in mid-October and granting them until April 1.

Unless otherwise indicated, prices in this chapter include service and taxes. Breakfast may or may not be included. Individual write-ups reflect various hotel policies about breakfast. All references in Portugal to "including breakfast" refer only to a continental breakfast of juice, coffee (or tea), croissants, butter, and jam. If you stay at an establishment and order bacon and eggs or other extras, you will likely be billed for these as à la carte items.

RESERVATIONS

Most hotels require at least a day's deposit before they will reserve a room for you. Preferably, this can be accomplished with an international money order, or, if agreed to in advance, with a personal check. You can usually cancel a room reservation 1 week ahead of time and get a full refund. A few hotelkeepers will return your money 3 days before the reservation date, but some will take your deposit and never return it, even if you cancel far in advance. Many budget-hotel owners operate on such a narrow margin of profit that they find just buying stamps for airmail replies too expensive by their standards. Therefore, it's most important that you should enclose a prepaid International Reply Coupon with your payment, especially if you're writing to a budget hotel. Better yet, call and speak to the hotel of your choice, or send a fax.

If you're booking into a chain hotel, such as Sheraton or Meridien, you can call toll free in North America and easily make reservations over the phone. Whenever such a service is available, toll-free 800 numbers are indicated in the individual hotel write-ups.

If you arrive without a reservation, begin your search for a room as early in the day as possible. If you arrive late at night, you may have to take what you can get, often in a much higher price range than you'd like to pay.

1. In the Center

VERY EXPENSIVE

Hotel Tivoli, Avenida da Liberdade 185, 1298 Lisboa Codex (tel. 01/53-01-81; fax 01/57-94-61), has enticing features. First, its location is choice, right on the main boulevard of Lisbon. Second, it's large enough to accommodate more than 600 guests—hence, its public facilities are bountiful. Third, its prices are not extravagant, considering its amenities. The two-story-high reception lobby has an encircling mezzanine lounge that is almost arena-size, with comfortable islands of furniture arranged on Oriental rugs. The wood-paneled O Zodiaco restaurant offers a buffet for both lunch and dinner. Meals are all à la carte. On the top floor, O Terraço offers a view of Lisbon. Here, à la carte meals are provided, with the emphasis on steaks and chops, which you select yourself and have cooked on a tile charcoal grill. Adjoining the restaurant is a homelike salon with a wood-burning fireplace, Oriental rugs, and restrained decor.

The air-conditioned rooms contain a mixture of modern and traditional furniture. All have private bath, TV, minibar, and phone. The regular room prices are scaled according to position—with the larger and more expensive ones facing the boulevard. Singles begin at 36,000$ ($241.20) daily, rising to 40,000$ ($268) in a double. Suites begin at 50,000$ ($335). Breakfast is included. A total of 297 bedrooms and 30 suites are rented. Guests have access to the Tivoli Club, surrounded by a lovely garden, with a swimming pool that can be heated when necessary, a tennis court, a solarium, a bar, and a restaurant where you can order light snacks. Services include laundry, 24-hour room service, and baby-sitting. There is a business center on the premises, along with shopping boutiques. It costs 1,250$ ($8.40) a day to park your car in the hotel garage. Subway: Avenida. Bus: 1, 2, 9, or 32. AE, DC, MC, V.

Le Meridien, Rua Castilho 149, 1000 Lisboa (tel. 01/69-09-00; fax 01/69-32-31), one of the most dramatic major hotels in Lisbon, opened in 1985. Each of the air-conditioned bedrooms has a wraparound window that overlooks the Edward VII Park and lets in the bright Iberian sunshine. Rooms contain minibars, TV, and phone. The hotel rents 331 bedrooms and 17 suites. Singles cost from 38,000$ ($254.60); doubles from 44,000$ ($294.80). Suites begin at 85,000$ ($569.50). All tariffs include an American buffet-style breakfast. The air-conditioned lobby glitters with white marble, polished chromium, and mirrors. A symmetrical entranceway frames the tile-bottomed fountains whose splashing rises to the top of the sunlit atrium.

You'll find lots of attractive and interesting public rooms, including a tearoom with Portuguese tiles, a ground-floor Brasserie des Amis with a view of the park and the adjacent boulevard, and the formal, glamorous Restaurant L'Atlantic upstairs. There's a piano bar, Le Nautique, upholstered in maroon velvet, and a health club is also on the premises, offering a sauna and massage service. The facilities are operated by a competent staff. Services include laundry/valet; baby-sitting; and 24-hour room service. There is also a business center. The hotel garage charges 2,000$ ($13.40) a night. Cars can be rented at a kiosk in the hotel lobby. Subway: Rotunda. AE, DC, MC, V.

Lisboa Sheraton Hotel & Towers, Rua Latino Coelho 1, 1097 Lisboa (tel. 01/57-57-57, or toll free 800/325-3535 in the U.S.; fax 01/54-71-64), the tallest hotel and one of the tallest buildings in Lisbon, is easy to spot from most of the city's major parks and gardens. The hotel contains 384 rooms and 7 suites, two restaurants, a health club, and one of the more enviable outdoor swimming pools in Lisbon. Originally built in 1972, but renovated several times since, it has its most desirable rooms in the tower. From there, views open onto either the longest bridge in Europe and the Tagus or the cityscape. Each air-conditioned room contains a private marble bath, phone, TV, and minibar. Singles range from 40,000$ ($268) to 50,000$ ($335) daily, with doubles costing from 45,000$ ($301.50) to 55,000$ ($368.50). Suites begin at 100,000$ ($670). Breakfast is another 1,500$ ($10.05). The night begins with live music played in The Lounge, followed by dinner in either the Caravela or the Alfama Grill Gourmet Restaurant, either serving a selection of Portuguese and continental dishes. You can enjoy drinks throughout the day and evening on the 26th floor, which has a panoramic view of Lisbon. The hotel has a garage, charging 2,000$ ($13.40) a night. Room service is available 24 hours a day, and laundry/valet and baby-sitting are also offered. Facilities include a sauna and solarium, a swimming pool, car-rental facilities, and shopping boutiques. Bus: 1, 2, 9, or 32. AE, DC, MC, V.

The Ritz, Rua Rodrigo da Fonseca 88, 1200 Lisboa (tel. 01/69-20-20 or toll free 800/327-0200; fax 01/69-17-83), was built in the late 1950s and is operated by Inter-Continental Hotels. Its 40 suites boast the finest decoration you'll see in any major Portuguese hotel. Slender mahogany canopied beds with fringed swags, marquetry desks, satinwood dressing tables with tip-mirrors, plush carpeting—no wonder the Ritz has been traditionally the preferred choice of celebrated guests. Some of the 260 modern rooms have terraces opening onto Edward VII Park. All are air conditioned and soundproof, each with marble bath with double basin, local and satellite TV, radio, and minibar. In a single the rate goes from 44,000$ ($294.80). For a double, the tariff ranges from 48,000$ ($321.60) daily. Suites begin at 100,000$ ($670). All prices include breakfast.

The main dining room, Veranda, is dignified and pleasant, and from May to October you can take meals outdoors on the attractive Veranda Terrace. The Grill Room is traditionally decorated (see my restaurant recommendations in Chapter 6). The Ritz Bar is a magnet. Lodged in a corner of the hotel, overlooking the terrace and park, it offers everything from a Pimm's No. 1 Cup to a mint julep. Baby-sitting, 24-hour rooms service, and laundry/valet are available. Facilities include a coffee shop, a tearoom, a disco, and a beauty parlor. The hotel's garage charges 2,000$ ($13.40) a night. Bus: 1, 2, 9, or 32. AE, DC, MC, V.

EXPENSIVE
Hotel Alfa Lisboa, Avenida Columbano Bordalo Pinheiro (without number), 1000 Lisboa (tel. 01/726-21-21; fax 01/726-30-31), removed from the commercial center of Lisbon, is a five-star hotel that has gained popularity with business travelers since it opened. The staff works hard to make visitors comfortable. Someone at the imposing reception desk in the marble-floored lobby will quote singles at 21,000$ ($140.70) to 26,000$ ($174.20) daily, and twins and doubles at 26,000$ ($174.20) to 32,000$ ($214.40). Suites begin at 45,000$ ($301.50). Breakfast is included. Rooms are air conditioned, with minibar, TV, and phone.

The occupants of the hotel's 355 well-furnished rooms and 38 junior suites can enjoy an array of drinking and dining facilities. The most formal is the Pombalino Restaurant, with an 18th-century Portuguese palatial decor and an international cuisine. The most popular and least expensive selection is A Aldeia, a coffee shop and restaurant decorated in regional Portuguese style. The Labirinto Bar with a piano player nightly is the most popular drinking spot. Room service is available 24 hours a day, and laundry/valet is offered, as is baby-sitting. Facilities include car-rental kiosks and a shopping gallery. The staff will direct you to the nearest places to go for a health club, jogging track, tennis, sauna, and horseback riding. Parking is free in the 80-car garage. Subway: Sete Rios. Bus: 16, 46, or 85. AE, DC, MC, V.

Hotel Altis, Rua Castilho 11, 1200 Lisboa (tel. 01/52-24-96; fax 01/54-86-96), is a luxurious modern hotel, with 307 attractively furnished bedrooms and 13 suites, right in the commercial and cultural center of Lisbon. The Portuguese hospitality offered by the staff and management, together with the refurnishing of the lobby, public areas, restaurants, and bars makes for an enjoyable five-star hotel. For example, you can order a drink or a meal night or day. Many services are provided, as befits a big-city hotel, and that includes a laundry and dry-cleaning service right in the hotel. Bedrooms are well equipped, with air conditioning, baths, color TVs with eight channels via satellite, radios, phones, and minibars, and are fitted with warm contemporary furnishings. Singles range from 26,000$ ($174.20) to 34,000$ ($227.80) daily, with doubles costing 32,000$ ($214.40) to 38,000$ ($254.60), including a buffet breakfast. Suites begin at 45,000$ ($301.50). Three meals a day are served in the Girassol Restaurant, and for lunch or dinner a guest can also choose the Don Fernando Grill. Continental dishes are featured along with Portuguese regional food. The Piano Bar has live music for dancing, and if you want to see the Lisbon skyline, you can take the elevator to the São Jorge Bar on the top floor. The indoor heated swimming pool and health club are other facilities offered by the hotel. The hotel offers 24-hour room service, laundry/valet, and baby-sitting. It costs 750$ ($50.25) a night to park your car. Bus: 1, 2, 9, or 32. AE, DC, MC, V.

Avenida Palace, Rua 1 de Dezembro 123, 1200 Lisboa (tel. 01/346-01-54; fax 01/342-22-884), is a link to the past, a world reflected in crystal and antiques. The second-floor drawing room attracts those partial to the age of silk-brocaded wall paneling, fringed velvet draperies, crystal chandeliers, marquetry tables, consoles, and hand-woven Portuguese carpets. Five tall windows in the dining room overlook the avenue. The location is noisy, right at the Rossio, minutes from fado clubs, restaurants, and some of Lisbon's major shops.

Major renovations have prevented the Avenida Palace from slipping into disrepair and deterioration. Most of the rooms have been redone. The redecorated bedrooms are furnished in a traditional manner, with 18th-century antiques or artwork and are air conditioned and centrally heated, with TVs, minibars, and phones. The spacious bathrooms are faced in Portuguese marble. The hotel rents 81 bedrooms, a single costing from 25,000$ ($167.50) daily, a double going for 30,000$ ($201). In addition, 10 suites are rented, beginning at 45,000$ ($301.50). An American buffet breakfast is included. The hotel offers 24-hour room service, laundry service, and baby-sitting. Facilities include a car-rental desk and limited private parking (free). Subway: Rossio. Bus: 1, 2, 36, or 44. AE, DC, MC, V.

Hotel Diplomático, Rua Castilho 74, 1200 Lisboa (tel. 01/56-20-41; fax 01/52-21-55), is a first-class hotel near the Ritz and the Edward VII Park. The two-story lobby and lounge is dominated by a mural by George Bramdeiro. Spread among the 11 floors are the 72 tasteful bedrooms, which often have small balconies. Singles cost 18,000$ ($120.60), and doubles 21,000$ ($140.70). The hotel also rents 18 luxurious suites, costing from 23,000$ ($154.10) per night. Tariffs include breakfast. The hotel also offers the Park Restaurante, serving an array of international dishes along with Portuguese regional specialties. Guitar music accompanies most meals. Services include 24-hour room service, laundry service, and baby-sitting, and facilities include a car-rental desk and free parking. Subway: Rotunda. Bus: 2. AE, DC, MC, V.

Dom Carlos, Avenida Duque de Loulé 121, 1000 Lisboa (tel. 01/53-90-71; fax 01/35-20-728), just off the Praça Marquês de Pombal, faces its own triangular park, dedicated to the partially blind Camilo Castelo Branco, a 19th-century "eternity poet." The curvy facade of the hotel is all glass, giving guests an indoor-outdoor feeling, reinforced by green trees and beds of orange and red canna. In summer, there is air conditioning; in winter, central heating. The hotel offers 56 bedrooms, plus 17 suites. The bedrooms, all with private baths, minibars, phones, and TVs, are paneled in reddish Portuguese wood. The Nordic-inspired furnishings are softened by an occasional hand-carved cherub. Singles rent from 13,500$ ($90.45) daily; doubles 16,500$ ($110.55) and suites begin at 21,500$ ($144.05). Breakfast is included. The lobby-lounge is satisfactory, but even more inviting is the mezzanine salon, where sofas and chairs face the park. In addition, there's a miniature bar, with leather chairs, ideal for a tête-à-tête. Breakfast is the only meal served. Services include laundry, baby-sitting, room service (6am to midnight), and the limited facilities include a car-rental desk. The staff will direct you to the nearest garage for parking. Subway: Rotunda. Bus: 1, 36, 44, or 45. AE, DC, MC, V.

Hotel Fenix, Praça Marquês de Pombal 8, 1200 Lisboa (tel. 01/53-51-21), enjoys a front-row position on the circular plaza dedicated to the 18th-century prime minister of Portugal. From most of its bedrooms you can view the trees on the avenue and in Edward VII Park. A modern hotel, the Fenix is run by the HUSA chain. The hotel is favored by many clients who return repeatedly. All its 122 air-conditioned bedrooms are equipped with private bath, phone, radio, TV, and minibar. In a double room, the daily rate is 18,700$ ($125.30); it's 15,500$ ($103.85) in a single, including breakfast. The brightly furnished and air-conditioned two-floor reception lounge, with a cozy bar-lounge on the mezzanine, is much favored. Another plus is the grill room in the hotel, the Bodegón, worthy of a separate recommendation as a restaurant. Subway: Rotunda. AE, DC, MC, V.

Hotel Lisboa Plaza, Travessa do Salitre 7, Avenida da Liberdade, 1200 Lisboa (tel. 01/36-39-22), is a charmer, right in the heart of the city. A family-owned and -operated four-star hotel, the Plaza has many appealing art nouveau touches, including its facade. My favorite place for a rendezvous is the 1900s-style bar, with its soothing olive colors and tufted leather chairs. The hotel was built in 1953, but completely overhauled in 1988. A well-known Portuguese designer, G. Viterbo, decorated it in a contemporary classic style. Modern amenities were added at the time. The rooms—87 bedrooms and 6 suites—have marble baths, hairdryers, minibars, air conditioning, direct-dial phones, color TVs, and in-house videos. They are all well styled and comfortable. Singles cost from 20,500$ ($137.35) to 25,000$ ($167.50) daily, with doubles renting for 24,500$ ($164.15) to 28,000$ ($187.60). Triples range from 28,500$ ($190.95) to 32,000$ ($214.40), with suites costing 40,000$ ($268). Tariffs include an American buffet breakfast. Through an art nouveau entrance you approach the Quinta d'Avenida Restaurant, which specializes in a traditional Portuguese cuisine. The multilingual staff will introduce you to the hotel, with its car-rental facilities, garage (750$, or $5.05, a night), business services, baby-sitting, 24-hour room service, and same-day laundry service. Subway: Avenida. Bus: 1, 2, 36, or 44. AE, DC, MC, V.

Hotel Lutecia, Avenida Frei Muguel Contreiras 52, 1700 Lisboa (tel. 01/80-31-21; fax 01/80-78-18), is in a shopping center, 5 minutes by subway (go to Roma station) from old Lisbon, toward the airport. It offers 151 air-conditioned rooms, plus 8 suites, that have distilled beauty and space and are without excessive adornment. The rooms are furnished with leather-and-wood armchairs, a desk and dressing table, a room-wide headboard, and walnut and leather paneling complete with pushbuttons, reading lights, minibar, TV, and phones. The baths are tiled, with a tub and shower combination, and large wraparound towels on heated rods. Breakfast, included in the rates, is available either on your private balcony or from the buffet in the roof restaurant. Singles rent for 14,500$ ($97.15) to 16,000$ ($107.20) daily; doubles for 16,500$ ($110.55) to 19,500$ ($130.65), with suites going for 35,000$ ($234.50).

Its 12 stories are set back from a busy thoroughfare, with a formal driveway entrance. The public lounges consume most of the first two floors, although you must take an elevator to the top for the open-view dining room. In the lobby, the Concorde Bar, with French decoration based on a picture of the Place de la Concorde in Paris at the beginning of the 20th century, is ideal for a drink. In the snack bar, a good meal costs around 1,600$ ($10.70). You can order a three-course menu in the restaurant for 2,800$ ($18.75) and up in the Panoramic Restaurant. Services include room service, laundry/valet, and baby-sitting. Car-rental facilities are on the premises, but there is no garage. Bus: 27. AE, DC, MC, V.

Mundial Hotel, Rua Dom Duarte 4, 1100 Lisboa (tel. 01/86-31-01; fax 01/87-91-29), is right in the heart of everything. The top-floor restaurant offers a view of St. George's Castle and the Alfama, and is a short walk from the Rossio, theaters, and shops. The staff is efficient, everything is properly manicured and polished, and the hotel is high on the preference list of European businesspeople. The 150 rooms, all with private bath, phone, and TV, are comfortable, spacious, and restrained in decor. The tile baths have bidets, shower/tub combinations, and plenty of mirrors and shelf space for toilet articles. Singles are 11,500$ ($77.05) to 13,800$ ($92.45) daily, doubles are 17,500$ ($117.25) to 19,000$ ($127.30), and triples are 16,500$ ($110.55) to 21,900$ ($146.75). All tariffs include breakfast. Subway: Rossio. AE, DC, MC, V.

Principe Real, Rua de Alegria 53, 1200 Lisboa (tel. 01/34-60-116; fax 01/34-02-104), is a modern hotel, reached after a long, steep climb from Avenida da Liberdade. Behind its rather impersonal facade lies a small world of fine living. Guests get acquainted in the bar. Selectivity and care are shown in the 24 individualized bedrooms, which are small but tasteful, with air conditioning, TV, and phone. The beds are reproductions of fine antiques, with excellent mattresses. Each room is color coordinated, a happy blending of floral fabrics. All units are doubles, costing from 18,000$ ($120.60) to 23,000$ ($154.10) per night, including an American buffet breakfast. The hotel's restaurant opens onto panoramic views of Lisbon, and serves an excellent Portuguese cuisine. There is also a cozy bar downstairs. No parking is available. Subway: Rotunda. Bus: 2. AE, DC, MC, V.

Hotel Rex, Rua Castilho 169, 1000 Lisboa (tel. 01/68-21-61; fax 01/68-75-81). Sandwiched between its neighbors in a desirable location a few steps from the Hotel Ritz and the Hotel Meridien, this retreat offers accommodations and a helpful staff at prices far below those of its more prestigious competitors. Many of the rooms have spacious balconies, whose panoramic vistas include views of Edward VII Park and the baroque Manueline church on its far edge. The 68 cozy bedrooms have minibars, TVs, radios, phones, tile baths, and built-in beds whose wide edges are covered in full-grain lengths of well-rubbed Iberian leather. If you're lucky enough to lodge in one of the nine suites, you'll enjoy a cozy sitting room with its own breeze-swept terrace, in addition to the comfortable bedroom. Singles cost from 20,500$ ($137.35) daily, doubles 24,000$ ($160.80), and suites from 38,000$ ($254.60), including breakfast. From the large front windows of the elegant lobby with its high coffered wood-and-plaster ceiling, an unusual bronze statue of women bearing baskets is visible. On the ground floor, a darkly intimate restaurant, Cozinha d'El-Rey, has two levels lined with provincial artifacts. The Panoramic Restaurant on the top floor offers a sweeping view of one of Lisbon's most beautiful parks, as well as the city far below. The hotel offers 24-room service, laundry service, and baby-sitting. Parking is free, and there are car-rental facilities on the premises. Subway: Rotunda/Marquês de Pombal. Bus: 2, 11, 12, 23, 48, or 53. AE, DC, MC, V.

Tivoli Jardim, Rua Julio Cesar Machado 7–9, 1200 Lisboa (tel. 01/53-99-71; fax 01/55-65-66), is under the same ownership as its neighbor, the previously recommended Hotel Tivoli. Set behind its namesake, avoiding the traffic noises from the Avenida da Liberdade, it features a free parking area for guests. The air-conditioned structure is adorned with cliff-hanging balconies, two shafts of elevators, and 119 well-styled bedrooms. The walls are white plaster and the furnishings basic built-in, with color TV, minibar, reading lights, phone, maid-summoning bells, and channel music, as well as comfortable armchairs, and a glass wall (curtained off at night) leading to the balcony. The baths have patterned tile, with a bidet, shower, and tub. Singles range from 19,900$ ($133.35) to 21,900$ ($146.75) daily, with doubles renting for 23,500$ ($157.45) to 28,500$ ($190.55), including breakfast.

There are adequate public lounges. Portuguese businesspeople have found the Jardim ideal for meeting clients in the cathedral-high lobby, with its wall of glass through which the Iberian sun pours in. Dominating everything is a ceiling-high tapestry in sunburst colors. The tile and marble floors are peacock blue and emerald green, the staircase leading to the mezzanine a blood red. The dining room is tasteful, with its white brick walls and green tables, its wall niches filled with Portuguese ceramics. Guests can use the facilities of the Tivoli Club in the Hotel Tivoli, with a swimming pool. Services include limited room service, laundry, and baby-sitting. Car-rental facilities are on the premises. Subway: Avenida. Bus: 1, 2, 9, or 32.

MODERATE
Hotel Botânico, Rua Mãe d'Água 16–20, 1200 Lisboa (tel. 01/32-03-92; fax 01/32-01-25), perches near a hilltop in a neighborhood dotted with parks and cafés, not far from the Botanical Gardens. A modern cement building with a tasteful wood-accented lobby, it was renovated recently. The 30 air-conditioned rooms, although small, are clean and convenient, and each contains a private bath, phone, TV, and radio. The rooms cost 11,500$ ($77.05) daily in a single, 17,000$ ($113.90) in a double. No meals other than breakfast are served. Bus: 1, 2, 9, or 32. AE, DC, MC, V.

Capitol Hotel, Rua Eça de Queirós 24, 1000 Lisboa (tel. 01/53-68-11; fax 01/352-61-65), is a fine little hostelry, just minutes from the top of the Avenida da Liberdade and the Praça Marquês de Pombal. It nestles on a quiet street, away from busy boulevards, and opens onto a wedge-shaped park with weeping willows and oaks. The Capitol places the emphasis on good, roomy chambers with private bath, all of which are simply furnished. Each of the 58 bedrooms is air conditioned and has a phone. The more desirable rooms open onto private balconies. Singles pay 12,700$ ($85.10) nightly; doubles, 13,900$ ($93.15). Breakfast is included. On the premises are a bar, snack bar, and restaurant. Bus: 1, 2, 9, or 32. AE, DC, MC, V.

Dom Manuel, Avenida Duque d'Ávila 189, 1000 Lisboa (tel. 01/57-61-60; fax 01/57-61-60), may be small, but it has high style, and for such an atmosphere the rates are moderate. It's a short distance from the very heart of Lisbon, on a tree-lined avenue. Its guest lounge, with an open fireplace, is like a private home in an estate. Flanking sofas are set on an Oriental area rug. On one wall is an Aubusson tapestry, and a picture window looks out onto an interior planter with subtropical greenery. On a mezzanine there is an intimate little cocktail lounge. You dine on the lower level, which is very Portuguese, with formal leather armchairs and elegant floor torchères. Each of the bedrooms is in a restrained modern style, with muted color coordination, built-in headboards, a desk and armchair, bed lights, all-tile baths, air conditioning, TV, and phone. The hotel rents 64 bedrooms, charging 13,500$ ($90.45) daily in a single, 17,000$ ($113.90) in a double, including a buffet breakfast. Laundry/valet service is available, as is 24-hour room service. There is no garage. Bus: 18 or 42. Subway: Saldanha or São Sebastião. AE, DC, MC, V.

Hotel Excelsior, Rua Rodrigues Sampaio 172, 1100 Lisboa (tel. 01/53-71-51; fax 01/57-87-79), enjoys a setting 1 block from Praça Marquês de Pombal, at the entrance to Edward VII Park. Right off the upper regions of Lisbon's major boulevard, it contains 81 good-sized bedrooms, each with its own private bath. Most of the rooms have a small sitting area, with a combination desk and dressing table. Singles rent for 11,500$ ($77.05) daily, with doubles costing 13,500$ ($90.45), including breakfast. All units contain TVs and radios. In addition to the air-conditioned bar and cocktail lounge with color TV, the hotel has a spacious breakfast room, which has large windows. Bus: 1, 2, 9, or 32. AE, DC, MC, V.

Hotel Eduardo VII, Avenida Fontes Pereira de Melo 5, 1000 Lisboa (tel. 01/53-01-41; fax 01/53-38-79), is a completely renovated 121-room hotel in a desirable location in the commercial and cultural center of Lisbon, 1 block north from Praça Marquês de Pombal.

It offers many amenities and much comfort. Each bedroom has air conditioning, phone, minibar, TV, and a private bath. All units are doubles, costing from 14,000$ ($93.80) to 16,400$ ($109.90) daily. Breakfast is an additional 800$ ($53.60). A lovely terrace-style restaurant with a greenhouse wall of windows offers good food and a sweeping view over the city. The restaurant specializes in both Portuguese and Brazilian dishes. Nearby, a posh bar offers relaxing end-of-the-day drinks. Bus: 1, 2, 9, or 32. AE, DC, MC, V.

Jorge V Hotel, Rua Mouzinho da Silveira 3, 1200 Lisboa (tel. 01/56-25-25; fax 01/56-25-69), is a neat little hotel of modern design, with amenities, moderate prices, and a choice location a block off the Avenida da Liberdade. Its facade contains rows of cellular balconies, roomy enough for guests to have breakfast or afternoon "coolers." A tiny elevator takes you to a variety of rooms. The 43 rooms aren't generous in size, but are comfortable in a compact way. All have small tile bathrooms, phones, air conditioning, TV, and radios. Singles rent for 10,000$ ($67) daily, with doubles costing 12,000$ ($80.40), including breakfast. Six suites are rented for 14,000$ ($93.80) each. Room service is provided until midnight. The reception lounge shares space with a bar. Most favored by guests is a regional-style combination bar/breakfast room of nicely melded aggregate stone and wood paneling. Subway: Avenida. AE, DC, MC, V.

Miraparque, Avenida Sidónio Pais 12, 1000 Lisboa (tel. 01/57-80-70; fax 01/57-89-20), is a first-class modern hotel on a secluded quiet street, opposite Edward VII Park. The lounges are furnished in simulated brown leather with wood-paneled walls. The tiny bar, with stools and lounge chairs, has a neat and comfortable ambience. The dining room, also wood-paneled, with contemporary chairs, has a wall-wide mural. Bedrooms have the same modified contemporary styling, with pastel colors. All units have private baths, minibar, TV, phone, and air conditioning. The hotel rents 100 bedrooms, charging from 9,000$ ($60.30) daily in a single or 10,200$ ($68.35) in a double. Triples rent for 12,700$ ($85.10). Rates include breakfast. Bus: 1, 2, 9, or 32. AE, DC, MC, V.

Presidente Hotel, Rua Alexandre Herculano 13, 1200 Lisboa (tel. 01/53-95-01; fax 01/35-20-272), is a small-scale establishment near Avenida da Liberdade on a busy street corner. It's recommended for families, as children under 9 are granted a 50% reduction; baby-sitting can be arranged. There's a laundry on the premises, and medical service. The general atmosphere, including the furnishings, is of good taste. The 59 bedrooms are small and nicely laid out, with built-in chestnut headboards, radios, bed lights, minibars, air conditioning, TVs, and phones. There are double-view windows, a small entry with two closets, bath tiled in bright colors, and even a valet stand. Single rooms cost from 12,000$ ($80.40) daily, with doubles going for 14,500$ ($97.15), including breakfast. Room service is provided until midnight. In the wood-paneled mezzanine lounge, only breakfast is served. The modest-size reception lounges are on three levels, connected by wide marble steps. Streetcar: 20. Bus: 1, 36, 44, or 45. Subway: Rotunda. AE, DC, MC, V.

Hotel Roma, Avenida de Roma 33, 1700 Lisboa (tel. 01/76-77-61; fax 01/793-29-81), one of the capital's largest reasonably priced hotels, is popular with commercial travelers. It is on a traffic-clogged boulevard on the northeast side of town. It has a turquoise-and-white tile facade, and recessed balconies extend out from the air-conditioned bedrooms. Each of these is comfortably filled with contemporary furnishings, sometimes with a gauzy curtain that coyly separates the sleeping alcove from the living room. The 265 rooms rent for 9,000$ ($60.30) daily in a single, 12,000$ ($80.40) to 13,000$ ($87.10) in a double room, and 14,000$ ($93.80) in a triple. The more expensive accommodations are spacious. Any last-minute shopping can be done in the array of shops that fill the marble-floored arcade near the reception desk. There's a swimming pool in the basement, plus a sauna and massage facilities. The hotel has restaurants on the ground floor and the 10th floor. Bus: 1, 2, 9, or 32. AE, DC, MC, V.

York House, Rua das Janelas Verdes 32, 1200 Lisboa (tel. 01/396-24-35; fax 01/67-27-93), mixes the drama of the past with the conveniences of the 20th century. York House was once a 16th-century convent and is outside the center of traffic-filled Lisbon, attracting those who want peace and tranquillity. Long known to the English and embassy personnel, it is almost opposite the National Art Gallery, sitting high on a hillside street overlooking the Tagus.

You go past an old iron gate and ascend a flight of stone steps past trailing ivy and rugged walls and enter through a garden cloister, where guests congregate under gnarled trees. Owned and run by José Telles, York House was tastefully furnished by one of the most distinguished designers for theater, opera, and villas in Lisbon. Each bedroom has antique beds, soft mattresses, and 18th- and 19th-century bric-a-brac. All of the 36 bedrooms have private baths. The charge is 20,400$ ($136.70) daily in a double. Singles go for 18,000$ ($120.60). Breakfast is included.

The guest book reveals that York House is favored by embassy staffs, artists, writers, poets, and professors.

In the public rooms are inlaid chests, coats of armor, carved ecclesiastical figures, paintings, and ornate ceramics. The former monks' dining hall has deep-set windows, large niches for antiques, and best of all, a combined French and Portuguese cuisine. Guests gather in the two-level lounge for before- or after-dinner drinks.

Mr. Telles has acquired a former town house at no. 47 (tel. 01/39-68-144; fax 01/67-27-93), down the street, adjacent to the museum. This aristocratic mansion of the 18th century was the home of the late Portuguese novelist Eça de Queirós. Here you can book larger, more luxurious rooms, with abundant closet space and large, tile bathrooms. Only breakfast is served here, and main meals are provided at the convent. A total of 17 bedrooms are rented, costing 15,700$ ($105.20) daily in a single or 17,000$ ($113.90) in a double, including breakfast. The lounge is Victorian, predominantly red, and evocative of turn-of-the-century Lisbon. Breakfast is brought on a tray to your room, to the lounge, or to the rear walled-in terrace which has an antique iron spiral staircase whose steps are filled with potted flowering plants. Bus: 27, 40, 49, or 54. AE, DC, MC, V.

INEXPENSIVE

Casa de São Mamede, Rua da Escola Politécnica 159, 1200 Lisboa (tel. 01/39-63-166). A blue-and-white tile mural on this establishment's facade depicts St. Mamede (a 12-year-old martyr in the early Christian church) between a lion and a bull. Originally built in the 1800s as a private villa for the count of Coruche, it was transformed into a hotel in 1945. Today, its 30 bedrooms are managed by the Marquês family. Breakfast is served in a sunny second-floor dining room decorated with antique yellow-and-blue tiles. Although renovated, the rooms retain an aura of their original high-ceilinged and slightly dowdy charm. Each has a phone, air conditioning, and a bath. Singles rent for 6,000$ ($40.20) daily, with doubles costing 8,500$ ($56.95). Breakfast is 350$ ($2.35) extra. Bus: 1, 2, 9, or 32. No credit cards.

Hotel do Reno, Avenida Duque d'Ávila 195–197, 1000 Lisboa (tel. 01/54-81-81; fax 01/54-67-86), opened in 1959, lies only about a 10-minute taxi ride from the heart of Lisbon. A three-star hotel, it enjoys heavy patronage by Germans and Scandinavians, but it also attracts English and American visitors. There is a large sitting room, and a pleasant bar is near the main entrance. The bedrooms are contemporary, each with a small sitting area that includes a desk and an armchair, a private bath, radio, phone, TV, and central heating. Most of the 54 rooms have balconies. Singles cost 8,500$ ($56.95) daily; doubles 9,500$ ($63.65), and triples 10,500$ ($70.35). All tariffs include breakfast. Children up to 8 years of age are granted a substantial reduction on the rates. Private parking is provided free. Babysitting can be arranged, as can laundry service. Bus: 16. Subway: São Sebastião. AE, DC, MC, V.

Residência América, Rua Tomás Ribeiro 47, 1000 Lisboa (tel. 01/352-11-77; fax 01/86-46-48), was built as a bank nearly 40 years ago and became a comfortable, unpretentious hotel through later renovation. Each of the 56 bedrooms contains a private bath. Fifty percent of the rooms are air conditioned and contain TVs. The 1950s-style accommodations all differ in layout and size. The quiet rooms are in back, though they tend to be slightly smaller and darker than those in front. Single rooms rent for 8,000$ ($53.60), including breakfast. No visitor to the América should leave without checking out the seventh-floor bar, whose leatherette furniture has been there so long that it is by now right in style. Having a drink here can be a lot of fun, adding a note of nostalgia to your stay. The América has no restaurant. Laundry service is provided, as is baby-sitting. Bus: 1, 36, 44, or 45. Subway: Picoas. AE, DC, MC, V.

Residência Imperador, Avenida 5 de Outubro 55, 1000 Lisboa (tel. 01/57-48-84), not far from the center, provides 43 rooms with private baths or showers costing 7,000$ ($46.90) daily in a single, 8,500$ ($56.95) in a double, including breakfast. The front entranceway, designed in Portuguese pinewood, is barely large enough to set down one's suitcase. However, the bedrooms and upper lounge are adequate in size. Opening onto balconies, the front bedrooms face a tiny private garden. The units are neatly planned with built-in beds and simple lines, and each has a phone. Muted colors are used on the walls and in the fabrics. On the top floor is a public room and terrace with a glass front, where breakfast is served. Streetcar no. 1 or 21 and the subway (Saldanha station) can whisk you into the city center. AE, DC, MC, V.

Residência Horizonte, Avenida António Augusto de Aguiar 42, 1000 Lisboa (tel. 01/53-95-26; fax 01/56-25-29). When it was built as an apartment house, the architect designed an impressively proportioned flight of stone steps leading up from the busy tree-lined boulevard outside. As you enter, the lower-level reception area is at the bottom of a short flight of stairs. What used to be an elegant lobby is a bit grim today. Nonetheless, the 52 rooms upstairs are clean and unpretentiously comfortable. A few have balconies. Each has a phone, and 50% have TVs. The units in the back are slightly less sunny than those at the front, but are much quieter. With breakfast included, singles rent for 7,000$ ($46.90) daily, while doubles go for 8,000$ ($53.60). Subway: Parque. Bus: 24 or 41. AE, DC, MC, V.

Residência Nazareth, Avenida António Augusto de Aguiar 25, 1000 Lisboa (tel. 051/54-20-16; fax 01/54-20-16). You'll recognize it by its dusty pink facade, on which some of the windows are surrounded with decorative arches raised in low relief. Take an elevator to the fourth-floor landing. There, far from the beauticians, hair stylists, and offices below, someone has re-created the look of the medieval vaulting you might find in a romanticized version of a Portuguese fortress. The distressed plaster and wrought-iron lanterns are obvious facsimiles, yet their undeniable charm somehow works wonders on a tired sightseer after a full day of exploring the capital. Even the spacious bar and TV lounge look like a vaulted cellar. Light floods in from the windows. Some of the simple bedrooms contain platforms, requiring guests to step up or down to the bathroom or to the comfortable bed. Each of the 32 units has a private tile bath, air conditioning, TV, and phone. Singles rent for 7,000$ ($50.25) daily; doubles 8,500$ ($56.95), including breakfast. Bus: 31, 41, or 46. Subway: São Sebastião. AE, DC, MC, V.

Hotel Principe, Avenida Duque d'Ávila 201, 1000 Lisboa (tel. 01/53-61-51; fax 01/53-43-14), over a quarter of a century old, is a favorite with visiting Spanish and Portuguese matadors. All of its large bedrooms have private baths and phones, and most of them open onto their own balconies. The hotel's eight floors are accessible by two elevators. Rooms contain TVs with music (three channels), and half of them are air conditioned. A single costs 9,000$ ($60.30) daily, and a double room goes for 10,000$ ($67), all rates including breakfast. Children up to 8 years of age are given a 50% reduction on the rates. The matadors do seem to like the Principe's dining room and bar. Don't confuse this hotel with the first-class Principe Real, recommended previously. Parking is free. Baby-sitting can be arranged, and laundry service is available. Room service is also offered until midnight. Bus: 16. Subway: São Sebastião. AE, DC, MC, V.

BUDGET

Residência Alicante, Avenida Duque de Loulé 20, 1000 Lisboa (tel. 01/53-05-14; fax 01/352-02-50). Its burnt-orange postwar facade curves around a quiet residential street corner in an undistinguished neighborhood. This hotel is nonetheless clean, welcoming, and safe. You register on the street level, with a kindly staff who speak little or no English; then you'll take a small elevator to one of the four upper floors. There, 26 rooms with bath are available and 16 without bath. Furnishings and size vary, but most budget-minded visitors find the Alicante an acceptable and reasonable headquarters for a stay in Lisbon. Units have TVs and phones. With breakfast included, rooms with private bath cost 5,800$ ($38.85) daily in a single and 6,800$ ($45.55) in a double. Without private bath, singles rent for 3,000$ ($20.10) daily and doubles cost 4,000$ ($26.80). The quieter rooms overlook an interior courtyard. Bus: 1, 2, 9, or 32. AE, DC, MC, V.

Residencial O Paradouro, Avenida Almirante Reis 106, 1100 Lisboa (tel. 01/81-53-256), occupies a somewhat inconvenient location on a busy traffic artery on the east side of town. Once you find it, amid a cluster of commercial and residential buildings, you'll take an elevator to the seventh-floor reception area. The 27 bedrooms are clean and comfortable, and 23 of these offer a private bath. Each room has a phone, although only 20% of them have a TV. Singles without bath cost 3,900$ ($26.15) daily or 6,200$ ($41.55) with bath. Doubles without bath rent for 4,500$ ($30.15) daily or 6,800$ ($45.55) with bath. Breakfast is included in these rates. Laundry service is provided, as is 24-hour room service. You'll be served breakfast while seated in a wrought-iron garden chair near a big window with a view over a 19th-century villa far below. A bar offers drinks throughout the afternoon. Parking is available in the basement for 450$ ($30.15). Subway: Arroios. No credit cards.

---

2. In the Chiado District

Borges Hotel, Rua Garrett 108, 1200 Lisboa (tel. 01/34-61-951; fax 01/86-78-96), has a beehive reception area as crowded as the 19th-century coffeehouse next door, A Brasileira, the traditional gathering spot for the Portuguese literati. On the second floor of the Borges, the dining room partially escaped modernization, its paneled walls and crystal chandeliers intact. The 100 bedrooms and 10 suites have been refurnished in a semicontemporary manner, with traditional draperies and counterpanes. All the rooms have private bath or shower, phone, and TV. Singles range from 7,500$ ($50.25) to 8,500$ ($56.95) daily, with doubles costing 8,500$ ($56.95) to 9,500$ ($63.65), including breakfast. The location is minutes from some of Lisbon's best-known restaurants and fado clubs, as well as the shops of Baixa. Subway: Rossio. AE, DC, MC, V.

---

3. In the Graça District

Hotel Albergaria da Senhora do Monte, Calçada do Monte 39, 1100 Lisboa (tel. 01/86-60-02; fax 01/87-77-83), is a special little hilltop hotel with a unique character. It's perched near a belvedere, the Miradouro Senhora do Monte, in the

Graça district—a spot where knowing Lisboans take their friends for a memorable nighttime view of the city, the Castle of St. George, and the Tagus. Built originally as an apartment house, the hotel has been converted into a clublike establishment, with lots of lavish touches for those seeking an unusual atmosphere. The living room is intimate, with large tufted sofas and oversized tables and lamps. Multilevel corridors lead to the excellent bedrooms, all 28 of which contain private baths and verandas. The rooms reveal a decorator's touch, especially the gild-edge door panels, the grass-cloth walls, and the tile baths with bronze fixtures. Accommodations contain air conditioning, TV, and phone. Singles range from 11,000$ ($73.70) to 12,500$ ($83.75) daily; doubles 14,000$ ($93.80) to 19,500$ ($130.65). The hotel also rents four suites, costing from 21,000$ ($140.70). Breakfast, the only meal served, is included in these rates. Room service is available, as is laundry and valet. Streetcar: 28. AE, DC, MC, V.

4. In the Belém District

Hotel da Torre, Rua dos Jerónimos 8, 1400 Lisboa (tel. 01/36-30-161; fax 01/64-59-95), is in Belém, a suburb of Lisbon, near an estuary of the Tagus. As such, it is suitable primarily for those who want to be in the belt of Lisbon's museumland. The renovated inn rises three stories, and is furnished in a regional style. The 50 bedrooms, with comfortable, modern furnishings, cost from 9,750$ ($65.35) daily in a single or from 12,250$ ($82.10) in a double, including breakfast. Rooms contain TV and phone but no minibar or air conditioning. The air conditioning is confined to the public rooms and the wood-paneled bar. The modern lobby contains sunken seating areas, overhead balconies, and large front windows. Regional food is served in the provincial restaurant, São Jerónimo. Laundry/valet service is provided. Bus: 28 or 43. Tram: 17.

LISBON DINING

Lisbon offers a wide range of dining spots, headed by such places as Gambrinus and Tágide. The cuisine in these establishments is of a high standard, ranking with that of Europe's leading restaurants. Here, you'll encounter the best of Portuguese dishes, intermixed with classics from the continental repertoire. In such establishments, a knowledgeable maître d'hôtel and a wine steward are at your elbow to guide your culinary decisions.

But you needn't pay high prices for top-quality food in Lisbon and its environs. There are many noteworthy regional restaurants offering Portuguese cooking, even foreign viands, at all price levels, from a simple beer-and-steak tavern to a formal town house–style dining room, to a cliffside restaurant with a panoramic view. Aside from the recommendations found in this chapter, you may also want to consider having your evening meal at one of the fado cafés (see Chapter 9).

Portuguese friends often confide that it takes two hours for people of their country to dine—"one hour to talk, another to eat."

1. In the Center

VERY EXPENSIVE
    Gambrinus, Rua das Portas de Santo Antão 25 (tel. 342-14-66), is one of the premier restaurants of Lisbon, the finest choice for fish and shellfish. It's in the congested heart of the city, off the Rossio near the rail station on a little square behind the National Theater. You can arrive early (providing you made a reservation) and enjoy an apéritif at the bar in front while munching on "sea creatures." Have your meal while sitting on leather chairs in the rear or under a cathedral-beamed ceiling, or select a little table beside a fireplace upon the raised end of the room. All is dominated by an impressionist tapestry along one wall. There is also an alcove with a stained-glass enclosure.

    There is a diversified à la carte menu, and you can also peruse the specialties of the day. The soups are good, especially the bisque of shellfish. The most expensive items on the menu are shrimp and lobster dishes. However, you might prefer conch with shellfish thermidor or sea bass minhota. If you don't fancy fish, and you like your dishes *hot*, ask for chicken piri-piri. The restaurant also offers elaborate desserts. Coffee with a 30-year-old brandy complements the meal perfectly. Expect to spend from 9,000$ ($60.30) to 12,000$ ($80.40). The restaurant is open daily from noon to 2am. Subway: Rossio. AE, MC, V.

Restaurant Aviz, Rua Serpa Pinto 12B (tel. 34-28-391). What is now the Aviz was saved from the demolition of the famed hotel of the same name, once (in pre-Ritz days) the only deluxe hotel in Lisbon. You ascend a staircase into the foyer lounge. While drinks are served, menu selections are made. Mahogany paneling, tufted black-leather chairs, green marble columns, and crystal create the ambience of a private club. The former hotel staff brought not only parts of the torn-down establishment with them, including all the silver, a meat trolley, and the wall torchères, but the recipes of the kitchen as well.

The cuisine is both Portuguese and international. For a beginning, try smoked swordfish. An alternative might be vichyssoise Rothschild, based on creamed prawns. A bevy of main dishes includes perdreau mode d'Alcantara, about which Bonaparte's Marshal Junot wrote, "It is the only positive factor that emerged from our ill-fated Iberian invasion campaign." Desserts include Aviz crêpes, flamed in kirsch at the table. A dinner costs from 8,000$ ($53.60) to 10,000$ ($67) and up, with the emphasis on up. Your table must be reserved in one of three intimate dining rooms, preferably the larger green-and-gold chamber, with its ornate bronze, frosted-glass, and globed chandelier. The Aviz is open from noon to 3pm and 7 to 10:30pm; closed at lunch Saturday and all day Sunday. Bus: 15. AE, DC, MC, V.

EXPENSIVE

António Clara, Avenida da República 38 (tel. 76-63-80). Even if it weren't one of the capital's best restaurants, this exquisitely crafted turn-of-the-century villa would still be famous as the former private home of one of Portugal's most revered architects. It was built in 1890 by Miguel Ventura Terra (1866–1918), whose photograph hangs amid polished antiques and gilded mirrors. The angled and tiled wings of the villa seem to embrace visitors as they approach the vaguely Moorish facade. The soaring height of the curved staircase and the elegant moldings serve as attractive backdrops for 17th-century wood carvings and belle époque porcelain. You might enjoy a before-dinner drink in the 19th-century saloon, where griffins snarl down from the pink-shaded chandelier. Even the service areas of this house, the ones rarely seen by visitors, contain ceiling frescoes. The dining room is one of the loveliest in Lisbon.

Full meals, priced from 6,000$ ($40.20), include such specialties as smoked swordfish, paella for two, chateaubriand béarnaise, codfish Clara style, and beef Wellington. The cuisine is both Portuguese and international and reservations are required. A well-coordinated group of wine stewards, headwaiters, and attendants make wine tasting a ceremony. The restaurant is open Monday to Saturday. Lunch is served from noon to 3pm and dinner from 7pm to midnight. There's a ground-floor bar, accessible through its own entrance, for an after-dinner drink if you're interested. The bar contains an art gallery with frequent special shows. Subway: Entre Campos. AE, DC, MC, V.

Clara, Campo dos Mártires da Pátria 49 (tel. 57-04-34). In a hillside location amid decaying villas and city squares, this green-tile house contains an elegant hideaway. You might enjoy a drink under the ornate ceiling of the bar, whose locale has functioned over the years as an antiques store, the living room of a private apartment, and the foyer of a palatial house. A piano plays softly at dinner. During lunch, however, you might prefer a seat near the plants and fountain of the garden terrace. At night, an indoor seat—perhaps near the large marble fireplace—is more appealing. Menu specialties include tournedos Clara, stuffed rabbit with red wine sauce, four different kinds of pasta, codfish Clara, filet of sole with orange, pheasant with grapes, and Valencian paella. The menu is both Portuguese and continental, and reservations are required. Full meals, costing from 5,500$ ($36.85) to 8,000$ ($53.60), are served Monday to Saturday throughout the year. Hours are noon to 3:30pm and 7pm to midnight. Subway: Avenida. AE, DC, MC, V.

Restaurante Tavares, Rua da Misericórdia 37 (tel. 34-21-112), is a gilt-and-crystal world. This slice of the past offers a palace-style setting and fine cuisine. White-and-gold paneled walls, three chandeliers, and Louis XV armchairs all keep intact the spirit of the 18th century. Actually, Tavares was originally a café founded in 1784. When the two Tavares brothers died in the 19th century, half a dozen waiters formed a partnership and took over the restaurant. It is still owned by a group of waiters, who continue its high standards. It is the oldest restaurant in Lisbon, attracting many diplomatic and government heads, as well as the literati. However, its reputation as an exclusive bastion of Portuguese society faded with the revolution. Drinks are served in the petite front salon, where you can plan your meal. The wine steward aids you in your selection (he tries to provide a pleasant wine and does not push the most expensive bottles).

A beginning might be crêpes de marisco. A main-course selection might be the sole in champagne, a real delicacy, or tournedos Grand Duc. Many continental dishes are scattered throughout the menu, including the classic scallops of veal viennoise. However, the restaurant nearly always serves such basic Portuguese dishes as sardines and salted codfish, so secure is it in its reputation. Expect to spend from 5,800$ ($38.85) to 8,000$ ($53.60). To complete your meal, why not try the chef's dessert specialty, a high-rise soufflé, followed by a café filtro? The restaurant is open from 1 to 3pm and 8 to 10:30pm. It's closed Saturday and for lunch on Sunday. Reservations are necessary. Bus: 15. AE, DC, MC, V.

MODERATE
A Gondola, Avenida de Berna 64 (tel. 79-70-426), is Lisbon's "Little Italy," serving perhaps the finest Italian specialties in town. The restaurant offers indoor dining as well as al fresco meals in the courtyard. Although the decor isn't inspired, the food makes the restaurant worth the trip out of the city center. A full dinner is offered for about 3,500$ ($23.45), quite a buy when you realize what you get. A first-course selection might be Chaves ham with melon and figs, followed by filet of sole meunière or grilled sardines with pimientos. This is followed by yet another course, ravioli or cannelloni in the Roman style, perhaps veal cutlet milanese. The banquet is topped off by fruit or dessert. The restaurant is open from 12:30 to 3pm and 7:30 to 10pm; closed Saturday for lunch and Sunday. This is a convenient choice if you're visiting the Gulbenkian Museum in the area. Reservations are necessary. Bus: 16 or 26. Subway: Praça de Espanha. V.

Bachus, Largo da Trindade 9 (tel. 34-21-260). Amusing murals cover the wood-paneled facade of this deluxe restaurant, and inside, the decor is elaborate and sophisticated. The ambience is somewhere between a private salon in a Russian palace, a turn-of-the-century English club, and a stylized Manhattan bistro. You can drop in for a drink or mount the brass staircase that winds around a column of illuminated glass to the dining room. If you're dining, call for a table. Menu specialties include a frequently changing array of dishes based on the market availability of their ingredients. Full meals, priced from 5,000$ ($33.50) per person, might include a mixed grill Bachus, chateaubriand with béarnaise sauce, mountain goat, beef Stroganoff, shrimp Bachus, or other daily specials. The wine list is extensive. Food is served daily from noon to 2am. Bus: 15. AE, DC, MC, V.

Bodegón, Hotel Fenix, Praça Marquês de Pombal 8 (tel. 52-91-55), is a first-class grill room attached to this previously recommended hotel, which serves Portuguese, Spanish, and international cuisine. A marble staircase descends to it from street level. After stopping for an apéritif in the bar, you dine in a tavern setting with beamed ceiling, tile floors, and wood-paneled pillars. Depending on availability you might enjoy quail, partridge, or fresh salmon from the north of Portugal. You can also order cultivated oysters, which are at their best after October. Among à la carte selections are fried squid, Valencian paella, and some Italian dishes. For dessert, try, if featured, the delectable fresh strawberries from Sintra. Expect to spend from 6,000$ ($40.20) for a meal, although a tourist menu costs 3,800$ ($25.45). Service is daily from 12:30 to 3pm and 7:30 to 10:30pm. Reservations are necessary. AE, DC, MC, V.

Casa da Comida, Travessa de Amoreiras 1 (tel. 68-53-76), is recognized by local gourmets as having some of the finest food in Lisbon. If you're in the city on one of the gray, rainy days that often occur December through March, this is an excellent choice for dining, with a roaring fire greeting and warming you. At any time of year, however, you will find the Portuguese food good and the atmosphere pleasant. The dining room is handsomely decorated, the bar is done in period style, and there's a charming walled garden. Specialties include roast kid with herbs, a medley of shell-fish Casa da Comida, and pregado with green pepper. French cuisine is also offered. An excellent selection of wines is available from the cellar. Meals cost from 5,000$ ($33.50) up. The restaurant is open from 1 to 3:30pm and 8 to 11pm. It's important to make a reservation here. The place is closed Saturday at lunch and on Sunday. Subway: Rotunda. AE, DC, MC, V.

Chester, Rua Rodrigo da Fonseca 87D (tel. 65-73-47), near the Ritz Hotel, is an attractive restaurant and bar, with a good cellar. Its specialty is grilled steaks, plus continental dishes. The peppersteak is tempting, as is the rib steak for two. Entrecôte with whisky sauce is hearty, and the fondue bourguignonne is prepared only for two persons. You might begin with a crab cocktail, finishing with flambéed pineapple. The tab is likely to range from 5,000$ ($33.50) to 6,000$ ($40.20) for a complete meal. Service is efficient, and reservations are suggested. Open Monday to Saturday from 12:30 to 3pm and 8:30 to 10:30pm, the restaurant is upstairs, and the cozy little bar lies below. Subway: Rotunda. AE, DC, MC, V.

Conventual, Praça das Flores 45 (tel. 60-91-96). In many ways this is one of my favorite Lisbon restaurants. That's due in large part to the taste and sensitivity of its gracious owner, Mrs. Dina Marques. It's on one of the loveliest residential squares in town, behind a discreetly plain wooden door. Once inside, you'll be treated to a display of old panels from baroque churches, religious statues, and bric-a-brac from Mrs. Marques's private collection in an attractively austere environment whose temperature is kept gratifyingly cool by the building's very old, thick stone walls and terra-cotta floor. If you select this place, you'll be in good company, since the prime minister of Portugal comes here. Lunch is served from 12:30 to 3:30pm and dinner from 7:30 to 11:30pm. As is appropriate in any establishment even resembling a convent, work stops on Sunday.

Many of the delectably flavored recipes were invented by the owner. They include a creamy coriander soup, stewed partridge in port, ox tongue in egg sauce, and a tempting form of grilled monkfish in a herb-flavored cream sauce, along with osso buco, frogs' legs in buttery garlic, and stewed clams in a sauce of red peppers, onions, and cream. The cuisine is Portuguese, and reservations are necessary. A fixed-price menu costs 3,800$ ($25.45), although most à la carte meals range from 4,000$ ($26.80) to 7,000$ ($46.90). Bus: 100. AE, DC, MC, V.

Escorial, Rua das Portas de Santo Antão 47 (tel. 34-64-429). You can dine here with Spanish flair. Right in the heart of Lisbon's restaurant district, this Spanish-owned establishment combines classic Spanish dishes with an inviting ambience. The dining room walls are paneled in rosewood, with frosted-globe lighting. Before dinner you can have a drink in a cocktail lounge called the Art Room that exhibits contemporary Portuguese artists. A menu is printed in English (always look for the course of the day). Your most expensive selection would be from the lobster tank. You might enjoy a sampling of Portuguese oysters or squid on a skewer. A selection of the chef's specialties is likely to include barbecued baby goat, beef Stroganoff, or partridge casserole. A dinner begins at 6,000$ ($40.20), and service is from noon to midnight daily. Reservations are advised. Subway: Rossio. AE, DC, MC, V.

Frei Papinhas, Rua Dom Francisco Manuel de Melo 32 (tel. 65-87-57), near Edward VII Park, lying off the Rua Castilho, is an easy walk from the Ritz and Meridien hotels. The restaurant was created by a group of writers and intellectuals who wanted a place where they could meet for really good food and enjoy vigorous conversation at their leisure. They ended up with their own attractive, cozy eating place, offering excellent service. The interior is done in sophisticated country style, relying on natural elements such as a wall of exposed stone, old brick behind the front bar, heavy black beams, and whitewashed walls.

In air-conditioned comfort, you can enjoy an array of international cookery, including fresh fish and game dishes. You might begin with one of the chef's soups, such as vichyssoise or gazpacho, followed by filet of swordfish or pork Alentejo. Racks of the best Portuguese wines are available. Meals cost from 5,000$ ($33.50) to 6,000$ ($40.20). Hours are daily from 12:30 to 3pm and 7 to 11pm. Reservations are needed. Subway: São Sebastião. AE, DC, MC, V.

Numero Um, Rua Dom Francisco Manuel de Melo 44A (tel. 68-43-26), is the "Number One" steak house of Lisbon. The location, on a somewhat hard-to-find street, is off the Rua Castilho, near Edward VII Park. English is spoken. The atmosphere and English decor are relatively subdued, but the platters sizzle. Gourmets often fault Portuguese beef, but this special restaurant imports its beef from Brazil. The main menu is filet steak, T-bone, rumpsteak, and kebab. Naturally, you can order it well done, medium, or rare. Most guests order a mixed salad to accompany their meat platter, finishing with a fruit salad. Every day the kitchen prepares a meal of Portuguese regional cooking, costing from 4,500$ ($30.15). On Friday a Brazilian meal is offered, usually a feijoada, at the same price. Otherwise, à la carte meals cost from 4,000$ ($26.80). Hours are from 12:30 to 3pm and 7:30 to 10:30pm. The restaurant is closed for lunch on Saturday and all day Sunday. Reservations are necessary. Bus: 31. Subway: São Sebastião. AE, DC, MC, V.

Pabe, Rua Duque de Palmela 27A (tel. 53-74-84), is the Portuguese name for pub, and that's what this cozy English-style place is. Convenient to the Praça Marquês de Pombal, the pub has done its best to emulate English establishments, with a soft carpet on the floor, mugs hanging over the long bar, a beamed ceiling, coats-of-arms, and engravings of hunting scenes around the walls. Two saloon-type doors lead into a wood-paneled dining room, where you can sup on meat specially imported from the U.S. A chateaubriand for two is about the most expensive dish. If you prefer local fare, start off with a shrimp cocktail, then Portuguese veal liver, or a supremo de galinha (chicken breast with mushrooms). Finish with sherbet. Meals cost from 4,000$ ($26.80) and up per person, plus drinks. The cuisine is both Portuguese and international, and reservations are necessary. The crowd tends to be a well-groomed Portuguese set as well as resident Yanks and Britons. The Pabe is open daily from noon to 1am. Subway: Rotunda. AE, DC, MC, V.

Restaurant 33, Rua Alexandre Herculano 33A (tel. 54-60-79), is a little discovery. Decorated in a style evocative of an English hunting lodge, it lies near many previously recommended hotels, including the Altis. It specializes in an array of Portuguese and international dishes, including shellfish rice served in a crab shell. You can also order smoked salmon or lobster Tour d'Argent, as well as peppersteak. Service is Monday to Saturday from 12:30 to 3pm and 8:30 to 10pm. On Saturday, only dinner is served. You can enjoy a glass of port in the small bar at the entrance while you peruse the menu. A full meal costs from 2,800$ ($18.75). Reservations are suggested. Subway: Rotunda. MC, V.

Sancho, Travessa da Glória 14 (tel. 346-97-80), is a cozy, rustic-style restaurant just off the Avenida da Liberdade, close to Praça dos Restauradores. The decor is in a classic Iberian style, with a beamed ceiling, a fireplace, and leather-and-wood chairs. The walls are stuccoed. In summer there is air conditioning. A classic Portuguese cuisine is served. A fish gratinée soup is the classic opener. Shellfish is the specialty, and it's always expensive. Main dishes are likely to include the chef's special hake or pan-broiled Portuguese steak. If your palate is made of asbestos, order churrasco de cabrito (goat) au piri-piri. For dessert, sample crêpes Suzette or perhaps a chocolate mousse. Meals cost from 2,500$ ($16.75), and service is Monday to Saturday from noon to 3pm and 7 to 10pm. Reservations are suggested. Subway: Avenida. AE, MC, V.

Sua Exceléncia, Rua do Conde 40–42 (tel. 60-36-14), is the creation of Francisco Queiroz, who was a travel agent in Angola before he settled in Portugal. In Lisbon, he has created his little dream restaurant, with a refined, sedate atmosphere, attracting a discerning clientele. Outside you'll see no sign. Just ring the bell to announce your arrival and the proprietor will greet you. The atmosphere he has created is somewhat like a fashionable drawing room, with colorful tables placed in an intimate Portuguese provincial decor, made cool by the terra-cotta floor and high painted ceiling.

Some dishes served are uncommon in Portugal. Specialties include prawns piri-

piri (not unreasonably hot), rollmop sardines, what he proclaims as the "best smoked swordfish in Portugal," and clams in at least five different recipes. One unusual specialty is "little jacks," a small fish eaten whole: heads, tails, everything. It's served with a well-flavored "paste" made from 2-day-old bread. Meals cost 3,500$ ($23.45) and up. Hours are 1 to 3pm and 8 to 10:30pm. The place is closed on Wednesday, on Saturday and Sunday at lunchtime in July and August, and for the entire month of September. The restaurant is just a block up the hill from the entrance to the National Art Gallery, so it could be visited on a tie-in museum/luncheon adventure, although its ambience is more charming in the evening. Reservations are needed. Bus: 27 or 49. AE, DC, MC, V.

Telheiro, Rua Latino Coelho 10A (tel. 53-40-07), means "The Roof" in Portuguese, and it's a bistrolike place not far from the Sheraton Hotel. The ceilings are beamed, and you sit on wooden chairs with heart shapes carved out of their backs. The waiters are clad in scarlet waistcoats. Peppers hang from the chandeliers. Pâté, butter, and rolls are placed on your table before you even order. The cuisine is from the various regions of Portugal. Different specialties are featured every day—perhaps gazpacho, a cabbage-and-potato soup, mussels, suckling pig, grilled fresh sea bass or sole, or seafood with rice in a casserole. For dessert, try the fresh Portuguese fruit. At the presentation of your bill, be prepared to pay 1,500$ ($10.05) to 2,000$ ($13.40). Tourist menus cost from 1,000$ ($6.70) to 1,500$ ($10.05). Hours are daily from noon to 3pm and 7 to 10:30pm. Reservations are suggested. Bus: 30. AE, DC, MC, V.

INEXPENSIVE

António Restaurante, Rua Tomás Ribiero 63 (tel. 53-87-80), was created especially for Portuguese businesspeople who want a relaxing ambience and good Portuguese and international food. A corner establishment, just a bit away from the din of central traffic, it is a refreshing oasis. The color scheme of blue and white prevails, with blue-and-white glazed earthenware tiles, a blue free-form ceiling, blue linen tops over white cloths, even crisp blue jackets on waiters. The menu is in English. You can start with shellfish soup. Orders of fish, garnished with vegetables, include filets with tomato sauce and baked sole. Arroz de marisco (rice with shellfish) is a specialty. Among the fowl and meat dishes, try an order of breaded chicken with spaghetti or pork with clams, in the Alentejana style. The owner-manager recommends his açorda de marisco, a stewlike, breaded dish of shellfish and eggs, which is a treat. The dessert list is extensive, with even a banana split. A full meal comes to 3,000$ ($20.10). Food is served daily from noon to 4pm and 7 to 10:30pm. Reservations aren't needed. Subway: Picoas. Bus: 30, 36, or 38. MC, V.

Bota Alta, Travessa da Queimada 35–37 (tel. 34-27-959), sits at the very top of a steeply inclined street in the Bairro Alto, and boasts a clientele which eagerly crams into its two dining rooms, sometimes standing at the bar waiting for a table to become available. Reservations are needed. Painted a shade of cerulean blue, it contains rustic artifacts as well as lots of original art and photographs. Full Portuguese meals cost from 2,500$ ($16.75) each. These might include beefsteak Bota Alta, several different preparations of codfish, and a frequently changing array of daily specials, including, for example, Hungarian goulash. The establishment is open Monday to Saturday from noon to 2:30pm and 7 to 11:30pm. Bus: 15, 24, or 30. AE, DC, MC, V.

Bonjardim, Travessa de Santo Antão 10 (tel. 34-27-424), quite rightly deserves the enthusiastic approval of a Boston traveler: "I was given the names of eight inexpensive restaurants, including Bonjardim, to try out in Lisbon during my 5-day stay. I ended up trying only two of them, as I took the rest of my meals at Bonjardim, sampling a different dish for lunch and dinner every day." Manuel Castanheira, who owns and manages the restaurant, caters mostly to families, providing wholesome Portuguese meals that fit most budgets. So successful has been the operation that he has taken over a building across the street, where the same menu is offered.

In the main restaurant, the second-floor air-conditioned dining room is in the rustic Portuguese style, with a beamed ceiling and a tile mural depicting farm creatures. The noonday sun pours in through seven windows. The street-floor dining room, with an adjoining bar for before-meal drinks, has walls of decorative tiles. During your dinner the aroma of fat chickens roasting to a golden brown on the charcoal spit can only persuade you to try one. An order of this house specialty, frango no espeto, is adequate for two persons, with a side dish of french fries. The cook also bakes hake in the Portuguese style. An alternative dish is pork fried with clams. For dessert, you can order a cassate. You can dine well here for less than 1,800$ ($12.05). The Bonjardim is open 7 days a week from noon to 11pm. Reservations aren't needed. Subway: Rossio. AE, DC, MC, V.

Bonjardim also has a nearby self-service cafeteria at Rua do Jardim do Regedor 41 (tel. 34-61-727). Sample Portuguese dishes: seafood soup, always a good choice; half a roast chicken with trimmings, traditional and reliable; garoupa fish a Bretone, the chef's specialty; and mousse, a velvety finish. A meal costs around 1,200$ ($8.05), excluding your drink. The decor is simple, plastic, and efficient. The cafeteria is near the Rossio. It's open daily from noon to 10pm. Closed: June. Reservations aren't needed. Subway: Rossio. No credit cards.

Choupal, Rua do Salitre 9 (tel. 54-29-63), is a stylized tavern, 1 minute from Avenida da Liberdade, where regional dishes are served family style. Its walls have aqua and olive tiles, combined with wood paneling, and the ceiling is in a warm brown cork. There is an English menu but the cuisine is Portuguese. The waiter brings a loaf of crusty bread and a little ceramic jar of mildly seasoned pâté with sweet butter to begin your meal. You might start with a shellfish soup or savory Spanish-style clams. Two main-dish specialties are roast chicken and lampreys, those tiny eellike creatures from the north of Portugal. The chef also does a special beef dish. A meal here costs from 2,500$ ($16.75), although a tourist menu is offered for only 1,250$ ($8.40). Lunch is Monday through Saturday from noon to 4pm and dinner is Monday through Saturday from 7pm to midnight. Reservations aren't needed. Bus: 1, 2, 44, or 45. AE, DC, MC, V.

Leão d'Ouro, Rua 1 de Dezembro 93 (tel. 34-26-195), stands beside the Estação do Rossio, the railway station best described as Victorian Gothic. The atmosphere of a large, old tavern prevails—high brick arches, a beamed ceiling, and a pictorial tile, depicting Portugal's liberation from Spain in 1640. In the late 1980s, this restaurant once more became the fine dining room it was once reputed to be. The waiters are again clad in formal black clothing with black bow ties. The cuisine is Portuguese, and reservations aren't needed. You can start your meal with a rich-tasting soup, such as crème de camarão (cream of shrimp) or sopa a alentejana (made with bread and garlic, among other ingredients). Among the meat dishes, try pork chops prepared in the Alentejana way or filet mignon. A fowl specialty is frango de churrasco (barbecued chicken). For dessert try the pêssegos (peaches). The average cost of a meal, including wine, is from 2,500$ ($16.75). Service is from noon to 3pm for lunch, 7 to 10pm for dinner. The restaurant is closed Sunday. Subway: Rossio. AE, DC, MC, V.

Lychee, Rua Barata Salguiero 37 (tel. 54-59-90), is a basement-level restaurant, with a decor inspired by the Portuguese colony of Macau. It is one of the finest Chinese restaurants in the city, serving daily from noon to 3pm and 7 to 11pm. Meals cost from 3,000$ ($20.10), and an array of specialties are presented for your selection. Typical dishes include shrimp in a hot pepper sauce, fish with black bean sauce, honey garlic chicken wings, and deep-fried banana chicken. Reservations are rarely needed. Subway: Rotunda. Bus: 1, 2, 36, 44, or 45. AE, DC, MC, V.

O Funil (The Funnel), Avenida Elias Garcia 82A (tel. 76-60-07), specializes in cozinha portuguesa (Portuguese cuisine) and does the cooking so well and so inexpensively that a line forms at the door, and it's often hard to get a table. You should reserve. You enter a street-floor tavern with crowded tables. But chances are you'll be directed to the lower level, where you can wait at a tiny bar while a table is made ready for you. The owners serve their own vinho da casa (wine of the house). Try their red Alijó. The kitchen buys good-quality meat and fresh fish daily. The most successful fish dishes are boiled codfish with a sauce made with eggs, flour, olive oil, milk, and cream, and eels stewed with a sausage of pickled pork, smoked ham, and slices of toast. The most favored meat dish is mutton stew with boiled potatoes, as well as a chicken stuffed with smoked ham. For dessert, try the chocolate pyramid and nut tart. Meals cost from 2,200$ ($14.75), and service is from noon to 3:30pm and 7 to 10:30pm. It is closed Sunday evening and Monday. Bus: 1, 36, 38, or 45. MC, V.

Tia Matilde, Rua Doutor Alvaro de Castro 12B (tel. 65-87-57), is a very large and busy place in the Praça de Espanha area. The service here is often hectic, and tourists are rare, but the Portuguese love this one. Here you can sample home cookery and the savory specialties of Ribatejo, that region of fighting bulls previewed in Chapter 14. Specialties include cabrito assado (roast mountain goat), arroz de frango (chicken with rice), bacalhau (codfish) a Tia Matilde, plus many other à la carte items. Chefs also make a pungent caldeirada, or fish stew. The restaurant is open from noon to 4pm and 7 to 10:30pm Monday to Saturday. Meals cost from 2,500$ ($16.75). Reservations aren't needed. Bus: 31. AE, DC, MC, V.

Toni dos Bifes, Avenida Praia da Vitória 50E (tel. 53-60-80), is an old Lisbon standby where hungry Portuguese and foreigners have been going for years to get a good, inexpensive, and copious meal. Near the Monumental cinema, the restaurant has a plain but pleasant decor, with a counter on one side of the dining room and small tables on the other. Some tables and chairs are placed outdoors as well, in French café style, with a glass enclosure. You begin with small portions of pâté, along with butter and toast, bread and roll, and then you can launch into the homemade tomato soup or perhaps a seafood omelet, followed by a Toni special beefsteak. Other specialties include Toni calamares (squid), grilled or meunière sole, pork Alentejana style, and roast duck. Finish with a melon with ham or a peach Melba. The final tab is a modest 1,800$ ($12.05). It is open daily from noon to 10:30pm. Reservations aren't needed. Subway: Picoas. No credit cards.

Velha-Goa, Rua Tomás de Anunciação 41B (tel. 60-04-46), evokes memories of the Portuguese empire. The Portuguese colony of Goa was forcibly annexed by India in 1961, but the aura still lingers in this restaurant. The background is Asian, and the cuisine is Goanese. All dishes are prepared according to the taste of the diners—that is mild, pungent, and *very* pungent. The meal begins with the appetizer, samuchas. House specialties include curries—prawns, chicken, Madrasta—but the chef also serves beef and pork chops in case you're dining with someone who doesn't like Indian food. Expect to pay 2,000$ ($13.40) for a meal in the dining hall. The restaurant is open from noon to midnight, and you must arrive before 10:30pm. Closed Monday and Saturday lunch. Reservations aren't recommended. Bus: 9. AE, DC, MC, V.

Xico Carreira, Parque Mayer (tel. 346-38-05). To reach it, you'll have to traverse the grounds of a famous but slightly seedy amusement park whose arcades, theaters, and restaurants open onto the Avenida da Liberdade. Even if the rides and the theaters are not operational at the hour of your visit, the site is evocative of small amusement parks around the world (tired children, cotton candy, and too many restaurants). Some Lisboans, however, head for what is probably the best restaurant within the theme park, the one most distantly removed from the cluster of other buildings in the park's center. Perched on a hillside overlooking the park below, scattered with bullfight memorabilia, and preceded with a steep flight of zigzagging concrete steps, it charges only 1,800$ ($12.05) for a simple and unpretentious meal from a limited but inexpensive menu. Menu items include beef of the house, pork cutlets, and such Portuguese specialties as grilled sardines and codfish with green sauce. The only appetizer might be a steaming bowl of such soups as caldo verde. The place is open daily from noon to midnight, and on Friday night, there's likely to be a fado performance. Reservations aren't needed. Subway: Avenida. No credit cards.

2. In the Chiado District

Tágide, Largo da Academia Nacional de Belas Artes 18–20 (tel. 34-20-720), has had a prestigious past. Once the town house of a diplomat, then a major nightclub, it now is one of Lisbon's leading restaurants. Its situation is colorful—up from the docks, on a steep hill on a ledge overlooking the old part of Lisbon and the Tagus. The dining room has view windows overlooking moored ships and the port. Set into the white plaster walls are large figures made of blue-and-white tiles, each depicting a famous queen; glittering above are crystal chandeliers.

Both Portuguese dishes and selections from the international repertoire are featured and are beautifully served. For an appetizer, I suggest the salmon pâté, cold stuffed crab, or smoked swordfish. Other specialties include suprême of halibut with coriander, pork with clams and coriander, and grilled baby goat with herbs. For dessert, I recommend the stuffed crêpes Tágide. Expect to spend from 6,000$ ($40.20) to 9,000$ ($60.30), plus the cost of your wine. Food is served from noon to 2:30pm and 7:30 to 10:30pm. The restaurant is closed Saturday and Sunday. Always call for a reservation. Bus: 15. AE, DC, MC, V.

3. In the Graça District

Restaurante O Faz Figura, Rua do Paraíso 15B (tel. 86-89-81), is one of the best and most attractively decorated dining rooms in Lisbon. When reserving a table, ask to be seated on the veranda, where you can order both lunch and dinner overlooking the Tagus. The restaurant lies in the heart of the Alfama, and it offers faultless service and typical Portuguese food along with international specialties. A complete meal will cost from 4,000$ ($26.80) to 5,000$ ($33.50). You are given a warm reception and then shown to your table unless you want to make a stop first for a before-dinner drink in the "international cocktail bar." The restaurant serves Monday to Saturday from 12:30 to 3pm and 8pm to midnight. Reservations are needed. Subway: Santa Apolónia.

4. In the Belém District

MODERATE

São Jerónimo, Rua dos Jerónimos 12 (tel. 64-87-97). A visit to this light-hearted and elegant restaurant could be combined with a trip to the famous monastery of the same name. The restaurant sits directly on the east side of the monastery, behind a big-windowed facade that floods the interior with sunlight. It takes its inspiration from the Roaring '20s, with a French-style decoration; chairs are by Philip Stark, and armchairs in the bar by Carbusier. The waiters wear striped shirts, gray waistcoats, and gray aprons. Hours are from 12:30 to 3pm and 7:30 to 11pm Monday to Saturday. The average price of a meal of Portuguese regional dishes or international specialties ranges from 3,000$ ($20.10) to 4,800$ ($32.15). Reservations are suggested. Bus: 27, 28, or 29. Streetcar: 16 or 17. AE, DC, MC, V.

INEXPENSIVE

Dionysos', Rua Belém 124 (tel. 64-06-32), is a good Greek restaurant out in the suburb of Belém, an ideal place for lunch if you're visiting the Coach Museum or the monastery nearby. Of course, it's also open for dinner. At the latter, while ensconced at a crowded table under a beamed ceiling on the second floor, you can dine by candlelight, enjoying good service. You might begin with a Greek salad for two. The popular souvlaki is featured, and you can also select from a varied menu of fish and meat dishes, finishing with a homemade dessert. Meals cost from 3,000$ ($20.10), although a tourist menu is offered for only 1,800$ ($12.05). Reservations are needed. Hours are Tuesday through Sunday for lunch from 12:30 to 3pm, and Tuesday through Sunday for dinner from 7 to 10pm. Bus: 27, 28, or 29. Streetcar: 16 or 17. AE, DC, MC, V.

---

5. In the Alfama

Michel, Largo de Santa Cruz do Castelo 5 (tel. 86-43-38), is a good French bistro with plenty of atmosphere and a hard-to-beat location right on the corner of a pocket-size plaza near St. George's Castle. It is considered one of the best restaurants in Lisbon. The restaurant is made up of three buildings: a barbershop, blacksmith's shop, and a wine tavern, all renovated and decorated in a tastefully rustic manner. Antique wood chests are used for coffee tables in the tavern portion, and a refectory table holding desserts stands in the walk-in fireplace. On the walls hangs everything from zithers to stirrups to ceramics. The chef-owner, Michel da Costa, an energetic host with a keen eye for food preparation and service, was trained in southern France. His restaurant provides French gourmet food with *cuisine moderne* overtones. You might begin with fish soup flavored with saffron or goat cheese coated in bread crumbs and tossed into a salad. Main-dish specialties include beef filet Santa Cruz and monkfish médaillons in a cognac sauce. An interesting selection of Portuguese cheeses is always ready to be brought out. However, most diners head immediately for the dessert list, called *sobremesas* in Portuguese, loaded with concoctions such as a parfait made with almonds from the Algarve with a hot chocolate sauce. The fresh fruit of the season is also presented, but I personally gravitate to the sorbet with champagne, the most soothing finish to such rich fare, which is likely to cost from 5,000$ ($33.50) to 6,000$ ($40.20). The restaurant is closed on Sunday and for lunch Saturday but open otherwise from 12:30 to 3pm and 8 to 11pm. A Portuguese fadista entertains at night. Reservations are imperative. Bus: 37. AE, DC, V.

---

6. In the Bairro Alto

Pap' Açorda, Rua da Atalaia 57–59 (tel. 346-48-11), lies behind a facade that was originally built for a bakery. It welcomes one of Lisbon's most diverse collection of iconoclasts (of all possible life-styles and sexual persuasions) into its pink-and-white interior. Most visitors order a predinner drink at the long and vaguely old-fashioned bar whose marble top dominates the front of the establishment. No one will object if you never get around to actually dining, but if you do, there are two different dining rooms in back, one of which is outfitted like a garden. Both are ornamented with Empire-style crystal chandeliers and an occasional decorative lattice set incongruously against a minimalist background. The cuisine is Portuguese. Full meals cost from 2,800$ ($18.75), and could include Spanish-style mussels, shellfish rice, sirloin steak with mushrooms, and a wide array of fish and shellfish dishes. The house specialty, after which the establishment was named, is a traditional dish incorporating coriander, bread, seafood, and eggs, called an *açorda*. Reservations in advance are a good idea. Subway: Rossio. MC, V.

Xêlê Banana, Praça das Flores 29 (tel. 395-25-15). Catering to a sophisticated and hip crowd of all possible persuasions, this stylish restaurant lies behind an anonymous-looking facade on a residential 18th-century square. The decor consists of wraparound green-and-brown murals of jungle plants evocative of the Brazilian rain forest, against a cream-colored background of art deco inspiration. Full meals cost around 3,000$ ($20.10) each, and might include oysters au gratin, rabbit mousse with walnuts, steak with Roquefort sauce, ox tongue with mushrooms, and several different preparations of partridge. Meals are served from 12:30 to 3pm and 8 to 11pm, except Saturday lunch and Sunday. Reservations are recommended. Metro: Restauradores. AE, DC, MC, V.

7. Specialty Dining

HOTEL DINING
Ritz Grill Room, Rua Rodrigo da Fonseca 88 (tel. 69-20-20), is in the Ritz Hotel, overlooking the terrace and Edward VII Park, but fortunately set apart from the main hotel lobby. This restaurant features a sophisticated menu of French, Portuguese, and international cuisine. Each dish is prepared with the freshest ingredients. You might begin with lobster and scampi salad with watercress and orange, or vegetable ravioli in a sauce made with morels. Bisque of fresh lobster is regularly featured. Fish courses include fresh salmon cooked in a papillotte with ginger or steamed kingfish stuffed with vegetables. Meat and poultry devotees might be attracted to tournedos with foie gras and Madeira sauce or duck breast with a custard apple vinegar. For dessert, a large variety of pastry is available from the trolley. For a finish, try filtered coffee. Service and taxes are included in the price, which is likely to be from 4,000$ ($26.80), plus the cost of your wine. Reservations are recommended. Hours are daily from noon to 3pm and 7:30 to 10:30pm. Subway: Rotunda. AE, DC, MC, V.

DINING WITH A VIEW
Casa do Leão, Castelo de São Jorge (tel. 87-59-62). My idea of the perfect way to visit the charmingly located Castle of St. George is to stop for a midday meal at this restaurant, which serves an international cuisine. It's in a low-slung stone building within the castle walls. You'll pass between a pair of ancient cannons before entering a sun-flooded vestibule where the splashing from a dolphin-shaped fountain and the welcoming voice of the uniformed maître d' provide the only sounds. Once seated in the spacious blue-tile dining room, beneath soaring brick vaulting, you'll enjoy a panoramic view of the Alfama and the legendary hills of Lisbon. There's even a baronial fireplace, which in cold weather provides an intimate retreat for an apéritif.

Regrettably, this establishment is open only for lunch, which it serves daily from 12:30 to 6pm. Full meals, which range upward from 4,500$ ($30.15), include roast duck with orange or grapes, pork chops St. George style, codfish with cream, smoked swordfish from Sesimbra, and an array of the chef's daily specials. Reservations are suggested. Bus: 37. AE, DC, MC, V.

LOCAL FAVORITES
Floresta do Ginjal, Ginjal 7 (tel. 275-00-87), overlooks the waterfront on the left bank of the Tagus in Cacilhas. Floresta is reached by ferryboat, from Praça do Comércio or from Cais do Sodré. You can buy tickets right on the boat.

You dine on some of the best-cooked fish dinners in the area, while overlooking the river life and the hills of Lisbon. The restaurant draws a thriving family trade from right-bank Lisbon families, especially on Sunday afternoon. While there is a complete Portuguese menu of meat and fowl dishes, the fish sets the pace. The fishermen's stew, or caldeirada, is a meal in itself. Another main course might be fried eels or turbot meunière. A dessert favorite is manjor de principe, made of eggs and almonds. You can also order strawberries with sugar. The average meal will cost from 3,000$ ($20.10). Food is served daily from noon to 3pm and 7 to 10:30pm. No credit cards.

BEER & SHELLFISH TAVERNS
Cervejaria Brilhante, Rua das Portas de Santo Antão 105 (tel. 34-61-407), is where to go if you enjoy seafood with beer. Lisboans from every walk of life stop off for a stein of beer and mariscos. Opposite the Coliseu, the tavern is decorated with stone arches, wood-paneled walls, and pictorial tiles of sea life. You can dine either at

the bar or at marble tables. The front window is packed with an appetizing array of king crab, oysters, lobster, baby clams, shrimps, even barnacles. And they aren't cheap. The price changes every day, depending on market quotations, and you pay by the kilo. A meal might cost 2,500$ ($16.75), unless you order some of the more expensive shellfish. A tourist menu, however, is priced at 1,240$ ($8.30). Hours are daily from noon to 1am. Reservations aren't necessary. Subway: Rossio. Bus: 1, 2, 36, 44, or 45. AE, DC, MC, V.

Cervejaria Ribadoura, Avenida da Liberdade 155 (tel. 54-94-11), is one of the typical shellfish and beer emporiums in central Lisbon, midway along the city's major boulevard at the corner of the Rua do Salitre. There's a minimum of decor in this tavern-style restaurant. The emphasis is on the varieties of fish: There are more than 50 fish and meat dishes, highlighted by the crustaceans and "sea fruit" recommendations. Try the bacalhau (codfish) à Bras. You can dine lightly as well, particularly at lunch, on such plates as shrimp omelet. Many diners often follow fish with a meat dish. However, only those who've been trained for at least 25 years on the most mouth-wilting Indian curries should try the sautéed pork cutlets with piri-piri, the latter made with red hot peppers from Angola. A wedge of Portuguese cheese "from the hills" finishes off the meal nicely. The place is open from noon to midnight daily. A typical meal costs 2,800$ ($18.75), and a tourist menu is offered for 2,400$ ($16.10). Reservations aren't necessary. Subway: Avenida. Bus: 1, 2, 44, or 45. AE, DC, MC, V.

Cervejaria da Trindade, Rua Nova de Trindade 20B (tel. 34-23-506), is a combination of a German beer hall and a Portuguese tavern—the oldest of them all, owned by the brewers of Sagres beer. Here you can order tasty little steaks and heaps of crisp french-fried potatoes. Many of the Portuguese prefer bife na frigideira—that is, steak with a mustard sauce and a fried egg accompaniment, all in a clay frying pan. The tavern features shellfish, which come from private fish ponds, and the house specialties are ameijoas (clams) à Trindade and the giant prawns. To go with your main course, a small stein of beer does nicely. For dessert, a good selection is a slice of queijo da serra (cheese from the mountains) and coffee. This restaurant was formerly a convent and later on a brewery. Its walls, which resisted the 1755 earthquake, are tiled with Portuguese scenes. Meals are served in the inner courtyard on sunny days. A typical meal costs 2,000$ ($13.40), and a tourist menu is featured for 1,400$ ($9.40). Hours are daily from 9am to 2am. Bus: 15, 20, and 100. AE, DC, MC, V.

FAST FOOD

The Big Apple, Avenida Elias Garcia 19B (tel. 79-75-575). Dozens of tongue-in-cheek accessories adorn the walls and menu of this American-style eatery on a tree-lined boulevard of a residential neighborhood. You'll find a Texan's map of the U.S. (Amarillo appears just south of the Canadian border), and a red, white, and blue checkerboard awning out front. It's simple, pleasant, and clean, and you can order any one of 18 variations of hamburgers, many constituting a meal in themselves. You can also select five kinds of dinner crêpes along with five kinds of temptingly sweet dessert crêpes. A meal costs from 1,800$ ($12.05), and the Apple is open daily from noon to 3pm and 7 to 11:30pm. Subway: Campo Pequeno. AE, DC, MC, V.

Hamburger House (The Great American Disaster), Rua Duque de Palmela 32 (tel. 51-61-45). Cramped and sometimes convivial, within a big-windowed room outfitted in theme-restaurant tones of red, white, and blue, it occupies a big-windowed room one floor above street level, at the corner of one of Lisbon's busiest intersections, about a block from the Ritz Hotel. To reach it, you'll enter an anonymous-looking commercial arcade within a building devoted to Varig Airlines, then climb a flight of winding steps to the second floor. Hamburgers, depending on their size and their garnishes, range from 550$ ($3.70) to 800$ ($5.35), although full meals, which can include more substantial fare such as platters of roast beef and daily specials, begin at around 1,200$ ($8.05) and up. The place is open from noon to 3pm and from 7 to 11pm daily. Reservations aren't needed. Subway: Rotunda. AE, MC, V.

Ritz Snack Bar, Rua Castilho 77C, in the Ritz Hotel (tel. 69-20-20), is a three-level dining establishment with a separate entrance facing Edward VII Park. A menu enticingly presents a variety of Portuguese and international specialties, including grilled fish and meats. Special emphasis is given to regional Portuguese dishes, which change on a daily basis. As a happy ending, the snack bar offers a goodly assortment of tarts, cakes, ice cream "coupes," and cheeses. Meals begin at 1,600$ ($10.70). The menu includes an English version. The snack bar is open daily from noon until 1:30am. Reservations aren't necessary. Subway: Rotunda. AE, DC, MC, V.

VEGETARIAN

A center of healthy eating and living is **Restaurante A Colmeia,** Rua da Emenda 10 (tel. 34-70-500). On the top floor of this corner building is this restaurant offering vegetarian and macrobiotic cuisine. In addition, you'll find a miniature shop where you can purchase such natural ingredients as nuts, raisins, herbs, even pastries and black breads. You enter on the street floor through an old hall with a stone floor, then ascend scrubbed wooden steps, with an old Portuguese tile dado. The top floor has a narrow hallway lined with shelves of books dealing with metaphysics as well as healthful living. At your left is a reception room where you can ask for the dishes of the day and learn the prices. Meals cost from 1,000$ ($6.70). Through the open doors of the two kitchens you'll see the aromatic pastries. Three dining rooms, each with large windows, are decorated differently. The restaurant is open Monday through Saturday from noon to 8:30pm. Reservations aren't necessary. Subway: Praça de Camões. No credit cards.

GAY RESTAURANTS

Restaurant Bizarro, Rua da Atalaia 133 (tel. 37-18-99), enjoys a certain cachet as a likable meeting spot for gay friends and lovers who appreciate its permissive charm. Lying on a narrow street of the Bairro Alto, it's an airy and spacious place with a sparse and spare decor and plenty of room between tables. À la carte meals cost from around 2,200$ ($14.75), although there is a fixed-price meal offered for 1,800$ ($12.05). Your meal might include grilled red snapper, codfish prepared in three different ways, and filet of wild boar in red wine sauce. The cuisine is Portuguese, and reservations are recommended. Subway: Rossio. MC, V.

Senhor Marquês, Rua da Horta Seca 42 (tel. 32-85-19). It lies on a residential street whose buildings are eerily quiet at night, within a trio of very old rooms whose ceilings are supported by the massive arches and ceiling beams of an 18th-century town house. Catering largely to a gay clientele, it serves predinner apéritifs from a small bar raised several steps above the floor of the dining room, and full meals priced from 2,800$ ($18.75) every day (except Saturday lunch) from 12:30 to 3pm and 7:30 to 11pm. The cuisine is both Portuguese and international. Specialties include shrimps with Pernod, grilled sole, fondue bourguignonne, Portuguese steak, and frogs' legs with curry. Reservations in advance are a good idea. Subway: Rossio. MC, V.

AFTERNOON TEA

Pastelaria Sala de Chá Versailles, Avenida da República 15A (tel. 54-63-40), is the most famous teahouse in Lisbon, declared part of the "national patrimony." Regulars meet here, and, it is claimed, some patrons have been coming here ever since it opened in 1932. In older days, the specialty was Licungo, the famed black tea of Mozambique; you can still order it, but nowadays many drinkers enjoy English brands. However, the Portuguese claim they—not the English—introduced the custom of tea drinking to the English court, after Catherine of Bragança married Charles II in 1662. The decor is rich with chandeliers, gilt mirrors, stained-glass windows, tall stucco ceilings, and black-and-white marble floors. You can also order milk shakes, mineral water, and fresh orange juice, along with beer and liquor. Snacks come in many varieties, including codfish balls and toasted ham-and-cheese sandwiches. A pot of tea with buttered toast costs 370$ ($2.50) and a pastelaria crema fina (cream cake) goes for 235$ ($1.60). No reservations are taken. It is open daily from 7:30am to 10pm. Subway: Campo Pequeno. No credit cards.

Pastelaria Bénard, Rua Garrett 104 (tel. 347-31-33), is considered the most fashionable teahouse in Lisbon. Dating from the 1800s, it lies in the heart of the Chiado and in fair weather sidewalk tables are placed outside. In the revolution of 1974, the waiters took it over but couldn't make a go of it until a dressmaker moved in, rescued it, and restored it, reopening it in 1981. Lunch is served in a back room, a full meal of Portuguese specialties such as codfish with almonds costing 3,000$ ($20). But most visitors come here for tea, served along with sandwiches and snacks. Desserts are famous, including one called duchesses (whipped cream cakes), costing 300$ ($2) per serving. Proper dress is required inside, although tourists in shorts sometimes occupy the outside tables. It is open Monday through Saturday from 8am to midnight, which makes it a good choice for breakfast as well. Fresh croissants cost from 65$ (45¢). A continental breakfast is only 175$ ($1.15). No credit cards are accepted, and no reservations taken. Metro: Rossio.

FOR BREAKFAST

See Pastelaria Bénard, above, under "Afternoon Tea."

COFFEEHOUSES

How can one go to Lisbon without visiting one of the traditional coffeehouses? It's like a trip to England without four o'clock tea, or to Munich without a stein in a beer hall. To the Portuguese, the coffeehouse is an institution, a democratic parlor where they can drop in for their favorite beverage, abandon their worries, relax, smoke a cigarette, read the paper, write a letter, or chat with friends about tomorrow's football match or last night's lover.

The coffeehouse in Portugal is no longer revered as it once was. The older and more colorful ones with their turn-of-the-century charm are rapidly being replaced by the 20th-century world of chrome and plastic.

One of the oldest coffeehouses in Lisbon is **A Brasileira,** Rua Garrett 120 (tel. 34-69-541), in the Chiado district. Behind an art nouveau facade, it's a 19th-century emporium, once a favorite gathering place of the literati. Today, it still remains dear to some diehard devotees. Guests sit at small tables on chairs made of tooled leather, while taking in the mirrored walls and marble pilasters. Aside from the architectural adornments, there is also a collection of paintings to admire. The café has the great Portuguese poet Fernando Pessoa—or rather his statue—sitting on a chair side by side with the customers. A demitasse costs 50$ (35¢) as does a simple glass of beer at the more recently created section on the sidewalk. The café is open Monday to Saturday from noon to 2pm and 7 to 9pm. Subway: Rossio.

Outside, the street speaks of past associations with men of letters. Garrett, a romantic dandy of the 19th century, was one of Portugal's leading poets (the street is named after him). The district itself, the Chiado, was named for another poet. On the square near the café a statue honors António Ribeiro, a 16th-century poet. Yet another poet, Bocage of Setúbal, used to frequent this coffeehouse. When once accosted by a bandit, he is said to have replied, "I am going to the Brasileira, but if you shoot me I am going to another world."

PORT WINE TASTING

A bar devoted exclusively to the drinking and enjoyment of port in all its known types is **Solar do Vinho do Porto,** 45 Rua de São Pedro de Alcantara 45 (tel. 34-75-707). The Solar is near the Bairro Alto, with its fado houses. You enter what appears to be a private living room. In the rear of a large building, it offers a relaxing atmosphere, the feeling enhanced by an open stone fireplace.

Owned and sponsored by the Port Wine Institute, it displays many artifacts related to the industry. But the real reason for dropping in here during the day is for its *lista de vinhos*—there are nearly 150 wines to choose from. You can have a glass (*cálice*) for anywhere from 100$ (65¢) to 800$ ($5.35). Hours are from 10am to 11:30pm Monday to Friday, from 11am to 10:30pm Saturday. Closed Sunday. The location is about 50 feet from the upper terminus of the Glória funicular. Bus: 15 or 100. AE, DC, MC, V.

PICNIC FARE & WHERE TO EAT IT

Lisbon has many "green lungs" (public parks) where you can go with your makings of a picnic. Of these, the finest is **Parque Eduardo VII,** at the top of Avenida da Liberdade, which has picnic tables.

A good place to stock up on supplies is **Charcutaria Brasil,** Rua Alexandre Herculano 90 (tel. 68-56-44), in the vicinity of the Largo do Rato. To accompany your sandwiches, you'll find a good selection of cheeses and wines, along with fresh fruits and breads. You can also order a roast chicken for 800$ ($5.35) per kilo (2.2 pounds). Hours are Monday through Friday from 8am to 9pm and Saturday from 8am to 2pm. Subway: Rotunda.

LISBON ATTRACTIONS

In Lisbon it's still a case of the frame competing with the picture. The Portuguese capital offers many worthwhile attractions, yet few can resist its environs. Many guests end by using Lisbon only as a base, while venturing forth during the day to Lord Byron's "variegated maze of mount and glen" at Sintra, to the sandy beaches along the Portuguese Riviera (Estoril and Cascais), to the monastery and royal palace at Mafra, even as far north as the fishing village of Nazaré or perhaps Fátima, where three shepherd children claimed to have seen a vision of the Virgin Mary.

One reason Lisbon gets overlooked is that enough time isn't budgeted for it. One or 2 days simply isn't adequate for Lisbon and the environs. A minimum of 5 days is needed. A second reason is that the attractions of Lisbon remain relatively unknown. Seemingly, every stone in Rome has been documented or recorded by someone. But in talks with literally dozens of visitors, the question most often asked is: "What does one do in Lisbon?"

This chapter hopes to answer that question, specifically with regard to sightseeing. If your time is limited, and you can cope only with the most important, then you should explore the **Coach Museum, Jerónimos Monastery,** and the **Alfama** and the **Castle of St. George.** At least two art museums, although not of the caliber of Madrid's Prado, merit attention: the **National Art Gallery** and the **Gulbenkian Center for Arts and Culture.**

Readers who enjoy more leisure time can visit the **Fundação Ricardo Espírito Santo** and watch reproductions of antiques being made, or books being gold-leafed; or you can see the gilded royal galleys at the **Naval Museum;** or wander through the **fish market;** or explore the arts and crafts of a **Belém folk museum;** and lots more.

More important, the Lisbon voyager will discover, just by walking its streets, a city unique in the world, a capital that extended its power across continents.

SIGHTSEEING STRATEGIES

If You Have 1 Day

Much too little time, but enough to take a walking tour (see below) of the Alfama, the most interesting district of Lisbon, visiting the **Sé** (cathedral) from the 12th century and taking in a view of the city and the River Tagus from the **Santa Luzia Belvedere.** Climax your visit with a call at the **Castelo São Jorge** (St. George's Castle). Taxi to Belém to see the **Mosteiro dos Jerónimos** (Jerónimos monastery) and the Torre de Belém. While at Belém explore one of the major sights of Lisbon, the **Museu dos Coches** (Coach Museum).

If You Have 2 Days

Spend Day 1 as above. On Day 2, head for **Sintra,** the single most visited sight in the environs of Lisbon—Byron called it "glorious Eden." You can spend the day there, as it has many attractions. Try at least to visit the **Palácio Nacional de Sintra** and the **Palácio Nacional da Pena.** Return to Lisbon for a night at a fado café.

If You Have 3 Days

Spend Days 1 and 2 as above, but on the third day get to see more of Lisbon. A morning passes quickly at the **Museu da Fundação Calouste Gulbenkian,** one of Europe's treasure troves of art. Have lunch at a *típico* restaurant in the Bairro Alto. In the afternoon see the **Fundação Ricardo Espírito Santo** (Museum of Decorative Art), and the **Museu Nacional de Arte Antiga.** To climax your day wander through Parque Eduardo VII.

If You Have 5 Days

Spend Days 1 through 3 as above. On the fourth day, take one of the most interesting excursions from Lisbon (it can be done on an organized tour—see below—for comfort, speed, and convenience). Visit the fishing village of **Nazaré** and the walled city of **Óbidos.** Catholic readers might also want to include a visit to the shrine at **Fátima,** although that would make for one very busy day. On the final day, slow your pace a bit, with a morning spent at the beach at **Estoril** on Portugal's Costa do Sol. Then continue along the coast to **Cascais** for lunch. After lunch wander around this old fishing village now turned into a major resort. Go to **Guincho,** 4 miles along the coast from Cascais, which is near the westernmost point on the European continent and has panoramic views.

---

1. The Alfama

The Lisbon of old lives on in the most typical quarter of the city. The wall built by the Visigoths and incorporated into some of the old houses is mute testimony to its ancient past. In East Lisbon, the Alfama was the Saracen sector of the city centuries before its conquest by the Christians.

Some of the buildings were spared from the earthquake of 1755, and the Alfama has retained much of its original charm, characterized by narrow cobblestone streets; cages of canaries chirping in the afternoon sun; fish in baskets balanced on the heads of *varinas;* strings of garlic and pepper inviting you inside a *típico* tavern; old street markets; and charming balconies.

The 19th-century Lisbon historian Norberto de Araújo wrote of "its perpetual resigned human tragedy from the habit of living it." In a colorful description he pointed up some of its elements: "labyrinth, confused, heaped up, multicolored; twisted and retwisted, lots of embracing narrow streets and kissing eaves; archways, backyards, blind alleys, stairways and terraces; commons and courtyards . . ."

The houses are so close together that in many places it's impossible to stretch your arms to their fullest length. That proximity was dramatically expressed by the poet Frederico de Brito: "Your house is so close to mine! In the starry night's bliss, to exchange a tender kiss, our lips easily meet, high across the narrow street."

Stevedores, fishmongers, and sailors occupy the Alfama. From the smallest houses, streamers of laundry protrude. The fishwives make early-morning appearances on their iron balconies, where they water their pots of geraniums.

But perhaps the most exciting sight is a little boy racing down a stone stairway in his droopy underwear (or wearing nothing at all) to hug his sailor father. The boy's mother will be preparing a steaming pot of caldeirada, the traditional fishermen's stew, for her family. When that same boy isn't racing to greet his father or isn't on an errand for his mother, he'll likely join one of Norberto de Araújo's "waves of little truants" who like to attach themselves to visitors. These children appear in ripples, always with an alert eye for a lost tourist. With hands outstretched and eyes soulfully pleading, they beg you to let them lead you to an open street market. Once there, you can wander in a maze of stacks of brightly colored vegetables from the country, bananas from Madeira, pineapple from the Azores, and fish from the sea.

Much of the charm of the Alfama lies in its armies of cats roaming the streets at will, asserting their unique rights. It is said that without these cats the sector would be rat infested. Occasionally, a black-shawled old woman, stooping over a brazier grilling sardines in front of her house, will toss one of these felines a fish head.

Once aristocrats lived in the Alfama, their memory perpetuated by the coats-of-arms of noble families slowly decaying on the fronts of some of the 16th-century houses. Some still do live there. One of the surviving members of an old family refuses to move, despite the pleadings of her relatives. "I will always live here," she said. "When I die, then you can remove my body." The best-known aristocratic mansion is the one once occupied by the Count of Arcos, the last viceroy of Brazil. Constructed in the 16th century and spared, in part, from the earthquake, it lies on Largo da Salvador.

On your exploration, you'll suddenly come upon a belvedere and be rewarded with an overall perspective of the contrasting styles of the Alfama, from a simple tile-roofed fishmonger's abode to a gaily decorated baroque church. One of the best views is from the belvedere of **Largo das Portas do Sol,** near the Museum of Decorative Art. It's a balcony opening onto the sea, overlooking the typical houses as they sweep down to the Tagus.

One of the oldest churches is that of **Santo Estevão** (St. Stephen), at the Largo de Santo Estevão. It was originally constructed in the 13th century. The present marble structure dates from the 18th century. Also of medieval origin is the **Church of São Miguel** (St. Michael), at Largo São Miguel, deep in the Alfama on a palm tree–shaded square. The interior is richly decorated, with 18th-century gilt and trompe l'oeil walls. The church was reconstructed after the earthquake.

Rua da Judiaria (The Street of Jews) is yet another reminder of the past. It was settled largely by refugees fleeing Spain to escape the Inquisition.

At night the spirit changes. Although the Bairro Alto is the traditional fado quarter of Lisbon, the Alfama also reverberates to the plaintive sound of the fadista. Amália and Celeste Rodrigues, two celebrated fadistas, got their start in the vicinity of the dockland, selling flowers to tourists arriving on boats.

The Alfama was well summed up by another Portuguese writer who called it ". . . a sort of old curiosity shop, under a veil of humility here and there, ever inclined to be romantic and childish."

A WALKING TOUR

Allow at least 2 hours for your walking tour of the Alfama, more if you can afford the sightseeing time. The streets are rarely suitable for a car; at times you must walk up steep stone stairs. A good point to begin your tour is **Largo do Salvador** (a taxi can take you to this point). Here you'll see a 16th-century mansion that once belonged to the count of Arcos.

From there, turn down Rua da Regueira, leading to **Beco do Carneiro,** the "cul-de-sac of rams." The lane couldn't be narrower. Families live in houses four feet (if that much) apart.

THE ALFAMA

0 ⊨⊨⊨⊨⊨⊨ 150 m
164 y

Rua da Veronica
Rua Cavaleiros
MOURARIA
Rua das Olarias
Rua da Voz do Operário
Calçada Santo André
Calçada da Graça
Campo de Santa Clara
Rua Marques Ponte de Lima
Rua São Vicente
Campo de Santa Engrácia
Rua da Costa do Castelo
Military
Museum
❸
❻
Rua das Escolas Gerais
❼ Rua dos Corvos
❶❶
SANTA CRUZ
Beco do Carneiro
❶❷
Mercado
Museu de Artes
Decorativas
Rua da Regueira
❷ ❶❼
Rua dos Remedios
Rua Jardim Tabaco
Rua Milagres Rua Loios Rua São Tiago
❶
❺
Beco de
Cardosa
Rua de São Mamede
❶❺
❽
Rua João Evangelista
Doca do Trigo
Rua da Madalena
❾
Rua Limoeiro
Rua de São Pedro
Terreiro do Trigo
❶❸
BAIXA
Rua A. Rosa
❹
❶❹
Rua des Judiaria
Rua da Prata
❶❻
Rua da Alfândega
Campo das
Cebolas
Rua Cais de Santarem
Praça da
Ribeira
Doca da Marinha
Praça do Comércio
(Terreiro do Paço)
Rio Tejo
Estação do
Sul e Sueste
Embarcadouro

PORTUGAL
LISBON
★
The Alfama

Beco de Cardosa ❶	Largo do Chafariz de Dentro ❶⓪
Beco do Carneiro ❷	Largo do Salvador ❶❶
Castelo São Jorge ❸	Pátio das Flores ❶❷
Cathedral (Sé) ❹	Rua da Judiaria ❶❸
Church of São Miguel ❺	Rua de São Pedro ❶❹
Largo das Portas do Sol ❻	Santa Luzia Belvedere ❶❺
Largo de Santo Estavão ❼	Santo António de Lisboa ❶❻
Largo de São Miguel ❽	Santo Estavão ❶❼
Largo de São Rafael ❾	

Church ✝

At the end of the alley, circle back via a flight of steps to your left to **Largo de Santo Estevão** named after the church on the site. Round the church and from the back proceed to the **Patio das Flores,** via a flight of steps, where you can see some of the most delightful little houses fronted with characteristic Portuguese tiles (*azulejos*). Walk down the steps to the Rua dos Remédios, cutting right to **Largo do Chafariz de Dentro,** where you're bound to see Alfama housewives busily gossiping in front of an old fountain.

From the square, you connect with **Rua de São Pedro,** which is perhaps the most animated street of the Alfama. Strolling deep into the street, you'll probably attract a trail of children.

Some local taverns will pass before you, and the most adventurous sightseers will venture inside to sample a glass of *vinho verde* (green wine). Later, your head reeling from several glasses, you'll step out onto the narrow street again, where you'll be virtually knocked down by an old fisherman with saffron and brown nets draped over his shoulder.

Rua de São Pedro leads into **Largo de São Rafael,** which convinces you that the 17th century never ended. You pass a *leitaria* (dairy), which now sells milk in the bottle instead of via the old-fashioned method (cows were kept right inside, as the women of the Alfama wanted to make sure their milk was fresh).

Right off the square is **Rua da Judiaria,** so called because of the many Jews who settled there after escaping the Inquisition in Spain.

Go back to Largo de São Rafael, crossing to rejoin Rua de São Pedro. Walk down that street to the intersection, forking left. You enter **Largo de São Miguel,** with its church richly decorated in the baroque style. From there, walk up Rua da São Miguel, cutting left into **Beco de Cardosa,** where from some flower-draped balcony a varina is bound to scream down hell and damnation to her street urchin son if he doesn't come up immediately.

At the end of the alley, you connect with Beco Sta. Helena, a continuation, which leads up several flights of steps to **Largo das Portas do Sol.** On this square is the Museum of Decorative Art, handsomely ensconced in one of the many mansions that used to grace the Alfama.

One of the most favored belvederes in the city opens onto this square. Called **Santa Luzia Belvedere,** it's really a balcony to view the sea, overlooking the houses of the Alfama, as they sweep down in a jumbled pile to the Tagus. How fitting to end your tour here.

Although best explored by day, the Alfama takes on a different spirit at night, when street lanterns cast patterns against medieval walls and the plaintive sound of the fadista is heard until the early-morning hours in the traditional cafés. But, regrettably, it can be dangerous to go wandering around the Alfama at night.

CASTELO SÃO JORGE

The local people speak of it as the cradle of their city. **Castelo São Jorge** in the Alfama district may well have been the spot on which the Portuguese capital began in times too distant to be known. Although it is believed to have predated the Romans, the hilltop was used as a fortress guarding the Tagus and its settlement below.

From the 5th century A.D. it was a Visigothic fortification, falling in the early 8th century to the Saracens. Many of the walls that still remain were erected during the centuries of Moorish domination. The Moors were in control until 1147, a historic year for the Portuguese, for it was then that Afonso Henriques, the first king of the country, chased the Moors out and extended his kingdom south. Even before Lisbon was made the capital of a newly emerging nation, the site was used as a royal palace.

For what many consider the finest view of the Tagus and the Alfama, walk the esplanades and climb the ramparts of the old castle. The structure takes its name, St. George, in commemoration of an Anglo-Portuguese pact dating from as early as 1371. (Portugal and England have been traditional allies, although their relationship was strained in 1961 when India, a member of the British Commonwealth, seized the Portuguese overseas territories of Goa, Diu, and Damão.)

Huddling close to the protection of the moated castle is a sector that appears almost medieval (many houses still retain their Moorish courtyards, while others have been greatly altered).

At the entrance to the castle, visitors pause at the Castle Belvedere. The Portuguese refer to this spot as their ancient window overlooking the Alfama, the Serras of Monsanto and of Sintra, Ponte 25 de Abril spanning the Tagus, Praça do Comércio, and the tile roofs of the Portuguese capital. In the square stands a heroic statue—sword in one hand, shield in the other—of the first king, Afonso Henriques.

Inside the castle grounds, you can stroll through a setting of olive, pine, and cork trees, all graced by the appearance of a flamingo. In bad weather when rain is sweeping the city, you'll focus on a cannon and think of the massacres that must have occurred on this blood-soaked hill. On a fair day, you'll perhaps notice that the willows weep or that oleander bloom. Swans with white bodies and black necks glide in a silence shattered by the bloodcurdling scream of the rare white peacock. Open every day from 7am to sunset, the castle may be visited without charge. Bus: 37.

THE CATHEDRAL (SÉ)

Even the tourist literature admits that the cathedral at Largo da Sé (tel. 86-67-52) is not very rich. Characterized by twin towers flanking its entrance, it represents an architectural wedding of Romanesque and Gothic. The facade is severe enough for a medieval fortress, and like many European cathedrals it has had many different architectural fathers. The devastation caused by the earthquakes of 1344 and 1755 didn't help either. At one point in its history the site of the present Sé was allegedly used by the Saracens as a holy mosque. When the city was captured by Christian Crusaders, led by Portugal's first king, Afonso Henriques, the structure was rebuilt. That early date in the 12th century makes the Sé the oldest church in Lisbon.

Inside are many treasures, such as the font where St. Anthony of Padua is said to have been christened in 1195. A notable feature is the Gothic chapel of Bartolomeu Joanes, constructed in the 14th century. Other things of interest are a crib by Machado de Castro (the 18th-century Portuguese sculptor who did the equestrian statue on Praça do Comércio); the sarcophagus of Lopo Fernandes Pacheco, dating from the 14th century; and the original nave and aisles.

To visit the sacristy and cloister requires a guide. The cloister, built in the 14th century by King Dinis, is of ogival construction, with garlands, a Romanesque wrought-iron grille, and tombs with inscription stones. In the sacristy are housed marbles, relics, valuable images, and pieces of ecclesiastical treasure from the 15th and 16th centuries.

Whether you're Catholic or not, you may want to attend a service here. If seen in the morning, the stained-glass reflections on the floor evoke a Monet painting. Admission is free, and hours are daily from 9am to noon and 2:30 to 6pm. Bus: 37. Streetcar: 28 (Graça).

SANTO ANTÓNIO DE LISBOA

St. Anthony of Padua was born in 1195 in a house that stood on this spot at Largo de Santo António de Sé (tel. 86-91-45). In the crypt, a guide will show you the spot where the saint was allegedly born.

Buried at Padua, Italy, this itinerant Franciscan monk remains the patron saint of Portugal. The devout come to this little church to light candles under his picture. He is known as a protector of young brides, and also has a special connection with the children of Lisbon. To raise money to erect the altar at the church, the children of the Alfama built miniature altars with a representation of the patron saint on them. June 12 of every year is designated as St. Anthony's Day, a time of merrymaking, heavy eating, and drinking. In the morning there are street fires and singing, climaxed by St. Anthony's Feast on the following day.

The original church was destroyed by the earthquake of 1755, and the present building was designed by Mateus Vicente in the 18th century. Hours are daily from 7:30am to 12:30pm and from 3 to 7:30pm. Admission is free. Bus: 37.

2. Belém

At Belém, where the Tagus (*Tejo* in Portuguese) meets the sea, the caravels were launched on their missions: Vasco da Gama to India, Ferdinand Magellan to circumnavigate the globe, Bartolomeu Dias to round the Cape of Good Hope.

Belém emerged from the Restélo, that point or strand of land from which the ships set sail across the so-called Sea of Darkness. As riches, especially spices, poured back into Portugal, Belém flourished. Great monuments, such as the Belém Tower and Jerónimos Monastery, were built and embellished in the Manueline style.

In time the royal family established a summer palace here. Much of the character of the district came about when wealthy Lisboans began moving out and erecting town houses. For many years Belém was a separate municipality. Eventually, however, it became incorporated into Lisbon as a parish.

Nowadays it's a major target for sightseers, as it's a virtual monument-studded museumland.

For most visitors, the first sight is the Torre de Belém.

TORRE DE BELÉM

This quadrangular Tower of Belém, Praça do Império (tel. 301-68-92), is a monument to Portugal's Age of Discovery. Erected between 1515 and 1520, the tower is Portugal's classic landmark, often used on documents and brochures as a symbol of the country. A monument to Portugal's great military and naval past, the tower stands on or near the spot where the caravels once set out.

In the Manueline style, its architect, Francisco de Arruda, blended Gothic and Moorish elements using such characteristic devices as twisting ropes carved of stone. The coat-of-arms of Manuel I rests above the loggia, and balconies grace three sides of the monument. Along the balustrade of the loggias, stone crosses symbolize the Portuguese Crusaders.

However, the richness of the facade fades once you cross the drawbridge and enter the Renaissance-style doorway. Gothic severity reigns; there are a few antiques, including a 16th-century throne graced with finials, and an inset paneled with pierced Gothic tracery. If you scale the steps leading to the ramparts, you'll be rewarded with a panorama of boats along the Tagus and pastel-washed, tile-roofed old villas in the hills beyond.

Hours are daily June through September from 10am to 6:30pm, when admission is 400$ ($2.70). October through May, it is open daily from 10am to 5pm, when admission is 200$ ($1.35). On Sunday year round its hours are from 10am to 2pm when it is free. It is closed on Monday. Bus: 27, 28, or 29.

Facing the Tower of Belém stands a monument in commemoration of the first Portuguese to cross the Atlantic by airplane (not nonstop). The date was March 30, 1922, and the flight took pilot Gago Coutinho and navigator Sacadura Cabral from Lisbon to Rio de Janeiro.

At the center of the Praça do Império at Belém is the **Fonte Luminosa**, the Luminous Fountain. The patterns of the water jets, estimated at more than 70 original designs, make an evening show lasting nearly an hour if you want to see all of them.

MEMORIAL TO THE DISCOVERIES

Like a prow of one of the Age of Discovery caravels, this memorial at Praça da Boa Esperança stands on the Tagus, looking as if it's ready at any moment to strike out across the Sea of Darkness. The Portuguese call it **Padrão dos Descobrimentos** (tel. 61-62-60). Memorable explorers, chiefly Vasco da Gama, are immortalized in stone along the ramps.

At this point where the two ramps meet stands a replica of Henry the Navigator, whose genius opened up new worlds. The memorial was unveiled in 1960, and one of the figures in stone is that of a kneeling Philippa of Lancaster, the English mother

LISBON ATTRACTIONS

0 [=====] 200 m
          220 y

The Alfama **6**
Castelo São Jorge **5**
Jardim Botânico **1**
Jardim de Estrêla **2**
Museu de Arte Contemporanea **12**
Museu de Arte Decorativas **11**
Museu Militar **10**
Museu Nacional de Arte Antiga **9**
Praça Rossio **4**
São Roque **13**
Sé Cathedral **7**
Teatro Nacional **3**
Teatro São Carlos **8**

Post Office ⊠   Church ✝

of Henry the Navigator. Other figures in the frieze symbolize the Crusaders (represented by a man holding a flag with a cross), navigators, monks, cartographers, and cosmographers. At the top of the prow is the coat-of-arms of Portugal at the time of Manuel the Fortunate. The space in front of the memorial is floored with a map of the world in multicolored marble, with the dates of the discoveries set in metal. The continents are in red marble, the oceans a gray-blue, and the caravels are in still another color marble. It can be viewed 24 hours a day, and admission is free. Bus: 27, 28, or 29.

MOSTEIRO DOS JERÓNIMOS

"Here, frozen forever in stone, is the blazing noontide of empire. Stylized hawsers writhe in the arches. Shells and coral and fish entwine in every column. Sanctuary lamps glow red above carved African lions." Or so wrote Howard La Fay.

In an expansive mood of celebration, Manuel I, the Fortunate, ordered this monastery built to commemorate the sailing of Vasco da Gama to India and to give thanks to the Lady Mary for its success. The style of architecture to which the king contributed his name, Manueline, combines flamboyant Gothic and Moorish influences with the dawn of the Renaissance in Portugal.

Opening onto Praça do Império (tel. 362-00-34) in Belém, the monastery was founded in 1502, partially financed by the spice trade that was to grow following the discovery of the route to India. Originally, a small chapel dedicated to St. Mary had been built on this spot by Henry the Navigator, and although the earthquake of 1755 damaged the monastery, it didn't destroy it. Extensive restoration, some of it ill-conceived, was carried out.

The decorated southern doorway is outstanding. Inside, the most interesting architecture is to be seen in the cloister. Every pillar is different, as each craftsman vied with the others in exuberance of motifs. From the cloister, doors lead to rooms about 7 feet long and 4 feet wide. You walk across the unmarked tombs of unnamed ghosts; other bodies were buried in the walls. The second tier of the cloister is approached by a stairway, where monks of old walked in meditation.

The interior of the church is divided into a trio of naves, noted for their fragile-looking pillars. Some of the ceilings, like those in the monks' refectory, have a ribbed barrel-vault ceiling. The "palm tree" in the sacristy is also exceptional.

Many of the greatest names in Portuguese history are said to be entombed at the monastery, but none is more famous than Vasco da Gama. The Portuguese also maintain that Luís Vaz de Camões is buried here. Both tombs rest on the backs of lions. Camões, of course, was the national poet of Portugal, author of *Os Lusíadas* (*The Portuguese*), in which he glorified the triumphs of his compatriots.

Camões' epic poetry is said to have inspired a young Portuguese king, Sebastião, to dreams of glory. The foolish king—devoutly, even fanatically, religious—was killed at Alcácer-Kibir, Morocco, in a crusade against the Muslims in 1578. Those refusing to believe that the king was dead formed a cult. Known as Sebastianism, it rose to minor influence, and four men tried to assert their claim to the Portuguese throne. Each maintained steadfastly, even to death, that he was King Sebastião. Sebastião's remains were allegedly entombed in a marble shrine built in the 16th century in the Mannerist style.

Finally, the romantic poet Herculano (1800–54) is buried at Jerónimos, as is Fernando Pessoa.

Open daily from 10am to 6:30pm from June through September and from 10am to 5pm from October through May. The monastery charges no entrance fee to the church, but admission to the cloisters costs 400$ ($2.70) in summer, 250$ ($1.70) October to May. Take bus no. 43 from Praça de Figueira or no. 27 or 43 from Praça Marquês de Pombal.

MUSEU DE MARINHA

The pageant and the glory that was Portugal on the high seas is evoked for posterity in this maritime museum, **Museu de Marinha**, Praça do Império (tel. 362-

00-19), one of the most important in Europe. Appropriately, it is installed in the west wing of the Monastery of Jerónimos.

These royal galleys re-create an age of opulence that never feared excess. Dragon heads drip with gilt; sea monsters coil with abandon; and, of course, assembling a large crew was no problem for kings and queens in those days. Surely Cleopatra sailing down the Nile on her barge would have recoiled with jealousy at the sight of the galley Queen Maria I ordered built for the marriage of her son and successor, Crown Prince João, to the Spanish Princess Carlota Joaquina Bourbon in 1785. Eighty dummy oarsmen, elaborately attired in scarlet- and mustard-colored waistcoats, represent the crew.

The museum contains hundreds of models of 15th- to 19th-century sailing ships, the transition from sail to steam, 20th-century warships, merchant marine vessels, fishing boats, river craft, and pleasure boats. In a section devoted to the East is a pearl-inlay replica of a Dragon Boat used in maritime and fluvial corteges. Other models include a large reproduction of the frigate *Ulysses,* dating from December 15, 1792, and an early-20th-century destroyer with two torpedo tubes.

A full range of Portuguese naval uniforms is displayed, from one worn at a military outpost in Mozambique in 1896 to a model worn as recently as 1961. In a special room can be seen the queen's stateroom as it was on the royal yacht of Carlos I, the Bragança king who was assassinated at Praça do Comércio in 1908. It was on this craft that his son, King Manuel II, and his wife, the queen mother, Amélia, escaped to Gibraltar following the collapse of the Portuguese monarchy in 1910.

Historical exhibits include a letter from Lord Nelson dated October 24, 1799. A large map traces the trail of Brito Capelo and Roberto Ivens through the African continent in 1884–85.

The Naval Museum also honors some of the early Portuguese aviators. On display is the aquaplane *Santa Cruz,* the first aircraft to cross the South Atlantic. The date was March 30, 1922 ("Aventura magnífica" hailed the press), and the captain was Commander Sacadura Cabral and the navigator Admiral Gago Coutinho, who invented a new sextant for use by airmen. The flight was from Lisbon to Rio de Janeiro, with stopovers en route. Also displayed is a 1917 airplane, the first one used by Portuguese aviators.

The museum charges 200$ ($1.35) admission for adults. Children up to 10 and adults over 65 are admitted free. It is open Tuesday through Sunday from 10am to 5pm. Bus: 27, 28, 43, and 49.

Annexed to the Naval Museum, the **Calouste Gulbenkian Plantarium** (Planetário Calouste Gulbenkian), also at Praça do Império (tel. 362-00-02), is open to the public April through September for sessions at 4, 5, and 6pm on Saturday and Sunday; October through March, the same days at 4 and 5pm. Sessions are held in Portuguese unless a previous request has been made for a special session in English. Admission is 250$ ($1.70) for adults, 150$ ($1) for children aged 6 and above. (Those under 6 are not allowed.)

MUSEU NACIONAL DOS COCHES

Visited by more tourists than any other attraction in Lisbon, the Coach Museum, at Belém's Praça Afonso de Albuquerque (tel. 363-80-22), is considered the finest of its type in the world. Founded by Queen Amélia, wife of Carlos I, it's housed in what was originally an 18th-century riding academy connected to the Belém Royal Palace.

The coaches stand in a former horse ring, and most of them date from the 17th to the 19th centuries. Drawing the most interest is an opulently decorated trio of gilded baroque carriages once used by the Portuguese ambassador to the Vatican at the time of Pope Clement XI (1716). Also displayed is a 17th-century coach in which the Spanish Hapsburg king, Phillip II, journeyed from Madrid to Lisbon to see his new possession.

Other coaches include the processional chariot of "Our Lady of Cabo," the coach of King João V, the coach of Queen Maria Ana de Austria, as well as Queen Maria's berlinda. Portuguese and foreign harnesses and trappings, all the gala livery, are exhibited on the second floor.

The portrait gallery belonged to the House of Bragança, which ended in 1910. Pictured are such notables as Maria I and a host of minor royalty.

The museum is open from 10am to 1pm and 2:30 to 5:30pm Tuesday to Sunday; closed holidays. It charges 400$ ($2.70) admission. Bus: 27, 28, 43, and 49.

MUSEU DE ARTE POPULAR

Nowhere are the folk arts and customs of the Portuguese displayed more dramatically than here at the **Folk Art Museum,** Avenida de Brasilia (tel. 301-12-82). The walls of the building, which previously housed the Regional Center during the 1940 Portuguese World's Exhibition, are painted by contemporary artists, some of the best in Portugal, including Carlos Botelho, Eduardo Anahory, Estrela Faria, Manuel Lapa, Paulo Ferreira, and Tomás de Melo. Their work is supplemented by enlarged photographs of the people of the provinces. The establishment of the Folk Art Museum in 1948 was a result of a campaign for ethnic revival directed by António Ferro. The collections, including ceramics, furniture, wickerwork, clothes, farm implements, and painting, are displayed in five rooms that correspond more or less to the provinces, each of which maintains its regional personality.

Entre-Douro and Minho are represented by flowers, musical instruments, goldsmith pieces, Barcelos painted pottery, and Vila Nova de Gaia painted earthenware dolls. Elaborate harnesses used for oxen are on display, along with farm implements. You can see models of regional boats, fishing tools, embroidered sweaters, Azurara stockings, rugs, a Viana do Castelo weaver's loom, and various items for the preparation of linen, for spinning, and for knitting. Bilros laces are also on exhibit.

The exhibition from Trás-os-Montes gives a survey of the activities of the northeast area. You'll see straw *escrinhos* (baskets), a Vila Real oxcart and a harrow for threshing corn, kitchen items (*transfogueiro* and a piece of furniture, *escano*), black earthenware, and a collection of bedspreads. *Chocalheiros,* the masks worn by men called by the same name who appear on feast days, are interesting displays.

The Algarve, well known to tourists, is represented by palm mats and baskets, a water cart, horse trappings, fishing nets, and a manually operated millstone, plus line-cut chimneys.

The room devoted to the Beiras contains a reproduction of the interior of a Monsanto country house, as well as a variety of wicker and straw baskets, fine Molelos black earthenware items, bedspreads, and rugs. Here too is a set of tools used in salt making from Aveiro. Of special interest is a *moliço* catcher's boat. Moliço is seaweed dredged up and used as fertilizer.

The fifth room, containing displays from Estremadura and Alentejo, holds a variety of objects, such as glazed pottery pieces from Leiria and Mafra; Nazaré fishing and clothing items, sculpture, and saints' registries; and a wax dummy modeling the garb of the *campino,* a herdsman who looks after the bulls on the plains. From Alentejo, you'll see a replica of a kitchen, glazed Redondo earthenware, Nisa earthenware, Estremoz polished and striped pottery, and earthenware painted dolls, together with items of shepherds' art and votive paintings.

The museum is open Tuesday to Sunday from 10am to 12:30pm and 2 to 5pm; closed holidays. Admission is 200$ ($1.35). Children up to 10 are admitted free. Buses no. 14 and 40 go there.

OTHER SIGHTS

If you have a car, drive up to **Restélo Chapel** before heading back to Lisbon. Here priests held masses, praying for the success of such epic voyages as that of Vasco da Gama. A chapel in the Manueline style stands on the spot. A belvedere overlooks the Tagus, offering good views of Belém Tower and Jerónimos Monastery.

Palácio Nacional de Ajuda, Largo da Ajuda, near Belém (tel. 363-70-95), built in the early 19th century, contains rooms that have not been changed since the days of royal supremacy in Portugal. The palace collection is extensive and of particular note are the Germain silver, the Sormani furniture, and the tapestries. The palace is open daily Thursday to Tuesday from 10am to 5pm. It charges 200$ ($1.35) admission. Children up to 10 years of age are admitted free. Take bus no. 29 or 40.

3. Museums & Galleries

Most of the major museums of Lisbon are at Belém, but two major attractions are found in the city: the National Art Gallery and the Gulbenkian Center for Arts and Culture, described below. For a survey of yet two more museums, the St. Roque gallery of ecclesiastical art and the Archeological Museum in the ruins of the Carmo Church, refer to "The Churches of Lisbon," below.

MUSEU NACIONAL DE ART ANTIGA

The country's greatest collection of paintings is housed in this **National Museum of Ancient Art,** Rua das Janelas Verdes 95 or Jardim 9 de Abril (tel. 396-41-51). The museum occupies two connected buildings—an ancient palace from the 17th century and an added edifice which was built on the former site of the old Carmelite Convent of Santo Alberto. The chapel of the convent was preserved and is a good example of the integration of ornamental arts, with gilt carved wood, glazed tiles (*azulejos*), and sculpture of the 17th and 18th centuries.

The museum has many notable paintings, including the famous polyptych from St. Vincent's monastery attributed to Nuno Gonçalves between 1460 and 1470. It contains sixty portraits of leading figures of Portuguese history. Other outstanding works are Hieronymus Bosch's triptych, *The Temptation of St. Anthony,* Hans Memling's *Mother and Child,* Albrecht Dürer's *St. Jerome,* and paintings by Velázquez, Zurbarán, Poussin, and Courbet. Paintings from the 15th through the 19th century trace the development of Portuguese art.

The museum also exhibits a remarkable collection of gold- and silversmiths' work, both Portuguese and foreign. Among these is the cross from Alcobaça and the monstrance of Belém, constructed with the first gold brought from India by Vasco da Gama. Another exceptional example is the French silver tableware from the 18th century, ordered by King José I. Diverse objects from Benin, India, Persia, China, and Japan reflect Portuguese expansion overseas. Two excellent pairs of screens depict the Portuguese relationship with Japan in the 17th century. Flemish tapestries, a rich assemblage of church vestments, Italian polychrome ceramics, and sculptures are also on display.

The museum is open Tuesday to Sunday from 10am to 1pm and 2:30 to 5pm. Admission is 200$ ($1.35); free on Sunday morning. Children up to 10 are free. Bus: 27 or 40.

MUSEU CALOUSTE GULBENKIAN

Opened in 1969, this museum, part of the Fundação Calouste Gulbenkian, houses what one critic called "one of the world's finest private art collections." It was deeded by the Armenian oil tycoon, Calouste Gulbenkian, who died in 1955. The modern multimillion-dollar center, at Avenida de Berna 45 (tel. 73-51-31), is in a former private estate that belonged to the Count of Vilalva.

From June to October it is open on Tuesday, Thursday, Friday, and Sunday from 10am to 5pm; on Wednesday and Saturday from 2 to 7:30pm (closed Monday and holidays). During other months of the year, it is open Tuesday to Sunday (closed Monday and holidays) from 10am to 5pm, charging an admission of 200$ ($1.35) except on Sunday, when it's free. Children under 10 are admitted free.

The collections cover Egyptian, Greek, and Roman antiquities; a remarkable set of Islamic art including ceramics and textiles of Turkey and Persia; Syrian glass, books, bindings, and miniatures, along with Chinese vases, Japanese prints, and lacquer work. The European displays include medieval illuminated manuscripts and ivories, 15th- to 19th-century paintings and sculpture, Renaissance tapestries and medals, important collections of 18th-century French decorative works, French impressionist painting, René Lalique jewelry, and glassware.

In a move requiring great skill in negotiation, Gulbenkian managed to make purchases of art from the Hermitage in St. Petersburg. Among his most notable acquisitions are two Rembrandts: *Portrait of an Old Man* and *Alexander the Great.*

Two other well-known paintings are a *Portrait of Hélène Fourment* by Peter Paul Rubens and Renoir's *Portrait of Madame Claude Monet*. In addition, I'd suggest you seek out Mary Cassatt's *The Stocking*. The French sculptor Jean-Antoine Houdon is represented by a statue of *Diana*. Silver made by François-Thomas Germain, once used by Catherine the Great, is here, as well as one piece by Thomas Germain, the father.

As a cultural center, the Gulbenkian Foundation sponsors plays, films, ballet, and musical concerts, as well as a rotating exhibition of works by leading modern Portuguese and foreign artists. Bus: 16 or 31. Streetcar: 24 or 27.

CENTRO DE ARTE MODERNA

Around the corner from the entrance to the Gulbenkian Museum, the **Center for Modern Art,** Rua Dr. Nicholau de Bettencourt (tel. 79-35-131), is the first major permanent exhibition center of modern Portuguese artists to open in Lisbon. The center shares park-like grounds with the Gulbenkian Foundation and was, in fact, a gift left in the legacy of the late Armenian oil magnate.

It is housed in a British-designed complex of clean lines and dramatically proportioned geometric forms, with a Henry Moore sculpture in front. The museum owns some 10,000 works of art. It displays the work of many modern Portuguese artists, some of whom enjoy world fame. These include Souza-Cardoso, Almada, Paula Rego, João Cutileiro, Costa Pinheiro, and Vieira da Silva. From June through September, hours are Wednesday and Saturday from 2 to 7:30pm; Tuesday, Thursday, Friday, and Sunday from 10am to 5pm. From October through May, hours are Tuesday to Sunday from 10am to 5pm. Admission is 200$ ($1.35) except on Sunday when it's free. Children under 10 are admitted free. Subway: Praça de Espanha. Bus: 16 or 31.

FUNDAÇÃO RICARDO ESPÍRITO SANTOS

The decorative arts school museum, **Museum of Decorative Art,** Largo das Porta do Sol 2 (tel. 86-21-84), is a foundation established in 1953 through the vision and generosity of Dr. Ricardo do Espírito Santo Silva, who endowed it with items belonging to his personal collection and set up workshops of handcrafts in which nearly all activities related to the decorative arts are represented. The handsomely furnished museum is in one of the many aristocratic mansions that used to grace the Alfama. The principal aim of the foundation is the preservation and furtherance of the decorative arts by maintaining the traditional character of the handcrafts while developing the craftspersons' skills and culture. In the workshops you can see how perfect reproductions of furniture and other objects are made in the purest styles. The foundation also restores furniture, books, and Arraiolos rugs. The workshops may be visited on Wednesday.

The museum has been given the appearance of an inhabited palace by placing objects in appropriate surroundings. Visitors can have a fairly accurate picture of what might have been the interior of an upper-class Lisbon home in the 18th and 19th centuries. There are outstanding displays of furniture, Portuguese silver, and Arraiolos rugs, all from the 17th through the 19th centuries, with 16th-century silver included.

The museum is open Tuesday to Saturday from 10am to 1pm and 2:30 to 5pm. Admission is 500$ ($3.35).

Close to the museum is a bar where visitors may have a rest, snacks, or a drink. To reach the museum, take streetcar no. 12 or 28 or bus no. 37.

MUSEU NACIONAL DE ARTE CONTEMPORÂNEA

Founded in 1911, the **National Museum of Contemporary Art,** Rua Serpa Pinto 6 (tel. 346-80-20), has collections of paintings and sculptures going back to 1850. The romantic and naturalistic schools of the 19th century, and modern styles from the beginning of the 20th century—surrealism, neorealism, abstractionism, and neofigurative works—are represented. This is perhaps the most important collection of Portuguese painting and sculpture from those centuries, consisting of more than 2,500 works of art.

The collection is displayed in rooms of the old Monastery of Saint Francis, where the Lisbon Royal Academy of Arts opened in 1836, the first school and art gallery in the capital. The first three directors, famous painters Carlos Reis (1863–1940), Columbano (1857–1920), and Sousa Lopes (1879–1944), organized and exhibited the initial grouping. At that time, the museum was mainly an artistic workshop.

This museum has closed temporarily for reorganization. Check with the tourist office to see if it has reopened before going there.

MUSEU MILITAR (NATIONAL MILITARY MUSEUM)

This museum, at Caminhos de Ferro (tel. 86-71-31), in front of the Santa Apolónia station, not far from Terreiro do Paço and São Jorge (St. George's) Castle, is on the site of a shipyard built during the reign of King Manuel I (1495–1521). Later, in the reign of King João III, a new foundry for artillery was erected which was also used for making gunpowder and to store arms to equip the Portuguese fleet. A fire damaged the buildings in 1726, and the 1755 earthquake destroyed them completely. Rebuilt at the order of King José I, the complex was designated as the Royal Army Arsenal. The museum, originally called the Artillery Museum, was created in 1851. Today the facility exhibits not only arms but also paintings, sculpture, tiles, and specimens of architecture.

The museum has one of the world's best collections of historical artillery. There are bronze cannons of various periods; one of these is from Diu, weighs 20 tons, and bears Arabic inscriptions. Some iron pieces date from the 14th century. Light weapons, such as guns, pistols, and swords, are displayed in cases. The museum is open Tuesday through Saturday from 10am to 4pm and Sunday 11am to 5pm. Admission is 150$ ($1). Children pay 75$ (50¢). Bus: 9, 12, or 46.

MUSEU NACIONAL DO TRAJE

A treasury of materials and clothing is contained within the **National Costume Museum,** Largo Julio de Castilho, Lumiar (tel. 758-27-39). Some of the fabric is from medieval times, and there is Oriental finery and a wide selection of wearing apparel from different parts of the world. As the textiles cannot be kept on constant display, different exhibits of costumes, modern tapestries, jewelry, and other collections are shown at various times. A part of the museum depicts various processes required to produce materials, including weaving, spinning, and hand-printing. The museum is open Tuesday through Sunday from 10am to 1pm and 2:30 to 5pm. From June through September, admission is 300$ ($2). From October to May, admission is lowered to 200$ ($1.35). Admission is free on Sunday morning, and children under 10 are always admitted free. Bus: 1 or 36.

Connected with the museum is the **Parque do Monteiro-Mor,** Largo Julio de Castilho, Lumiar, one of Lisbon's most beautiful botanical gardens, where you'll find a restaurant (tel. 759-03-18). The park is open June through September from 10am to 6pm and October through May from 10am to 5:30pm. Admission is 100$ (65¢), except on Sunday, when it is free. Children under 10 are admitted free. Bus: 1 or 36.

MUSEUM RAFAEL BORDALO PINHEIRO

Rafael Bordalo Pinheiro was a ceramicist and caricaturist in the 19th century, and this museum at Campo Grande 382 (tel. 759-08-16) honors his memory. Actually, it's one of the most esoteric museums in Lisbon and is of little interest to the average North American visitor, unless he or she knows something about Bordalo Pinheiro's day—that is, 19th-century Portuguese life and the scandals of the literati. In his caricatures he poked fun at some of the most distinguished people of his day.

Bordalo Pinheiro's crustacean and reptilian ceramics are marvelous caricatures. Search out the portrait of Bordalo Pinheiro, by Columbano, the outstanding Portuguese painter who died in 1929.

The museum is open from 10am to 1pm and 2 to 6pm Tuesday to Sunday. Admission is 150$ ($1), except on Sunday, when it is free. Children up to 18 years of age are also admitted free. Bus: 1 or 36.

4. The Bairro Alto

Like the Alfama, the Bairro Alto (the upper city) preserves the characteristics of the Lisbon of yore. It once was called the heart of the city, probably for both its location and its houses, streets, and inhabitants. Many of its buildings were left intact during the 1755 earthquake. Today it is the home of some of the finest fado cafés in Lisbon, making it a center of nightlife, but it is also a fascinating place to visit during the day, when its lasting charm of narrow, cobblestone streets and alleys, lined with ancient buildings, can be enjoyed.

The Bairro Alto, originally called Vila Nova de Andrade, was started in 1513, when part of the huge Santa Catarina farm was sold to the Andrade family, who sold the land as plots for construction. Early buyers were carpenters, merchants, ship caulkers, who must have been astute businessmen: At least some of them immediately resold their newly acquired land to aristocrats, and little by little noble families moved to the quarter. The Jesuits followed, moving from their modest College of Mouraria to new headquarters at the Monastery of São Roque, where the *Misericórdia* (social assistance to the poor) of Lisbon is still carried on today. As often happens, the Bairro Alto gradually became a working-class quarter. Today the quarter is also the domain of journalists, since most of the big newspapers have their plants here. Writers and artists have been drawn here to live and work, attracted by the ambience and the good cuisine of local restaurants.

The area is a colorful one. From the windows and balconies, streamers of laundry hang out to dry, and here and there are cages of canaries, parrots, parakeets, and other birds. In the morning the street scene is made up of housewives coming out from their homes to shop for food, probably attracted by the cries of the varinas (fishmongers) and other vendors, some pushing creaky, heavily laden carts, and some, usually women, trudging by with baskets of fresh vegetables. Women lounge in doorways or lean on windowsills to watch the world go by.

The Bairro Alto blooms at night, luring with fado, food, discos, and small bars. Lisbon's budget restaurants, the tascas, proliferate here, together with more deluxe eateries. Victorian lanterns light the streets, where people stroll leisurely along.

5. The Churches of Lisbon

"If you want to see all of the churches of Lisbon, you'd better be prepared to stay here for a few months," the guide told a tourist. What follows is a selection of the most interesting churches.

PANTEÃO NACIONAL (IGREJA DE SANTA ENGRÁCIA)

When a builder starts to work on a Portuguese house, the owner often chides, "Don't take as long as St. Engrácia." Construction on this Portuguese baroque church with its four square towers began in the 1600s, and it resisted the earthquake, but wasn't completed until 1966. Now the **National Pantheon,** the **Church of Santa Engrácia** is at Campo de Santa Clara (tel. 87-15-29). The church is so well planned and built that relief and architectural idiosyncrasies would have been welcomed. The completed building appears pristine and cold, and the state has fittingly turned it into a neoclassic National Pantheon, containing memorial tombs to Portuguese heads of state and other greats.

Memorials honor Henry the Navigator; Luís Vaz de Camões, the country's greatest poet; Pedro Álvares Cabral, discoverer of Brazil; Afonso de Albuquerque, viceroy of India; Nuño Álvares Pereira, warrior and saint; and Vasco da Gama, of course. Entombed in the National Pantheon are presidents of Portugal and several writers; Almeida Garrett, the outstanding 19th-century literary figure; João de Deus, lyric poet; and Guerra Junqueiro, also a poet.

THE BAIRRO ALTO

Academia das Ciencas
Rua do Século
Rua N. do Loureiro
Rua S. Boaventura
Rua de São Pedro Alcântara
Belvedere
Funicular
Estaçao do Rossio
Rua Soriano
Rua da Rosa
Trav. da Queimada
Rua Santa Catarina
Rua da Atalaia
Rua da Barroca
Rua do Norte
Rua das Gáveas
Rua da Misercórdia
BICA Funicular
Rua das Chagas
Rua das Flores
Pr. Luis de Camões
Rua Nova da Trindade
Largo do Carmo
Rua Trindade
Largo do Chiado
Rua Garrett
Rua de São Paulo
Rua do Alecrim
Rua Duque de Bragança
Rua Vitor Cordon
Rua Serpa
Pr. Duque da Terceira
Pr. do Municipio
Rua do Ouro
Rua Augusta

Church ◼ ✝
Post Office ⊠
Information ◯

PORTUGAL
LISBON

Biblioteca National ❼
Elevador de Santa Justa ❺
Igreja de São Roque ❶
Igreja do Carmo ❸

Museu de Arqueologia ❹
Museu de Arte Contemporâneo ❽
Teatro São Carlos ❻
Teatro Trindade ❷

The National Pantheon is closed on Monday and holidays. Otherwise, it is open to the public from 10am to 5pm. Ask the guards to take you to the terrace for a beautiful view over the river. Admission is 150$ ($1), except on Sunday when it is free. Children under 10 are admitted free. Bus: 9 or 46.

A visit to the pantheon can be combined with a shopping trip to the Flea Market (walk down the Campo de Santa Clara, heading toward the river).

ARQUEOLÓGICO DA ASSOCIAÇÃO DOS ARQUEOLÓGOS PORTUGÊSES

Standing in its ruins today, you can only imagine the glory of this former 14th-century Carmo Church, Largo do Carmo (tel. 346-04-73). On the morning of November 1, 1755, the church was crowded for All Saints' Day. The roof cracked and buckled. It was the Lisbon earthquake. When the debris was cleared, only a Gothic skeleton remained. For some reason, the Carmo Church was never reconstructed.

Silhouetted against the Lisbon sky are the chancel, apse, and the Great Door, a section of which has been converted into an archeological museum. This museum contains collections of prehistoric weapons and implements. Roman and Visigothic pieces, pottery, statues, azulejos, and South American mummies, among other treasures. There are a great number of stone inscriptions in Latin, Hebrew, Arabic, and Portuguese.

The museum is best reached by taking the Santa Justa elevator from the Rua do Ouro below or else take bus no. 15 or 100. Hours are May through September from 10am to 6pm and October through September from 10am to 1pm and 2 to 5pm. Admission is 250$ ($1.70). Children under 10 are admitted free. It is closed on Sunday.

MUSEU ST. ROQUE

The St. Roque Church (tel. 346-03-61) was founded in the closing years of the 16th century by the Jesuits. To reach it, head for the Largo Trindade Coelho on bus no. 15 or 100 or streetcar no. 24.

The church, with its painted wood ceiling, contains a celebrated chapel honoring John the Baptist by Luigi Vanvitelli. The chapel was assembled in Rome in the 18th century with such precious materials as alabaster and lapis lazuli, then dismantled and shipped to Lisbon, where it was reassembled. It was ordered by the Bragança king João V, 9 years before the end of his reign in 1750. The marble mosaics look like a painting. You can also visit the sacristy, rich in paintings illustrating scenes from the lives of the Society of Jesus saints. The Jesuits held great power in Portugal, at one time virtually governing the country for the king.

The St. Roque Museum is visited chiefly for its collection of baroque jewelry. A pair of gold-and-silver torch-holders, weighing about 840 pounds, is considered among the most elaborate in Europe. The gold embroidery from the 18th century is a rare treasure, as are the vestments. The paintings are mainly from the 16th century, including one of a double-chinned Catherine of Austria, another of the wedding ceremony of Manuel I. Look for a remarkable 16th-century *Virgin (with Child) of the Plague* and a polished conch shell from the 18th century that served as a baptismal font.

The museum lies in the Bairro Alto section and is open Tuesday to Sunday from 10am to 5pm. From June through September, it stays open until 6pm. Admission is 25$ (20¢) for adults, and free for children under 10.

IGREJA DA SÃO VICENTE DE FORA

In this Renaissance church, **St. Vincent Outside the Walls,** Largo de São Vicente (tel. 86-25-44), the greatest names and some forgotten wives of the House of Bragança were placed to rest. It's really a pantheon. Originally a convent from the 12th century, the church was erected between 1582 and 1627. At that time it was outside the walls of Lisbon. On the morning of the earthquake of 1755, the cupola fell in.

The Braganças assumed power in 1640 and ruled until 1910, when the Portuguese monarchy collapsed and King Manuel II and the queen mother, Amélia, fled to England. The body of Manuel II was subsequently returned to Portugal for burial. Amélia, the last queen of Portugal, died in 1951 and was also entombed here, as are her husband, Carlos I, the painter king, and her son, Prince Luís Felipe, both killed by an assassin at Praça do Comércio in 1908.

Aside from the royal tombs, one of the most important reasons for visiting St. Vincent is to see its azulejos (the glazed earthenware tiles), some of them illustrating the fables of La Fontaine. I suspect no one's officially counted them, but their number is placed at one million. Look for a curious ivory statue of Christ, carved in the former Portuguese province of Goa in the 18th century.

The church may be visited from 9am to 1pm and 3 to 5pm for 150$ ($1) admission. Children under 10 are admitted free. Closed: Monday. Bus: 12 or 28.

MUSEU NACIONAL DO AZULEJOS (NATIONAL MUSEUM OF TILES)

An outstanding characteristic of Portuguese churches is the architectural device of lining the walls with azulejos. Dutch blue and white usually predominate in the color scheme. Some of the finest azulejos decoration is found in this former convent founded by Queen Leonor in 1509. There is also a rich collection of 17th- and 18th-century oil paintings. The small sacristy of the church is lined with polychrome azulejos (Portuguese work), and there you can also see the retable of Sta. Auta, of the 16th-century Flemish school.

Near the riverside, at Rua Madre de Deus 4 (tel. 814-77-47), it is open from 10am to 5pm except Monday and public holidays. Admission is 200$ ($1.35). It is free on Sunday, when it is open from 10am to 2pm. Children under 10 enter free. Bus: 13A, 18, or 42. Tram: 3 or 16.

---

6. A Bullfight Spectacle

Bullfighting in Portugal was once the sport of noblemen. In Portuguese bullfights, the bull is not killed, a prohibition instituted in the 18th century by the prime minister, Marquês de Pombal, after the son of the Duke of Arcos was killed in the sport. The Portuguese bullfight differs in other respects from the Spanish version. The drama is attended with much ceremony and pageantry, and the major actors are the elegantly costumed *cavaleiros,* who charge the bull on horseback, and the *macos de forcado,* who grapple with the bull in face-to-face combat—for many, the most exciting event.

Warning: The bullfight is not for everyone. Even though the animal is not killed, many readers find the spectacle nauseating and take strong objection to the idea that it is beautiful, or an art form. The spears that jab the neck of the bull produce blood, of course, making the unfortunate animal visibly weaker. The so-called fight has been labeled "no contest!" One reader wrote, "The animals are frightened, confused, and badgered before they are mercifully allowed to exit. What sport!"

The season is from Easter until around mid-October. The 8,500-seat **Campo Pequeno** (reached on the subway to that stop) in Lisbon is the largest ring in the country, and usually presents fights on Thursday and Sunday afternoons in season. These *touradas* and the names of the stars are announced well in advance, so your hotel concierge can be of help to you (many arrange tickets).

Another major bullring is the **Monumental de Cascais,** at Cascais (tel. 73-66-01), the resort lying west of Estoril on the Costa do Sol. The electric train from Lisbon ends its run in Cascais; from the station, an inexpensive taxi will take you to the bullring, just outside the center of town. The best place to buy tickets is, of course, right at the ticket office at the arenas. However, for the best seats, it is perhaps advisable to pay the usual 10% commission to an agency. The best ones are Agência de Bilhetes para Espectáculos Públicos, whose offices are at Avenida da Liberdade 140 (tel. 32-75-24), Praça dos Restauradores (tel. 36-95-00), and Parque Mayer (tel. 37-25-94).

7. Other Sights

Those sights in and around Lisbon that could not be categorically listed else-where are highlighted below. Some reveal much about the nation's natural resources, geography, climate, inhabitants, and life-style, and it is the knowledge of these things that makes you far more than just a tourist passing through.

MARKETS

The big market of **Ribeira Nova** is as close as you can get to the heart of Lisbon. Near the Cais do Sodré, where trains are boarded for the Costa do Sol, an enormous roof shelters a collection of produce stalls, where you'll see the produce you'll be eating later at one of Lisbon's fine restaurants. Foodstuffs are brought in each morning in bulging wicker baskets filled with oversize carrots, cabbages big enough for shrubbery, and stalks of bananas. Some of the produce arrives by donkey; some by truck; some balanced on the heads of Lisboan women in Mediterranean fashion— all from yesterday's field. The rich soil produces the juiciest of peaches, the most aromatic tomatoes.

"Seeing-eye" fishing boats, many believed to have been based on Phoenician designs, tie up at the dock at dawn with their catch. The fish are deposited on long marble counters: cod, squid, bass, hake, swordfish. Soon the varinas take wicker baskets of the fresh catch, balancing them on their heads, and climb the cobbled streets of the Alfama or the Bairro Alto to sell fish from door to door.

At the market, the mounds of vegetables, fruit, and fish are presided over by hearty, outgoing Portuguese women gaily clad in voluminous skirts and calico aprons. On cue the vendors begin howling out the value of their wares, stopping only to pose for an occasional snapshot.

Adjoining the market, away from the river, cut-stone streets are flanked with shops selling inexpensive Portuguese clothing. The best buy, if you can locate one, is a distinctively styled cape from the Alentejo district. In three tiers, these capes are often capped with red-fox collars.

ESTUFA FRIA (THE GREENHOUSE)

The Portuguese call it their **Estufa Fria** in Parque Eduardo VII (tel. 68-22-78). It's in the handsomely laid out Edward VII Park, named after Queen Victoria's son to commemorate his three trips to Lisbon. Against a background of streams and rocks, tropical plants grow in such profusion that some writers have called it a "sylvan glade"; so luxuriant is its growth that it evokes a rain forest.

The park lies at the top of the Avenida da Liberdade, crowned by a statue of the Marquês de Pombal, with his "house pet," a lion. There's a 57$ (40¢) admission charge to the greenhouse, which is open daily from 9am to 6pm April through September, from 9am to 5pm daily October through May. Subway: Rotunda.

BRITISH CEMETERY

Up the Rua da Estrêla at one end of the Estrêla Gardens lies the British Cemetery. It's famous as the burial place of Henry Fielding, the English novelist (*Tom Jones*) and dramatist. A sick man, Fielding went to Lisbon in 1754 for his health, and the story of that trip is narrated in the posthumous tract *Journal of a Voyage to Lisbon*. Reaching Lisbon in August, he died 2 months later. A monument honoring him was erected in 1830.

THE AQUEDUCT

An outstanding baroque monument, the **Aguas Livres Aqueduct** runs from the Aguas Livres River in Caneças to the Casa da Agua reservoir in Amoreiras. The aqueduct, built under King João V in the early 18th century, runs for about 11 miles. Part of it is underground, but the aboveground section allows some of the 109 stone arches to be seen. For the best view, visitors can see the 14 arches stretching across the valley of Alcantara from Serafina to the Campolide hills.

SANTA JUSTA ELEVATOR

For a splendid rooftop view of Lisbon, take the Santa Justa Elevator, Rua de Santa Justa, an ornate concoction often attributed to the man who built that tower in Paris, the French engineer Alexandre-Gustave Eiffel. However, the elevator was actually built by a Portuguese engineer, Raoul Mesnier de Ponsard, born in Porto in 1849, son of French immigrants. He graduated in mathematics and philosophy at Coimbra, then studied in France, Germany, and Switzerland. The elevator goes from Rua Aurea, in the center of the shopping district near Rossio Square, up to the Carmo Church. It operates daily from 7am to 11pm. A ticket costs 28$ (20¢) for everyone except children under 4. Subway: Rossio.

---

8. Cool for Kids

JARDIM ZOOLÓGICO

The **Zoological Garden,** Parque dos Laranjeiras (tel. 72-68-041), with a collection of some 2,000 animals, enjoys a flower-filled setting in the 65-acre Park of Laranjeiras, about a 10-minute subway ride from the Rossio (disembark at Sete Rios). You can also take bus no. 15, 31, or 46. The Children's Zoo, with its miniature houses in small gardens, is exceptional. There are also a small tram, rowboats, a roller-skating rink, elephant and pony rides, films, and puppet shows presented on Sunday.

AQUÁRIO VASCO DA GAMA

With a museum in addition, the **Vasco da Gama Aquarium,** Rua Diretio, Dafundo (tel. 419-80-52), on the N6, near Algés on the Cascais railway line, has been in operation since 1898. Live exhibits include a pavilion containing eared seals, plus a vast number of tanks for fish and other sea creatures from all over the world. A large portion of the exhibits in the museum consists of zoological material brought back by King Carlos I on oceanographic expeditions. They include preserved marine invertebrates, water birds, fish, mammals, and some of the king's laboratory equipment. The aquarium is open daily from June through October from 10am to 6pm and from November through May daily from 10am to 5:30pm. Admission June through September is 300$ ($2), lowered to 150$ ($1) October through May. It is free on Wednesday. Children under 10 and those over 65 are admitted free. Take bus no. 23 or streetcar no. 15 or 17.

---

9. Organized Tours

Lisbon travel agents will book you on organized tours. One of the most popular agencies is **Star,** the representative of American Express at Avenida Sidónio Pais 4A (main office, tel. 53-98-71), close to Eduardo VII Park-South (Praça Marquês de Pombal), the starting point of the tours. It also has a downtown branch office at Restauradores 14 (tel. 34-62-501).

Touristic Lisbon has two daily departures year round—one at 9:30am, another at 2:30pm. This tour takes in all the highlights, including St. George's Castle and Belém. The cost is 3,950$ ($26.45) per person.

A full-day Lisbon/Mafra/Estoril/Queluz Tour, also operated year round, costs 9,000$ ($60.30), including lunch. Departures are at 9:30am. A half-day tour takes in the highlights of Sintra and Estoril, with departures at 9:30am and 2:30pm, costing 4,450$ ($29.80). A full-day tour to Óbidos, Nazaré, and Fátima departs at 8:30am, costing 10,000$ ($67), including lunch.

LISBON SHOPPING

1. THE SHOPPING SCENE
2. SHOPPING A TO Z

Portuguese handcrafts often have exotic influences because of the versatility of the Portuguese and their skill in absorbing other styles. The best showing of their work is in Lisbon. The shopkeepers and their buyers hunt out unusual items in the Madeira Islands and the Azores as well as in their own country.

If you want to bargain it is still possible in Lisbon, although it is not looked on kindly in the more prestigious shops. Use both your sixth sense and common sense. A good yardstick is whether or not a store is owner managed, as smaller ones usually are. In owner-managed stores you might work out a deal.

1. The Shopping Scene

SHOPPING AREAS
Baixa is the major area for browsing, but shops are spread all over the city. Baixa is the district forming downtown Lisbon. *Rua do Ouro* (Street of Gold, where the major jewelry shops can be found), *Rua da Prata* (Street of Silver), and *Rua Augusta* are Lisbon's three principal streets for shopping. The Baixa shopping district lies between the Rossio and the River Tagus.

Rua do Carmo is another major shopping artery, found in the Chiado, site of many of the more upmarket shops of Lisbon. Many of these shops were destroyed in a major fire in 1988, and several have not reopened. To reach the area, you can take the Santa Justa Elevator near the Rossio.

Antique lovers gravitate to the Rua Dom Pedro V in the Bairro Alto, although other streets with antique stores include Rua da Misericórdia, Rua São Pedro de Alcantara, Rua da Escola Politécnica, and Rua do Alecrim.

HOURS, SHIPPING & TAXES
Most stores open at 9am, closing at noon for lunch. They reopen at 2pm, closing for the day at 7pm. However, many shopkeepers like to take lunch from 1 to 3pm, so check before making the trip. On Saturday, most stores in Lisbon, and elsewhere in Portugal for that matter, are often closed.

Many establishments will crate and ship bulky objects. Any especially large item, such as a piece of furniture, should be sent by ship. Every antique dealer in Lisbon has lists of reputable maritime shippers. For most small and medium-size shipments, air freight isn't much more expensive than ship. TAP, the Portuguese airline, offers shipping service from Portugal to New York. At any of its gateway cities, TAP can arrange to have your purchase transferred to another airline for shipment.

Remember that all your air cargo shipments will need to clear Customs after they're brought into the United States, Canada, or your home country. This involves some additional paperwork and perhaps a trip to the airport near where you live. It's usually wiser to hire a commercial Customs broker to do the work for you.

Emery Worldwide, a division of CF Freightways, can clear your goods for around $100 for most shipments. For information, you can call toll free in the U.S.: 800/443-6379.

If you wish to send a package home—usually of a smaller variety—you can do so by packing it in your luggage unless you're worried about possible breakage. If you are afraid of going beyond your luggage allowance, you can send a package home at most major post offices. Appear with your merchandise at the post office along with string and tape. There are limitations on the duty-free goods you can bring back to the United States. Packages go to the U.S. Customs office upon arrival in the States.

Goods valued at less than $50 can be delivered by the postman. If the value of your package is more than $50, you must pay the amount the Customs people assess. Your postman is entitled to collect the additional charges. It is illegal, incidentally, to ship liquor to the United States through the mails.

Items carried with you and purchased abroad are duty free up to $400. Anything beyond that is assessed a duty of 10% up to the nearest $1,000. For example, if you bring back purchases of $1,400, you are allowed a $400 exemption but must pay another $100 for the additional $1,000 of goods you're bringing in.

Value Added Tax (called IVA in Portugal) is about 16% on most items. Foreigners with valid passports can get a refund on their purchases if their purchases in one store add up to about 11,700$ ($78.40). To be granted this refund, ask the shop at which you purchased the merchandise to fill out a Tax Free Check.

When you leave Portugal, show your purchases (which must be carried by hand and not checked with your luggage) to the Portuguese Custom officials, along with your passport. If everything is in order, your Tax Free Checks will be stamped and you can redeem them at a Tax Refund counter for cash. Tax Refund offices are found both at the airport and the harbor of Lisbon.

BEST BUYS

Especially good handcrafts buys from the Azores and Madeira Islands can be found in Portugal, including handmade embroideries, such as blouses, napkins, tablecloths, and handkerchiefs; products made of cork, from placemats to cigarette boxes; and *azulejos* (decorative glazed tiles). From Vista Alegre there is porcelain and china; three are fishermen's sweaters from Nazaré; local pottery; and, of course, fado records.

Considered a good buy in Portugal, gold is strictly regulated by the government, which requires jewelers to put a minimum of 19¼ karats in jewelry made of this expensive metal. Filigree jewelry in gold and silver is all the rage not only in Lisbon but elsewhere in Portugal. This art of ornamental openwork made of fine gold or silver wire dates back to ancient times. The most expensive items—often objets d'art—are fashioned from 19¼-karat gold. Depictions of caravels are one of the forms this art expression takes. However, less expensive trinkets are often made of sterling silver, perhaps sterling silver that has been dipped in 24-karat gold.

Portugal is also famous for its Arraiolos carpets. Later when we explore Alentejo and Ribatejo, you can actually visit the little town of Arraiolos where these fine woolen rugs, which have earned an international reputation, are sold. Legend says these rugs were first made by Moorish craftsmen expelled from Lisbon in the early 16th century. The designs were said to be in imitation of those from Persia. Some of these carpets eventually find their way into museums.

2. Shopping A to Z

ANTIQUES

Along both sides of the narrow street Rua de S. José are treasure troves—shops packed with antiques from all over the world. Antique dealers from America come here to survey the wares. You'll find ornate spool and carved beds, high-back chairs, tables, wardrobes with ornate carving or time-seasoned woods, brass plaques, copper pans, silver candelabra, crystal sconces, and chandeliers, plus a wide selection of old wooden figures, silver boxes, porcelain plates, and bowls. But don't count on super bargains.

Rua Dom Pedro V is another street of antique shops, of which my personal favorite is **Solar,** Rua Dom Pedro V 68–70 (tel. 34-65-522). It is stocked with antique tiles salvaged from some of Portugal's historic buildings and manor houses. The condition of the tile varies, of course. Many go back as far as the 15th century. The store also sells antique furniture and pewterware.

ART GALLERIES

One of the leading art galleries of Lisbon is **Galeria Sesimbra,** Rua Castilho 77 (tel. 56-02-91), near the Ritz Hotel. It is operated by one of the most distinguished art dealers of Iberia. Mainly Portuguese artists are displayed here, but foreign artists "who have lived in Portugal long enough to get a feeling for the country" are also exhibited. The finest of Portuguese paintings, sculpture, and ceramics are sold here. Its best-known works for sale, however, are Agulha tapestries. The Agulha tapestry is composed of a controlled variation of stitching, giving it an advantage over those made on looms. Many artists have turned to this new medium for depth and movement in their work. Size can range from 10 square feet to the "longest tapestry in the world."

Galeria 111, Campo Grande 13A (tel. 79-77-418), is recognized as one of the major art galleries of Lisbon, a distinction it has shared since 1964. Some of the leading contemporary artists of Portugal are on display here in a wide-ranging exhibition of sculpture, paintings, and graphics. It also sells drawings, etchings, silk screens, lithographs, art books, and postcards. Annual closing is from August 10 to September 8.

BOOKS

A corner bookstore, **Libraria Bertrand do Chiado,** Rua Garrett 73–75 (tel. 34-20-081), in the Chiado district, has a large selection of titles in English. They also have travel material such as good maps of Portugal.

CARPETS

In Lisbon the showcase for the Arraiolos carpet is **Casa Quintão,** Rua Ivens 30–34 (tel. 34-65-837). Rugs here are priced by the square foot, according to the density of the stitching. Casa Quintão can reproduce intricate Oriental or medieval designs in rugs or tapestries, and create any custom pattern specified by a client. The shop also sells materials and gives instructions on how to make your own carpets and tapestry-covered pillows. The staff seems genuinely willing to help.

CHINA & GLASSWARE

Unparalleled for china and glassware, **Vista Alegre,** Largo do Chiado 18 (tel. 34-75-481), numbers royalty and diplomats, or whoever demands the very best, among its clientele. The colorful porcelain from Ilhavo, with many of the figurines depicting regional costumes, is of special interest to the casual shopper. Professional and do-it-yourself decorators are drawn to the porcelain figures and birds. They are amazingly lifelike, but also alarmingly high-priced. If you're bargain hunting, you'd do better buying a fruit bowl or a set of dishes.

CORK PRODUCTS

For something typically Portuguese, try **Casa das Corticas,** Rua da Escola Politécnica 4–6 (tel. 34-25-858). "Mr. Cork" became somewhat of a legend in Lisbon for offering "everything conceivable" that could be made of cork, of which Portugal controls a hefty part of the world market. Mr. Cork is long gone now, but the store carries on. You'll be surprised at the number of items that can be made from cork, including a chess set or a checkerboard. Perhaps a set of six placemats in a two-tone checkerboard style will interest you. For souvenirs, the cork caravels are immensely popular. Other items include a natural cutting board and ice bucket.

EMBROIDERY

A good place to shop is **Madeira Superbia,** with a branch at the Ritz Hotel and a somewhat larger store at Duque de Loulé 75A (tel. 53-69-68), an outlet for one of the best embroidery factories on the Madeira Islands. The exquisite craft they display, not inexpensive, includes tapestries, linens, and women's apparel, such as petit-point handbags and blouses. Often, high-quality fabrics are imported from Switzerland and Ireland, then embroidered on the islands. The collection of hand-embroidered napkins, tea cloths, pillowcases, and sheets is exceptional. Beautiful placemats often come in organdy with a linen appliqué (some are double-edged with shadow work embroidery). One of the most popular items is monogrammed linen handkerchiefs.

Madeira House, Rua Augusta 131–135 (tel. 32-69-13), a competitor, also specializes in a good selection of high-quality cottons, linens, and small gift items, and does so equally well. Its other locations in Lisbon are at Rua Aurea 246, Rossio 44, and Avenida da Liberdade 159, and there is a shop at Rua das Padarias 2 in Sintra. At one of these shops you can purchase a hand-embroidered top sheet with two matching pillowcases in linen or cotton. The store also stocks wheat-colored 6-by 8-foot linen tablecloths from the Minho district in north Portugal.

Casa Regional da Ilha Verde, Rua Paiva de Andrade 4 (tel. 34-25-974), specializes in handmade items, especially embroideries from the Azores. That's why it's called the Regional House of the Green Island. Each piece carries a made-by-hand guarantee. Some of the designs used on the linen placemats with napkins have been in use for centuries. You can get some good buys here.

Principe Real, Rua da Escola Politécnica 12–14 (tel. 34-65-945), specializes in linens elegant enough to grace the tables of monarchs, including, in days gone by, that of Princess Grace of Monaco. This family-run store produces some of Europe's finest tablecloths and sheets in cotton, linen, and organdy. Although the Rockefellers have purchased items here from its owner and designer, the merchandise (especially with beneficial escudo exchange rates) is not beyond the means of a middle-class tourist. About two dozen staff members can execute a linen pattern to match a client's favorite porcelain, or else the owner can create one of her own designs.

MARKETS

Here is a place where you can haggle and enjoy the fun of getting a bargain. Called the **Feira da Ladra,** this open-air street market is like the flea markets of Madrid and Paris. Nearly every possible item that can be purchased is seen here in the street stalls. For the finest pickings it's best to go in the morning. The vendors peddle their wares on Tuesday and Saturday.

About a 5-minute walk from the waterfront, in the Alfama district, the market sits in back of the Military Museum adjoining the Pantheon of São Vicente. Start your browsing at the Campo de Santa Clara. Portable stalls and individual displays are lined up on this hilly street with its tree-lined center.

You can often pick up a bargain here, but you must search diligently through masses of cheap clothing and lots of junk to find it. Everything from brass scales, oil lamps, portable bidets, cow bells, and old coins, to Macau china, antique watches, and Angola wood carvings is on display. Take bus no. 12 from Santa Apolónia Station.

SHOPPING MALLS

There are some 150 boutiques, shops, and snack bars installed in four of the five floors of the **Rossio Railway Station,** in the heart of downtown Lisbon. The fifth floor is where the trains arrive and depart. Banks of escalators whisk you from floor to floor, and shopping in the maze of small shops is easier than walking on the congested streets. Conveniently, the shops are open every day of the year from 9am to midnight. The street floor is deceptively shabby—ignore it and take the escalator to the boutiques. You'll find apparel for men, women, and children, as well as shops specializing in jewelry, fado records, and so forth. There are a pharmacy for "naturalists," beauty parlors, hairdressers, bookstores, leather goods, sweaters, and Portuguese handcrafts.

The most spectacular shopping complex in Lisbon is the **Amoreiras Shopping Center de Lisboa,** Avenida Duarte Pacheco (tel. 69-25-58), the largest in Iberia and the fourth biggest in Europe. You can wander through this Oriental fantasy, exploring the contents of more than 300 shops and boutiques. A huge array of merchandise is offered for sale, including Portuguese fashion, leather goods, crystal, and souvenirs. In addition to several restaurants and snack bars, there is also a health center. The location is on a hill at the entrance to Lisbon, lying in back of the old reservoir called Aguas Livres. The blue-and-pink towers rise 19 stories and have already changed the skyline of Lisbon. The mall is open daily from 10am to midnight. Take bus no. 11, 15, or 23.

Apolo 70, Avenida Julio Dinis 10 (tel. 79-71-594), near the bullring, is a self-contained unit that includes everything from an interior sidewalk café to a cinema and a leather shop. Wander for an hour or two among the 38 shops, making purchases at a teenage boutique, getting your photograph blown up to poster size, or having your hair styled by experts, after which you can stop in the cozy bar for a cooling drink, on the lower level. Also on the lower level is a restaurant that vaguely evokes a merry-go-round. Subway: Campo Pequeno.

SILVER, GOLD & FILIGREE

At the foot of the Santa Justa Elevator, **W. A. Sarmento,** Rua Aurea 251 (tel. 342-67-74), has been in the hands of the family that owns it for well over a century. The shop has been the favorite place for Lisboans to buy treasured confirmation and graduation gifts, and it has customers among the Costa do Sol aristocracy as well as movie stars and diplomats. They are the most distinguished silver- and goldsmiths in Portugal, specializing in lacy filigree jewelry. For additions to your charm bracelet, Sarmento is the place to go. There are literally dozens of choices. The shop is a member of the tax-free-for-tourists system.

Well on its way to being a century old, **Joalharia do Carmo,** Rua do Carmo 87B (tel. 34-24-041), is the best place in Lisbon to shop for filigree work. Some of the gold pieces here have been further adorned with either precious or semiprecious stones.

SUEDE

Diagonally across from the Ritz Hotel, **Caprice,** Rua Joaquim António de Aguiar 45 (tel. 53-85-27), sells a fine line of suede items, such as long coats, suits, and skirts. It is owned by Philippe L. Gaulier, whose mother was a Lanvin stylist. He apparently inherited her good taste. Both he and his wife are English-speaking and will offer you an assortment of Alcantara suede (an acrylic called "ultrasuede," which is machine-washable) in both dresses, two-piece suits, and coats as well as men's safari shirts. The suede comes in a wide assortment of interesting colors, including pink, dark chocolate, navy, aqua, and caramel. In addition, the Gauliers present a selection of hand-crocheted suits and dresses, but, unfortunately, these items are so expensive to produce that they don't fall within the average person's price range.

TILES

Founded in 1741, **Sant'Anna,** Rua do Alecrim 95–97 (tel. 34-22-537), is Portugal's leading ceramic center. Famous for its azulejos (glazed tiles), Sant'Anna is in the Chiado section. The showroom is at the Rua do Alecrim location, but you can also visit the factory at Calçada da Boa Hora 96; however, you must telephone ahead to make an appointment. Some of the designs that decorate the tiles are created by artisans who are among the finest in Europe, and many of them employ designs in use since the Middle Ages. Bargains I bought recently include a group of framed scenic azulejos, a two-holder candelabrum, an hors d'oeuvres tray (tiled), and a ceramic umbrella stand that is three feet high.

A rival to Sant'Anna, **Fábrica Cerâmica Viúva Lamego,** Calçada do Sacramento 29 (tel. 34-69-692), sells contemporary tiles, mostly reproductions of old Portuguese motifs, and also pottery, including an interesting selection of planters and umbrella stands. When you reach the address, you'll know you're at the right place: Its facade is decorated with these colorful azulejos with figures in their rich plumage and dress.

TOYS

Parents seeking new and unusual toys for their children will find the best selection at **Biagio Flora,** Rua do Ouro 136 (tel. 34-60-691). Thousands of toys are displayed at this location in the center of town. Their specialty is electric trains.

LISBON NIGHTS

•

If you have only one night in Lisbon, spend it at a fado club. That same sentiment holds true if you have two or even three nights. The nostalgic sounds of fado, Portuguese "songs of sorrow," are heard at their best in Lisbon, as the Portuguese capital attracts the greatest fadistas (fado singers) in the world. (A fado singer, male or female, is called fadista.)

For more information about fado, refer to "Music" in Chapter 2, "Getting to Know Portugal."

Don't go to hear fado and plan to carry on a private conversation. It's considered bad form.

Most of the authentic fado clubs are clustered near one another in the Bairro Alto or in the Alfama, between St. George's Castle and the docks. You can "fado hop" between these two typical quarters. Alfama-bound hoppers can ask the taxi driver to deliver them to **Largo do Chafariz,** a small plaza a block from the harbor, and Bairro Alto devotees can get off at **Largo do S. Roque.** Most of my recommendations lie only a short walk from either of these squares.

Fado outshines all other nighttime entertainment in Lisbon. However, for a change of pace, I've included suggestions for other tastes, including discos, bars, even vaudeville-type places.

Lisbon, especially in the autumn and winter, also enjoys a rich cultural life (see "The Performing Arts," below), although because of its smaller size its cultural presentations obviously can't equal that of some of the more gilded capitals of Europe, such as London and Paris.

For more information about nighttime attractions, go to the tourist office, which has a list of major events being staged in Lisbon. Another helpful source is the **Agência de Bilhetes para Espectáculos Públicos** in the Praça dos Restauradores. It is open daily from 9am to 10pm, and you should show up in person instead of trying to call for information. This agency sells tickets to most theaters and cinemas, except the Teatro Nacional de São Carlos. For that you should go to the theater's own box office (see below).

To obtain information, consult a copy of *What's On in Lisbon,* available at most newsstands. Your hotel concierge is also a good bet for information, since one of his or her duties is reserving seats.

The local newspaper, *Diário de Notícias,* carries all cultural listings, but the information is presented only in Portuguese. No special discount tickets are offered, except students get 50% off on tickets purchased for the national theater (see "Theater," below).

1. The Performing Arts

OPERA & BALLET

The **Teatro Nacional de São Carlos,** Rua Serpa Pinto 9 (tel. 346-84-08), attracts opera and ballet aficionados from all over Europe. Top companies from around the world perform at this 18th-century theater. The season begins in mid-December and extends through May. Opera tickets cost from 450$ ($3) to 7,500$ ($50.25). The box office is open daily from 1 to 7pm. There are no special discounts.

CLASSICAL MUSIC

From October through June, concerts and recitals—and occasional ballet—are performed at the **Museu da Fundacão Calouste Gulbenkian,** Avenida de Berna 45 (tel. 73-51-31). Sometimes jazz concerts are also presented here. You'll have to inquire locally about what is happening at the time of your visit. Ticket prices depend on the event.

Chamber-music concerts and symphony presentations are performed at the **Teatro Municipal de São Luis,** Rua António Maria Cardoso 40 (tel. 36-52-59).

THEATER

Teatro Nacional de D. Maria II, Praça Dom Pedro IV (tel. 32-37-46), is the most famous theater in Portugal. Its season usually begins in the autumn, lasting through spring. It presents a repertoire of both Portuguese and foreign plays, and as a national theater performances are strictly in Portuguese. Tickets range from 500$ ($3.35) to 3,000$ ($20.10), but students with valid ID get a 50% discount.

2. The Club & Music Scene

A NIGHTCLUB/RESTAURANT

Café Alcantara, Rua Maria Luisa Holstein (tel. 363-71-76), is currently the most fashionable nighttime rendezvous in Lisbon. The premises were adapted from a converted cannery along the waterfront. The owners, Pedro Luz and Raul Rodriguis, have turned it into the chicest nightclub and restaurant in the capital. Guests enjoy their drinks in a setting of classical sculptured torsos or even in the shadow of trees. The menu is both French and Portuguese, including such classic dishes as grilled fish with vegetables from the market (whatever was fresh that day). Dinner begins at 3730$ ($25). The restaurant serves food Wednesday through Monday from 8pm to 12:45am. Most guests stay to enjoy the dance club which swings into action Wednesday through Sunday from 11:30pm to 6am.

DANCE CLUBS

Among disco devotees in Lisbon, **Banana Power,** Rua Cascais 53 (tel. 363-18-15), generates a lot of youthful enthusiasm. An old warehouse was converted into a disco in the Alcântara section, lying between the heart of the city and the suburb of Belém. Hundreds of Lisboans, all young, pour in here to enjoy the bands. A cover charge of 1,500$ ($10.05) is levied only on Friday and Saturday; otherwise, there is no charge. This cover includes the price of two drinks. A beer costs 500$ ($3.35) and a mixed drink 650$ ($4.35). Hours are 8pm to 4am Monday through Saturday. Streetcar: 16, 17, or 18. Bus: 12, 13, 14, or 32.

Ad Lib, Rua Barata Salgueiro 28 (tel. 56-17-17), is a posh disco dreamed up by a clique of chaps who wanted an elegant place to drink and dance. On the top floor of a modern building, it doesn't call attention to itself with a sign outside. A uniformed attendant at the formal entrance checks on the intercom system to weed out undesirables. If you're well groomed and not drunk or drugged, you stand a good chance of scaling the citadel; even so, it's wise to telephone in advance.

Upstairs, you'll enter a penthouse with a bar on one level, tables and a dancing area on another. A plant-filled terrace provides a view of Lisbon by night. The decor is Oriental, with fine stone Buddhas from Macau, mirrors, and candles in red bowls. A disc jockey plays the newest continental and American records. Hours are Monday through Saturday from 11pm to 6:30am. The cover charge of 7,000$ ($46.90) includes the price of your first drink. Mixed drinks cost 850$ ($5.70); beer, 600$ ($4). Subway: Avenida.

Kremlin, Escadinhas da Praia 5 (tel. 60-87-68). For at least a part of its history, its cellar-level premises served as a stables for neighborhood horses and the supplies required to feed them. Today, it's the most energetic and iconoclastic of Lisbon's discos, welcoming a very hip crowd of electronic music lovers who come in costumes whose inspiration probably comes from counterculture circles throughout Europe. The decor changes about once a month: At press time the walls were covered with masks in dozens of different variations. Entrance varies from 1,000$ ($6.70) to 5,000$ ($35), depending on the "whim" of the doorman when you happen to arrive. Beer costs 500$ ($3.50), a whisky with soda, 700$ ($4.70). It is open nightly from 11:30pm to 4am. Tram: 15, 16, 17, 18, 29, or 30. Bus: 14, 28, 32, 40, or 43.

Loucuras, Avenida Pedro Alvares Cabral 35 (tel. 68-11-17), was originally built as a movie theater. Its spacious perimeter welcomes a well-dressed crowd of affluent young people who converse, meet, mingle, and dance to music imported from the recording studios of London, Los Angeles, and New York. The crowd is somewhat more conservative than that within the previously recommended Kremlin, although usually in their 20s and 30s, with lots of available energy for conversing with newcomers from abroad. The club is open Friday and Saturday from 4 to 8pm when it caters to a mainly teenage market. It reopens on Friday and Saturday from 11pm to 4am, attracting patrons mostly in their 20s and 30s. Bus: 9, 20, or 22.

Springfellows, Avenida Oscar Monteiro Torres 8B (tel. 79-32-944), is one of the most elegant discos in Lisbon. A disc jockey rides between a trio of floors while encased in a glass cage. After 10pm, suppers are served, costing from 3,000$ ($20.10). The cover charge of 1,200$ ($8.05) includes the price of two drinks. Mixed drinks cost 650$ ($4.35) with beer going for 500$ ($3.35). Hours are daily from 10pm to 4am.

Whispers, Edifício Aviz, Avenida Fontes Pereira de Melo 35 (tel. 57-54-89), lies next to the Sheraton Hotel. It has long been a standard on the dance-club circuit of Lisbon. The latest recorded music is played here for gyrating crowds. It is open daily from 11pm to 4am. An admission of 5,000$ ($33.50) is charged, but you are allowed to drink up to that amount once you're inside. Otherwise, you then pay extra for drinks, with beer costing 400$ ($2.70) or a mixed drink priced at 600$ ($4). Subway: Picoas.

Elefante Branco, Rua Luciano Cordeir 8A (tel. 57-98-11), is a luxurious disco with a piano bar and restaurant. A supper costs from 6,000$ ($40.20). The admission of 5,000$ ($33.50) includes two drinks. Otherwise, mixed drinks cost 1,000$ ($6.70), with beer going for 750$ ($5). Hours are daily from 8:30pm to 4am. Bus: 23. Streetcar: 20, 25, or 26.

---

3. The Fado Clubs

In the clubs listed below, it isn't necessary always to have dinner. You can always go later and order just a drink. However, you often have to pay a minimum consumption charge. The music begins between 9 and 10pm, but it's better to arrive after 11pm. Many of the clubs stay open till 3am, others, till dawn.

Lisboa à Noite, Rua das Gaveas 69 (tel. 346-85-57). Electricity fills the air—the tempestuous Fernanda Maria is about to make her first appearance of the evening. Tossing down a shot of whisky offered by a waiter, she stands quietly, tensely clutching her black shawl. Then she comes forward, pauses, scans the audience, and pours forth all the fiery intensity of fado. You too may fall under her spell. Success has come to Fernanda—she owns the club.

The 17th-century-style setting is rustic, yet luxurious (once this Bairro Alto club was a stable). Creating its present ambience are thick stone-edged arches, heavy hand-hewn beams, blue-and-white tile walls, a round well with its original bucket, a collection of old engravings, antique guns, and pewter and copper. When it's cold, scented eucalyptus logs crackle in a high fireplace. In the rear is an open kitchen and charcoal grill, with an assemblage of spices, sausages, garlic pigtails, and onions hanging from the beams. It's customary to go here for dinner, enjoying such house specialties as dry codfish Fernanda Maria, named after the owner, or steak Lisboa à Noite flambé, named after the club. The cover charge is 2,000$ ($13.40), including the cost of two drinks. If you go for dinner, the price of an average meal is 8,000$ ($53.60). Hours are Monday through Saturday from 8pm to 3am. Bus: 15 or 100. Streetcar: 20 or 24.

Cota D'Armas, Beco de São Miguel 7 (tel. 86-86-82). Nightclub cookery isn't always the best in Lisbon (is it anywhere?), but there is one restaurant that would rank among the top 10 in Lisbon, even if it didn't present a nightly program of "fado and folklore." The elegantly decorated Cota D'Armas is one of the leading attractions on the nighttime circuit for those wishing to venture into the Alfama at night. You can arrive early for dinner, enjoying drinks in the bar decorated in the style of a regional stable. The dining room is upstairs, and it's graced with a hand-painted ceiling. The coat-of-arms (the English translation of the restaurant's name) is depicted on the export china of the East India Company. In winter this setting is made even more inviting by an open fireplace. During dinner, a well-seasoned group of fadistas and guitar players entertain you with Portuguese songs and music. You can also go for lunch, except on Sunday, when it's closed all day. Dinner is served Monday to Saturday. Hours are 12:30 to 3pm and 7:30 to 11:30pm. There is no admission charge, and meals begin at 5,000$ ($33.50). If you go for drinks, the cost is 400$ ($2.70) for mixed drinks or 200$ ($1.35) for beer. Streetcar: 3 or 16. Bus: 9, 12, or 18.

A Severa, Rua das Gaveas 49–57 (tel. 346-40-06). Good food and careful selection of fadistas make this the perennial favorite. Before he became president, Richard Nixon selected it for a night on the town with his wife, Patricia, leading a congalike line between tables, warbling the refrain, "Severa . . . Severa . . . Severa." Every night top singers, both male and female, appear at the Bairro Alto nightspot, accompanied by guitar and viola music, alternating with folk dancers. In a niche you'll spot a statue honoring the club's namesake, Maria Severa, the legendary gypsy fadista of the 19th century. After midnight tourists seem to recede a bit in favor of loyal Lisbon habitués, who request and sometimes join in on their favorite fado number.

The kitchen turns out regional dishes based on recipes from the north of Portugal. For dinner, the favorite main-dish selection is chicken cooked in a clay pot. Before that, you might like to order *caldo verde,* a green cabbage soup. Another house specialty is stuffed squid. Those less experimental may request the steak of the house, fried in a clay dish. Expect to spend from 5,000$ ($33.50) to 8,000$ ($53.60) for a meal with wine. You can also visit just for drinks. The 2,400$ ($16.10) admission charge entitles you two drinks. Otherwise, drinks cost 900$ ($6.05) apiece. The club is open Friday through Wednesday from 8pm to 3:30am. Bus: 20 or 24. Streetcar: 20 or 24.

Adega Machado, Rua do Norte 91 (tel. 346-00-95), has passed the test of time and is today one of the favored fado clubs of Portugal. Formerly you could perhaps spot Edward G. Robinson or Vittorio de Sica listening to the incomparable Amália Rodrigues. Alternating with its fadistas are folk dancers, whirling, clapping, singing their native songs in colorful costumes. The evening dinner hour starts at 8pm and the doors don't close till 3am, when the last fadista aficionado trails out humming his or her favorite song. The club is open daily; from November to March it is closed on Monday.

Dinner is à la carte, and the cuisine is mostly Portuguese, with any number of regional dishes. House specialties include chicken in a pot, stuffed squid, steak Machado, roasted baby goat, and pork with clams. For dessert, I'd suggest almond cake made with nuts from the Algarve. Expect to spend 4,500$ ($30.15) to 6,000$ ($40.20) for a complete meal. Guests often join the singers and folk dancers, carrying arched garlands of flowers, as they parade around the crowded tables, singing the "Marcha do Machado." The club charges an admission of 2,100$ ($14.05), entitling a patron to two drinks. Otherwise, drinks cost from 800$ ($5.35). Bus: 15 or 100. Streetcar: 20 or 24.

Parreirinha da Alfama, Beco do Espírito Santo 1 (tel. 86-82-09). Seemingly, every fadista worth her shawl has sung at this old-time café, just a 1-minute walk from the dockside of the Alfama. It's fado and fado only that enthralls here, not folk dancing. You can order a good regional dinner beginning early, but it's suggested that you go toward the end of the evening and stay late. It's open from 8pm to 3am daily. In the first part of the program, fadistas get all the popular songs out of the way, then settle in to their own more classic favorites.

You can order a filling dinner for 4,500$ ($30.15) and the menu includes specialties from nearly every region of Portugal. The atmosphere is self-consciously taverna, and the walls are hung with all sorts of Portuguese provincial oddities along with photos of famous people who've been here. The singers selected by the management are first-rate. It's possible to visit just for drinks. The cover charge is 1,500$ ($10.05), including one drink. After that, mixed drinks cost from 800$ ($5.35). Streetcar: 3 or 16. Bus: 9, 12, or 18.

Luso, Travessa da Queimada 10 (tel. 342-22-81), has long been one of the most famous and enduring fado and folkloric clubs of the Bairro Alto. On a crowded street—often filled with waiting taxis and the sound of honking horns—the entertainment and the regional food are presented Monday to Saturday nights to some 160 patrons. Most guests come here for the fado and the entertainment. But full dinners are served, costing 4,000$ ($26.80) and likely to include such specialties as *vieiras de peixe* (fish stuffed in a scallop shell) and *frango na Púcara* (chicken in a casserole). In air-conditioned comfort, guests can enjoy the dinner and music nightly from 8pm to 3am.

---

4. The Bar Scene

In addition to its role as a restaurant, **Bachus,** Largo da Trindade 9 (tel. 342-12-60), offers one of the capital's most convivial watering spots. In an environment filled with Oriental carpets, fine hardwoods, bronze statues, intimate lighting, and uniformed, very polite waiters, you can hobnob with some of the most glamorous names in Lisbon. Late-night suppers are served in the bar by candlelight. The array of drinks is international, costing from 550$ ($3.70), and the spot is a good one in which to unwind in privileged circumstances. Open from noon to 2am daily.

Metro e Meio, Avenida 5 de Outubro 174 (tel. 79-75-997), is spotted easily. A giant yellow ruler forms its facade. In renovating, the management discovered several grottolike rooms that had been hidden for decades. Now guests have a choice of a maze of rooms, with a central fireplace. The decor is formed by hand-loomed wall hangings, gilt mirrors, statues, hanging lamps, Victorian fringed shades, and contemporary paintings. Recordings are piped in. Whiskies begin at 400$ ($2.70), and you can order an omelet for 400$ ($2.70) also. The bar stands near the Gulbenkian Museum and can be reached by bus no. 1, 44, or 45. Hours are Monday through Saturday from 6pm to 2am.

Procópio Bar, Alto de San Francisco 21A (tel. 65-28-51), could easily become your favorite watering hole in Lisbon—that is, if you can find it. The street it lies on rarely appears on Lisbon maps. However, the location is just off Rua de João Penha, which itself is off the landmark Praça das Amoreiras. The café is a social center for many politicians and journalists. In a turn-of-the-century atmosphere, it leans heavily on nostalgia. Guests sit on red tufted velvet, enjoying the atmosphere of stained and painted glass, ornate brass hardware—and a piano awaiting an amateur player. It's like being in àn intimate living room where the guests know each other. It is open Monday through Saturday from 10pm to 3:30am except in August. A mixed drink costs 700$ ($4.70), with a beer going for 350$ ($2.35). Bus: 9, 15, or 20. Streetcar: 10, 20, or 24.

Passport, Rua Nova do Carvalho (tel. 346-15-07). The flashing neon sign in front promises bright lights and dancing. Once you're inside, the lights are cooler and the furniture more Iberian than you might have expected. In many ways the leather, wood, and masonry accents imply a Portuguese village, and there's always the chance to meet new friends. The club is open daily from 9:30am to 3:30am. Beer costs 300$ ($2); mixed drinks 600$ ($4). Bus: 1, 44, or 45.

Bora-Bora, Rua da Madalena 201 (tel. 87-20-43). A Polynesian bar might seem out of context in Lisbon, but its concept is all the rage in Iberia these days. If, therefore, you have a yearning for the kind of fruited, flaming, and rum-laced drinks you thought you'd left behind on the West Coast, you'll find imaginative variations here. The couches are comfortable and inviting, and you can take in the Polynesian art on the walls. Hamburgers and other fare are available to accompany your Pacific Ocean nectars as well. Hours are Monday through Saturday from 6pm to 2am. Beer costs 450$ ($3); mixed drinks 800$ ($5.35). Subway: Rossio.

The **Panorama Bar,** Lisboa Sheraton Hotel, Rua Latino Coelho (tel. 57-57-57), lies on the uppermost floor of one of Portugal's tallest buildings, the 30-story Lisboa Sheraton Hotel. Consequently, the view by day or night ingests the old and new cities of Lisbon, the mighty Tagus, and many of the towns on the river's far bank. Amid a decor of chiseled stone and stained glass, a polite uniformed staff will serve you. You'll pay from around 1,000$ ($6.70) for a whisky and soda. The bar is open Monday to Friday from 10am to 1:30am, Saturday and Sunday from 4pm to 1:30am.

Texas Bar, Rua Nova do Carvalho 24 (tel. 346-36-83). Remember those movies of port cities, showing red neon lights flashing, drunken sailors staggering down labyrinthine narrow streets, a mixed bag of human flotsam unmatched since Jean Genêt wrote of his "whores, thieves, pimps, and beggars." These rip-roaring scenes live on in Lisbon, in the little streets near the dock area, where sailors hang out at bars named after western American states: Arizona, California, Texas.

The most popular, occasionally drawing some of the Ritz crowd, is the Texas Bar, a gutsy tavern under a bridge. A singer usually warbles a Portuguese version of an old country-and-western hit.

If you're a man alone (if you're a woman alone, stay away), you'll be surrounded on entering by the wildest assemblage of Gravel Gertie look-alikes this side of Barcelona or Marseilles. "Speak English?" is the typical query. One young man trying to escape answered a resounding, "No, Svenska," but a girl was found who spoke lilting Swedish. The Texas Bar accommodates all. When the fleet's in, and some fleet from some port is likely to be in all the time, this waterfront hotspot can be very rowdy. It is open daily from 11:30am to 3:30am. There is a cover charge of 640$ ($4.30). Once inside, you can order mixed drinks for 600$ ($4), or a beer for 320$ ($2.15). Bus: 1, 7, 15, or 44. Streetcar: 20.

GAY BARS

Xeque Mate Bar, Rua de São Marçal 170 (tel. 347-28-30), mingles the down-home earthiness of an English pub with the futuristic black-and-silver trappings of a high-tech disco. Set behind a discreet brass plaque on a steeply sloping street lined with elegant 18th-century villas, it imposes no cover charge. Beer costs from 400$ ($2.70), whisky and soda from 500$ ($3.35). Xeque Mate is open 7 nights a week from 10pm to between 1:30 and 2am. A taxi is recommended.

Memorial, Rua Gustavo de Matos Sequeira 42 (tel. 396-88-91), is near the narrow streets of the Bairro Alto and is considered a "household word" among the gay community of Lisbon. This disco caters mostly to gay men. Both Spanish and Portuguese are spoken by most of the staff, and newcomers will usually be able to strike up a conversation with one of the regular patrons. It's open Tuesday to Sunday from 10pm to 4am. You'll pay a cover charge of 900$ ($6.05), after which a beer costs 450$ ($3).

Trumps, Rua da Imprensa Nacionale 104B (tel. 67-10-59), lies near (but not in) the Bairro Alto. Although it tries to cater to both heterosexual and homosexual tastes, most of its clientele is composed of male homosexuals. Contained within a large room on the street level of its building, it has a prominent dance floor, a spacious bar, and a staff that speaks French and Spanish. You'll pay 1,200$ ($8.05) at the door only on Friday and Saturday nights. A beer costs 450$ ($3). Trumps is open Tuesday to Sunday from 11am to 3:30am. The bar is run by David C. West, who was born in Oxford and today is the master of ceremonies, presiding over the most sophisticated gay bar in Lisbon.

---

5. More Entertainment

MOVIES
Major motion pictures are shown in Lisbon in their original languages, usually at one of the big cinema houses along Avenida da Liberdade. First-run movie houses include **São Jorge,** Avenida da Liberdade 175 (tel. 57-91-44).

VAUDEVILLE
Just off the Avenida da Liberdade, in the **Parque Mayer,** is a cluster of vaudeville and music halls, each offering a *revista,* a Portuguese revue similar in some respects to a Spanish zarzuela. In the park are a few restaurants and Coney Island–style fun-and-chance stalls, where Lisboans throw darts and win dubious prizes. Here you can feel the entertainment pulse of the people, seeing everything from popular singers to fadistas to acrobats to ballet dancers. Matinees are staged on Sunday at 4pm, and show time is nightly at 9:45pm. Tickets range from a low 600$ ($4) for the worst seats in the house (definitely not recommended) to 1,500$ ($10.05) for a grand perch. One reader warns, "Ticket buyers should make sure they're seeking the vaudeville entertainment, and not something else. We were at first misdirected to one of the pornographic skin flicks in the same area."

ORGANIZED TOURS
Transtejo (Transportes Tejo), Rua Aurea 181 (tel. 87-50-58), offers a nighttime tour of the River Tagus, departing daily from the Praça do Comércio at 9pm and returning at 11pm. Adults pay 3,500$ ($23.45) for the tour. Children up to 6 years of age go free. Live music is played as the boat cruises along the river, and a small buffet is offered, although most people have eaten dinner before joining the cruise.

ESTORIL, CASCAIS & SINTRA

The environs of Lisbon are so intriguing that many fail to see the capital itself, lured by **Guincho** (near the westernmost point in continental Europe), the **Mouth of Hell,** and Lord Byron's "glorious Eden" at **Sintra.** A day could be spent drinking in the wonders of the library at the monastery-palace of **Mafra** (Portugal's El Escorial), dining in the pretty pink rococo palace at **Queluz,** or enjoying seafood at the Atlantic beach resort of **Ericeira.**

However, the chief magnet remains the **Costa do Sol,** that string of beach resorts, such as **Estoril** and **Cascais,** that form the Portuguese Riviera on the northern banks of the mouth of the Tagus. In fact, if you arrive in Lisbon when the sun is shining and the air balmy, you should consider seeking lodgings along this cabana-studded shoreline. So near to Lisbon is Estoril that it's easy to dart in and out of the capital on sightseeing jaunts or fado sprees, while ensconced in a hotel by the sea. An inexpensive electric train leaving from the Cais do Sodré in Lisbon makes the trip frequently throughout the day and evening, ending its run in Cascais.

The sun coast is sometimes known as A Costa dos Reis, the coast of kings, because of all the deposed royalty who have settled there—everybody from exiled kings to pretenders, marquesses from Italy, princesses from Russia, and baronesses from Germany. These people may live simply, as did a virtual recluse in an unpretentious villa, the late Princess Elena of Romania (Magda Lupescu); or they may insist on rigid court ambience, as did Umberto, the 1946 1-month-king of Italy, who was forced into exile when a plebiscite went against the monarchy. Tending his cows in "baggy trousers and muddy boots" in Sintra was the Count of Paris, the pretender to the throne of France; a descendant of Louis Philippe, he was the son of the Duke of Guise. In 1969 another pretender, Don Juan, Count of Barcelona, was shortchanged the Spanish throne when his son, Don Juan Carlos, was named successor by the late Generalísimo Franco. The count was once an officer in the British navy and is now a noted yachtsman. Other nobility include Joanna, the former queen of Bulgaria, and the Infanta Dona Maria Adelaide de Bragança, sister of the Portuguese pretender.

The Riviera is a microcosm of Portugal. Ride out on the train, even if you don't plan to lodge there. Along the way you'll pass pastel-washed houses, with red tile roofs and facades of antique blue-and-white tiles; miles of modern apartment dwellings; rows of canna, pines, mimosa, and eucalyptus; swimming pools; and in the background green hills studded with villas, chalets, and new homes.

Regrettably, the coast, like all major beach coasts in Europe, has become much too overbuilt, which detracts greatly from its antique charm. It has less traffic on weekdays than it does on Saturday and Sunday when much of Lisbon drives out. If you have a choice, try to avoid weekends, especially from June through September.

1. Carcavelos

On the road between Lisbon and Estoril, this seaside town boasts the longest stretch of beach along the Costa do Sol. Often considered the coastal gateway, it commands a view of the white Manueline-style Tower of Belém. Carcavelos was noted for its fortress, **São Julião,** which once held prisoner left-wing radicals during the Miguelite wars. The fortress, with its pale-yellow walls and unusual turrets, is of a unique design that is attributed to the theories of Sebastien Le Prestre de Vauban, a French engineer.

The resort lies 13½ miles west of Lisbon and 9 miles south of Sintra and is easily reached on the electric train from the Cais do Sodré. Even if you don't go to Carcavelos, you may want to sample some of its full-bodied wine, praised by the Duke of Wellington.

There is no local tourist office. The nearest tourist office is in Estoril (see below).

WHERE TO STAY & DINE

Moderately priced accommodation is provided by the **Hotel Praia-Mar,** Rua do Gurué 16, Carcavelos, 2775 Parede (tel. 01/247-31-31; fax 01/247-31-30). You'll recognize this 1967 building from a distance because of its angular design and dramatically recessed balconies. When you get closer, you'll appreciate the private world that unfolds behind the plant-bordered walls separating the elliptical swimming pool from the street outside. Unlike some of the other hotels on the coast, Praia-Mar is in a quiet neighborhood a few blocks away from the four-lane highway along the coastline.

Only the public areas are air conditioned, not the bedrooms. The lobby has large windows leading toward the sun-flooded swimming pool. There's a bar near the roof and another blue-and-white version in a remote corner of the lobby, graced with an imposing statue of an Amazon brandishing a ferocious-looking infant. Each of the 158 bedrooms contains a balcony, usually with a view toward the sea, along with a combination of contemporary and Iberian-inspired furniture. All have individual safes, private baths, radios, and phones. The in-house restaurant on the eighth floor serves well-prepared meals costing from 3,000$ ($20.10). Singles cost from 12,000$ ($80.40) daily, while doubles rent for 14,000$ ($93.80), with breakfast included. The hotel also rents five first-class suites, costing from 26,000$ ($174.20) a night. Free parking is provided, and the hotel offers laundry service. AE, DC, MC.

2. Estoril

This chic resort along the Portuguese Riviera has long basked in its reputation as a playground of kings. Fading countesses arrive at the railway station, monarchs in exile drop in at the Palácio Hotel for dinner, the sons of assassinated dictators sunbathe by the pool—and an international joie de vivre pervades the air.

Once Estoril was a figment of the imagination of Fausto Figueiredo, the founding father of the deluxe Palácio and the Casino. Before the First World War, Fausto Figueiredo envisioned hundreds of people strolling through the marble corridors and down mosaic sidewalks to the ocean as he gazed out over scrub pines and sandy hills. Before the Second World War, Estoril was firmly entrenched in the resort sweepstakes. As Nazi troops advanced across Europe, many collapsed courts fled to Estoril to wait out the war in a neutral country.

Parque Estoril, in the center, represents magnificent landscaping, a subtropical setting with the plants swaying in the breeze. At night when it's floodlit, fashionable guests go for a stroll. The palm trees studding the grounds have prompted many to call it "a corner of Africa." At the top of the park sits the **Casino,** offering not only gambling, but international floor shows, dancing, and movies.

Across the railroad tracks is the beach, where some of the most fashionable women in Europe sun themselves on the peppermint-striped canvas chairs along the Tamariz Esplanade. The atmosphere is cosmopolitan, and the beach is sandy, unlike the pebbly strand at Nice. If you don't want to swim in the ocean, you can check in at an oceanfront swimming pool for a plunge instead.

To the east is **São João do Estoril,** which also boasts a beach and many handsome private villas. Most visitors go here to dine and dance.

The **Estoril Tourist Office** is at Arcadas do Parque (tel. 468-01-13).

GETTING THERE

Estoril lies 15 miles west of Lisbon and 8 miles south of Sintra and is reached by an electric train from the waterfront Cais do Sodré. The cost is 135$ (90¢) for a one-way ticket, the ride taking 20 minutes. By private taxi, count on spending about 4,000$ ($26.80). If you're driving, Estoril is approached by the coastal road.

SPORTS & RECREATION

In the foothills of Sintra, a 3-minute drive from the Casino, lies the **Clube de Golf do Estoril,** Avenida da República (tel. 01/468-01-76). An attraction for international sports figures, it offers a fairway set against a vista of pine and mimosa. The quality of the course is so acclaimed as one of the finest in Europe that it is selected for international championship matches. Both a 9-hole and an 18-hole course are offered. Golfers play from around 7:30am till sunset daily. Guests of the Estoril Palácio Hotel are entitled to a 50% reduction on the greens fees, which are 6,000$ ($40.20) for 18 holes.

WHERE TO STAY

Very Expensive

Palácio Hotel, Parque Estoril, 2765 Estoril (tel. 01/468-04-00; fax 01/468-48-67), is legendary as a retreat for exiled royalty and as a center of World War II espionage. At its debut in 1930, the Palácio received the honeymooning Japanese crown prince and his new bride. In time other royalty would follow: Umberto of Italy; Don Juan, the Count of Barcelona. In World War II, when people escaped with a case of jewels and the clothes on their back, diamonds, rubies, and gold were accepted instead of money.

The reception rooms are Pompeian, with sienna-colored marble pillars, bold bands of orange, and handmade carpets. Ideal for a tête-à-tête are the series of intimate salons. In the classic central drawing room, with black-and-white marble checkerboard floors, groups of antique furnishings are arranged for guests to have after-dinner coffee.

Starting early in the morning, guests gather at the terrace overlooking the pool, which is encircled by a reflecting pool. A buffet luncheon is served on a chaise lounge or at a table beside the pool. An asset of the Palácio is the Restaurant-Grill Four Seasons (see my dining recommendations, below). You can also enjoy regional and international dishes in the Atlântico Restaurant, preceded by a drink in the Bar Estoril, which features piano entertainment.

The bedrooms are traditional, with fine furnishings plus baths with bidets and heated towel racks. Each room also is air conditioned, with TV and phone. The hotel, which is in the center of Estoril near the casino, charges 30,000$ ($201) to 35,000$ ($234.50) daily in a single and from 35,000$ ($234.50) to 39,000$ ($261.30) in a double, including a buffet breakfast. The hotel also rents 31 luxurious suites, charging from 50,000$ ($335) to 65,000$ ($435.50) per night. Room service is available 24 hours a day. Baby-sitting and laundry/valet are also offered. There is free outdoor parking for 150 cars.

The hotel opens onto the side of Estoril Park, capped by the casino. The beach is only a short walk away. Seven clay-surface championship tennis courts are next door to the hotel, with three courts floodlit for night play. Guests of the hotel are offered special privileges as its own international championship golf course. AE, DC, MC, V.

Moderate

Estalagem Belvedere, Rua Dr. António Martins 8, 2765 Estoril (tel. 01/466-02-08; fax 01/467-14-33). Built as a private villa during the Edwardian age, and converted into a charming hotel some 25 years ago, this establishment offers 24 bedrooms, each with private bath and phone. Some contain TVs, but none has air conditioning. Singles cost 4,500$ ($30.15) to 7,500$ ($50.25) daily, and doubles go for 6,500$ ($43.55) to 11,500$ ($77.05), with breakfast included. It sits in a gracious neighborhood of faded 19th-century residences, among century-old trees and gardens. Inside, the comfortable public rooms contain Iberian furnishings, a cozy bar filled with rustic bric-a-brac, and a dining room serving dinner only, from 7:15 to 10pm daily. The cuisine is both French and Portuguese. Free parking is provided, and laundry and valet services are available, as are limited room service and baby-sitting. Facilities include a swimming pool, sauna, and solarium. MC, V.

Hotel Alvorada, Rua de Lisboa 3, 2765 Estoril (tel. 01/468-00-70; fax 01/468-72-50), opened its doors late in 1969 to provide Iberian pousada–style living on a small scale, opposite the casino and the formally styled Estoril Parque. Just a 3-minute trek from the sands, it is recommended to those desiring well-styled bedrooms, which rent for 13,900$ ($93.15) daily in a double, 8,400$ ($56.30) in a single. There are 55 rooms in all, each with private bath and balcony and phone. The public rooms are personalized and well conceived. Off the reception area, the drinking lounge is decorated with modern Portuguese paintings and provincial-style furnishings. The top-floor solarium offers a panoramic view of the sea. Parking is free, and only breakfast is served. AE, DC, MC, V.

Hotel Estoril-Praia, Estrada Marginal, 2765 Estoril (tel. 01/468-18-11; fax 01/468-18-15), was built next door to its glamorous neighbor, the Palácio. Its seven floors with walls of glass soar high, about half the rooms boasting good-sized balconies overlooking a view of the water and the casino with its formal gardens. Only a minute or so from the seafront and the electric train station, it is in the center of Estoril's boutique district. The upper-floor dining room provides unobstructed vistas of the sea and the nearby hills studded with villas. On many evenings a white-capped chef stands in front of his specialty display table. In the marble-floored lounge and bar, good contemporary design prevails, with plenty of museumlike space. Soft tufted-leather chairs are gathered at marble-topped tables. Live music is played in the Bar Estoril every night from 6pm to midnight, and there is also a disco in the hotel. A hairdressing salon is among the facilities offered.

The 91 bedrooms are not only trim, utilitarian, and uncluttered, but many have sitting areas, with wood-grained pieces. French doors open onto balconies in most of the rooms. All have phones and shiny tile private baths with a shower. Singles rent for 17,800$ ($119.25) to 19,500$ ($130.65) daily, and doubles go for 20,200$

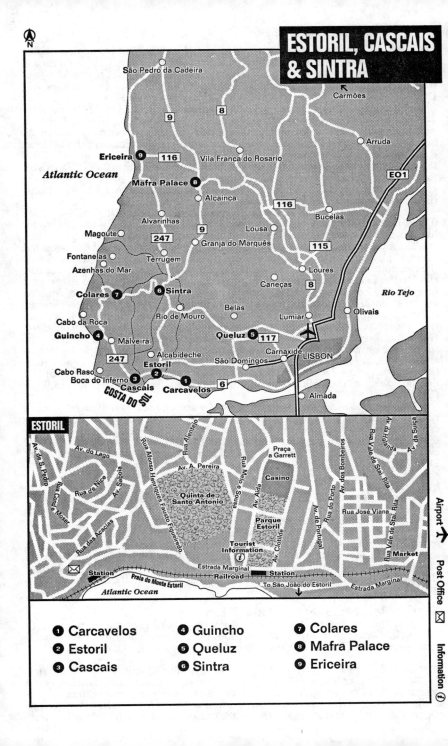

($135.35) to 23,600$ ($158.10), the prices including breakfast. Portuguese cuisine is served, and sometimes live piano music is provided in the bar. There is no garage, but parking is free on the street. Laundry service and baby-sitting are provided, and room service is available 24 hours a day. Car-rental facilities are on the premises. AE, DC, MC, V.

Hotel Lido, Rua do Alentejo 12, 2765 Estoril (tel. 01/468-41-23; fax 01/268-36-65), is a five-story white concrete cube set into a residential neighborhood on a hill above town. Each of its functional and comfortable bedrooms, 62 in all, benefits from a recessed balcony. Each room contains air conditioning and a phone. Rates, including breakfast, are 10,400$ ($69.70) daily in a single, rising to 13,750$ ($92.15) in a double. Portuguese and continental meals cost from 2,000$ ($13.40). Parking is free. The decor of the public rooms, whose floors are covered with slabs of gray-and-white marble, is modern and just a bit sterile. The hotel's large, plant-ringed swimming pool is one of its most attractive features. AE, DC, MC, V.

Lennox Country Club, Rua Eng. Alvaro Pedro Sousa 5 (tel. 01/468-04-24; fax 01/267-08-59). Partially because of its emphasis on golf, this hillside hotel is a lot like a corner of Scotland. As you complete the steep climb to the reception desk you'll notice a series of Portuguese tiles depicting kilted bagpipers and plaid-covered "bairns" playing golf, in almost a tongue-in-cheek comment on the juxtaposition of the two cultures. There's even a map of the golf course at St. Andrews near the bar, close to the autographed photos of the many championship golfers who have stayed here. The hydrangeas and the herbaceous borders in the gardens outside, coupled with the sunshine, make this place a potent attraction. Some of its comfortably attractive accommodations are scattered among a collection of buildings a short walk from the reception area. The most desirable are contained within the main building, which was formerly a private home. Self-caterers might be interested in one of the suites, each of which is equipped with a kitchenette. The hotel rents 34 bedrooms and 5 suites, each with private bath, minibar, and phone. Rooms are not air conditioned. Charges are 13,700$ ($91.80) daily in a single or 19,800$ ($132.65) in a double, plus another 500$ ($3.35) for breakfast. Suites cost from 25,000$ ($167.50).

The hotel provides free transport to nearby golf courses, as well as to the area's riding stables. There's a kidney-shaped heated swimming pool, adorned with intricate mosaics, terraced into a hillside near the main villa. Parking is free, and room service, baby-sitting, and laundry are provided. A barbecue is served around the pool every other week, and there is a band or a folkloric group performing for clients. AE, DC, MC, V.

Inexpensive

Pensão Residential Smart, Rua José Viana 3, 2765 Estoril (tel. 01/468-21-64). Set on a hillside, in a grandly faded neighborhood of 19th-century villas, this 13-room hotel offers well-scrubbed accommodations and plenty of quiet. Don't expect opulent furnishings or glamour. What you get is a low-key welcome and unpretentious solitude. Rooms are not air conditioned, but each has a private bath or shower and a few also offer TV. Singles cost from 5,000$ ($33.50) to 5,500$ ($36.85) daily, with doubles going for 5,500$ ($36.85) to 6,000$ ($40.20), including breakfast. The hotel, lying about a 7-minute walk from the rail station, offers free parking and a bar. No credit cards.

Nearby Places to Stay in Monte Estoril

A satellite of Estoril, Monte Estoril lies directly to the west on the road to Cascais, half a mile away. Built across the slope of a hill and containing many moderately priced hotels, it opens onto a vista of Cascais Bay and the Atlantic beyond.

EXPENSIVE Estoril Eden, Avenida Sabóia 209, Monte Estoril, 2765 Estoril (tel. 01/467-05-73; fax 01/467-08-48), is a four-star, 161-apartment hotel open all year. Built in 1985, this white-walled tower sits on a rocky knoll above the road paralleling the edge of the sea. An outdoor swimming pool, protected from the noise of the coastal road by its altitude and the wall, is one of the establishment's main attractions. The apartments, ranging from one-bedroom units to a two-bedroom penthouse suite, are soundproof, air conditioned, and elegantly decorated. Each accommodation has a kitchenette, private bath, direct-dial phone, radio, TV, in-house video, and a balcony opening onto a view of the sea. In the studio apartments, the beds are "in-wall," allowing larger living space during the day. A single rental costs 20,000$ ($134) daily, with doubles going for 23,500$ ($157.45), plus another 1,000$ ($6.70) for breakfast. Live music is presented every Wednesday. Parking is provided for 800$ ($5.35) per night, and facilities include a sauna, health club, solarium, indoor swimming pool, and bar. There is no room service, but laundry is provided. Dining facilities include the Garden Patio, offering both regional and international cuisine served either à la carte or buffet, and a poolside café bar, Le Bistrot. You can stock up on food supplies in a mini-market. AE, DC, MC, V.

Grande Hotel, Avenida Sabóia (without number), Monte Estoril, 2765 Estoril (tel. 01/468-46-09; fax 01/468-48-34), is a modern, 71-bedroom compound, just a few minutes up from the beach. It offers seven floors of spacious rooms with private bath, about half of which have balconies large enough for breakfast and sunbathing. Guests relax and swim in its covered pool opening off a cocktail terrace, with a view of eucalyptus and palm trees. The air-conditioned main dining room is undistinguished, yet still serves adequate meals. The large sitting room is popular, with a fireplace and groupings of comfortable furniture. International visitors wander into the open wood-paneled lobby and into the chestnut-fronted drinking lounge.

The bedrooms are furnished in blond modern (bedside tables, chest-desk combinations), the severity lightened by simple color schemes. Each room has a private bath and phone. The hotel charges 14,500$ ($97.15) daily in a single, 24,000$ ($160.80) in a double. Children under 8 are given a 50% reduction if they share a room with their parents. A few rooms have sitting areas, for which you'll pay more, of course. The better rooms open onto sea views. Portuguese cuisine is served. Laundry service and baby-sitting are provided, and room service is available until 10pm. Facilities include a bar and a swimming pool. AE, DC, MC, V.

Hotel Atlântico, Estrada Marginal 7, Monte Estoril, 2765 Estoril (tel. 01/468-02-70; fax 468-36-19), is a self-contained playground, almost directly on the sandy beach. The hotel's separated from the beach by the electric train tracks from Lisbon. Its disadvantages are the whizzing coastal-road traffic in front, the clatter of the train in the rear. However, if you get a room high enough up facing the sea, you can be assured of quiet. Between the lower floor of the hotel and the tracks is a wide sun terrace, with a seawater swimming pool. The dining room, built cavelike under the width of the hotel, has a view through an all-glass wall overlooking the pool and the sea. One TV lounge has video; another lounge offers live music in the evening.

The 175 bedrooms are medium sized and moderately well furnished, with built-in headboards, reading lights, telephones, Swedish-style desks and armchairs, and tile baths and showers. Each room is a double, costing 25,000$ ($167.50) a night, including breakfast. Parking is free. AE, DC, MC, V.

MODERATE Aparthotel Vale do Sol, Rua do Viveiro (without number), Monte Estoril, 2765 Estoril (tel. 01/468-33-85; fax 01/468-44-70), is a modern 85-unit apartment-house complex with accommodations for two or four persons. All are fully equipped with kitchenette, bath, terrace, phone, radio, air conditioning, and TV upon request. Laundry service is available, and there are a supermarket, hairdresser, and restaurant on the premises. An apartment for two costs 11,000$ ($73.70) daily. An apartment for three or four guests rents for 15,000$ ($100.50). Guests prepare their own breakfast, which is not included in the rates. In July and August, guests are entertained by international singing and guitar playing. Facilities include an outdoor swimming pool and a bar. Baby-sitting can also be arranged. There is no room service; parking is free. AE, DC, MC, V.

Hotel Zenith, Rua Belmonte 1, Monte Estoril, 2765 Estoril (tel. 01/468-11-22; fax 01/468-11-17). You'll find comfortable modern accommodations inside this white-and-moss-green tower jutting skyward from a neighborhood of 19th-century villas above town. The ground-floor bar, encased in burnished tones of hardwood, offers a big-windowed rendezvous point to relax in air-conditioned comfort. Each of the 48 bedrooms contains a phone, radio, and private bath, plus access to the rectangular swimming pool whose waterside plants are sheltered from the wind by the bulk of the hotel itself. Singles rent for 11,000$ ($73.70) daily, and doubles go for 15,100$ ($101.15), including breakfast. There's a TV lounge with a fireplace, along with a basement-level snack bar and restaurant, where meals cost from 1,850$ ($12.40). AE, DC, MC, V.

WHERE TO DINE

Expensive

For fine food, go to the **Four Seasons,** Hotel Palácio, Parque Estoril 4 (tel. 468-04-00). Its connection with one of Portugal's most famous hotels adds a vivid cachet to this restaurant. But even if it were independently operated, it would still be one of the finest—and also one of the most expensive—restaurants in the country.

The menus and the service of the Four Seasons depend on just that—the seasons. Dishes, uniforms, linen, china, and glasses are changed four times a year. Other than the handful of intimate tables set imperially on the upper mezzanine, each of the elaborately decorated tables is grouped around a beautiful but purely decorative Iberian kitchen, whose copper pots and blue tiles lend an appealingly rustic touch to an otherwise sophisticated decor. The hushed quiet, the candles, and the rich colors almost invite comparison to an elegant home in 19th-century Russia. However, the discreet charm and polite manners of the well-trained staff are distinctively Portuguese.

The international cuisine is superb. For example, you might select the three-cheese crêpes as an appetizer. Or you might be tempted by lobster bisque or chilled mussel soup, following with chateaubriand, mussels in cream sauce, grilled beef and monkfish on a skewer, shrimps in garlic butter, or roast duckling with orange sauce. Reservations are necessary for full dinners, served daily from 7:30 to 11pm and costing from 5,500$ ($36.85). You can enter this place directly from the street or from the hotel lobby after enjoying a drink among the international clientele at the bar. AE, DC, MC, V.

Moderate

English Bar, Estrada Marginal (tel. 468-12-54). Many couples come here just to watch the sunsets over the Bay of Cascais. Its mock-Elizabethan facade may lead you to think of steak-and-kidney pie and tankards of ale, yet the food is essentially Portuguese, and it's well prepared. Many international dishes are also served.

Try for a window seat in the handsome dining room, with its wide-plank floors, comfortable leather-backed wood chairs. There are numerous English-style decorations: heraldic symbols, horsey prints, and bric-a-brac. From the à la carte menu, you can sample such highly recommended dishes as a savory *crème de mariscos* (cream of shellfish soup). The chef's specialty is *cherne na canoa,* a turbot dish served with baby clams and a succulent sauce. In season you can order *perdiz Serra Morena* (roast partridge). An excellent dessert is a mousse made with nuts. For a complete meal, expect to spend from 3,000$ ($20.10). Food is served daily from noon to 4pm and 7:30 to 10:30pm; closed Sunday. AE, DC, MC, V.

Pak Yun, Centro Comercial, Estoril Parque 5 (tel. 467-06-92), is one of the best Asian restaurants along the Costa do Sol. Across from the main entrance to the casino, it lies right off Praça José Teodoro dos Santos in the heart of Estoril. The chef is skilled at preparing such fare as shark's-fin soup, Peking duck, steamed fresh fish, along with steamed seasonal vegetables in oyster sauce. A tourist menu costs 2,500$ ($16.75), with an à la carte meal averaging 4,000$ ($26.80). The Oriental decor is attractively modern, and hours are Tuesday to Sunday from noon to 3pm and 7pm to midnight. Reservations aren't needed. Closed: January. AE, DC, MC, V.

Tamariz, on Estoril Beach (tel. 468-35-12), is the most popular gathering spot on the beach. Bathing attire is not only permitted but encouraged. Some of the most attractive visitors on the Estoril coast fill some of the most imaginative bathing suits from the boutiques of Europe. They sit for hours at canopied tables on a terrace projecting out toward the beach. Light fare and snacks are the order of the day, including a hamburger, combination plates, coffee, and a milk shake. Meals, served daily from 9am to 7pm, cost from 3,500$ ($23.45). Shower facilities and lockers adjoin, and the swimming pool is open from April to October. Service may be a bit slow, but who's in a hurry? AE, DC, MC, V.

EVENING ENTERTAINMENT

Gambling

The glamour hub for international society is the **Casino,** Parque Estoril (tel. 468-45-21). Occupying a position on the rise of a hill, it opens onto the formal gardens of the Parque Estoril, which sweep toward the water. The glass walls suggest an international museum of modern art, and enclose an inner courtyard, with tile paths, a fountain and pool, and borders of lilac-colored petunias and red carnations.

Off the main lobby are various bars, a motion-picture theater, an art gallery, and groups of boutiques. The five-star magnet, of course, is the Casino, which accepts your money daily from 3pm to 3am (passport required). An adjoining salon is for one-armed bandits. In the main room you can take your chance at roulette, French banque, chemin de fer, baccarat, blackjack/21, craps, and slot machines. A nonresident pass is given for 600$ ($4).

Other diversions include the **Grand Salon Restaurant,** really a supper club offering Portuguese and international cuisine daily from 9pm. There's a cover charge of 2,000$ ($13.40), plus another 6,500$ ($43.55) to 8,000$ ($53.60) charged if you want dinner. Specialties include smoked swordfish, pâté, grilled prawns, calves' kidneys flambéed with cognac, and pressed duck. A tea dance is staged every Sunday afternoon at 5. The extravaganza stage show commences at 11:15pm and 1am. On the arena stage, leggy, feathered, and bejeweled dancers strut their wares to good advantage in billowing trains and bespangled bras.

A small movie theater shows films daily. There's also an art gallery selling contemporary paintings, and a few boutiques offering apparel and souvenirs.

Dance Clubs

The very young meet in a very old setting in **Forte Velho** (Old Fort), Estrada Marginal, São Pedro Cadaveira, São João do Estoril (tel. 468-13-37). The disco was ingeniously conceived, capturing a 17th-century fortress on a cliff above the ocean. It's built of solid rock and offers a central room with fireplace.

Dancing is to records only, and there's an adjoining bar with stools and cozy banquettes, ideal for hand-holding couples. For a change of pace, drinks are carried out on the terrace to the parapet, where imbibers gasp at the steep drop to the surf below. The fun commences at 10pm, though it doesn't really warm up till around midnight. The Old Fort rides the crest until closing at 4am Tuesday to Sunday. You pay a minimum charge of 1,500$ ($10.05), which can be used up in drinks once you're inside. A mixed drink costs 600$ ($4).

---

3. Cascais

In the 1930s Cascais was a tiny fishing village, attracting artists and writers to its little cottages. But its history as a resort is old. In fact, it was once known as a royal village, because it enjoyed the patronage of Portugal's royal family. When the monarchy died, the military moved in. Gen. António de Fragoso Carmona, president of Portugal until 1951, the man responsible for naming Dr. Salazar as minister of finance, once occupied the 17th-century fort guarding the Portuguese Riviera.

That Cascais is growing is an understatement. It's leapfrogging! At one entrance to the resort, someone penciled in the word "City" after Cascais. Even if not officially recognized as such, it is well on its way. Apartment houses, new hotels, and the finest restaurants along the Costa do Sol draw a never-ending stream of visitors every year.

However, the life of the simple fisherman still goes on. Auctions, called *lotas,* at which the latest catch is sold, still take place on the main square, though a modern hotel has sprouted up in the background. In the small harbor, rainbow-colored fishing boats must share space with pleasure craft owned by an international set that flocks to Cascais from early spring until autumn.

The tie that Cascais has with the sea is old. If you speak Portuguese, any of the local fishermen, with their weather-beaten faces, could tell you that one of their own, Afonso Sanches, discovered America in 1482, that Columbus learned of his accidental find, stole the secret, and enjoyed the subsequent acclaim.

Cascais lies only 4 miles west of Estoril, 18 miles west of Lisbon. It's reached by the electric train that begins its run at the Cais do Sodré waterfront station, ending it in the center of town. Trains to and from Lisbon leave every 15 minutes.

Many visitors, both foreign and domestic, drive out to Cascais on a road-clogged summer Sunday to attend the bullfights at the **Monumental de Cascais,** a ring outside the "city" center.

The most popular excursion outside of Cascais is to the **Boca de Inferno** (Mouth of Hell). Reached by heading out the highway to Guincho, then turning left toward the sea, the Boca deserves its ferocious reputation. At their peak, thundering waves sweep in with such power and fury that they have long ago carved a wide hole, or boca, in the cliffs. However, if you should arrive when the sea is calm, you'll wonder why it's called a cauldron. The Mouth of Hell can be a windswept roar if you don't stumble over too many souvenir hawkers.

The **Cascais Tourist Information Office** is at Alameda Combatentes da Grande Guerra 25 (tel. 486-82-03).

WHERE TO STAY

Cascais has a number of accommodations in all price ranges. Reservations are vital in July and August.

Very Expensive

Hotel Albatroz, Rua Frederico Arouca 100, 2750 Cascais (tel. 01/483-28-21; fax 01/284-48-27). The wandering albatross, of course, is a bird noted as a master of gliding flight, capable of staying airborne on motionless wings for hours on end. What an appropriate symbol for this treasure along the Costa do Sol. Whether you're seeking rooms or food, the hotel is your "good luck" choice. Positioned on a ledge of rocks just above the ocean, it is centered around a neoclassic villa which was originally built as a luxurious holiday retreat for the Duke of Loulé. It was later acquired in the 19th century by the Count and Countess de Foz. Sometime in this century it was converted into an inn, and in time received such famous guests of long ago as Anthony Eden, Cary Grant, Chief Justice Warren Burger, the Duke and Duchess of Bedford, Claudette Colbert, William Holden, Amy Vanderbilt, and the former queen of Bulgaria. Prince Rainier and the late Princess Grace visited on more than one occasion.

Today the hotel has benefitted from a tastefully elegant refurbishing which incorporates a lavish use of intricately painted tiles in garlanded patterns of blue and yellow, acres of white latticework, and sweeping expanses of glass. The stone-trimmed 19th-century core has been expanded with a terraced series of balconied additions, each of which contains some of the 37 pristin, elegant bedrooms. Singles range from 27,500$ ($184.25) to 32,500$ ($217.75) daily, with doubles costing from 32,500$ ($217.75) to 37,500$ ($251.25). Each room is air conditioned, with phone, TV, and minibar. The hotel also rents three suites ranging in price from 48,000$ ($321.60) to 53,000$ ($355.10). Room service is 24 hours a day, and baby-sitting and laundry/valet service are provided. The à la carte restaurant, serving Portuguese and international cuisine, is one of the finest along the coast (see "Where to Dine," below). Parking is provided free, and there's an oval-shaped swimming pool nestled alongside a sun terrace midway between the old and new wings. AE, DC, MC, V.

Estoril Sol, Parque Palmela, 2750 Cascais (tel. 01/483-28-31; fax 01/483-22-80), is a luxury high-rise holiday world, perched on a ledge, with the coastal highway and electric train tracks separating it from the beach. It represents a dream come true for its late owner, José Teodoro dos Santos, a self-made man, who originally arrived in Lisbon with less than a dollar in his pocket. A modern land of resort living has been created: a gymnasium, an Olympic-size pool for adults, a smaller one for children, a complete sauna, a health club with squash courts, facilities for horseback riding, waterskiing, a shopping arcade, a garage and service station, and public rooms large enough for a great invasion of sun-seeking visitors.

The air-conditioned Estoril Sol ended up as one of the largest hotel in Portugal, with 317 bedrooms and 18 suites overlooking the sea or the hills beyond. Single rooms range from 25,000$ ($167.50) to 32,000$ ($214.40) daily; doubles 29,000$ ($194.30) to 36,000$ ($241.20). Each room has a phone, minibar, and TV. Rates include breakfast. Suites range from 50,000$ ($335) to 60,000$ ($402). Room service is available 24 hours a day, and laundry/valet and baby-sitting can be arranged. It boasts a spacious main lounge (a traffic cop would be helpful here), the most expansive veranda on the peninsula, and a beach reached by an underground passageway. The dining facilities include the Ain Restaurant and the Grill and Coffee Shop, each serving both Portuguese and French cuisine. A piano player entertains in the grill at dinner. The hotel also has a nightclub and disco. Parking is 750$ ($5.05) a night. Facilities include a health club, sauna and solarium, and a swimming pool. AE, DC, MC, V.

Moderate

Estalagem Farol, Estrada da Boca do Inferno 7, 2750 Cascais (tel. 01/483-01-73; fax 01/284-14-47). When it was built in the late 19th century, its stone walls housed the entourage of the Count of Cabral. Today its once-aristocratic interior has been converted into an inn whose allure is only slightly dimmed by the dozens of Portuguese families who make it the center of their vacation holidays. The owners have converted the gardens in back into a stone-ringed concrete slab with a small swimming pool in the center, a few steps from the sea.

One of the favorite places is the richly masculine bar area, where a water view and the handcrafted paneling create an elegant rendezvous point. The restaurant is outfitted with Iberian charm. The 14 bedrooms are tastefully furnished and comfortable. Each has a phone, minibar, and TV, but no air conditioning. Singles range from 14,000$ ($93.80) to 15,500$ ($103.85) daily; doubles 17,500$ ($117.25) to 19,500$ ($130.65), including breakfast. Laundry and baby-sitting can be arranged. Parking is free on the street. AE, DC, MC, V.

Estalagem Senhora da Guia, Estrada do Guincho, 2750 Cascais (tel. 01/486-97-85; fax 01/486-92-27). One of the loveliest hotels in the region was opened only a few years ago by the Ornelas family, who returned to their native Portugal after a sojourn in Brazil. They settled on the former country villa of one of the most famous fortunes of Portugal, the Sagres brewery family. The house was originally built as recently as 1970, but its thick walls, high ceilings, and elaborately crafted moldings give the impression of a much older building.

A trio of blond, blue-eyed, multilingual siblings embarked on the task of restoring the house to its former state. Today each of the 28 elegant bedrooms and 4 suites is tastefully outfitted with reproductions of 18th-century Portuguese antiques, thick carpets, louvered shutters, spacious modern bathrooms, and many extras. Single rooms range from 12,500$ ($83.75) to 15,500$ ($103.85) daily; doubles 13,000$ ($87.10) to 16,000$ ($107.20); with suites costing from 20,000$ ($134). A buffet breakfast is included. Rooms have TVs and phones, but no air conditioning. The sun-washed bar is one of the more alluring rooms in the house. It's filled with some of the family antiques, many of them English and acquired during their years in Madeira. Upholstered sofas provide quiet corners, and there is a fireplace for cold weather.

Sports lovers receive a 20% discount at a nearby golf and tennis club, while horseback riding can be arranged on short notice. Because of the villa's position on a bluff above the sea, the views are excellent. Breakfast is served buffet style under parasols at the edge of the swimming pool. Lunches and dinners are offered beneath a ceiling of African hardwood in a formal dining room which remains cool even on the hottest days. AE, DC, MC, V.

Hotel Cidadela, Avenida 25 de Abril, 2750 Cascais (tel. 01/483-29-21; fax 01/486-72-26). Architecturally and decoratively, this hotel is a citadel of high taste. It is elegantly furnished in a restrained way, spacious in concept both in its private and public rooms, and gracious in its reception and amenities. Many Riviera-bound guests have deserted their old favorites for this holiday rendezvous.

You can reserve a first-class room, built into the central block with balconies, or else the Cidadela will place you in womblike comfort in one of its twin-bedded, terraced suites or one of its apartmentlike duplexes, the latter usually sheltering three to six persons. The hotel rents 130 bedrooms, plus 10 suites and apartments, each with air conditioning, minibar, TV, and phone. Singles range from 11,000$ ($73.70) to 19,500$ ($130.65) daily, with doubles costing 13,000$ ($87.10) to 22,000$ ($147.40). Suites and apartments are priced from 45,000$ ($301.50). The rear rooms, sheltered from the noise of traffic, are preferable. Two wings of rooms and duplexes face a garden with a large open swimming pool.

The duplexes are as complete as an apartment: a living room, dining room, and a fully equipped kitchenette on the lower floor, with a staircase leading to the upstairs bedrooms, two or three each, with private bath. Each floor opens onto verandas with garden furniture.

The three major public rooms are pleasantly decorated, the main living room with low modern groups of furniture in warm colors. In the good-sized dining room, the sturdy armchairs, upholstered with Portuguese fabric, seat many diners desiring top-quality cooking. You can take lunch or dinner here for 3,200$ ($21.45) extra per person. However, nearby is a supermarket for those wanting to whip up their own concoctions. The intimate bar is done in blue and gray with "medievalesque" helmets and breast plates. On the premises are a garage, a boutique, a hairdresser, plus a concierge skilled at arranging boating and fishing trips, tennis games, a day at the golf course, horseback riding, or a ticket for the bullfight. Room service is available from 8am to 10pm daily, and laundry/valet service is also provided. Parking is free. A pianist entertains Wednesday to Monday in the bar. The hotel divorces itself from the hustle-bustle of summering Cascais, and is reached by heading out on a tree-shaded avenue, past restaurants, boutiques, and nightclubs. AE, DC, MC, V.

Hotel Nau, Rua Dr. Iracy Doyle 14, 2750 Cascais (tel. 01/483-28-61; fax 01/483-28-66). The hotel's 53 rooms are popular with Europeans on a budget holiday —consequently there might be a tour bus pulled up near the concrete front. You'll find this place behind a balconied facade, a few steps from the town's rail station. A bar is on the second floor, and other facilities include a sun terrace on the roof and a dining room. The simple and functional bedrooms, which tend to be quieter in the back, offer balconies, phones, private bathrooms, and a well-scrubbed look. Single rooms cost 14,495$ ($97.10) daily, with doubles renting for 15,950$ ($106.85). All tariffs include breakfast. The hotel is next to one of the biggest garages in town, where parking is free.

Inexpensive

Albergaria Valbom, Avenida Valbom 14, 2750 Cascais (tel. 01/486-58-01). The white concrete facade with its evenly spaced rows of recessed balconies doesn't offer anything architecturally distinctive. Nonetheless, the interior is warmly and comfortably decorated, and the staff is helpful and polite. You'll find a spacious sienna-colored bar on the premises, along with a sun-washed TV lounge ringed with engravings of fish, and 40 conservatively decorated bedrooms, each with private bath, air conditioning, and phone. Singles rent for 7,500$ ($50.25) to 8,500$ ($56.95) daily, with doubles costing 10,500$ ($70.35) to 11,500$ ($77.05). Breakfast is another 400$ ($2.70) per person. Parking is an additional 500$ ($3.35). The quieter accommodations look out over the back. The Valbom lies on a commercial-residential street close to the center of Cascais, near the rail station. AE, DC, MC, V.

Casa Pergola, Avenida Valbom 13, 2750 Cascais (tel. 01/484-00-40). Originally built in the 18th century behind a deep and well-planted garden, this elegant villa offers some of the most charming interiors in Cascais. In the center of town, it stands in a neighborhood filled with restaurants and shops. Inside, the wall surrounding its flowers and hanging vines provides a calm from the hectic life outside. This is the domain of Maria de Luz, whose genteel Portuguese staff proudly displays a collection of antique furniture and blue-glazed tiles which surround the elegant second-floor sitting room. Eight of the establishment's 12 well-furnished bedrooms contain private baths. Each accommodation is suitable for one or two persons, and comes with breakfast in the price of 9,000$ ($60.30) in a room without bath or 12,000$ ($80.40) in a room with bath. Parking is another 500$ ($3.35). No credit cards.

WHERE TO DINE

Outside of Lisbon, this sprawling resort offers the heaviest concentration of high-quality restaurants in all of Portugal. Even if you're based in the capital, you should trek out to Cascais to sample the viands—both Portuguese and international dishes. Once you've tasted cognac-simmered lobster, mint-flavored shellfish soup, stuffed cuttlefish, shrimp pâté, even southern fried chicken, you may become a total refugee from your hotel dining room.

Regrettably, from the customer's—not the owner's—point of view, many of the restaurants in Cascais tend to be overcrowded in summer, as they are so popular and quite reasonably priced. However, since many are excellent, press on to the next recommendation if you can't find a seat at your first choice. What follows is a wide-ranging survey of the best of the lot, in all price ranges.

Expensive

Restaurant Albatroz, Rua Frederico Arouca 100 (tel. 483-28-21). One of the finest dining experiences along the Costa do Sol can be found at this elegantly decorated restaurant, part of the most famous hotel along the coast (see my previous recommendation). Its summer-style decor is inviting year round. It's best to begin with an apéritif on the covered terrace high above the sea.

Afterward you'll be ushered into a glistening dining room. There, between walls pierced by large sheets of glass, under an alternately beamed and lattice-covered ceiling, you can enjoy some of the finest Portuguese and international cuisine in Cascais. Your repast might include poached salmon, partridge stew, chateaubriand, or a savory version of stuffed sole with shellfish. For dessert, your choice will range from crêpes Suzette to an iced soufflé. Accompanying your meal will be a wide selection of Portuguese and international wines. Full meals cost from 4,200$ ($28.15) to 6,000$ ($40.20) per person, and reservations are necessary. Hours are daily from 12:30 to 3pm and 7:30 to 10pm.

Restaurant O Pescador, Rua das Flores 9 (tel. 483-20-54). The name (the Fisherman), the lane (the Street of Flowers), and the proximity to the fish market may lead you to expect a simple café. Pescador is, however, considered the best restaurant in Cascais for fish. Its *caldeirada la lagosta com frango,* on which the tab fluctuates daily, is made with fresh lobster and tender chicken, simmered in a base sauce of cognac and rum with the natural juices, then served in a crockery pot. Even if you decide to forgo the house specialty, you may not want to pass up *sopa marisco* (shellfish soup), which is prepared with a savory tomato base and flavored with a sprig of mint. One appealing recommendation is *bacalhau* (codfish) *à pescador.* Finally, another Portuguese dish is *espeteda de lulas com gambas* (shrimp). If you forgo the high-priced lobster, your tab is likely to range in price from 6,000$ ($40.20). Food is served from 12:30 to 3pm and 7:30 to 11pm.

The decor is tavern style, with hand-hewn beams, iron lanterns, cork-and-wood paneling, lobster baskets, ships' models, smoked fish and meats, and strings of garlic, red pepper, and onions. An appetizing table in the front displays a selection of prepared foods, fruit, wines, and cheeses. Reservations are necessary. AE, DC, MC, V.

Visconde da Luz, Jardim Visconde da Luz (tel. 486-68-48). The location of this well-known restaurant is one of its most appealing features. It sits within a low-slung bungalow at the edge of a park in the center of Cascais. The view from the windows encompasses rows of lime trees and towering sycamores where flocks of birds congregate at dusk (so be duly warned if you're walking under these trees). Inside, the decor is a modernized form of art nouveau, complete with mirrors, touches of scarlet, and a polite, uniformed staff eager to cater to your wishes. Before you enter, you might be interested in looking at the blue-and-white tile kitchen. The Portuguese food is well prepared with fresh ingredients. A meal, costing from 5,000$ ($33.50), might include fried sole, shellfish, pork with clams, seafood curry, and clams in garlic sauce, finished off with an almond cake for dessert. Open from noon to 4pm and 7pm to midnight. Closed Monday. Reservations are needed. AE, DC, MC, V.

Moderate

Baluarte, Avenida Dom Carlos I (tel. 486-54-71). This airy and contemporary restaurant often attracts a chic clientele, who understand that a meal here can be expensive, but is usually worth the escudos. It stands across the street from the waters of the port, behind a glass-fronted facade whose windows are separated from the sidewalk by a small but well-maintained cluster of flowerbeds. Inside you can enjoy a drink on one of the white barrel-shaped chairs of the bar before heading for the dining room. Full international meals, priced from 4,000$ ($26.80), might include sea bass Ribatejo style, sole with almonds, Florentine-style snapper, ravioli carbonara, lobster bisque, and a large variety of shellfish dishes, including mixed seafood au gratin. Good service and fresh ingredients are the norm here, to be experienced daily from noon to 3pm and 7:30 to 11pm. Reservations are needed. AE, DC, MC, V.

Gil Vicente, Rua dos Navegantes 22–30 (tel. 483-20-32). This is the kind of bistro you usually find on a back street in a town along the Côte d'Azur. Set on the rise of a hill above the harbor, it was converted from a fisherman's cottage. Both the Portuguese and French cuisine and the ambience reflect the mood of its owner, who sees to it that excellent meals are served. Hours are from 12:30 to 3pm and 7pm to 1am; closed Wednesday. The restaurant is closed in February. The name of the tavern, Gil Vicente, honors the 16th-century father of Portuguese drama, virtually the Iberian Shakespeare, if you will. The decor of the restaurant is simple—a setting of plaster walls, an old stone fireplace, windows recessed with pots of greenery. An ornate iron washstand has been adapted for condiments, and the walls contain heads of old iron bedsteads, gaily painted.

You may be won over by the cooking (pâté, crêpes, shellfish, or grilled chicken and steaks)—and the reasonable tariffs. To whet your appetite, try the assortment of hors d'oeuvres, the pâté maison, or the bisque of shellfish. At least three main dishes hit the mark every night: sole Colbert, sole delicia, and grilled steak with mushrooms. Among the desserts, you can order a fruit salad, a chocolate mousse, or a banana flambé. You can dine well for 3,500$ ($23.45) and up. Reservations are needed. AE, DC, MC, V.

John Bull (Britannia Restaurant), Largo Luís de Camões 4A (tel. 483-01-54). With its black-and-white timbered Elizabethan facade, this centrally located pub and restaurant is a wedge of England. In the street-floor pub, the John Bull, you can order an iced pint of lager. The setting is appropriate—wood paneling, oak beams, a fireplace, crude tavern stools and tables, pewter pots, and ceramic jugs. The meals at the second-floor Britannia Restaurant feature a medley of English and Portuguese, even American, dishes. Southern fried chicken and T-bone steak are familiar Yankee favorites. For English tastes, specialties include cottage pie. An average meal here will cost from 3,500$ ($23.45). Reservations are necessary. Hours are daily from 12:30 to 3:30pm and 7:30 to 11:30pm. AE, DC, MC, V.

Os Doze, Rua Frederico Arouca 71 (tel. 483-53-94), is an intimate tavern restaurant behind a stone facade and a thick wooden door on a busy pedestrian street in the center of town. The heart and soul of the place rest in the attentions of its owner, who will happily compose a Portuguese menu selection for you if you are at all undecided about what to order. Within his small enclave, you can enjoy a seafood curry, avocado with shrimp, fresh oysters, chicken piri-piri (it's hot), or entrecôte bordelaise. He always has a wide selection of fresh fish, and you might try his delectable grilled sole or whiting sautéed in bread crumbs. Full meals, costing from 3,200$ ($21.45), are served from noon to 2:30pm and 7 to 10:30pm; closed Tuesday evening and all day Wednesday. Reservations are needed. AE, DC, MC, V.

Reijos Restaurant, Rua Frederico Arouca 35 (tel. 483-00-11). First, you should be warned that it's likely to be crowded, and that you'll either have to wait for a table or abandon all hope in high season. This intimate, informal bistro is that good. The fine foods of two countries, the United States and Portugal, are combined on the menu, and the result is altogether pleasing. An American citizen, Ray Ettinger, long ago teamed up with a Portuguese, Tony Brito, pooling their talents in the running of this successful enterprise.

At times, to the homesick Mr. Ettinger, nothing is more delectable than roast beef à l'inglese or Salisbury steak with mushroom sauce. Other popular items include lobster thermidor, peppersteak, and shrimp curry. From Macau, two Chinese dishes are prepared at your table: beef with garden peppers, and shrimp and cucumbers. Fresh seafood includes sole, sea bass, garoupa, and fresh salmon, as well as the famous *bacalhau à Reijos* (dry codfish baked in the oven with a cheese sauce). Unlike many European restaurants, Reijos serves fresh vegetables at no extra cost with its main dishes. In addition, it has an outstanding selection of desserts made on the premises by Mr. Ettinger from fresh seasonal ingredients. The service is excellent. Be prepared to spend from 3,000$ ($20.10) per person for dinner. Lunch is served Monday through Saturday from 12:30 to 3:30pm; dinner, 7 to 11pm Monday through Saturday (telephone first). Closed from December 20 to January 20. AE, DC, MC, V.

Inexpensive

Restaurante Alaúde, Largo Luís de Camões 8 (tel. 483-02-87). The blue tile facade of this convivial restaurant opens onto a square teeming with vacationing Europeans. Its famous neighbor, the John Bull, frequently serves as the cocktail lounge for clients who eventually stroll over to Alaúde for dinner. The square onto which it opens is sometimes so crowded that it's referred to as "the living room of Cascais," offering plenty to see from the vantage point at one of this restaurant's outdoor tables. If you prefer, you can select a seat inside, enjoying one of several well-prepared Portuguese and international specialties. These include sardines in olive oil with tomatoes, several preparations of scampi, clams of the house, and a grilled mélange of shellfish. Full meals cost upward from 2,100$ ($14.05). The establishment is open from 10am to midnight 7 days a week. Reservations are a good idea. AE, DC, MC, V.

Eduardo, Largo das Grutas 3 (tel. 483-19-01), is a rustic restaurant that offers good value. It's named for its French owner, Eduard de Beukelaer, who turns out a selection of savory Portuguese and French meals. The food is well-prepared, especially the French dishes. Specialties are monkfish gratin, crayfish in butter with capers, and beef Stroganoff. The average meal costs from 2,000$ ($13.40). Reservations are recommended. Eduardo is open from noon to 3pm and 7pm to midnight Thursday to Tuesday. AE, DC, MC, V.

Restaurante O Batel, Travessa das Flores 4 (tel. 483-02-15), fronts the fish market. Styled as a country inn, it doesn't overdo with touristy gimmicks. The atmosphere is semirustic, with rough white walls and beamed ceilings. A display indicates the ingenuity of the chef, his wares enhanced by a basket of figs, plums, peaches, and fresh flowers. The prices are reasonable, and that, balanced with the superb Portuguese cuisine, explains why the tiny tables are usually filled at every meal. Lobster thermidor and lobster stewed in cognac are the house specialties, but the price on these items changes daily. For something less expensive, I recommend Cascais sole with banana, a savory dish of clams with cream, and mixed shellfish with rice. For an appetizer, you can try prawn cocktail. To complete your meal, such desserts as pineapple with Madeira wine are offered. *Wine tip:* Order a Casal Mendes rosé, a cool choice. Tabs run from 2,800$ ($18.75) to 4,000$ ($26.80). A fixed-price meal costs 3,000$ ($20.10). The restaurant serves daily from noon to 3pm and 7 to 10:30pm. Reservations are needed. AE, DC, MC, V.

O Pipas, Rua das Flores 1B (tel. 486-45-01). If you order shellfish here, a meal can be very expensive. Otherwise, this popular restaurant offers well-prepared food at acceptable prices. Many diners consider it the finest independent (outside the hotels) restaurant at the resort. It stands on a teeming street whose pavement is covered with black-and-white mosaics. The decor is Portuguese bistro style, with racks of exposed wine bottles, and big picture windows letting in sunlight and views of the busy street outside. The Portuguese menu items include lobster, clams, shellfish of all kinds (including oysters), and several preparations of sole, along with a few meat dishes, especially beef O Pipas. Full meals cost from 3,000$ ($20.10) to 4,200$ ($28.15). Hours are daily from noon to 3:30pm and 7 to 11:30pm. Call for a table. AE, DC, MC, V.

EVENING ENTERTAINMENT

Discos
Palm Beach, Praia da Conceição (tel. 483-08-51), is a hillside disco and restaurant with a rather swank atmosphere—and a doorman to weed out undesirables. The disco lies a 10-minute walk from the Cascais rail station. It rides the crest of the wave along the Costa do Sol, drawing a young, fun-loving crowd that's well mannered enough to please the management. The club is positioned below the coastal road, its wide windows overlooking the bay at Cascais. You lounge comfortably on banquettes and chairs when not dancing on the mini-size floor. The atmosphere is informal, not dressy, and only records are played. The minimum charge at the disco is 1,000$ ($6.70), with beer going for 300$ ($2) and hard drinks from 600$ ($4). The restaurant, which has a maritime decor and a profusion of plants, overlooks the bay. Here you can order excellent shellfish and local fish dishes, a meal costing from 2,500$ ($16.75). The Palm Beach also has a pub–cocktail lounge, set up to look like the bridge of a steamboat. Hours are daily from 10:30pm to 4am.

Van Gogo, Travessa Alfarrobeira 9 (tel. 483-33-78), is a chic playground. Modestly hidden in a corner stone building, it was transformed from a simple fisherman's cottage into a disco, lying a 10-minute walk from the Cascais rail station. A doorman carefully evaluates those who would cross the threshold, using some inner radar I don't understand. You'll encounter a young crowd similar to the one at Juan-les-Pins, France. A seductive atmosphere is created by the black-glass walls, and the customers can rock and roll. You pay a steep 3,000$ ($20.10) as an entrance minimum, unless they know you. Once inside, you're entitled to buy that amount in drinks. The Van Gogo opens its doors year round at 11pm, closing at 4am.

Fado
Rodrigo, Forte Dom Rodrigo, Estrada de Birre (tel. 485-13-73). Amália Rodrigues is still the leading fadista of Portugal, but since she doesn't sing that much anymore, one of the most popular young fadistas in the country today is a singer known only as "Rodrigo." His club lies just outside the resort of Cascais, along Estrada de Birre. Some of the most fashionable people in Lisbon drive out here just to hear Rodrigo sing—he's that good. His voice is haunting and melancholy. The nightclub opens at 8:30pm for dinner, costing from 4,000$ ($26.80) to 6,000$ ($40.20), but that is much too early to go, as Rodrigo himself rarely appears before 10pm. Closing time is 4am. A minimum of 2,000$ ($13.40) is imposed, and be prepared to pay in cash, as credit cards aren't accepted. The cover charge includes two drinks. Closed Monday.

The Bar Scene
Mr. Busby's Bar and Pub, Avenida Sabóia 3A (tel. 468-09-75). The place is fun, a bit rowdy, and popular with a fickle crowd of music lovers. You'll find it on a steep hillside street a short distance above Estoril. Illuminated through large sheets

of plate glass, the high ceilings are covered with beer banners. Few of them get noticed when video movies are screened. In addition to drinks and beer, sandwiches are served. Hot dishes begin at 300$ ($2), and mixed drinks cost from 200$ ($1.35). The establishment is open from 4pm to around 2:30am every day.

The most popular bar is the **Pickwick Pub,** Avenida Biarritz 3 (tel. 468-67-26). The Pickwick is decorated like an old English pub, complete with carpeted floor, mugs hanging over the bar, and plenty of cozy nooks and crannies where you sit in subdued lighting. Soft music is provided from a disc jockey sitting in an adjoining room. You can play darts, have light meals, and while away a couple of hours chatting with the locals and foreigners. It's open daily from noon to 2am. Beers cost from 400$ ($2.70).

An interesting watering spot, **Ray's Cocktail Bar & Lounge,** Avenida Sabóia 425 (tel. 468-01-06), in Monte Estoril, is popular with American expatriates, many of whom make it their private club, including the original Ray now that he's retired and has turned it over to Rafael Neves. It's a souped-up decorator extravaganza. Inside you're likely to find a completely catholic assemblage of elements—a fátima hand from Tangier, a glass ruby-colored newel post finial, chandeliers dripping with crystal, antique benches, and provincial chairs, plus a heterogeneous mixture of modern art. Everyone seemingly enjoys the drinks (many enjoy quite a few of them). Most strong drinks cost from 400$ ($2.70). The bar is open daily from 6pm to 2:30am.

Spirits Piano Bar, Rua Alexandre Herculano 3 (tel. 438-38-64). When you ring the doorbell of this chic rendezvous, a tuxedoed employee will open the speak-easy door if you look appropriate. Once inside, you descend a flight of stairs into a slightly cramped, but very intimate hideaway accented with ceiling beams, black mosaic floors, and thick stucco walls. Live music is presented on Saturday and Sunday. Otherwise the bar is open from 7pm to 4am every night. Somewhat difficult to find, the bar is on a terrace a few feet above a street running into one of the corners of the triangular Jardim Visconde da Luz. A whisky costs 500$ ($3.35).

---

4. Guincho

Guincho means caterwaul, screech, shriek, yell—the cry that swallows make while darting among the air currents over the wild sea. These swallows at Guincho are to be seen all year, unlike their fickle fair-weather counterparts at San Juan Capistrano, California. Sometimes at night the sea, driven into a frenzy, howls like a wailing banshee, and that too is guincho. The settlement is near the westernmost point on the European continent, known to the Portuguese as **Cabo da Roca.** The beaches are spacious and sandy; the sunshine, incandescent; the nearby promontories, jutting out amid white-tipped Atlantic waves, spectacular. The windswept dunes are backed by wooded hills, and to the east the Serra de Sintra is silhouetted upon the distant horizon.

Praia do Guincho draws large beach crowds each season. The undertow is treacherous—be forewarned. It's wise to keep in mind the advice of Jennings Parrott, writing in the *International Herald Tribune:* "If you are caught up by the current, don't fight it. Don't panic. The wind forces it to circle, so you will be brought back to shore." A local fisherman, however, advises that you take a box lunch along. "Sometimes it takes several days to make this circle."

Guincho lies 4 miles north of Cascais, 6 miles north of Estoril. To reach it, you have to either drive or take a bus from Cascais. One of the primary reasons for coming to Guincho is to sample its seafood restaurants, described below. You can try, for example, the crayfish-size, box-jaw lobsters known as *bruxas,* which in Portuguese means sorcerer, wizard, witch doctor, even a nocturnal moth. To be totally Portuguese, you must also sample the barnacles, called *percêbes,* meaning to perceive, to understand, to comprehend. After devouring these creatures, many foreign visitors fail to comprehend or perceive their popularity with the Portuguese. The fresh lobsters and crabs are cultivated in nearby shellfish beds, a fascinating sight.

If you're staying over at one of the recommendations described below, the night calls of the "sirens" may enrapture you. The nearest tourist office is in Cascais.

WHERE TO STAY

A fine choice is the **Hotel do Guincho,** Praia do Guincho, 2750 Cascais (tel. 01/285-04-91; fax 01/285-04-31). In the 17th century an army of local masons built one of the most forbidding fortresses along the coast, within a few hundred feet of the most westerly point in Europe. The twin towers that flank the vaguely Moorish-looking facade still stand sentinel amid a sun-bleached terrain of sand and rock. Today, however, the inhabitants are more likely to be well-heeled representatives of a more glamorous world. In the past they've included Orson Welles, who was reportedly fascinated by the mist and the surging roar of the waves as they dashed upon the nearby cliffs. The late Princess Grace also found the place intriguing, as have prime ministers of both Italy and Portugal.

You'll enter through an enclosed courtyard, where there's a well that used to provide water for the garrison. The public rooms are filled with all the antique trappings of an aristocratic private home. In cold weather a fire might be blazing in one of the granite-framed fireplaces, illuminating the thick carpets and the century-old furniture. Each of the small but comfortable bedrooms, 31 in all, is sheltered behind a thick pine door, heavily banded with iron. Each room has a vaulted stone ceiling, the keystone of which is carved into one of the 36 different heraldic shields. In addition to the wealth of 17th-century trappings, every room contains a color TV, minibar, air conditioning, private bath, and phone. Singles cost 25,500$ ($170.85) daily, while doubles rent for 30,000$ ($201). Three small but elegant suites, some with their own fireplaces, cost from 35,000$ ($234.50). Half board is priced at another 4,500$ ($30.15) per person daily. Parking is free.

If you're exploring the coast, the hotel also makes an ideal luncheon or dinner stop. Some celebrities have declared that many of their most perfect meals in Portugal were served here on a sunny afternoon, within sight of the surf a short distance away. The chef prepares such specialties as pâté of pheasant with morels, seafood salad, lobster Newburg, grilled black grouper with tartare sauce, and roast suckling pig Portuguese style. Full à la carte meals begin at 4,000$ ($26.80) and are served every day of the week from 12:30 to 3pm and 7:30 to 11pm. AE, DC, MC, V.

Estalagem do Forte Muchaxo, Praia do Guincho, 2750 Cascais (tel. 01/285-02-21; fax 01/285-04-44), was begun some four decades ago as a simple straw hut set up on rugged wave-dashed rocks, with the founding father selling brandy and coffee to the fishermen. Gradually, the senior Muchaxo started to cook for them. In time, beach-loving Germans discovered the place, and eventually even royalty arrived wanting to be fed. Nowadays the new has absorbed the old, yet the straw shack remains to please traditionalists. The Muchaxo family operates this overblown hacienda, placing emphasis on the rustic blended with a mild dose of the contemporary. The estalagem is rectangular in shape, with windows of bedrooms overlooking either the courtyard or the nearby coast and hills. At one side, thrust out onto rock walls, is a swimming pool with terraces and diving boards. After a day of swimming, guests gather in the chalet living room to warm themselves at the huge raised stone fireplace.

There's a choice of two dining rooms, one modern, the other with bamboo ceiling, staccato black-and-white covered tables, and hand-painted provincial furniture. People drive from miles around just to sample the Portuguese and French cuisine, highly praised by such discriminating Iberian travelers as author James A. Michener. The adventurous will begin their meals with barnacles, described previously. The house specialty is lobster, Barraca style, but the price is likely to change daily. An order of grilled sea bass is decidedly less expensive. A dish worth recommending is the chateaubriand. However, unless your throat is lined with asbestos, avoid ordering the chicken with piri-piri sauce made with hot pepper from Angola. One diner is said to have fainted after tasting this concoction. An excellent finish to a meal would be banana fritters. A typical meal here will cost 5,000$ ($33.50) to 6,000$ ($40.20).

Those who want to stay for the night will find a choice of 23 rooms and 1 suite

—the best units overlooking the sea. A single costs from 14,800$ ($99.15) nightly. Two persons can stay here for 15,600$ ($104.50). All rooms have private baths, phones, and central heating. Each unit is unique, although most of them have basic stark white walls with beamed ceilings. Suites cost from 21,000$ ($140.70). Breakfast is included. The inn has an outdoor swimming pool. Laundry service is available, as is room service until midnight. Parking is free. AE, DC, MC, V.

WHERE TO DINE
Restaurante Porto de Santa Maria, Estrada do Guincho (tel. 01/285-02-40). If you decide to drive to the isolated stretch of roadside where this restaurant is located, you won't be alone. Hundreds of vacationing Europeans and Portuguese might decide to join you, especially in summer. This restaurant is one of the most appealing of its type along the coast, and it also serves some of the best seafood. A doorman will usher you into the low-lying seafront building, where large windows take in views of the sometimes-treacherous surf.

The beige-and-white decor is highlighted with an enormous aquarium made from white marble and thick sheets of glass, within which trapped crustaceans such as lobsters wave their claws. A central serving table is laden with fruits and flowers. The polite staff serves every conceivable form of shellfish, priced by the gram, as well as such house specialties as grilled sole. Shellfish rice, known as *arroz de mariscos,* is the most popular specialty, and it's usually served to two persons. Full meals cost from 3,500$ ($23.45). You'll probably want to taste the rondelles of pungent sheep's-milk cheese that await the arrival of guests at each table. Hours are daily from 12:15 to 3:30pm and 7 to 10:30pm. Reservations aren't needed. AE, DC, MC, V.

---

5. Queluz

Back in Lisbon, we strike out this time on quite a different excursion. On the highway to Sintra, 9½ miles northwest of Lisbon, **Palácio de Quelez,** Largo do Palácio, 2745 Lisboa (tel. 01/435-00-39), shimmers in the sunlight, a brilliant example of the rococo in Portugal.

Pedro III ordered its construction in 1747, and the work dragged on until 1787. The architect Mateus Vicente de Oliveira was later joined by French decorator and designer Jean-Baptiste Robilon. The latter was largely responsible for planning the garden and lakeland setting.

Pedro III had actually adapted an old hunting pavilion that had belonged to the Marquis Castelo Rodrigo. Later the pavilion came into the possession of the Portuguese royal family. Pedro III liked it so much that he decided to make it his summer residence. What the visitor of today sees is not exactly what it was in the 18th century. Queluz suffered a lot during the French invasions, and almost all of its belongings were transported to Brazil with the royal family.

A fire in 1934 destroyed a great deal of Queluz, but tasteful and sensitive reconstruction has restored the light-hearted aura of the 18th century.

The topiary effects, with closely trimmed vines and sculptured boxhedges, are highlighted by blossoming mauve petunias and red geraniums. Fountain pools on which lilies float are lined with blue azulejos and reflect the muted facade, the statuary, and the finely cut balustrades.

Inside, you can wander through the dressing room of the queen, lined with painted panels depicting a children's romp; stroll through the Don Quixote Chamber (Dom Pedro was born here and returned from Brazil to die in the same bed); pause in the Music Room, complete with a French grande piano-forte and an 18th-century English harpischord; and stand in the mirrored throne room adorned with crystal chandeliers. The Portuguese still hold state banquets here.

Festooning the palace are all the eclectic props of the rococo era—the inevitable chinoiserie panels (these from the Portuguese overseas province of Macau), Florentine marbles from quarries once worked by Michelangelo, Iberian and Flemish tapestries, Empire antiques, indigo-blue ceramics from Delft, 18th-century

Hepplewhite armchairs, porcelains from Austria, carpets from Rabat, Portuguese Chippendale furnishings, and wood pieces (jacaranda) from Brazil—all of which are of exquisite quality. When they visited Portugal, Presidents Eisenhower, Carter, and Reagan were housed in the 30-chambered Pavilion of D. Maria I, as was Queen Elizabeth II on two occasions, and the Prince and Princess of Wales. These storybook chambers, refurbished by the Portuguese government, are said to have reverberated with the rantings of the grief-stricken monarch Maria I, who, it is alleged, had to be strapped to her bed at times. Before becoming mentally ill, she was a bright, intelligent, and brave woman who did a great job as ruler of her country in a troubled time.

The palace is open Wednesday to Monday except holidays from 10am to 1pm and 2 to 5pm. From June through September, admission is 400$ ($2.70). During other months, the charge is 200$ ($13.40). It is free Sunday morning. It costs only 50$ (35¢) if you wish to visit only the gardens. Children are admitted free. From Lisbon, you can visit Queluz by a train departing from the central station at the Rossio, costing 90$ (65¢) for a one-way ride.

WHERE TO DINE

If you have only two or three meals in all of Portugal, take one of them at **Cozinha Velha** (Old Kitchen), Palácio Nacional de Queluz, Largo do Palácio (tel. 435-07-40). Once it was the kitchen of the palace, built in the grand style; now it has been converted into a colorful dining room that finds favor with gourmets, royalty, and the average visitor seeking a romantic setting for a fine dinner.

The entrance is through a garden patio. The dining room is like a small chapel, with high stone arches, a walk-in freestanding fireplace, marble columns, and the original spits. Along one side is a 20-foot marble chef's table that's a virtual still life of the culinary skill of the chef, augmented by baskets of fruit and vases of flowers. You sit on ladderback chairs in a setting of shiny copper, oil paintings, and torchères.

Fortunately, Portuguese and international meals are served 7 days a week (luncheon, noon to 3pm; dinner, 7:30 to 10pm). I suggest the hors d'oeuvres for two persons, followed by such main courses as filet steak, poached sea bass, grilled pork on a spit, or whiting with capers. To finish, you might try the island cheese or a vanilla soufflé for two. Expect to spend from 7,000$ ($46.90), including your drink, for a complete meal. Reservations are needed. AE, DC, MC, V.

---

6. Sintra

"It is indeed a fairytale setting and gives one the feeling that this is where Sleeping Beauty must have rested all those years." These were the words of a publicist singing the praises of Sintra. Writers have been doing that ever since Portugal's greatest poet Luís Vaz de Camões proclaimed its glory in *Os Lusíadas (The Portuguese)*. Lord Byron called it "glorious Eden" when he and John Cam Hobhouse included Sintra in their grand tour of 1809. English romantics thrilled to its description in the poet's autobiographical *Childe Harold's Pilgrimage.*

Picture a town on a hillside, decaying birthday-cake villas covered with azulejos coming loose in the damp mist hovering like a veil over Sleeping Beauty. What would Sintra be without its luxuriant vegetation? It's all here: camellias for melancholic romantics, ferns behind which lizards dart, pink and purple bougainvillea over garden trelliswork, red geraniums on wrought-iron balconies, eucalyptus branches fluttering in the wind, lemon trees studding the groves, and honey-sweet mimosa scenting the air. Be duly warned: There are those who visit Sintra, fall under its spell, and stay forever.

Sintra is one of the oldest towns in the country. When the Crusaders captured it in 1147, they fought bitterly against the Moors firmly entrenched in their hilltop castle, the ruins of which remain today.

The town, 18 miles northwest of Lisbon, is on the northern slope of the granite

Sintra Range. A 45-minute train ride from the neo-Manueline railway station at the Rossio in Lisbon will deposit you here. A train bound for Sintra leaves every 16 minutes from Lisbon's Rossio Railway Station. Service is daily until 2am. The bus from Lisbon is not recommended, because the service is too slow and too many stops are made en route. However, visitors staying in the Costa do Sol hotels can make bus connections at both Cascais and Estoril. Sintra is also visited on many organized tours departing from both Lisbon and Sintra. But this latter method allows no time for personal discovery, which is essentially what Sintra is all about. The **Sintra Tourist Office** is at Praça da República 3 (tel. 923-11-57).

SPECIAL EVENTS

During June and July the **Sintra Festival** attracts a large number of music lovers, owing to the quality of the artists and the program, which is entirely made up of a piano repertoire from the Romantic period, with the best interpreters of the present international music milieu. The various concerts (about 12) usually take place in churches, palaces (Palácio da Vila, Palácio da Pena, and Palácio de Queluz), as well as in parks and country estates of the region. The tourist office (see above) will furnish complete details.

WHAT TO SEE & DO

The specific sights of Sintra are set forth below, but the task of selection is difficult. Byron put it well: "Ah me! What hand can pencil guide, or pen, to follow half on which the eye dilates."

Horse-drawn carriages are available for rent between the town and the serra. It is well worth trying this means of transport, for a most agreeable trip under shady trees to the "glorious paradise" of which Byron wrote. The carriages start from and return to the large square in front of the National Palace of Sintra.

National Palace of Sintra

Palácio Nacional de Sintra, Largo da Rainha D. Amélia (tel. 923-00-85), was a royal palace until 1910. Its last royal inhabitant was Queen Maria Pía, the Italian grandmother of Manuel II, the last king of Portugal. Much of the palace was constructed in the days of the first Manuel, the Fortunate.

The palace opens onto the central square of the town. Outside, two conically shaped chimney towers form the most distinctive landmark on the Sintra skyline. Long before the arrival of the Crusaders under Afonso Henriques, this was a summer palace of Moorish sultans, filled with dancing harem girls who performed in front of bubbling fountains. The original was torn down, and the Moorish style of architecture was incorporated in latter-day versions of the palace. The entire effect is rather a conglomeration of styles, with Gothic and the Manueline predominant. The glazed earthenware tiles, or azulejos, lining many of the chambers are among the best you'll find in Portugal.

The Swan Room was a favorite of João I, one of the founding kings, father of Henry the Navigator, and husband of Philippa of Lancaster. It is said that one day the English queen came upon her king embracing one of the ladies of the court. Apparently she did not hold a grudge against him for this one indiscretion, but it grew into a court scandal of which the king became painfully aware. Hoping to end speculation and save his wife further embarrassment, he called in his decorators and gave them a secret mission. The room was locked. When the doors were finally opened to the ladies of the court, they marched in, only to discover that the ceiling was covered with magpies. The symbol of the chattering birds scored a point, and a new subject of gossip was discovered. Guides now call the salon the Chamber of the Magpies.

The Room of the Sirens or Mermaids is one of the most elegant in the palace. In the Heraldic or Stag Room, coats-of-arms of aristocratic Portuguese families and hunting scenes are depicted. From most of these rooms, wide windows look out onto attractive vistas of the Sintra mountain range. Tile-fronted stoves are found in the Old Kitchen, where the feasts of yore were held, especially game banquets in the reign of Carlos I, the king assassinated in 1908.

The palace is rich in paintings and Iberian and Flemish tapestries. But it is at its best when you wander into a tree- and plant-shaded patio and listen to the water of a fountain. Perhaps the young king Sebastião sat here lost in the dreams of glory that would one day take him and his country on an ill-fated mission to North Africa, a mission that would cost him his life.

As you approach the palace, you can buy a ticket at the kiosk on your left. The cost is 200$ ($1.35) from October to May and 400$ ($2.70) June to September. Children up to 10 years pay 100$ (65¢). Visiting hours are daily from 10am to 1pm and 2 to 5pm.

The Pena Palace

Towering over Sintra, the **Palácio Nacional de Pena,** Estrada de Pena (tel. 923-02-27), appeals to special tastes. From its perch on a plateau about 1,500 feet above sea level, it stands like a medieval fortress on one peak, looking at the ruins of the old Moorish castle on the opposite hill. Part of the fun of visiting it is the ride up the verdant winding road, through the Parque das Merendas.

At the top you come upon a castle that was called a "soaring agglomeration of towers, cupolas, and battlemented walls" by *National Geographic.* The inspiration behind this castle in the sky was Ferdinand of Saxe-Coburg-Gotha, the husband of Maria II.

Of course, Ferdinand needed a German to help him build this fantasy. While dreams of the Middle Ages danced in his head, Baron Eschwege arrived. You can still see a sculptured likeness of the baron by looking out from the Pena at a huge rock across the way. Romantically, the architect fancied himself a soldier, armed with a halberd.

In the early 16th century Manuel the Fortunate had ordered a monastery built on these lofty grounds for the Jerónimos monks. Even today you can visit a cloister and a small ogival chapel that the latter-day builders decided to preserve.

Crossing over a drawbridge, you'll enter the palace proper, whose last royal occupant was Queen Amélia. On a long-ago morning in 1910, she clearly saw that monarchy in Portugal was drawing to an end. Having already lost her husband and her soldier son 2 years before, she was determined not to lose her second offspring, King Manuel II. Gathering her most precious possessions and only the small family heirlooms that could be packed quickly, she fled to Mafra where her son waited. Behind she left Pena Palace, not to see it again until 1945 when she returned to Portugal under much more favorable conditions. Pena has remained much as Amélia left it, and that is part of its fascination; it emerges as a rare record of European royal life in the halcyon days preceding World War I.

For an entrance fee of 400$ ($2.70), you can visit the palace from 10am to 1pm and 2 to 4:30pm, except on Monday when it is closed. Children up to 10 years are admitted free.

Pena Park was designed and planted in a four-year span beginning in 1846. Again, Ferdinand was the controlling factor behind the landscaping. What he achieved was one of the most spectacular parks in Portugal, known for the scope of its plant and tree life. For an eye-opening vista of the park and the palace, you can make the ascent to **Cruz Alta.**

If you're not driving, you can take a taxi or the bus that departs from the main square of Sintra from May to September, heading for the palace, a 20-minute run. If you choose to walk, be warned that it's an arduous trip from the square, taking about 2 hours even if you're in good walking condition.

The Moorish Castle

The fortification **Castelo dos Mouros,** reached along Calçada dos Clérigos, had been around for a long time when Scandinavian crusaders in 1147 besieged and successfully captured it from its Moorish occupants. It was built sometime between the 8th and 9th centuries at a position 1,350 feet above sea level. The consort of Maria II, Ferdinand, the German responsible for Pena Palace, attempted restoration in the 19th century, but was relatively unsuccessful.

There's a parking area for your car, and a guide will send you in the right direction. From the royal tower, the view of Sintra, its palace and castle, and of the Atlantic coast is spectacular. The castle is open from 9am to 5pm from October to April. From May to September it stays open until 6pm. Admission is free.

Monserrate

An Englishman, Sir Francis Cook, set out between 1846 and 1850 to make Lord Byron's dream of a glorious Eden a reality. Bringing in landscape artists and flora from everywhere from Africa to Norway, he planned a botanical garden, the rival of which is not to be found either in Spain or Portugal. It lies along the Estrada de Monserrate.

The garden scales the slope of a hill—paths cut through to hidden oases—and you need to give it the better part of the afternoon. Walking back is rough for all but seasoned hill scalers. However, it's worth the descent.

At the bottom, Cook built his **Palácio de Monserrate.** It seemed that in his Eden, only a Moorish temple would do. But when Cook died, Monserrate faced a troubled future. An English manufacturer purchased the property and set out virtually to destroy Cook's dreams. He began by selling the antiques in the palácio, and it's said that he made so much money on the sale that he was paid back for all the cash he sank into Monserrate. He wasn't satisfied. When news leaked out to Lisbon that he was going to subdivide the park and turn it into a housing development of villas, the government belatedly intervened, and well that it did. When you see Monserrate, you'll surely agree that it belongs to all the people, preserved and well maintained.

Lilies float on cool fountains, flowers scent the air, ferns scale the hillside, northern spruce grows tall, and flora from Africa thrives as if it were in its native habitat. Admission is free. The park is open daily from 10am to 6pm.

To reach Monserrate, go out Route EN375 and follow the signs.

Convento de Santa Cruz dos Capuchos

Dom Alvaro de Castro ordered that this unusually structured convent be built along the Estrada de Pena for the Capuchins in 1560. Cork was used so extensively in its construction that it is sometimes known as the cork monastery.

You walk up a moss-covered path, like a wayfarer of old approaching for his dole. Ring the bell, and a guide (not a monk) will appear to show you in and out of the miniature cells. The convent is in a secluded area, 4½ miles from Sintra.

It appears forlorn, forgotten. Even when it was in use, it probably wasn't too lively. The Capuchins who lived here, perhaps eight in all, had a penchant for the most painstaking of detailed work. For example, they lined the walls of their monastery with cork-bark tiles and seashells. They also carved a chapel out of rock, using cork for insulation.

A hospital was even installed into the most cramped of quarters. Their monastery is perhaps the coziest in the world. Outside, one of them found time to fresco an altar in honor of St. Francis of Assisi.

In 1834, they left suddenly; but fortunately the monastery they left behind wasn't destroyed by vandals. From April to October, it is open daily from 9am to 6pm. The rest of the year, it is open from 9am to 5am. Admission is 75$ (50¢). For information, phone 923-01-37. It's best reached by taking a taxi from Sintra's main square. There is no bus.

WHERE TO STAY

Expensive

Hotel Palácio de Seteais, Rua Barbosa do Bocage, Seteais, 2710 Sintra (tel. 01/923-32-00; fax 01/923-42-77), is a palace converted into a hotel. Lord Byron worked on *Childe Harold* in the front garden. The palace is approached via a long private encircling driveway, past shade trees, a wide expanse of lawn, and yew hedges. The stone architecture is formal, dominated by an arched entryway. Seteais looks older than it is, having been built in the late 18th century by a Dutch

Gildmeester. It was subsequently taken over and restored by the fifth Marquês de Marialva, who sponsored many receptions and galas for the aristocrats of his day.

The palácio is on the crest of a hill, with most of its drawing rooms, galleries, and chambers overlooking the formal terraces, flower garden, and vista toward the sea. Upon entering there is a long galleried hall and a staircase with white-and-gilt balustrades and columns, leading to the lower-level dining room, drinking lounge, and garden terraces. Along the corridor are tapestries, groupings of formal antique furniture, and hand-woven decorative carpets. On the left is a library and an adjoining music room, furnished with period pieces. The main drawing room is decorated with antiques and a fine mural extending around the cove and onto the ceiling. Large bronze chandeliers with crystal add to the luster. The guest book reads like a *Who's Who.*

Don't just drive up to the entrance and expect to be given shelter. There are only 30 rooms (all with private bath and phone), so advance reservations are definitely needed. Some units are air conditioned and contain a minibar. Housed in a beautiful room furnished with antiques or reproductions, you'll pay from 35,000$ ($234.50) daily for one person to 38,000$ ($254.60) for two. A continental breakfast is included. The hotel has a swimming pool and two tennis courts. Parking is free.

Lunch or dinner is special, in the restaurant Monserrat, and it's possible to come here just for your meal if you make a reservation. In summer, the tables are graced with clusters of pink or blue hydrangea from the garden, and each is set with stemware and silver. The set meal for 8,000$ ($53.60), consists of four courses, with continental and regional dishes. The hors d'oeuvres are among the best, especially the crayfish and fish mousse. The dessert trolley is intriguing—pastries with light rich cream blended with a flaky crust and fruits. After-dinner coffee is taken on the adjoining terrace and loggia or in the dining room. Food is served daily from 12:30 to 2:30pm and 7:30 to 9:30pm. A pianist, harpist, and violinist often entertain. AE, DC, MC, V.

Moderate

The finest hotel in Sintra is the modern, airy **Hotel Tivoli Sintra,** Praça da República, 2710 Sintra (tel. 01/923-35-05; fax 01/923-15-72), opened in 1981. It lies only a few doors to the right of the Central Hotel (recommended below) and the National Palace. The hotel offers an abundance of modern conveniences, including a garage (most important in Sintra). Parking is free. However, the decorator stuck to the typical Portuguese style, and the combination of modern with traditional is successful. In the cavernous lobby the floors are made of marble. Brass lamps are used, and many earth tones are among the colors chosen. The 75 air-conditioned bedrooms are spacious and comfortably furnished, with complete bath, phone, color TV, video, radio, minibar, large beds, and big easy chairs for relaxation. The balconies and the public rooms look out onto a wooded hill, with views of some of Sintra's *quintas* (manor houses). The sight, according to readers Peter and Cynthia Hecker, of Berkeley, California, "could have inspired mad Ludwig of Bavaria or at least Walt Disney." Two persons can stay here for 16,500$ ($110.55) to 18,000$ ($120.60) daily, the price including breakfast. Singles cost 13,500$ ($90.45) to 15,000$ ($100.50). The hotel has a restaurant with panoramic views, the Monserrate, a bar, a beauty parlor, and a travel agency. Room service is available to midnight, and laundry and baby-sitting can be arranged. AE, DC, MC, V.

Estalagem Quinta da Capela, Monserrate, 2710 Sintra (tel. 01/929-01-70), a complex of two-story stone buildings, was built in the 16th century as a private home for the duc de Cadaval. Much later, the American ambassador to Portugal used it as his weekend retreat before being recalled from his assignment. Today, it is a country inn of 11 rooms and 3 suites, each with private bath and phone. Ten rooms contain TVs. Including breakfast, the single rate is 14,000$ ($81.74), rising to 17,000$ ($101.75) in a double. Suites begin at 19,000$ ($121.75). No meals, other than breakfast, are served. The gardens of Monserrate are visible from the breakfast room. A basement level health club and gym are available, as is a spring-fed swimming pool in the gardens. Follow the signs toward Seteais from Sintra, passing both the hamlet and gardens of Monserrate, after which you'll detect the stone columns and the sign marking the hotel's entrance. Parking is free. AE, DC, MC, V.

Quinta de São Thiago, Estrada de Monserrate, 2710 Sintra (tel. 01/923-29-23), is one of the most desirable places to stay in the Sintra area. Reached along a difficult road, it edges up a side of Sintra mountain. Its origins as a quinta go back to some time in the 1500s, and it's always been a private home. Now, in its role as an inn, it's been refurbished and handsomely furnished with antiques. Visited by Lord Byron in 1809, it enjoys a woodland setting. Rooms are not air conditioned nor do they have phones, but many of the 10 units open onto views of the Valley of Colares and the water beyond. On a hot day a special delight is the swimming pool, with its views of Monserrate and the coastline along the Atlantic.

In the finest British tradition, tea is offered in the parlor, which was transformed from the original kitchen. Dances are held in summer in the music room, and summertime buffets are a feature. Dinner is like eating in the private home of a Portuguese family. The cuisine is both regional and continental. Modern plumbing has been installed, and the quinta bedrooms are comfortably furnished and attractively decorated. Rates range from 15,000$ ($100.50) to 20,000$ ($134), including breakfast. Each room is suitable for a single or double. It's also recommended that you book ahead for a satisfying dinner in a lovely setting, at a cost of 5,000$ ($33.50), including your wine. Parking is free. No credit cards.

Budget

Central Hotel, Largo da Rainha D. Amélia 35, 2710 Sintra (tel. 01/923-09-63), should be given a heavy check with your pencil if you prefer a charming family-owned and -operated village inn offering personalized accommodations and good food. The hotel opens onto the main square of Sintra, facing the National Palace. Because of its location, accommodations facing the square are noisy. The facade is inviting, with decorative blue-and-white tiles and an awning-covered front veranda with dining tables. The interior, especially the bedrooms, reflects an English background. Each of the 14 rooms is furnished individually, with a reliance on fine old pieces—polished wood, inlaid desks. The baths, one to nearly every room, are well designed, with tiles and cheerful colors, and each unit has a phone. The cost for one person in a room with bath is 9,800$ ($65.65) nightly, increasing to 10,500$ ($70.35) for two. Breakfast costs 600$ ($4) extra.

The restaurant of the Central offers a choice of dining on the veranda overlooking the village, or in one of the large interior rooms. The cooking is primarily Portuguese, with such main courses as escalopes of veal in a Madeira sauce, veal cutlet milanese, beef Portuguese, and chateaubriand for two. A traditional dessert, homemade caramel pudding, makes a smooth finish. You can enjoy a complete dinner for 3,500$ ($23.45) and up. Food is served from 12:30 to 3pm and 8 to 9pm daily. AE, DC, MC, V.

Estalagem da Raposa, Rua Alfredo Costa 3, 2710 Sintra (tel. 01/923-04-65; fax 01/923-57-57), formerly was a private home that belonged to an old Sintra family. It's been run as an inn for 40 years, and is centrally located, within walking distance of the railroad station. The house is set back from the street in a fenced and flowered yard. The inn is owned by a Lisbon family who make you feel at home immediately. They keep a careful eye on the housekeeping and upkeep of the nine high-ceilinged rental units. Rooms all have tile baths, and they're furnished with old-fashioned pieces that are homey and comfortable. A double room with breakfast rents for 5,300$ ($35.50) in winter, 6,700$ ($44.90) in summer. The maid who keeps the rooms in spotless condition is polite, and she runs right up with a ring of keys to open your door the moment she hears you on the carpeted stairs. You can enjoy regional specialties in the tearoom. Parking is not available. AE, DC, MC, V.

A Nearby Place to Stay

At Alcabideche, **Sintra Estoril Hotel,** No. 9 ão km 6 (Junto ão Autodromo), 2765 Alcabideche (tel. 01/269-07-21; fax 01/269-07-20), is a crescent-shaped hotel between Sintra, Cascais, and Estoril. On the outside it looks like a stadium, with encircling balconies. It's not unlike a modern museum inside, with its bedroom balconies opening onto a large playground area, Olympic-size swimming pool, and tennis and volleyball courts. Its lounges are varied, lofty, and warmly colored. A few public rooms have drama, with shimmering mirrored walls, circular sofas, or a wall of abstract sculpture. Even the 187 bedrooms have their own contemporary character, with built-in headboards, phones, TV, radios, and piped-in music. All have two double beds, air conditioning, a terrace, and tile bath; some contain minibars. A single rents for 16,000$ ($107.20) daily, rising to 18,000$ ($120.60) in a double. The hotel also rents five suites, costing from 35,000$ ($234.50). Breakfast is included, live music is played nightly in the bar, and every Friday evening a folkloric show is presented. The restaurant serves an international cuisine. Room service is available 24 hours, and baby-sitting and laundry can be arranged. The hotel also has a sauna. AE, DC, MC, V.

WHERE TO DINE

The most reliable choice is the **Hotel Tivoli Sintra,** Praça da República (tel. 923-35-05). Because of its concealment within the concrete-and-glass walls of the town center's most desirable hotel, many visitors might overlook its impressive possibilities as a dining spot. Actually, it serves some of the finest food in town, priding itself on its associations with two hotels of note in nearby Lisbon. Staffed by a battalion of uniformed waiters, the place is capped with a shimmering metallic ceiling, ringed with dark paneling, and illuminated along one side with floor-to-ceiling panoramic windows. Full Portuguese and international meals, priced from 5,000$ ($33.50), are served daily from 12:30 to 2:30pm and 7:30 to 9:30pm. Specialties include tournedos Rossini, a delectable version of fish soup, filet of turbot elegantly prepared house style with mushrooms and garlic, and seafood. Reservations are suggested. AE, DC, MC, V.

Galeria Real, Rua Tude de Sousa, in São Pedro de Sintra (tel. 923-16-61), is a unique mixture of antique galleries and an 18th-century-style restaurant. The Galeria Real is one of the most impressive-looking places in Portugal. On the ground floor is a cocktail lounge as well as eight shops crammed with antiques, busts, and paintings. Going up a balustraded staircase, you come to further antique shops and a sumptuous restaurant. The main dining room has a hand-painted beamed ceiling, tile floors, small wooden-frame windows, and candles and flowers on each table. All this is a perfect setting for gracious dining on Portuguese cuisine. Lunch and dinner might start with a melon cocktail, followed by a filet of sole or a *queijada de bacalhau* (a codfish soufflé, which is a specialty of the house). The final course might be veal cutlets or a steak, topped by assorted desserts. On the à la carte menu, expect to spend 6,000$ ($40.20). A tourist menu costs 5,000$ ($33.50). Food is served from 12:30 to 2:30pm and 7:30 to 10pm; closed Monday night. Reservations are needed. AE, DC, MC, V.

Restaurante Solar S. Pedro, Praça Dom Fernando II 12, off the Largo da Feira in São Pedro de Sintra (tel. 923-18-60), is run by the helpful and hospitable Francisco Freitas, who speaks English. His place is a popular rendezvous, as diners are drawn not only to his personality but to his good selection of Portuguese cuisine, as well as Italian and French specialties. The lobster crêpes are a favorite, and another specialty is a flavorsome filet of sole. Trout with cream and toasted almonds is perfectly balanced. Also excellent is the steak Café Paris. Many of the beef specialties are distinguished as well, including the peppersteak and the entrecôte with mushrooms. Dinners cost 3,100$ ($20.75) to 4,500$ ($30.15). Hours are noon to 3pm and 7:30 to 10pm. A lovely windowless room, the restaurant is decorated with tiles, wrought-iron, and regional artifacts. Reservations are advised. It's closed Wednesday. AE, DC, MC, V.

Tacho Real, Rua da Ferraria 4 (tel. 923-52-77). Sometimes Portuguese diners come all the way from Lisbon to enjoy a well-prepared meal at this restaurant. Fish and meat dishes are deftly handled in the kitchen, which turns out an array of Portuguese regional food and international specialties. Service is efficient and polite. It is open Thursday to Tuesday from 12:30 to 3pm and 7:30 to 10pm. An average meal costs from 3,000$ ($20.10) to 4,000$ ($26.80). Reservations are advised. AE, DC, MC, V.

A Tiborna, Largo da Rainha D. Amélia 6 (tel. 923-48-03), is one of the most popular cafés in Sintra (it's also a small restaurant), in an easy-to-find location on the main square, Praça da República. There's a well-stocked bar against one wall, but most drinkers try to secure one of the tables that spill out onto the sidewalk, where you can watch the eternal international parade. Or else you can retreat to the rear to enjoy the chef's array of dishes for the day from a Portuguese cuisine. The bill of fare is likely to include roast veal Sintra style, escalope of veal with mushrooms, or filet of fish with a shellfish sauce. Expect to spend from 1,700$ ($11.40) for a complete à la carte meal. A tourist menu is offered for 1,350$ ($9.05). Hours are 9am to 11:30pm Tuesday to Sunday. No credit cards.

Restaurant Alcobaça, Rua dos Padarias 7 (tel. 923-16-51). Popular with English visitors, this shop-size restaurant occupies two floors of a centrally located building on a steep and narrow pedestrian street. The place is *very* local, and consequently provides one of the cheapest meals in town. As you'd expect, Alcobaça serves typical Portuguese cuisine, including roast sardines, caldo verde, hake filet with rice, octopus, Alcobaça chicken, and many other dishes. Meals cost from 1,500$ ($10.05). It is open Thursday to Tuesday from noon to 4pm and 7 to 10pm. It is closed in December. No credit cards.

---

7. Colares

At the end of the Serra de Sintra toward the sea is Colares, a small town with winding streets, old quintas, bright flowers, and vineyards. It is known for its white and red wines produced from grapes grown on the surrounding sandy soil. The good soil and sea breezes help assure the fundamental ingredient for some of the best wine of the country.

Colares lies 22 miles west of Lisbon and 5 miles west of Sintra. Many visitors drive here just to see the wineries, but others seek accommodations, preferring the quiet town to more crowded Sintra (where you'll find the nearest tourist office).

WHERE TO STAY

Pensão Residential do Conde, Rua Quinta do Conde, Colares, 2710 Sintra (tel. 01/929-16-52), was originally built as a farmhouse in 1737. In the 1950s it was greatly expanded by a German family as their vacation home. Set on a cul-de-sac in the upper reaches of Colares, it lies just north of the center. It sports 2 acres of garden, a flagstone-covered terrace, and a sophisticated ownership by Yorkshire-born Dave and Jean Tinsley. It is decorated in a rustic style with a fireplace and regional furniture. The property opens onto a view of the faraway sea, lemon groves, and the hilltops of Sintra. It rents 11 bedrooms, including a garden cottage with its own bath. It is open February through October. The inn charges from 7,600$ ($50.95) daily in a single and 8,600$ ($57.60) in a double, plus 100$ (65¢) for a continental breakfast. Each room contains a private bath, but TVs and radios are deliberately not included to achieve tranquillity for guests. There is no air conditioning. Parking is free. No credit cards.

About 1¼ miles outside Colares stands the **Hotel Miramonte,** Estrada Nacional 155, Pinhal da Nazaré, Colares, 2710 Sintra (tel. 01/929-12-30). What a visitor sees from the road appears to be an attractively maintained modern hotel, with an accommodating front porch and a screen of flowers and vines. You'll soon discover that this well-directed hotel stretches almost endlessly through a series of flower-ringed patios, pine-shaded terraces, and one of the most beautifully landscaped swimming pools in the region; there's even a Japanese garden. The 89 well-organized bedrooms are usually inhabited by a quiet, often British, group of vacationers eager to take in the beauty of the surrounding countryside. Each unit has a private bath and phone. Singles cost 9,000$ ($60.30); doubles 12,500$ ($83.75), including breakfast. Half board ranges from 9,000$ ($60.30) to 14,000$ ($93.80) per person daily. A bus running between Sintra and Azenhas do Mar stops in front of the hotel. There's mini-golf on the property, plus disco dancing at the hotel three times a week. Parking is free. No credit cards.

---

8. Mafra Palace

Palácio Nacional de Mafra, 2640 Mafra (tel. 523-32), baroque chef d'oeuvre of precision craftsmanship, is an ensemble of discipline, grandeur, and majesty. At the peak of its construction, it is said to have employed a working force of 50,000 Portuguese men. A small town was built just to house the workers. Its master model was El Escorial, that Daedalian maze constructed by Philip II outside Madrid. Mafra's corridors and complex immurements may not be as impressive, nor as labyrinthine, but the diversity of its contents is amazing. The end product was 880 rooms, housing 300 friars, who could look through 4,500 doorways and windows.

That devout king of "peace and prosperity," João V, seemingly couldn't sire an heir, and court gossips openly speculated that he was sterile. One day he casually mentioned to a Franciscan that if he were rewarded with an heir, he would erect a monastery to the order. Apparently the Franciscans, through what the king considered "divine intervention," came through. João produced his heir and Mafra was born, the work beginning in 1717. Originally it was to house 13 friars, but that figure rapidly mushroomed into 300.

It is said that Mafra, 13 years in the making, was built with gold and diamonds pouring in from the new colony of Brazil. Seeing it now, and considering building methods in those days, one wonders how such a task was ever completed in so short a time.

Its more than 110 chimes, made in Antwerp, can be heard from a distance of 12 to 15 miles when they are played at Sunday recital. Holding the chimes are two towers which flank a basilica, capped by a dome that has been compared to that of St. Paul's in London. The inside of the church is a varied assortment of chapels, 11 in all, expertly crafted with detailed jasper reredos, bas-reliefs, and marble statues from Italy. In the monastery is the pride of Mafra, a 40,000-volume library with tomes 200 and 300 years old, many gold-leafed. Viewed by some more favorably than the world-famed library at Coimbra, the room is a study in gilded light, decorated in what has been called grisaille rococo. In the Museum of Religious Art, the collection of elaborately decorated vestments is outstanding.

Following the omnipresent red Sintra marble, you enter the monks' pharmacy, hospital, and infirmary, the beds without mattresses. Later you can explore the spacious kitchens and the penitents' cells, with the flagellation devices used by the monks.

The summer residence of kings, Mafra was home to such members of Portuguese royalty as the banished Queen Carlota Joaquina. In addition to his love of painting, Carlos I, the Bragança king assassinated at Praça do Comércio in 1908, was also an avid hunter. In one room, he had chandeliers made out of antlers and upholstery of animal skins. His son, who ruled for 2 years as Manuel II, spent his last night on Portuguese soil at Mafra before fleeing with his mother, Amélia, to England.

You can wander through the trompe l'oeil–ceilinged audience room, the sewing room of Maria I, and the music room of Carlos. Throughout the apartments hang decaying tapestries, taking their place among antiques, ceramics, and silverware.

The charge for admission is 300$ ($2) from June to September and 200$ ($1.35) from October through May. Hours are from 10am to noon and 2 to 5pm Wednesday through Monday. An RN bus from Lisbon runs to Mafra, lying 25 miles west of the Portuguese capital.

WHERE TO STAY & DINE

For good accommodations, I recommend the **Hotel Castelão,** Avenida 25 de Abril, 2640 Mafra (tel. 061/812-050; fax 061/51-698), which has 34 comfortable rooms furnished with easy chairs, reading lamps, and carpeted floors, all having complete baths, TVs, radios, minibars, and phones. Guests can relax in a reading room. Singles cost from 6,500$ ($43.55) daily, and doubles run from 8,300$ ($55.60). The hotel has four bars and a typical wine cellar. The restaurant, where well-prepared meals cost from 1,500$ ($10.05), has a panoramic view over the main street of the village. The location of the hotel is excellent, right in the heart of Mafra. AE, DC, MC, V.

---

9. Ericeira

Some 32 miles northwest of Lisbon and a quick 13 miles west across the countryside from Sintra, this fishing port nestles on the Atlantic shore. Its narrow streets are lined with whitewashed houses, accented by pastel-painted corners and window frames. To the east, the mountains of Sintra appear.

The sea has been giving life to Ericeira for 700 years and continues to do so today. Not only do the fishermen pluck their food from it, but it is the sea, especially the beach, that lures streams of visitors every summer, adding a much-needed shot in the arm to the local economy. Along the coast lobsters are bred in cliffside nurseries, *serração*. Anyplace in Ericeira, lagosta is la specialité de la maison.

In 1584 Mateus Álvares arrived in Ericeira from the Azores, claiming to be King Sebastião (The Desired One), who was killed (some say disappeared) on the battlefields of North Africa. Álvares and about two dozen of his chief supporters were finally executed after their defeat by the soldiers of Philip II of Spain; but he is today remembered as the king of Ericeira. It wasn't until an October day in 1910 that the second monumental event occurred at Ericeira. From the harbor, the fleeing Manuel II and his mother, Amélia, set sail on their yacht to a life of exile in England.

For such a small place, there are quite a few sights of religious and historic interest. The **Church of São Pedro** (St. Peter) and the **Misericórdia** (charitable institution) both contain rare 17th- and 18th-century paintings. The **Hermitage of São Sebastião,** with its Moorish designs, would seem more fitting in North Africa. There is one more hermitage honoring **St. Anthony.**

The chloride-rich spring waters of **Santa Maria** attract health-spa enthusiasts. But it is the crescent-shaped sandy **Praja do Sol** that is the favorite of Portuguese and foreign visitors alike. Ericeira maintains bus connections with both Sintra and Lisbon (you can also take the train from Lisbon to Mafra, where connections can be made).

The **Ericeira Tourist Office** is at Rua Mendes Leal (tel. 631-22).

WHERE TO DINE

If you're passing through for the day, a good restaurant stopover is **Parreirinha,** Rua Dr. Miguel Bombarda 12 (tel. 621-48). Lots of seafood dishes, as expected, appear on the Portuguese menu, but I always gravitate to their tender pork cooked with baby clams. Steak, which is the most expensive item on the menu, is cooked with a special hot sauce, the recipe for which is known only to the chef. The service is accommodating. You'll want to stick around for supper. Everything tastes better when washed down with a bottle of vinho verde. Meals cost from 2,000$ ($13.40), and a tourist menu goes for 1,500$ ($10.05). The restaurant is closed Tuesday and in November. Hours are noon to 3:30pm and 7:30 to 10pm. Reservations aren't needed. No credit cards.

O Poço, Calçada da Baleia 10 (tel. 636-69), is another good place to eat. You are served a wide range of cookery, with Portuguese and international specialties, especially seafood, predominating. Some 50 diners can pack in here, taking a table overlooking the esplanade and paying from 2,500$ ($16.75) for a good and filling à la carte menu. A tourist menu costs 1,600$ ($10.70). Specialties include tournedos in a Madeira sauce with fried banana, monkfish with prawns and potatoes, and sole Ericeira style. Food is served daily from noon to 4pm and 7 to 10pm. The restaurant is closed Wednesday in winter. Reservations aren't needed. AE, DC, MC, V.

SOUTH OF THE TAGUS

As 19th-century continental travelers from Victorian England crossed the Tagus by boat and headed for the scenic wonders on the left bank of Lisbon, chances are, under one arm they carried a gold-leafed copy of a work by Robert Southey, England's poet laureate. After all, this Lake poet, a much-traveled gentleman, did more than anyone to publicize the glories that awaited his compatriots on the other bank. He virtually made the trek famous when he wrote: "I have never seen such a sublime panorama as the Arrábida Mountains afford, which, constantly changing as we go our way, offer us new beauties at every turn."

Nowadays the narrow isthmus south of the Tagus is fast booming into a major attraction. Behind the upsurge of interest is the Ponte 25 de Abril, the longest suspension bridge in Europe. It has speeded traffic and development to the area, and now it is possible to cross the Tagus in minutes, then head rapidly across good roads through pine groves to the vertices of the triangle known as "The Land of the Three Castles": Sesimbra, Setúbal, and Palmela. Of course, traditionalists still prefer taking the ferry from Praça do Comércio in Lisbon, docking in Cacilhas.

The isthmus, long cut off from the Portuguese capital, is wild, rugged, lush, and productive. The strip of land plummets toward the sea, stretches along for miles of sandy beaches, and rolls through groves heavy with the odors of ripening oranges and vineyards of grapes used to make muscatel. With craggy cliffs and coves in the background, the crystalline waters of the Atlantic are ideal for swimming and skindiving, or for fishing for tuna, swordfish, and bass.

Sandy beaches double as the sites of fish auctions and leisurely sunbathing. Farther up from the sardine-canning center of Setúbal, the coastline roughens where the Serra of Arrábida meets the sea, resulting in an abundance of caves, grottoes, and precipitous crags.

The land possesses vivid reminders of its past, reflected in Moorish architectural influences, Roman ruins and roads, traces of the Phoenicians, and Spanish fortresses. Mighty castles and humble fishermen's cottages alike shook on a November day in 1755 when the earthquake brought Lisbon to its knees. Signs of that catastrophe are still evidenced in the ruins of the hamlet of Palmela, and the lonely walls of Coina Castle.

Its proximity to Lisbon (Setúbal is only 25 miles south of the capital) makes it ideal for a 1-day excursion. But its unusual inns and moderate tariffs mark it as a place where the budget-minded reader will want to linger.

1. Azeitão

This sleepy village lies in the heart of quinta country. In Portuguese, a *quinta* means a farm, villa, or country house. At its most meager, it is a simple farmhouse surrounded by lands. At its best, it is a mansion of great architectural style filled with art decorations. Azeitão boasts the best.

It is said that King Manuel I started the concept of quintas in the early 16th century when he built the **Quinta de Bacalhoa** at Vila Fresca de Azeitão (tel. 208-00-11). The king's mother once lived there. In time it was taken over by the son of Afonso de Albuquerque. At one point in its history the building was owned by the Braganças, eventually falling into disrepair, as many of its decorations, specifically its antique tiles, were carted off by vandals.

Before World War II the mansion was purchased by an American woman who worked for years restoring it as much as possible to its original condition. The architecture is characterized by loggias, pavilions, half-moon domes that suggest a Moorish influence, and a trio of pyramided towers. One of the panels of 16th-century azulejos (tiles) depicts an innocent Susanna being hotly pursued by lecherous Elders. Some architectural critics have suggested that the palace is the first sign of the Renaissance in Portugal. Bacalhoa is a private villa, but its gardens are open to the public upon request from 1 to 5pm, except Sunday and holidays. Admission is 50$ (35¢).

The farmland of the quinta is devoted to vineyards, owned by J. M. da Fonseca, International-Vinhos, Lda., makers of Lancers wine. There are two J. M. da Fonseca wineries half a mile apart: the "mother house," as it is called, and a newer plant characterized by white domes. The original winery and warehouses are in the center of Azeitão, as is the classic 19th-century house that was the Fonseca family home. A little museum and public reception room can be visited on the ground floor of the house. The century-old Fonseca wineries have made their product from grapes grown on the slopes of the Arrábida Mountains since the early 19th century, and the fine muscatel for which they have long been known is used in the flavoring and sweetening of white Lancers. Of course, the Fonseca vintners produce other wines you might like to try besides the popular Lancers, much of which is exported. Their top product is a muscatel called Setúbal, rarely sent abroad but considered delectable by wine connoisseurs.

Another 16th-century mansion, **Quinta das Torres,** is open not just for visits —you can stop for a meal or even spend the night (see below).

Azeitão makes a good base for trekkers, especially those who want to scale the limestone Serra of Arrábida by foot. Others settle for long walks through scented pine woods or silvery olive groves. To cap your day, you can order some Azeitão cheese and a bottle of local muscatel. The village lies 9½ miles north of Setúbal, 15½ miles south of Lisbon.

There is no local tourist office and the nearest tourist office in Setúbal is not likely to have any information.

WHERE TO STAY & DINE

A 16th-century baronial mansion of deteriorating elegance, **Quinta das Torres,** Estrada Nacional 5, Azeitão, 2900 Setúbal (tel. 065/208-00-01), has been kept intact on purpose for those desiring to live quietly, stepping back in time. It has been owned by the same family for many generations. The estate is approached through large gates and along a tree-lined driveway. Gradually, a pair of square peaked towers framing the entrance terrace comes into view. Ten bedrooms, all with private bath, have been set aside for paying guests. Each is quite different, ranging from smaller chambers to a ballroom-size suite dominated by princess-style brass beds, with a high tester and soft, flouncy ruffles. Some of the rooms have high shuttered windows, time-mellowed tile floors, antique furnishings, vases of fresh flowers, oil lamps, and niches with saints or madonnas. A single room, with breakfast, goes for 9,000$ ($60.30) daily, a double for 13,000$ ($87.10).

The dining room of the Quinta has a covered ceiling, a tall stone fireplace where log fires are lit on chilly evenings, plus elaborate scenic tiles depicting "The Rape of the Sabine Women" and "The Siege of Troy." The rich-tasting, heavy cuisine is well recommended, and a meal will cost around 3,000$ ($20.10). The bill of fare is likely to include smoked filet of pork, steak au poivre, and giant prawns. Food is served daily from 1 to 3pm and 7 to 9pm.

---

2. Sesimbra

Among the Portuguese, Sesimbra used to be a closely guarded secret. With justification, it was considered one of the most unspoiled fishing villages in the country. Nowadays, rapid new building and growth have occurred. High-rise buildings overshadow the old life. However, the varinas and fishermen still go about their time-honored task of plucking their livelihood from the Atlantic. Against a backdrop of rocky cliffs, sardines, shellfish, whiting, and the scabbard fish, with its whip-shaped body and daggerlike teeth, lie stretched out in the sun. When the fleet comes in, the day's catch is auctioned at a lota at the harbor (Porto Abrigo).

Far down the beach, beyond the boat-clogged harbor, is the 17th-century **Fortress of St. Teodosio,** built to fortify the region against the pirates who plagued and plundered, carting off the most beautiful women and young girls.

A walk along the ruined battlements of the five-towered **Castle of Sesimbra** reduces the village to a nearly immobile miniature. The castle was captured from the Moors in 1165 and rebuilt following the 1755 earthquake, which sent sections of its crenellated walls tumbling to the ground. Enclosed within is a 12th-century church, the oldest monument in Sesimbra. Sesimbra also enjoys popularity as an angling center.

The resort lies 19 miles south of Lisbon, 17 miles west of Setúbal. Sesimbra is connected by bus to Lisbon. Departures are from the Praça de Espanha in Lisbon, and the trip takes 1 hour. You can also get to Sesimbra by taking the ferry from Praça do Comércio wharf, then a bus from Cacilhas. The nearest train station is in Setúbal (see below).

From Sesimbra, you can head east to the headland of **Cape Espichel,** with its arcaded pilgrim hospices dating from the 1700s. Often violently windswept with sea gulls circling overhead, this strip of land has been called the "Land's End of Portugal," a reference to the far western extremity of England. A pilgrimage church, Santuario Nossa Senhora do Cabo, in a state of disrepair, occupies space in this melancholy atmosphere. You can go inside, inspecting its baroque interior with gilded wood and sculpture. Later, you can walk to the edge of the cliffs in back of the church for a spectacular view. Beware: There's no guard rail, and it's a sheer drop of 350 feet to the ocean waters. Modern sculpture is placed about in this forlorn setting. At the southern end of the Arrábida chain, this pilgrimage site has been popular since the 13th century. It was here in 1180 that Fuas Roupinho routed the Moors at sea, his forces capturing several ships of the enemy.

The **Sesimbra Tourist Office** is at Largo de Marinha (tel. 223-57-43).

SPECIAL EVENTS
The year's festivities begin with "Carnaval"—"Mardi Gras" (Shrove Tuesday/Pancake Tuesday), when there is always a cortege that attracts a great number of young people. There is also the typical "Cegadas," consisting of a kind of popular burlesque theater, usually made only by men, where the political, economic, or just daily-life events of the town, government, or country are satirized.

In April (no fixed date) to promote Sesimbra's gastronomy, there is "Festa do Peixe e do Marisco." Apart from special dishes based on fish and shellfish, this event has several other activities: music, exhibitions, and contests.

From May 3 to 5, there is a religious festivity: "Festas em Honra do Senhor Jesus das Chagas"—the celebration of the patron saint of the fishermen. On May 4 is a procession and the blessing of the sea. As it is common in Portuguese religious festivities, it has an exuberant side: a town fair.

From June 23 to 30, the Festivities of the Popular Saints are presented. During this period the streets are gaily decorated. At night bonfires, marches, and sometimes fado give a joyful atmosphere to the event.

From July 25 to 28, the celebration of the town's patron saint, S. Tiago, takes place. The event is marked by several cultural events, including dance.

In the last Sunday of September there is another religious feast: "Our Lady of the Cape," with a procession and a small fair.

In October (no fixed date) there is the "Festival do Mar," an event with cultural, sports, and gastronomic activities.

WHERE TO STAY

One of the most unusual self-contained beach-resort hotels south of the Tagus, **Hotel do Mar,** Rua General Humberto Delgado 10 2070 Sesimbra (tel. 01/223-33-26; fax 01/223-38-88), is a beehive construction of units spreading from a high cliff to the water below. The passageways are like continuous art galleries, with contemporary paintings and ceramic plaques and sculpture, and the main lobby houses a glassed-in aviary with tropical birds. During the day one can soak up sun at the beach or at the circular swimming pool. The 120 bedrooms each have their own bath, phone, and private terrace, with a view of the ocean and gardens sweeping down the hillside. Furnishings are streamlined and well selected; the rooms are airy, with breakfast served on a flower-filled terrace. Singles cost from 24,700$ ($165.50) daily and doubles, from 25,500$ ($170.85), including breakfast. Children under 8 sharing a room with their parents get a 50% reduction.

The hotel restaurant is warmed with wood-grain paneling and overlooks the sea. If you're stopping off on a day-trip from Lisbon, you can order a meal for 3,500$ ($23.45) and up. The before-dinner gathering point is a rustically styled bar; after dinner guests congregate in a living room, with a fireplace. The concierge will arrange for everything from fishing to hairdressing appointments to excursions by private boats. There are two tennis courts on the premises. The hotel operates transfer services. Parking is free. AE, DC, MC, V.

Hotel Espadarte, Avenida 25 de Abril 11, 2970 Sesimbra (tel. 01/22-33-189), is named after the swordfish which once flourished in local waters. The five-floor hotel is right on the esplanade, and below the incline ramp are boats and seamen mending their nets. Open all year, the hotel receives guests in its 80 bedrooms, each with private bath or shower and phone. Most of the accommodations also have private balconies overlooking the sea. Room furnishings, a sort of 1960s decor, are simple but comfortable. Including breakfast, singles rent for 6,700$ ($44.85) daily, with doubles costing 9,500$ ($63.65). The Concha do Mar restaurant specializes in seafood, and there's also a self-service section. In the Bar Miami, guests can dance or watch a movie. There is also a solarium, along with laundry facilities and individual safes. Parking is free. AE, DC, MC, V.

WHERE TO DINE

In the square near the town hall, **Chez Nous,** Largo do Município 11–13 (tel. 223-01-41), is an attractive restaurant behind a handful of sidewalk tables. When the owner, José P. Costa, founded it, he brought back to Portugal some of the culinary techniques he had learned during his stay in Mozambique. The walls of the interior are covered with dark green lattice, creating a garden effect around the bistro-style tables that sit close to one another with a view of the exposed kitchen. There, an array of employees concoct such Portuguese specialties as grilled prawns, rice with seafood, mussels Chez Nous, kebabs of squid, filet of catfish, and peppersteak, which cost from 4,000$ ($26.80), although a tourist menu is presented for 1,900$ ($12.75). Call for a reservation. The restaurant serves food from noon to 3pm and 7 to 11pm. It is closed Monday for lunch and in November. AE, DC, MC, V.

Restaurante Ribamar, Avenida dos Náufragos (tel. 223-48-53), serves some of the best Portuguese cookery in the area, specializing in fish and shellfish, most of it freshly caught in local waters. Its location is in front of the sea, a short stroll from the beach, with a view of the bay. There is space for about 60 seats outside and 80 inside. The chef's specialty is a platter of mixed fish and shellfish (served for two persons). Downstairs are two large aquariums where guests can "catch" their own lobster, crayfish, or crab. A typical meal here averages 3,000$ ($20.10) to 4,500$ ($30.15), and service is daily from noon to 3pm and 7 to 10:30pm. Reservations are recommended. MC, V.

---

3. Portinho da Arrábida

The limestone Arrábida Mountains stretch for about 22 miles, beginning at Palmela, and rolling to a dramatic end at Cape Espichel on the Atlantic. At times the cliffs and bluffs are so high that it seems you have to peer through the clouds to see the purple waters of the Atlantic below.

A Swiss botanist once said the mountain range contained "the most amazing flora to be seen in Europe." The foliage that rims the cliffs and the surrounding areas is lush, subtropical, and wide ranging, with everything from holm oaks, sweet bay, pines, laurel, juniper, cypress, araucaria, magnolia, lavender, myrtle, and pimpernels. A riot of color and fragrance carpets the mountains.

The serra is riddled with numerous caves and grottoes, the best known of which is the **Lapa de Santá Margarida.** Of it, Hans Christian Andersen wrote: "It is a veritable church hewn out of the living rock, with a fantastic vault, organ pipes, columns, and altars."

Perched on a hillside like a tiara over Portinho da Arrábida, the **New Convent** dates from the 16th century. You can go to the gate and ring for the caretaker, who may or may not show you around the precincts.

Plummeting down to the sea, you arrive at Portinho da Arrábida, at the foot of the sêrra. This is a favorite oasis with many families from Lisbon who rent little multicolored cottages on the beach. If you take a car down here in July and August, you do so at your own risk. There is virtually no parking space, and the road should be one way but isn't. You can be stranded for hours trying to get back up the hill. The other problem is this: to walk down and back could qualify you for the Olympics. Portinho da Arrábida, which can be approached from either Setúbal or Sesimbra, lies about 23 miles south of Lisbon. By public transportation, you must make RN bus connections in Sesimbra or Setúbal.

WHERE TO DINE

In summer, as mentioned, it is both frustrating and dangerous to take a car down the narrow, winding road whose edges are jammed with cars. More knowing visitors try to park on a wider road above the port, and then negotiate the hordes of summer visitors on foot. The walk back is steep and only for the hearty. However, a meal at **Restaurante Beira-Mar** (without street name), Portinho da Arrábida (tel. 208-05-44), can be your reward for the trek. The most sought-after warm-weather tables at this airy restaurant are set out on a concrete balcony, a few feet above the still waters of the port, near the many fishing vessels. White paper usually serves as the napery for the savory but unpretentiously informal Portuguese meals that are the rule here. Full meals, costing from 2,800$ ($18.75) each, include pork with clams, roast chicken, fish stew, grilled sardines, several preparations of codfish, grilled sole, shellfish rice, and several regional wines. A tourist menu is featured for 1,650$ ($11.05). Food is served daily from noon to 9:30pm, except Wednesday from October to April. The restaurant shuts down in December. No credit cards.

4. Setúbal

On the right bank of the Sado River, 25 miles south of Lisbon, lies one of Portugal's largest and most ancient cities, said to have been founded by the grandson of Noah. Motorists often include it on their itineraries because of an exceptional inn, the **Pousada de São Filipe**, installed in a late-16th-century fort overlooking the sea (see below).

Setúbal is known as the center of Portugal's sardine industry and for the production of the most exquisite muscatel wine in the world. As far back as the days of the Romans and the Visigoths, the aromatic and hearty grapes of this region were praised by connoisseurs.

Orange groves (a jam is made from the fruit), orchards, vineyards, and outstanding beaches (a popular one, **Praia da Figueirinha**) compose the environs of Setúbal. And the white pyramidal mounds you see dotting the landscape are deposits of sea salt drying in the sun, another major commercial asset of this seaside community.

Many artists and writers have come from Setúbal, none more notable than the 18th-century Portuguese poet Manuel Maria Barbosa du Bocage, a forerunner of romanticism. At Praça do Bocage, a monument honors him.

In Setúbal is the late 15th-century **Convento de Jesus** (tel. 52-47-72), first example of the Manueline style of architecture. Of particular interest are the main chapel and the ornate decorations on the main doorway and the Arrábida marble columns. Each of the latter is actually three columns twisted together like taffy to form a cable or rootlike effect. Somehow they don't seem to hold up the vaulted ceiling, but give the illusion of appendages grown down to the floor. Raymond Postgate wrote that the columns "look as if they had been twisted and wrung by a washerwoman," and Hans Christian Andersen recorded that the monument was "one of the most beautiful small churches that I have ever seen." The church has been heavily restored, the latest wholesale renovation in 1969–70. Adjoining is the unpretentious **Museu da Cidade** (Town Museum) housing some early 16th-century Portuguese paintings, as well as some Spanish and Flemish works and a contemporary art section. The museum has since 1983 a Temporary Exhibitions Gallery where you can see different works. The church-museum is at the Praça Miguel Bombarda, off Avenida 22 de Dezembro (no phone). The museum is open Tuesday to Sunday from 9am to noon and 2 to 5pm, with no admission charged.

To reach this port, where windmills still clack in the countryside, roosters crow, and the "girls of the sardines" seem to speak Portuguese with Arabic accent, take the ferry from Lisbon to Barreiro. There, you can board a train for the rest of the way.

WHERE TO STAY

Pousada de São Filipe, Castelo de São Filipe, 2900 Setúbal (tel. 065/52-38-44; fax 065/52-38-44), is a fortress-castle, dating back to 1590. It was built by an Italian architect who came to Portugal during the ill-fated reign of the young king Sebastião. The builder perched it on a hilltop overlooking the town and the harbor. You wind your way up a curving mountain road, passing through a stone arch, by towers to the belvedere. Rooms that once were for the soldiers and the governor have been tastefully and richly furnished with antiques and reproductions. In earlier days there were guns and ammunition, but they have given way to soft beds and ornate Portuguese crafted headboards. The walls of the chapel and the public rooms contain tile dados, depicting scenes from the life of São Filipe and the life of the Virgin Mary. Nearby there is a small chapel decorated with tiles that depict the life of São Filipe. They are dated 1736 and signed by Policarpo de Oliveira Bernardes.

The 14 bedrooms are individually decorated, each with private bath and TV. Some rooms are air conditioned. They are reached via what seems like miles of plant-filled corridors, up wide, worn stone steps. To stay here on a bed-and-breakfast basis costs 22,500$ ($150.75) daily in a double room, 19,700$ ($132) in a single. One suite is rented at 28,700$ ($192.30) a night.

Dining is pleasant, sitting in Windsor-style armchairs. Six alcoved windows open onto a panoramic view. Against a background of tile dado, a primitive tapestry, and photostated engravings, a luncheon or dinner, including many fish specialties, is served. Most guests take this meal when they stop over on a day-trip from Lisbon, paying from 3,300$ ($22.10) to 4,000$ ($26.80). The clients seem to gravitate to the medieval-style lounge, with its coved and arched ceiling, pierced-copper hanging lanterns, tile bar, and husky brass-studded armchairs. The sitting rooms are also intimate, with tile walls, antiques, bowls, engravings, chests, and copper artifacts in the niches. Parking is free, and laundry service is provided. The Pousada is reached by taxi from Setúbal, as it is too far for most people to walk. AE, DC, MC, V.

Esperança Hotel, Avenida Luisa Todi 220 (tel. 065/251-51), stands in the heart of Setúbal, on the main inner street. It's a modern six-story hotel, with basic amenities, a clean-cut lounge, plus a reception area with streamlined furnishings, all in a restrained design. Each bedroom is done in pastel colors and has built-in headboards, a dressing table, bedside lighting, and all-tile bath. The 64 rooms all contain phones. Singles run 7,700$ ($51.60) daily; doubles 8,300$ ($55.60), including breakfast. Twelve suites have TVs and cost 11,000$ ($73.70) a night. There is a dining room on the top floor that provides a panoramic view of the area, including the Sado River. The hotel also has a bar and nightclub. Laundry service is provided, and parking is free. Room service is available 24 hours. Bus: 2, 7, 8, or 20. AE, DC, MC, V.

WHERE TO DINE

In the center of town, **O Beco,** Largo da Misericórdia 24 (tel. 52-46-17), is entered through a narrow passageway that leads to two dining rooms, decorated in a typical style with old ovens, regional artifacts, and a fireplace. The service is efficient, the Portuguese food excellent. The quantities could be smaller and nobody would leave hungry. Shellfish soup is the classic opener. Pork chops are from the acorn-sweetened variety in Alentejo, and a special beefsteak is offered. *Cabrito* (goat) is also good. Two more recommendable regional dishes include a Portuguese stew, *cozido,* and paella. More adventurous seafaring palates will order the grilled squid. A typical dessert is the orange tart. Count on spending 1,500$ ($10.05) to 2,200$ ($14.75). Food is served from noon to 4pm and 7:15 to 11pm; closed Tuesday. Bus: 2, 7, 8, or 20. Closed from September 15 to October 2. Reservations aren't needed. AE, DC, MC, V.

Restaurante Bocage, Rua da Marqueza do Faial 8–10 (tel. 52-25-13). Old Portugal comes alive to visitors who approach the faded facade of this pink-walled town house, whose doors open onto a corner of the traffic-free main square of town. Inside you'll find a no-nonsense decor of 1950s-era ceiling fans, a coffered white ceiling, and a green-and-white terrazzo floor. Most patrons order a fruity muscatel to accompany the array of fresh fish served here. In deference to their almost exclusively local clientele, regional Portuguese cookery is emphasized. A meal is traditionally topped off with a taste of muscatel brandy, and full dinners cost from 2,800$ ($18.75). Hours are 12:15 to 3:30pm and 7:15 to 10:30pm daily. The restaurant is closed every Monday night and all day Tuesday. Reservations are not accepted. AE, DC, MC, V.

---

5. Tróia

Tróia is a long, sandy peninsula, across the Sado River estuary from Setúbal, which lies 25 miles south of Lisbon. The pine-studded strip of land is the site of one of Portugal's largest tourist enterprises, featuring the Torralta tourist complex with high-rise apartment hotels and a par-72, 6,970-yard, 18-hole golf course designed by Robert Trent Jones.

At **Cetóbriga,** ruins of a thriving Roman port have been discovered, with excavations beginning in the mid-19th century. The city, dating from the 3rd and 4th centuries, was destroyed by the ocean, but traces have been unearthed of villas, bathing pools, a temple decorated with frescoes, and a place for salt preservation of fish. There is also evidence that those long-ago seafarers, the Phoenicians, inhabited the peninsula at one time. Cetóbriga's ruins are about 1½ miles from the site of the present development of Tróia. Come here to enjoy the resort. Don't come looking for the ruins, as they are fenced off and not open at present for viewing by tourists. However, conditions may change.

You can reach Tróia by road, traveling on the N10 and the N120, turning toward the ocean in the vicinity of Comporta. Watch for the signs.

The best way to get there, however, is to go from Setúbal by car-ferry. The car-ferry leaves from near the commercial port in Setúbal every half hour in summer, every hour the rest of the year, taking about 20 minutes to cross.

WHERE TO STAY

An island resort, **Aparthotel Tróia,** Tróia, 2900 Setúbal (tel. 065/44-221), is a tourist development that's part of the Torralta golf course and high-rise complex with 397 apartments. Against a white background, most of the rooms have strong colors, wide, low white couches and lounge chairs, white globe lights, large paintings, dining room areas, complete kitchens, and private baths along with phones. Bedrooms are stark but attractive. Each apartment will house two to four persons. Rates range from 11,000$ ($73.70) to 16,500$ ($110.55) daily. There is no breakfast service and no room service. The view of the coastline is special, and there are encircling sandy beaches. It's complete with all the resort amenities. AE, DC, MC, V.

Torralta has several other apartment hotels in the complex, including **Rosamar and Magnóliamar,** Tróia, 2900 Setúbal (tel. 065/44-151), both in magnificent settings of sea and sand with the golf course close by. Like the Tróia, they are furnished in contemporary style, with many amenities to make a complete resort vacation. The Rosamar rents 138 apartments with no amenities such as phones or air conditioning. Apartments for two to three persons cost 15,900$ ($106.55), rising to 19,400$ ($130) for four. At the 128-unit Magnóliamar, units have phones and TVs, costing 19,750$ ($132.35) for two to three persons; 27,500$ ($184.25) for up to four guests. Laundry is provided, and the Magnóliamar also has 24-hour room service. The complex also offers an outdoor swimming pool. AE, DC, MC, V.

---

6. Palmela

The village of Palmela lies in the heart of a wine-producing region, in the foothills of the Arrábida Mountains 27 miles south of Lisbon and 5 miles east of Setúbal. It is famous for its fortress, from which, at a vantage point of 1,200 feet, you'll be rewarded with one of the most extensive and varied views in all of Portugal. Over sienna-hued valleys and vineyards heavy with grapes, one sees the capital to the north, the estuary of the Sado to the south.

The position of **Palmela Castle** has long been a strategic point in securing control of the lands south of the Tagus. It was from Palmela that Afonso Henriques, the first king of Portugal, drove out the Moors and established his new nation's domination of the district. The fortress was built in the 12th century, and was, in its day, a splendid example of medieval military architecture. It is further believed that the Celts founded a castle on this spot in 300 B.C.

Of special interest is the Roman road discovered behind the castle by archeologists. It is the only such road to be unearthed in Portugal, and makes for speculation as to its relationship with the Roman beach colonies of Tróia, off Setúbal. You can scale the hill to the castle any time of the day.

WHERE TO STAY & DINE

One of the last remaining segments of the 12th-century castle is the **Pousada do Castelo de Palmela,** 2950 Palmela (tel. 01/235-12-26; fax 01/235-04-10). It was built as a monastery within the castle walls in 1482 on orders of King João I and dedicated to St. James. The change to use as a pousada kept it from falling into complete ruin. The conversion was done skillfully and unobtrusively, so that the classic look and feel of a cloister has been preserved. It is located on the high crest of a hill, overlooking the valley and sea in the distance. It's traditional in design, a huge, square building opening into a large courtyard. The lower-level arches have been glassed in and furnished with lounge chairs.

Each of the 25 bedroom cells has been opened up, enlarged, and given a glamorous up-to-date ambience. The rooms are furnished in the Portuguese manner, with hand-carved pieces, fine fabrics, tile baths, TVs, and phones. Most of them open onto views. Rates are 19,700$ ($132) daily in a single and 22,500$ ($150.75) in a double. The inn also rents two suites, costing from 28,700$ ($192.30) to 43,400$ ($290.80). There is a comfortable drawing room near the dining room with a noteworthy washbasin once used by the monks for their ablutions.

The dining room, once the refectory of the monastery, is stately yet informal. The pulpit used for the reading of prayers during meals is still standing. The room is large and long, with terra-cotta tile floors, and large windows. The effect is beautiful, light, and elegant. The service is efficient. Portuguese cuisine is offered, and meals cost from 3,300$ ($22.10) to 4,000$ ($26.80). Food is served daily from 12:30 to 2:30pm and 7:30 to 9:30pm. Laundry service is provided, as is room service to midnight. Parking is free. AE, DC, MC, V.

ESTREMADURA

The first flowers of the Portuguese empire bloomed in these lands north of Lisbon hundreds of years ago, and the beauty has not been diminished by time. Like the once-white limestone of Battle Abbey (Batalha), this land has been gilded in the sunlight of the passing years.

Estremadura is a land of contrasts. The Atlantic smashes the coast of Guincho, while farther up it can hardly muster a ripple in the snug cover of São Martinho do Pôrto. These coastal regions are teeming with seafood: nursery-bred lobster, shrimp, crabs, squid, tuna, barnacles, and albacore. The sea is never far from any spot in Estremadura. From many a village's bastion, its shimmer can be seen, a reminder of the source of the land's bounty. In the many examples of Manueline architecture, especially at Batalha, the tie with the sea remains unbroken. The basic nautical designs—ropes, cables, armillary spheres, seascape effects—acknowledge the debt.

If it is impossible for you to spend several days exploring Estremadura, you can dip into it on 1-day trips from Lisbon: first to Óbidos, 58 miles north of Lisbon; then to Alcobaça, 67 miles north of Lisbon; on to Nazaré, 81 miles north of Lisbon; back to Batalha, 73 miles north of Lisbon; and finally a stop at Fátima, 87 miles north of the capital. Traveling to these five major places will take you through the heartland of Estremadura.

1. Óbidos

Years after Afonso Henriques drove the Moors out of Óbidos, the poet king, Dinis, and his saintly wife, Isabella of Aragón, passed by the walls of this medieval borough and were struck by its beauty. The queen likened the village, with its extended walls and gleaming plaster-faced houses, to a jewel-studded crown. Anxious

ESTREMADURA

0 ‒‒‒‒‒ 12 mi / 19.2 mi

Atlantic Ocean

COSTA PRATA

Leiria
Caranguejeira
N242
N113
Pataias
Maceira
Batalha 9
Alperdiz
São Mamede
10 **Fátima**
Porto de Mos
8 **Nazaré**
Aljubarrota 6
N1
5 **Alcobaça**
N243
Mendiga
Minde
Serra de Aire
7 **São Martinho do Pôrto**
N8
Parque Natural das Serras de Aire Candieiros
Monsanto
Berlenga Island 4
Foz do Arelho
Benedita
Alcobertas
Alcanede
Vaqueiros
N3
Caldas da Rainha 2
Serra dos Candieiros
N362
Peniche 3
Baleal
Lagoa de Óbidos
N114
Rio Maior
Tremes
N114
1 **Óbidos**
N115
Romeira
Póvoa de Santarém
João da Ribeira
E3
N114
Praia da Areia Blanca
Bombarral
Cadaval
Cercal
Almoster
Santarém
Rio Maior
Lourinha
N8
N115
Serra de Montejunto
Vale de Santarem
Rio Tejo
Campelos
Cabanas de Tôrres
Ereira
Vimeiro
Pontével
Cartaxo
Praia de Santa Cruz
Matial
Ventosa
Ota
Aveiras de Cima
N3
Muge
Torres Vedras
N9
Merceana
N1
Turcita
N115
Alenquer
Azambuja
N118
N9
Sobral de Monte-Agraço
Carregado
Santo Isidoro
Gradil
Salvaterra de Magos
Benavente
Ericeira
N116
Mafra
Samora Correia
Vila Franca de Xira
Ribeira de Sorto
N116
Bucelas
Athandra
N10
Magoito
N9
Lousa
N1
Alverca do Ribatejo
N18
N115
N10
Sânto Estevão

PORTUGAL
Estremadura
★ **LISBON**

1 Óbidos
2 Caldas da Rainha
3 Peniche
4 Berlenga Island
5 Alcobaça
6 Aljubarrota
7 São Martinho do Pôrto
8 Nazaré
9 Batalha
10 Fátima

to please, Dinis made her a present of this gemlike village ribboned by a defensive wall. A tradition was established. Instead of giving precious stones, Portuguese royal bridegrooms presented Óbidos to their spouses—and it didn't cost them a penny. And what queen could complain at getting such a gift?

Entered through a tile-coated gatehouse, Óbidos rises on a sugarloaf hill, above a valley of vineyards. Its golden towers, its ramparts (rebuilt in the 12th century and subsequently restored), and its crenellated battlements contrast with bright white houses and the rolling countryside where windmills clack in the breeze. Inside its confines, you will have traveled back hundreds of years. The narrow streets are either cobbled or made of roughly hewn flagstones. Green shoots lodge in the crannies of the walls, and vines climb the sides of tile-roofed houses. A loom hums in a candlelit vaulted workshop. It's a living piece of history.

In the Renaissance **Parish Church of Santa Maria,** Afonso V, at the age of 10, exchanged marriage vows with his cousin, only 8. Inside, the church is lined with blue-and-white azulejos. Pause long enough to admire a Renaissance tomb and the paintings of Josefa of Óbidos, a 17th-century artist. In the Chapel of St. Lawrence are contained relics of saints' hands.

The castle has been converted into a tourist inn *(pousada)*. From its ramparts you can bask in views of Estremadura, the scene so unspoiled one can imagine Afonso Henriques' retinue marching over the hills.

Save some time for browsing through the shops, searching out thick-woven fabrics, regional rugs (both hand- and machine-made), raffia and handmade bags, and the local lace.

This well-preserved national monument village lies 58 miles north of Lisbon. Trains leave the Rossio station in Lisbon. A 7:40am train leaves Lisbon daily, arriving in Óbidos at 9:29am.

There are also bus connections to Lisbon, but service is more awkward. Buses leave from Avenida Casal Ribeiro in Lisbon, going to Caldas da Rainha. From there, you have to transfer to another bus to Óbidos.

You'll find the Óbidos tourist office on Rua Direita (tel. 062/952-31).

WHERE TO STAY

For excellent accommodations, I recommend **Pousada do Castelo,** 2510 Óbidos (tel. 062/95-91-05; fax 061/95-91-05). This Manueline-trimmed stone palace lodged on the ramparts of the walls of Óbidos is firmly rooted in Portugal's history, and today, with the supervision of the government, it is one of the best pousadas in the country. Reached via twisting cobblestone streets through the village, the entrance is through a thick Gothic archway. You ascend farther, into a wide sunny forecourt, and up a grand stone stairway to the main hall. Through the Manueline door, you can go to Foz do Arelho beach, a pleasant resort where the British writer Graham Greene used to spend his vacations.

There are several well-furnished lounges, but regrettably, only six double bedrooms, plus three suites. The fortunate few who stay here enjoy the character of the bedchambers, furnished with antiques or fool-the-eye reproductions. Deeply set windows have tiny monk ledges, where you can squat to enjoy the view of the surrounding countryside. Homelike cretonne fabrics cover the beds, and a few rooms contain desks with brass church lamps, armchairs, and ecclesiastical wall plaques. Each room has a private bath and a phone. Singles cost 19,700$ ($132); doubles 22,500$ ($150.75), and suites 28,700$ ($192.30). Fellow guests gather in one of two drinking lounges for sundown drinks.

Most wayfarers stop off just for the day, partaking of the 3,300$ ($22.10) to 4,000$ ($26.80) luncheon or dinner. I particularly recommend the roast suckling pig and the chicken cooked in an earthenware pot with a red wine sauce. Try for a table near one of the view windows. The dining room is in the Portuguese quinta style, almost grand, yet nicely provincial, with old oak beams, tile dado, a fireplace, wrought-iron chandeliers, and leather chairs. If you're not staying at the pousada, call ahead for summertime dining reservations. Food is served daily from 12:30 to 3pm and 7:30 to 9:30pm. Laundry is provided, and room service is available until 10pm. Parking is free. AE, DC, MC, V.

Estalagem do Convento, Rua Dom João de Ornelas, 2510 Óbidos (tel. 062/ 95-92-14; fax 061/95-91-59), is an old village nunnery turned inn. Outside the town walls, it is owned by a chemist, Luís de Sousa Garcia. The reception lounge is surely the tiniest on the Iberian Peninsula, with a fireplace, 17th-century chest, tor-chères, and a pair of gilt angels. The 30 rooms have furniture to complement the structure. Although the beds are old, the mattresses are more recent, and tile bath-rooms have been sneaked in. The bedchambers open off rambling corridors with chests and benches large enough to hold the trousseaus of a dozen brides. Each room has a phone and minibar. The cost for one person is 11,000$ ($73.70) daily with breakfast; a double, also with breakfast, is 13,000$ ($87.10).

Dinner guests from the outside are welcomed, and can order a 3,400$ ($22.80) table d'hôte or specialties from the à la carte menu, including French onion soup, peppersteak, and crêpes Suzette. The dining room decor consists of heavy black beams, an open corner stone fireplace, and a brick oven. On sunny days guests dine on the rear patio, in a garden with a moldy stone wall and tangerine and orange trees. Food is served from 12:30 to 2:30pm and 7:30 to 9:30pm daily. In addition to a bar with hand-hewn beams, there's a living room with leather armchairs, old paintings, an 18th-century desk, and a brass-studded chest dating from 1827. A for-mer wine cellar has been turned into a typical pub. Parking is free. AE, DC, MC, V.

Albergaria Josefa d'Óbidos, Rua Dom João de Ornelas, 2510 Óbidos (tel. 062/95-92-28), is of recent construction although it looks much older. It is placed just outside the fortifications of the old town. Each of its 40 air-conditioned bed-rooms contains a private bath, minibar, TV, radio, and phone; some have wall-to-wall carpeting. Singles rent for 6,000$ ($40.20) daily, with a double going for 8,000$ ($53.60), including breakfast. There is a disco on the ground floor. Because the inn is set on a hillside, it is entered through two separate main doors. It also has a typical restaurant with a private terrace, which you may want to patronize even if you're not staying there. Meals cost from 2,000$ ($13.40). Service is daily from 12:30 to 3pm and 7:30 to 10pm. You can have an apéritif in the bar, which is deco-rated with reproductions of the works of the artist who is the namesake of this albergaria. Parking is free. AE, DC, MC, V.

Albergaria Rainha Santa Isabel, Rua Direita, 2510 Óbidos (tel. 062/95-91-15; fax 062/95-91-15). Except for the necessity of negotiating a parking space, many visitors prefer this above many of the other hostelries in town. It's on a narrow cobblestone-covered street running through the center of town. It opened as a hotel in 1985, but the building itself, once a private home, is many centuries old. The high-ceilinged lobby is covered with blue, white, and yellow tiles. There's a comfort-able and sunny bar area filled with leather-covered sofas and Victorian-style chairs. An elevator carries you to one of the 20 bedrooms, each of which is equipped with a private bath, TV, and phone. Singles cost from 6,500$ ($43.55) daily and doubles from 8,000$ ($53.60). Most guests drive through the town, and deposit their lug-gage at the reception desk before moving on to park free on the square in front of the village church, about 100 feet away. AE, DC, MC, V.

Pensão Martim de Freitas, Estrada Nacional, Arrabalde, 2510 Óbidos (tel. 062/95-91-85), is outside the walls on the road that leads to Alcobaça and Caldas da Rainha. The accommodating hosts rent six simply furnished rooms at prices rang-ing from 6,500$ ($43.55) to 7,500$ ($50.25) daily for two persons with bath to 4,500$ ($30.15) for a double without bath. Everything is spotless in this establish-ment, which is generally cited by the tourist office to those seeking low-cost accom-modations. Breakfast, included in the rates, is the only meal served. Parking is free. MC, V.

WHERE TO DINE

Most visitors to Óbidos like to dine at the pousada, previously recommended. However, you get far better value, less formality, and more local color at one of the typical little restaurants that exist either inside or outside the walls.

My favorite within the walls is the **Restaurante Alcaide,** Rua Direita (tel. 95/ 92-20). On a narrow street leading up to the pousada, this little restaurant is known for its regional cookery and good and inexpensively priced wines. Decorated in a

Portuguese tavern style, it opens onto a balcony where the lucky few quickly fill up the tables. Meals cost from 2,500$ ($16.75), and as many as 50 guests can be seated for one time. The restaurant serves Tuesday to Sunday. In the afternoon, you can drop in for either tea or a drink. Hours are 12:30 to 3:30pm and 7:30 to 9:30pm. The restaurant takes a holiday in November. AE, DC, MC, V.

Restaurant Dom João V, Largo da Igreja Senhor da Pedra (tel. 95-91-34), just outside Óbidos, specializes in the regional cuisine of Estremadura, accompanied by good Portuguese wines. The dining room is spacious and clean, and you're invited to look into the kitchen, so that you can make your own selection if you find the menu confusing. The helpful staff adds to the enjoyment of dining here, where the food is not fancy but tasty and good value for your money. A complete meal will cost from 2,700$ ($18.10). A tourist menu is offered for 2,250$ ($15.10). The restaurant serves from noon to 4pm and 7 to 11pm daily. Parking is possible, an important item in Óbidos. Closed in October. AE, DC, MC, V.

EVENING ENTERTAINMENT

You can spend a pleasant, Portuguese evening at **Bar Abrigo da Biquinha,** Rua da Biquinha (tel. 95-94-49), a little bar just outside the city walls. The building, which dates from the 15th century, has whitewashed walls and several floor levels. One has a bar with stools and houses the liquor supply and refrigerator; another is equipped with a balcony for fado entertainers and is furnished with tables and chairs; and still another has a large table made from an old millstone, surrounded by stools of padded kegs. The bar has a fireplace, two fountains built into the walls, and a little courtyard where you can enjoy your drinks in summer. The greeting here is warm, and the local people don't mind sharing their enjoyment with visitors. Hours are 6pm to 2 or 3am daily. A beer costs 150$ ($1.05), and you can order a mixed drink for 400$ ($2.70). Sandwiches are available for 200$ ($1.35).

---

2. Caldas da Rainha

After a bad night's sleep, the sister-queen of Manuel the Fortunate one day set out from Óbidos to Batalha. Passing through a small village en route, the rheumatic Leonor is said to have seen peasants bathing in fetid pools off to the side of the road. When told of the therapeutic value of these springs, she had her ladies-in-waiting clear the area to protect her modesty. A screen of fabric was draped around her, and she descended partially dressed into a foul sulfur bath.

So great was her relief from her ailment that she returned to Caldas da Rainha again and again—in fact, she pawned her personal wealth in rubies and gold jewelry (many gems given to her by her deceased husband, the Perfect Prince, João II) to construct a hospital and an adjoining church. The chapel, **Nossa Senhora do Pópulo,** was built at the dawn of the 16th century in the Manueline style, then at its apex, and is graced with a well-executed landmark belfry. Inside are handsome 300-year-old glazed earthenware tiles in buttercup yellow and marine blue. Today a classic green bronze statue of Leonor stands at Largo do Conde de Fontalva; and the town has been a spa ever since, enjoying a particular chic in the 19th century. It is open daily from 9am to 12:30pm and 2 to 5pm.

The spa park is studded with palm trees, weeping willows, flowers, and statues on its green lawns, with lagoons breaking the patterns. In the park, you can visit the **Museu de José Malhoa,** Parque Dom Carlos I (tel. 062/83-19-84), which contains the painting of the popular artist José Malhoa, portraits by Columbano, art pottery and the Passion Christ statues by Bordalo Pinheiro, as well as works by other painters and sculptors. Malhoa, Columbano, and Bordalo worked in the latter 19th and early 20th centuries. The museum is open from 10am to 12:30pm and 2 to 5pm Tuesday to Sunday; closed holidays. Admission is 200$ ($1.35). Children under 12 are admitted free.

Caldas da Rainha is also noted for its ceramics, especially the cabbage-leaf designs on soup tureens and accompanying bowls. Inside the town and outside along the road to Alcobaça you can stop at many roadside stands and purchase these ceramics at far cheaper prices than you'd pay in Lisbon. However, you'll have to carry them back to the capital with you and arrange shipment there. These primitively painted reproductions of cabbage, fruit, shellfish, and lizards are made from the local clay, and many of them, especially the reptilian and crustacean specialties, evoke the designs of the ceramist and caricaturist Rafael Bordalo Pinheiro. He had a studio at Caldas da Rainha during its heyday as a 19th-century resort.

Caldas da Rainha is also a thriving market town, the activity centering on the Praça da República where you'll see what surely must be the world's largest cabbages. Women with weather-beaten faces sell wild hares in the shop stalls, and at day's end, trudge wearily home. In winter, men in fur-trimmed coats walk around clutching red hens, much to the pleasure of camera-happy tourists. The town is 60 miles north of Lisbon, and is usually visited after Óbidos, 4 miles to the east.

Nine trains a day arrive from Lisbon, the trip taking 2¼ hours and costing 275$ ($1.85) for a one-way ticket. Fourteen buses a day come in from Óbidos (see above). Trip time is 20 minutes, and a one-way fare costs 150$ ($1.05).

The **information office** is at Praça da República (tel. 062/345-11).

WHERE TO STAY & DINE

A good choice is the **Hotel Malhoa,** Rua António Sérgio 31, 2500 Caldas da Rainha (tel. 062/84-21-80), widely acknowledged as the newest and most dramatic modern building in town. Behind its eight-story bulk, an elliptically shaped swimming pool offers an encircling terrace to hotel guests. You'll find an attractive series of tiled and polished rooms: a bar, a restaurant, a sauna, a bingo room, and a disco. The unpretentious, comfortable bedrooms each contain a radio, air conditioning, and phone. There's a free parking garage on the premises. The 110 rooms rent for 6,800$ ($45.55) daily in a single, 8,000$ ($53.60) in a double, with breakfast included. Lunch or dinner costs from 1,800$ ($12.05). AE, DC, MC, V.

3. Peniche

The town of Peniche, 57 miles north of Lisbon, stands on a high peninsula, with wide, sandy beaches at the foot of the rocky cliffs. It is an important fishing port, where fish canning and packing, plus a dockyard, are the economic backbone of the community. The making of bobbin laced by hand was once an important cottage industry here, and efforts have been made to revive the method and quality of the traditional product through a school for apprentices at the **Industrial and Commercial School,** Avenida 25 de Abril. You can visit the school and see a display of samples of the beautiful lacework. The making of lace can be viewed at the **Work House of the Daughters of Fishermen** on Rua do Calvario, and the product can be purchased at a shop on Avenida do Mar.

Originally an island, Peniche and the mainland were connected when a channel was filled in with silt by the 15th century. There are traces of an ancient fortress at a point called Peniche-de-Cima, as well as indications that the Phoenicians landed here, founding a commercial outpost across the channel from the then-existing island. Greeks, Lusitanians, and Romans also landed and settled here.

A strong fortress begun in 1557 and finished in 1570 was built to defend Peniche, and became part of a coastline defense network. Today the warlike aspects have faded into history, and **Peniche harbor** is a striking place to visit, with its view of high peaked rocks and the activity of fishermen putting out to sea and returning with their loads of fish.

The **citadel,** intended to prevent landings by enemy troops and pirates that ravaged Peniche, was ordered constructed by King João I. It underwent many modifications, being used as a prison until 1974 and then as a temporary haven for people forced to flee former Portuguese colonies in Africa. You can see the water hole in the courtyard, the casemates, and the air grilles of the dungeons, as well as engraved stones and inscriptions.

The largest church in Peniche, the **Igreja de São Pedro,** Largo Castilho, is a 16th-century building extensively altered through the centuries. The interior, with three naves, is still worth seeing, particularly the chancel with four enormous paintings depicting stages in the life of St. Peter.

Another house of worship worth visiting in the area is the Roman-Gothic **Church of St. Leonardo** at Atouguia da Baleia, on the coast just north of Peniche. Of great historical and architectural interest, it dates from the 13th century. The three naves are formed by ogival arches and covered with wood, while the chancel has a stone-ridged vault. Five paintings on wood on the lateral wall of one of the naves are from the 16th century. One of the two chapels is decorated with colorful 17th-century tiles. A 14th-century bas-relief sculpture in limestone, depicting the Nativity, is of interest for its naïve realism.

Perhaps the major reason most visitors go to Peniche is to explore **Cabo Carvoeiro** on the peninsula, about 1½ miles east of the town, which offers breathtaking views of the surf smashing into the wild rock formations hundreds of feet below the road. A *farol* (lighthouse), built in 1779, is some 80 feet high and affords a magnificent panorama over the archipelago of the Berlengas and Nau dos Corvos. The lighthouse stands at the end of the Cabo road. One reader, Robert M. Levine of Long Island, New York, says that "in many ways, the view ranks with that at the Grand Canyon."

The **tourist office** is at Rua Alexandre Herculano (tel. 062/79-571). Rodoviária Nacional buses run from Lisbon daily at 7am, 8:30am, 9am, and 10am, taking 2 hours. The one-way cost is 600$ ($4), and the trip takes 2½ hours. Nine buses a day also arrive from Caldas (see above). The trip takes 1 hour and costs 265$ ($1.80) one way. Caldas is the nearest rail link.

WHERE TO DINE

For a dining room with a view, go to the **Restaurante Nau Dos Corvos,** Cabo Carvoeiro (tel. 062/72-410). It's difficult to miss this glass-walled restaurant, since it's one of the few buildings at the end of the tip of land overlooking the rocks of Peniche. To some observers the handful of towering rocks isolated in the offshore surf look like petrified giants who didn't quite make it to shore before being turned to stone. Many Portuguese travel for miles for a view of the seascape, then later enjoy a meal in this restaurant, seating 122 patrons. Service is Tuesday to Sunday from noon to 3pm and 7 to 10pm. Reservations aren't needed. Menu items feature both continental and regional specialties, including an array of fish and shellfish, plus several pork and beef dishes. Everything is accompanied by a good selection of Portuguese wines, both red and white, which the waiter or steward will be happy to recommend. Meals cost from 2,800$ ($18.75) à la carte or 1,400$ ($9.40) for a tourist menu. There is space for parking and the restaurant can at times get quite busy on a summer day. Closed in November. No credit cards.

---

4. Berlenga Island

Berlenga, a granite rock set in the Atlantic, is an island hideaway and nature reserve. Seven miles out in the ocean west of Peniche, a medieval fortress once stood sentinel over the Portuguese coastline. The reddish granite mass of Berlenga is the largest island in a little archipelago made up of three groups of rocky rises known as the Farilhões, the Estelas, and the Forcades. Berlenga draws skindivers and fishermen, intrigued by the undersea fauna, the long-finned tunny (albacore), jackfish, and varieties of marine crustaceans. It has numerous coves and underwater caves.

The medieval fortress was destroyed in 1666 when 28 Portuguese tried to withstand some 1,500 Spaniards who bombarded it from 15 ships. Rebuilt toward the end of the 17th century, it now houses a hostel. You can take a stairway from the fortress to the lighthouse, stopping along the way to look over the panorama of the archipelago. A cobblestone walk from the top of the lighthouse site takes you down to a little bay with fishermen's cottages along a beach.

You can arrange a boat trip around the island. On the way, to the south of the hostel, you can see the **Furado Grande,** a long marine tunnel that leads to a creek walled in by the granite cliffs. Under the fortress is a cave the locals call the **blue grotto,** except that its pool is more emerald green in color.

Between June and September there is regular boat service to Berlenga Island from the Peniche peninsula, operated by the Viamar Company, whose office is on the Peniche harbor. The crossing takes about an hour and costs 1,500$ ($10.05) per person round-trip. The boat makes one round-trip a day in June and September, three round-trips a day in July and August (two in the morning and one in the afternoon). You can also rent equipment for underwater fishing and skindiving at Peniche, which is 57 miles north of Lisbon, jutting out into the Atlantic.

For tourist information ask at the office in Peniche (see above).

WHERE TO STAY

If you'd like to live in an offshore fortress, you can try for an accommodation at the already-mentioned hostel. It's the **Casa Abrigo São João Batista,** Berlenga Island, 2520 Peniche (tel. 062/720-21). To stay on this islet separated from the main body of land, you have to love the sea and savor the thrill in your bones of living in a converted fortress from the Middle Ages. Its stone walls, towers, and turrets rise up sturdily on its own rocky islet. Open only from June 1 to September 20, it was built as a far-out bulwark in the coastal defense of Portugal.

Still standing firmly on its granite foundation, it is prepared for a different invasion today—the tourist thrilling to ocean waves lashing and spraying below his or her windows. The fortress turns its outer stone walls against the elements, opening its interior courtyards to those who relax in the sun. Umbrella tables are set on stone pavements. Individual rooms are very basic, and some dorm accommodations are available as well. Lodgers take care of themselves, as there is no maid service. Guests must bring in their food and linen, cook their meals, make their beds, even clean the place. A deposit of 50% of the total cost of the stay must be sent in with the application for a reservation. A boarder can't stay at the hostel for more than 7 days. The rates per person are from 500$ ($3.35) daily, and the place can accommodate about 50 travelers in 11 accommodations. Baths are shared. No credit cards.

---

5. Alcobaça

At the apex of its power in the Middle Ages, the Cistercian **Mosteiro de Santa Maria** was one of the richest and most prestigious in Europe. Begun around 1152, it was founded to honor a vow made by Portugal's first king, Afonso Henriques, should he be victorious over the Moors at Santarém. Alcobaça, at the confluence of the Alcoa and Baça rivers, was built to show his spiritual indebtedness to St. Bernard of Clairvaux, who inspired (others say goaded) many crusaders into battle against the infidel.

Today the monastery, in spite of its baroque facade and latter-day overlay, is a monument to simplicity and majesty. Somehow a sense of other-worldliness pervades as you walk down the 350-foot-long nave. Tall chalk-white clustered columns, like trees, hold up a vaulted ceiling nearly 70 feet high. The transept of Alcobaça shelters the Gothic tombs of two star-crossed lovers, the Romeo and Juliet of Portuguese history. They were Pedro the Cruel and the ill-fated Spanish beauty, Inês de Castro, his mistress and (later perhaps) his wife. The work of an unknown sculptor, their sarcophagi (although damaged) are considered the greatest pieces of sculpture from 14th-century Portugal.

The oval-faced Inês is guarded and protected by angels hovering over her. Her tomb rests on sculpted animals with human faces, said to represent the assassins who slit her throat. Inês was buried at Alcobaça following a ghoulish ceremony in which the king had her decaying body exhumed and forced his courtiers to kiss her rotted hand and honor her as "the queen of the realm." Around the tomb are panels depicting scenes from the Last Judgment.

Pedro hoped to rise on that day of Resurrection to greet Inês emerging from her sleep of centuries. On a wheel of fortune at his tomb, a sculptor, following his mandate, carved the words *ate o fim do mundo,* meaning "until the end of the world." Guarded by angels, his feet nestled on a dog, Pedro lies in a tomb supported by lions, symbols of his timeless rage and vengeance.

There is much to see at Alcobaça, certainly the Cloisters of Silence, with their delicate arches, favored by Dinis, the poet king. He sparked a thriving literary colony at the monastery, the monks busily engaged in translating ecclesiastical writings. But aside from the tombs and cloisters, the curiosity is the kitchen, through which a branch of the Alcoa River was routed. As in most Cistercian monasteries, the reason for a flowing brook was one of sanitation. Chroniclers have suggested that the friars fished for their dinner in the brook, later washing their dishes in it. In the huge chimneyed pit, five or six steers or oxen were roasted at the same time. A 6-ton marble table resting here would probably have accommodated Gargantua and Pantagruel.

In the dining room are found niches where the monks prayed while the hierarchy ate. In honor of an old tradition, Queen Elizabeth II was fêted at a luncheon here. In front of the dining room is a fountain, where Portuguese girls wet their fingers, putting the water to their cheeks. The old women of the village predict that by so doing the young girls will soon get married.

Finally, in the 18th-century Salon of Kings are niches with sculptures of some of the rulers of Portugal (many fell from their resting places and were damaged in the 1755 earthquake). An air of melancholy is lent to the scene by the empty niches left waiting for the rulers who were never sculpted. The tiles in the room depict, in part, Afonso Henriques' triumph over the Moors. Hours are daily April to September from 9am to 7pm; from 9am to 5pm October to March. Admission is 350$ ($2.35) April to September, or 250$ ($1.70) off season.

After your visit, you can explore the nearby market, said to sell the best fruit in all of Portugal, especially succulent peaches grown in surrounding orchards originally planted by the Cistercian monks. Many stalls also sell the blue-and-white pottery of Alcobaça.

Trains depart from Lisbon's Rossio station, 67 miles to the south. The nearest rail connection is at Valado dos Frades, 3 miles away lying halfway between Nazaré and Alcobaça. About 11 buses a day connect Nazaré with Alcobaça, a one-way ticket costing 150$ ($10.05). The **Alcobaça Tourist Office** is at Praça 25 de Abril (tel. 062/423-77).

WHERE TO STAY

The most attractive modern hotel in town, **Hotel Santa Maria,** Rua Francisco Zagalo, 2460 Alcobaça (tel. 062/432-95), is on a sloping street just above the flower-dotted plaza in front of the monastery. Its position in a quiet but central part of the historic city is ideal. The combination TV salon, bar, and breakfast room are interconnected on the ground floor. Each is filled with paneling cut into well-polished geometrical shapes and comfortable contemporary chairs, some of which look out over the monastery. If parking is a problem, the 31-room hotel will open its garage free. With breakfast included, singles rent for 5,500$ ($36.85) daily, while doubles cost 8,500$ ($56.95). Each contains a private bath, phone, and radio. Some chambers contain balconies looking out over the square. Only breakfast is served. MC, V.

WHERE TO DINE

Trindade, Praça Dom Afonso Henriques 22 (tel. 062/423-97), is the most popular restaurant in town. It opens onto a side of the monastery, fronting a tree-shaded square. In fair weather, tables are placed on this square, and harried waiters rush back and forth across the street carrying cooling drinks. Trindade has both a full restaurant service and snack bar facilities. If you're dining here, count on spending from 2,500$ ($16.75) for a complete Portuguese meal, likely to include shellfish soup, roast rabbit, or the fresh fish of the day. Roast chicken is also available. A tourist menu costs only 1,400$ ($9.40). Hours are noon to 3:30pm and 8 to 10pm daily. It is closed on Saturday in winter and from September 25 to October 26. V.

---

6. Aljubarrota

Against a backdrop of mountain scenery, the extensive green fields on the Aljubarrota plateau are considered "the birthplace of Portugal." Between Alcobaça and Batalha, on August 14, 1385, near the village of Aljubarrota, Portuguese independence was secured. João I, the founder of the Aviz dynasty, and his young captain, Nuño Álvares—fortified by scythe- and shovel-bearing peasants and some English archers—defeated the Castilian soldiers.

A story of the battle relates how during the heat of conflict the king and his army were consumed by thirst under a blazing sun. He vowed that never would a voyager pass this way again without access to water. Today, outside the village, a small chapel offers a pitcher of fresh water in a niche in honor of that ancient commitment. Motorists can take the N3, 4 miles east of Alcobaça. The nearest rail connection is at Valado dos Frades, 7 miles away, to which there is a bus connection.

WHERE TO STAY & DINE

A comfortable hacienda, **Casa de Padeira,** Route N8, Aljubarrota 2460 Alcobaça (tel. 062/482-72; fax 062/48-272), is the private domain of a local professor of philosophy, Figueiredo Ventura, who with his charming wife and three children create an extension of their private home in each of the establishment's well-furnished modern bedrooms, eight in all. Each of the units contains some form of antique bed, as well as a scattering of family heirlooms. Some of them are Portuguese spool beds; others are well-rubbed art nouveau fantasies. Regardless of their style, they dominate each of the attractive rooms with their well-oiled beauty. The bedrooms each contain a private bath. All rooms are doubles costing 10,500$ ($70.35), including breakfast. Breakfast is served at a Sheraton dining table between 8 and 10am daily. It's most generous, including a fruit gâteau, eggs, and an array of local fruits. Meals other than breakfast are prepared on request for 2,800$ ($18.75) per person.

The casa has a swimming pool and another room where guests can play snooker, table tennis, or watch videos and slides about the Aljubarrota plateau. The Venturas will distribute handmade maps of the region, with multilingual descriptions of the nearby beaches, monuments, and places of interest. In winter, a fire is likely to be blazing in the stone fireplace of the guest lounge.

The Casa da Padeira was named after a local heroine who in 1385 is said to have single-handedly killed seven marauding Spanish soldiers with a baker's shovel. The legend is grisly, but a humorous version of it is displayed in blue-and-white tiles on the bar of the Ventura's comfortable salon and breakfast room. Parking is free. MC, V.

---

7. São Martinho do Pôrto

This seaside village nestles between pine-covered foothills and the ocean. Its main attraction is an almost landlocked sandy beach, brightly scalloped into the terrain. The waters are calm and clear, the days gently descending from May to October.

For many, São Martinho do Pôrto makes a good base for touring: Óbidos is 12½ miles to the south; Alcobaça, 11 miles to the east; Fátima, 28 miles to the east; and Batalha, 22 miles to the northeast. It is 72 miles by rail north of Lisbon, and only a short run north to the fishing village of Nazaré. A coastal road skirts the village, and buses run regularly into Nazaré.

WHERE TO STAY & DINE

Old-fashioned and gracious, **Parque Hotel,** Avenida Marechal Carmona 3, 2465 São Martinho do Pôrto (tel. 062/985-05), is set in its own small private garden. Ideal for families who want to live pleasantly and inexpensively near the beach, it is surrounded by trees, with summer furniture set out for relaxation. It's especially favored by economy-minded English tourists who like the 37 large bedrooms and homelike furniture.

Open only from March to October, it has installed a private bath in each of its bedrooms. They cost from 6,500$ ($43.55) daily in a single; from 11,500$ ($77.05) in a double. Breakfast is included. You eat in a turn-of-the-century hall, with an elaborate ceiling and an old chandelier. In all, the hotel is a world of polished floors and well-scrubbed rooms. On the grounds are two tennis courts. Parking is free. AE, DC, MC, V.

Since the hotel doesn't serve meals, you may want to go instead to the **Apartamentos Turísticos São Martinho,** Rua Dr. Rafael Graça 31 (tel. 062/98-93-35; fax 062/98-99-343), which does. It offers both continental and regional cuisine. Service is efficient and polite, and full Portuguese meals cost from 2,500$ ($16.75). Try for a shellfish and rice dish, or any of the grilled catches of the day. Service is daily from 12:30 to 2:30pm and 7:30 to 10pm. This popular tourist complex also has a bar and disco. It rents 81 comfortably furnished apartments, costing from 11,000$ ($73.70). Each has a phone and air conditioning. Room service is available 24 hours a day, and parking is free. AE, DC, MC, V.

---

8. Nazaré

The inhabitants of Portugal's most famous fishing village live in a unique, tradition-bound, ageless world. Many have never been to Lisbon; indeed, many have never left their village, except perhaps to make the pilgrimage to nearby Fátima.

The people remain insular, even though their village blossoms into a big resort in summer. White tents filled with international visitors dot the crescent-shaped beach. Yet the natives go about their time-honored tasks, perhaps pausing to pose for cameras. Nazaré was originally discovered by writers and painters; but in the 1960s seemingly everyone arrived. For that reason, the young who have grown up in a tourist-oriented economy will probably not follow the time-honored folkways of their forebears.

Nazaré is best viewed in winter, because, chances are, you won't get to see it in summer. You'll be too busy looking for a parking place (virtually impossible to find) or fighting for a place on the beach in a seething mass of humanity. The problem was that Nazaré was advertised as "the most picturesque" and "the most quaint" fishing village of Portugal. With advertising like that, the hordes arrived and now have almost engulfed the village itself. That, coupled with high-rise construction on every foot of available land, has made people wonder what happened to the fishing village. It's still there. You just have to look harder for it.

Don't expect stunning architectural styles or historic sights. The big attraction is its people and their boats. Claiming descent from Carthaginian and Phoenician ancestors, many of the natives are characterized by aquiline noses and dark brows. They are a gentle, hard-working folk whose classical features are marked and lined by sad, yet noble, countenances.

The clothes of the villagers are patch quilts of sun-faded colors. The rugged-looking men appear in rough woolen shirts and trousers, patched in kaleidoscopic rainbow hues, resembling Scottish plaid. Although the origin of this apparel remains unknown, one explanation ventured is that the fishermen picked up the designs from Wellington's troops who passed this way during the Napoleonic wars. On their heads the men wear long woolen stocking caps, in the dangling ends of which they keep their valuables—a favorite pipe, even a crucifix.

The women are mostly barefoot, wearing embroidered handmade blouses and pleated skirts also made of plaid woolens patched many times. It is customary for married women to don black as a traditional sign of mourning—black tasseled shawls, black capes or cowls; whereas the unmarried girls of the village are traditionally attired in seven petticoats. The government has made it illegal to count these petticoats, as many tourists were fond of doing in the 1950s.

The boats of the fishermen are Phoenician in design, elongated, slender, and decorated in bold colors. Crudely shaped eyes often appear on the high knifelike prows, eyes supposedly imbued with the magical power to search the deep for fish and to avert storms. Powered by oars, the boats contain lanterns for the dangerous job of fishing after dark. During the gusty days of winter, or at high tide, the boats are hauled in and lined up along the waterfront promenade.

While the men are at sea, the women wait, passing their time mending nets, drying sardines on the beach, perhaps nursing children, darning socks, or sewing patches on articles of clothing. At sundown they squat in circles, waiting on the somber shore. When their men come in, the business of sorting out the fish begins. The women trudge up toward the shoreline with heavy baskets balanced precariously on their heads. Some hang nets to dry in the night air; some slice entrails from the silver bodies upon the beach; others chase away pestering children . . . and some wait.

Nazaré is divided into two sections, the fishing quarter and the Sítio, the latter being the almost exclusively residential upper town. Near the beach, you'll find handcraft shops, the markets, restaurants, hotels, and boardinghouses. The main square opens directly onto the sea, and narrow streets lead to the smaller squares, evoking a Medina in a Moorish village. Simple shops hang objects outside their doors, indicating what they sell (for example, a carved wooden cow head would be a butcher shop). At the farthest point from the cliff and square are the vegetable and fish markets, where auctions are held.

Jutting out over the sea, the promontory of the Sítio is a sheer drop to the ocean and the beach below. It is reached either by a funicular or by a goat-steep cobblestone pathway. At the Sítio the Virgin Mary supposedly appeared in 1182. A young horseback-riding nobleman, Faus Roupinho, was pursuing a wild deer dangerously near the precipice, shrouded in mist. The fog lifted suddenly to reveal the Virgin and the chasm below. In honor of this miracle, the nobleman built the **Chapel of Memory.** Today, near the spot, you can go inside the 18th-century structure honoring that long-ago event.

Eight miles northwest of Alcobaça, Nazaré lies 82 miles north of Lisbon. From the capital, take the 3-hour train ride to the nearest station of Valado, where bus connections into Nazaré can be made. Coaches depart from Lisbon's Rossio station.

The **Nazaré Tourist Office** is at Rua Mouzinho de Albuquerque 72 (tel. 062/511-20).

WHERE TO STAY

The leading hotel in town (where the competition is not keen) is the **Hotel Praia,** Avenida Vieira Guimarães 39, 2450 Nazaré (tel. 062/514-23). Built at the end of the 1960s, just when Nazaré was being put on the tourist maps of the world, the hotel is a 41-bedroom structure, rising six floors and decorated in a modern style. All rooms are equipped with private bath, TV, and phone, and the location is about a 3-minute walk to the sandy beach where the fishing boats and bathing cabins lie. A single with breakfast rents for 10,500$ ($70.35) per day, with a double going for 11,000$ ($73.70). The hotel doesn't have a restaurant on the premises, but guests can patronize the Mar Bravo (see below), which it owns. The hotel remains closed for December. AE, DC, MC, V.

Hotel Da Nazaré, Largo Afonso Zuquete, 2450 Nazaré (tel. 062/513-11; fax 062/532-38), is the runner-up. This hotel will not please everybody (and hasn't in the past), yet many patrons count themselves lucky if they can get a room here on a hot summer day. The location is on a busy street set back from the water, about a 3-minute walk from the promenade. The hotel opens onto a tiny plaza, and many of its front bedrooms have private balconies. Open all year, it rents 52 small bedrooms which are very simply furnished. With room and breakfast, the single rate is 7,500$

($50.25) per day, going up to 10,500$ ($70.35) in a double. A rooftop terrace for sun-lounging puts Nazaré and the clifftop Sítio in perspective. Frankly, the best feature of this hotel is its fourth and fifth floors, which contain dining and restaurant facilities. The dining room opens onto window walls peering out over the village housetops, the rugged cliffs, and the harbor where tomorrow's sardines are being hauled in. Specializing in fish dishes, this dining room is open to the general public. Featured dishes include lobster thermidor, grilled crab, shrimps, and clams in a savory sauce. Meals cost from 2,500$ ($16.75). AE, DC, MC, V.

Pensão-Restaurante Ribamar, Rua Gomes Freire 9, 2450 Nazaré (tel. 062/55-11-58), is a genuine old-fashioned village inn, with a traditionally styled dining room where candlelit meals are served at night. It's right on the water, with most of its 23 double rooms opening onto balconies from which guests watch the beaching of the sardine-filled boats. Or you can watch (without being caught staring) the multipetticoated women or the tasseled stocking caps of the men. Even if you're passing through just for the day, you may want to try a regional meal in the oak-beamed dining room. A meal is offered for 2,000$ ($13.40) and includes specialties such as cream of shellfish soup, fish stew (*caldeirada*) in the Nazaré style, and roast kid. The atmosphere is genial, with ornate tiles, brown chairs, and stark white cloths. Food is served daily from 12:30 to 3pm and 7 to 10pm.

A twisting stairway in the rear leads to the old-style bedrooms, with rattan baskets of pine cones on each landing. Each bedroom is individually decorated, comfortable, and immaculately maintained with private bath. Doubles cost 7,500$ ($50.25) to 9,000$ ($60.30) daily, including breakfast. AE, DC, MC, V.

Hotel Maré, Rua Mouzinho de Albuquerque 8, 2450 Nazaré (tel. 062/56-12-26; fax 062/56-17-50), has a modern lobby sheathed in vertical planks of wood, with black-and-white photographs of the fishermen of Nazaré. The hotel is right in the heart of the fishing port, and its 36 rooms are furnished simply, all with private bath, phone, minibar, and TV. The site is a block from the beach. Including breakfast, a double room costs 16,000$ ($107.20) daily, and a single goes for 12,500$ ($83.75). The hotel also rents three suites, costing from 19,000$ ($127.30). Usually the person at the desk speaks some English. The hotel's sun-flooded restaurant is on the fourth floor, offering a panoramic view. From 12:30 to 3pm and 7 to 10pm daily, guests enjoy meals for 1,800$ ($12.05), including such fare as steak in a cream sauce, escalopes of veal in Madeira, and sea bass prepared fisherman's style. On the fifth floor is a bar with comfortable tables. At least half of the floor space is devoted to an outdoor sun terrace. Laundry service is provided, and room service is available until midnight. AE, DC, MC, V.

A three-star boardinghouse, the **Pensão Madeira,** 2450 Nazaré (tel. 062/56-14-23), is simple but adequate. Its 11 bedrooms, each with private bath, face the sea. A single with bath and breakfast costs 8,000$ ($53.60) daily, a double with the same amenities going for 10,500$ ($70.35). AE, DC, MC, V.

WHERE TO DINE

One of the most frequented of the dozens of restaurants in this bustling village is **Mar Bravo,** Praça Sousa Oliveira 75 (tel. 55-11-80), on the corner of the town's busy square overlooking the ocean. The decor is tile, with a huge photo of the Nazaré beach covering the back wall. A complete meal costs from 2,200$ ($14.75) and consists of soup, followed by a fish or meat dish, and bread. There's a menu in English. À la carte specialties are bass caprice, fish stew Nazarena, and grilled pork. Dessert might be a soufflé, a fruit salad, or a pudding. The cuisine is Portuguese and reservations aren't needed. Hours are daily from noon to 4pm and 7 to 10pm. Upstairs is a second dining room, with an oceanside view. AE, DC, MC, V.

Beira-Mar, Avenida da República 40, 2450 Nazaré (tel. 062/55-14-58), is one of the best restaurants in the port. In a modern building, it offers typical Portuguese dishes, including the "day's catch." Meat dishes are also available, along with regional soups, but Neptune is king. Meals cost 1,800$ ($12.05) and up, and are served daily from noon to 3pm and 7 to 10pm. More than 75 diners can crowd in here on a busy day in summer.

Opening onto the beach, this popular place is also one of the more reasonable inns in town if you're seeking modest accommodations at modest prices—from 10,500$ ($70.35) daily for one of the 15 simply furnished double rooms. Guests are received only from March through November. AE, DC, MC, V.

Restaurante Maresia, Avenida Manuel Remigio (tel. 55-12-01), is one of the special restaurants of Nazaré. Maria José Conde Sousa and her daughter run this place, specializing in lobster, which is displayed in a tank at the entrance. Overlooking the beach and the waterfront promenade, the restaurant serves excellently prepared Portuguese food with a natural emphasis on the sea. Try any of their dishes—shellfish rice, fish stew, roasted sardines, or codfish prepared in a number of ways. Meals cost from 2,000$ ($13.40) and can be enjoyed at one of the sidewalk tables in fair weather. A tourist menu goes for 1,350$ ($9.05). Food is served daily from noon to 3pm and 6:30pm to midnight. AE, DC, MC, V.

SHOPPING

Even if they aren't worn by the actual fishermen of Nazaré, Portuguese fishermen's sweaters have become attractive and fashionable garments in the United States. These bulky, hand-knit pullovers are usually wheat-colored wool, with elaborate chain-stitching on the front, back, and sides. Aficionados of Portuguese lore claim that the regional origin of each sweater can be determined by the designs knitted into it.

Fishermen's sweaters are also available cardigan style, at dozens of stores in Nazaré. Watch out for acrylic blends, as even Portugal is becoming more industrialized. Because of irregular sizes, try on anything you fancy before buying it. Also for sale in Nazaré are wool tartan shirts (which the fishermen do wear), woolen caps and scarves, all bargains at dozens of shops throughout the town. Feel free to bargain at all shops. I've always managed to get discounts ranging from 20% to 35% (on one winter day when business was bad, 65%).

For an all-around preview of the merchandise offered in Nazaré, visit **Perola da Nazaré,** Avenida da República 49 (tel. 062/55-16-49), along the waterfront, opening onto the beach. At this English-speaking shop, you'll come across a wide range of fishermen's sweaters, along with handcrafts made not only in the environs but throughout Portugal. They also sell embroidery from the island of Madeira and lace from the Azores. It is open daily from 9am to midnight.

---

9. Batalha

The founder of the House of Aviz, João I, vowed on the plains of Aljubarrota in 1385 that if his underequipped and outnumbered army defeated the powerful invading Castilians, he would commemorate his spiritual indebtedness to the Virgin Mary. The result is the magnificent **Mosteiro de Santa Maria da Vitória,** Batalha. Designed in the splendid Gothic-Manueline style, it appears as an imposing mass of steeples, buttresses, and parapets when approached from its western facade. Much restored, it is a jewel case of fine cut gems in stone, bearing the stamp of the English masons who built it.

The western porch, ornamented by a tangled mass of Gothic sculpture of saints and other figures, is capped by a stained-glass window of blue, mauve, and amber. The hue of the limestone has supposedly changed through the ages; today it is a light burnished beige, similar to the color of the facade of the Convent of Christ at Tomar. Napóleon's irreverent army used the stained-glass windows for target practice, turning the nave into both a latrine and a bordello.

In the Founder's Chapel, completed in 1435, João I and his English queen, Philippa of Lancaster, daughter of John of Gaunt, lie in peaceful repose, their hands entwined. Near that of his parents is the tomb of Prince Henry the Navigator, whose fame eclipsed their own even though he never sat on the throne but spent a great part of his life at the School of Navigation at Sagres, on the southern coast of Portugal. Henry's sculpted hands are clasped in prayer. Three of the other princes are also entombed here under a ceiling resembling snow crystals. The Royal Cloister is attributed to Afonso Domingues. These cloisters reveal the beginnings of the nautically oriented Manueline architecture. (Still a second cloister, called the Meditation Cloister, dates from the 15th century.)

The magnum opus of the monastery is the Chapter House, a square chamber whose vaulting is an unparalleled example of the Gothic style, bare of supporting pillars. When originally built by a French architect it collapsed, but a Portuguese redesigned it and slept under it for 8 days to prove its soundness. The two tombs of Portugal's Unknown Soldiers from World War I are guarded by sentinels and the glow of an eternal flame. In one part of the quadrangle is the Unknown Soldiers Museum, housing gifts to the fallen warriors from the people of Portugal and from other countries, including a presentation from Maréchal Joffre. Beyond the crypt are the remains of the old wine cellars.

The filigree designs ornamenting the coral-stone entrance to the seven unfinished chapels is stunning. The *capelas,* under an inconstant "sky ceiling," are part of one of the finest examples of the Manueline style of architecture, a true extravaganza in stone. It seems a pity that construction was abandoned here so that workers and architects for Manuel I could help build his Monastery at Belém. Originally, the chapels were ordered by Dom Duarte, the son of João I, but he died before they could be completed.

Outside in the forecourt, a heroic statue was unveiled in 1968 to Nuño Álvares, who fought with João I on the plains of Aljubarrota. The monastery is open daily from 9am to 6pm May through September. It closes at 5pm October through April. Admission is 400$ ($2.70) from May through September, 250$ ($16.75) off-season. Batalha stands 73 miles north of Lisbon, reached by taking a train to Valado where bus connections are made to Batalha. Three *expressos* buses a day also arrive from Lisbon, taking 2 hours and costing 850$ ($5.70) one-way.

WHERE TO STAY & DINE

Filling a big accommodation gap in this part of the country is **Pousada do Mestre Afonso Domingues,** Largo Mestre Afonso Domingues, 2440 Batalha (tel. 044/962-61). It stands right across the square from the Batalha, accommodating guests in good comfort in 21 rooms and 1 suite. The hotel is extremely well kept, and everything is modern. Rooms are of good size, and all contain a well-equipped private bath, phone, and air conditioning. The manager has wisely employed a helpful staff. A double rents for 16,200$ ($108.55) daily, with singles costing from 14,300$ ($95.80). The suite costs 21,300$ ($142.70). Even if you're not staying overnight in Batalha, you can patronize the first-class dining room, enjoying typically Portuguese fare for 2,750$ ($18.45) to 3,650$ ($24.45) for a complete meal. Food is served daily from 12:30 to 3pm and 7:30 to 10pm. Laundry service is offered, and room service is available to 10pm. Parking is free. AE, DC, MC, V.

---

10. Fátima

This is a world-famous pilgrimage site. Thorny bushes, dwarfed holly, gnarled and twisted olive trees, a stray oak—the terrain around Fátima is wild, almost primitive, with an aura of barren desolation hanging over the countryside. But if you should go on the 13th of May or the 13th of October, the drama that unfolds is remarkable. Beginning on the 12th of each of those months, the roads leading to Fátima are choked with pilgrims traveling in donkey-pulled carts, on bicycles, or in automobiles. Usually, however, they go on foot, some even walking on their knees in penance. They camp out till day breaks. In the central square, larger than St. Peter's in Rome, a statue of the Madonna passes through the crowd. In the breeze 75,000 handkerchiefs flutter, like thousands of peace doves taking flight.

Then, as many as are able crowd in to visit a small slanted-roof shed known as the Chapel of the Apparitions. Inside stands a single white column marking the spot where a small holm oak once grew. It is alleged that an image of the Virgin Mary appeared over this oak on May 13, 1917, when she is said to have spoken to three shepherd children. The oak has long ago disappeared, torn to pieces by souvenir collectors. The oak that now stands near the chapel existed in 1917, but was not connected with the apparition. The original chapel constructed here was dynamited on the night of March 6, 1922, by skeptics who suspected the church of staging the so-called miracle.

While World War I dragged on in Europe, the three devoutly faithful children —Lúcia de Jesus and her cousins, Jacinto Marto and Francisco—claimed they saw the first appearance of "a lady" on the tableland of Cova da Iria. Her coming had been foreshadowed in 1916 by what they would later cite as "an angel of peace," who is said to have appeared before them.

Attempts were made to suppress their story, but news of it spread quickly, eventually generating worldwide enthusiasm, disbelief, and intense controversy. During the July appearance, the lady was reported to have revealed three secrets to them, one of which prefigured the coming of World War II, another connected with Russia's "rejection of God." The final secret, recorded by Lúcia, was opened by church officials in 1960, but they have refused to divulge its contents.

Acting on orders from the Portuguese government of the time, the mayor of a nearby town threw the children into jail and threatened them with torture, even death in burning oil. Still, they would not be intimidated, sticking to their original story. The lady was reported to have made six appearances, the final one on October 13, 1917, when the children were joined by an estimated 70,000 people who witnessed the famous Miracle of the Sun. The day of October 13 had broken to pouring rain and driving winds. Observers from all over the world testified that at noon "the sky opened up" and the sun seemed to spin out of its axis and hurtle toward the earth. Many at the site feared that the Last Judgment was upon them. Others later reported that they thought the scorching sun was crashing into the earth and would consume it in flames. Many authorities, and certainly the faithful pilgrims, agreed that a major miracle of modern times had occurred. Only the children reported seeing "Our Lady," however.

In the influenza epidemic that swept over Europe after World War I, both Francisco and Jacinto died. Lúcia became a Carmelite nun in a convent at the university city of Coimbra. She returned to Fátima to mark the 50th anniversary of the apparition, when the pope flew in from Rome.

A cold, white, pristine basilica in the neoclassic style was erected at one end of the wide square. If you want to go inside, you may be stopped by a guard if you're not suitably dressed. A sign posted outside reads: "The Blessed Virgin Mary, Mother of God, appeared in this place. Therefore, women are asked not to enter the sanctuary in slacks or other masculine attire." Men wearing shorts are also excluded.

Fátima lies 36 miles east of Nazaré and 88 miles north of Lisbon. A train from Lisbon arrives daily. From the rail station, coaches connect with the pilgrimage site. Outside of Fátima, in the simple and poor village of Aljustrel, you can still see the houses of the three shepherd children.

When you arrive, everything at first seems to be either a souvenir shop, boardinghouse, or a hotel. But on the days of the major pilgrimages, it's virtually impossible to secure a room unless you've reserved months in advance. Those visiting at other times of the year may find the following recommendations suitable.

The **tourist office** is at Avenida Dom José Alves Correia da Silva (tel. 049/531-39).

WHERE TO STAY

Rated three stars by the government, the **Hotel de Fátima,** Rua João Paulo II, 2495 Fátima (tel. 049/53-23-51; fax 049/53-26-91), is a leading accommodation. Many of its 133 rooms and 9 suites overlook the sanctuary. The ever-increasing invasion of pilgrims to the shrine forced the hotel to enlarge. All rooms have natural wood furnishings in the provincial Portuguese style, with private bath, central heating, and phone. Some rooms have minibar, TV, and air conditioning. The building has three floors, serviced by two elevators. A single costs 7,500$ ($50.25), a double 10,500$ ($70.35), and a suite 14,000$ ($93.80), including breakfast. On the main floor is a cozy little sitting room with a brick fireplace, a reception lounge, a large sitting room, plus a dining room where you can order a two-course table d'hôte luncheon or dinner for 2,100$ ($14.05). Parking costs 1,000$ ($6.70). AE, DC, MC, V.

Hotel Três Pastorinhos, Rua João Paulo II, 2495 Fátima (tel. 049/53-23-39; fax 049/53-24-49), is translated as the Hotel of the Three Shepherd Children. The three-star facility is designed in a holiday style, with its most recently added bedrooms opening onto private balconies overlooking the sanctuary. All 92 rooms have modern facilities, including a private bath, air conditioning, and phone. One person pays from 5,800$ ($38.85) daily for a room; two persons are charged 8,500$ ($56.95). Breakfast is included. If you're just passing through, you can come in for a multicourse meal costing 2,000$ ($13.40). The breakfast rooms open onto raised sun terraces, edged with pots of flowering plants. Parking is free. AE, DC, MC, V.

Estalagem Dom Gonçalo, Rua Jacinto Marto 100, 2495 Fátima (tel. 049/53-22-62; fax 049/53-20-88), is a modern, clean, 42-room hotel set in a large garden at the entrance to town and serving some of the best food in Fátima, with the biggest portions. Once it was known as the Pensão Zéca, but it has been considerably remodeled and improved upon. Rooms are comfortably and attractively furnished, costing from 5,500$ ($36.85) daily in a single, from 7,500$ ($50.25) in a double, these tariffs including breakfast. The restaurant has an à la carte menu, a typical repast going for around 1,800$ ($12.05). You can order the usual selection of fish and meat dishes, along with a mixed salad or perhaps a tasty omelet. Food is served daily from noon to 3pm and 7:30 to 9:30pm. AE, DC, MC, V.

Hotel Santa Maria, Rua de Santo António, 2495 Fátima (tel. 049/53-10-15; fax 049/53-21-97), is a comfortable modern hotel set on a quiet side street just a few steps east of the park surrounding the sanctuary. Inside you'll find a lobby floored with gray-and-white marble, lots of exposed wood, and a sunny lounge area with plants that thrive in the light streaming through stained-glass windows. The well-trained staff charges 7,000$ ($46.90) daily in a single, 10,000$ ($67) in a double, breakfast included. Each of the 56 modern rooms contains a private bath, balcony, phone, and radio. Meals cost 2,000$ ($13.40). Parking is free. AE, MC, V.

Hotel Dom José, Avenida Dom José Alves Correia da Silva, 2495 Fátima (tel. 049/53-22-15; fax 049/53-21-97). Set beside one of the busiest streets in Fátima, within walking distance of the sanctuary, this modern balconied hotel is large and urban, with 63 bedrooms. A uniformed staff will register you in the marble-floored lobby, after which you proceed by elevator to a comfortable room. Much that this hotel offers, including its bar and dining room, seems to have a bit more style than some of the other more Spartan hotels in town. Each room has a private bath, phone, radio, and central heating. Six also contain TVs. There's also a free parking garage. Singles cost from 7,000$ ($46.90) daily, while doubles go for 10,000$ ($67), including breakfast. Lunch or dinner is another 2,000$ ($13.40). AE, MC, V.

Hotel Regina, Rua Dr. Gonego Manuel Formigão, 2495 Fátima (tel. 049/53-23-03; fax 049/53-23-03), is a good bet for a conservative, relatively unexciting, yet perfectly adequate hotel. It sits just east of the street bordering the sanctuary. Many of your fellow guests are likely to be elderly Portuguese pilgrims spending a slow-paced holiday. There's a very clean lobby, with an adjacent bar and TV room, which is popular just before bedtime. Many guests enjoy their simple meals in the hotel's dining room. Each of the 86 comfortably outfitted bedrooms contains a private bath, air conditioning, TV, and phone. Rates are 4,500$ ($30.15) daily in a single, 6,250$ ($41.90) in a double, and 7,800$ ($52.25) in a triple. Two suites rent for 9,000$ ($60.30). Tariffs include breakfast. Laundry service and 24-hour room service are available. Parking is free, but there is no garage. AE, DC, MC, V.

Hotel Cinquentenário, Rua Francisco Marto 175, 2495 Fátima (tel. 049/53-28-60; fax 049/53-29-92), is built onto a corner lot a short walk east of the sanctuary. This balconied structure offers comfortable accommodations throughout the year. Inside, a heavily patterned series of carpets and wallpapers provide a warmly agreeable, slightly angular decor. Each of the 115 bedrooms contains a private bath, radio, phone, and central heating. Some also provide TVs. There's a bar on the premises, plus a dining room, serving special Portuguese food. Singles rent for

4,950$ ($33.15), and doubles cost 6,200$ ($41.55), including breakfast. Parking is free. AE, DC, MC, V.

WHERE TO DINE

Fátima has many reliable hotels but few independent restaurants, mainly because those hotels have garnered most of the business. If you'd like an independent eatery, however, try **Grelha,** Rua Jacinto Marto 76 (tel. 53-16-33), which is one of the best in town. It offers not only regional specialties, but is known for its grills, and you can enjoy meals for 2,000$ ($13.40). A tourist menu is offered for 1,495$ ($10). In the cooler months the fireplace is an attraction, and the bar is kept busy year round. Meals are served Friday to Wednesday from noon to 3pm and 7 to 10:30pm. Reservations aren't needed. Closed from September 1 to 15. AE, DC, MC, V.

NEARBY ATTRACTIONS

Just 8 miles from Fátima, the caverns in and near the village of Mira de Aire offer visitors a glimpse at another kind of miracle: the miracle of nature. The first of these subterranean marvels are the **Alvados Caves,** which are a series of caverns naturally segmented into many smaller caves dotted with lakes. The favorite of these is the Lake of Pearls, with rock formations unique in Europe, including even the remains of an ancient stag preserved in stone.

Mira de Aire Caves, opened in 1974, boast the only Portuguese cavern with an underground river, the Rio Negro, which forms the *Grande Lago* (Great Lake). Fountains and lighting add to the beauty of the underground wonderland, with its sparkling jewel room, the great hall, the red room, and the majestic Dome of the Second Shaft. Various formations have been given such names as jellyfish, Martian, the crib, and the Chinese hat. The return to the surface from the Great Lake is via a modern elevator.

Saint Anthony's Cave, Serra de St. António, opened in 1969, was the first Portuguese cave to become a tourist attraction. Its main feature is a single chamber about the size of a football field whose walls, ceiling, and floor are covered with unusual rock formations. Sound-and-light equipment are used here as in the other caverns to make the tour both enjoyable and educational. Atop the cave is a restaurant whose windows offer a panorama of the rolling hillsides around Mira de Aire.

Fourth in the cave circuit are the **Grutas da Moeda** (Coin Caves) of São Mamede, discovered in 1971 by two hunters searching for a fox that had gone underground. In their exploration, they found the Shepherd's Hall, as they named it, full of fantastic limestone formations. Other sections of the caves since opened to the public are the waterfall, the crib, the red cupola, the unfinished chapel, and the wedding cake, among others. The caves took the name "Coin Caves" from an old legend of a wealthy man who was the victim of robbers. The story goes that he was murdered but when he fell into a steep declivity in the earth, his coins fell with him, to the dismay of the thieves.

The caves are open from 9am daily, closing at 6pm in January through March and October through December, at 7pm April through June, and at 8pm July through September. Admission to St. Anthony's Cave is 300$ ($2). You can visit these caves and those of Alvados for 500$ ($3.35) admission. To visit both Mira de Aire and Moeda costs 300$ ($2) each. For information, call 044/440-32.

THE ALGARVE

In the ancient Moorish town of Xelb (today called Silves), a handsome and sensitive vizier is said to have once lived. During one of his sojourns into northern lands, he fell in love with and won the hand of a beautiful blond Nordic princess. Marrying her, he brought her back to the Algarve. Soon the young princess began to pine, finding no solace in the Moor's rose castle. Her young husband finally learned that his new bride's melancholy came from her longing for the snow-covered hills and valleys of her native land. Issuing a decree, the vizier demanded that thousands of almond trees be planted throughout his realm. From that day on, pale white almond blossoms have blanketed the Algarve in late January and early February. The sight healed the heart of the young princess. On seeing the blossoms, she found she could finally fulfill her marital duties and lived happily ever after in her vizier's sun-drenched kingdom with its sweet-smelling artificial winters . . . or so the story goes.

The maritime province of the Algarve, often called the Garden of Portugal, is the southwesternmost part of Europe, its coastline stretching a distance of 100 miles, all the way from Henry the Navigator's Cape St. Vincent to the border town of Vila Real de Santo António, fronting a once-hostile Spain.

Called Al-Gharb by the Moors, the land south of the *serras* (hills) of Monchique and Caldeirão remains a spectacular anomaly that seems more like a transplanted section of the North African coastline. The temperature in winter averages around 60° Fahrenheit, increasing to an average of 74° in summer. During the day the sky is a pale blue, deepening in the evening to a rich cerulean. The countryside abounds with vegetation: almonds, lemons, oranges, carobs, pomegranates, and figs, the latter sending their branches across the ground like the tentacles of an octopus.

Expanses of sun-drenched golden sands contrast harmoniously with sinuous scored rock passageways that open up into high-ceilinged grottoes and sea caves with natural pillars supporting ponderous arches above inrushing waters. The variety of the coastline provokes wonder: sluggish estuaries, sheltered lagoons, low-lying areas where the cluck of the marsh hen can be heard, long sandy spits, the pounding surf breaking upon pine woods, and promontories jutting out into the whitecapped aquamarine foam.

Even though most of the towns and villages of the Algarve are more than 150 miles from Lisbon, the great earthquake of 1755 was felt here as well. Entire communities were wiped out; however, there remain many Moorish (even Roman) ruins. In the character of its fret-cut chimneys, mosquelike cupolas, and cubist houses, a distinct oriental flavor prevails. However, much of that flavor is gone forever, swallowed by a sea of dreary high-rise apartment blocks surrounding most towns. Years ago Portuguese officials, looking in horror at what happened to Spain's Costa del Sol, promised more limited and controlled development so they wouldn't make "Spain's mistake." That promise, in my opinion, was not kept.

The marketplaces in the shaded arcades of Algarvian villages sell esparto mats, copper work, pottery, and almond and fig sweets, sometimes shaped like birds and fish. Through the narrow streets comes the fast sound of little accordions pumping out the rhythmical corridinho.

Many small fishing villages dot the Algarvian coast, their names tongue twisting: Carvoeiro, Albufeira, Olhão, Portimão. The black dress of the varinas (with embroidery on their apparel, flower-studded hats on their heads), the healthy ruddy faces of the "bullfighters of the sea," the fishing-craft—all create a living bridge with tradition in a land known to Phoenicians, Greeks, Romans, Visigoths, Moors, Christians, and now foreign visitors of every hue, who have changed the old landscape forever.

Sports activities can be pursued year round in the Algarve, and the six championship golf courses between Faro and Lagos lure players from all over the world. Near Almansil is the 27-hole Quinta do Lago course, which is acknowledged to be one of Europe's top ten. Hotels have tennis courts, and horseback riding can be arranged with any of a number of stables quite near the beaches and in wooded mountain areas. Deep-sea fishing in the ocean waters, beach activities, and surfing attract thousands of vacationers to the Algarvian coast.

A NEW RIVIERA

Clearly a new Riviera has come to be.

Excellent accommodations are provided in nearly all price levels, the list topped by luxury hotels (some of which have their own championship golf course). The hotels scattered along the coast from Monte Alvor to the Vale do Lobo often have reciprocal meal arrangements.

Budgeteers seek out bargains in the pensions (boardinghouses) and estalagems (inns), some of them in converted mansions and villas. The government owns two pousadas—one on the sea at Sagres, the other in the mountains (São Brás de Alportel). In July and August the Algarve peaks in popularity, and accommodations without reservations made far in advance are difficult to obtain. The population of the Algarve in summer jumps from 300,000 to 800,000 and above, which causes strain almost to the breaking point on water and electrical supplies—and on traffic and tempers.

I find the area much more inviting in the low season, with February and March especially attractive, both because of the scenery and the cheaper, less crowded accommodations.

The flight from Lisbon to the Algarvian airport at Faro takes about 30 minutes. There are daily flights all year leaving Lisbon, with two daily return flights also. You can also go by one of the three daily trains. Take the ferryboat at Praça do Comércio in Lisbon, disembarking at Barreiro on the opposite bank of the Tagus, where Algarve-bound trains can be boarded. Three times a week there's a first-class-only special run. A daily motorcoach also leaves from Barreiro to the Algarve, and a drive in your own rented car takes about 5 or 6 hours.

ALONG THE WAY—SINES

On the somewhat barren route from Lisbon to the Algarve, attractions are rare. However, 99 miles south of the capital, almost exactly midway between there and Cape St. Vincent, sits Sines. The side road to the promontory of Sines runs through a land swept by sea breezes. Along the 11-mile route from the cutoff point at Santiago do Cacém, pine forests rise along the horizon, the scent from the resin-filled barrels permeating the air.

The origin of Sines is lost. Many of the natives, like those at Nazaré, trace their ancestry to the Phoenicians. The town sits upon the crest of a high inclined surface, its little houses trimmed in cobalt blue blending into the sky. Below the residential district, a natural rock looms over the tiny harbor. Off the coast is a small island, Pessegueiro, on which the crumbled ruins of a fortress remain. Vasco da Gama was born at Sines in 1469, and his house, long ago torn down, has been reconstructed in the original style. Anglers are attracted to Sines because of the bass and swordfish. Sand dunes rise along the extensive beaches, which are private, remote, seldom sharing their tranquil beauty with the Algarve-bound motorist.

SANTIAGO DO CACÉM

On the main road to the Algarve, about 60 miles south of Setúbal, the village of Santiago do Cacém, dedicated to St. James, is crowned by the ruins of a castle built by medieval knights upon the foundation of a Moorish fortress. At the castle walls there is a fine view of the sea and the cypress-studded countryside, from which a low hum and clack of windmills can be heard.

Two Pousadas

Algarve-bound vacationers or returning suntanned tourists like to stop off for a luncheon at the **Pousada de Saõtiago,** Estrada de Lisboa, 7540 Santiago do Cacém (tel. 069/224-59). This salmon-pink hilltop villa is approached via a climbing road through pine and fir trees, seemingly like a private estate. Guests walk around the terraced garden or take a dip in a pool surrounded by lawns and rows of cypress trees, plus a classic piece of sculpture in a coved niche. In the chalet-style dining room (or on a wide terrace where tables are set under an arbor of magenta bougainvillea), you can order table d'hôte two-course luncheons at 3,200$ ($21.45). You get a bowl of soup from the tureen, fish caught that day at Sines, meat with vegetables, then seasonal fruit. Sinking into the sofa, you can take coffee in the lounge in front of a 15-foot inglenook. This combination lounge and dining room is decorated in the provincial style, with a collection of handmade ceramic figures and jugs. Food is served daily from 12:30 to 2:30pm and 7:30 to 9:30pm.

Seven bedrooms are furnished comfortably with antiques or good reproductions. Each accommodation contains a private bath. Guests are assigned rooms in both the main building and the annex. Rates range from 10,500$ ($70.35) daily in a double. Singles cost 9,500$ ($63.65), including breakfast. Parking is free. AE, DC, MC, V.

THE ALGARVE

0 | 12 mi / 19.2 km

1 Sagres
2 Lagos
3 Portimão
4 Serra de Monchique
5 Praia da Rocha
6 Praia dos Três Irmãos & Alvor
7 Praia do Carvoeiro

8 Silves
9 Armação de Pêra
10 Albufeira
11 Praia de Quarteira
12 Vilamoura
13 Vale do Lobo
14 Faro

15 Loulé
16 São Brás de Alportel
17 Estói & Milreu
18 Olhão
19 Tavira
20 Monte Gordo
21 Vila Real de Santo António

PORTUGAL

LISBON

The Algarve

Continuing south, we come upon the **Pousada Santa Clara,** at Barragem Marcello Caetano, 7665 Santa Clara-a-Velha (tel. 083/98-250), overlooking the large lake and dam of the Rio Mira. The charming pousada is a most convenient stopover on the Lisbon-Sagres road to the Algarve. There are 18 pleasant rooms with bath and phone. A double with breakfast included rents for 10,500$ ($70.35) daily, and a single goes for 9,500$ ($63.65). If you stop for just a meal, the tab is 2,500$ ($16.75), served daily from 12:30 to 2:30pm and 7:30 to 9:30pm. An ideal place for swimming and fishing, the inn has spacious lounges and good food, such as roast kid done to a turn or fish freshly caught from the lake. Parking is free. AE, DC, MC, V.

---

1. Sagres

At the extreme southwestern corner of Europe, Sagres is a rocky escarpment jutting out into the Atlantic, the ocean beating itself into an aquamarine froth on the steep cliffs. It was here that Henry the Navigator, the Infante of Sagres, "dreamed dreams no mortal ever dared to dream before." He also proved that they could come true, launching Portugal and the modern world upon the seas of explorations. At Sagres, Henry, son of João I and Philippa of Lancaster, established his School of Navigation.

He died (1460) before the great discoveries of Columbus and Vasco da Gama, but those explorers owed a debt to him. A virtual ascetic, he assembled the best navigators, cartographers, geographers, scholars, sailors, and builders he could muster, infusing them with his rigorous devotion and methodically setting Portuguese caravels upon the Sea of Darkness.

Today, at the reconstructed site of his windswept fortress upon Europe's Land's End (nicknamed that after the narrowing westernmost tip of Cornwall, England), you can see a huge stone compass dial that he is alleged to have used in the naval studies pursued at Sagres.

At a simple chapel here, restored in 1960, sailors are said to have prayed for help before setting out into uncharted waters. To the left of the chapel is the villa where Henry lived (inquire at the tourist office nearby if you want to visit the interior). On what is believed to have been the site of the School of Navigation, a youth hostel has been installed. In the Auditorium of Sagres, a film is shown daily depicting the story of Henry the Navigator.

Three miles away is the promontory of **Cape St. Vincent.** The cape is so named because, according to legend, the body of St. Vincent arrived mysteriously here on a boat guided by ravens. Others claim that the body of the patron saint, murdered at Valencia, Spain, washed up upon the shores of Lisbon. A lighthouse stands here. Sea gulls glide upon the air currents; and on the approach, a few goats graze on a hill where even the trees are bent from the gusty wind.

Both the cape and Sagres (especially from the terrace of the pousada), offer a view of the sunset. To the ancient world, the cape was the last explored point, although in time the Phoenicians pushed beyond it. Many mariners thought that when the sun sank beyond the cape, it plunged over the edge of the world. To venture around the promontory was to face the demons of the unknown.

Sagres lies 174 miles south of Lisbon; from Lisbon's Praça do Comério you can take a ferry across the Tagus to Barreiro. From there, it's possible to make connections with the Southern Line Railway on its run to Lagos. At Lagos, buses go back and forth between that town and Sagres. The accommodations at Sagres are limited, but good.

The **Sagres Tourist Office** is at Promotó Rio de Sagres (tel. 641-25).

WHERE TO STAY & DINE

Pousada do Infante, Ponta da Atalaia, 8650 Sagres (tel. 082/642-22), seems like a monastery once built by ascetic monks who wanted to commune with nature —the rugged beauty of the rocky cliffs, the pounding surf, the sense of the infinity of the ocean. The glistening white-painted government-owned tourist inn with a tile roof is spread along the edge of a cliff, protruding rather daringly over the sea. It boasts a long colonnade of arches with an extended stone terrace set with garden furniture, plus a second floor of accommodations with private balconies. There are 21 bedrooms, and each has a private tile bath and is furnished with traditional pieces. All rooms have direct-dial phones, and most of them also have minibars and satellite TVs. Rates are 15,500$ ($103.85) daily in a single, rising to 17,900$ ($119.95) in a double, including breakfast. Two suites are rented at 23,800$ ($159.45) a night.

The public rooms are generously proportioned, gleaming with marble and decorated with fine tapestries depicting the exploits of Henry the Navigator. Large velvet couches flank the fireplace with tall brass floor lamps. In the dining room, the walls are lined with azulejos, and in the corner rests a cone-shaped fireplace with a mounted ship's model. Sitting in Portuguese provincial chairs, guests can order the traditional luncheon or dinner of the pousadas, costing 2,700$ ($18.10) to 3,650$ ($24.45) and including homemade bread, homemade soup, a fish course, meat with vegetables, and dessert. Have a before-dinner drink on the terrace, and watch the oceangoing vessels make their way around the point, heading for faraway ports of call. Other facilities include an outdoor saltwater swimming pool and a tennis court. Room service is provided until midnight, and parking is free. AE, DC, MC, V.

In a ship's-bow position, **Hotel da Baleeira,** Sagres, 8650 Vila do Bispo (tel. 082/642-12; fax 082/57-467), is a first-class whaleboat (its name in Portuguese), spread out above the fishing port with boats tied up in the harbor, it affords a view of the shoreline. Even its angular saltwater swimming pool is thrust out on a ledge, surrounded by a flagstone terrace. It's almost like swimming in the ocean, only you're perched high on a cliff. The largest hotel on this land projection, it offers 118 bedrooms, all with private bath, phone, and seaview balcony. The hotel has nearly doubled the number of its bedrooms in recent years, although the older ones are quite small, as are the baths. The bedrooms are on the lower level. You pay from 10,000$ ($67) daily in a single, 11,500$ ($77.05) in a double, including a buffet breakfast.

If you're exploring the Algarve and are in Sagres just for the day, you can stop off and order a 2,200$ ($14.75) luncheon or dinner in a dining room cantilevered toward the sea, where everyone gets a view seat. The chef has his own private lobster tanks (no frozen lagosta here), and the meals are well prepared and served in a efficient manner.

The atmosphere is that of a private world, as the hotel has its own sandy beach, free car park, cocktail lounge, and nearby hairdresser. AE, DC, MC, V.

Residência Dom Henrique, Sítio da Mareta, 8650 Sagres (tel. 082/641-33), is a sunny two- and three-story hotel with a restaurant, situated dramatically on the *promontório,* the viewpoint above the beach. The view of the cliffs, beach, and sea from this hotel is so magnificent that it's featured on postcards sold in the area. More like a country house, it is a white stucco building stretched along a small garden. There are 15 rooms, each with private bath and phone. A single room with a private bath goes for 3,600$ ($24.10) to 5,800$ ($38.85). The most expensive doubles open onto the water. Lunch or dinner is another 2,200$ ($14.75) per person. The staff can arrange for boats, waterskiing, and bike rentals. It's also an informal place for afternoon tea, where you can sample some of the regional cakes. Parking is free. No credit cards.

Nearby Places to Stay & Dine

A hospitable place, **Motel and Restaurant Gambozinos,** Praia do Martinhal, 8650 Vila do Bispo (tel. 082/643-18), has 17 large, well-furnished rooms, modern baths, and an excellent restaurant. The room charges depend on the view: sea, land, or none to speak of. The rent for a room for two persons is 8,500$ ($56.95) to 11,500$ ($77.05) per night. The restaurant is charming and the food is tasty, with the sea platter (a lobster salad with other assorted seafood) a specialty. Other dishes include grilled fish, preceded by gazpacho. You can dine inside or on the sea terrace. Meals cost from 1,800$ ($12.05). The beach is secluded, and is used almost exclusively by hotel guests. To find Gambozinos, turn off the road from Lagos to Sagres about 2 miles east of Sagres where a sign says "Martinhal—1 kilometer," where you'll also see a sign for the motel. Parking is free. Closed November through February. MC.

For those who want an escapist retreat, **Estalagem Infante do Mar,** Praia da Salema, 8650 Vila do Bispo (tel. 042/651-37; fax 042/57-451), lies 11 miles east of Sagres, set back from the main coastal road along the Algarve. A four-star accommodation, it was built on the crest of a hill, looking down onto the fishing village of Praia da Salema. It is bright and immaculately kept, and the welcome is gracious. The hotel rents 30 bedrooms, each with private bath and phone. Most are quite spacious and well furnished, often with private balconies overlooking the fishing village and the sea beyond. A single costs 7,900$ ($52.95) daily, a double 8,400$ ($56.30), plus another 500$ ($3.35) for breakfast. The hotel has a bar, TV, swimming pool, and a private free car park. Even if you're just driving along the Algarve coast, you might want to drop in for a meal, as the food is well prepared and served in bountiful portions. Expect to spend around 2,200$ ($14.75) to dine here. No credit cards.

Restaurante Cabo de S. Vicente, Fortaleza do Beliche, Vila do Bispo, 8650 Sagres (tel. 082/641-24), stands near the lighthouse on the road to the cape. The restaurant is in the middle of the ancient fort, right close to the cliff's edge, and it offers a complete menu—soup, fish, meat, and dessert—for 2,500$ ($16.75) and up. Specialties are grilled squid and grilled swordfish. Hours are daily from 12:30 to 2:30pm and 7:30 to 9:30pm. Reservations aren't needed. No credit cards.

---

2. Lagos

What the Lusitanians and Romans called Locobriga, and the Moors knew as Zawaia, was to become, under Henry the Navigator, a private experimental shipyard of caravels. Edged by the *Costa do Ouro* (Golden Coast), the Bay of Sagres at one point in its epic history was big enough to allow 407 warships to maneuver with ease.

An ancient port city (one historian traced its origins back to the Carthaginians three centuries before the birth of Christ), Lagos was well known by the sailors of Nelson's fleet. From Liverpool to Manchester to Plymouth, the sailors spoke wistfully of the beautiful, green-eyed, olive-skinned women of the Algarve. Eagerly they sailed into port, looking forward to drinking the heady Portuguese wine and to carousing.

Actually, not that much has changed since Nelson's day, and few go to Lagos wanting to know of its history. Rather, the mission is to drink deeply of the pleasures of table and beach. In winter, the almond blossoms match the whitecaps on the water, and the climate is often warm enough for sunbathing. In town, the flea market sprawls through narrow streets, the vendors selling such articles as rattan baskets, earthenware pottery, fruits, vegetables, crude furniture, cutlery, knitted shawls, and leather boots.

Less than a mile down the coast, the hustle-bustle of market day is forgotten as the rocky headland of the **Ponta da Piedade** (Point of Piety) appears. This beautiful spot is considered by many the best on the entire coast. Dotted among the colorful cliffs and secret grottoes carved by the waves are the most flamboyant examples of Manueline architecture.

Much of Lagos was razed in the 1755 earthquake, at which time it lost its position as the capital of the Algarve. Today only ruins remain of its former walls of fortification. However, traces of the old are still to be discovered on the back streets. On Rua Silva Lopes, just off the waterfront, sits the 18th-century **Igreja de Santo António** (Church of St. Anthony). Decorating the altar are some of Portugal's most notable rococo gilt carvings. Begun in the 17th century, they were damaged in the earthquake, but subsequently restored. What you see today represents the work of many artisans—at times, each of them apparently pursuing a different theme.

Nearby the **Museu Municipal Dr. José Formosinho,** Rua General Alberto Carlos Silveira (tel. 082/72-23-01), containing replicas of the fret-cut chimneys of the Algarve, three-dimensional cork carvings, 16th-century vestments, ceramics, 17th-century embroidery, ecclesiastical sculpture, a painting gallery, weapons, minerals, and a numismatic collection. An oddity is a sort of believe-it-or-not section, displaying among other things an eight-legged calf. In the archeological wing are Neolithic artifacts, along with Roman mosaics found at Boca do Rio near Budens, fragments of statuary and columns, and other remains of antiquity from excavations along the Algarve. Charging an admission of 200$ ($1.35), the museum is open Tuesday to Sunday from 9:30am to 12:30pm and 2 to 5pm; closed holidays.

The old **Customs House** on Praça Infante Dom Henriques stands as a painful reminder of the Age of Exploration. The arcaded slave market, the only one of its kind in Europe, looks peaceful today, but under its four Romanesque arches captives taken from their homelands were sold to the highest bidder. The house opens onto a peaceful square, dominated by a statue of Henry the Navigator.

The Algarve's most westerly golf course is signposted left off EN125 at Odéaxere. Five of this course's 18 holes are on sand dunes bordering the beach. The address is **Clube de Golfe de Palmares**, Companhia de Empreendimentos Turísticos de Lagos, Monte Palmares, Meia Praia (tel. 082/76-29-61).

Lagos is 21 miles east of Sagres, 164 miles south of Lisbon, and 49 miles west of Faro. To reach it by rail from Lisbon, take the ferryboat at Praça do Comércio across the Tagus to Barreiro. There, connections to Lagos can be made on the Southern Line Railway.

The **Lagos Tourist Office** is at Largo Marquês de Pombal (tel. 082/76-30-31).

WHERE TO STAY

A 20th-century castle, **Hotel de Lagos,** Rua Nova da Aldeia 1, 8600 Lagos (tel. 082/76-99-20), has its own ramparts and moats (a swimming pool and a paddling pool). This first-class hotel is spread out over 3 acres of hilltop overlooking Lagos, so no matter which room you're assigned, you'll have a view, even if it's one opening upon a sun-trap courtyard with semitropical greenery. The main room has a hacienda atmosphere, with a background of bone-white plaster walls, enlivened by sunny colors. Guests gather here in one of the clusters of soft built-in sofas set on carpets. In a corner logs burn in a fireplace in chilly weather. Excellent meals are served in an expansive harborview room, decorated in wood paneling. There is also a coffee shop, plus a piano bar.

Some of the 318 bedrooms have patios on the ground level, but most are on the upper six floors, all with private baths. The rooms offer a choice of standard or deluxe. All rooms are doubles, costing from 19,000$ ($127.30) to 22,600$ ($151.40) a night, including a buffet breakfast. Single occupancy of one of these double rooms costs from 15,650$ ($104.85) to 17,450$ ($116.90). Eleven suites are also rented, costing from 28,000$ ($187.60). The average bedroom has a background of stark white walls contrasted with warm Oriental colors. Most rooms open onto a wedge-shaped balcony where you can eat breakfast. Amenities include game rooms, a restaurant, a poolside bar, two lounge bars, and complete air conditioning.

The Hotel de Lagos also owns Duna Beach Club on Meia Praia Beach, with a saltwater swimming pool, a restaurant, a snack bar, and three tennis courts. Guests of the hotel are given a free membership during their stay. A private motorcoach makes regularly scheduled trips to the beach club, only 5 minutes from the hotel. Arrangements can be made for golf at nearby Palmares 18-hole course, where hotel guests get a 20% reduction on greens fees; for skin diving and sports fishing in the waters along the coast; for horseback riding through nature's garden; for sailing in the bay; and for international floor shows and gambling in the Algarve's casinos. Parking is free. Room service is available 24 hours a day. AE, DC, MC, V.

Hotel São Cristovão, Avenida dos Descrobrimentos, 8600 Lagos (tel. 082/76-30-51), may have been a simple inn at one point, but that is now history. The rather modest beginnings have given way to style. At the edge of town, almost within sight of the harbor, the hotel sits on a busy parkway junction of the coastal highway and the road to Lisbon. There is a solarium.

The 76 bedrooms are inviting in their uncluttered design. Each room opens onto a private terrace and contains a private bath. The price of a single is 7,050$ ($47.25) daily. Doubles cost 9,460$ ($63.40). Breakfast is included in the tariffs. The hotel also rents four suites, costing 15,890$ ($106.45).

Opening off the reception are public lounges. The largest uses natural pine slats for the ceiling, cube lighting, and pillars. One part on a lower level makes for intimate seating around a freestanding black fireplace. Before-dinner drinks are available in the cocktail lounge, which opens onto an inner patio with a fountain waterfall. The hotel closes from November through March. Parking is free, and laundry service is provided. Room service is available until midnight. AE, DC, MC, V.

Hotel da Meia Praia, Meia Praia, 8600 Lagos (tel. 082/76-20-01), lies 2½ miles northeast of Lagos. This first-class hotel is for those who want sand, sun, and good food rather than an exciting decor. The hotel, containing 66 bedrooms, all with private bath, stands at a point where a hill begins its rise from the sea. Surrounded by private gardens, it fronts railway tracks and a wide sandy beach, 4 miles long. The guests play tennis on two professional hard courts, linger in the informal garden where white wrought-iron outdoor furniture is scattered under the olive and palm trees, or loll by the large pools, one for adults, another for children. The oceanside bedrooms have balconies with partitions for sunbathing. The furnishings in the rooms are uncluttered, functional, and modern. The best rooms have sea views. All rooms are doubles, costing from 13,260$ ($88.85). Across the entire all-glass front of the hotel are the dining room, lounge, and cocktail bar. The establishment is open from May to October. Parking is free. AE, DC, MC, V.

Hotel Riomar, Rua Cândido dos Reis 83, 8600 Lagos (tel. 082/76-30-91), is a modern structure in the center of town. It has a pleasant downstairs lounge, a cozy bar, and tasteful decor. The hotel has 42 comfortably furnished bedrooms, each with private bath. Singles cost 6,000$ ($40.20) daily, with doubles going for 12,000$ ($80.40), including breakfast. Many of the bedrooms open onto terraces. Furnishings are in a typical Portuguese style. Rooms have telephones, but a TV is available only in the lounge. Only the public rooms are air conditioned, and there is no parking. AE, DC, MC, V.

Casa de São Gonçalo da Lagos, Rua Cândido dos Reis 73, 8600 Lagos (tel. 082/76-21-71). This pink town villa, with its fancy iron balconies, dates back to the 18th century. At the core of Lagos, close to restaurants and shops, the antique-filled home is almost an undiscovered gem. Most of the public lounges and 13 bedrooms turn, in the Iberian fashion, to the inward peace of a sun-filled patio. Here, surrounded by bougainvillea climbing up balconies, guests order their breakfast, sitting under a fringed parasol and enjoying the splashing of the fountain. All the furnishings are individualized: delicate hand-embroidered linens, period mahogany tables, silver candlesticks, chests with brass handles, inlaid tip-top tables, fine ornate beds brought from Angola, even crystal chandeliers. Singles cost 7,000$ ($46.90); doubles 12,000$ ($80.40), including breakfast. In the restoration of the house, modern amenities were added, so that each room contains a private bath and phone.

The luxury pension is in a rambling *casa* (house), with various stairways leading to corridors with fine old prints, engravings, and Portuguese ceramic bowls of flowers set on aged hand-carved chests. Guests enjoy get-togethers in the large living room with its comfortable armchairs drawn up around a fireplace. Here, again, the furnishings are personalized, with a preponderance of antiques. Closed from the end of October to April. Parking is free. AE, DC, MC, V.

WHERE TO DINE

A Lagosteira, Rua 1 de Maio 20 (tel. 76-24-86), has long been a mecca for knowledgeable diners in Lagos. Its decor is simple and there's a small bar on one side. On the à la carte menu, the best opener for a big meal is a classic Algarvian fish soup. The most savory opening, however, is clams Lagosteira style. After the fishy beginning, you might happily settle for a sirloin steak grilled over an open fire. Expect to spend 1,800$ ($12.05) to 3,500$ ($23.45) for a meal. The restaurant is open from 12:30 to 3pm and 6:30 to 10:30pm; closed Sunday and January 10 to 31. Reservations are recommended. AE, DC, MC, V.

One of the most elaborate and sophisticated menus along the Algarve is offered at **Alpendre,** Rua António Barbosa Viana 71 (tel. 76-27-05). The food is tasty, but portions aren't large. Service tends to be slow, so don't come here if you're rushed. *Gourmet* magazine called the Alpendre "the most celebrated and luxurious restaurant in Lagos." Your afternoon or evening might begin in the downstairs bar where you can have a before-dinner drink, sampling crunchy Algarvian almonds and olives. Later, you can order your Portuguese cuisine meal, selecting from among excellent soups, such as onion au gratin, following with one of the house specialties, such as peppersteak or filets of sole, sautéed in butter, then flambéed with cognac, and served with a sauce of cream, orange and lemon juices, vermouth, and seasonings known only to the chef. Two dessert features are the mixed fruits flambé or crêpes flambés with coffee, both of which are for two persons. Meals are served daily from 12:30 to 3pm and 7 to 11pm, costing 5,000$ ($33.50). A tourist menu is offered for 2,500$ ($16.75). Reservations are advised. AE, DC, MC, V.

Don Sebastião, Rua 25 de Abril 20 (tel. 76-27-95), is a rustically decorated tavern, considered among the finest dining choices in Lagos. Run by Portuguese, it offers a varied menu of local specialties, particularly shellfish dishes such as clams and shrimp. Live lobsters are kept on the premises. Often feverish with activity in summer, it features filling and tasty meals at prices ranging from 1,800$ ($12.05) to 3,200$ ($21.45). Meals, including grills, are accompanied by one of the best selections of Portuguese vintage wines in the town. Hours are noon to 3pm and 6:30 to 10pm. It is closed Sunday from November through March. Reservations are recommended. AE, DC, MC, V.

Galeão, Rua de Laranjeira 1 (tel. 76-39-09), in air-conditioned comfort, offers a wide range of local and continental dishes, and you can "oversee" the action through an exposed kitchen, which gets very busy in season. Meats are savory, and the fish dishes are well prepared and tasty. Try such dishes as king prawns and garlic, a gratinée of seafood, lobster thermidor, and salmon trout in a champagne sauce. You can also order such meat dishes as pork médaillons in a curry sauce and sirloin steak Café de Paris. Count on spending 2,500$ ($16.75) to 3,200$ ($21.45) for a filling repast. Hours are 1 to 3pm and 7 to 10pm. It is closed Sunday and in December. AE, DC, MC, V.

Mandarin, at Calicas (tel. 76-04-24), is good to know about if you're seeking some change-of-pace fare. It is outside Lagos on the road to Meia Praia. In an attractive structure, it is run by helpful people. Parking is available, and from one of the 40 seats in the well-run restaurant you can enjoy panoramic views. There is a bar if you'd like to go early for a drink. Lunch is served by the swimming pool daily in summer from noon to 2:30pm, costing from 2,000$ ($13.40). A traditional English roast meal is available on Sunday. Dinner, from 7 to 11pm daily, costs from 3,000$ ($20.10). The specialty is Peking duck with five spices and some of the ingredients are flown in from Taiwan. Reservations are needed only for the Sunday roast. No credit cards.

O Trovador, Largo do Convento da Senhora de Glória (tel. 76-31-52), is run by Marion (she's from Germany) and Dave (he's English). It's especially nice off-season, when comfortable chairs are placed around a log-burning fireplace. But at any time of the year you get a pleasant atmosphere, good service, and good food. The location is up the hill behind the Hotel de Lagos (follow the signs from Rua Vasco da Gama). The cuisine is international. Among the recommended appetizers are homemade chicken liver pâté, an octopus cocktail, a fish pâté with a delicate salmon taste, and escargots bourguignons. Shellfish dishes are prepared in unique Trovador style. Main courses also include Dave's special—a beef casserole cooked in black beer. You might also enjoy Portuguese swordfish. The desserts are all good, but I especially like the homemade cheesecake (not baked) and the coupe Trovador. Expect to spend from 2,200$ ($14.75). The restaurant is open from 7pm to midnight Tuesday to Saturday. Reservations are recommended. MC, V.

Pouso do Infante, Rua Alfonso d'Alméida 11 (tel. 76-28-62), is a pleasant tavern restaurant, with an iron chandelier, walls decorated with local craftwork, and rustic chairs painted green with straw seats. The Portuguese fare is not experimental in any way, but it's quite tasty. For example, for an appetizer, you're usually faced with a homemade vegetable soup (generous portions) or a classic Portuguese shrimp cocktail. For a main course, you might order that Portuguese oddity, sole with banana, or veal scaloppine with spaghetti. Also worthy as a main-course choice is chicken curry with rice (not always offered) and, my personal favorite, lamb in wine sauce. For dessert, the typical Algarvian selection is a smooth almond cake. Expect to spend 3,000$ ($20.10) à la carte or 1,550$ ($10.40) for a tourist menu. Hours are Monday to Saturday from 12:30 to 3pm and 6 to 11pm. Closed from mid-December to mid-January and on Wednesday from October to June. Reservations are necessary. AE, DC, MC, V.

---

3. Portimão

Go here only if you prefer the life of a bustling fishing port and commercial city instead of a hotel perched right on the beach. Ever since the 1930s, Praia da Rocha, 2 miles away, has snared sun-loving traffic. But the Algarve is so popular in summer that Portimão long ago developed a base of tourists.

The wafting aroma of the noble Portuguese sardine permeates every street and café nook. As a fish-canning center, Portimão leads the Algarve, but it doesn't outpace Setúbal in production. Still, for a change of pace, this town, on an arm of the Arcade River, makes a good stopover center (it also has some fine dining recommendations). Stroll through its gardens, its shops (especially noted for their pottery), drink the wine of the cafés, and roam down to the quays where you will see sardines roasting on braziers. The routine activity of the Algarvians is what gives the town its charm. On its left bank the little whitewashed community of **Ferragudo** is unspoiled, but tame, with a castle.

Between 9:30 and 10:30am the fishermen can be seen unloading their boats by tossing up wicker baskets full of freshly caught fish. Fish, fruit, and vegetable markets are held every morning except Sunday in the market building and open square, closing at 2pm. On the first Monday of every month, a day-long, gigantic regional market is held with gypsies selling local artifacts, pottery, wicker, even snake oil. Boutiques offering the Algarve's best selection of hand-knit sweaters, hand-painted porcelain, and pottery abound.

Many of the buildings in the old quarter of town date back to the mid-18th century when the town was rebuilt after the devastating earthquake of 1755. Roaming the streets, you can peer into delightful hidden courtyards, some with bread ovens built into the 3-foot-thick walls, blacksmith stables, tinsmiths, sardine-canning factories where sardines are still cleaned and packed by hand, and carpenters' shops.

Portimão is a perfect escape from the summer rush of visitors (mostly European) in the oceanfront towns, and the room rates are considerably cheaper. A bus runs to the beach at Praia da Roche, mentioned above. Buses or trains leave Portimão for all parts of the Algarve and Portugal. An express bus to Lisbon makes a 4½-hour run.

Portimão lies 180 miles southeast of Lisbon, 11 miles east of Lagos, and 38 miles west of Faro. The **Portimão Tourist Office** is at Largo 1° de Dezembro (tel. 082/236-95).

WHERE TO STAY

In the heart of the old town, **Hotel Globo,** Rua 5 de Outubro 26, 8500 Portimão (tel. 082/221-51; fax 082/831-42), is an island of contemporary living. A first-class hotel, it is recommended for its clean-cut, well-thought-out design. Snug modern balconies overlook the tile rooftops crusted with moss. In 1967 the owner-manager imported an uninhibited architect to turn his inn into a top-notch hotel. Each of the 71 bedrooms, with private bath and phone, enjoys good taste in layout and furnishings: matching ebony panels on the wardrobes, built-in headboards, and marble desks. Singles cost 12,000$ ($80.40) daily and doubles 15,000$ ($100.50), including breakfast.

On the ground floor is an uncluttered, attractive lounge with an adjoining bar. Crowning the top floor is a dining room, the Aquarium, encircled by four glass walls that permit unblocked views of the harbor, ocean, or mountains, its tables set with crystal stemware and flowers. Guests can also enjoy a rooftop cocktail bar and lounge, Al-Kantor. Parking is free. AE, DC, MC, V.

Albergaria Miradoiro, Rua Machado Santos 13, 8500 Portimão (tel. 082/230-11; fax 082/41-50-30), benefits from a charmingly central location, on a quiet square opposite an ornate Manueline church. Its modern facade is banded with concrete balconies. A few of the 26 simple bedrooms contain terraces, and each has a private bath and phone. You're likely to meet an array of European backpackers here, any of whom seem eager to converse and share travelers' stories. With breakfast included, doubles cost 9,000$ ($60.30) daily, while singles go for 7,000$ ($46.90). The hotel is open throughout the year, and motorists can usually find a parking space in the square just opposite the hotel. V.

WHERE TO DINE

Alfredo's, Rua Pe da Cruz 10 (tel. 83-102), is in the old tavern style, on the ground floor of a modern building. Against a backdrop of chalk-white walls, new and old provincial artifacts are combined decoratively. From the dining room, you can see an ornately tiled open kitchen, with a charcoal grill, crocks of lobster, baskets of mushrooms, cabbage, salad greens, even a glass case of fresh fish. You dine on high-back chairs with rush seats, where you can see the carved refectory table laden with cheeses, baskets of fruits, special desserts, and a tall scale. A candle in a brass holder is lit by the waiter, and you make your choice from a Portuguese à la carte menu. The fish soup, *ameijoas* (clams) a Alfredo's, *pescada* (hake) a marinheira, and tournedos Rossini are recommended. A light and creamy chocolate dessert finishes off a meal nicely at 4,500$ ($30.15) and up. A tourist menu goes for 3,000$ ($20.10). Open Tuesday to Sunday from noon to 3:30pm and 6pm to midnight. Reservations are necessary. Closed November 15 to December 15. AE, DC, MC, V.

One of the oldest restaurants on the Algarve, **Cachemire,** Rua Judice Fialho 42 (tel. 233-25), has a Moorish look, provided by arched corridors and doorways. The Portuguese and Indian menu is of a later era, however, offering such main courses as lamb kidneys in Madeira sauce, marinated wild boar, *cataplana* (a regional specialty of quality clams with pork cooked in white wine), chicken and prawn curry Madras, and Portuguese breast of turkey. If you prefer, you can enjoy fresh lobster, rock lobster, crab, and other seafood which can be chosen from the aquarium in the bar. Dinner costs from 2,600$ ($17.40) and is served Monday to Saturday from 6 to 11pm. A tourist menu is offered for 1,600$ ($10.70). The bar has been rebuilt with local stone, marble, and clay brick. Reservations are necessary. AE, DC, MC, V.

Mariners, Rua Santa Isabel 28 (tel. 258-48). Masses of bougainvillea fill the corners of this restaurant's garden patio. Even without the flowers, you still might be tempted by the vaulted and tile-lined inner room for more formal dining. The owners illuminate much of this place with candlelight, whose glow sparkles on the fine china, good linen, and soothingly repetitive ceiling arches. A relaxing Portuguese dinner costs from 2,500$ ($16.75) and is likely to include peppersteak, filets of plaice in a Mornay sauce, a mixed grill, lasagne, or a hot Indian curry. Lunches, less elaborate, and costing from 1,200$ ($8.05), offer such dishes as beefburgers and fish-and-chips, served on the patio or in the bar and dining room upstairs. Hours are Monday to Saturday from noon to 3pm and 7 to 10:30pm. Mariners closes from October through March. Reservations aren't needed. No credit cards.

O Bicho Restaurant, Largo Gil Eanes 12 (tel. 229-77), is one of the best places in the Algarve to order cataplana, a typical regional dish consisting of clams, pork, green pepper, tomatoes, and spices, including hot pepper, garlic, and bay leaf. All this is cooked in a special copper pot, also called cataplana, which has a lid that seals the mixture in tightly to steam. The owner of this simple eating place has made O Bicho popular with locals and discerning tourists who enjoy the typical Portuguese food. A meal will cost from 1,800$ ($12.05) to 2,800$ ($18.75), served daily from noon to 3pm and 7 to 10:30pm. It is best to reserve. Closed January 10 to 20. AE, DC, MC, V.

Nearby Places to Dine

Outside of Portimão, one of the best places for dining on both a Portuguese and international cuisine is **O Gato**, Urbanização da Quintinha, Lote 10-rc, Estrada de Alvor (tel. 082/276-74). Daily from noon to 3pm and 7 to 11pm, the skilled chefs turn out a selection of dishes that are first-rate in both their preparation and choice of ingredients. Its international menu selection is reflected by such classic main dishes as duckling in orange sauce. However, care also goes into regional favorites, including rabbit stew, one of the most savory main courses. A good cataplana is also served, or you may prefer any number of fish and shellfish dishes, along with peppersteak and beef Stroganoff. To begin with, try a refreshing soup such as gazpacho, or razor-thin swordfish which has been smoked and is served with some of the same accompaniments that usually go with caviar. Meals cost from 3,200$ ($21.45) to 5,500$ ($36.85) and are served against an attractive backdrop of white walls and mahogany-beam trim. If you're feeling expansive, you can end your repast with one of the flambé desserts. Reservations are needed. AE, DC, MC, V.

O Leão de Porches, Porches (tel. 082/523-84), lies in a small village, a 3-minute drive from Lagoa on the road (N25) to Faro. Its experienced owner and manager, John Forbes, ran a restaurant in London that enjoyed a worldwide reputation, and he brought his expertise to this place. His cuisine is international, including such dishes as cataplana, roast duck with orange and Cointreau sauce, and fresh fish. You might finish off with Irish coffee or one of the homemade ice creams. Meals cost from 2,500$ ($16.75) and service is Monday through Saturday from 7:15 to 10pm. Closed mid-November to mid-February. Reservations are needed. MC, V.

---

4. Serra de Monchique

The Monchique range of hills is the Algarve at its cool and verdant height. The rocky peak of the range, some 3,000 feet high, looks down on forested slopes and green valleys, burgeoning with cork-oak, chestnut, pine, and eucalyptus trees, orange groves, Indian corn, heather, mimosa, rosemary, and oleander bushes. Icy water springs from the volcanic rock that makes up the range, flowing down to the towns that lie in its foothills.

The towns of Monchique produce many handcrafts in wood, including chairs, benches, decorated canes, and carved wooden spoons. Other articles made by local artisans are wicker baskets, wool sweaters and stockings, and macramé lace made with linen. A typical industry of the people of the Monchique is the making of charcoal, although this activity is slowly disappearing.

The largest town in the borough is also named **Monchique,** lying on the east side of Mount Fóia, 16 miles north of Portimão. The town was once engaged in the manufacture of wooden casks and barrels and the making of oakum and rough cloth. The town has a Manueline-style parish church from the 16th century, with an interesting radiated door-facing. Colorful decorated tiles and carved woodwork grace the interior, along with a statue of Our Lady of the Immaculate Conception, an 18th-century work attributed to Machado de Castro. The Convent of Nossa Senhora do Desterro is in ruins, but you can take a look at the curious fountain with decorative tiles and the impressive old magnolia tree in its grounds.

Caldas de Monchique was discovered in Roman days and turned into a spa. The waters, coming from springs in volcanic rock, are still considered good treatment for respiratory disorders, accompanied as they are by the clear air of the highlands.

Nearly 8 miles from the town of Monchique, **Alferce,** nestling among trees and mountains, has traces of an ancient fortification. There is also an important handcraft center here. In the opposite direction, west of Monchique about 8 miles by the road is **Fóia,** the highest point in the Algarve at almost 3,000 feet. From here you have splendid views of the hills and the sea, seeing all the way to Cape St. Vincent and Sagres on clear days. A TV tower and a restaurant stand on the height. The nearest tourist office is in Portimão.

WHERE TO STAY & DINE

A small inn in the town of Monchique, **Estalagem Abrigo de Montanha,** 8550 Monchique (tel. 082/921-31), is set amid a botanical garden. With all those camellias, rhododendrons, mimosa, banana palms, and arbutus blooming, plus the tinkling waterfalls, you'd never believe the hot Algarve coast was in the same province. The inn has eight rooms, each complete with bath. The bedrooms, each a double, are furnished in a typical Portuguese motif. Rates are 11,000$ ($73.70) a night, including breakfast. On chilly evenings, guests gather before a fireplace in the lounge. In the attractive restaurant, good food is served daily from 12:30 to 3pm and 7:30 to 9:30pm. A main meal costs from 2,500$ ($16.75) to 4,000$ ($26.80). Reservations aren't needed. AE, DC, MC, V.

---

5. Praia da Rocha

This creamy yellow beach has long been the most popular seaside resort on the Algarve. The beauty of its rock formations led English voyagers to discover it around 1935. At the outbreak of World War II there were only two small hotels on the Red Coast, interspersed with a few villas, many built by wealthy Portuguese. Nowadays Praia da Rocha is booming, as many have fallen victim to the spell cast by its shoreline and climate.

It is named the Beach of the Rock because of the sculptural formations of the rock. At the end of the mussel-encrusted cliff, where the Arcade flows into the sea, the ruins of the **Fort of St. Catarina** lie, the location offering many views of Portimão's satellite, Ferragudo, and of the bay.

To reach Praia da Rocha, you go first to Portimão (see above), where you can catch a bus to Praia da Rocha, 1½ miles to the south on the beach.

WHERE TO STAY

Praia da Rocha is endowed with accommodations in all price ranges, the leader of which is the **Algarve Hotel,** Avenida Tomás Cabreira, Praia da Rocha, 8500 Portimão (tel. 082/41-50-01; fax 082/41-50-01), which is strictly for those who love glitter and glamour. With a vast staff at one's beck and call, a guest is ensconced in luxury within an elongated block of 220 rooms poised securely on the top ledge of a cliff. On a lower terrace is a huge kidney-shaped heated swimming pool (plus another one for children), with a sun deck cantilevered over still another cliff, projecting above rugged rocks, caves, and a sandy cove.

The main lounge is like a sultan's palace: gold velvet chairs, Oriental carpets, brass-and-teak screens, antique chests, and deep sofas set around a copper-hooded fireplace. The bedrooms have white walls, colored ceilings, intricate tile floors, mirrored entryways, indirect lighting, balconies with garden furniture, and baths with separate showers. Everything is air conditioned and centrally heated. In April, May, and October, the bed-and-breakfast cost of a single is 18,000$ ($120.60), rising to 25,000$ ($167.50) in a double. In June, the rate in a single is 20,000$ ($134), 27,000$ ($180.90) in a double. From July through September, the rate in a single is 27,000$ ($180.90), going up to 35,000$ ($234.50) in a double. Twenty suites are rented, beginning at 45,000$ ($301.50). The Yachting, Oriental, Presidential, and Miradouro suites are each a decorator's tour de force in originality.

Portuguese chefs, with French backgrounds, provide gourmet meals on the à la carte menu served either in the Grill Azul or Das Amendoeiros. Meals in Das Amendoeiras range from 2,600$ ($17.40) to 3,800$ ($25.45), whereas those in the specialty restaurant, Grill Azul, cost from 5,000$ ($33.50) to 6,000$ ($40.20). Buffet luncheons in season are served by the swimming pool. A one-of-a-kind nightclub books top-flight entertainers (even Amália Rodrigues on one occasion), in addition to their regular troupe of folk dancers. The club is like an Oriental grotto dug out of a cliff, with three stone walls and a fourth allowing for an oceanic backdrop. Extra services include a sauna, hairdresser, barbershop, manicurist, laundry and dry cleaning, baby-sitting, boutiques, and 24-hour room service. There's even a social director who plans personalized activities, such as fishing parties on the hotel boat (with seafood stews), games of bridge, barbecues on the beach, mini-golf, volleyball, tennis competitions, plus waterskiing and deep-sea fishing. Parking is free. AE, DC, MC, V.

Bela Vista, Avenida Tomás Cabreira, Praia da Rocha, 8500 Portimão (tel. 082/240-55; fax 082/41-53-69), is an old mansion built in the Moorish style during the last century by a wealthy family, for use as a summer home. As well as a minaret-type tower that flanks its facade, there's also a statue of the Virgin set into the masonry of one of the building's corners. Since 1934 it's been a special kind of hotel, ideal for those who respond to the architecture of the past. Rated first class, it's set on the oceanside, atop its own palisade, with access to a sandy cove where you can swim. The villa is white, with an ornate tower and terra-cotta tile roof, a coastal landmark spotted by fishermen bringing in their boats at sundown. It's flanked by the owner's home and a simple cliff-edge annex shaded by palm trees.

The attractive structure and its decorations have been preserved, but plastic furniture has been placed into the public lounges. The entry hallway has an art nouveau bronze torchère and a winding staircase, with walls almost covered with 19th-century blue-and-white tiles depicting allegorical scenes from Portuguese history. Guests enjoy get-togethers around a baronial fireplace with a tile facade. In the high-ceilinged dining hall, meals combine Portuguese cuisine with a continental flair. The 14 bedrooms each contain TV, private bath, and phone. Those facing the sea, the former master bedrooms, are the most desirable, though all rooms have character. The main house is preferable to the annex. For a room and breakfast, the price is 20,000$ ($134) daily in a single, 21,000$ ($140.70) in a double. Decorations vary from a tile inset shrine of the Virgin Mary to crystal sconces. Parking is free. AE, DC, MC, V.

Júpiter, Avenida Tomás Cabreira, Praia da Rocha, 8500 Portimão (tel. 082/41-50-41; fax 082/41/53-19), occupies what might be the most prominent street corner in this bustling summer resort. There's a wraparound arcade filled with boutiques and a spacious lobby where guests relax, sometimes with drinks, on comfortable couches. The hotel is just across the street from a wide beach, but it has a swimming pool, covered and heated. The Night Star disco provides late-night diversion beneath a metallic ceiling, while a semiformal restaurant, an informal pub, and a cocktail bar offer food and drink. You can enjoy snacks and light lunches at poolside during the summer. The 180 comfortably modern and air-conditioned accommodations contain balconies, as well as radios and phones, with views over either the river or the sea. Singles range from 16,000$ ($107.20) daily, and doubles go for 18,000$ ($120.60), including breakfast. Parking is free. AE, DC, MC, V.

Pensão Tursol, Rua Engenheiro Francisco Bivar, Praia da Rocha, 8500 Portimão (tel. 082/240-46). This simple but charming hotel is fronted by a garden rich with flowering vines and shrubs. You'll find it on a street running parallel to the main road beside the beach. It's in a quiet part of the resort, not far from the center. The establishment contains a cool, basement bar and TV room filled with leatherette chairs. The staff is helpful. In winter a fire warms a corner of the dining room. But the rest of the year the windows are thrown open for a view of the surrounding landscape. Singles rent for 6,600$ ($44.20) daily, while doubles cost from 8,000$ ($53.60). Each of the 23 accommodations comes with private bath and phone, and breakfast is included. The inn is closed in December and January. Parking is free. No credit cards.

Residencial Sol, Avenida Tomás Cabreira 10, Praia da Rocha, 8500 Portimão (tel. 082/240-71). Partly because of its location near the noisy main street, the painted concrete facade of this establishment appears somewhat bleak. In this case, however, appearances are deceiving, since the 21 bedrooms offer some of the cleanest and most unpretentious, attractive accommodations in town. Each of the units is designed for two guests, and contains a private bath, phone, radio, and exposed wood. The rooms in back are quieter, but the terrace-dotted front units look across the traffic toward a park filled with bougainvillea. The breakfast lounge doubles as a TV room. Singles rent for 6,000$ ($40.20) daily, with doubles costing 6,500$ ($43.55). The hotel rents two suites—suitable for two to three guests—costing from 8,000$ ($53.60). Breakfast is included, and private parking is free. Laundry service is provided, and room service is available until midnight. AE, DC, MC, V.

Residencial Solar Penquin, Avenida Tomás Cabreira, Praia da Rocha, 8500 Portimão (tel. 082/24-308). The foundations of this well-placed hotel were originally those of an ancient Moorish fort. Later, they supported the thick walls of a private house whose red tile roof still juts up near a public park festooned with bougainvillea and dotted with café tables. As the hotel sits on a cliff jutting out over the sands below, it offers the resort's best view of the beach. The establishment contains 14 simple bedrooms, each with bath and suitable for two people. With breakfast included, these rent for 7,000$ ($46.90) to 8,000$ ($53.60) daily. The hotel is open March through October. Parking is free. No credit cards.

WHERE TO DINE

Complete with gilt and crystal, the **Titanic,** Edifício Colúmbia, Rua Engenheiro Francisco Bivar (tel. 223-71), is the most elegant restaurant in town. It also serves the best food, an array of international specialties, including live shellfish and flambé dishes. In spite of the fact that it is named after the ill-fated luxury liner, it is not on the water, but lies in a modern residential complex. For 2,500$ ($16.75) to 3,300$ ($22.10), you can dine very well here, ordering such appealing dishes as the fish of the day, pork filet with mushrooms, prawns *a la plancha* (grilled) and sole Algarve. Service is among the best at the resort. The 100-seat Titanic, which is air conditioned, sails daily from noon to 2pm and 7 to 11pm. It closes from the end of November until the end of December. The kitchen is in open view, and diners should make a reservation, especially in summer. AE, DC, MC, V.

Safari, Rua António Feo (tel. 082/235-40), is a Portuguese-run restaurant with a "taste of Africa" in its cuisine, as its name suggests. Many of its specialties were inspired by the former Portuguese colony of Angola. Built on a cliff overlooking the beach, this third-category restaurant has a glass-enclosed terrace. It is known for its fresh fish and seafood, and many guests in neighboring hotels like to escape the board requirements of their accommodation just to sample one of Safari's good home-cooked meals. The fare includes such delectable dishes as curry Safari, steak Safari, swordfish steak, and shrimp Safari. It's customary to begin your meal with a bowl of savory fish soup. Meals, served from noon to midnight, cost from 2,800$ ($18.75), and you get good value here. A tourist menu is only 1,600$ ($10.70). Reservations are required. It closes in November and December.

Bamboo Garden, Edifício Lamego, Avenida Tomás Cabreira (tel. 830-83), which has a classic Asian decor, serves some of the best Chinese food along the coast. In air-conditioned comfort, diners can select from a large menu that includes everything from squid chop suey to prawns with hot sauce. After deciding on a soup or appetizer (try the spring roll), guests can make their selections from various categories, including chicken, beef, duck, squid, and prawns. You might, for example, prefer fried duck with soybean sauce or chicken with almonds from the Algarve. Meals cost from 2,200$ ($14.75) and are served daily from 12:30 to 3pm and 6pm to midnight. Reservations are recommended. AE, DC, MC, V.

---

6. Praia dos Três Irmãos & Alvor

PRAIA DOS TRÊS IRMÃOS

Go here for the beach, 9 miles of burnished golden sand, broken only by an occasional crag riddled with arched passageways. Just 3 miles southwest of

Portimão, the Beach of the Three Brothers has been discovered by skin divers who explore its undersea grottoes and shoreside cave.

Its neighbor is the whitewashed fishing village of **Alvor,** where Portuguese and Moorish arts and traditions have mingled since the Arabs gave up their 500 years of occupation. Alvor was a favorite coastal haunt of King João II. The gambling casino, the **Casino de Alvor** (tel. 231-41), is modest in size compared to the one at Estoril, but it does feature roulette, blackjack, and craps. A restaurant features good food and also offers a floor show at 11pm and 1am. It is open nightly. The nearest tourist office is in Portimão, which you can reach by public transportation (see above). From Portimão, you can reach either Praia dos Tres Irmãos and Alvor by public bus which runs frequently throughout the day.

Where to Stay

Alvor Praia, Praia dos Três Irmãos, 8500 Portimão (tel. 082/45-89-00; fax 082/45-89-00). "You'll feel like you're loved the moment you walk in the door," said a well-dressed woman visitor from the Midwest. This citadel of hedonism seems to have more joie de vivre than any hotel on the Algarve. Its position is ideal, as are the building, bedrooms, decor, service, and food. On a landscaped crest, the luxury hotel has many of its bedrooms and public rooms exposed to the ocean view, the gardens, and the free-form Olympic-size swimming pool. Gentle walks (or else an elevator) lead down the palisade to the sandy beach and the rugged rocks that rise out of the water.

The 183 accommodations are quite varied, everything from a cowhide-decorated room evoking Arizona's Valley of the Sun, to typical Portuguese accommodations with provincial furnishings. Many of the rooms contain private balconies where guests take breakfast facing the view of the Bay of Lagos.

The rooms contain oversize beds, plenty of clothing space, a long desk-and-chest combination, and well-designed baths with double basins and lots of towels. Each room is air conditioned, with a phone, minibar, and TV. Singles cost from 16,000$ ($107.20) to 21,400$ ($143.40) daily; doubles, 22,950$ ($153.75). The hotel also rents 18 suites beginning at 30,600$ ($205). Breakfast is included.

The hotel is so self-contained you may never stray from the premises. Inside, a wide, domed airborne staircase leads to a lower level, encircling a Japanese garden and lily pond. The main dining room is on two levels, with three glass walls so that every guest has an ocean view. The Maisonette Grill is considered separately as a restaurant recommendation (see below). Like an exclusive club, the main drinking lounge is equipped with deep leather chairs and decorated with a cubistic modern ceiling. You can get reduced greens fees on a nearby 18-hole golf course. Other sports include horseback riding, waterskiing, and tennis. On the lower level of the hotel are boutiques, a newsstand, hairdressers, and a Finnish sauna. Other facilities include a solarium, health club, and outdoor swimming pool. Baby-sitting and laundry service are arranged, and room service is 24 hours a day. Parking is free. AE, DC, MC, V.

Delfim Hotel, Praia dos Três Irmãos, 8500 Portimão (tel. 082/45-89-01; fax 082/45-89-70). The developers of this hotel chose their site wisely. The Delfim sits near the beach on a scrub-covered hillside whose sands offer a sweeping view of the Algarvian coastline and its dozens of high-rises. With its central tower and its identical wings splayed back like a boomerang in flight, the hotel is one of the most dramatically modern buildings in the region. In spite of its proximity to the beach, many guests prefer the parasol-ringed swimming pool whose circumference encloses a swim-up bar marooned like an island in its midst. Tennis courts are nearby, as well as an assortment of shops, restaurants, and bars. Each of the 300 well-furnished rooms contains a private terrace, bath, TV, minibar, radio, and phone. Singles cost from 10,800$ ($72.35) to 13,500$ ($90.45) daily; doubles, 15,520$ ($104) to 19,400$ ($130). The hotel also rents 13 suites, costing from 27,900$ ($186.95). Only the suites are air conditioned. Portuguese and international cuisine is served, with meals costing from 2,800$ ($18.75). Piano bar entertainment is offered. Laundry service is provided, as is baby-sitting, and room service is 24 hours a day. Parking is free. AE, DC, MC, V.

Where to Dine

Maisonette Grill, Hotel Alvor Praia, Praia dos Três Irmãos (tel. 45-89-00), takes its rightful place alongside other distinguished restaurants connected with luxury hotels, such as the Ritz Grill in Lisbon. It is among the smartest places for gourmet cuisine along the Algarve coast. The grill, in spite of its spaciousness, has an intimate atmosphere, allowing you plenty of time to peruse the à la carte Portuguese and international menu. You might begin your meal with vichyssoise. Main courses are likely to include poached turbot with hollandaise and a broiled rib of beef prepared for two persons. The dessert menu has such delicacies as Rothschild soufflé and crêpes Suzette. Meals, served nightly from 8pm to midnight, cost from 6,000$ ($40.20). Reservations are necessary. The grill is closed on Thursday in summer. AE, DC, MC, V.

Restaurante O Búzio, Aldeamento da Prainha, Praia dos Três Irmãos (tel. 45-85-61), stands at the end of a road that encircles a resort development dotted with private condos and exotic shrubbery. In summer there are so many cars lining the narrow blacktop road that you'd be well advised to park near the resort's entrance, then walk the downhill stretch toward the restaurant.

Lunch and dinner are served in two separate locations. From noon to 3pm daily, lunch is offered on a shaded hillock overlooking one of the best-landscaped pools on the Algarve. Many visitors enjoy the grassy lawns sloping toward the pool so much that they pay an entrance fee and spend the rest of the day beside its waters. If you come only for lunch, there is no entrance fee. For 2,200$ ($14.75), you can enjoy a light meal, which might include omelets, salads, hamburgers, or fresh fish. The real allure of the place, however, is after dark when dinners are served near the resort's administrative offices. In a room whose blue curtains reflect the color of the shimmering ocean at the bottom of the cliffs, you can enjoy dinner at prices beginning at 4,200$ ($28.15). Reservations are necessary for international meals, which might include fish soup, gazpacho, Italian pasta dishes, boiled or grilled fish of the day, peppersteak, and lamb kebabs with saffron-flavored rice. Dinner is every night from 7:30 to 10pm. In winter, when it's too cold to eat outside, you can also have lunch in this restaurant. Closed in November. AE, DC, MC, V.

MONTES DE ALVOR

Where to Stay & Dine

The first deluxe hotel on the Algarve was the **Penina Golf Hotel,** Montes de Alvor, 8502 Portimão (tel. 082/41-54-15; fax 082/41-50-00), between Portimão and Lagos, founded by a group of hotel entrepreneurs. Nowadays, of course, it has much competition from the other luxury choices. Golfing fans remain loyal to the Penina, however, as it is a major sporting mecca. A 36-hole championship golf course was designed by Henry Cotton between the hotel and the sea. Those not sunning themselves by the pool are transported to the hotel beach, with its own snack bar and changing cabins. The ground level of the Penina is devoted to changing rooms, lockers, and a golf school and shops. Other facilities include a sauna, billiard room, a beauty parlor, and a barbershop. Five hard tennis courts are offered. Guests enjoy the Grill Room or the dining room (table d'hôte meals in the latter) for a well-prepared repast, capped by dancing.

Most of the 188 bedrooms contain picture windows and honeycomb balconies providing views of the course and swimming pool or vistas of the Monchique hills. The standard bedrooms are furnished in a pleasant style, combining traditional pieces with Portuguese provincial spool beds. The rooms are spacious enough for off-the-course relaxation, and contain good-sized beds and tile baths. Each room is air conditioned, with phone, TV, and minibar. Singles cost 21,800$ ($146.05) to 24,500$ ($164.15) daily, with doubles going for 32,000$ ($214.40) to 34,500$

($231.15). Fourteen suites are rented, costing from 64,000$ ($428.80). Tariffs include breakfast. Laundry and baby-sitting can be arranged, and room service is available 24 hours. Parking is free. AE, DC, MC, V.

---

7. Praia do Carvoeiro

One of the little whitewashed beach fishing villages along the Algarve coast has been turned into an expatriate colony, with many sophisticated Europeans finding it the most ideal place along the coast. It has not been overbuilt (as of yet), and it has a number of excellent restaurants. Accommodations, as of this writing, were still extremely limited, including only one major hotel and time-share units.

Lying 3 miles south of the wine-rich town of Lagoa, and 189 miles southeast of Lisbon, the sandy beach nestles between two rock masses, creating a solarium. The shadows of the cliffs are cooling, the sea calm. East of the beach on a steep slope is a **belvedere,** dedicated to Our Lady of the Incarnation (*Nossa Senhora da Encarnação*), from which you have a commanding view of the sea and surrounding cliffs. Not far from the belvedere, you can reach the fascinating **Algar Seco,** a collection of huge reddish stones carved by the sea into interesting shapes and a number of sea caves, often underwater. You go through mazes of rock and down some 134 steps to reach the site. The sea caves can be visited by boat in summer. Ask in the town.

Incidentally, before venturing down to the little commune of Praia do Carvoeiro, you may want to stop off at **Lagoa,** on the main coastal highway. If you announce yourself at the door to the big warehouse here, chances are you'll be allowed to visit the wine cellars.

The **tourist information office** is at Largo da Praia, Praia do Carvoeiro (tel. 082/577-28). You can get a bus from Silves or Portimão, which will take you to Lagoa, where connections run to Praia do Carvoeiro.

WHERE TO STAY

A few steps from the sheltered but sandy harbor, **Hotel Dom Sancho,** Largo da Praia, Praia do Carvoeiro, 8400 Faro (tel. 082/357-30; fax 082/37-72-11), is in a hard-to-miss spot on the main square of the port. If this folkloric village becomes, as its devotees predict, the Portuguese St. Tropez, this comfortable hotel will probably be one of its social centers. Its major drawback is that you may not be able to get in, as tour operators have been known to book every room for a whole season. This is a pity for the independent traveler, as the Dom Sancho is the only real hotel in town, although you may find a little guest room or boardinghouse, perhaps a time-share unit on the hill.

The hotel's thick white walls, angular windows, and flat roof remind visitors of Pueblo dwellings in the American Southwest. The brick-covered courtyard and the vaulted dining room, however, are pure Iberian, as is the polite attention of the well-trained staff. Bedrooms are air conditioned, containing radios, phones, and unpretentious modern furnishings. Some of the units have private balconies overlooking the port. The 47 rooms rent for 8,800$ ($58.95) daily in a single, 14,400$ ($96.50) for double occupancy, with breakfast included. The hotel also rents three suites, costing from 16,400$ ($109.90). The restaurant serves good Portuguese cuisine, and sometimes guests are treated to live music and folkloric exhibitions. Laundry service and baby-sitting can be arranged, and room service is provided until midnight. The hotel also has an outdoor swimming pool, and parking is free. AE, DC, MC, V.

WHERE TO DINE

A pleasant place to go for dinner is **O Castelo,** Rua do Casino (tel. 35-72-18). If you're fortunate enough to obtain a table on the outdoor terrace or near one of the establishment's small windows, you'll have a view over the sea. It's actually an Algarve house, whose entrance sits beside the steep road skirting the edge of a harborside cliff. The ambience is relatively sophisticated, and the youthful waiters somehow seem to anticipate your needs. The international meals are reasonably priced at 2,800$ ($18.75). Lunch isn't served, but for dinner you might enjoy such specialties as peppersteak, grilled prawns, piri-piri, assorted shellfish au gratin, shrimp kebab, and fish cataplana. For dessert, you can order almond cake. Dinner is served Monday to Saturday from 7 to 10pm. Closed January 15 to March 1. Reservations aren't needed. AE, DC, MC, V.

THE BAR SCENE

Right in the center of the resort, **Long Bar,** Rua dos Pescadores (tel. 35-74-35), as its name implies, has the longest bar in town. You might select one of the scattering of outdoor tables, but the heart and soul of the place is visible only from within its British pub-style interior. There, you can order a Sagres beer to accompany a pub lunch or dinner. You might, after a round of drinks or two, decide to order such fare as a baked potato, an omelet, a hamburger, or a sandwich. Meals cost from 1,200$ ($8.05). Drinks cost from 300$ ($2). The bartender specializes in liqueur coffees. Hours are daily from 10am to 2am. Closed January 15 to February 15.

Smiler's Bar, Rua do Barranco (tel. 35-73-04). A sampling of the assorted youth of Europe is likely to be crammed between the thick white arches of this bar on a summer night. The place is British owned, and it's the most popular bar in town. Its regulars also claim that it serves the best beer. Hard drinks cost 400$ ($2.70), with beer going for 150$ ($1). Hours are 10:30pm to 2am. It is closed in December.

---

8. Silves

When you pass through the Moorish-inspired entrance of this hillside town, you quickly become aware that Silves is unlike the other towns and villages of the Algarve. It lives in the past, recalling its heyday when it was known as Xelb, the seat of Muslim culture in the south before it fell to the crusaders. Christian warriors and earthquakes have been rough on Silves. But somehow the **Castle of Silves,** crowning the hilltop, has held on, although it's seen better days. Once the blood of the Muslims, staging their last stand in Silves, "flowed like red wine," as one Portuguese historian put it. The cries and screams of women and children resounded over the walls. Nowadays the only sound you're likely to hear is the loud rock music coming from the gatekeeper's house.

The red sandstone castle may date back to the 9th century. From its ramparts you can look down the saffron-mossed tile roofs of the village houses, down the narrow cobbled streets where roosters strut and scrappy dogs sleep peacefully in the doorways. Inside the walls, the government has planted a flower garden, adorning it with golden chrysanthemums and scarlet poinsettias. In the fortress, water rushes through a huge cistern and a deep well made of sandstone. Below are dungeon chambers and labyrinthine tunnels where the last of the Moors hid out before the crusaders found them and sent them to their deaths.

The 13th-century former **Cathedral of Silves** (now a church), down below, was built in the Gothic style. You can wander through its aisles and nave, noting perhaps beauty in their simplicity. Both the chancel and transept date from a later period, having been built in the flamboyant Gothic style. The Christian architects who originally built it may have torn down an old mosque. Many of the tombs contained here are believed to have been the graves of crusaders who took the town in 1244. The Gothic structure is considered one of the most outstanding religious monuments in the Algarve.

Outside the main part of town, near an orange grove (one of the local Silves boys will surely volunteer as your inexpensive guide), a lonely open-air pavilion shelters a 15th-century stone lacework cross. This ecclesiastical artwork is two-faced, depicting a pietà (the face of Christ is destroyed) on one side, the Crucifixion on the other. It has been declared a national monument of incalculable value.

Trains from Faro pull into the Silves train station, which is 1 mile from the center of the town. The bus station is on Rua da Cruz de Palmeira, where eight buses a day arrive from either Silves or Portimão. Trip time is 45 minutes. The **Silves Tourist Office** is on Rua 25 de Abril 26–28 (tel. 082/422-55).

WHERE TO DINE

Silves is most often visited on a day-trip from one of the beach towns to the south. For that reason, many visitors find themselves in Silves at lunchtime. Restaurants here are very simple but also very cheap.

One of the best is **Rui,** Rua Comendador Vilarim 27 (tel. 44-31-06), which is known for its shellfish, such as lobster, and its superb grills. In fact, the owners of this restaurant have their own shellfish nursery. They serve good-tasting Portuguese meals along with regional wines for 2,500$ ($16.75) and up per person. A tourist menu is offered for 1,400$ ($9.40). Rui is the largest restaurant in town, and can take as many as 120 diners on its busiest day. You can sample arroz de mariscos, (shellfish rice), clams na cataplana, and carré de borrego (lamb). It is open daily from noon to 4pm and 6 to 11pm. Reservations aren't needed. AE, DC, MC, V.

Ladeira, Ladeira de São Pedro (tel. 44-28-70), is smaller, seating 40 diners. It is also cheaper, charging from 2,000$ ($13.40) for a filling meal. A tourist menu costs 1,200$ ($8.05). Regional specialties are featured, and the place is known for its "home-cooking." Steak Ladeira and mixed-fish cataplana are specialties. Service is from noon to 3pm and 6 to 10pm. It is closed Sunday. Reservations aren't needed. AE, DC, MC, V.

---

9. Armação de Pêra

Squat fishermen's cottages make up the core of this ancient village. It rests almost at water's edge on a curvy bay that comes near its Golden Beach, one of the largest along Portugal's southern coast. In the direction of Portimão are rolling low ridges, toward Albufeira's rosy cliffs. Because Armação de Pêra has such a fine beach, it has almost become engulfed in a sea of high-rise buildings, which have virtually eliminated its once rather charming character.

Once Armação de Pêra was utilized by the Phoenicians as a trading post and stopping-off point for cruises around Cape St. Vincent. Near the center of the village is a wide beach where fishing boats are drawn up on the sands when a fish auction (*lota*) is held.

While at the resort, you may want to walk out to **Nossa Senhora da Rocha** (Our Lady of the Rock), a Romanesque chapel on a 95-foot-high stone that sticks out into the ocean like the prow of a boat. Underneath are the cathedral-size **Sea Grottos** (*Furnas*). To visit these, you have to call at the tourist office, Avenida Marginal (tel. 082/321-45), and make arrangements to go out in a boat, but they're certainly worth the effort. Unique in the Algarve, the sea caves are entered through a series of arches that frame the sky and ocean from the inside. In their galleries and vaults, where pigeons nest, the splashing and cooing reverberate in the upper stalactite-studded chambers.

The nearest railway station is at the village of Alcantarilha, 5 miles away. Five trains arrive daily from Lisbon, requiring a change of trains at Alcantarilha. Trip time ranges from 5 to 6 hours. About five buses a day also arrive from Lisbon, the trip taking 4 hours. Armação de Pêra lies 195 miles southeast of Lisbon and 28 miles west of Faro.

WHERE TO STAY

A deluxe establishment, **Hotel Viking,** Praia da Senhora da Rocha, 8365 Armação de Pêra (tel. 082/31-48-76; fax 082/31-28-26), lies about a mile southwest of the resort, with many signs directing you. It rises in a mass of gray stone and buff-colored concrete between two spits of land jutting into the sea. The hotel has many and diverse amenities, including a replica of a 19th-century café set into the windbreak of a cobblestone courtyard, an English pub, a large cocktail bar leading into an enormous dining room, a TV room filled with card tables, a basement-level disco, and an array of in- and outdoor bars. My favorite place within the grounds is the clifftop pair of swimming pools. There, within a view of the rugged geology marking this region of Portugal, you can stretch out under bamboo parasols, between the shades of large terra-cotta pots festooned with geraniums and trailing strands of ivy.

Even the geodesic dome of the lobby's skylight illuminates a splashing fountain ringed with glistening slabs of white marble. Each of the comfortably contemporary and air-conditioned rooms, 109 in all, contains a private balcony angled toward a view of the sea, and each has a marble-covered bath, wall-to-wall carpeting, a minibar, radio, and phone. Singles cost 22,400$ ($150.10) daily, with doubles going for 27,600$ ($184.90). The hotel also rents 69 suites, costing from 28,800$ ($192.95). Breakfast is included. The Viking also contains tennis courts, puts out lavishly decorated buffets, and has a wide array of "above and below" water sports, as well as a beauty salon, a sauna, massage facilities, and a Jacuzzi. Laundry and baby-sitting are arranged, and parking is available free. Room service is offered until midnight. AE, DC, MC, V.

Vilalara, Praia das Gaivotas, 8365 Armação de Pêra (tel. 082/31-49-10; fax 082/31-49-56), is a luxury apartment complex on a cliffside, with a sandy beach— all in all, a self-contained miniature resort 1 mile west of Armação de Pêra. International magazines have acclaimed its good taste, which has attracted diplomats, movie stars, members of royalty, as well as business executives. Curving with the contour of the coast, the apartments are built in a serpentine fashion, two floors of one-, two-, and three-bedroom units, each with a private sun-pocket terrace balcony. That balcony is furnished in bamboo and rattan. A long continuous flower box softens the look at the railing. Each apartment is spacious and delightful, with a living room, a fully equipped kitchen, a veranda with a southern view, and each bedroom has its own tile bath. At total of 86 apartments and 50 junior suites are rented. Junior suites cost 35,880$ ($240.40) daily, with two-bedroom apartments going for 62,000$ ($415.40).

The major dining focus is the Vilalara Restaurant, recommended separately. The hotel contains what it calls a club, with dining and wining facilities, as well as tennis courts, three swimming pools (one for children), and a disco. The snack bar/ grill restaurant is near the pool. The complex has an indoor-outdoor informality that is casually chic. Other facilities include a health club and solarium. Laundry service is provided, and room service is offered until midnight. Parking is free. AE, DC, MC, V.

Hotel do Garbe, Avenida Marginal, 8365 Armação de Pêra (tel. 082/31-21-94; fax 082/31-20-87), is a self-contained resort dominating the top of a cliff, with a sandy beach at its feet. Stone steps lead through the terraced palisade to the hotel, built block fashion, its white walls, bedroom balconies, and public terraces shining in the summer sun. The public rooms, on several levels, are modern, but warmed by their colors and natural wood. In the main sitting room, with its open fireplace, furnishings are grouped with an eye to the sea view; likewise, the dining hall turns to the sea. If you're just passing through, you can order a luncheon or dinner for 2,200$ ($14.75).

The 90 bedrooms combine Nordic and Algarvian features. Often a room will have window seats, beds set on pine frames, an occasional white skin throw rug, a red parasol on a private patio, and leather-toned tile floors. Amenities include phone, TV, and private bath. Only the public rooms are air conditioned. Rates range from 10,000$ ($670) to 16,800$ ($112.55) daily in a single, 16,800$ ($112.55) to 18,800$ ($125.95) in a double, including breakfast. Nineteen suites are also rented, costing from 19,250$ ($129). The hotel also has an outdoor swimming pool, and laundry and baby-sitting can be arranged. Parking is free. AE, DC, MC, V.

Hotel do Levante, 8365 Armação de Pêra (tel. 082/31-49-00; fax 082/31-49-99). Many repeat visitors consider this their favorite hotel on the Algarve. It's contained within a Mediterranean-style villa set on a hill away from the congestion of the resort. From a position near the lobby, visitors have a sweeping view of the sea, the high-rises along the coast, and a pair of swimming pools dug into the shrub-bordered terraces. The hotel opened in 1967. Some of the 41 bedrooms open onto enclosed courtyards, where pines glimmer with festoons of colored lights. Others have a view of the sea, and each contains a radio, phone, TV, private bath, minibar, air conditioning, and a private balcony or terrace. Singles cost 13,500$ ($90.45) daily, with doubles renting for 19,400$ ($130), including breakfast. Perhaps, best of all, a formal garden, laid out in a star-shaped pattern, includes the name of the hotel spelled out amid the greenery. A haciendalike dining room, replete with leather-backed chairs and pure white walls, serves well-prepared meals to a largely English or German clientele. Laundry and baby-sitting can be arranged, and room service is offered 24 hours a day. Parking is free. AE, DC, MC, V.

WHERE TO DINE

It's worth the effort it takes to get to the **Panorama Sol Grill** (tel. 082/31-24-24). You'll find it on a road west of town leading to the Hotel do Levante and the Hotel Viking. At first you might think that the only available seating is on the simple benches, under sunscreens that have been set up on the outdoor walled-in terrace. No one will object if you want to sit there. However, you'll be rewarded if you continue to climb past the outdoor grill to the top of the stairs, entering a baronial dining hall. There, within view of a huge stone fireplace, you can eat in more dignified circumstances.

Regardless of where you choose to sit, you'll have to give your menu order at the grill, where the day's catch, as well as an array of meats, is laid out in a refrigerated case for your inspection. Average meals cost from 3,500$ ($23.45) and might include silver bass, fresh asparagus, and several preparations of beef, veal, or pork, plus live lobster from the restaurant's aquarium. The cuisine is Portuguese, and reservations are necessary. A tourist menu costs only 1,800$ ($12.05). The establishment is open for lunch from 12:30 to 3pm and dinner from 6:30 to 10pm every day in summer. Between February and the end of April it is closed every Wednesday, and between November and February it is completely closed. AE, DC, MC, V.

Vilalara, Praia das Gaivotas (tel. 31-49-10), 1 mile west of Armação de Pêra, was recommended previously as a hotel. In this luxury apartment complex, with its splendid flower gardens, Vilalara also serves some of the finest Portuguese, English, and international food on the Algarve. The restaurant is open only for dinner, which is served nightly from 8 to 10:30pm and costs from 7,000$ ($46.90) à la carte, although a tourist menu costs only 4,000$ ($26.80). Service, which is deluxe, is in a restaurant that has a big-windowed panoramic view of the sea and black painted bamboo chairs and black-and-white décor. The chefs use only top-quality ingredients and prepare dishes with flair. These include the freshest of seafood. An indoor and outdoor grill and its adjacent snack bar are often closed for part of the year, but the restaurant is open all year. Reservations are necessary. AE, DC, MC, V.

Santola, Largo 25 de Abril (tel. 31-23-32), has long been established. Its faithful patrons remember Armação de Pêra when it was just a fishing village. At the edge of the beach, "The Crab" specializes in a wide range of Portuguese and international dishes, placing the emphasis on seafood. It does excellent charcoal grills and has several continental specialties to tempt diners, who pay from 4,000$ ($26.80) for a good-tasting meal. Service is daily from noon to 3pm and 7pm to midnight. From one of its tables you can enjoy a panoramic view. In winter a fireplace adds the proper glow, and all year round the bar is popular. AE, DC, MC, V.

---

10. Albufeira

This cliffside town—once a fishing village—is the St. Tropez of the Algarve. The lazy life, sunshine, and beaches make it a haven for young people and artists, although the old-time villagers still haven't quite made up their minds as to what they think of the invasion that began in the late 1960s. That migration turned

Albufeira into the largest resort in the region. Some of them, however, open the doors of their cottages to those seeking a place to stay. Those without the money often sleep in a tent on the cliff, or under the sky.

The big, bustling resort retains characteristics more readily associated with a North African seaside community. Its streets are steep, the villas staggered up and down the hillside. Albufeira rises above a sickle-shaped beach that shines in the bright sunlight. A rocky grottoed bluff separates the strip used by the sunbathers from the working beach, where brightly painted fishing boats are drawn up on the sand. Access to the beach is through a tunneled rock passageway.

In accommodations, the resort is well supplied. The tariffs in many of the establishments are more suited to the middle-class pocketbook than that of the young people who favor the place so much.

Albufeira lies 202 miles southeast of Lisbon and 23 miles west of Faro. Its **tourist information office** is on Rua 5 de Outubro (tel. 089/521-44).

Trains connect Albufeira with Faro (see below) from which good connections can be made to Lisbon. The train station lies 4 miles from the center, but frequent buses run back and forth from the station to the resort every 30 minutes, a one-way ticket costing 60$ (40¢).

WHERE TO STAY

Expensive
Hotel Boa-Vista, Rua Samora Barros 6, 8200 Albufeira (tel. 089/58-91-75; fax 089/58-69-98). Built in the Algarvian style, and set high above the sea outside the center, the "Residence of the Good View" offers two different modes of living: one in its amenity-loaded main building, another in its block of furnished efficiencies across the street. The style, the welcome, the level of taste are set by a private hotel chain called Glitter Hotels.

International cuisine is served in the panoramic restaurant/grill bar with a view of the bay. The 89 rooms open onto balconies, from which you can look down upon the whitewashed, orange tile–roofed cottages to the bay below. The private baths are superb, in gray and white with marble. Traditional wickerwood decor is used, with matching carpets and ceramics. Each accommodation has air conditioning, private bath, phone, and TV. Singles cost 16,000$ ($107.20) daily; doubles 21,000$ ($140.05) and the two suites rent for 24,000$ ($160.80), including an American buffet breakfast. A small band plays 3 nights a week. Facilities include a bar and a sauna, plus both an indoor and outdoor swimming pool. Laundry service is available, as is room service 24 hours a day. Parking is free. AE, DC, MC, V.

The leading candidate, **Hotel Montechoro,** 8200 Albufeira (tel. 089/85-94-23; fax 089/85-99-47), is generally conceded to be the finest hotel in the area for the individual traveler not wanting to stay at the nearby Club Med. The Montechoro, looking like a hotel you might encounter in North Africa, lies 2 miles northeast of the center of Albufeira. It's a fully equipped resort complex, a four-star hotel with ample facilities such as a pair of swimming pools, professional tennis courts, four squash courts, a sauna, and a gymnasium. You might get lost here, as it contains 302 bedrooms. Rooms are often done in an extremely modern style, each with private bath, air conditioning, phone, and TV. The most elegant way of staying here is to book into one of the 48 well-furnished suites. A single rents for 18,000$ ($120.60) daily, with a double costing 22,000$ ($147.40), and suites going for 28,000$ ($187.60) and up, all tariffs including breakfast. Dining facilities include the Restaurant Montechoro, the rooftop Grill Das Amendoeiras, and the coffee shop, Aquarium. Guests gather in the evening in the Almohade piano bar. Laundry and dry-cleaning service are available, as is 24-hour room service. Parking is free. AE, DC, MC, V.

Moderate
Aparthotel Auramar, Praia dos Aveiros, 8200 Albufeira (tel. 089/58-76-07; fax 089/533-27), at the edge of Albufeira, sits on a low cliff overlooking a sandy

beach, like a fortress facing the ocean. Close to the sea cliff is an outstanding recreation area, with the finest swimming pool in the area. There's an informal snack bar, and the main building has a restaurant providing Portuguese and an international cuisine. Essentially an apartment house, the Auramar offers meals as well as a bar lounge. The 282 apartments have living room furnishings in addition to a kitchenette and terrace for sunbathing. Each accommodation has a phone, radio, private bath, and air conditioning. Singles cost 11,000$ ($73.70) daily, with doubles renting for 15,200$ ($101.85), plus another 800$ ($5.35) for a buffet breakfast. Children under 8 receive a 50% reduction. Facilities include two tennis courts, two swimming pools (one reserved for children), and a bookshop, plus a mini-market. Parking is free. Live entertainment is presented 4 nights a week, and rent-a-car service is available.

Clube Mediterrâneo de Balaia, Praia Maria Luisa, 8200 Albufeira (tel. 089/58-66-81; fax 089/53-78-47). Tiers of roughly hewn balconies rise sky high, and the public rooms seem to flow one into another, with connecting passageways. Above the central core, corridors lead to the 408 bedrooms, all of which are uncluttered, with furnishings coordinated in simple textured fabrics. The hotel accepts both individuals and groups. Bookings are made through Clube Mediterrâneo de Viagens, Avenida António Augusto de Aguiar 24A in Lisbon (tel. 01/53-83-09). Reservations are accepted only for a minimum of a week's stay. There are about nine different rates depending on the time of the year. The tariffs per week begin at 162,000$ ($1,085.40) per person, based on double occupancy and including full board. Add 20% to these tariffs if you desire single occupancy.

The manager has arranged a number of social and sporting activities through the sports shop, from waterskiing to clay-pigeon shooting (an 18-hole golf course is nearby). Most guests, however, like to lounge by the heated swimming pool, enjoying a buffet luncheon. The drawing rooms and salons are too numerous to itemize. Also on the premises is a disco, featuring occasional fado and folklore entertainers.

The resort is 4 miles east of Albufeira on hilly land, encompassing a shoreline or rugged rock formations and a series of coves for surf swimming. Facilities include an outdoor swimming pool, a health club, and a sauna. Laundry is provided, as is babysitting. There is no room service, however. Parking is free. AE, DC, MC, V.

Estalagem do Cerro, Rua Samora Barros, 8200 Albufeira (tel. 089/58-61-91; fax 089/58-61-94), captures Algarvian charm yet doesn't neglect modern amenities. Its English name is the "Inn of the Craggy Hill" and it is located at the top of a hill overlooking Albufeira's bay, about a 10-minute walk down to the beach. An older, regional-style building has been recently renovated, but its character has been maintained. It is joined to a modern structure in a similar Moorish style. The 82 bedrooms have private bath and a veranda overlooking the sea, pool, or garden. Each is tastefully furnished and contains such necessities as a phone and TV. Singles rent for 14,350$ ($96.15) daily, with doubles costing 14,950$ ($100.15). The hotel also rents three suites for 16,300$ ($109.20). All tariffs include breakfast. A panoramic dining room provides good meals for 1,950$ ($13.05). Here you are served both regional dishes and international specialties in air-conditioned comfort. Before or after dinner, guests gather in a comfortable, modernized bar or its patio. On most nights, guests can dance to disco music, but fado and folkloric shows are also presented on some nights. The inn has an outdoor heated swimming pool in a garden setting. Other facilities include a hairdressing salon, sauna, massage facilities, solarium, Jacuzzi, and Turkish bath. There's also a fully equipped gym. The inn is rated four stars, which is the equivalent of a three-star hotel. Laundry and baby-sitting are available, and the hotel provides room service until midnight. Parking is free. AE, DC, MC, V.

Hotel de Aldeia, Avenida Dr. Francisco Sá Carneiro, Areias de São João, 8200 Albufeira (tel. 089/58-88-61; fax 089/58-864), is a complete holiday complex, where you have the advantage of an apartment, suite, or hotel room. It's in the holiday village of Areias de São João, near Golden Beach, about a mile from Albufeira. You'll find adequate recreation facilities—a tennis court, mini-golf, sun terraces, and a snack bar, plus a piano bar and live entertainment weekly. Across the road is a restaurant if you don't want to cook a meal in your own kitchen. The apartments have one or two bedrooms, accommodating a maximum of six guests. All units have fully equipped kitchens, and maid service includes dish washing, cleaning, and making of beds. Suites and apartments are handsomely decorated, using strong colors and natural wood furniture with rattan and bamboo. Built-in headboards hold telephones and provide background music and light switches. You have a choice of sea, pool, or mountain view. The complex rents 133 units, each with private bath, air conditioning, and TV. Singles cost 11,500$ ($77.05) daily, with doubles renting for 18,000$ ($120.60). Suites and apartments begin at 24,000$ ($160.80). Full board is another 4,000$ ($26.80) per person daily. Lunch or dinner, if ordered separately, costs from 2,300$ ($15.40). Parking is free. There is an outdoor swimming pool, plus one reserved for children. Service includes laundry and baby-sitting. AE, DC, MC, V.

Hotel Sol e Mar, Rua Bernardino de Sousa, 8200 Albufeira (tel. 089/58-67-21; fax 089/58-70-36), has captured the prime position within the center. It deceives you with its two-story entrance on the upper palisade. When you walk across the spacious, sun-filled lounges to the picture windows and look down, it's a six-story drop. Hugging the cliff are bedrooms and a wide stone terrace with garden furniture and parasols. On still a lower level is a sandy beach. There are 74 bedrooms, only six of which are singles. All contain private balconies, phones, and air conditioning. The twins have wooden headboards, locally painted seascapes, slimline armchairs, and plenty of wardrobe space. Singles or doubles cost 17,500$ ($117.25) daily, including breakfast.

Guests are a continental crowd with a sprinkling of Americans. Diners take their meals in a two-level room, opposite a drinking lounge, a room for card players, and a television room. After-dinner concerts are played on the electric organ till long past midnight. During the day, guests take the elevator to the lower sun terrace to find swimming, sunbathing, and the Esplanade Café, designed as a Portuguese tavern with Madeira stools, decorative tiles, and hanging anchors. Tuesday to Sunday nights, guests dance at the Disco Sol e Mar to the latest records. Facilities include two pools (one for children). Laundry service and baby-sitting are available, as is room service until 12:30am. Parking is free. AE, DC, MC, V.

Inexpensive

Apartamentos Albufeira Jardim, Cerro da Piedade, 8200 Albufeira (tel. 089/58-69-72; fax 089/58-79-77), is becoming increasingly popular with visitors who like to stay in one place for a while before resuming their touring. Standing on a hill overlooking the resort, it rents 440 attractively furnished studio apartments that are ideal for families. Each unit includes a fully equipped kitchen, private bath, and phone. The good news is that you don't have to do your cleaning, as the management provides daily maid service. A studio for two guests cost 10,950$ ($73.35) daily, and an apartment for four rents for 17,500$ ($117.25), with an apartment for six going for 29,100$ ($194.95). Breakfast is not served. Balconies from the apartments open onto the ocean and a view of Albufeira. As a further enticement, there are two restaurants, two coffee shops, three bars, three tennis courts, and five pools (including two baby pools). Laundry service is provided, as is baby-sitting. Parking is free. AE, DC, MC, V.

Hotel Baltum, Avenida 25 de Abril, 8200 Albufeira (tel. 089/58-91-02; fax 089/58-61-46), is a 1-minute walk from the main beach strip. The hotel offers modern accommodations. In the main building, the Baltum rents 53 rooms, each with central heating, private bath, and phone, and some offer a private balcony. Cozy sitting areas—furnished with leather chairs, blond coffee tables, and couches—are available to those willing to spend a few more escudos. A total of 47 accommodations is offered, plus 6 suites. Singles rent for 5,800$ ($38.85) daily, with doubles costing 9,000$ ($60.30) and suites renting for 13,000$ ($87.10), including breakfast. The solarium-terrace with its little bar has music. Lunch or dinner costs another 1,700$ ($11.40), and the cuisine is Portuguese. Facilities include a solarium, and laundry service is available. Parking is free. AE, DC, MC, V.

Hotel Rocamar, Largo Jacinto d'Ayet, 8200 Albufeira (tel. 089/58-69-90; fax 089/58-69-98). Depending on how much wine you've had for lunch, this cubistic hotel might look alternately like an updated version of a Moorish castle, a well-ordered assemblage of building blocks, or the partially excavated side of a stone quarry. It rises seven stories above the tawny-colored cliffs that slope down to one of the most inviting beaches along the Algarve. Many of its windows, and all of its balconies, benefit from the view this provides. The hotel is within walking distance of the attractions of town, yet its more secluded location enables guests to relax within the sun-washed confines of their 91 simple but comfortable bedrooms. Singles cost from 6,500$ ($43.55) to 8,250$ ($55.30) daily, with doubles renting for 11,500$ ($77.05) to 14,000$ ($93.80), including breakfast. Rooms contain private baths and phones. An Iberian-style dining room serves conservative but well-prepared meals, and a contemporary bar offers the possibility of a congenial tête-à-tête. Laundry service and baby-sitting are provided, and room service is available until midnight. Parking is free. AE, DC, MC, V.

Mar a Vista, Cerro da Piedade, 8200 Albufeira (tel. 089/58-63-54; fax 089/58-63-54). From the crow's-nest vantage point of this estalagem, you can gaze out over the rooftops of the resort below, the beach dotted with bright tents for bathers. The rooftop breakfast room of this first-class 34-unit inn, decorated in a provincial style with blond paneling, takes advantage of the view. The estalagem is composed of two buildings. The principal structure, covered with climbing plants, has bedrooms, a bar, and the breakfast room. The second building contains four bedrooms. There is a well-tended walled garden and plenty of space to park cars. Most of the rooms contain private balconies, and each has a private bath and phone. The walls are hung with interesting prints; the furnishings, although not sumptuous, are typical and comfortable. The hotel charges 6,000$ ($40.20) daily in a single, rising to 8,000$ ($53.60) in a double, including breakfast. Laundry service and baby-sitting are available, and room service is provided until midnight. The hotel is closed from October through March. Parking is free. AE, DC, MC, V.

Villa Recife, Rua Miguel Bombarda 6, 8200 Albufeira (tel. 089/58-67-47), is a self-catering hotel entered through a café that fills its front garden. Sometimes a live band entertains here on a wooden platform near an encircling wall. The establishment was originally built as a private home. Today the palms and bougainvillea that the original owners planted tower over the entranceway, whose walls are covered with blue, white, and yellow azulejos. A cabana bar dispenses tropical drinks. The hotel has been expanded to include a total of 92 accommodations, about 20 of which are contained within the original villa. The majority, however, are found in a modern rear wing, whose design is invisible from the front garden. There, studio apartments all contain a tiny terrace, oak cabinets, and a kitchenette. Each unit has a private bath, phone, and minibar. Singles cost 7,500$ ($50.25) daily, with doubles renting for 9,500$ ($63.65), including breakfast. Facilities include an outdoor swimming pool. Laundry service is available, and room service is offered until midnight. No parking is provided. AE, DC, MC, V.

WHERE TO DINE

Expensive

The pleasant **Alfredo,** Rua 5 de Outubro 9–11 (tel. 51-20-59), serves what are really banquets. Just a minute's stroll from the market square, it is housed in an old building that looks as if it's always been an inn. It's full of atmosphere, with crude wooden tables and chairs just made for leisurely drinking. The second-floor restaurant is a heavily beamed room with a marble slab floor and simple wooden tables. Ceiling fans create a cooling breeze, and a semivisible kitchen provides all the visual entertainment many diners require. Your Portuguese meal might include tuna salad, cataplana clams, and bream or swordfish, as well as tournedos with mushrooms or Portuguese-style steak. The wine of the house, Regengos, is sold by the glass. A meal usually costs around 4,500$ ($30.15) with a tourist menu going for 2,500$ ($16.75). Reservations are required. The restaurant is open daily from noon to 3pm and 6 to 11pm. AE, DC, MC, V.

A Ruina, Cais Herculano (tel. 51-20-94), sits opposite the fish market. From the arcaded dining room, with its long, wooden, candlelit tables, you can peer at the fishermen mending their nets. Another cavelike room has more tables and a bar. The decor is unpretentious, and the seafood is fresh. The cuisine is Portuguese. A bowl of good-tasting soup will get you going, then it's on to one of the fish specialties, perhaps grilled fresh tuna. The fish stew, caldeirada, is the chef's specialty. Desserts tend to run to custard and mousse. A complete meal will come to around 5,000$ ($33.50) à la carte, while a tourist menu costs 3,000$ ($20.10). The restaurant is open daily from 12:30 to 3pm and 7 to 11pm. Reservations are needed. No credit cards.

O Montinho, at Montechoro (tel. 51-39-59), is the finest restaurant in the area, lying 2 miles northeast of Albufeira. Set behind the already-recommended Hotel Montechoro, this Portuguese quinta has a red-tile roof and a covering of ivy and oleander, along with white stucco walls. Its terrace design looks almost fortified against the parking lot outside. You get an old Iberian feeling here, with raftered ceilings, carved chairs, and Algarvian accents. A host of international visitors comes here nightly (except Sunday) for dinner from 7 to 11pm. The cuisine is French, and reservations are necessary. The chef's specialties include hot fish and herb pâté with a shellfish sauce, monkfish escalopes with "melted" leeks, and duckling confit or filet of duckling with fruit. Other dishes are changed regularly to offer novelty to the regular clients. A menu dégustation of four courses costs 3,750$ ($25.15), or else you can order à la carte for 4,000$ ($26.80). Closed November 15 to December 15 and January 8 to February 8. AE, MC, V.

Moderate

Fernando, Avenida 25 de Baril, on the main square (tel. 51-21-16), with a large terrace, temptingly displays good-value tourist menus. There's a pleasant indoor dining room as well. I always go here for the fish of the day, never knowing what I'm going to get. You can always count on a good soup, most often fish based, and, if you're tired of fish, the chef will fix you a simple steak or perhaps a Portuguese specialty such as clams with pork. Desserts aren't special but very fattening. For an average meal, the tab will range from 3,5000$ ($23.45). A tourist menu costs 2,500$ ($16.75). Hours are daily from noon to 3pm and 6:30 to 10:30pm. Reservations aren't needed. No credit cards.

La Cigale, Olhos d'Água (tel. 50-16-37), stands right on the beach, 4½ miles from Albufeira; its terrace makes it a romantic choice at night. Here is your cliché of the sunny southern coast of Europe. Fortunately, the Portuguese food matches the atmosphere, enough so that the place draws a lot of diners who have villas on the Algarve—hence, reservations are important. The wine list is fairly distinguished, in keeping with the impressive food. The management seems to operate everything with amiable efficiency. Specialties include clams à la Cigale, sea bass, filet mignon, and a selection of fresh fish depending on the day's catch. An à la carte meal costs 3,000$ ($20.10), and a tourist menu is offered for 2,500$ ($16.75). Hours are daily from 7 to 11pm. The restaurant is closed from November through January. AE, DC, MC, V.

O Dias, Praça Miguel Bombarda (tel. 51-52-46), near the Beach Basket (recommended below), is a Portuguese-run restaurant with good food and reasonable prices, with meals costing from 2,800$ ($18.75). A tourist menu goes for 2,450$ ($16.40). An outside terrace overlooks the sea, and this is, of course, the most desirable setting. Main dishes include various versions of fresh fish and shellfish, including lobster and squid. The charcoal grills are among the most delectable. The restaurant is open from 12:30 to 2:30pm and 7 to 10:30pm Friday to Wednesday. Reservations aren't needed. Closed in January. No credit cards.

Inexpensive

Beach Basket (O Cabaz da Praia), Praça Miguel Bombarda 7 (tel. 51-21-37), near the Sol e Mar Hotel, sits on a colorful little square near the Church of São Sebastião, which is now a museum. In a former fisherman's cottage, the restaurant has an inviting ambience and good French food. With its large, sheltered terrace, it offers diners a view over the main Albufeira beach. Main courses, including such favorites as cassolette of seafood, salade océane, and papillotte of salmon, are served with a selection of fresh vegetables. The restaurant is renowned for its lemon meringue pie. Expect to pay 2,300$ ($15.40) for a meal. Hours at this popular restaurant are daily from noon to 11pm. Reservations are needed. Closed in December. MC, V.

Café Doris, Avenida Dr. Francisco Sá Carneiro, Areias de São João (tel. 51-24-55), is a rôtisserie-crêperie and restaurant, German operated, which does some well-prepared German specialties in crêpes, home-baked cakes, and ice creams. Ice cream comes in many flavors, including one delectable cup with fresh strawberries at 450$ ($3). To begin your meal, a rich-tasting goulash meat soup is always offered. You might follow with the roast pork with onion sauce or a good steak, accompanied by a mixed salad with cream sauce and herbs and lyonnaise potatoes. In addition, Doris has an unusual selection of hot drinks, including coffee Algarve (with Medronho). From October to June, a different special dish is offered every night from 7 to 10pm. Expect to spend from 1,800$ ($12.05). You can visit from 10am to 10pm; closed Thursday and in November. Reservations are needed in summer. MC, V.

THE BAR SCENE

In the center of the village, **Harry's Bar** (tel. 51-40-90) is on the market square. This bar is a center for any bloke who has abandoned his Cotswold tweeds for the lighter threads of the Algarve. Converts swear that Sir Harry's is their Algarvian "local," and after about a quarter of a century, it has earned the reputation of being the Algarve's most popular international rendezvous. The bar merges the ambience of a black-and-white timbered village pub with the coziness of a Portuguese fisherman's cottage.

Beneath the low natural beams, a comfortable array of Savonarola chairs, crude tables, and wooden settles are found on two levels, divided by wrought-iron railings. The collection of rifles, steins, gleaming copper pots and pans, and earthenware water jugs provides a genuine sense of the past. A bar of herringbone brick and timbers has heel-propping stools, attracting those drawn to the center of the action. Most drinks, such as a rum and Coke, go for 400$ ($2.70), and a beer for 250$ ($1.70). Hearty sandwiches and other bar snacks are served as well. It's open daily all year from 9am to 2am.

---

11. Praia de Quarteira

Between Albufeira and Faro, this once-sleepy fishing village used to be known only to a handful of artists who provided amusement for the local fishermen and their varinas. Now with the invasion of outsiders, the traditional way of life has been upset. What was Quarteira has been swallowed up in a sea of high-rise buildings and the place is now a big, bustling overgrown resort. The big attraction, of course, is one of the longest beaches along the Algarve, filled in summer not only with vacationing Portuguese but with hordes of Europeans who descend on Quarteira, also supplying a much-needed boost to the local economy.

Surprisingly, Praia de Quarteira has very few hotels. Most of its accommodations are apartment blocks that visitors from the north, from the Midlands of England to Frankfurt, book for a week or two for their holiday. I feel the typical North American visitor will find more charm elsewhere. But for those who want to give it a try, here are some recommendations.

Golfers who don't want to pay the high tariffs at Vale do Lobo or Vilamoura (both of which have 18-hole golf courses) can stay inexpensively in Quarteira at one of the accommodations listed below. The above-mentioned courses are only a 10-minute drive away, and Quarteira lies about 7 miles from the Faro Airport.

If you're dependent on public transportation, take a plane, bus, or train from Lisbon to Faro (see below), then catch one of the frequent connecting bus links between Faro and Quarteira. Quarteira lies 191 miles southeast of Lisbon and 14 miles west of Faro.

The **tourist information office** is along Avenida Infante de Sagres (tel. 089/ 322-17).

WHERE TO STAY

One of the most popular hostelries in town is **Hotel Dom José,** Avenida Infante de Sagres, 8125 Quarteira (tel. 089/30-27-50; fax 089/30-27-55). Travel agents in Britain consider the amenities offered by this three-star hotel considerably better than its official status dictates. Consequently, it is (deservedly) often heavily booked even in low season. Its pool is separated from the portside promenade of town by a low wall, behind which a well-developed subculture thrives among the largely British clientele. At its tallest point, the hotel has nine balconied stories. The outlying wings are shorter, of course. The velvet sofas of the public rooms are filled every evening with convivial holiday-makers, enjoying drinks, the live music, and the air-conditioned view of the sea beyond. An aquarium bubbles behind the darkly exotic-looking bar. In another corner of the ground floor, a lattice-covered room contains a wide-screen TV and a garden-style list of salad and sandwich treats. There's even a disco, as well as a seaview restaurant.

Each of the 146 comfortably furnished rooms contains a private bath, phone, and radio, but only 12 are air conditioned. With breakfast included, doubles peak at 15,000$ ($100.50) daily, with singles costing 12,000$ ($96.50). Breakfast costs 500$ ($3.35). Parking is free. AE, DC, MC, V.

Atis Hotel, Avenida Paralela a Infante de Sagres, 8125 Quarteira (tel. 089/38-97-71; fax 089/38-97-74). The main artery on which this hotel is located is so completely lined with high-rise apartment blocks that comparisons are sometimes made to the canyons of Wall Street. Fortunately, many of its 73 balconied rooms look out over the beach, which is just a short walk away. Horizontal bands of bare concrete curve sinuously around the jutting balconies, many of which are accented with white stripes. A tiny outdoor swimming pool is separated from the sidewalk by a fence. However, many clients prefer to bathe at the beach instead. There's a snack bar, along with a darkly paneled bar, plus a TV room on the ground floor. Each bedroom contains a private bath, air conditioning, phone, and TV. Singles cost 9,900$ ($66.35) daily; doubles 12,000$ ($80.40), with 10 suites renting for 15,000$ ($100.50), including breakfast. Laundry and baby-sitting are offered, and the hotel provides room service until midnight. Parking is free. AE, DC, MC, V.

WHERE TO DINE

About 2 miles from Quarteira on Estrada de Loulé, **Etons** (tel. 31-53-26) stands in the pines. The international menu changes nightly, so what is presented below should only suggest the type of cuisine offered. Usually there's a rich good-tasting soup, or you might begin your meal with smoked swordfish, which looks like smoked salmon but, to me at least, tastes even better. The leg of lamb is often excellent. Expect to pay about 2,000$ ($13.40). The restaurant serves meals from noon to 3pm and 7 to 11pm daily. It closes in January. Reservations are recommended. AE, DC, MC, V.

Restaurante Atlântico, Avenida Infante de Sagres 91 (tel. 31-51-42). You'll find the protective awning of this portside restaurant on the main promenade of town, sitting near a cluster of other restaurants that look very much alike. The place is crowded and popular (often when the others are empty), and it's patronized by an array of international and often scantily clad diners. The hosts direct a staff of waiters who bring out such Portuguese specialties as fish soup Algarve style, king prawns Atlântico, peppersteak, clams in their shells, and other regional dishes. An à la carte menu costs 2,300$ ($15.40) with a tourist menu featured for 1,500$ ($10.05). Hours are Monday to Saturday from noon to 3:30pm and 6:30 to 11pm. Reservations are necessary. AE, DC, MC, V.

Restaurante O Pescador, Largo Cortés Real (tel. 31-47-55), is an unpretentious spot across the parking lot from the fish market, just west of the straw market. Beneath a wooden lattice-accented ceiling, diners enjoy friendly service and impeccably fresh fish and vegetables. A clean display case contains some of the ingredients that go into the meals. The cuisine is typically Portuguese, including steak, grilled filet of pork, grilled gray mullet, grilled prawns, and fresh hake. An à la carte meal costs 2,800$ ($18.75), with a tourist menu offered for 1,500$ ($10.05). Service is from 1 to 3pm and 7 to 10pm Friday to Wednesday. Reservations are not needed. The restaurant closes in December. No credit cards.

Bonnie's Wine Bar, Avenida Infante de Sagres (tel. 31-43-12). This outpost of Britain thrives within a cocoon of pine paneling, comfortable banquettes, mugs of beer, and assorted banners from soccer teams. This is more a pub than a wine bar, where the accents are more Cockney than Iberian and where any Anglophile will feel at home. You can order such light Portuguese and English meals as omelets, a ploughman's lunch, and steak-and-kidney pie. Various kinds of meat and fish are grilled. Wine is sold by the glass or bottle, but many customers prefer to drink beer. An à la carte meal averages 2,000$ ($13.40), but you can order a tourist menu for only 1,000$ ($6.70). Service is Friday to Wednesday from 11am to 3pm and 6:30pm to midnight. Reservations are recommended. The wine bar closes in November. No credit cards.

---

12. Vilamoura

Although the remains of a Roman villa were discovered when builders were working on the marina, the history of this settlement is yet to be written. At a central point on the Algarve coast, only 11 miles west of Faro Airport, Vilamoura is an expansive land-development project, the largest private tourist "urbanization" in Europe. Plans call for a city larger than Faro and an interior lake linked with the bay and ocean by two canals. One can sum up the Vilamoura situation by comparing it to the weather of New England: "If you don't like it now, wait a minute!" There is already a 1,000-boat marina for pleasure boats. At the moment it is filled with what are called "holiday villages," along with apartment complexes. Sports get much attention here: two 18-hole golf courses, along with water sports, tennis courts, and a riding center. The yachting set is attracted to the marina, especially in summer, and shops and other tourist facilities, including restaurants and bars, can occupy many a day.

More than 100 hotels are projected, but at the moment you'll have to make do with a more limited selection.

Vilamoura has bus links with Quarteira (see above) and Faro (see below). The nearest tourist office is at Quarteira.

WHERE TO STAY

A five-star choice, **Vilamoura Marinotel,** Vilamoura, 8126 Quarteira Codex (tel. 089/88-99-88; fax 089/88-98-69), is considered by some the finest deluxe hotel on the Algarve. It has some 324 employees for its 389 guest rooms. Operated by a Spanish company, HUSA International Hotels, the Marinotel was a dream long in coming true. Originally launched in 1974, construction was delayed because of the revolution and the tight-money situation, but by spring of 1987, the hotel was officially opened and has proved just as popular with the Portuguese as with international visitors. During the slower winter months it becomes a convention hotel, but in summer is overrun with holiday-makers. The hotel mainly employs young Algarvians on its staff.

Rising like a massive pile, the rectangular hotel sits next to the Vilamoura Marina. Each of its attractive and well-furnished bedrooms provides a view, either of the marina or the ocean. A large swimming pool stands between the ocean and the hotel, and there is direct access to the beach. The interior, with lounge space for 500 guests, is decorated with both traditional and modern designs. It is characterized by high ceilings and wide-open staircases, with an effective use made of silver, red, and white. Each room is well equipped with phone, air conditioning, minibar, TV, and private bath, of course. Singles cost 22,000$ ($147.40) daily, with doubles renting for 30,000$ ($201). The hotel also offers 21 suites, beginning at 83,400$ ($558.80). Tariffs include an American buffet breakfast in the main restaurant.

Its dining facilities (see below) are among the best at Vilamoura. Health-club devotees will find good facilities here, including a Jacuzzi and a sauna. Fado, folk dancing, fashion shows, and occasional barbecues round out the program. Baby-sitting, laundry, and 24-hour room service are provided, and parking is free. AE, DC, MC, V.

One of the most stylish hostelries at this resort is **Hotel Atlantis Vilamoura,** Vilamoura, 8125 Quarteira (tel. 089/325-35; fax 089/326-52). A Moorish flavor is imparted by the pointed arches accenting the facade. Set away from the congested section of Vilamoura, the style is Iberian contemporary, with gleaming marble, coffered wooden ceilings, and polished mirrors. The sophisticated decor of the bar is dimly lit, with a piano providing evening music. A large, wind-shaded terrace is filled with plants, and a big indoor pool is covered with a dome decorated with bas-reliefs. A coffee shop remains open throughout the day, while a more formal restaurant caters to a more elegant clientele.

Each of the 302 well-furnished rooms and the 8 suites contain a TV, minibar, private bath, phone, and a seaview veranda, among other amenities. Singles rent for 22,000$ ($147.40) daily, with doubles costing from 30,000$ ($201), and suites beginning at 38,000$ ($254.60), including breakfast. Hotel patrons receive a 20% discount at a nearby golf course. A health club is on the premises, as well as three tennis courts and an outdoor pool for bathers wishing to avoid saltwater swimming. A sandy beach lies away from the hotel. Room service, laundry, and baby-sitting are provided. Parking is free. AE, DC, MC, V.

Dom Pedro Golf Hotel, Vilamoura, 8125 Quarteira (tel. 089/38-96-50; fax 089/31-54-82), is a large hotel of first-class comfort, right in the tourist complex of Vilamoura. The 262-room center stands near the casino, and there is a choice of three swimming pools, including one for children. The public rooms are sleekly styled, and the private rooms are pleasantly furnished and carpeted, with private terraces, private baths, phones, TVs, minibars, and air conditioning. Singles cost 17,600$ ($117.90) daily, with doubles renting for 22,400$ ($150.10), including breakfast. Nine suites are also rented for 29,500$ ($197.65) and up. Three tennis courts are available, and after a game guests can enjoy a bar overlooking the pool. Other facilities include a sauna, massage, and hairdresser. The staff at the hotel arranges for guests to go deep-sea fishing or riding from its fine stable of horses, as well as reduced greens fees at various golf courses in the Algarve. The hotel's band plays for nightly entertainment. There's a restaurant serving both Portuguese and international specialties, and there is also a grill room. Laundry and baby-sitting are provided, and room service is available 24 hours a day. Parking is free. AE, DC, MC, V.

Vilamoura Golf Motel, Vilamoura, 8125 Quarteira (tel. 089/30-29-75; fax 089/30-29-76), is for golf enthusiasts, among others. It is located on a Frank Pennink championship golf course surrounded by pine trees. Only minutes from the ocean and a marina, it enjoys a tranquil setting that forms part of the biggest tourist complex on the Algarve. Operated by Sointal Casinos do Algarve, it offers 52 well-furnished bedrooms, 31 of which are suites, each with private terrace and tile bath. Rooms contain phones, air conditioners, and TVs. Singles cost 9,150$ ($61.30) daily, with doubles renting for 10,600$ ($71), and suites costing from 22,000$ ($147.40) and up, including breakfast. The hotel has many facilities, including a large patio with two swimming pools. The complex is designed in a typical modern Algarvian style, with much use made of local materials including dark woods, polished tiles, and Portuguese mosaics. Guests heavily patronize the nearby diversions, including an 18-hole golf course (6,877 yards), tennis courts, and the casino. Parking is free. Laundry and room service are provided. AE, DC, MC, V.

Estalagem da Cegonha, Centro Hípico de Vilamoura, Vilamoura 8125 Quarteira (tel. 089/30-25-77), stands at Poco de Boliqueime, Vilamoura, about 4½ miles from the golf course, casino, marina, and beach, on the national road between Portimão and Faro. The ancient inn lies in a peaceful setting, adjoining the riding stables (which charge reasonable rates, incidentally). There are only 10 rooms, but they are large and cozily decorated, each containing a private bath and phone. Singles rent for 8,500$ ($56.95) daily, doubles for 9,000$ ($60.30), including breakfast. The decoration is in a *típico* Portuguese style. The chef at the inn has won an award for regional food; before or after dinner, you can enjoy drinks in one of the comfortable bars. A horse-jumping contest is held every year in September. Room service is provided until 10pm. Parking is free. AE, DC, MC, V.

WHERE TO DINE

A shopping and dining complex, the Centro Comercial da Marinha, across from the marina, is filled with restaurants, many of dubious quality. Nevertheless, many are popular more for their colorful location than for their cuisine. The best food is consistently served at the already-recommended **Vilamoura Marinotel** (tel. 38-99-88). The most exclusive—and most expensive—dining spot here is the Sirius Grill on the main floor. It is separated from a chic rendezvous center, the Bar Castor, by a grand piano on a dais. Live music filters into both areas. This drinking and dining establishment is the most elegant in Vilamoura. The bar—stylish, modern, and monochromatic—offers a large variety of drinks and is open daily from 11am to 11pm.

Overlooking the marina, the Sirius Grill is high-ceilinged, with a sophisticated, unfussy decor. The chefs prepare a splendid Portuguese and international cuisine, and the service is formal. You might begin with assorted smoked fish and follow with one of the seafood specialties such as lobster cassolete, turbot in seafood sauce, sea bass flambé with fennel, or stuffed trout. Meat dishes use only the finest cuts, as reflected by the T-bone steak or the tournedos stuffed with shrimps and scallops and served with a béarnaise sauce. Meals cost 7,000$ ($46.90) and up and are served daily from 12:30 to 3pm and 7:30 to 10pm.

The food is also excellently prepared in the large, airy Aries dining room, also at the Vilamoura Marinotel. This dining room is built on two levels and opens onto the swimming pool and ocean. Lavishly decorated with tiles, it is elegantly appointed, with one of the finest young staffs on the Algarve. A set menu for 4,500$ ($30.15) changes daily, and selections can be made from an à la carte list. Traditional dishes and Iberian regional specialties are the main fare. Specific dishes are likely to include chicken breast Oscar, roast pork with garlic, or grilled swordfish, preceded by one of the soups or appetizers. Hours are daily from 12:30 to 2:30pm and 7:30 to 10pm. Reservations are needed at both places. AE, DC, MC, V.

EVENING ENTERTAINMENT

Close to the Vilamoura Golf Club is the **Vilamoura Casino** (tel. 30-29-99), one of the finest, featuring a gambling salon with roulette, blackjack, French banque, and baccarat. A separate salon is devoted to slot machines. There is a 250-seat supper club, with a floor show at 10:45pm nightly. The casino is open from 4pm to 3am every day of the year. Tourists must present their passports and pay a fee of 100$ (65¢). A tourist menu in the restaurant costs 6,000$ ($40.20), with an à la carte meal averaging 8,000$ ($53.60). Drinks cost from 650$ ($4.35). Admission to the nightclub is 2,000$ ($13.40).

Skipper's Disco Club, Loja 38, Centro Comercial da Marinha (tel. 31-42-51), in a restaurant and shopping complex close to the marina, is the most popular stopover on the nighttime rounds. Guests drink at street level at the vaguely nautical bar before descending to dance in the basement to the latest in recorded music. The entrance fee is 1,000$ ($6.70). Drinks cost from 600$ ($4), although the first drink is included in the admission price. You can also order snacks such as beefburgers and sandwiches. Hours are daily from 10pm to 5am.

---

13. Vale do Lobo

The name Valley of the Wolf suggests some forlorn spot, set amid bleak terrain. Hardly likely! The *Vale,* west of Faro, about a 20-minute drive from the airport, is the site of a golf course designed by Henry Cotton, the British champion. Some of the holes are played by the sea, resulting in many an anxious moment when a shot may hook out over the water a precarious distance from the green. Another nine-hole course and a nine-hole par-three course, a putting green, and driving range have been installed.

Reached through fig orchards, cork forests, and a valley of tufted pines, the seaside strongly evokes Carmel, California. Pale golden cliffs jut out over sandy beaches that stretch brilliantly in the distance until they disappear into a faint haze.

The two resorts below, Vale do Lobo and Quinta do Lago, are near the town of Almancil, which lies 190 miles southeast of Lisbon and 7 miles west of Faro. Vale do Lobo lies 4 miles southwest of Almancil and Quinta do Lago lies 6 miles south of Almancil.

None of these places has a tourist information office, but some information is available at Faro (see below). To reach the resorts by public transportation, go by bus, plane, or train from Lisbon to Faro, then take a connecting bus bound for Almancil.

WHERE TO STAY

At Vale do Lobo

A citadel of ostentatious living, **Hotel Dona Filipa,** Vale de Lobo, Almancil, 8106 Loulé (tel. 089/39-41-41; fax 089/39-42-88), is a deluxe golf hotel, with such touches as gold-painted palms holding up the ceiling. The grounds are impressive, embracing 450 acres of rugged coastline with steep cliffs, inlets, and sandy bays. The exterior of the hotel is comparatively uninspired, but a greater dimension was brought to the interior by Duarte Pinto Coelho. Green silk banquettes, marble fireplaces, Portuguese ceramic lamps, old prints over baroque-style love seats—the flair is lush. Aside from a Chinese room for card playing, the most popular meeting point is the Gothic Bar, with its cathedrallike stools, wooden decorations, and matching floor and upholstery fabric in tile patterns.

There are 135 air-conditioned rooms—each with bath, phone, TV, and minibar, and most with balcony. A single rents for 28,400$ ($190.30) daily, rising to 37,800$ ($253.25) in a double. All prices include breakfast. The hotel also rents nine junior suites and six deluxe suites.

Dining is formal and gracious, with a knowledgeable maître d'hôtel and wine steward guiding you on your selections. Meals average 6,000$ ($40.20). At the beach is a disco, where international records are played for dancing (occasionally, folk artists and fadistas perform). Laundry and 24-hour room service are provided. Three tennis courts are floodlit at night, and the swimming pool is suitable for both adults and children. Other facilities include a gambling room, and the hotel also has a hairdresser. Greens fees are free to hotel guests at the São Lorenzo Golf Course. Parking is free. AE, DC, MC, V.

At Quinta Do Lago

A pocket of posh living is **Quinta do Lago,** Quinta do Lago, Almancil, 8100 Loulé (tel. 089/39-66-66; fax 089/39-63-93), a sprawling 1,600-acre estate that sells private plots within it. The hotel is an investment of Saudi Arabian Prince Faisal, but he has wisely turned over management to the Venice-Simplon Orient Express staff, which is also a hotel chain. The resort offers a riding center, one of the best in southern Europe; a 27-hole golf course, designed by American course architect William F. Mitchell, and recognized among the top six in Europe; tennis courts; the Patio Club, the Algarve's sophisticated disco; the luxurious Quinta Park Country Club Apartments, overlooking the seawater lake and provided with modern comforts. The quinta offers 141 bedrooms and 9 suites. Singles rent for 30,000$ ($201) to 34,000$ ($227.80) daily, and doubles for 40,000$ ($268) to 44,000$ ($294.80). Suites cost from 75,000$ ($502.50). All rates include breakfast.

The Pergola Restaurant is for those who prefer an informal grill room. It overlooks a swimming pool for both children and adults. There's a modern clubhouse with a restaurant and bar close to the golf driving range and overlooking the Bermuda green of the B1 fairway. The Beach Pavilion (at the beach, of course) offers a menu of snacks, light meals, and drinks. A specialty restaurant serves Italian cuisine, and the Navegador Restaurant offers a varied menu, including several traditional Portuguese game dishes. The hotel offers an outdoor swimming pool, a health club, a solarium, and an indoor swimming pool. Laundry and baby-sitting can be provided, and room service is available 24 hours. Parking is free. AE, DC, MC, V.

WHERE TO DINE

At Quinta Do Lago

An excellent dining choice nearby, which is not part of Quinta do Lago management, is **Shepherds Casa Velha,** Quinta do Lago (tel. 39-43-57), which is open for dinner Monday to Saturday from 7 to 10:30pm. Full meals cost from 7,500$ ($50.25). The restaurant is renowned for its fine Portuguese and international food and impeccable service. Chateaubriand for two persons, a rack or saddle of lamb persillé (also for two persons), délices of sole, sea bass Quinta do Lago, fishermen's soup, and smoked swordfish with horseradish sauce are recommended. The dessert specialty is crêpes. Dinners are eaten to the sound of piano and guitar music. Reservations are accepted. AE, DC, MC, V.

---

14. Faro

Flowers brought in from the countryside are plentiful. In the blue lagoon sailing enthusiasts glide by. A typical old quarter flanks the ruined ramparts that proved all too vulnerable in the past. At the yacht harbor starlings and sparrows flutter nervously, while children run noisily to the pastry shops to buy stuffed figs and almond cakes. Beyond the waterfront lie the tree-studded avenues and cobbled alleyways of the city.

Once loved by the Romans and later by the Moors, Faro is the capital of the Algarve. Sit at a café sampling the wine and you'll watch yesterday and today pass by. An old man walks ahead, pulling a donkey on which a parasol-shaded girl in a white dress is sitting. Brushing past is a German student in shorts, tanned golden by the sun. Faro is a hodgepodge of life and activity: It's been rumbled, sacked, and "quaked" by everybody from Mother Nature to the Earl of Essex (Elizabeth I's favorite).

Since Afonso III drove out the Moors for the last time in 1266, Faro has been Portuguese. On its outskirts an international jet airport brings in thousands of visitors every summer. The airport has done more than anything else to speed tourism not only to Faro but to the Algarve in general, as jet planes make it possible to reach Faro from Lisbon in 30 minutes. For flight information, phone 089/242-01. Bus no. 18 leaves daily from the railway station in Faro every 45 minutes, heading for the airport, from 7:45am to 7:45pm. The cost is 100$ (65¢). Six times a day trains arrive from Lisbon, the trip taking 7 hours and a one-way ticket costing 1,645$ ($11). For rail information in Faro, call the train station at Largo Estação (tel. 089/226-53). Three buses a day from Lisbon, after a 7-hour journey, pull into the Faro bus station, Avenida da República (tel. 089/299-92). A one-way ticket costs 1,150$ ($7.70).

The most bizarre attraction is the *Capela d'Ossos* (Chapel of Bones), entered from the rear of the **Igreja de Nossa Senhora do Monte do Carmo do Faro,** via a courtyard. Erected in the 19th century, this chapel is completely lined with the skulls and bones of human skeletons, an extraordinarily ossicular rococo. In all, it's estimated there are 1,245 human skulls. Hours are 9:30am to 12:30pm and 3 to 5pm daily.

The church, built in 1713, contains a gilded baroque altar. Likewise, its facade is baroque, with a bell tower rising from each side. Topping the belfries are gilded mosquelike cupolas, connected by a balustraded railing. The windows of the upper levels are latticed and framed with gold; statues stand in each of the niches on either side of the main portal.

Other religious monuments include the old **Sé** (cathedral), built in the Gothic and Renaissance styles (originally a Muslim mosque stood on this site); the **Church of St. Francis,** with panels of glazed earthenware tiles in milk white and Dutch blue, depicting the life of the patron saint; and the **Convent of Our Lady of the Assumption,** declared a national monument and noted for its Renaissance portal and cloister.

But most visitors don't come to Faro to look at churches, regardless how interesting they are. Rather, they take the harbor ferry to the wide, white sandy beaches called the **Praia de Faro,** on an islet. The ride is available only in summer. The beach is also connected to the mainland by bridge, a distance of about 31½ miles from the town center. Once there, you can waterski and fish or just rent a deck chair and umbrella and lounge in the sun.

Faro lies 192 miles southeast of Lisbon and 160 miles southeast of Setúbal. The **Faro Tourist Office** is at Rua da Misericórdia 8–12 (tel. 089/254-04).

WHERE TO STAY

Dominating the harbor like a fortress is the **Eva,** Avenida da República, 8000 Faro (tel. 089/80-33-54; fax 089/80-23-04), a modern, eight-floor hotel occupying an entire side of the yacht-clogged harbor, providing direct sea views from most of the 150 bedrooms. Bedrooms are air conditioned, furnished in a restrained style, and have private baths. Double rooms rent for 12,000$ ($80.40) to 15,000$ ($100.50) daily. There are no singles. Breakfast is included. The better rooms open onto the water. The Eva's best feature is a penthouse restaurant and rooftop swimming pool, supported on 16 posts, with sun terraces and a bar. Dancing is offered at the hotel's disco 5 nights a week. Other facilities include a snack bar, three cocktail bars, a hairdresser, and a boutique. Laundry, room service, and baby-sitting can be arranged. Parking is free. AE, DC, MC, V.

Hotel Faro, Praça D. Francisco Gomes, 8002 Faro Codex (tel. 089/80-32-76; fax 089/80-35-46), is a first-class hotel with 52 rooms opening right onto the bustling harbor, a prime position. The furnishings in the rooms are comfortable but uninspired, and many contain balconies opening right onto the square which tends to be noisy until late at night. Singles rent for 8,500$ ($56.95) daily, with doubles costing 11,000$ ($73.70). Rooms have phones, and some are air conditioned. Breakfast is included. The four suites have a small sitting room with a sofa bed, suitable for a third person. These cost from 14,500$ ($97.15). In a light and spacious room, the restaurant serves French and Portuguese dishes complemented by a well-coordinated wine list. The bar provides drinks, which you can order from the mezzanine while surveying the scene below. Parking is free. AE, DC, MC, V.

Casa de Lumena, Praça Alexandre Herculano 27, 8000 Faro (tel. 089/80-19-90; fax 089/80-40-19), was once the town house of a reigning sardine family of Faro, but now it's an English-run pensão with central heating, and a bar and restaurant, the Grapevine, where the international community often meets at lunchtime. The restaurant serves a Portuguese cuisine slightly modified for the international palate. The inn sits on a square shaded by jacaranda trees. Built at the edge of the sidewalk with wrought-iron gratings at its windows, the Lumena offers 12 renovated and upgraded accommodations, all with private baths and phones. The rooms are of different shapes and furnished in part with pieces inherited with the casa. Throughout are antiques, carved chests, satinwood tables, painted dressers, and armoires. Singles cost 6,000$ ($40.20) daily, with doubles renting for 9,000$ ($60.30), including breakfast. Only street parking is available. AE, DC, MC, V.

Hotel Albacor, Rua Brites Almeida 25, 8000 Faro (tel. 089/80-35-93). A few of the 38 rooms in this well-located hotel contain small balconies. Each of them has a tile bath, phone, and a comfortably unpretentious decor that is spotlessly clean. This is a good choice for a budget hotel, and because of that, is likely to be full of a loyal repeat clientele unless you make reservations in advance in high season. There's a bar on the ground floor, plus an elevator. The English-speaking staff is most helpful.

Doubles cost from 7,000$ ($46.90) daily, while singles go for 6,200$ ($41.55), with breakfast included. Parking is free. AE, DC, MC, V.

WHERE TO DINE

The leading restaurant in town is **Restaurante Cidade Velha,** Rua Domingos Guieiro 19 (tel. 27-45). It used to be one of the best-located private homes in Faro. Today it serves as a very charming culinary hideaway. You'll find it behind the cathedral, behind thick stone walls built at least 250 years ago. You'll be invited to enjoy an apéritif in the tiny bar near the entrance.

Your meal will be served in one of a pair of rooms, each with a vaulted brick ceiling. Reservations, which are important, can either be phoned in or left in person early in the day with one of the vested waiters. Full meals, priced at 2,500$ ($16.75) and up, might include Portuguese and international items such as crab cakes or smoked swordfish with horseradish sauce, followed with roast rack of lamb with rosemary and mint sauce or roast duck with an apricot sauce. Lunch is served from 12:30 to 2pm Monday to Friday, and dinner from 7:30 to 11:30pm Monday to Saturday. Closed Sunday. MC, V.

Café Chelsea, Rua de Francisco Gomes 28 (tel. 284-59), on a stone-paved street thronged with pedestrians, offers a well-preserved Algarvian and international cuisine. You can select a table in the open air or between the colorful tile walls of the ground-floor interior. Diners, however, looking for a different kind of atmosphere will press on to the upper-level dining room, where the style is art nouveau, with a decor that includes varied stripes of blue-and-white tiles, touches of scarlet, bentwood chairs and tables, a prominent bar, and big windows looking out over the street. Full meals in any of the restaurant's seating areas cost from 2,200$ ($14.75) each. Specialties include Portuguese beefsteak, pork filet, Chelsea hamburgers, Spanish omelets, and an array of pasta dishes, and Indian curried prawns, plus an array of salads. The establishment's open for both lunch and dinner from noon to 4pm and 6pm to midnight. Reservations aren't needed. AE, DC, MC, V.

Dois Irmãos, Largo do Terreiro do Bispo 18 (tel. 233-37), is a popular Portuguese bistro, founded in 1925, with a no-nonsense atmosphere. Yet it has its devotees. The Portuguese menu is as modest as the establishment and its prices, but you get a good choice of fresh fish and shellfish dishes. Ignore the paper napkins and concentrate on the fine kettle of fish placed before you. Clams in a savory sauce is a favorite, and sole is regularly featured. But, of course, everything depends on the catch of the day. Service is slow and amiable, and no one seems in a hurry. For a seafood dinner, your bill is likely to run from 1,700$ ($11.40). Open daily from 10am to 11pm. Reservations are necessary. AE, DC, MC, V.

EVENING ENTERTAINMENT

The most popular disco in town, **Sheherazade,** Hotel Eva, Avenida da República (tel. 80-33-54), is just off the lobby of the leading hotel in Faro. It is open daily from 10pm to 4am. It's often packed with young Algarvian people who mingle with tourists. Guests can also enjoy the afternoon tea dances from 4 to 7pm Saturday and Sunday. There is regional folk dancing every Thursday night, followed by a program of typical Portuguese fado and guitars on Friday night. There is no admission, and drinks cost from 450$ ($3).

WHERE TO STAY & DINE NEARBY

The only *Relais & Châteaux* member in Portugal, **Hotel La Reserve,** Estrada de Esteval, Santa Barbara de Nexe, 8000 Faro (tel. 089/904-74), is near a hamlet about 7 miles west of Faro. It offers luxury accommodations in a modern and elegant country-estate atmosphere. The hotel has two swimming pools and a tennis court. It lies in its own 6-acre parkland. Each of the 20 handsome suites has a southern sea view and private terrace, radio, TV, minibar, direct-dial phone, and air conditioning. Singles cost 30,000$ ($201) daily; doubles, 36,000$ ($241.20). All tariffs include breakfast. The hotel has a snack bar, two bars for drinks, and an international restaurant. Parking is 1,000$ ($6.70) a night.

The restaurant, **La Reserve,** is in a building adjacent to the hotel structure. It is operated by a U.S./Swiss alliance—Victor and Katja Fuchs. It is the finest dining room in the Algarve, although some have complained of the reception received here. Their international dinners are carefully presented, and they care about the freshness of their meats, fish, and produce. A specialty is smoked swordfish, which is as fine as any served at Lisbon's more famous Avis. Along with this dish, served in razor-thin slices, it is customary to drink a glass of chilled vodka. Try also the Oriental shrimp served on a bed of rice with a fried banana. Local duckling, crisp on the outside and tender inside, makes a good main course. The duck is served with potato croquettes and red cabbage.

The best Portuguese wines are on the wine list, including the well-known *vinho verde* (green wine) of the north. Expect to spend from 6,500$ ($43.55) per person for a meal, which you can be sure will be worth it. The restaurant is open from 7 to 11pm Wednesday to Monday. It's important to call for reservations. No credit cards.

Drive out of Faro on the N125 (toward the airport) for 4 miles and you will come to a sign "Loulé" straight ahead. Follow this direction and drive for a further 1 mile to Esteval where there is a right turn signed "Santa Barbara de Nexe." Turn right here and after 1 mile you have La Reserve on the right side of the road.

---

15. Loulé

Loulé, 9½ miles north of Faro and 185 miles southeast of Lisbon, is a market town in the heart of the chimney district of the Algarve. If you ever thought that chimneys couldn't excite you, you haven't seen the ones here. From many of the houses and cottages, these fret-cut plaster towers rise. You may even see one on the house of a very discriminating dog. They resemble fine lacework or filigree in stone; others are as delicately contrived as forms of snow crystals blown against glass.

Loulé and villages around it are among areas of the Algarve known for their handcrafts, producing work in palm fronds and esparto, such as handbags, baskets, mats, and hats. Loulé artisans also make copper articles, bright-colored harnesses, delicate wrought-iron pieces, clogs, cloth shoes and slippers, tinware, and pottery. Products are displayed in workshops at the foot of the walls of an old fortress and in other showrooms. The medieval castle is in the center of town.

In Loulé, you may want to visit the Gothic-style **Parish Church,** which was given to the town in the latter 13th century, and the **Church of the Misericórdia,** looking like a wedding cake, especially its Manueline entrance. The town also contains the remains of a fortress-castle that Afonso III captured from the Moors.

Bus service is good during the day, with about 40 buses arriving from various parts of the Algarve, mainly Faro. Trains from Faro arrive at Loulé rail station at the rate of five per day. The station is 3 miles from the center of town. There are bus connections to the center of town from the station or you can use a taxi.

The **Loulé Tourist Information Office** is at Edifício do Castelo (tel. 089/639-00).

WHERE TO STAY

Loulé Jardim Hotel, Praça Manuel de Arriaga, 8100 Loulé (tel. 089/41-30-94; fax 089/63-177), became the first hotel of a high standard ever to open in Loulé. (Until this place opened, Loulé was visited mainly on a day-trip from Faro because of its lack of any really fine accommodations.) In the center of town, this yellow-and-white structure is built in a typical Algarvian style, with local chimneys. The decorations are modern with Algarvian regional overtones. The hotel also has a swimming pool. Each bedroom is well furnished and beautifully maintained, costing 8,500$ ($56.95) daily in a single and 12,500$ ($83.75) in a double, including breakfast. Fifty-two bedrooms are rented, each with private bath, phone, and TV. The hotel also has two bars and an excellent restaurant, serving Portuguese specialties. Parking is free. MC, V.

Pensão Residencial Iberica, Avenida Marcal Pacheco 157, 8100 Loulé (tel.

089/41-41-00), is simplicity and modesty itself. However, ever since it was mentioned in the *New York Times*, visitors from northeast America have shown up at its door. Double rooms cost 5,000$ ($33.50) daily, and singles go for 4,000$ ($26.80). Breakfast is served. A laundry service is provided. DC, MC, V.

WHERE TO DINE

For meals, you can go to **O Avenida,** Avenida José da Costa Mealha 13 (tel. 62-106), which is on the main street of Loulé, very close to the traffic circle. It is one of the finer restaurants along the Algarve. The restaurant is attractively decorated in tavern style. It serves Monday to Saturday from noon to 3pm and 7 to 10pm. The cuisine is Portuguese. Reservations aren't necessary. In air-conditioned comfort, you can enjoy an apéritif at its bar before being shown to a table. Its specialty is shellfish cooked cataplana style. You can also order beefsteak à Avenida or sole meunière. Meals cost from 3,000$ ($20.10), a tourist menu going for 2,500$ ($16.75). Occasional live entertainment is featured. Closed Sunday and for most of November. AE, DC, MC, V.

Outside of town, about 2½ miles along the road to Faro (EN-125-4) is the **Outside In,** Sítio de Valados (tel. 904-43), a converted country house with panoramic views of 15½ miles of coastline. The French chef and the owner, also a chef, prepare the most savory and freshest viands in the entire area; they've recently received several international awards for their efforts. Knowing vacationers come here nightly, as the fame of its *cozinha francesa* (French cuisine) has spread to the up-market beach resorts. Specialties include langoustines au gratin, sole Véronique, and fantail of duck, along with la tulip aux trois sorbets. The place has an enormous wine cellar. Expect to pay from 4,500$ ($30.15) for a meal. Food is served from 7:30 to 10pm Tuesday to Sunday. Reservations are necessary. MC, V.

---

16. São Brás de Alportel

Traveling north from Faro for 12½ miles, you'll pass through groves of figs, almonds, and oranges, through pine woods where resin collects in wooden cups on the tree trunks. At the end of the run, you'll come upon isolated São Brás de Alportel, one of the most charming and least-known spots on the Algarve.

Far from the crowded beaches, it attracts those wanting pure air, peace, and quiet—a bucolic setting filled with flowers pushing through nutmeg-colored soil. Northeast of Loulé, this whitewashed, tile-roofed town rarely gets lively except on market days. Like its neighbor, Faro, it is noted for its perforated plaster chimneys. Lying at the foot of the Serra do Caldeirão, the whole area has been called one vast garden.

The nearest tourist office is in Faro. Buses journey here from Faro and Loulé.

WHERE TO STAY & DINE

A change of pace from the seaside accommodations is offered at **Pousada de São Brás,** Estrada de Lisboa, N2, 8150 São Brás de Alportel (tel. 089/84-23-05). The government-owned inn is a hilltop villa, with fret-cut limestone chimneys and a crow's-nest view of the surrounding serras. It's approached through a fig orchard in which stones have been painted with welcomes in many languages.

Many visitors arrive just for lunch or dinner (served daily from 12:30 to 2:30pm and 7:30 to 9:30pm), returning to the coastline by night, but a knowing few remain for the evening. In the dining room, rustic mountain-tavern chairs and tables rest on hand-woven rugs. The soft sofa before the wood-burning fireplace is a perfect place for lingering over a cup of coffee. The 2,750$ ($18.45) table d'hôte dinner offers soup, a fish course, a meat dish, vegetables, and dessert. The cuisine is plain, but good. After dinner you may want to retire to the beamed-ceilinged sitting room to watch the embers of the evening's fire die down. Then trundle upstairs, past the large ornamented, tasseled donkey collar for a night's sleep in cozy beds in a room cooled by highland breezes. The 22 bedrooms contain private baths and phones. Singles rent for 14,300$ ($95.80) daily and doubles for 16,200$ ($108.55), including breakfast. The inn also rents a suite, costing from 21,300$ ($142.70). The place has an outdoor swimming pool as well. Laundry service is provided, and room service is offered until 10pm. Parking is free. AE, DC, MC, V.

17. Estói & Milreu

A little village some 6 miles northeast of Faro, **Estói** is still mainly unspoiled by throngs of tourists. Those who come here are objects of some interest, stared at by old women sheltered behind the curtains of their little houses. Begging children are likely to follow sightseers around. Sometimes you may even see women washing their clothing in a public trough. Garden walls are decaying here and the cottages worn by time and the weather.

The principal sight in Estói is the Palácio do Visconde de Estói, with a baroque, salmon-pink facade. Built in the late 18th century for Francisco José de Moura Coutinho, and rescued from near ruin by José Francisco da Silva between 1893 and 1909, today it could use a massive infusion of cash. A palm-lined walk leads to terraced gardens set with orange trees along the balusters. Statues, busts, vases, and ornamental lakes adorn the terraces; azulejos and Roman mosaics adorn the gardens. Stairways, fountains, and belvederes rise beside cypresses, magnolia trees, patches of lavender, and climbing roses. This has been called a "cross between Versailles and the water gardens of the Villa d'Este near Rome."

The villa is not open to the public, but the grounds can be visited. To enter, ring a bell at the iron gates outside the palm-lined walk. A caretaker will guide you to the gardens. There is no entrance fee, but the caretaker should be tipped.

About half a mile west of Estói is **Milreu,** which was the Roman town of Ossonoba in the 1st century A.D. Two broken capitals and some fluted columns stand on ground blanketed by buttercups. In classical times the Roman soldiers, seeing the gardens of the Algarve in the spring, decided that a Temple of Venus was in order here, and you see its remains. Around the temple, ruins of baths and houses have been uncovered, with mosaics of interest. Little excavation has been done, however. There is no admission charge, just a lonely field where once a thriving spa existed.

18. Olhão

Olhão has been called a living re-creation of a Georges Braque collage. This is the famous cubist town of the Algarve, so long beloved by painters. In its heart, white blocks stacked one upon the other, with flat red-tile roofs and exterior stairways on the stark walls, evoke the aura of the casbahs of North African cities.

But let us not paint too romantic a portrait. Many readers have found it disappointing. J. L. Busey writes: "It turned out to be dirty, dusty, very poverty-stricken in appearance, and almost entirely without any eating facilities." Another reader, Mrs. Jules Berman of Kensington, Maryland, writes: "Olhão has almost disappeared before the onslaught of modern commercialism. Apartments have almost obliterated this famous cubist town. Yes, we finally found some fishermen on the beach!"

I totally agree with these assessments. If you do go there, I hope you'll be able to attend the fish market near the waterfront when a *lota* (auction) is under way. Olhão is also known for its bullfights of the sea, in which fishermen wrestle with struggling tuna trapped in nets and headed for the smelly warehouses along the harbor.

For the best view, climb **Cabeça Hill,** its grottos punctured with stalagmites and stalactites, or perhaps **St. Michael's Mount,** offering a panorama of the Casbah-like Barreta. Finally, for what is perhaps one of the most idyllic beaches on the Algarve, take a 10-minute motorboat ride to the **Ilha de Armona,** a nautical mile away. Olhão is 6½ miles west of Faro.

WHERE TO DINE

Restaurants tend to be very simple but they are reasonably priced, and nearly all of them feature fresh fish.

Escondidinho, R. J. P. Leonardo (tel. 70-26-74), attracts devotees of Portuguese home-cooking. Stick to the fish dishes and, chances are, your bill will rarely run more than 2,000$ ($13.40). A tourist menu costs 1,300$ ($8.70). Specialties include fried sole, red mullet, and other fresh fish dishes, nothing grilled. The chef makes a savory caldeirada (fish stew) and also specializes in roast meat (carne assada). It is open Monday to Saturday from noon to 3pm and 7 to 9:30pm. Reservations aren't necessary. No credit cards.

---

19. Tavira

An Algarvian gem, Tavira is approached through green fields studded with almond and carob trees, the latter producing a dry pod of hard seeds in sweet pulp (eaten by both people and animals). Sometimes called the Venice of the Algarve, Tavira lies on the banks of the Ségua and Gilão rivers, which meet under a seven-arched Roman bridge. In the town square, palms and pepper trees rustle amid the cool arches of the arcade.

A tunny fishing center, Tavira is cut off from the sea by an elongated spit of sand, the **Ilha de Tavira,** which begins west of Cacela and runs all the way past the fishing village of Fuzeta. On this sandbar, reached by motorboat, are two beaches: the **Praia de Tavira** and the **Praia de Fuzeta.** Others prefer to go to the beach at the tiny village of **Santa Luzia,** about 2 miles from the heart of town.

In spite of modern encroachments, Tavira, 195 miles southeast of Lisbon, is festive looking, with floridly decorated chimneys topping many of the houses, some of which are graced with emerald-green tiles and wrought-iron balconies capped by finials. Many doorways are adorned with fretwork. The liveliest action, however, centers on the fruit and vegetable market on the river esplanade. The town lies 19 miles east of Faro.

The **Tavira Tourist Office** is at Praça da República (tel. 081/225-11). Tavira has frequent bus connections with Faro throughout the day.

WHERE TO STAY

A choice place to stay is **Eurotel,** Quinta das Oliveiras, 8800 Tavira (tel. 081/220-41; fax 081/22-171). The grounds of this sprawling white-walled hotel are incorporated into one of the Algarve's many residential vacation developments. Visitors will find two tennis courts and a full array of water sports. Set on the edge of the sea, on a flat terrain dotted with trees, the hotel's concrete wings, with their arches, Iberian balconies, and wooden balustrades, are visible from far away. The establishment includes two bars, a snack bar, and a restaurant. Much of the social life here revolves around one of the two swimming pools. Well-furnished singles peak at 6,500$ ($43.55) daily, with doubles going for 9,600$ ($64.30). Tariffs include a breakfast. The hotel lies midway between Tavira and Cabanas Beach, about 1¼ miles from each. Parking is free. AE, DC, MC, V.

WHERE TO DINE

The English Rose, Avenida Dom Matheus Teixeira d'Azevedo 14 (tel. 222-47), is the finest dining choice within the town. It not only has the most beautiful name of any restaurant in the vicinity, it dispenses continental and Portuguese cuisine with flair and style. The staff serves dinner daily from 7:30 to 11:30pm. For dinner, you are likely to spend from 2,000$ ($13.40) up. A tourist menu costs 1,350$ ($9.05). Try the tuna fish steak or the swordfish in a garlic sauce. In the tavern and carvery, bar snacks are also offered. AE, DC, MC, V.

Restaurante Imperial, Rua José Pires Padinha 22 (tel. 223-06), is a small, air-conditioned place off the main square, where you can order regional food, including sarrabulho of shellfish, shellfish rice, pork a camponesa, chicken na caçarola, and other Portuguese dishes, accompanied by vegetables, and good local wines. A local favorite here is pork and clams with french fries, topped off with a rich egg-and-almond dessert. Meals cost from 2,200$ ($14.75) per person, including wine. A tourist menu is 1,600$ ($10.70). Food is served daily from noon to 3pm and 7 to 10pm. Reservations aren't needed. No credit cards.

---

20. Monte Gordo

Monte Gordo is the last in a long line of Algarvian resorts, lying 2 miles west of the frontier town of Vila Real de Santo António at the mouth of the Guadiana River. The location is 310 miles southeast of Lisbon. Its wide beach, one of the finest along the southern coast of Portugal, is backed by lowlands studded with pines.

Sadly, this was once a sleepy little fishing village. But nowadays, the varinas urge their sons to work in the hotels instead of the sea, fishing for tips instead of tunny. Monte Gordo has succumbed to the high-rises, often attracting Spaniards from across the border. One reader described it as a "compact version of Ocean City, Maryland." Nevertheless, it has many good hotels, and a number of Europeans use it as their place in the Algarvian sun.

The nearest tourist office is at Vila Real de Santo António (see below). Ten buses a day run from Faro to Vila Real (trip time: 1 hour and 20 minutes). Stops are made at Monte Gordo before the approach to Vila Real. Trains from Lisbon continue beyond Faro to Vila Real, from which bus connections can be made to Monte Gordo.

WHERE TO STAY

Hotel Alcazar, Rua de Ceuta, Monte Gordo, 8900 Vila Real de Santo António (tel. 081/421-84; fax 081/42-242), is considered the best hotel in town. Its palm-fringed facade alternates rust-colored brick with curved expanses of white balconies. A free-form pool is built on terraces into the retaining walls that shelter it from the wind and extend the hot-weather season late into the autumn. The interior design is a vaguely Arab-style series of repetitive arches and vaults crafted from distressed concrete. The resulting niches offer dozens of intimate cavelike retreats, which at night sparkle from the pinpoint lighting of table lamps handcrafted from sheets of perforated copper. Each of the 95 units contains its own sun terrace, a private bath, phone, radio, and air conditioning. Each unit is a double, costing from 11,000$ ($73.70) to 15,000$ ($100.50), including breakfast. Three suites are also rented, and these contain minibar and TV. Suites cost from 17,500$ ($117.25).

There's a disco in the basement for nighttime roving. One of the sunken living rooms off the main lobby shows recently released video movies. Near the bar, live music ushers in the night from 6pm to midnight. One of the hotel's most alluring spots is under the soaring ceiling of the in-house restaurant, where formal meals are served by a polite staff in a modern setting. The hotel isn't located on the beach, but the sea is within walking distance. Entertainment is presented at various times throughout the week. Laundry and baby-sitting are provided, as is room service. Parking is free. AE, DC, MC, V.

Hotel Vasco da Gama, Avenida Infante Dom Henriques, Monte Gordo, 8900 Vila Real de Santo António (tel. 081/443-21; fax 081/44-321). Its entrepreneurs know what their northern guests seek—lots of sunbathing and swimming. Although it enjoys a position on a long, wide, sandy beach, it also offers an Olympic swimming pool with high-dive board, and nearly an acre of flagstoned sun terrace. Inside is a sky-high oceanfront dining room, with additional tables on the mezzanine, plus several well-furnished lounges with many groupings of chairs. Other conveniences include two drinking bars, and a boîte where it's possible to dance to records or combos several nights a week. All the rooms are furnished conservatively, and glass doors open onto balconies. A total of 160 bedrooms are rented, each with private bath and phone. Singles cost from 9,240$ ($61.90) to 12,080$ ($80.95) daily, with doubles renting for 12,320$ ($82.55) to 14,780$ ($99), including breakfast. The hotel also rents five suites costing from 17,250$ ($115.60). Folkloric exhibitions are staged Monday and Saturday. Laundry service and baby-sitting are possible, as is room service until 11:30pm. Parking is free. AE, DC, MC, V.

Hotel dos Navegadores, Monte Gordo, 8900 Vila Real de Santo António (tel. 081/424-90; fax 081/448-72). The sign in front of this large hotel is so discreet you might mistake the building for an apartment house. The establishment is popular with vacationing Portuguese and British families, who congregate under the dome covering the atrium's swimming pool, a short distance from the reception desk. In some ways the hotel evokes a Caribbean retreat. You'll find an open bar willing to serve you a fruit-laden drink, along with an array of semitropical plants scattered throughout the wide expanses of the clean and functional public rooms. About three-quarters of the 346 bedrooms have a private balcony. Each room has a private bath, air conditioning, and phone. Singles rent for 8,500$ ($56.95) daily; doubles 12,500$ ($83.75), including breakfast. The beach is only 5 minutes away by foot. There's an array of boutiques in a corridor near the swimming pool, along with a hairdresser. There's a children's center to amuse children between the ages of 3 and 12. The hotel will also procure baby-sitters in the evening if you request it. Laundry service is provided, and parking is free. AE, DC, MC, V.

The **Casablanca Inn,** Rua 7, Monte Gordo, 8900 Vila Real de Santo António (tel. 081/424-44; fax 081/420-99), is not directly on the beach, but its frontage on a flower-dotted downtown park makes up for it. Owner Carlos Fernandes and his family designed it to look a lot like something you might find in a wealthy part of Morocco. There's a lush flower garden in front, a series of arched and recessed balconies, and a format similar to one that a modern Humphrey Bogart might have built in an updated version of *Casablanca* — in fact the lobby-level bar is called Rick's and is covered with movie photos of Hollywood's most romantic couple. The 42 bedrooms each contain a terrace, a private bath, a radio, and phone. At night the bar is popular with younger people, especially on Wednesday when live fado music begins at 10:30pm. You can enjoy the bar's café terrace for simple lunches every day from 11am to 2pm and for drinks in the evening between 5:30pm and 1am. Live organ music is part of the weekly entertainment. With breakfast included, singles range from 10,100$ ($67.65) daily, while doubles cost 15,000$ ($100.50). The beach is about a 10-minute stroll away. Parking is free. AE, DC, MC, V.

Albergaria Monte Gordo, Avenida Infante Dom Henriques, Monte Gordo, 8900 Vila Real de Santo António (tel. 081/421-24), is a modern, streamlined building, open to sea and sky, emulating Pueblo architecture. It is across the road from an immense sweep of beach, clean and colorful with the local fishin boats. Each room has a private bathroom. Of the 49 bedrooms, 27 also contain private phones, but no air conditioning. Singles rent for 5,500$ ($36.85) daily, with doubles costing 6,500$ ($43.55), including breakfast. The atmosphere is informal, the staff helpful. Many speak English. Decorative touches to the public rooms include fabric and needlework hangings. There is a lively bar and a good restaurant, known for its soups and local fish dishes. Nonresidents may enjoy its seaview location and fine service. The peaceful winter atmosphere makes this a place ideal for writers, painters, or people looking for the simple life. Parking is free. No credit cards.

WHERE TO DINE

Copacabana, Avenida Infante Dom Henriques 13 (tel. 424-64). Because of its Oriental roof and its vivid pink bougainvillea, this indoor/outdoor restaurant looks almost like a piece of Macau-made porcelain. Its entrance is flanked with a pair of feathery pine trees, which give a sparse shade to a few of the tables set out in the courtyard. Under an Oriental arcade, you can watch the chefs working in the heat of an exposed grill. Many patrons prefer to sit outdoors within view of the sea, which lies just across the street. Others retreat to the interior, which is walled in wood. You can order such Portuguese specialties as fondue of fish for two, grilled chicken, steak Diane, grilled suckling pig, bread-and-egg soup, or swordfish Copacabana, as well as grilled kid and even chiliburgers if that is your desire. Full meals cost from 2,800$ ($18.75) and are served at lunch from noon to 3pm and at dinner from 7 to 10pm 7 days a week. A tourist menu costs 1,200$ ($8.05). Reservations are necessary. AE, DC, MC, V.

21. Vila Real de Santo António

Twenty years after the Marquês de Pombal rebuilt Lisbon, which had been destroyed in the great earthquake of 1755, he sent architects and builders to Vila Real de Santo António where they reestablished the frontier town on the bank opposite Spain. It took only 5 months to build the town. Pombal's motivation was jealousy of Spain. Much has changed, of course, although the Praça de Pombal remains. An obelisk stands in the center of the square, which is paved with inlays of black-and-white tiles radiating like rays of the sun, and filled with orange trees. Separated from its Iberian neighbor by the Guadiana River, Vila Real de Santo António offers a car-ferry between Portugal and Ayamonte, Spain.

A long esplanade, the Avenida da República, lines the river, and from its northern extremity you can view the Spanish town across the way. Gaily painted horse-drawn carriages take you sightseeing past the shipyards, the lighthouse, or to the bullfights in July and August.

A short drive north on the road to Mértola takes you to the gull-gray castle-fortress of **Castro Marim.** This formidable structure is a legacy of the old border wars between Spain and Portugal. The ramparts and walls watch Spain across the river. Afonso III, who expelled the Moors from this region, founded the original fortress, which was razed by the 1755 earthquake. Inside the walls are the ruins of the Church of São Tiago, dedicated to St. James.

Thirteen buses a day arrive straight from Lisbon, and there are 10 buses a day from Faro in the west. Trip time from Faro is 1 hour and 20 minutes. Four trains also arrive daily from Lisbon, taking about 6 hours. The **tourist office** is at Avenida da República (tel. 081/432-72).

WHERE TO STAY

The best accommodation in town is **Hotel Apolo,** Avenida dos Bombeiros Portuguêses, 8900 Vila Real de Santo António (tel. 081/444-48), on the western edge of town as you enter Vila Real from Monte Gordo or Faro. Near the beach and the river, it attracts vacationers as well as travelers who don't want to cross the Spanish border at night. The hotel is attractive inside, with a spacious marble-floored lobby leading into a large and tastefully congenial bar scattered with comfortable sofas and flooded with sunlight. Each of the 42 simply furnished bedrooms has a private balcony and bath. With breakfast included, singles rent for 8,500$ ($56.95) daily, and doubles cost from 10,000$ ($67). Parking is free. AE, DC, MC, V.

WHERE TO DINE

Edmundo, Avenida da República 55 (tel. 446-89), has long been known in the Algarve, attracting Spaniards from across the river who often visit just for the day "for a glimpse of Portugal." One of the most popular restaurants in Vila Real, it overlooks the river and Spain across the water, a view you will enjoy if you get a sidewalk table. The people who run this place are friendly, and they are proud of their repertoire of local cuisine, especially fresh fish. You might begin with a shrimp cocktail, then follow with fried sole, crayfish, or sautéed red mullet. You can also order meat dishes, such as lamb cutlets and veal filet. Count on spending 3,000$ ($20.10) à la carte or 1,500$ ($10.05) for a tourist menu. Hours are daily from noon to 3pm and 7 to 10pm. Reservations are recommended. AE, DC, MC, V.

ALENTEJO & RIBATEJO

The adjoining provinces of Alentejo and Ribatejo are the heartland of Portugal. But while Ribatejo is a land of bull-breeding pastures, Alentejo is characterized as a plain of fire and ice.

Ribatejo is the country of the river, where the Tagus, coming from Spain, overflows its banks in winter. It is famed for bluegrass, Arabian horses, and black bulls. The most striking feature, however, is a human one: the *campinos,* the sturdy horsemen of the region in their stocking caps. Theirs is the job of harnessing the Arabian pride of their horses and searching out the intangible quality of bravery in the bulls. Whether visiting the château of the Templars, rising in the middle of the Tagus at Almourol, or attending an exciting *festa brava,* when the hooves of horses and the rumble of bulls reverberate in the streets of Vila Franca de Xira, you'll marvel at the passion of the people of Ribatejo. Their fadistas have long been noted for intensity.

The cork-producing plains of Alentejo (literally, beyond the Tagus) compose the largest province in Portugal—so large, in fact, that the government has divided it into Alto Alentejo in the north (capital: Évora), and Baixo Alentejo in the south (capital: Beja). Even today it's difficult to reach. Take the Ponte 25 de Abril across the Tagus via Setúbal, or go all the way north to Vila Franca de Xira, then head east.

In Alentejo the locals have insulated themselves in whitewashed houses with tiny windows that keep in heat in the cold winters, coolness during the scorching summers. The least populated of Portuguese provinces, Alentejo possesses seemingly endless fields of wheat, and is the world's largest producer of cork (the trees can be stripped only once in 9 years).

In winter the men are a dramatic sight in their characteristic capes, which are long brown coats with two short tiered capes, often adorned with a red fox collar. The women are even more colorful, especially when they are working in the rice paddies or wheatfields. Their skirts and patterned undergarments are short so they can wade barefooted into the paddies. Over a knitted cowl, with a "peek through" for their eyes, is a brimmed felt hat usually studded with flowers.

From our last stopover in the Algarve, we head north once again, approaching the cities of the plains.

---

1. Beja

The capital of Baixo Alentejo, founded by Julius Caesar and once known as *Pax Julia*, rises like a pyramid above the surrounding fields of swaying wheat, only 116 miles southeast from Lisbon and 47 miles south of Évora.

The fame of Beja rests on what many authorities believe to be a literary hoax. In the mid-17th century, in the Convent of Conceição, a young nun named Soror Mariana Alcoforado is said to have fallen in love with a French military officer, identified as the Chevalier de Chamilly. He was believed to have seduced her, then to have left Beja never to return again.

The girl's outpouring of grief and anguish found literary release in the *Five Love Letters of a Portuguese Nun*. Published in Paris in 1669, they created a sensation and have remained an epistolary classic of self-revelation and remorse ever since. In 1926, F. C. Green wrote "Who Was the Author of the *'Lettres Portugaises'?*" claiming that their true writer was the Comte de Guilleragues. However, a modern Portuguese study has submitted evidence that the *Lettres Portugaises* were in fact written by the nun, Sister Alcoforado.

Five trains per day make the 4-hour journey from Lisbon to Beja, a one-way ticket costing 780$ ($5.25). There are also six daily trains arriving from Évora (see below). This journey takes only 1 hour, a one-way ticket costing 415$ ($2.80). If you're in the Algarve (see Chapter 13), you can take one of two trains per day from Faro to Beja, taking 5½ hours and costing 975$ ($6.55) for a one-way ticket. Four *expressos* (express buses) per day run between Lisbon and Beja, taking 3 hours and costing 775$ ($5.20) for a one-way ticket. There are also 3 buses per day from Évora, taking 2 hours and costing 455$ ($3.05) for a one-way ticket, and 2 buses per day from Faro, taking 3½ hours and costing 660$ ($4.40) for a one-way ticket.

The **Beja Tourist Office** is at Rua Capitão João Francisco de Sousa 25 (tel. 084/236-93).

WHAT TO SEE & DO

Museu Rainha D. Leonor, Largo da Conceição (tel. 084/233-51), was founded in 1927–28 and occupies presently three different buildings in the city of Beja: the Convento da Conceição and the churches of Santo Amaro and São Sebastião. The main building was an ancient convent, founded in 1459 by the parents of the Portuguese King Manuel I. Favored by royal protection, it became one of the richest and most important convents of that time. Nevertheless, the Convento da Conceição is famous throughout the world because of its nun, Mariana Alcoforado, who is said to have written here the *Lettres Portuguaises,* love letters to the French Chevalier de Chamilly, in the 17th century.

One of the most important features of the building is precisely what is left of the ancient convent: the church with its baroque decoration and the cloister and chapter house, which present one of the most impressive collections of Spanish and Portuguese tiles from the 15th to the 18th centuries. Also displayed are statuary and silverwork belonging to the convent patrimony, a good collection of Spanish, Portuguese, and Dutch paintings (15th to the 18th centuries), and the "Escudela de Pero de Faria," a piece of Chinese porcelain dating from 1541 and unique in the world. In the first floor of the building there is a permanent archeological exhibition with various artifacts from the region of Beja—it shows the importance of this area from prehistoric to modern times.

Santo Amaro church is one of the oldest churches of Beja, maybe an early Christian foundation. It houses the most important Porguguese Visigothic collection (from the city of Beja and its surroundings).

The **church of São Sebastião** is a small temple with no great architectural interest. It houses part of the museum's collection of architectural goods from Roman to modern times. It is not open to the public but only to those who ask to visit it as a special request.

The museum is open from 9:45am to 1pm and 2 to 5:15pm Tuesday to Sunday. The regular admission is 25$ (15¢).

Crowning the town is **Castelo de Beja,** which King Dinis built in the early 14th century on the ruins of a Roman fortress. Although some of its turreted walls have been restored, the defensive towers are gone, save for a long marble keep. Traditionally the final stronghold in the castle's fortifications, the old keep appears to be battling the weather and gold fungi. The walls are grown over with ivy, the last encroachment upon its former glory. From the keep, you can enjoy a view of the provincial capital and the outlying fields. The castle opens onto the Largo Dr. Lima Faleiro.

WHERE TO STAY

Many visitors consider the **Residencial Cristina,** Rua de Mértola 71, 7800 Beja (tel. 084/230-35; fax 084/298-74), the best place to stay in Beja. A friendly management rents 42 simply furnished rooms, making the Cristina the largest hostelry in town. Rooms contain private bath, phone, and TV. Everything is immaculately kept and the price is very low; from 4,500$ ($30.15) daily in a single, rising to 6,200$ ($41.55) in a double. Breakfast, included in the tariff, is the only meal served. Parking is free. AE, DC, MC, V.

Santa Barbara, Rua de Mértola 56, 7800 Beja (tel. 084/220-28), is a little oasis in a town that has few suitable accommodations. The residência is a bandbox building, shiny clean and well kept. It's all small scale, with only a whisper of a reception lobby and elevator. There are two street-level salons, each partially covered with elegant blue-and-yellow tiles. The 26 compact rooms are adequate, with carpeting, good beds, phones, tile baths with showers, and central heating in the winter. The cost of staying here is low: 3,000$ ($20.10) daily for one person, 4,200$ ($28.15) for two. No meals are served except breakfast, which is included in the price. Parking is free. Laundry service is provided. AE, DC, MC, V.

WHERE TO DINE

Beja is rather lacking in first- or even second-class restaurants. However, at the **Luís da Rocha,** Rua Capitão João Francisco de Sousa 63 (tel. 231-79), on the same street as the tourist office, you can sit downstairs in the café where the whole town seems to congregate for coffee and pastries, or go upstairs where a spacious neon-lit dining room features a complete menu for 1,800$ ($12.05) if you order à la carte. A tourist menu costs 1,200$ ($8.05). The cuisine is Portuguese. You might begin with one of the cream soups, prepared fresh daily, then follow with boiled or fried fish or

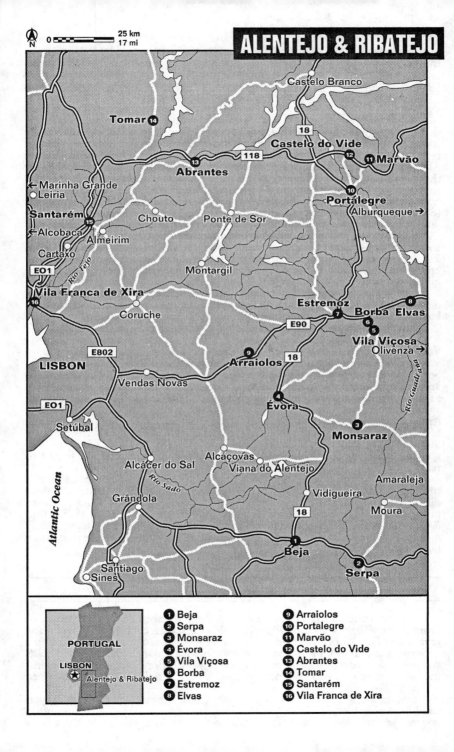

pork with clams in the Alentejo style. Reservations aren't needed. Hours are daily from noon to 3:30pm and 7 to 10pm. Closed Sunday in summer. No credit cards.

2. Serpa

Serpa is a walled town with defensive towers. Its origins go back to 1295 when it was incorporated into the kingdom of Portugal after having belonged to the Infante of Serpa, Dom Fernando, brother of Dom Sancho II. Overlooking the vast Alentejo plain, Serpa is a town of narrow streets and latticed windows, famous for the cheese that bears its name, as well as for pork sausage and sweets. Silvery olive trees surround the approaches to the town, and the whiteness of the buildings contrasts with the red-brown of the plains. The wild beauty of the Guadiana River, endless fields of grain, and cork-oak groves mark the landscape. In the town, you can see unique painted furniture, an archeological museum, and several ancient churches.

Serpa lies only 20 miles west of Vila Verde de Ficalho (the Spanish frontier). To the east at a distance of 18½ miles stands Beja. It is 137 miles southeast of Lisbon. Today Serpa has become a stopping-off place for lunch or just a rest stop for travelers on the way to and from Spain, and many motorists like to spend the night here at the hilltop pousada.

The nearest rail link is Beja (see above), to which Serpa is linked by three bus departures a day. It's also possible to take a bus directly from Lisbon to Serpa. A bus leaving Lisbon at 7:30am arrives at Serpa at 1:30pm in time for lunch.

The **Serpa Tourist Office** is at Largo D. Jorge de Melo 2 (tel. 084/903-35).

WHERE TO STAY & DINE

A government-owned tourist inn, **Pousada de São Gens,** Alto de São Gens, Serpa, 7830 Beja (tel. 084/903-27), is set at the crown of the hill of São Gens, in keeping with the Portuguese love of vistas. On clear nights guests can see all the way to Spain. Although a long way from the Algarve, the architecture is Moorish inspired, almost a pueblo villa with white walls easily seen as you ascend the winding road past olive trees. The pousada is family run and has a homelike atmosphere. Each of the 16 bedrooms has a private bath, tiled in aqua and white. The furnishings are modern, making use of bold colors. Doubles cost 14,300$ ($95.80) daily, and singles run 12,700$ ($85.10). Breakfast is included in all the tariffs. The hotel also rents two suites, costing from 21,300$ ($142.70).

In winter dinner is served in a salon with a coved ceiling; in the warmer months the wide veranda is also used by diners. A Portuguese cuisine is offered, with many dishes of the region featured. A complete meal, including soup, a fish course with potatoes, a meat dish with vegetables, and dessert, goes for 2,750$ ($18.40) to 3,650$ ($24.45). Food is served from 12:30 to 2:30pm and 7:30 to 9:30pm. Before dinner, you can have a drink in the gold-and-white bar or in one of the stark white living rooms. Parking is free. AE, DC, MC, V.

3. Monsaraz

The old fortified town of Monsaraz lies 32 miles east of Évora on the way to Spain. It's a village of antique whitewashed houses, with cobbled lanes and many reminders of the Moors who held out here until they were conquered in 1166. Some of the women still wear the traditional garb: men's hats on their shawl-covered heads and men's pants under their skirts. This was obviously done as a protection against the sun. The town overlooks the Guadiana Valley, forming the border between Spain and Portugal.

Still walled, Monsaraz can easily be visited in an afternoon from Évora. As you stroll its streets, look for the original coats-of-arms on the 17th- and 18th-century houses. As you scale the ramparts, you'll have a view over what looks like a cross between a bullring and a Greek theater. The highlight of the town is a visit along the main street, **Rua Direita,** which has the most distinguished architecture, along with wrought-iron grilles, balconies, and outside staircases. The former **Tribunal** is noted for its fresco depicting "true" and "false" justice, and the town has a church with a 16th-century marble tomb along with a more recent pillory nearby (it dates from the 1700s). Opposite the parish church is the 16th-century **Misericord Hospital,** with a lovely assembly hall on the second floor. King Dinis in the 1200s rebuilt the town **castle,** which saw later fortified additions in the 17th century.

Two buses a day run between Évora (see below) and Monsaraz going via Reguengos de Monsaraz. Évora is both the nearest rail link and has the nearest tourist office.

WHERE TO STAY & DINE

If you'd like to dine or stay over in the town, your choice is **Estalagem de Monsaraz,** Largo de São Bartolomeu, 7200 Reguengos de Monsaraz (tel. 066/551-12). Overlooking the valley, this antique-filled inn is most often visited by "day trippers" for lunch. There, in the heat of the afternoon, they enjoy the gardens and scented arbors. Under a beamed ceiling, guests might begin with a robust vegetable soup or Chaves ham. For a main course, they can select sole meunière or acorn-sweetened pork with a savory baby-clam sauce. You might skip the regular desserts and opt instead for one of the fresh fruits of the region. Its melons have been compared to "the taste of Château d'Yquem," and its oranges have been called "candy sweet." Meals cost from 1,800$ ($12.05) and are best sampled with local Borges branco wine.

For those wishing to stop over, the estalagem offers seven tiny but attractively decorated bedrooms, each with striped rugs and hand-painted headboards along with private bath. A double room rents for 6,000$ ($40.20) nightly, a single for 3,000$ ($20.10) including breakfast. Parking is free. AE, V.

---

4. Évora

The capital of Alto Alentejo is a historical curio. Considering its size and location, it is something of an architectural phenomenon, its builders freely adapting whatever they desired from Mudejar to Manueline, from Roman to rococo. Évora lives up to its reputation as the Museum City. As it lies only 96 miles east of Lisbon, it is often visited on a day-trip from the capital, but that's a long trek. It is 63 miles southeast of the Spanish frontier city of Badajoz.

Nearly every street in Évora is filled with 16th- and 17th-century houses, many with tile patios. Cobblestones, labyrinthine streets, arcades, squares with bubbling fountains, whitewashed houses, a profuse display of Moorish-inspired arches characterize the town, all of which used to be enclosed behind medieval walls.

Many conquerors have passed through, and several have left architectural remains. To the Romans at the time of Julius Caesar, Évora was known as Liberalitas Julia. Perhaps its heyday was in the 16th century, during the reign of João III, when it became the Montmartre of Portugal, and avant-garde artists congregated under the aegis of royalty. Included among them were the playwright Gil Vicente.

Évora today is a sleepy provincial capital, perhaps self-consciously aware of its monuments. One local historian actually recommended to an American couple that they must see at least 59 monuments. Rest assured that you can capture the essence by seeing only a fraction of that number.

The major event in Évora is the **Feira de São João,** which is a folkloric and musical extravaganza, when all the handcrafts of the area, including fine ceramics, are displayed as hundreds of people from the Alentejo region come into the city. The event occupies the last 10 days of June. Ostensibly the festival is to celebrate the arrival of summer. Food stalls sell specialties of the region, and regional dances are presented. The tourist office will supply more details.

The Évora train station (tel. 066/221-25 for information) lies 1 mile from the center. Four trains per day arrive from Lisbon, taking 3 hours and costing 550$ ($3.70) for a one-way ticket. Three trains arrive from Faro in the Algarve, taking 5½ hours and costing 960$ ($6.45) for a one-way ticket, and 3 trains per day pull in from Beja (see above), taking 2 hours and costing 450$ ($3) for a one-way ticket. Rodoviária Nacional, Rua da República (tel. 066/221-21), provides bus service for the area. Five buses per day arrive from Lisbon, taking 2½ hours and costing 740$ ($4.95) for a one-way ticket, and 1 bus per day comes in from the Faro in the Algarve, taking 5 hours and costing 975$ ($6.55) for a one-way ticket. Two buses per day connect Beja with Évora. Trip time is 1½ hours and a one-way ticket costs 455$ ($3.05).

WHAT TO SEE & DO

The major monument in Évora is the **Temple of Diana,** in the Praça do Giraldo, directly in front of the government-owned pousada (see below). Dating from either the 1st or 2nd century A.D., it is a light, graceful structure, with 14 granite Corinthian columns topped by marble capitals. Of course, no one can prove that it was actually dedicated to the goddess, but it is a good guess. Incidentally, the temple withstood the earthquake of 1755, and there is evidence that it was once used as a slaughterhouse. Don't fail to walk through the garden for a view of the Roman aqueduct and the surrounding countryside.

A short stroll along Rua 5 de Outubro leads to the **Sé (cathedral)** (tel. 066/29-160). Bulky and heavy, the church of Évora was built in the Roman-Gothic style between 1186 and 1204, although notably restored and redesigned over the centuries. The stone facade is flanked by two square towers, both topped by cones, one surrounded by satellite spires. The interior consists of a nave and two aisles. The main altar, from the 18th century, is the finest in town, made of marble in tones of pink, black, and white.

At the sculptured work *The Lady of Mothers,* young women pray for fertility. A French couple, whose marriage had produced no children, prayed here and the wife found herself pregnant by the time she returned to Paris. The next year the couple returned to Évora, bringing their new child.

The museum, charging an admission of 150$ ($1), is open from 9am to noon and 2 to 5pm; closed Monday. It houses treasures from the church, the most notable of which is a 13th-century Virgin carved out of ivory (it opens to reveal a collection of scenes from her life). A reliquary is studded with 1,426 precious stones, including sapphires, rubies, diamonds, and emeralds. The most valuable item is a piece of wood said to have come from the True Cross.

In the 14th-century cloister, the medallions of the Apostles include the Star of David, incongruous in a Catholic church. A cross in the ceiling, called the Key of the Cloister, marks the last stone to be set into place.

The **Igreja Real de São Francisco,** Rua da República, is visited by those wanting to see its ghoulish Chapel of Bones (Capela dos Ossos). The chancel walls and central pillars are lined with human skulls and other parts of skeletons. Alternate legends have it that the bones came either from soldiers who died in a big battle, or from plague victims. Over the door is the sign: "Our bones who stay here are waiting for yours!" The stone chapel dates from the 16th century. The church was built in the Gothic style with Manueline influences between 1460 and 1510. Admission is 25¢ (15¢). Hours are 9am to 1pm and 2:30 to 6pm Monday to Saturday, from 10 to 11:30am and 2:30 to 6pm Sunday.

The **Church of Our Lady of Grace** (Igreja Nossa Senhora de Graça), Largo da Graça, is visited chiefly for its baroque facade, with huge classical nudes over the pillars. Above each group of lazing stone giants is a sphere with a flame atop. These pieces of sculpture are often compared to works by Michelangelo. The church was built in Évora's heyday in the reign of João III. The central window shaft is flanked by columns and large stone rosettes, the lower level supported by ponderous neoclassic columns.

You may want to visit the **Ancient University** (Universidade de Évora). In 1559, as a result of the cultural flowering of Évora, a university was constructed and placed under the tutelage of the Jesuits. It flourished until the Jesuit-hating Marquês de Pombal closed it in the 18th century. The baroque structure is double tiered and built around a large quadrangle. The arches are supported by marble pillars, the interior ceilings constructed with brazilwood. The inner courtyard is lined with blue-and-white tiles. Other azulejo representations, depicting women, wild animals, angels, cherubs, and costumed men contrast with the austere elegance of the classrooms and the elongated refectory. The compound is no longer used as a university, although pupils (the equivalent of high-school students in America) attend class here. It is open (but ask permission first) from 9am to 12:30pm and 2 to 5pm Monday to Friday.

Facing the Temple of Diana is the **Church of St. John the Evangelist,** Praça do Giraldo. Next door to the government-owned pousada, this private Gothic-Mudejar church is connected to the palace built by the dukes of Cadaval. However, it is open to the public—in fact, it is one of the gems of Évora, although seemingly little visited. It contains a collection of azulejos from the 18th century. A guide will show you a macabre sight: an old cistern filled with neatly stacked bones removed from tombs. In the sacristy of the chapel are some paintings, including a ghastly rendition of Africans slaughtering a Christian missionary. A curiosity is a painting of a pope that not only has moving eyes, but moving feet. In addition, you can see part of the wall that once completely encircled Évora.

Museum of Ancient Art (Museu de Évora), Largo Conde de Vila Flor (tel. 066/226-04), is in the 16th- and 17th-century episcopal palace. Roman, medieval, Manueline, and Luso-Moorish sculptures are displayed on the ground floor. Here you'll see a remnant of a vestal virgin in marble, a 14th-century marble *Annunciation,* and a Holy Trinity in Ança stone, dating from the 1500s. On the floor above, of major interest is a 16th-century Flemish-school polyptych depicting the life of the Virgin, panels of an altarpiece, also from the Flemish school, on the subject of Christ's Passion, and pictures by Portuguese artists of the 16th and 17th centuries. The museum is open from 10am to 12:30pm and 2 to 5pm Tuesday to Sunday. Admission is 200$ ($1.35). Children up to 10 years of age are admitted free.

WHERE TO STAY

Expensive

One of the finest government-owned tourist inns in Portugal is **Pousada dos Lóios,** Largo Conde de Vila Flor, 7000 Évora (tel. 066/240-51). It occupies Lóios Monastery, built in 1485 on the site of the old Évora Castle which was destroyed during a riot in 1384. A powerful noble, Don Rodrigo Afonso de Melo, founded the monastery and carried two baskets of soil and the first stone for the foundation ceremony on his back. Kings João II, IV, and V used to visit the monastery. The chapter room, with doorways in Moorish-Portuguese style, dating from the beginning of the 16th century, was the place where the official Inquisition reports were kept. After the 1755 earthquake, extensive work was done to repair and preserve the structure. Through the years it was used as a telegraph station, a primary school, an army barracks, and offices. The opening of the pousada in 1965 made possible the architectural restoration of the monastery. Its position in the museumlike center of Évora is prime, between the cathedral and the ghostlike Roman Temple of Diana.

There's a salon in white and gold (a one-time private chapel), with an ornate Pompeian-style decor and frescoes. It's decorated with antique furnishings, hand-woven draperies, crystal chandeliers and sconces, and painted medallion portraits. There are 32 rooms. All have private bath and phone. They're furnished in a traditional provincial style, with a blending of antique reproductions. Double rooms cost 22,500$ ($150.75) daily and singles rent for 19,700$ ($132). The hotel also rents one suite for 28,700$ ($192.30). Breakfast is included in this tariff. Ask for a room in the interior.

Even if you're not bedding down for the night, like a pilgrim of old, you should at least stop for a regional meal of Alto Alentejo. In winter, meals are served in the main dining hall, with its heavy chandeliers. But in fair weather most guests dine in and around the cloister, at tables set under the Manueline fan-vaulted ceiling and an ornate Moorish doorway leading to the Chapter House. You pay 3,600$ ($24.10) to 4,200$ ($28.15) for a complete luncheon or dinner. For this, you get a basket of freshly baked bread and butter, a bowl of hot soup, followed by a fish dish, such as sole prepared in a herb-flavored tomato sauce and accompanied by mashed potatoes. For your main course, try the acorn-sweetened pork cooked with clams in the manner of Alentejo. For dessert, a trolley of assorted pastries is wheeled by. Food is served daily from 12:30 to 2:30pm and 7:30 to 9:30pm. Parking is free. Laundry service is available, and room service is provided until midnight. AE, DC, MC, V.

Moderate

Albergaria Vitória, Rua Diana de Lis 5, 7000 Évora (tel. 066/271-74). Set inconveniently near the beltway surrounding the old city, this modern concrete-walled hotel juts above a dusty neighborhood of villas. Its location is on the southeastern edge of the city, about a mile from the cathedral, but it could be a handy address in summer when all the central hotels are full. Built in 1985, it contains 48 doubles but only 3 singles, each with balcony, private bath, phone, radio, and air conditioning. Singles with breakfast included rent for 7,200$ ($48.25) daily and doubles for 9,500$ ($63.65). Only breakfast is served in the dining room, but the Vitória has a bar on the premises. Parking is free. AE, DC, MC, V.

Hotel Planicie, Rua Miguel Bombarda 40, 7000 Évora (tel. 066/240-26). Its symmetry, its stone window frames, and its severe facade make it resemble an old Tuscan villa. Inside, a tasteful modernization added hundreds of slabs of glistening marble but retained many of the best features of its original construction. Especially appealing is the vaulted brick ceiling of the basement bar. A member of the Best Western reservation system, the hotel contains 33 bedrooms, each of which has a private bath, heating, TV, and phone. With breakfast included, singles cost 8,000$ ($53.60) daily, doubles 9,000$ ($60.30). Well-prepared meals, each costing from 2,200$ ($14.75), are served in the street-level dining room daily from noon to 3pm and 7 to 10pm. Parking is free. DC, MC, V.

Residencial Riviera, Rua 5 de Outubro 49, 7000 Évora (tel. 066/233-04; fax 066/20-467), was built beside the cobblestones of what is said to be the most charming street in town, about 2 blocks downhill from the cathedral. Originally designed as a private villa, it has retained many handcrafted details from the original building, including stone window frames, ornate iron balustrades, and the blue-and-yellow tiles of its foyer. Each of its 22 comfortable bedrooms contains a bath, TV, and phone, and comes with breakfast included in the price. Singles rent for 6,500$ ($4.35) daily, and doubles cost 10,000$ ($67). Parking is free. AE, DC, MC, V.

Inexpensive

O Eborense, Largo da Misericórdia 1, 7000 Évora (tel. 066/220-31), is a delightful guesthouse with a touch of grandeur in the form of a stone staircase leading up to an entrance lined with plants and decorated with tiles. Your hosts are Mr. and Mrs. Serrabulho, who have recently improved the building, making the bedrooms more comfortable but keeping the original and antique atmosphere. They offer 29 rooms, all in the main building, all clean, traditional, and quite pleasant. Each room has a private bath and phone. Singles range from 5,500$ ($36.85) daily, and doubles from 7,500$ ($50.25). Breakfast is included. The guesthouse also rents one suite for 12,000$ ($80.40). You can sit on the terrace nursing a drink and peering through the cloisterlike, mullioned veranda. An adjoining rooftop garden-café attracts sun-worshipers. Parking is free. No credit cards.

Farther away, **Santa Clara,** Travessa da Milheira 19, 7000 Évora (tel. 066/241-41), is another good bet, especially if your requirements are simple. Near the free city car park, it is within walking distance of the major sightseeing attractions of Évora. The management rents 29 well-kept bedrooms at modest prices, ranging from 6,200$ ($41.55) in a single and from 8,000$ ($53.60) in a double. Units contain private bath, phone, and TV. The hotel has a good restaurant, serving regional specialties and local wines, with meals priced from 2,000$ ($13.40). Parking is free. AE, DC, MC, V.

WHERE TO DINE

The most atmospheric restaurant in Évora is the **Cozinha de St. Humberto,** Rua da Moeda 39 (tel. 242-51). Hidden away in a narrow side street leading down from the Praça do Giraldo, it is rustically decorated with old pots, blunderbusses, standing lamps, a grandfather clock, and kettles hanging from the ceiling. Carnations stand on each table, and you sit in rush chairs or on divan-settees. The cuisine is typically Portuguese. In warm weather, you can enjoy a gazpacho alentejana, followed by fried fish with tomato and garlic or pork Évora style (a real meal in itself), topped off by regional cheese. A bottle of Borba wine is a good companion with most meals. A complete meal costs 3,000$ ($20.10). Food is served daily from noon to 3:30pm and 7 to 10:30pm. The restaurant is closed in November. Reservations are necessary.

Fialho, Travessa Mascarenhas 14 (tel. 230-79), is considered the most traditional restaurant at Évora. Its entrance is unprepossessing, but the interior warms considerably. The decoration is in the style of a Portuguese tavern, and the cookery is both regional and international. You get good shellfish dishes along with such fare as pork with baby clams in a savory sauce. In season you might also be able to order partridge. Seating 80 patrons, the restaurant is air conditioned and serves meals from noon to midnight (closed Monday). The cost ranges from 2,800$ ($18.75) to 4,200$ ($28.15) à la carte. A tourist menu costs 2,400$ ($16.10). The restaurant is likely to be closed for most of September. Reservations are recommended. AE, DC, MC, V.

Guiao, Rua da República 81 (tel. 23-071), is a regional tavern that appears on most lists as one of the best three or four restaurants of Évora. It lies a short distance off the main square, the Praça do Giraldo. Dining is on two levels. The decor is filled with Portuguese charm, including a beamed ceiling and antique blue-and-white tiles. Family run, it offers local wines and Portuguese specialties. Meals—hearty and robust fare—are most filling, costing from 2,200$ ($14.75) to 2,800$ ($18.75) à la carte. A tourist menu goes for 1,800$ ($12.05). A typical bill of fare includes grilled squid, grilled fish, swordfish steak, and clams with pork in the Alentejo style. At certain times of the year the kitchen prepares partridge. Hours are daily from noon to 3pm and 7 to 11pm. Reservations aren't needed. AE, DC, MC, V.

---

5. Vila Viçosa

This borough was the near-private dominion of the Dukes of Bragança, the last royal rulers of Portugal. Thirty-four miles northeast of Évora, Vila Viçosa has been a ducal seat since 1442. But what cast it into worldwide prominence was when one of its members journeyed to Lisbon in 1640 to be declared the head of a new royal dynasty. Ruling as João IV, he freed Portugal from 60 years of Spanish domination.

Ironically, one of the last of the Bragança kings, Carlos I, spent his last night dining under his favored antler chandeliers before making the journey to Lisbon. His staff, lined up at the Terreiro do Paço, waved him and his older son good-bye. But when they arrived at another Terreiro do Paço (this one in Lisbon), the reception was less friendly. Both died by an assassin's bullets.

The nearest rail connection and tourist office is in Évora. Public transportation to Vila Viçosa includes two buses a day which connect with Évora via Reguengos de Monsaraz. A bus from Lisbon to Elvas passes through Vila Viçosa.

The **Paço Ducal de Vila Viçosa,** Terreiro do Paço (tel. 068/986-59), remains as a memorial to the Braganças. You'll see pictures of the last king, Manuel II, who fled with his mother, Amélia, into exile in 1910. The uniforms of Carlos I are here as well. Perhaps the most remarkable personal exhibit is a gallery of Carlos's (known as the painter king) paintings and watercolors. As one critic put it, he was a better artist than a king.

The inside of the palace and its furnishings are a collage of faded mementos, foreign art influences, and nostalgic specters of a once-royal life. As with a fine tapestry, separating the diverse treasures is difficult. They include a frescoed Salon of Hercules, tapestries based on Rubens's cartoons, 16th-century Persian carpets, 17th-century armor, an oratory with grotesque motifs, a Medusa chamber, Louis XVI furnishings, hand-carved armoires, a chapel faced with pink marble, a sword and shield collection (even spears from Angola), and cloisters dating from the early 16th century. The kitchen is filled with copper pots and utensils used by the royal family (a spit for roasting the big game Carlos I was fond of hunting), and a Coach Museum, containing some 80 carriages, from the 18th, 19th, and 20th centuries, with equipment, and a sedan chair. After your visit, you can stroll through the Garden of the Duchesses.

In the archives you can see the bequest of Manuel II: his priceless library of printed books from the 15th and 16th centuries, including editions of *Os Lusíadas* by Luís de Camões. The music archives contain what remains from the Schola Cantorum instituted by the dukes in the 17th, 18th, and 19th centuries. The palace is open daily, charging an admission of 400$ ($2.70); free for children 13 and under. Hours in winter are 9:30am to 1pm and 2 to 5pm, in summer to 6pm; closed Monday and holidays.

Today the white town of Vila Viçosa rests unchanged in the midst of the olive-green carpeted marble hills which are spotted with orange trees. The town is guarded by a walled castle (tel. 981-28) dating from the 14th century, with a quartet of tall towers and crenellated walls. It is a natural extension of the museum in the palace. There is also an archeological museum with artifacts from Paleolithic, Neolithic, Iron Age, and Roman civilizations found around Vila Viçosa. There are 22 churches in Vila Viçosa, many almost casually containing treasures, but only the most dedicated of visitors seek them out.

WHERE TO STAY

A 16th-century palace, **Casa dos Arcos,** Praça Martim Afonso de Sousa 16, Vila Viçosa, 7000 Évora (tel. 066/98-518), has Renaissance lines and balcony windows. Lying only a 2-minute walk from the palace, and located behind an aristocratically severe facade, it overlooks a cobblestone square. There is a quiet neighborhood feeling to the place. The wall decorations are neoclassic, and there is a family oratory adorned with canvas paintings and frescoes. Pillars of white stone support the graceful arcade outside and decorate a small indoor courtyard. You can have a comfortable and relaxed stay here. The hotel rents three bedrooms and four apartments, each with air conditioning and private bath. Singles are 8,000$ ($53.60) daily, with doubles costing 10,000$ ($67). Apartments for two to four persons begin at 12,000$ ($80.40), including breakfast. Laundry service and baby-sitting are provided. Parking is free. AE, DC, MC, V

WHERE TO DINE

Near the football field, **Ouro Branco,** Campo da Restauração 43 (tel. 985-56), has a warm and cozy ambience. You get good Portuguese local fare. Occasionally some of the coffee- and brandy-drinking Alentejo "cowboys" show up. Even though inland, the restaurant is known as a *marisqueira,* which in Portuguese designates a place where fresh shellfish is available. The regional fare is savory. Your meal might begin with a bowl of soup made from a rich stock of turnips, greens, and red beans, and follow with garlic-flavored pork. Seating 80, with a bar, the restaurant serves from noon to 4pm and 6:30 to 11pm Tuesday to Sunday. Meals cost from 2,500$ ($16.75) à la carte. A tourist menu goes for 1,500$ ($10.05). Reservations are recommended. AE, DC, MC, V.

---

6. Borba

The town that marble built, Borba lies on 2½ miles northeast of Vila Viçosa. You'll need a car to get here. On the way there you'll pass quarries filled with black, white, and multicolored deposits. In the village, marble is king. Along the streets many cottages have door trimmings and facings of marble, and the women get down on their hands and knees to scrub their doorways, a source of special pride to them.

On **Rua S. Bartolomeu** sits a church, also dedicated to S. Bartolomeu. It contains a groined ceiling; walls lined with azulejos in blue, white, and gold; and an altar in black-and-white marble. The richly decorated ceiling is painted with four major medallions, one depicting decapitation. As Portuguese churches go, this one isn't remarkable. What is remarkable, however, are eight nearby antiques shops (amazing for such a small town), which are filled with interesting buys. Borba is also a big wine center, and you may want to sample the local brew at a café.

On the outskirts is a remarkable sight, **Museu de Cristo,** on the main road to Estremoz at Vila Lobos. It lies almost 2 miles from Borba and 5½ miles from Estremoz. The entrance is inauspicious, on a farm by the side of the road. In front is an antiques shop filled with a hodgepodge of wares, including many pieces from Alentejo. In the rear, the museum is the most intimate and personal one in Portugal. It's owned by the Lôbo family.

Started more than four decades ago, the collection includes 3,000 crucifixes. One would suspect that this figure will change, as the Museum of Christ is still making acquisitions. The late founding father of the family started collecting primitive crucifixes from the country people, bartering his excess farm produce, picking up more figures in his travels to North Africa, Angola, and Spain.

The present collection spans about 13 centuries, 42 countries, and countless artistic traditions. Some of the figures were hollowed out to hide money in the 16th century. One of the finest is from 18th-century Florence, showing a skull and crossbones at the bottom. In the other rooms of the museum are regional artifacts and furnishings. The museum may be viewed from 8am to 10pm in summer (to 6pm in winter). You should make a contribution.

The nearest tourist office is in Évora.

WHERE TO STAY & DINE

In Borba, the best kitchen is the **Restaurant Lisbeto,** Rua Mateus Pais 31, Borba, 7000 Évora (tel. 066/943-32). Don't expect grandeur or culinary finesse. What you get is a warm welcome from the António Ganito family, along with solidly filling regional fare. You pass through a long and narrow anteroom, whose wood-trimmed walls are warmed by a tiny potbellied stove. Gregarious diners request a stand-up apéritif at the bar before heading into the tiled blue-and-white dining room, where imprints of horseshoes fill in the spaces of the otherwise unadorned plaster. Full Portuguese meals are served daily from noon to 4pm and 7:30 to 10:30pm, costing from 2,300$ ($15.40). A tourist menu goes for 1,200$ ($8.05). Menu choices are recited orally, and are likely to include codfish Lisbero style, sopa a alentejana, and loin of pork. Four simple bedrooms, each with private bath, are also rented out if you'd like to spend the night in Borba. The rate ranges from 3,000$ ($20.10) daily, either single or double occupancy. Parking is free. The restaurant is closed Saturday and on Sunday for dinner. No credit cards.

---

7. Estremoz

Rising from the Alentejo plain like a pyramid of salt set to dry in the sun, fortified Estremoz is in the center of the marble-quarry region of Alentejo, 108 miles east of Lisbon and 28½ miles from Évora. Cottages and mansions alike utilize the abundant marble in making windows and apertures or in fashioning balustrades and banisters.

The Estremoz bus station is at Rossio Marquês de Pombal (tel. 068/222-82). Six buses arrive here daily from Évora, taking 1 hour, a one-way ticket costing 360$ ($2.40). Five buses per day also arrive from Portalegre, taking 1½ hours and costing 430$ ($2.90) for a one-way ticket. At present there is no train service.

The **Estremoz Tourist Office** is at Largo da República 26 (tel. 068/22-538).

WHAT TO SEE & DO

From the ramparts of its **castle,** dating from the 13th-century reign of King Dinis, the plains of Alentejo are spread before you. Although one 75-year-old British lady is reported to have walked it, it's best to drive your car to the top of the Upper Town, bringing it to a stop on the Largo de Dom Dinis. The stones of the castle, the cradle of the town's past, were decaying so badly that the city leaders pressed for its restoration in 1970.

The large imposing keep, attached to a palace, dominates the central plaza. Dinis's saintly wife, Isabella, died in the castle. Isabella was unofficially proclaimed a saint by her local followers; even in life, however, one of her detractors wrote, "Poor Dinis!" Also opening onto the marble- and stone-paved largo are two modest chapels and a church. As in medieval days, soldiers still walk the ramparts, guarding the fortress.

With enough promenading Portuguese soldiers to man a garrison, the open quadrangle in the center of the Lower Town is called the **Rossio Marquês de Pombal.** The **Town Hall,** with its twin bell towers, opens onto this square, and the walls of its grand stairway are lined with antique azulejos in blue and white, depicting hunting, pastoral, and historical scenes.

The **Estremoz Potteries** turn out the traditional earthenware of the region. It is famous for *moringues,* wide- or narrow-mouthed jars with two spouts and one handle. A type associated with royalty, called "kings' jugs," is decorated with marble inlays. Primitive figurines of religious and lay characters are interesting, as well as those of animals.

The **Museu Rural,** Rossio Marquês de Pombal (tel. 068/225-38), has displays showing the life of people of the Alentejo through models and crafts. It is open for guided tours from 10am to 1pm and 3 to 6pm (to 5:30pm in winter) Tuesday to Sunday. Admission is 50$ (35¢).

In the **Church of St. Mary,** dating from the 16th century, you'll see pictures by Portuguese primitive painters. The church formed part of the ancient fortress.

Another church worth a stop is about a mile south of the town on the road to Bencatel, the **Church of Our Lady of the Martyrs** (Nossa Senhora dos Mártires), with beautiful azulejos and an entrance marked by a Manueline arch. Dating from 1844, the church has a nave chevet after the French-Gothic style of architecture.

WHERE TO STAY

The best of the government-owned tourist inns is the **Pousada da Rainha Santa Isabel,** Largo de Dom Dinis, 7100 Estremoz (tel. 068/226-18; fax 068/239-82). Within the old castle dominating the town, and overlooking the battlements and the Estremoz plain, it is a deluxe establishment, with gold leaf, marble, velvet, and satin mingling with antiques in the bedrooms and corridors. Before his departure for India, Vasco da Gama was received by Dom Manuel in the salon of this castle. In 1698 a terrible explosion followed by fire destroyed the royal residence, but ostentatious alterations were carried out. It became an armory and later was adapted to serve as a barracks, and then an industrial school, but its transformation into a castle-pousada has restored it as a historical monument. In perfect style, comfort is provided within the framework of history. Therefore, don't be surprised that prices differ from those of the less regal pousadas.

There are three suites and 23 bedrooms, all with bath, minibar, air conditioning, and phone. Singles cost 14,900$ ($99.85) daily, with doubles going for 19,700$ ($132), including breakfast. Suites begin at 28,700$ ($192.25). The vaulted dining room is cavernous but elegant. The menu is both international and regional. Try, for example, braised duck with olive sauce, or perhaps partridge stuffed with vegetables. If featured, you might want to be daring and order the grilled wild boar with a hot pepper sauce. A meal costs 3,300$ ($22.10) to 4,000$ ($26.80). Food is served daily from 12:30 to 3pm and 7:30 to 10pm. Laundry service is provided, and parking is free. Room service is offered until midnight. AE, DC, MC, V.

Residência Carvalho, Largo da República 27, 7100 Estremoz (tel. 068/227-12), is clean, simple, and inexpensive, just what you may be looking for in an emergency. Singles without bath range from 1,800$ ($12.05) daily, with doubles costing 3,500$ ($23.45) without bath to 5,800$ ($38.85) with bath. Seventeen rooms are rented, 12 with bath and 8 with phone. Breakfast, the only meal served, is included. The Carvalho is a possible stop in case the pousada is full and you're tired, two likely possibilities. Parking is free. No credit cards.

WHERE TO DINE

Good food in a pleasant ambience is offered at **Agulas d'Ouro,** Rossio Marquês de Pombal 27 (tel. 221-96). The Golden Eagle faces the largest square in Estremoz, its mosaic and marble balconied facade suggesting a doge's palace. On the second floor are several connecting dining rooms with rough white plaster walls under ceramic brick ceilings, heavy sumptuous black leather armchairs and white-draped tables. Your Portuguese meal begins with a dish of homemade pâté with rye bread. Dishes include a large bowl of spinach-and-bean soup with crispy croûtons floating on top. Main dishes include stuffed partridge and pork and clams. The chocolate mousse is the featured dessert. A complete meal costs from 2,300$ ($15.40), while a tourist menu goes for 1,600$ ($10.70). It is open daily from noon to 3pm and 7 to 11pm. Reservations are needed. AE, DC, MC, V.

8. Elvas

The city of the plums, known for its crenellated fortifications, is less than 7 miles west of Badajoz, Spain, and 138 miles east of Lisbon. The walled town is characterized by narrow cobblestone streets (pedestrians have to duck into doorways to allow automobiles to inch by), and is surely an anachronism, so tenaciously does it hold on to its monuments and history. The town was held by the Moors until 1226. It later was frequently assaulted and besieged by Spanish troops, being defeated in the War of the Oranges in 1801, which was ended by a peace treaty signed at Badajoz. Elvas remained part of Portugal, but its neighbor, Olivença, became Spanish. The Elvas ramparts are an outstanding example of 17th-century fortifications. There are fortified gates, curtain walls, moats, and bastions, with sloping banks (glacis) around them.

Lining the steep hilly streets are tightly packed gold- and oyster-colored cottages topped by tile roofs. Many of the doors leading to the houses are only 5 feet high. In the tiny windows are numerous canary cages and flowering geraniums. Water is transported to Elvas by the four-tier **Amoreira Aqueduct,** built between 1498 and 1622, coming from about 5 miles southwest of the town.

In the Praça Dom Sancho II (honoring the king who reconstructed the town) stands the **Sé (cathedral),** forbidding and fortresslike. Under a cone-shaped dome, it is decorated with gargoyles, turrets, and a florid Manueline portal. The cathedral opens onto a black-and-white-diamonded square. A short walk up the hill to the right of the cathedral leads to the **Largo Santa Clara,** a small plaza on which was erected an odd Manueline pillory, with four wrought-iron dragon heads.

On the south side of Largo Santa Clara is the **Church of Our Lady of Consolation** (Igreja Nossa Senhora de Consolação), an octagonal, 16th-century Renaissance building with a cupola lined with 17th-century azulejos.

The **castle** built by the Moors and strengthened by the Christian rulers in the 14th and 16th centuries, is open from 9:30am to 12:30pm and 2:30 to 7pm Friday to Wednesday (closes at 5:30pm from October 10 to April 30). From the top of the castle's ramparts, you have a panoramic view of the town and its fortifications, as well as the surrounding country.

The Elvas train station is at Fontainhas (tel. 069/628-16), 2 miles north of the city. Local buses connect the station to the Praça da República in the center. Four trains a day arrive from Lisbon, taking 5 hours and costing 900$ ($6.05) for a one-way ticket. From Évora, there is train service twice a day taking 1½ hours and costing 280$ ($1.90) for a one-way ticket. From Badajoz in Spain, there is only one train per day, taking 1 hour and costing 135$ (90¢) for a one-way ticket. The Elvas bus station is at Praça da República (tel. 069/628-75). Five buses per day arrive from Lisbon, taking 4 hours and costing 875$ ($5.85) for a one-way ticket. From Évora, three buses a day arrive, taking 1½ hours and costing 495$ ($3.30) for a one-way ticket. From Badajoz there are frequent buses through the day.

The **Elvas Tourist Office** is at Praça da República (tel. 068/62-22-36).

WHERE TO STAY

A major link in the government-inn circuit is the **Pousada de Santa Luzia,** Avenida de Badajoz, 7350 Elvas (tel. 068/62-21-94), a hacienda-style building just outside the city walls at the edge of a busy highway (Estrada N4). It was built some 50 years ago as a private hotel, lying about a 5-minute walk east of the center of town. The bone-white stucco villa faces the fortifications. The entire ground floor is devoted to a living room, an L-shaped dining salon, and a bar—all opening through thick arches onto a Moorish courtyard with fountain, lily pond, and orange trees.

There are some bedrooms on the upper floor, but you can also stay in the nearby annex, a villa with a two-story entrance hall and an ornate staircase. The hotel offers only 15 bedrooms, so getting in here without a reservation could be difficult. Each room has a private bath, phone, and air conditioning. Singles peak at 14,300$ ($95.80) daily and doubles at 16,200$ ($108.55), including breakfast. One suite is rented for 21,300$ ($142.70). Meals cost from 2,750$ ($18.45) to 3,650$ ($24.45) and are served daily from noon to 4pm and 8 to 10pm. The menu is extensive. Noteworthy are the fish dishes, including grilled red mullet and fresh oysters. The restaurant in the pousada is reputed to be the finest in the area. Laundry service is provided, and room service is available until 10pm. Parking is free. AE, DC, MC, V.

Since the pousada is likely to be full, you might try instead **Estalagem Dom Sancho II,** Praça da República 20, 7350 Elvas (tel. 068/62-26-84; fax 068/62-47-17), which sits proudly on the main square of Elvas. The location is perfect for walking around the village. Some of the rooms open onto the old square, and from your window you can look down upon the former town hall and, to the north, the old cathedral. However, one of the rooms in the rear would be much quieter. The hotel is furnished in period pieces, offering 26 small but still quite adequate units, each with private bath and phone. A double costs 7,500$ ($50.25) daily, and singles go for 6,000$ ($40.20), these tariffs including breakfast. The hotel offers an excellent dining room that serves Portuguese specialties every day; a complete meal costs from 2,500$ ($16.75) per person. A solarium is offered, and room service is provided until midnight. Parking is free. AE, DC, MC, V.

In terms of general amenities, the best selection—certainly the largest in town —is **Dom Luís,** Avenida de Badajoz (along the N4), 7350 Elvas (tel. 068/62-27-56; fax 068/62-07-33), which is a well-run hotel with 69 rooms furnished in a modern style, each with private bath, phone, TV, and air conditioning. Prices are reasonable too, ranging from 8,500$ ($56.95) per day in a single to 9,800$ ($65.65) in a double, including breakfast. Three suites are rented for 18,000$ ($120.60). The hotel also has a good restaurant, serving regional wines and local dishes, with prices beginning at 2,200$ ($14.75). Seating 130, the restaurant is air conditioned in summer. Meals are served daily from 12:30 to 2:30pm and 7:30 to 10pm. Laundry service is available, and room service is offered until midnight. Parking is free. AE, DC, MC, V.

WHERE TO DINE

Many guests will want to take their meals at the pousada, previously recommended. However, a more adventurous choice is the **Estalagem Don Quixote,** Route N4, Pedras Negras (tel. 62-20-14), about 2 miles west of Elvas. This isolated compound is the end point for many a gastronomic pilgrimage in the area. The place is especially busy on weekends, when it adopts a holiday feeling, with lots of convivial chatter and a kind of frenzied table service. You can order a drink in the leather-upholstered English-style bar near the entrance. The sprawling and sunny dining room greets newcomers with the sight of rows of fresh fish arranged on ice behind glass cases. Amid an Iberian traditional decor you can order full Portuguese meals costing 1,800$ ($12.05) to 2,500$ ($16.75), served daily from noon to 3pm and 7 to 10:30pm. Specialties include shellfish rice, grilled sole, grilled swordfish, roast pork, beefsteak alentejano, and at least five different kinds of shellfish. Reservations are recommended. AE, MC, V.

Restaurante O Estribo, Rua da Cadeia 33 (tel. 62-29-83), on the square, is a pleasant place to eat, offering good, filling Portuguese meals at reasonable prices. You can feast on fish dishes, lamb, or a tasty goatmeat stew after starting with a soup such as gazpacho (in deference to neighboring Spain) or an appetizer. The fruits served here are excellent conclusions to your meal, as is the regional cheese. Expect to spend from 2,200$ ($14.75) for a satisfactory à la carte meal, served from noon to 4pm and 7 to 10pm Monday to Saturday. A tourist menu costs 1,550$ ($10.40). The restaurant is clean, and the staff provides good service. No reservations are needed. AE, DC, MC, V.

---

9. Arraiolos

This small village has been famous since the 13th century for its carpets. Early designs were imitations of Persian designs, but were soon developed and expanded by the craftspeople until the 18th century, when the creative impulse seemed to cease. The present rugs follow the old designs religiously. They are made of heavy wool (the yarns tinted by natural dyes), are handmade, and often contain elaborate needlework. Many of the most elegant are displayed at the Museum of Antique Art in Lisbon. Even if you can't stop off at Arraiolos, you may want to see a wide-ranging display for sale at the **Casa Quintão,** Rua Ivens 30 in Lisbon (tel. 34-65-837).

In Arraiolos, **Tapetes de Arraiolos Condestave,** Rua Bombeiros Voluntarios 7 (tel. 066/424-23), is open from 9am to 1pm and 2 to 7pm Monday to Saturday and 2 to 7pm Sunday. You can visit the workshop Monday to Friday from 8am to noon and 1 to 6pm. This shop has a branch in Évora.

Arraiolos is most often visited on a day-trip from Évora. It lies a 30-minute bus ride to the northwest of Évora, and there are four buses a day going each way. The nearest tourist office is in Évora.

WHERE TO DINE

This rug town has never been known for its restaurants. However, if you are a collector and are passing through on a shopping trip, you might try **Arca de Noe,** Rua St. Condestavel 23 (tel. 424-27). This place, patronized almost exclusively by locals, is inexpensive, with meals costing from 1,800$ ($12.05). A tourist menu goes for 1,100$ ($7.35). For that you get regional cookery and wines, served Wednesday to Monday from noon to 10pm. Typical Portuguese dishes include a hearty vegetable soup, the inevitable salt cod, and fried fish of the day. Reservations aren't needed. Closed in September. AE, DC, MC, V.

---

10. Portalegre

Portalegre is more than 13 miles west of the border post at Marvão, providing motorists with the shortest route between Lisbon and Madrid. It is 148 miles east of Lisbon and 46 miles west of Badajoz, Spain. Three miles away lies the mountain of São Mamede. The town, a center for cork production, is filled with baroque mansions, particularly on Rua 19 de Junho. In the 16th century it was known for its tapestries. Silk mills were started in Portalegre in the late 17th century.

Trains (phone 045/961-21 for information) arrive 8 miles south of the city. There are infrequent bus connections from the station into the city of town. Four trains per day arrive from Lisbon, taking 6½ hours and costing 1,000$ ($6.70) for a one-way ticket. From Évora there are four trains per day, taking 4 hours and costing 510$ ($3.40) for a one-way ticket. Buses pull into the Rua Nuno Alvarez Pereira bus station. Five buses per day arrive from Lisbon, taking 5½ hours and costing 1,000$ ($6.70) for a one-way ticket. From Évora, there are only two buses per day, taking 2½ hours and costing 580$ ($3.90) for a one-way ticket.

The **Portalegre Tourist Office** is at Estrada de Santana 25 (tel. 045/218-15).

WHAT TO SEE & DO

Manufactura de Tapeçarias de Portalegre (Tapestry Workshops), Parque da Corredoura (tel. 045/232-83), in the old Jesuit monastery, can be visited Monday to Saturday from 9:30 to 11:30am and 2:30 to 5:30pm. Go up the stairs from the ground floor and ring the bell at the left-hand door. Visitors are taken through the weaving room with its hand-looms, studios where designs are worked out, and the display room.

The **cathedral** has a fine altarpiece in one of its chapels. The sacristy walls are covered with azulejos. The interior of the building, from the 16th century, is behind an 18th-century facade with wrought-iron balconies, granite pilasters, and marble columns at the door.

Casa Museu José Régio, Rua do Poeta José Régio, near Praça da República (tel. 045/236-25), has collections of folk and religious art of the region, including 300 crucifixes. Antique pottery and statuettes of St. Anthony are included in the collection, along with wrought-iron and forged-iron pieces. Many regional artifacts, such as powder horns, are also exhibited. Guided tours, costing 100$ (65¢), are conducted from 9:30am to 12:30pm and 2 to 6pm; closed Monday.

Museu Municipal de Portalegre, Rua José Maria da Rosa (tel. 045/216-16), Portalegre's Municipal Museum, near the cathedral in the former seminary, is open from 9:30am to 12:30pm and 2 to 5:30pm Wednesday to Monday. Here you can see treasures of sacred art, including a gilded wooden Spanish pietà from the late 15th century, a polychrome terra-cotta altarpiece and gold and silver church plate from the 16th century, as well as a number of other examples of ecclesiastical art. Arraiolos carpets from the 17th and 18th centuries are on exhibit, plus antique furniture, pottery, and porcelain. Admission is 100$ (65¢). Children 10 and under are admitted free. Close to the museum is the **Yellow Palace** with delicate wrought-iron grillework.

WHERE TO STAY

The best place to stay in Portalegre is the **Hotel D. João III,** Avenida de Liberdade, 7300 Portalegre (tel. 045/211-93). A modern hotel, its decor makes use of regional materials, including stone. The 60 bedrooms all have private baths, phones, and balconies, some looking out onto a town park. Thirty percent of the rooms are air conditioned. A single rents for 5,500$ ($36.85) daily, a double for 6,400$ ($42.90), including breakfast. Two suites are rented for 15,000$ ($100.50) to 20,000$ ($134) each. The hotel has a swimming pool (in use from May to October), a bar, and elevators. The dining room on the top floor has a panoramic view of the town and the amphitheater of hills in the distance. Meals cost 2,200$ ($14.75) and up. The hotel dining room, in fact, is one of the most reliable choices for dining in the area, and you can do so daily from 12:30 to 3pm and 7:30 to 10pm. Parking is free. Room service is available until midnight. AE, DC, MC, V.

WHERE TO DINE

Alpendre, Rua 31 de Janeiro 21 (tel. 216-11), is among the best of the local eateries, with a modern decor. It dispenses a typical Portuguese cuisine (try the pork with clams), along with a good selection of wines. You might begin with "little shark soup," then follow with grilled pork loin. Nearly 100 patrons can be accommodated, enjoying air conditioning in summer and a fireplace in winter. Meals, costing from 2,500$ ($16.75), are served daily from noon to midnight. A tourist menu costs 1,350$ ($9.05). Reservations aren't needed. AE, DC, MC, V.

Another suitable candidate is the **Quinta da Saúde,** Serra de Portalegre (tel. 223-24), which also offers regional specialties, national dishes, and good wines. Try little shark cooked in garlic wine, clam soup, pork loin flavored with saffron, and acorn-flavored pork roast. Try for a table with a panoramic view. Meals are served daily from noon to 11pm. The restaurant is located less than 2 miles from the center of town. The typical à la carte meal costs 2,700$ ($18.10), although a tourist menu is offered for 2,000$ ($13.40). Reservations aren't necessary. AE, DC, MC, V.

---

11. Marvão

This ancient walled hill town, lying close to Castelo de Vide, is well preserved and is visited chiefly for its spectacular views. Just under 4 miles west of the Spanish frontier, the once-fortified medieval stronghold retains a rich flavor of the Middle Ages. Those with limited time who can explore only one border town in Portugal should make it this one. It's that panoramic.

You get to Marvão by following a road around the promontory on which the little town was built, past the Church of Our Lady of the Star, the curtain walls, watchtowers, and parapets. Arcaded passageways, balconied houses with wrought-iron grillwork and Manueline windows, and a number of churches can be seen along the hilly streets.

The castle, built in the 13th century, stands at the western part of the rocky promontory. You can walk along the parapet, taking in a panoramic view of the surrounding country, all the way to the Spanish mountains in the east, as well as a vast sweep of Portuguese mountain ranges.

The population of Marvão is small. If you arrive in the afternoon, you may think you're in a ghost town. Most of the inhabitants are working in the fields outside the walls.

Marvão lies 12 miles northwest of Portalegre and 140 miles east of Lisbon. If you're coming by train, you go first to Beira, 6 miles from Marvão, which is the Portuguese border stop on the Madrid/Lisbon rail line. From Beira, there are connecting buses to Marvão. There is also a bus link between Portalegre and Marvão.

The **Marvão Tourist Office** is on Rua Dr. Matos Magalhães (tel. 045/932-26).

WHERE TO STAY & DINE

There is really only one recommendable choice. It's **Pousada de Santa Maria de Marvão,** Marvão, 7330 Portalegre (tel. 045/932-01), which stands in the upper levels of town sandwiched between two impossibly narrow cobblestone streets. With a total of 12 bedrooms, it is a small pousada, but one of the most charming and interesting in Portugal. Bedrooms are attractively furnished in a regional style, each with private bath, air conditioning, and phone. Singles cost 15,500$ ($103.85) daily, with doubles renting for 17,900$ ($119.95), including breakfast. One suite is also available for 23,800$ ($159.45). The pousada was created when the Portuguese government combined three antique houses into one graceful unit, staffing it with competent employees, and adding rows of panoramic windows to encompass one of the most breathtaking views in Iberia.

The establishment's social center lies within the combined living and dining room, where a cozy and intimate bar, a tile-surrounded hearth, deep, comfortable sofas, and carefully decorated tables create an undeniable charm. Service is from 12:30 to 3pm and 7:30 to 10pm daily, with meals costing 2,800$ ($18.75) to 4,800$ ($32.15). Typical menu choices include grilled prawns piri-piri, partridge, scampi, or clams Alentejo. Laundry service is provided, and room service is available until 10pm. Parking is free. AE, DC, MC, V.

12. Castelo de Vide

At an altitude of 1,800 feet, this spa town lies at the foot of a castle. Nature has endowed Castelo de Vide with therapeutic waters. Inside its walls stand white-washed houses, some on squares little changed since the 15th and 16th centuries. A view of pine woods, chestnuts, and oak trees gives the town a resort atmosphere. Cromlechs in the area testify to the ancient origin of the town. It was conquered by the Romans in A.D. 44 and destroyed by Vandals in 411.

Praça Dom Pedro V is the main square, on which stands the Church of Santa Maria, the late-17th-century town hall, the Santo Amaro Hospital of the same era, and a handsome 18th-century mansion.

The **castle** was built outside the walls. A 12th-century round tower leads to the keep, damaged in the early 18th century by an explosion. You can get a view of the town from a room with a Gothic cupola. The castle has played a part in the history of Castelo de Vide for a long time. It was rebuilt by the Arabs in 1299. At this fortress the contract for marriage of King Dinis to Dona Isabella of Aragón was signed.

The **Judiaria,** or Jewish Quarter, is a sector of narrow alleyways and small houses, with the richest collection of ogival doors in Portugal. This quarter also abounds with cats. A medieval synagogue has been restored. Below the Jewish Quarter is an attractive little square with a baroque fountain.

Castelo de Vide lies 12 miles due north of Portalegre, 7 miles west of Marvão, and 132 miles east of Lisbon. The nearest rail connection is at Beira, 6 miles from Marvão. From Beirã, it is possible to continue by bus to Castelo de Vide. The **Castelo de Vide Tourist Office** is at Rua Bartolomeu Alvares de Santa 81 (tel. 045/913-61).

WHERE TO STAY

Castelo de Vide has a number of modest but acceptable lodgings if you're planning to stay overnight.

At the **Hotel Sol e Serra,** Estrada de São Vicente, 7320 Castelo de Vide (tel. 045/913-01; fax 045/913-37), the building's modern lines contrast with the antique architecture of the town surrounding it. It lies near the center within a white stucco facade pierced with evenly spaced rows of recessed loggias like the kind you find on the Mediterranean. Built in 1983, the hotel contains 51 reasonably comfortable bedrooms. Each of these offers a private bath, radio, TV, and phone, and many also open onto private balconies. Singles rent for 8,000$ ($53.60) daily, with doubles going for 10,500$ ($70.35). A fixed-price meal in the dining room goes for 3,000$ ($20.10). Parking is free. AE, DC, MC, V.

Albergaria Jardim and **Estalagem S. Paulo,** Rua Sequeiro Sameiro 6, 7320 Castelo de Vide (tel. 045/912-17), combine to offer the visitor a total of 40 simply furnished but clean bedrooms. The rates, which include breakfast, are 5,500$ ($36.85) daily in a single, 7,000$ ($46.90) in a double. Each room has a private bath or shower, but only the albergaria has phones. The estalagem complex also has one of the best restaurants in town, charging from 2,500$ ($16.75) for a regional meal with wine. Food is served daily from 1 to 2pm and 8 to 9:30pm. Guests can swim in the pool or play squash on the courts of the complex. Laundry service is provided. Parking is free. No credit cards.

WHERE TO DINE

Dom Pedro V, Praça Dom Pedro V (tel. 912-36). It is generally conceded that this restaurant, outside the hotels, is the best eatery in town. In air-conditioned comfort, some 80 guests can select from a varied menu of regional dishes with good and inexpensively priced wines. The chef's specialty may be too much for you. It's sarapatel, a meal cooked with bits of pork, including the liver and blood. If that doesn't appeal to you, you can also order steak Dom Pedro. An à la carte meal averages 2,500$ ($16.75), although a tourist menu is priced at only 1,700$ ($11.40). Service is Tuesday to Sunday from 12:30 to 3:30pm and 7:30 to 10:30pm. The restaurant also has a bar and disco. Reservations aren't needed. The restaurant closes in July. AE, DC, MC, V.

13. Abrantes

After passing a dramatic view of the Tagus at Rodão, you arrive at Abrantes in central Portugal. The location is 88 miles east of Lisbon, and 38 miles northeast of Santarém. A town of whitewashed stone, it lies on the bank of the Tagus. The river must be crossed again to gain entrance to the town. Here, you see the ruins of a Roman bridge extending into the water.

High on a hill, the old **fortress** was rebuilt during the reign of King Dinis. It was already dilapidated by the beginning of the 19th century. To reach the fortifications, you must go through a labyrinth of narrow streets. Once at its belvedere, a panoramic view of the valley, mountains, and foothills unfolds.

There's a small **museum** in the Church of Santa Maria, already ancient when it was rebuilt in the 15th century. Here you can see a 15th-century statue of the Virgin and Child on the high altar. Of some interest is the 16th-century carving in stone of the Trinity. The museum is open from 10am to 12:30pm and 2 to 5pm Tuesday to Sunday; closed holidays. No admission is charged.

From Portalegre (see above), five trains a day run to Abrantes (trip time: 1 hour and 40 minutes). There are also three trains a day from Elvas, taking 2 hours and 50 minutes. Six daily buses also link Abrantes to Santarém (see below), taking 1 hour and 25 minutes. The **Abrantes Tourist Office** is at Largo de Feira (tel. 041/ 225-55).

WHERE TO STAY

Standing on a plateau above the town, **Hotel de Turismo,** Largo de Santo António, 2200 Abrantes (tel. 041/212-61; fax 041/252-18), overlooks the town on one side and the castle and mountains on the other. It's a pink-stucco concrete building, somewhat resembling an elementary school. A total of 40 comfortable bedrooms is offered, each with private bath, TV, phone, and air conditioning. Singles rent for 9,400$ ($63) daily and doubles for 11,500$ ($77.05), including breakfast. The dining room offers panoramic views, with meals served from 12:30 to 3pm and 7:30 to 10pm. Typical dishes are gazpacho, cannelloni Piedmont, and Portuguese loin of pork, perhaps a mixed grill on a brochette. A complete meal is offered for 2,000$ ($13.40) to 3,000$ ($20.10). An Olympic-size swimming pool belonging to the town is near the hotel. Parking is free. AE, DC, MC, V.

WHERE TO DINE

Pelicano, Rua Nossa Senbora Conceição (tel. 223-17), is one of the best bets for good and low-cost regional cookery. Seating nearly 50 diners, it serves Friday to Wednesday from noon to 3pm and 7 to 10:30pm. In air-conditioned comfort but with a fairly modest decor guests can enjoy meals for 1,500$ ($10.05). Service is polite and efficient. Reservations aren't needed. No credit cards.

14. Tomar

Divided by the Nabão River, historic Tomar lies 85 miles northeast of Lisbon, 40 miles north of Santarém. Tomar was integrally bound to the fate of the notorious quasi-religious order of the Knights Templar. In the 12th century these powerful and wealthy monks established the beginnings of the **Convento de Cristo** (Convent of Christ; tel. 049/31-34-81) on a tree-studded hill overlooking the town. Originally a monastery, it evolved into a kind of grand headquarters for the Templars. These knights, who swore a vow of chastity, had fought ferociously at Santarém against the Moors. As a result of their growing military might, they built a massive walled castle at Tomar in 1160. The ruins, especially the walls, can be seen today.

By 1314 the pope was urged to suppress their power, as they had made many enemies, and their great riches were coveted by others. King Dinis allowed them to regroup their forces under the new aegis of the Order of Christ. Henry the Navigator became the most famous of the grand masters, using much of their money to subsidize his explorations.

From its inception the monastery underwent five centuries of inspired builders, including Manuel I (the Fortunate). It also saw its destroyers, notably the overzealous troops of Napoléon in 1810 who turned it into a barracks. What remains on the top of the hill, however, is one of Portugal's most brilliant architectural accomplishments.

The portal of the Templars Church is in the Manueline style, depicting everything from leaves to chubby cherubs. Inside, you enter an octagonal church with eight columns, said to have been modeled after the Temple of the Holy Sepulchre at Jerusalem. The effect is like a mosque, linking Christian with Muslim culture, as in Córdoba's Mezquita. Howard La Fay called it "a muted echo of Byzantium in scarlet and dull gold." The damage done by the French troops is much in evidence. On the other side, the church is in the Manueline style with rosettes. Throughout you'll see the insignia of the Templars.

The monastery embraces eight cloisters in a variety of styles. The most notable one, a two-tiered structure built in 1557 by Diogo de Torralva, exhibits perfect symmetry, the almost severe academic use of the classical form that distinguishes the Palladian school. A guide will also take you on a brief tour of a dormitory where the monks lived in cells.

The monastery possesses some of the greatest Manueline stonework. An example is the grotesque west window of the Chapter House. At first, you may be confused by the forms emanating from the window; but a closer inspection reveals a meticulous symbolic and literal depiction of Portugal's sea lore and power. Knots and ropes, mariners and the tools of their craft, silken sails wafting in stone, re-created coral seascapes, all delicately interwoven in this chef d'oeuvre of the whole movement.

The monastery is open daily from 9:30am to 12:30pm and 2 to 6pm (to 5pm off-season). Admission is 300$ ($2); free for children 14 and under.

Tomar has many other sights of interest. On the way up the hill, you can stop off at the **Chapel of Our Lady of Conception,** crowned by small cupolas and jutting out over the town. Reached via an avenue of trees, it was built in the Renaissance style in the mid-16th century, and its interior is a forest of white Corinthian pillars.

In the heart of town, the **Church of St. John the Baptist** opens onto the Praça da República, built by Manuel I, with black-and-white diamond mosaics. Dating from the 15th century, the church contains a white-and-gold baroque altar (a chapel to the right is faced with antique tiles). In and around the church are the narrow cobblestone streets of Tomar, where shops sell dried codfish, and wrought-iron balconies are hung with bird cages and flowerpots.

The Tomar train station is at Combatentes da Grande Guerra (tel. 049/31-28-15). Eleven daily trains arrive from Lisbon, taking 2 hours and costing 580$ ($38.85) for a one-way ticket. Five trains also arrive from Porto, taking 4½ hours and costing 875$ ($5.85) for a one-way ticket. The Tomar bus station is also on Avenida Combatentes da Grande Guerra right next to the train station. Here six buses a day arrive from Lisbon, taking 2 hours and costing 740$ ($4.95) for a one-way ticket.

The **Tomar Tourist Office** is at Avenida Dr. Cândido Madureira (tel. 049/31-32-37).

WHERE TO STAY

The modern four-story **Hotel dos Templários,** Largo Cândido dos Reis 1, 2300 Tomar (tel. 049/31-21-21; fax 049/31-21-91), seems incongruously placed in such a small town. Pooling their know-how, in 1967 five local businessmen created this five-floor structure set on the banks of the river. Facilities include wide sun terraces, a riverside swimming pool fed by a fountain, a tennis court, and even a greenhouse.

The interior is spacious, including the lounges. There is a terraceview dining room. The 84 bedrooms are suitable, containing private baths, plus air conditioning, TV, and phone. Doubles rent for 11,400$ ($76.40) daily. Singles go for 7,700$ ($51.60), including breakfast. Children up to 8 years old are accommodated in their parents' room for half price. Most guests have breakfast either in their room or in a sunny salon overlooking the river. In the evening they gather around the huge living room fireplace for drinks. If you're passing through, you can stop in for a table d'hôte luncheon or dinner for 3,200$ ($21.45) and up. Hours are daily from 1 to 2:30pm and 8 to 9:30pm. Parking is free. AE, DC, MC, V.

Hotel Residencial Travador, Rua Dr. Joaquim Ribeiro, 2300 Tomar (tel. 049/31-15-67; fax 049/31-61-94). Only an inspection of its 30 bedrooms will reveal the high value of a stopover here. Each is outfitted with conservatively patterned wallpaper, a tile bath, TV, phone, and lots of well-scrubbed comfort. With breakfast included, singles cost 6,000$ ($40.20) daily and doubles from 9,000$ ($60.30). Built in 1982 by the polite family who still own it today, the hotel contains a basement with disco music, and a breakfast-only policy that most visitors find appealing. The location is near the commercial center of town in a neighborhood of apartment buildings. Parking is free. AE, DC, MC, V.

Nearby Places to Stay

Pousada de São Pedro, Castelo de Bode, 2300 Tomar (tel. 049/38-11-75). When it was built in the 1950s, it was used to house teams of engineers working on the nearby dam at Castelo de Bode. After the dam was completed in 1970, the government coverted it into one of the country's most unusual pousadas. From the flagstone-covered terrace in back you get a closeup view of Portugal's version of Hoover Dam. It curves gracefully against a wall of water, upon which local residents sail, swim, and sun themselves.

The pousada has a scattering of Portuguese antiques, some of them ecclesiastical, in its stone-trimmed hallways. These corridors lead to 15 unpretentious bedrooms, each with private bath and phone. Singles cost 9,500$ ($63.65) daily, with doubles renting for 11,000$ ($73.70), including breakfast. The hotel also rents one suite for 16,700$ ($111.90). The public rooms are more alluring than the bedrooms. The breeze-filled bar near the terrace is decorated a lot like an elegant private living room, with well-upholstered sofas and a fireplace. The pousada serves some of the best food in the area, both international and regional specialties, with meals costing from 2,470$ ($16.50) to 3,250$ ($21.80). Hours of service are daily from 12:30 to 2:30pm and 7:30 to 9:30pm. The pousada is between Tomar and Constância. The exact location is 9 miles southeast of Tomar. Room service is provided until 10pm, and laundry can be arranged. Parking is free. AE, DC, MC, V.

Estalagem Vale da Ursa, Estrada N238, 6100 Cernache do Bonjardim (tel. 074/99-511; fax 074/995-94), lies 20 miles northwest of Tomar, 35 miles from the shrine of Fátima, and 100 miles north of Lisbon. Situated near the bridge, over the lake, Castelo de Bode, the hotel is a tranquil choice, where you can use such facilities as a swimming pool and tennis courts and also fish from the lake's edge. It offers 12 pleasantly furnished bedrooms, each with bath and private terrace overlooking the lake. Singles rent for 9,800$ ($65.65) daily, and doubles for 12,000$ ($80.40), including breakfast. The kitchen offers an international as well as a regional cuisine, with meals costing from 2,400$ ($16.10). Parking is free. AE, MC, V.

WHERE TO DINE

Bella Vista, Rua Marquês de Pombal and Rua Ronte do Choupo (tel. 31-28-70), is, as its name indicates, a restaurant with a pretty view of the town and a small canal. You can dine outside, under a bower, or in rustic dining rooms decorated with plates, flowers, plants, and racks to hang your hat on. Meals are simple but plentiful, the prices low. Usually the cook makes a fresh pot of vegetable soup every day. For your main course, the Portuguese fare includes fried trout or sole, and always pork chops with potatoes. About the only exotic item you'll find is chicken curry with rice. Round off your meal with some of the local cheese. Everybody who dines here always orders a carafe of the local wine. Count on spending from 2,400$ ($16.10) for your meal. A tourist menu is 1,400$ ($9.40). Hours are noon to 3pm and 7 to 10pm; closed Monday dinner, Tuesday, and in November. Reservations aren't needed. No credit cards.

15. Santarém

The Portuguese use the words "noble" or "Gothic" in describing this town, 49 miles north of Lisbon and 97 miles west of Portalegre. The garrison here, set on a spur of land overlooking the river, has always been a key fortification. Afonso Henriques, the country's first king, drove out the Moors in 1147, and ordered the construction of the Cistercian monastery at Alcobaça to commemorate that feat.

Santarém still overlooks the low-lying lands devoted to cattle, vineyards, olive groves, even corn. It seems as if the whole of Ribatejo is spread out before one's eyes from the vantage point of the **Portas do Sol** (the Gates of the Sun), a park of tile fountains, flowering plants and bushes, statuary, red benches, and globe lamps. At times the river is so shallow that sandy islets appear; at other moments, it overflows its banks. The gardens are reached by heading out the Avenida 5 de Outubro.

One of the main squares is **Praça de Sá da Bandeira,** lying right off the Garden of the Republic. Opening onto the largo is the **College of the Patriarchal See,** whose multiwindowed, niched, and statuary-studded facade takes up an entire side of the plaza. Inside, the main altar is decorated with marble and alabaster inlays, and flanked by four serpentine columns. Alabaster statues of saints, azulejos, and a baroque trompe l'oeil ceiling add to the lushness. Across the way from the seminary (entrance at the end of the Rua Cidade da Covilha) sits the octagonal, domed **Chapel of Our Lady of Pity,** whose neoclassic style is enhanced by trompe l'oeil paintings.

One of the town's most interesting churches, **São João de Alporão,** right off the Rua São Martinho, en route to the Portas do Sol, has been converted into an **Archeological Museum.** Built in the Romanesque-Gothic style, probably in the 12th century, it is graced with a rose window and multiple-arched doorway. Inside is the elaborate tomb of Dom Duarte de Menezes, built by his wife after he died at the hands of the Moors. So badly mutilated was the body that the remains consisted of a lone tooth. The collection of Roman sarcophagi is more interesting. The museum is open from 10am to noon and 2 to 5pm Tuesday to Sunday.

Nearby, the Gothic **Church of Graça,** dating from 1380, has a rose window carved from a single stone. At the corner of Calçada da Graça and the Rua Vila de Belmonte, it has been completely restored and contains some carved tombs, and an architecture characterized by simple arches.

The Santarém train station lies a mile from the center, but a connecting bus runs into town every 30 minutes, with a fare of 100$ (65¢). Trains from Lisbon arrive during the day at the rate of one every 30 minutes, taking 1 hour and costing 315$ ($2.10) for a one-way ticket. There are also six trains per day from Tomar going via Entroncamento. Trip time is 1½ hours, a one-way ticket costing 295$ ($2). The bus station is along Avenida do Brasil (tel. 043/220-01). Here buses from Lisbon pull in during the day at the rate of one every 30 minutes, taking 1½ hours and costing 525$ ($3.50) for a one-way ticket. There are also six buses a day from Tomar, taking 1½ hours and costing 500$ ($3.35) for a one-way ticket.

The **Santarém Tourist Office** is at Rua Capelo Ivens 63 (tel. 043/231-40).

WHERE TO STAY

Rated second class, **Hotel Abidis,** Rua Fuilherme de Azevedo 4, 2000 Santarém (tel. 043/220-17), offers a good night's sleep. Although the reception area is small, the 28 bedrooms are personalized, with old-style furnishings and matching fabrics at the windows, on the beds, and at the dressing tables. Six of the bedrooms have private baths and phones. Singles or doubles without bath cost

7,000$ ($46.90) daily, whereas singles or doubles with bath rent for 8,000$ ($53.60). Breakfast is another 450$ ($3) and it's the only meal served. Parking is free. No credit cards.

You might also seek accommodations at the **Victoria,** Rua 2 Visconde de Santarém 21, 2000 Santarém (tel. 043/225-73), which has 21 simply furnished rooms rented at modest prices: 4,000$ ($26.80) daily in a single and 6,000$ ($40.20) in a double. The Victoria doesn't have a restaurant, but breakfast is included in the tariffs. Rooms have private baths, phones, and TVs. Parking is free. V.

WHERE TO DINE

Portas do Sol, Jardim das Portas do Sol (tel. 295-20), offers the most scenic location in a garden. Try for a terrace table opening onto a panoramic view. One of the best restaurants in Santarém, it serves meals, costing from 2,400$ ($16.10), from 12:30 to 3pm and 7:30 to 10pm. It is closed on Sunday night and all day Monday. A tourist menu goes for 1,600$ ($10.70). Good regional cookery and wines are offered and the place is fairly intimate, holding only about three dozen diners. Specialties include entrecôte with rice, dried codfish with boiled potatoes, and fresh fish. Reservations aren't necessary. No credit cards.

---

16. Vila Franca de Xira

Vila Franca de Xira is the Pamplona of Portugal, a reference to the Spanish city of the Pyrénées famous for its "running of the bulls" festival featured in Ernest Hemingway's *The Sun Also Rises*. Twice a year the frenzied community ordeal of the *festa brava,* the running of the bulls, is staged. The Red Waistcoat is held the first week of July, and the Annual Fair the first week of October. Bullfights are also held at these events. In the countryside around Vila Franca, 20 miles north of Lisbon, are pasturelands that are breeding grounds for the black bulls. There's a modern speedway to take you there.

At the festivals, a herd of black bulls, fresh and primed for the rings of Lisbon or Cascais, are let loose in the main street of town. With the smaller side streets heavily barricaded, the *corrida* is ready to begin. When the *campinos* (Ribatejo cowboys with their traditional stocking caps) first turn the bulls loose in the streets, the animals appear bewildered and confused.

The crowds hoot and holler, trying to make the massive bulls break rank. When one inevitably does, melees and frantic dashes follow, with occasional displays on the part of some young aspirant matador of virtuosity with the cape. The cape, incidentally, is likely to be an old piece of sackcloth or a quilt. The bulls are rarely intimidated by those who taunt them. Many a hopeful matador has been pulled by his arms to the safety of a spectator-filled wrought-iron balcony. Numerous injuries result, and the hospital staff is reinforced by recruits from Lisbon.

Attacked by many who consider it barbaric, the pagan custom is still well preserved on the streets of Vila Franca de Xira on at least two occasions of the year.

The **Museu Etnográfico de Vila Franca de Xira** (Ethnographic Museum of the Arenas) has some sculptures and pictures pertaining to the local region and to the art of bullfighting, as well as traditional 19th-century costumes of cattle breeders, fishermen, and peasants. It's open Tuesday to Sunday (closed holidays) from 10am to 12:30pm and 2 to 6pm.

Two miles north, along a road called António Lucio Baptista that passes under the motorway, watch for **Monte Gordo Belvedere** (Miradouro), up a hill between two windmills. From that spot, you have a panoramic view of hills, vineyards, quintas, and the plain of Ribatejo.

Frequent trains from Lisbon run throughout the day to Vila Franca de Xira (trip time: 25 minutes). Buses from Lisbon arrive every 30 minutes throughout the day, the trip taking only 30 minutes.

The **Vila Franca de Xira Tourist Office** is at Avenida Almirante Cândido dos Reis 147 (tel. 063/317-66).

WHERE TO STAY

The most desirable place to stay is the **Quinta São Jorge,** Estrada de Monte Gordo, 2600 Vila Franca de Xira (tel. 063/221-43), just over a mile north of Vila Franca de Xira. The road leading to this enclosed quinta will take you around some hairpin turns and over tortuous dirt roads. Finally you'll arrive in front of an iron gate. Behind this lies a sprawling compound of impressively proportioned buildings, some of them pink, others buff in color. They look as if they might have served as anything from a monastery to a prosperous but now attractively faded seat of a large Portuguese country estate. Unless the gate is open, you'll have to ring a hand-pulled bell to alert the staff to your arrival. Guests enjoy use of the quinta's luxurious living rooms. There are four double rooms and four singles, each with private bath. Doubles rent for 10,000$ ($67) daily, and singles go for 6,000$ ($40.20). Residents of the quinta can order dinner, costing from 1,600$ ($10.70) per person. There is a swimming pool, plus a riding ring. Parking is free. No credit cards.

WHERE TO DINE

In town, the best restaurant is **O Redondel,** Praça de Touros (tel. 229-73), along the Estrada de Lisboa (the road to Lisbon). At the bullring, it is filled to overflowing on the days of a fight, but otherwise it's more subdued. The cookery is regional, and it's washed down with plenty of local wines. Specialties include pigs' feet with a coriander sauce, squid with shrimp on the spit and açorda de savel (shad cooked with bread). There's a bar, and some 70 patrons can enjoy the air conditioning. The restaurant serves Tuesday to Sunday from noon to 3pm and 7 to 10pm. If you order à la carte, meals average 2,500$ ($16.75), and a tourist menu is offered for 1,900$ ($12.75). Reservations aren't needed. AE, DC, MC, V.

COIMBRA & THE BEIRAS

To many observers, the three provinces of the Beiras, encompassing the university city of **Coimbra,** are the quintessence of Portugal. *Beira* is a Portuguese word meaning edge or border. The trio of provinces includes **Beira Litoral** (coastal), **Beira Baixa** (low), and **Beira Alta** (high).

Embraced in the region is the **Serra da Estrêla,** Portugal's highest landmass and haven for skiers in winter, cool retreat in summer. The Mondego River, the main stream of the region, is navigable, and the only major artery in Portugal that has its source within the boundaries of the country.

The granite soil produced by the great range of serras blankets the rocky slopes of the Dão and Mondego river valleys and is responsible for the wine of the region: the ruby red or lemon-colored Dão.

The Beiras are a subtle land, a sort of Portugal in miniature.

1. Leiria

About 20 miles north of Alcobaça, on the road to Coimbra, the town of Leiria rests on the banks of the Liz and spreads over the surrounding hills. From any point you can see the great **Castle of Leiria** (Castelo de Leiria), once occupied by Dinis, the poet king, and his wife, called Saint Isabella. Tower-topped and imposing still, it has been extensively restored.

The castle church, as well as the palace, is Gothic. From an arched balcony, the city and its surroundings can be viewed. The castle lies on the summit of a volcanic outcrop. It was practically inaccessible to invaders. The Moors had their defense redoubt on this hill while they were taking possession of the major part of the Iberian Peninsula. The fortress was first taken for Portugal by its first king, Afonso Henriques, in the 12th century, and was twice recovered by him after the Moors had retaken it, the last recovery being definitive.

To reach the castle, you may take a car right to the front door. On the way to the castle, you might also visit St. Peter's Church, dating from the 12th century. The fortress is open from 9am to 7pm April to October, 9am to 6pm during other months. Admission is 50$ (35¢).

Around Leiria is one of the oldest state forests in the world. In about 1300 Dinis began the systematic planting of the **Pinhal do Rei**, with trees brought from the Landes area in France. He hoped to curb the spread of sand dunes, which ocean guests were extending deep into the heartland. The forest, still maintained today, provided timber used to build the caravels to explore the Sea of Darkness.

Many motorists find Leiria a convenient stopping point for the night.

Leiria is reached after a train ride of 3 hours and 45 minutes from Lisbon. At least two trains a day make the journey to Leiria from Lisbon. Twelve express buses from Lisbon journey to Leiria in just 2 hours, a one-way ticket costing 675$ ($4.50). You can also take one of eight buses arriving from Coimbra (see below) every day, taking 1 hour and costing 525$ ($3.50) for a one-way ticket.

The **Leiria Tourist Office** is at Jardím Luís de Camões (tel. 044/327-48).

WHERE TO STAY

An 11-story, well-styled hostelry, **Hotel Eurosol,** Rua D. José Alves Correia da Silva, 2400 Leiria (tel. 044/81-22-01; fax 044/81-12-05), competes in position with the stone castle crowning the opposite hill. All 135 bedrooms offer views, and rank successfully with those of any first-class hotel in the north. They are smart yet simple, making use of built-in headboards and wardrobe walls of wood paneling. All of them contain private baths, phone, minibar, TV, and air conditioning. Singles cost 10,000$ ($67) daily, with doubles renting for 11,000$ ($73.70), plus another 600$ ($4) for breakfast.

The hotel is the social hub of Leiria, attracting businesspeople to its rooftop lounge bar and dining room. Individual lunches or dinners cost 2,500$ ($16.75) on the four-course table d'hôte. Lighter meals are offered in an adjoining snack bar. The restaurant entrance lounge is decorated with a contemporary wall hanging, depicting the story of the building of the castle. Time your visit to enjoy a dip in the open-air swimming pool, with its tile terrace. There's a lower-level boîte for after-dinner diversions. Parking is free. AE, DC, MC, V.

Residencial São Francisco, Rua São Francisco 26, 2400 Leiria (tel. 044/251-42), lies on the top floor of a 10-story building in the center of town, a short walk from the river. Some of the bedrooms offer pleasant views of Leiria. Each is furnished with private bath, radio, phone, patterned wallpaper, and a collection of leatherette furniture. The 18 well-maintained bedrooms rent for 6,500$ ($43.55) daily in a single, rising to 9,000$ ($60.30) in a double, including breakfast. A cubbyhole bar in one of the public rooms serves drinks, but no meals other than breakfast. Parking is free. MC, V.

Ramalhete Residencial, Rua Dr. Correia Mateus 30, 2400 Leiria (tel. 044/

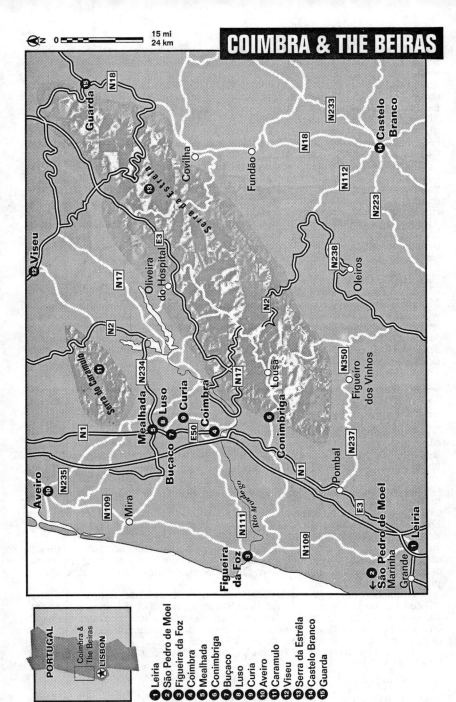

COIMBRA & THE BEIRAS

15 mi
24 km

PORTUGAL

Coimbra &
The Beiras

★ LISBON

- ❶ Leiria
- ❷ São Pedro de Moel
- ❸ Figueira da Foz
- ❹ Coimbra
- ❺ Mealhada
- ❻ Conimbriga
- ❼ Buçaco
- ❽ Luso
- ❾ Curia
- ❿ Aveiro
- ⓫ Caramulo
- ⓬ Viseu
- ⓭ Serra da Estrêla
- ⓮ Castelo Branco
- ⓯ Guarda

268-21; fax 044/250-99). Whoever decorated this pleasant hotel did so with a sense of hospitality and good taste. Many guests claim that their favorite retreat within the establishment is inside the wood-paneled bar, where subtle lighting from downward-directed wall sconces give an added coziness to the comfortable leather-covered chairs and partially mirrored ceiling. A reading room, with an occasionally used card table, provides a cozy environment for reading or quiet conversation. The 30 comfortable bedrooms each contain a private bath, minibar, phone, TV, and simple furnishings. Singles cost from 6,200$ ($41.55) daily, and doubles are 8,000$ ($53.60), including breakfast. No other meals are served at this second-floor inn. Parking is 300$ ($2) a night. AE, DC, MC, V.

Hotel São Luis, Rua Henrique Sommer, 2400 Leiria (tel. 044/81-31-97; fax 044/81-38-98), is one of the best budget accommodations in Leiria. Ranked only two stars by the government, it is spotlessly maintained. Some of the 47 accommodations are quite spacious, with a private bath, balcony, phone, TV, and air conditioning. You don't get a lot of frills here, but you do get comfort and convenience at a good price: 5,000$ ($33.50) in a single, 6,500$ ($43.55) in a double. A good breakfast, including ham and fresh fruit along with juice and freshly baked bread, costs another 400$ ($2.70) per person. Breakfast, incidentally, is the only meal served. Laundry service is provided and parking is free. AE, DC, MC, V.

WHERE TO DINE

Considered the best independent restaurant in Leiria, **Reis,** Rua Wenceslau de Morais 17 (tel. 248-34), is a fairly large place, seating 120, with faithful devotees who like both its food and its inexpensive prices. The chef specializes in grills, along with good regional fare such as hearty soups, fresh fish from the sea, and meats. Meals, costing from 1,800$ ($1.20), are served Monday to Saturday from noon to 3pm and 7 to 10pm. In winter, a fireplace makes the Reis more inviting. Reservations aren't needed. No credit cards.

---

2. São Pedro de Moel

If you care to relax before plunging into the Coimbra heartlands, São Pedro de Moel is an undiscovered place. The bracing Atlantic breezes pervade the little village, perched on a cliff above the water. New villas have sprung up, yet the old quarter retains its cobblestoned streets.

The scattered rocks offshore create controlled beach conditions, rolling breakers and rippling surf. The beaches are white and sandy, running up to the village's gray-walled ramparts. Paths border the cliffside, leading to the coastal lighthouse and a panoramic view. Centuries ago this was a small natural seaport, set between King Dinis's pine forest and the Atlantic. Today fishermen and divers find ideal conditions here, with a variety of fish to be caught.

The emerging resort is 14 miles west of Leiria and 84 miles north of Lisbon and can be reached via a 6-mile drive toward the sea from the glass-manufacturing center at Marinha Grande. Along the way you'll pass donkeys laden with twigs, the scent of pine mingling with salt air.

Public transportation to São Pedro de Moel is rather erratic. Leiria is the nearest rail connection but buses from Leiria to São Pedro de Moel are rather infrequent, although service is increased in the summer months to accommodate the beach crowds. If you're visiting São Pedro de Moel on a day-trip, the last bus back to Leiria departs at 6pm. Buses involve a change at Marinha Grande.

The **São Pedro de Moel Tourist Office** is at Praça Eng. José Lopes Viera (tel. 044/591-52).

WHERE TO STAY

On a palisade above the beach at the residential edge of the village, **Hotel Mar e Sol,** Avenida de Liberdade 1, São Pedro de Moel, 2430 Marinha Grande (tel. 044/59-91-82; fax 044/59-91-83), is a stark white, three-story, modern hostelry. Its vantage point gives about half of its 42 bedrooms views overlooking the ocean. It's for sun-and-sea addicts only, as there are no extravagant lounge facilities and only a minimum-size dining room. The compact bedrooms, all with private bath and air conditioning, are simply furnished with a mixture of contemporary and traditional pieces. The cost for two people is 12,000$ ($80.40) daily. Singles pay from 7,500$ ($50.25). This second-class hotel is immaculate and comfortable. Parking is free. MC, V.

Hotel de São Pedro, Rua Adolfo, Leitão, São Pedro de Moel, 2430 Marinha Grande (tel. 044/59-91-20), is another desirable place to stay. It is larger than the Mar e Sol, containing a total of 52 simply but comfortably furnished bedrooms. Singles rent for 8,000$ ($53.60) daily, while doubles cost 9,000$ ($60.30), including breakfast. One suite is rented for 17,300$ ($115.90). The modern hotel has provided private baths for all its rooms, along with phones. You can also visit just for a meal, paying from 2,200$ ($14.75). The hotel is located between the ocean and the pinewoods named after King Dinis. Laundry service is provided, and room service is available until midnight. AE, DC, MC, V.

WHERE TO DINE
O Pai dos Frangos, Praia Velha, 2430 Marinha Grande (tel. 59-91-58), does more than provide chicken on its menu, as its name suggests. Open all year, it is a good selection for Portuguese cuisine. The chef does many savory fish dishes, none more notable than arroz de mariscos (shellfish rice) and a bubbling caldeirada. Meals cost from 2,500$ ($16.75) à la carte, including wine of the region and are served daily except Monday in winter from noon to 10pm. A tourist menu costs 1,600$ ($10.70). The restaurant is large, seating 200 patrons, who enjoy the panoramic ocean view. Reservations aren't needed. AE, DC, MC, V.

---

3. Figueira da Foz

Old villas on the sea compete with apartment houses. On the north side at the Beach of Brightness, Portuguese families frolic, the wealthier ones hitting the gambling casino at night. Back in the Old Town fishermen dry cod in the sun. Others make their living by reclaiming salt from the marshes, and having their wives scoop it up and carry it back to town in wicker baskets on their heads.

At the mouth of the Mondego River, Figueira da Foz literally means Fig Tree at the Mouth of the River. How it got that name is long forgotten. North of Cascais and Estoril, Fig Tree is the best-known and oldest resort along the Atlantic coastline of Iberia. Aside from its climate (city leaders claim that the sun shines 2,772 hours annually), the most outstanding feature is the town's golden sandy beach, stretching for more than 2 miles.

Those who don't like the beach can swim in a pool sandwiched between the Grande Hotel da Figueira and the Estalagem da Piscina on the main esplanade. Should the beach crowds get you down, you can always go for a trek into the **Serra da Boa Viagem,** a range of hills whose summit is a favorite vantage point for photographers and sightseers.

Most visitors don't come to Figueira to look at museums, but there is an exceptional one, the **Casa do Paço,** Largo Prof. Victor Guerra 4 (tel. 033/221-59), the head office of the Associação Comercial e Industrial, a 1-minute walk from the post office and esplanade. It contains one of the world's greatest collections of Delft tiles, numbering almost 7,000 and most often depicting warriors with gaudy plumage (some blowing trumpets). The puce-and-blue tiles are detailed and subtly executed. The casa was the palace of Conde Bispo de Coimbra, D. João de Melo, who came here in the last century when Figueira was frequented by royalty, like San Sebastián in Spain. The tiles may be viewed from 9:30am to 12:30pm and 2 to 5pm daily (no admission is charged).

Bullfights are popular in season. The old-style bullring operates from mid-July to September.

Grande Casino Peninsular, Rua Bernardo Lopes 54 (tel. 033/220-41), features shows, dancing, a nightclub, and, of course, gambling salons. Admission to the games rooms is 1,500$ ($10.05), and a passport is required. The price of admission includes one drink; after that, mixed drinks begin at 700$ ($4.70). You can also dine here, an à la carte menu averaging 5,000$ ($33.50). A tourist menu costs 2,200$ ($14.75). The casino show begins at 10:30pm. From May to October, the club is open from 4pm to 4am, and in winter hours are 3pm to 3am.

Just 2 miles north of Figueira, bypassed by new construction and sitting placidly on a ridge near the sea, is **Buarcos,** a fishing village far removed from casinos and beaches. From the central square to the stone seawalls, it is unspoiled. Cod dries in wire racks in the sun, streets faintly move with activity, and native women with loaded baskets on their heads, arms akimbo, look out with bright eyes from under dark scarfs.

Figueira lies 80 miles south of Porto, 125 miles north of Lisbon, and 25 miles west of Coimbra. It is well supplied with accommodations.

Trains arrive at the Largo Estação (tel. 033/230-95), near the bridge. There are frequent rail connections through Coimbra (see below), with 27 trains per day arriving from that university city. Trip time is 40 minutes, and a one-way ticket costs 310$ ($2.05). The bus station is the Terminal Rodoviário (tel. 033/230-95), on Largo Luís de Camões. Here two buses per day from Lisbon arrive, the trip taking 3½ hours and costing 1,000$ ($6.70) for a one-way ticket.

The **Figueira da Foz Tourist Office** is at Avenida 25 de Abril (tel. 033/226-10).

WHERE TO STAY

The leading choice is **Grande Hotel da Figueira,** Avenida 25 de Abril, 3080 Figueira da Foz (tel. 033/221-46; fax 033/224-20), lying on the seafront promenade overlooking the ocean. Just walk across the esplanade and you have a clean sandy beach at your disposal. Or, as a guest of the hotel, you have free entrance to the adjoining Olympic-size saltwater swimming pool. The interior of the hotel is a world of marble and glass, more like a big city hotel than a resort accommodation. A few of the rooms on the sea have glass-enclosed balconies. Most rooms have open balconies. In all, 91 bedrooms are rented, each with private bath, TV, radio, and phone. Two persons pay from 16,700$ ($111.90) daily, with singles costing 9,400$ ($63), including breakfast. Other facilities include an à la carte restaurant, a piano bar, and a game room. The hotel is open all year. Parking is free. AE, DC, MC, V.

Hotel International, Rua da Liberdade 20, 3080 Figueira da Foz (tel. 033/220-41; fax 033/224-20), lies on a quiet street bordered by trees near the beach and the casino and shopping area. This three-star hotel with 50 well-furnished bedrooms offers clean and contemporary comfort to both businesspeople and vacationers. Rooms contain private baths and phones. Singles rent for 8,000$ ($53.60) daily, with doubles costing 10,500$ ($70.35). There's a swimming pool nearby for guests who prefer not to go to the beach. The hotel receives guests all year. Parking is free. AE, DC, MC, V.

Aparthotel Atlântico, Avenida 25 de Abril, 3080 Figueira da Foz (tel. 033/240-45; fax 033/224-20), is a towerlike structure rising aside the Grande Hotel, with panoramic views over the ocean, the Mondego River, and the beach. Seventy fully equipped apartments are rented, each with living room, bedroom, full bath, kitchenette, phone, and radio. Two persons in an apartment pay from 9,000$ ($60.30). Two to four guests can rent an apartment on a daily basis for 12,500$ ($83.75) to 14,000$ ($93.80). Breakfast is not served. Guests often book in here for a week, shopping for provisions in the nearby supermarket and walking across the busy street to the wide sandy beach. Guests are admitted free to the Olympic-size swimming pool nearby. Laundry service is available, as is baby-sitting. Parking is free. AE, DC, MC, V.

Estalagem de Piscina, Rua Santa Catarina 7, 3080 Figueira da Foz (tel. 033/221-46; fax 033/224-20). This "inn of the swimming pool" is a bargain for the resort. An intimate and small hotel, it offers 20 comfortable bedrooms, each with private bath, phone, and balcony opening onto the swimming pool and sea. The swimming pool area includes a restaurant and snack bar. Doubles range from 10,500$ ($70.35) daily, and singles cost 8,000$ ($53.60), including breakfast. The inn is open only from May to October. Laundry and baby-sitting can be arranged, and room service is available until midnight. Parking is free. AE, DC, MC, V.

Costa de Prata, Largo Coronel Galhardo 1, 3080 Figueira da Foz (tel. 033/266-10; fax 033/266-10), is a pleasant 66-room hotel built on a square that was terraced above the traffic-clogged beachside road running through town. Its peaceful but central location is one of its strongest points. It rises seven stories above the concrete in a series of beige and white balconies. There's no restaurant, but good drinks are served in the wood-paneled lobby bar. The well-furnished bedrooms each contain a private bath and phone, costing from 10,000$ ($67) daily in a double and from 8,000$ ($53.60) in a single with breakfast included. Parking is free. No credit cards.

WHERE TO DINE

People come to the **Restaurante Tubarão,** Avenida 25 de Abril (tel. 234-45), for the food, not the decor. You dine in a large room filled with cloth-covered tables and cooled by revolving ceiling fans. There is a sweeping view of the beach across the esplanade. Some of the tables spill onto the sidewalk, yet because of pedestrian traffic there they are often empty. A café in an adjoining room serves drinks throughout the day and night. A battery of hurried waiters will serve you full meals, costing from 2,500$ ($16.75) à la carte, with a tourist menu going for 1,500$ ($10.05). The Portuguese specialties include gambas à la plancha (grilled shrimp), grilled codfish, shellfish-flavored rice, seafood soup, and a variety of crab, lobster, and shrimp, priced by weight. Hours are daily from noon to 4pm and 7 to 11pm. Reservations aren't needed. No credit cards.

Restaurante Julio, Rua Dr. Francisco Dinis 30 (tel. 279-92). The unprepossessing building that contains this establishment lies in the old part of town, away from the beach. However, it is still eagerly sought out by many visitors because of its reputation for serving some of the best and most reasonably priced Portuguese food in the resort. Full meals cost 2,500$ ($16.75) à la carte and might include stuffed squid, cod casserole, stuffed veal, tripe with beans, rabbit, and young goatmeat. A tourist menu costs 1,600$ ($10.70). Open daily from noon to 3pm and 7 to 10pm. It is closed Monday in winter and in November. Reservations aren't needed. V.

NEARBY PLACES TO STAY & DINE

A *restaurant avec chambres,* **Restaurante-Pensão Teimoso,** Estrada do Cabo Mondego, 3080 Figueira da Foz (tel. 033/227-85; fax 033/210-17), is a regional fish restaurant right on the shore, with a wing of modern rooms reserved for overnight guests. The *Teimoso* (a Portuguese word meaning stubborn or mulish) is family operated. This place started many years ago with a simple waterfront restaurant. As business grew, the owner added more rooms. He attracts visitors and locals alike who know of his bountiful Portuguese meals: his shellfish soup, regional dishes such as fresh bass baked in a tomato sauce, roast kid, and suckling pig. Clams are served in a savory broth, and the roast veal is reliable. Desserts are not spectacular. Expect to spend from 2,500$ ($16.75). The dining room decor is barren, but the room has a fine view of the water. Food is served daily from noon to 3:30pm and 7:30 to 10:30pm.

There are 14 double rooms, all with private bath. Tariffs for doubles range from 6,000$ ($40.20) daily, including breakfast. Some of the newer rooms, prettily decorated and equipped with private sun terraces overlooking the ocean, may go a little higher. It's hard to get in from July through September, so make reservations. Parking is free. AE, MC, V.

More charming, and a half mile closer to town, is the **Tamargueira,** Estrada do Cabo Mondego, Buarcos, 3080 Figueira da Foz (tel. 033/225-14; fax 033/210-67), where you dine in an oval-shaped room with chandeliers made of ships' steering wheels. There's a fireplace at one end of the room, and the walls are decorated with typical plates and fishermen's nets. In good weather you can sit on the spacious terrace, from which you have a view of the sea. Portuguese cuisine specialties are caldeirada a mista a pescador (a mixed fish stew) and arroz de mariscos (rice with shellfish). You can finish with a mousse or custard. Expect to pay from 2,500$ ($16.75) for a meal, which can be served anytime from 8am to 1am daily. There are also 88 rooms available, furnished in a simple New England style, all with baths, air conditioning, and phone. Doubles cost 10,500$ ($70.35) daily, and singles go for 9,500$ ($63.65), including breakfast. Parking is free.

MONTEMOR-O-VELHO

Between Figueira da Foz and Coimbra, overlooking the fertile Mondego River valley, is the historic village of Montemor the Old. Dating from the 8th century, the ruins of the **Castle of Montemor-O-Velho,** Montemor-O-Velho 3140 (tel. 039/ 683-80), built by the Moors, crown the hilltop. The main road runs scenically past villas, shrines, high walls, and churches. Narrow cobblestone streets will lead you to the restored walls and ramparts, from which there is a fine vista of the valley.

The castle became a royal palace under Sancho I in the 12th century, and stood until it was destroyed by the French during the first invasion by Napoléon. It witnessed many moments in Portuguese history—perhaps the most infamous being when Afonso IV sanctioned (according to historian Pero Coelho) the plot to kill Inês de Castro, mistress of the king's son. The castle is a moving medieval setting, especially when sparrows play in the air over its time-worn stones. It is open for visitors from 10am to 12:30pm and 2 to 5pm Tuesday to Sunday. Admission is free. Buses run here from Figueira da Foz.

---

4. Coimbra

Coimbra, the most romantic city in Portugal, was the inspiration for the popular song "April in Portugal." On the weather-washed right bank of the muddy Mondego, Coimbra is also the educational center of the country, its university having been founded at Lisbon in 1290.

The students of Coimbra band together in republics, usually renting cramped buildings in the old quarter, some up many flights of winding stairs. The republic isn't very democratic, run as it is on a strict seniority basis. A typical evening's bill of fare in a republic is likely to include grilled sardines, bread, and a glass of wine.

An invitation to one of these student dormitories will give you an insight into Coimbra rarely experienced by the foreign visitor. If you get an invitation, I hope the evening will be capped by the students presenting you with a fado concert. To show your gratitude, if you should happen onto an invitation, cigarettes are much appreciated.

The Coimbra rail station is the Estação Coimbra (tel. 039/349-98), where 14 trains from Lisbon arrive per day, taking 3 hours and costing 850$ ($5.70) for a one-way ticket. From Figueira da Foz (see above), there are 16 trains per day, taking 1½ hours and costing 180$ ($1.20) for a one-way ticket. The Coimbra bus station is at Avenida Fernão de Magalhães (tel. 039/270-81). Here seven buses per day arrive from Lisbon, taking 5 hours and costing 825$ ($5.55) for a one-way ticket. Eleven buses per day come in from Porto (see Chapter 16). Trip time is 2 hours, and a one-way ticket costs 650$ ($4.35).

The **Coimbra Tourist Office** is at Largo da Portagem (tel. 039/255-76). Coimbra lies 123 miles north of Lisbon and 73 miles south of Porto.

WHAT TO SEE & DO

Coimbra's charms and mysteries unfold as you walk up Rua F. Borges, under the Gothic **Arch of Almedina,** with its coat-of-arms. From that point, you can continue up the steep street, past antique shops, to the old quarter.

The focal point for most pilgrims, of course, is the **University of Coimbra,** established in the town in 1537 on orders from João III. Among its alumni are Luís Vas de Camões (the country's greatest poet, author of the national epic, *Os*

Lusíadas); St. Anthony of Padua (also the patron saint of Lisbon); even the late Portuguese dictator, Dr. Salazar, once a professor of economics.

If you'll ignore the cold statuary and architecture on the Largo de Dom Dinis, you can pass under the 17th-century **Porta Pérrea** into the inner core of the academy. The steps on the right will take you along a cloistered arcade, **Via Latina,** to the **Sala dos Capelos,** the site of graduation ceremonies. You enter into a world with a twisted rope ceiling, a portrait gallery of Portuguese kings, walls of red damask, and the inevitable azulejos. Afterward you can visit the **University Chapel,** decorated with an 18th-century organ, 16th-century candelabra, a painted ceiling, 17th-century tiles, and a fine Manueline portal.

Of course, the architectural gem of the entire town is the baroque **Biblioteca Geral de Universidade** (University Library) next door, with its chinoiserie motifs and elaborate decoration. Established between 1716 and 1723 and donated by João V, it shelters more than a million volumes. The interior is composed of a trio of high-ceilinged salons walled by two-story tiers of lacquer-decorated bookshelves. The pale jade and sedate lemon marble inlaid floors complement the jeweled gold and emerald of the profuse gilt. The library tables are ebony and lustrous rosewood, imported from the former colonies in India and Brazil. Three-dimensional ceilings and the zooming telescopic effect of the room structure focus on the large portrait of João V, set against a backdrop of imitation curtains in wood. The side galleries, with their walls of valuable books in law, theology, and humanities of the 16th to the 18th century, the supporting pillars, the intricate impedimenta—all are dazzling, even noble. You may want to save the library for last; after viewing this masterpiece, other sights pale by comparison. Admission free, it is open daily from 9am to 5:30pm. For information call 255-41. Take bus no. 1.

To wind down after leaving the library, walk to the end of the belvedere for a panoramic view of the river—equal to scenes on the Rhine—and the rooftops of the old quarter. On the square stand a statue of João III and the famous curfew-signaling clock of Coimbra, known as "cabra," meaning goat.

A short walk from the university square leads you to **Machado de Castro National Museum,** Largo Dr. José Rodrigues (tel. 237-27). Named after the greatest Portuguese sculptor of the 18th century, this museum is one of the finest in the north. Built over a Roman building as the Paço Episcopal in 1592, it houses a collection of ecclesiastical sculpture, especially polychrome, much of which dates from the 14th to the 18th centuries. The other exhibits include vestments, a relic of Saint Isabella, paintings, antiques, coaches, silver chalices, old jewelry, embroideries, retables, and 16th-century ceramic representations of the Apostles and Christ. The museum is open from 9:30am to 12:30pm and 2 to 5pm, charging an admission of 200$ ($1.35). Children 16 to 18 must be accompanied by a family member, and then a joint ticket costs 300$ ($2). Children 15 and under are not allowed inside. Closed Monday. Take bus no. 1.

Across the way is the **New Cathedral (Sé Nova),** with its 17th-century cold, neoclassic interior. More interesting is the **Old Cathedral (Sé Velha).** At Largo da Sé Velha, the cathedral, founded in 1170, enjoys associations with Saint Anthony of Padua. Crenellated and staunch as a fortress, it is entered by passing under a Romanesque portal. Usually a student is there, willing to show you (for a tip, of course) the precincts, including the restored cloister. The pride of this monument is the gilded Flemish retable over the main altar, with a crucifix on the top. To the left of the altar is a 16th-century chapel designed by a French artist, and containing the tomb of one of the bishops of Coimbra.

Reached by going up Rua Visconde da Luz, the **Santa Cruz Church** is a former monastery, founded in the late 12th century when Afonso Henriques, Portugal's first king, ruled. However, its original Romanesque style gave way to Manueline restorers in 1507. The much popularized "Romeo and Juliet" story of Portugal, involving Pedro the Cruel and Inês de Castro reached its climax in this church. It was here that Pedro forced his courtiers to pay homage to her royal corpse and kiss her hand.

The lower part of the walls inside are decorated with azulejos. Groined in the profuse Manueline manner, the interior houses the Gothic sarcophagi of Afonso

Henriques, his feet resting on a lion, and that of his son, Sancho I. The pulpit nearby is one of the achievements of the Renaissance in Portugal, carved by João de Ruão in the 16th century. The choir stalls preserve, in carved configurations, the symbolism, mythology, and historical import of Portuguese exploration. With its twisted columns and 13th-century tombs, the two-tiered Gothic-Manueline cloister is impressive.

The facade makes Santa Cruz one of the finest monuments in the land. Decorated like an architectural birthday cake, it is topped with finials and crosses, its portal top-heavy with a baroque porch, an unusual blending of styles. It's overadorned, but fascinating.

Attractions Across the Mondego

On the left bank lie four of the most interesting but least visited attractions of Coimbra. On the silt-laden banks of the Mondego stand the gutted, flooded, and crumbling remains of **Santa Clara-a-Velha,** a Gothic convent built in the 14th century. This church once housed the body of Coimbra's patron saint, Isabella, although her remains were transferred to the New Convent higher up on the hill. Rising out of the inrushing river, the Roman arches are reflected in the canals, evoking a Venetian scene. You can walk through the upper part only, as the river has already reclaimed the floor. The former convent is reached by crossing the Santa Clara Bridge, and turning left down the cobblestone street (Rua de Baixo).

Commanding a view of right-bank Coimbra, the **Convent of Santa Clara-a-Nova** provides a setting for the tomb of St. Isabella. Built during the reign of João IV, the convent is an incongruous blend of church and military garrison.

The church is noted for a rich baroque interior and Renaissance cloister. In the rear, behind a grille, is the tomb of the saint (usually closed except on special occasions). When her body was removed in 1677, her remains are said to have been well preserved, even though she died in 1336. Instead of regal robes, she preferred to be buried in the simplest habit of the order of the Poor Clares. At the main altar is the silver tomb (a sacristan will light it for you), which the ecclesiastical hierarchy considered more appropriate after her canonization.

At least for youngsters, the main attraction of Coimbra is **Portugal dos Pequenitos,** Jardím do Portugal dos Pequenitos (tel. 039/81-30-21). "Portugal for the Little Ones" is reached by crossing Ponte de Santa Clara and heading out Rua António Agusto Gonsalves. It's a mélange of miniature houses from every province of Portugal, including Madeira and the Azores, even the distant foreign lands of Timor and Macau. It gives one the impression of a Gulliver strolling across a Lilliputian world. The recreations include palaces, an Indian temple, a Brazilian pavilion (with photos of gauchos), a windmill, a castle, and the 16th-century House of Diamonds from Lisbon. From April to September, hours are daily from 9am to 7pm; otherwise, from 9am to 5pm. Entrance for adults is 250$ ($1.70) for the garden, 200$ ($1.35) for the museum, children pay 50$ (35¢) for the garden, 50$ (35¢) for the museum.

Farther up the road is the final attraction, the **Quinta das Lágrimas** (the Garden of Tears; tel. 039/44-16-15). In "sweet Mondego's solitary groves," in the words of Camões, lived Inês de Castro, mistress of Pedro, and their three illegitimate children. Although they are the property of the Osôrio Cabral family since the 18th century, the gardens are visited by romantics from many countries. You can't go inside the house, but you can wander through the greenery to the spring fountain, known as the Fonte dos Amores. It was at the quinta on Camões' "black night obscure" that the Spanish beauty was set upon by assassins hired by her lover's father. Pedro returned, finding her in a pool of blood, her throat slit.

So classic and enduring a Portuguese love story is it that who would want to suggest that it wasn't true, or that the murder didn't happen at the Garden of Tears? You can visit from 9am to 7pm daily. Admission is 100$ (65¢).

WHERE TO STAY

Unfortunately, Coimbra is far better supplied with attractions than it is with hotels and restaurants. But there are the following recommendations.

Dom Luís, Quinta da Verzea, 3000 Coimbra (tel. 039/44-25-10; fax 039/81-31-96). Built in 1989, this is the newest and most stylish hotel in the Coimbra area. About half a mile south of the city, it lies on the road heading toward Lisbon. It has a pleasing modern design, brown marble floors, a restaurant, and 100 air-conditioned bedrooms. Each of these contains a private bath, phone, minibar, and TV. Classified as a three-star hotel, it contains amenities that might conceivably justify a four-star rating. Singles cost 10,800$ ($72.25) daily, doubles 13,000$ ($87.10), including breakfast. Parking is free. AE, DC, V.

Hotel Bragança, 10 Largo das Ameias, 3000 Coimbra (tel. 039/221-71), is a bandbox five-floor hotel, built next door to the railway station. Primarily catering to businesspeople, it does a thriving trade in the summer season. A few of its bedrooms open onto balconies overlooking the main road. All of the 83 units contain private baths, phone, and air conditioning; the furnishings are utilitarian. The rooms vary in size. Two persons pay 8,500$ ($56.95) daily. Singles are priced at 7,150$ ($47.90). Breakfast is included, and Portuguese meals are served for 1,800$ ($12.05). Nearby parking places are scarce. MC, V.

Hotel Oslo, Avenida Fernão de Magalhães 25, 3000 Coimbra (tel. 039/290-71; fax 039/20-614), lies on one of the busiest streets of town, and offers 33 comfortably modern accommodations, each with private bath and phone. The design, as its name suggests, is a somewhat chilly form of Scandinavian modern. The unpretentious contemporary bedrooms offer safe overnight accommodations (if you're a light sleeper, ask for a room in the rear). Doubles cost from 8,900$ ($59.65) daily and singles go for 7,700$ ($51.60), including breakfast. The hotel also rents three suites costing from 11,500$ ($77.05). There's a bar and restaurant on the fourth floor specializing in Portuguese cuisine. Laundry service is provided, and room service is available until 10pm. Parking is free. AE, DC, MC, V.

Pensão Residencial Alentejana, Rua Dr. Henriques Seco 1, 3000 Coimbra (tel. 039/259-24), is one of the best boardinghouses in this university city. All its 16 accommodations are with private bath and phone, and some are furnished with antiques. This boardinghouse is located in a reconstructed old villa, near Praça da República in the center of Coimbra. The accommodations are on the second and third floors. On the first or ground floor is a store. The Alentejana charges 4,000$ ($26.80) daily in a single and 4,750$ ($31.85) in a double, including breakfast. One suite is rented for 5,000$ ($33.50). Laundry service is available, and parking is free. AE, DC, MC, V.

Domus, Rua Adelino Veiga 62, 3000 Coimbra (tel. 039/285-84), lies above an applicance store on a narrow commercial street near the train station. Its facade is covered with machine-made golden-brown tiles, and its rectangular windows are trimmed with slabs of marble. The reception desk is at the top of a flight of stairs, one floor above ground level. The staff will check you into one of the 20 usually large and clean rooms. Many of them are filled with contrasting patterns of carpeting and wallpaper, creating a functional but cozy family atmosphere. Each accommodation has a small private bath, and 15 rooms have phones. A stereo system plays in the TV lounge, which also doubles as the breakfast room. With breakfast included, singles rent for 5,350$ ($35.85) daily, and doubles go for 5,800$ ($38.85). Parking is free. No credit cards.

Residencial Larbelo, Largo da Portagem 33, 3000 Coimbra (tel. 039/290-92). The lime-green, heavily ornamented facade sits on a statue-centered square just to the side of the river in the heart of town, near the tourist office. In the narrow reception area, a polite receptionist (who might speak very little English) will check you into a relatively clean and simple bedroom. The hotel rents 17 bedrooms, with either bath or shower. Singles cost 3,500$ ($23.45), with doubles going for 4,500$ ($30.15), including breakfast. Parking is free. No credit cards.

Hotel International, Avenida Emidio Navarro 4, 3000 Coimbra (tel. 039/255-03), is clean and very simple. It's unabashedly Portuguese in its mentality and decor. A few steps from the train station, it occupies a once-grand 19th-century building whose interior has, over the years, been updated. The insignificant lobby is staffed by members of the family who own the property. English is definitely not their second tongue. After registering, you climb a steep series of staircases to 28 rooms that are often tiny. The furniture is vintage 1920s and no unit has a private bath. But what a welcome relief to find any room in hotel-scarce Coimbra. Singles cost from 3,300$ ($22.10) daily, doubles go for 3,900$ ($26.15). Breakfast is not served. Parking is free. No credit cards.

WHERE TO DINE

Considered the best restaurant in Coimbra, **Piscinas,** Rua Dom Manuel 2E (tel. 71-70-13), is hard to reach, lying on the eastern side of town in a sports complex. It's best to go there by taxi, though parking is easily available. On the second floor, the air-conditioned restaurant, seating 230 patrons, opens onto a panoramic view. Portuguese and continental specialties are served from noon to 3pm and 7 to 10pm Tuesday to Sunday. Meals cost 1,800$ ($12.05) to 2,800$ ($18.75). You might begin with shellfish soup or escargots, then follow with one of the main-dish specialties, including beef Piscinas, grilled sole, peppersteak, pork piri-piri, or fondue bourguignonne. To finish your repast, why not an Irish coffee? Piano music is played at night. Reservations are recommended. AE, DC, MC, V.

Dom Pedro, Avenida Emidio Navarro 58 (tel. 291-08), stands across the street from the bank of the river, near a congested part of town. After negotiating a vaulted hallway, you'll find yourself in an attractive room whose tables are grouped around a splashing fountain. Above the fountain, a high ceiling is supported by four thick columns connected to one another by a series of arches. This, plus the random tile patterns of birds, animals, and flowers, contribute to an Iberian ambience. In winter a corner fireplace throws off some welcome heat. In summer the thick walls and terra-cotta floor provide a kind of air conditioning. Full Portuguese and continental meals, costing from 1,650$ ($11.05) to 3,000$ ($20.10), might include codfish Dom Pedro, trout meunière, peppersteak, and pork cutlet milanese. Hours are noon to 3:30pm and 7 to 10:30pm Tuesday to Sunday. Reservations are recommended. DC, MC, V.

O Alfredo, Avenida João das Regras 32 (tel. 44-15-22), lies on the less populated side of the river on the street that funnels into the Santa Clara bridge. This unobtrusive pink-fronted restaurant looks more like a snack bar than a formal dining establishment. The ambience is pleasant, albeit simple. Full Portuguese meals, costing 2,500$ ($16.75), might feature pork in the style of Alentejo, rice with shrimp, an array of shellfish, Portuguese-style stew, several types of clam dishes, grilled steak, and regional varieties of fish and meat. A tourist menu costs 1,750$ ($11.75). Hours are daily from noon to 3pm and 7 to 10pm. Reservations aren't needed. No credit cards.

Pinto d'Ouro (Golden Chicken), Avenida João das Regras 68 (tel. 44-12-3), is one of the most favored local dining rooms in the district. A bar serving snacks is alluring, though the little tables in the nook adjoining the dining room are preferred. A typically Portuguese cuisine is served. A good dish is clams in a wine garlic sauce. On one recent occasion I began a fine regional repast with caldo verde, followed by a large portion of roast *cabrito* (goat) with french fries, rice, and salad, concluding with a huge amount of vine-ripened strawberries sprinkled with sugar, as well as coffee. Vinho verde accompanied the meal, and, as an added surprise, I enjoyed fresh goat cheese as an appetizer. Service was fast, and the entire bill came to only 2,300$ ($15.40) à la carte. A tourist menu is available for 1,500$ ($10.05). Hours are daily from noon to 4pm and 6:30 to 11pm. Reservations aren't needed. AE, DC, MC, V.

Café Nicola, Rua Ferreira Borges 35 (tel. 220-61), is a plain but modern little second-floor restaurant over an old-fashioned delicatessen and pastry shop. It's Spartan inside, even the flowers are usually wilted, but tradition is to be respected. Students gather here for strong coffee. The window tables provide box seats for looking at the teeming street. The Portuguese food is good but plain, and the platters of fish or meat are usually large enough to be shared by two. The cuisine, as might be expected, is regional. A nourishing bowl of the soup of the day begins most meals. After that you can order filet of fish, roast chicken, chicken cutlets, or veal croquettes. Open for lunch from 12:30 to 2pm and for dinner from 7:30 to 10pm, the establishment charges from 3,000$ ($20.10) for a full meal. A tourist menu costs only 1,250$ ($83.75). Closed Sunday. Reservations aren't needed. No credit cards.

Democrática, Travessa do Rua Nova 7 (tel. 237-84), is a stark budget restaurant popular with students and travelers on a shoestring budget. This place couldn't be simpler, with a little dining room, tiles on the walls, and the kitchen in the back. The servings are large. The soup has the hearty flavor of the fertile fields of central and north Portugal (it's usually a caldo verde). Most likely the fish will be hake, and it's often served with greens and potatoes. A typical dessert would be rice pudding. Everybody orders a carafe of the local wine, and the final tab is around 1,500$ ($10.05). It opens at 9:30am, but starts serving lunch at 11:30am, lasting until 3pm. Dinner is from 7 to 10pm. Closed Sunday. Reservations aren't needed. No credit cards.

A Café

The most famous coffeehouse in Coimbra, perhaps in the north of Portugal, is **Café Santa Cruz,** Praça 8 de Maio (tel. 336-17). It's in a former auxiliary chapel of the cathedral, and has a high ceiling supported by flamboyant stone ribbing and vaulting of fitted stone. There's a paneled waiters' station with a marble top handsome enough to serve as an altar in its own right. Now a favorite gathering place in Coimbra, day or night, it has a casual mood. Cigarette butts are tossed on the floor. Scores of students and professors come here to read the daily newspapers. There's no bar to stand at, so everyone takes a seat at one of the hexagonal marble-topped tables, sitting on an intricately tooled leather chair. If you order cognac, the shot will overflow the rim of the glass. But most patrons ask for a big glass of coffee with milk, costing 75$ (50¢) at a table. In winter, the café is open from 7am to 11pm in summer, hours are 7am to 2am. Closed Sunday and in September. Take bus no. 3 or 4. No credit cards.

---

5. Mealhada

The little hamlet of Mealhada, off the main road 12 miles north of Coimbra, is devoted to selling roast suckling pig. The porcine pièce de résistance appears on menus in Portuguese as *leitão assado*.

WHERE TO STAY

For accommodations, I recommend **Quinta dos Três Pinheiros,** Estrada Nacional 1, 3050 Mealhada (tel. 031/223-91; fax 031/234-17). This property once contained only a farmhouse and a few outbuildings. Today it has grown into a rambling string of motellike accommodations, as well as what has become the most famous disco in the entire region. You won't lack for entertainment if you check in here. The disco opens every night at 8. Its urban decor includes the kind of accessories you'd expect to find in New York or Paris, including clouds of vapor, wraparound sounds, and what has been labeled the most sophisticated light show of any disco in Portugal.

The in-house dining room sits in what used to be the estate's wine press. Today, with the stone of its original walls exposed, the building serves well-prepared regional specialties, including roast suckling pig, shellfish rice, blanquette of veal, and a wide array of fresh fish. Full meals begin at 2,800$ ($18.75) to 4,000$ ($26.80) and are served daily from noon to 4pm and 7 to 10:30pm. The motel also has 60 well-furnished rooms. With breakfast included, singles go for 8,500$ ($56.95) daily, and doubles cost from 10,800$ ($72.35). Parking is free. AE, DC, MC, V.

WHERE TO DINE

Restaurants specializing in the tasty pork dish line the highway, and everyone seems to go to **Pedro dos Leitões,** Estrada Nacional 1 (tel. 220-62), for reasons I don't fully understand. I can't detect the difference between the suckling pig served here from that at other establishments. However, tradition prevails. Pedro dos

Leitões is usually mobbed on a summer day—even if you arrive before noon (which is considered early for Portugal). The place seats 220 patrons from noon to 4pm and 7 to 10:30pm, and it's open all year except on Monday and in September.

The name of the restaurant means "Pete of the Suckling Pigs." The decor is simple, and the service frantic and rushed. Suckling pig is priced by the kilo. If you don't want the house specialty, you can order such dishes as grilled sole or veal scallops with Madeira sauce. Enjoy your meal, which will cost from 2,700$ ($18.10), with the local sparkling wine, like a champagne, called Bomfinal. The pigs are spit-roasted over coals, and you can watch the cooking process if you wish. A tourist menu costs 1,800$ ($12.05). Reservations aren't needed. V.

---

6. Conimbriga

One of the great Roman archeological finds of Europe, the village of Conimbriga lies 10 miles southwest of Coimbra. Conimbriga, the site of a Celtic settlement established in the Iron Age, was occupied by the Romans in the late 1st century. Since then and up to the 5th century A.D., the town knew a peaceful life. The site lies near a Roman camp, but the town never served as a military outpost, although it was on a Roman road connecting Lisbon (Roman Olisipo) and Braga (Roman Bracara Augusta). Visitors walk from a small **museum** (Museu Monográfico) along the Roman road to enter the ruins. The museum contains artifacts from the ruins, including a bust of Augustus Caesar that originally stood in the Augustan temple of the town.

Roman mosaics in almost perfect condition have been unearthed in diggings in the area. The designs are triangular, octagonal, and circular—executed in blood-red, mustard, gray, sienna, and yellow. Motifs include beasts from North Africa and delicately wrought hunting scenes. Mosaics displaying mythological themes can be seen in one of the houses. Subjects include Perseus slaying the Medusa and the Minotaur of Crete in his labyrinth.

The diggings display to good advantage the complex functional apparatus of Roman ingenuity. Columns form peristyles around reflecting pools, and the remains of fountains stand in courtyards. There are ruins of temples, a forum, patrician houses, water conduits and drains. Feeding the public and private baths of the town were special heating and steam installations with elaborate piping systems. Conimbriga even had its own aqueduct.

The **House of Cantaber** is a large residence, in the remains of which the life of the Romans in Conimbriga can be traced. The house was occupied until the family of Cantaber was seized by invaders, who also effectively put an end to the town in the middle of the 5th century.

Another point of interest is the **House of the Fountains,** constructed before the 4th century, when it was partially destroyed by the building of the town wall. Much of the house has been excavated, and visitors can see remains of early Roman architecture as it was carried out in the provinces. Visits are possible from June through September from 10am to 1pm and 2 to 6pm daily. In off-season, it is open from 10am to 1pm and 2 to 5pm; closed Monday. Admission is 300$ ($2) in summer, 200$ ($1.35) in winter. For information, call 039/94-11-77. If you don't have a car, you can reach the site by taking a bus from Coimbra to Condeixa. The bus, Avic Mondego, leaves Coimbra at 9am returning at 1 and 6pm. Conimbriga lies about a mile away, reached either by walking (through an olive grove) or by hiring a taxi in the village.

---

7. Buçaco

The rich, tranquil beauty of the forests of Buçaco, 17½ miles north of Coimbra and 144 miles north of Lisbon, were initially discovered by a humble order of barefoot Carmelites, following the dictates of seclusion prescribed by their founder. In 1628 they founded a monastery at Buçaco, and built it with materials from the surrounding hills. Around the forest they erected a wall to further isolate themselves and to keep women out.

These barefoot friars had a special love for plants and trees, and each year they cultivated the natural foliage and planted specimens sent them from distant orders. Buçaco had always been a riot of growth: ferns, pines, cork, eucalyptus, and pink and blue clusters of hydrangea. But the friars introduced such exotic additions as the monkey puzzle, a tall Chilean pine with branches so convoluted it confuses monkeys that climb in it. The pride of the forest, however, remains its stately cypresses and cedars.

Such was the beauty of the preserve that a papal bull, issued in 1643, threatened excommunication to anyone who destroyed a tree. Even though the monastery was abolished in 1834, the forest has been preserved. Filled with natural spring waters, the earth bubbles with many cool fountains, the best known of which is **Fonte Fria** (cold fountain).

The forest of Buçaco was the battleground where Wellington defeated the Napoleonic legions under Marshal André Masséna. The Iron Duke slept in a simple cloister cell right after the battle. A small **Museum of the Peninsular War** reconstructs much of the drama of this turning point in the Napoleonic invasion of Iberia. It's about a half mile from the hotel. The very slim museum collection consists of engravings plus a few guns.

In the beginning of the 20th century, a great deal of the Carmelite monastery was torn down to make way for the royal hunting lodge and palace hotel of Carlos I and his wife, Queen Amélia. He hardly had time to enjoy it, as he was assassinated in 1908. Luigi Manini, an Italian architect, masterminded this neo-Manueline structure of parapets, buttresses, armillary spheres, galleries with flamboyant arches, towers, and turrets. After the fall of the Braganças, wealthy tourists took their afternoon tea by the pools underneath the trellis hung with blossoming wisteria.

One of the best ways to savor Buçaco is to make the 1,800-foot ride to **Cruz Alta** (high cross) by car through forests, past hermitages. At the summit is a view considered by many to be the best in Portugal.

The **tourist office** is at Posto de Turismo Luso (tel. 031/931-33).

Buçaco is best explored by car. However, if you're depending on public transportation, you can visit the forest on a day-trip from Coimbra. Buses from Coimbra bound for Viseu make a detour from Luso through the forest and stop at the hotel below.

WHERE TO STAY & DINE

Guests can stay in elegant surroundings at the **Palace Hotel do Buçaco,** Mata do Buçaco, Buçaco, 3050 Mealhada (tel. 031/931-01; fax 031/936-09). "Goodbye forever," Queen Amélia said on her last visit to Buçaco in 1945. The government had permitted her a sentimental journey (in a limousine with ladies-in-waiting) to visit all the places where she had spent her reigning years before her flight to England in 1910. The palace is an architectural fantasy. The designer borrowed heavily from everywhere: the Jerónimos Monastery at Belém, the Doge's Palace at Venice, the Graustark Castles of Bavaria. One of the most resplendently grandiose palaces in Europe, it is set in the center of a 250-acre forest. The structure is still intact and impressive, especially its grand staircase with ornate marble balustrades, 15-foot-wide bronze torchères, and walls of frescoes, some painted by Carlos. There are several drawing rooms and salons, a potpourri of architectural whims.

In 1910, the Swiss head of the kitchen, the king's cook, persuaded the government to let him run the palace as a hotel. There are 60 bedrooms, of which the most spectacular is the Queen's Suite, which has its own private parlor, dressing room, sumptuous marble bath, and even a private dining room. In some cases the baths were once the adjoining rooms for a valet or maid. Doubles with breakfast included range in price from 18,000$ ($120.60) to 22,400$ ($150.10) daily, with singles going for 14,600$ ($97.80) to 17,400$ ($116.60). The Royal Suite costs 60,000$ ($402).

The dining room is a theatrical success, the tables set with fine stemware and silver. Of note is the wooden Gothic ceiling and the view through two 20-foot-wide arched windows onto the gardens and the encircling neo-Manueline terrace. Even if you're not staying here, you should stop in for lunch or dinner, costing 4,500$ ($30.15) for a table d'hôte. A typical repast begins with gnocchi, then follows with sea bass and vegetables. For a third course, perhaps filet of veal, tender and sweet, will be served with a rosette of potatoes, topped by dessert, an assortment of cheese and crackers, and the fresh fruit of the season. In the cellars below, the palace stores more than 100,000 bottles of its own wine, both red and white. It is open all year. Parking is free. AE, DC, MC, V.

---

8. Luso

Luso is a little spa town 19½ miles north of Coimbra and 143 miles north of Lisbon on the northwestern side of the Buçaco mountain, boasting a mild climate and thermal waters for both drinking and bathing. The radioactive and hypotonic water, low in mineral content, is said to have great efficacy in the treatment of kidney ailments, alimentary complaints, and circulatory problems, as well as allergies of the respiratory tract or of the skin.

Besides the health-giving aspects of the spa, it is also a resort area, sharing many of its facilities with Buçaco, just 2 miles away. During the spa season, festivities and sports events are held at the casino, nightclub, and tennis courts, as well as on the lake and at the two swimming pools, one of which is heated. Thermal spa enthusiasts flock here generally from June through October.

Five buses a day from Coimbra run to Luso, taking 1 hour and costing 275$ ($1.85) for a one-way ticket. Beginning at 7:45am, departures are about every 2½ hours.

The **Luso Tourist Office** is at Rua Emidio Navarro (tel. 031/931-33).

WHERE TO STAY

With a backdrop of rolling forests, **Grande Hotel das Termas,** Rua dos Banhos, Luso, 3050 Mealhada (tel. 031/934-50; fax 031/936-68), nestles in a valley in the midst of abundant foliage. It is a sprawling establishment adjacent to the spa, offering 173 roomy units, each with private bath and phone. Forty-one rooms have TVs. Habitués praise its thermal spa facilities. The emphasis is on good health. You can swim in a 150-foot Olympic-size pool, lounge and sunbathe on the surrounding grassy terrace, or relax under the weeping willows and bougainvillea arbor. There are hard tennis courts, mini-golf, and, at night, a boîte for dancing.

The accommodations are comfortable in well-proportioned bedrooms, with matching furnishings. Some of the rooms open onto private terraces, with views of the tree-covered valley. The bed-and-breakfast rate in a double room is from 9,500$ ($63.65) to 10,700$ ($71.70) daily; in a single, from 8,500$ ($56.95). Lunch or dinner is an extra 2,950$ ($19.75). The meals are large (the cuisine is both regional and international), and they are served in a mural-decorated dining room. Try a bottle of full-bodied Messias and wine from nearby Mealhada. Parking is free. AE, DC, MC, V.

Hotel Eden, Rua Emidio Navarro, Luso, 3050 Mealhada (tel. 031/931-71). This attractive 57-bedroom hotel opened in 1983. The tone is set by the modern lobby with its Picasso-style mural covering one of the walls. It was the work of a Portuguese artist, Jorge do Açor. The Eden stands on a hill above the flowering central garden near what used to be the town's belle époque casino. The bedrooms are pleasantly and comfortably furnished, containing private baths, TV, phone, air conditioning, and balconies. Singles cost 7,000$ ($46.90) daily, with doubles renting for 8,800$ ($58.95), with breakfast included. The hotel also has a restaurant, serving good food and wine, a complete meal costing from 1,600$ ($10.70). Parking is free. AE, DC, MC, V.

WHERE TO DINE

Restaurant O Cesteiro, Rua Dr. Lúcio Pais Abranches (tel. 93-93-60), is an unpretentious restaurant on the road leading outside of town in the direction of Mealhada. It occupies a spacious room whose facade is covered with a simple sign and plain brown tiles. Inside is a popular bar that does a brisk business with local artisans and farmers. Full Portuguese meals are served at lunch from noon to 2:45pm and dinner from 7 to 9:45pm everyday. The price for a full meal is 2,200$ ($14.75) à la carte, and the fare is likely to include duck stew, roast goat, pimiento-flavored pork, and an array of fish dishes, including cod. A tourist menu costs 1,600$ ($10.70). Reservations aren't necessary. No credit cards.

---

9. Curia

Forming a well-known tourist triangle with Luso, 7 miles to the east, and Buçaco, 16 miles to the east, is Curia, in the foothills of the Serra de Estrêla. Lisbon is 142 miles to the south. Its spa has long been a draw to people seeking the curative properties of medicinal waters in a secluded spot. Among its recreation facilities, there are tennis courts, swimming pools, roller-skating rinks, boating on the lake, cinemas, and teahouses. The season for taking the waters here—calcium sulfated, slightly saline, sodium and magnesium bicarbonated—is from April through October, although June 1 sees the beginning of the largest influx of visitors.

In the Bairrada wine-growing district, Curia offers the fine wines of the region as well as such famous local cuisine as roast suckling pig, roast kid, and sweets.

Bus connections are made daily from Luso (see above).

The **Curia Tourist Office** is at Largo da Rotunda (tel. 031/522-48).

WHERE TO STAY & DINE

Receiving guests since 1926, **Palace Hotel de Curia,** 3780 Anadia (tel. 031/521-31), is still an elegant accommodation. As you drive past the town's tourist office, you can catch a glimpse of this hotel's facade through a protective grouping of shrubbery. Four female faces, almost outlandishly oversized, gaze enigmatically over the gardens and parasols of the front garden. Their presence, along with the thousands of pounds of stone ornamentation, imply life on a grand scale.

Between the twin towers of the hotel's Italianate facade are sandwiched 120 bedrooms, many of them quite spacious and each with private bath. The hotel is open only between April 2 and October 30. With breakfast included, singles are priced from 7,500$ ($50.25) to 13,000$ ($87.10) daily and doubles from 8,000$ ($53.60) to 14,000$ ($93.80).

There's a rectangular swimming pool on the grounds, as well as tennis courts. Horseback riding can also be arranged. Perhaps best of all, the hotel seems to exude a benign air of self-confidence, based on its having served as a temporary retreat for dozens of prestigious cosmopolites over the decades. Parking is free. MC, V.

Hotel das Termas, Curia, 3780 Anadia (tel. 031/521-85), is approached via a curving dirt road leading through a parklike setting with lacy shade trees—quiet and secluded. Open all year, it offers facilities for health and relaxation, including a free-form swimming pool encircled with orange trees and umbrella tables. In the park a rustic wooden bridge leads over a lake to walks and the tennis courts. The lounge is relaxed and casual, furnished with provincial pieces and hand-loomed rugs. The dining hall, with its parquet floors and brick fireplace is like a tavern, especially when filled with guests who aren't hesitant to chat from table to table. Even the bedrooms have a homelike feeling; with lots of floral chintz, wooden beds, and walls of wardrobe space. The 36 rooms contain private baths, air conditioning, TV, and phone. Rates range from 9,700$ ($65) daily in a single, from 13,500$ ($90.45) in a double, including breakfast. One commentator likened the Hotel das Termas to the Raffles Hotel in Singapore a few decades ago, with its British colonial atmosphere, along with a decor featuring lots of brass and wicker. Parking is free. AE, DC, V.

Pensão Lourenço, Curia, 3780 Anadia (tel. 031/522-14). Throughout the spa, a series of signs points motorists to this simple inn, which you'll eventually find in a tree-lined hollow away from the center of the town. It occupies a pair of buildings set on either side of a narrow road, almost forming its own miniature village. One of the buildings operates a ground-floor café whose tables and whose patrons sometimes spill over into the road. Most of the clients are elderly, many of them pensioners who come to Curia season after season. They form a closely knit community of shared interests and needs. The pension is open only between June and September. Rooms cost 3,500$ ($23.45) daily in a single, 5,000$ ($33.50) in a double, including breakfast. Rooms are air conditioned, with private bath. Parking is free. No credit cards.

---

10. Aveiro

The town on the lagoon, Aveiro is crisscrossed by myriad canals, spanned by low-arched bridges. At the mouth of the Vouga River, it is cut off from the sea by a long sandbar protecting clusters of islets. The architecture is almost Flemish, a good foil for a setting of low willow-reed flatlands, salt marshes, spray-misted dunes, and rice paddies.

On the lagoon, brightly painted swan-necked boats traverse the waters. Called *barcos moliceiros,* these flat-bottomed vessels hold fishermen who harvest seaweed used for fertilizer. They are ever on the lookout for eels, a specialty of the region, which they catch in the shoals studded with lotus and water lilies. Outside the town are extensive salt pits, lined with pyramids, fog-white in color.

The surrounding lagoons and many secret pools dotting the landscape make a boat excursion, which is reminiscent of a trip into bayou country in Louisiana. Inquire at the **tourist office,** Praça da República (tel. 034/236-80). The town is quite congested, and many readers have expressed their disappointment upon visiting here, citing the incessant whine of the Vespa, as well as the relatively stagnant canal water, which is foul smelling. Others, however, find it worth the journey.

Aveiro is 35 miles north of Coimbra and 42 miles south of Porto. The town's rail station is at Largo Estação (tel. 034/244-85). At least 30 trains per day from Porto (see Chapter 16) make the 30-minute run to Aveiro, a one-way ticket costing 455$ ($3.05). There are 22 trains arriving daily from Coimbra, taking 1 hour and costing 370$ ($2.50) for a one-way ticket. There are also five trains per day from Viseu, taking 4 hours and costing 625$ ($4.20) for a one-way ticket. The nearest Rodoviária (national express bus company) station is at Águeda, 12 miles from Aveiro. Buses connect Águeda with the train station at Aveiro.

WHAT TO SEE & DO

The **Convent of Jesus,** at Praça do Milenário, is hailed as the finest example of the baroque style in Portugal. At the convent, the Infanta Santa Joana, sister of João II and daughter of Afonso V, took the veil in 1472. Her tomb, an inlaid rectangle of marble quarried in Italy, attracts many pilgrims. Its pale delicate pinks and roses lend it the air of a cherub-topped confection.

The convent, owned by the state and now the **Museu de Aveiro** (tel. 034/232-97), displays a lock of the saint's hair, her belt and rosary, and a complete pictorial study of her life. A portrait of her, painted in intonaco, is exceptional. But what characterizes the convent is its carved giltwork, lustrous in the chapel, despite the dust.

In this setting is an assortment of 15th-century paintings, royal portraits of Carlos I and Manuel II (the last two Bragança kings), antique ceramics, and 16th-,

17th-, and 18th-century sculptures. There are also some well-preserved 18th- and 19th-century coaches and carriages. After viewing all this, you can walk through the cloisters with their Doric columns. The museum is open from 10am to 12:30pm and 2 to 5pm, charging 350$ ($2.35). Closed Monday.

On the same square is the 15th-century **Church of St. Domingos,** with its blue-and-gold altarpieces and egg-shaped windows flanking the upper part of the nave. The facade, in the Gothic-Manueline style, is decorated with four flame finials. To the right (facing) is a bell tower. There are other churches as well, especially the **Chapel of Senhor Jesus das Barrocas,** built in the shape of an octagon in 1722.

After a meal of stewed eels and a bottle of the hearty Bairrada wine, you might wish to explore some of the settlements along the lagoon, specifically **Ilhavo,** 3 miles south of Aveiro. Here you can stop off at the **Municipal Museum of Ilhavo,** Rua Serpa Pinto 13 (tel. 034/32-17-97), an unpretentious gallery that offers an insight into the lives of people who live with the sea. Inside you can see seascape paintings, boating paraphernalia, fishing equipment, ship models, and other exhibits. Hours are 9am to 12:30pm and 2 to 5:30pm except Sunday and Tuesday when it opens at 2, closing at 5:30pm. Admission is 100$ (65¢).

From Ilhavo, drive along an avenue of olive trees to **Vista Alegre,** the village of the Vista Alegre porcelain works. Founded in 1824, the establishment is noted for its delicate decorated china. To visit it on a tree-shaded square, you must write in advance to the director of the factory at Lugar da Vista Alegre, 3830 Ilhavo (tel. 034/32-23-65. A museum of the porcelain works is open from 9 to 11:30am and 2 to 5:30pm daily. Admission is free.

WHERE TO STAY

The best place in town is **Hotel Afonso V,** Rua Dr. Manuel das Neves 65, 3800 Aveiro (tel. 034/251-91; fax 034/38-11-11). A recent enlargement and renovation turned its original core into a glossy contemporary structure. If you're driving, you'll find small but well-placed signs directing you to the establishment. It stands in a residential neighborhood lined with trees. The facade is lined with small sea-green tiles. Inside, the lobby is a marble-floored haven operating from 10pm to 4am. The hotel has a disco and an English-style pub, as well as an adjacent pair of restaurants (see my dining recommendations, below). With breakfast included, 80 well-furnished singles rent for 7,400$ ($49.60) and doubles cost 9,400$ ($63). Rooms contain private bath, TV, and phone. Parking is free. AE, V.

Hotel Imperial, Rua Dr. Nascimento Leitão, 3800 Aveiro (tel. 034/221-41; fax 034/241-48), attracts the youth of the community who gravitate to the lower-lounge social center for drinks and TV, or the open and airy dining room with its two glass walls. They look forward to their Sunday dates here—the 1,900$ ($12.75) dinners or the drinks on the open terrace. Many of the 107 bedrooms and each of the lounges overlook the Ria de Aveiro and the garden of the Aveiro Museum, the old convent described earlier. All the rooms contain private bath, satellite TV, and direct-dial phone, as well as individually controlled central heating. A double costs from 11,000$ ($73.70) daily, and a single rents for 9,000$ ($60.30), including breakfast. The furnishings are contemporary, with many built-in features, and the color schemes are soothing. Meals cost from 1,800$ ($12.05). Parking is free. AE, DC, MC, V.

Arcada Hotel, Rua Viana do Castelo 4, 3800 Aveiro (tel. 034/230-01; fax 034/218-86), enjoys an enviable position in the center of Aveiro, with a view of the river traffic in the canal out front. In the summer, from your bedroom window you can see the white pyramids of drying salt on the flats. The hotel has been modernized, but the classic facade of beige and white has remained. Many of the rooms open onto balconies, and the rooftop is decorated with ornate finials. The hotel occupies the second, third, and fourth floors of the old building. There are 50 bedrooms, each with bath, phone, TV, and central heating. Doubles rent for 7,900$ ($52.95) daily, and singles go for 6,900$ ($46.25). Breakfast, included in the rates, is the only meal served. Parking is 500$ ($3.35). AE, DC, MC, V.

Paloma Blanca, Rua Luís Gomes de Carvalho 23, 3800 Aveiro (tel. 034/268-02). The design of what used to be an aristocratic private villa is Moorish. An iron fence encloses the three-sided courtyard in front, where a splashing fountain is surrounded by mature trees, trailing vines, and hand-painted gold-and-white tiles. The best rooms look out over the third-floor loggia onto a goldfish-filled basin in the garden. You'll find this well-preserved house—known in Portuguese as an *antiga moradia senhorial*—on a busy downtown street leading into the city from Porto. Well-furnished and often old-fashioned singles rent for 7,300$ ($48.90) daily, and doubles go for 10,800$ ($72.35), including breakfast, the only meal served. Rooms are air conditioned, with private bath, TV, and phone. French and Italian, as well as Portuguese, cuisine is served, meals costing from 1,800$ ($12.05). AE, DC, MC, V.

WHERE TO DINE

The location of **A Cozinha do Rei,** Hotel Afonso V, Rua Dr. Manuel das Neves 65 (tel. 268-02), in the newest hotel in the city, adds to its appeal. You'll face a choice as you enter. On the right is an informal snack bar/luncheonette arrangement. Meals in the snack bar, costing from 2,000$ ($13.40), might include cream of seafood soup, a range of omelets, squid, beefsteak Henri IV, veal cutlets with cream, and several kinds of grilled fish. A refrigerated case near the bar displays the day's catch of fresh fish and shellfish. Across the hallway, on the left as you enter, a more formal restaurant dispenses top-notch Portuguese meals at 3,200$ ($21.45) and up in a modernized and sun-washed elaboration of a grand restaurant. Service is among the best in town. Open daily from noon to midnight. Reservations aren't needed. AE, V.

Restaurante Centenário, Largo do Mercado 9 (tel. 227-98), stands at the side of Aveiro's version of Les Halles. From the restaurant's front door, you can see the teeming covered market, whose laborers often stream up to the elongated bar after their early-morning unloadings of fresh produce. Most visitors, however, will gravitate to a napery-covered table for a well-prepared lunch or dinner of Portuguese dishes. The modern, high-ceilinged room contains lots of well-polished wood and has a large window opening onto the street. A less-often-used name for the restaurant is "A Casa da Sopa do Mar." As anyone can guess, that shellfish-laden soup is the house specialty. In addition to a steaming bowlful, you can also order grilled pork or veal, fried or grilled sole, codfish "brasa," and an array of other specials. Full meals begin at a reasonable 1,800$ ($12.05), going up to 2,500$ ($16.75). Hours are daily from 9am to midnight. Reservations aren't needed. MC, V.

Galo d'Ouro, Travessa do Mercado 2 (tel. 234-56), also stands near the covered market, just off a sidewalk with the most amusing cobblestone patterns in town. You step down into a high-ceilinged modern room, darkly illuminated with a cubbyhole bar serving drinks throughout the afternoon. A handful of tables, covered with clean white napery, is available for full meals, costing from 2,000$. Main Portuguese dishes include fried eels, grilled sole, and grilled whiting, and you might finish off with the cheese of the country or pineapple in port wine. The wine of the house is inexpensive and flavorful, and the chef's specialty is beef Gala d'Ouro. The restaurant serves from noon to 5pm and 7pm to midnight Monday to Saturday. Reservations aren't needed. AE, DC, MC, V.

NEARBY PLACES TO STAY & DINE

The government operates a pousada in the area, lying about 18½ miles from Aveiro. It's the **Pousada da Ria,** Bico do Muranzel, 3870 Torreira-Murtosa (tel. 034/483-32), which stands on a promontory surrounded on three sides by water. Between the sea and the lagoon, it is a contemporary building where the architect made much use of glass, with rows of balconies on its second floor. You can reach it by going by boat from Aveiro (passengers only) or else by taking a long drive via Murtosa and Torreira until you reach this sandy spit. Along the way, you pass Phoenician-style boats in the harbor, sand dunes, and pine trees, not to mention a lot of trucks.

At the pousada, a waterside terrace opens onto views of fishing craft. The inn is popular with Portuguese families on holiday, who often book all its 16 bedrooms, which rent for 14,300$ ($95.80) daily in a single, 16,200$ ($108.55) in a double, including breakfast. The rooms are compact, furnished with built-in pieces, and each has a private bath and phone. Three suites rent for 21,300$ ($142.70). If you're stopping for a meal, the cost is 2,750$ ($18.40) to 3,650$ ($24.45). The chef's specialty is *caldeirada a ria,* a savory fish stew. A sunny Sunday is likely to be bedlam; otherwise, it's a peaceful haven. Parking is free. AE, DC, MC, V.

Set beside the highway, **Hotel João Padeiro,** Rua da República 13, Cacia, 3800 Aveiro (tel. 034/91-13-26; fax 034/91-13-26), is a sienna-colored building concealing an elegant accommodation. It used to be an unpretentious village café until the Simões family transformed it more than a decade ago. It can serve as an elegantly perfect weekend retreat. You enter a velvet-covered reception area filled with family antiques. A polite staff member will usher you via elevator to the brick-vaulted upstairs hallways and then to your room, 27 in all. Each unit is different, usually containing some form of antique four-poster bed. Most of the beds are cornered with spindle-turned posts, and flanked with elaborately crafted headboards. Each room contains a tastefully modern bath, phone, TV, exuberantly flowered wallpaper, and a coved ceiling, as well as a hand-crocheted bedspread. With breakfast included, singles rent for 5,100$ ($34.15) daily, while doubles cost from 6,800$ ($45.55). Four suites go for 8,500$ ($56.95) for two people. Laundry service is available, and rooms service is offered until 10pm.

The true flavor of the establishment, however, isn't appreciated until dinnertime. You might enjoy an apéritif in the Iberian-style bar, where well-rubbed leather covers the walls and where the ceiling is carefully crafted. In cold weather, a sweeping expanse of flagstones, fashioned into a curved fireplace, warms a distant corner of the restaurant. Meals are served in a blue-and-white dining room, with massive Portuguese chests, leather-upholstered chairs, and fresh flowers. The paintings ringing the walls of the room are the work of a well-known Portuguese artist, João de Sousa Araujo.

Meals from a distinguished Portuguese menu are priced from 4,000$ ($26.80). Specialties are likely to include a shellfish omelet, house-style filet of sole, goat cooked in wine, fried eels, and lobster curry, finished off with a walnut tart. The restaurant is open daily for lunch from 12:30 to 3pm and for dinner from 7:30 to 10pm. Closed Christmas.

Cacia is 4½ miles from Aveiro. Parking is free. AE, DC, MC, V.

On a rise above the Vouga River stands the **Pousada de Santo António,** Mourisca de Vouga, 3750 Aguedo (tel. 034/52-12-30), a large villa in a fine location near the main Lisbon-Porto highway. The meadowlands and river valley are lush, filling the dining and living-room windows with the picture postcard colors. Large natural flagstones make up the front courtyard, ushering you into a renovated villa decorated like a warm provincial inn. All 12 rooms have their own bath and phone and contain striped rugs and floral bedspreads. High headboards on the country-style beds and patterned stone floors give an air of simple comfort. Rates are 14,300$ ($95.80) daily for a single, 16,200$ ($108.55) for a double, including breakfast. One suite costs from 21,300$ ($142.70).

Meals are served daily from 12:30 to 3pm and 7:30 to 10pm. At dinner, whether you begin with a caldeirada or caldo verde, be sure to request, if available, the veal or bacalhau (codfish), followed by the fruits of the valley. A meal costs from 2,750$ ($18.45) to 3,650$ ($24.45). An outdoor swimming pool is an inviting attraction for guests, as is the tennis court. Laundry service is offered, and room service is available until 10pm. AE, DC, MC, V.

The pousada is about 157 miles north of Lisbon, 30 miles north of Coimbra and 48 miles south of Porto. Caramulo and Talhada's mountains are in the background.

---

11. Caramulo

Set against a background of mimosa and heather-laden mountains, this tiny resort is a gem and a good vantage point for going to see striking views of the surrounding country. About 2 miles north from town, at the end of a dirt road to the left, is a watchtower from which a panoramic view of the **Serra do Caramulo** unfolds.

From the tip of this mountain, about 4½ miles from town at Caramulinho, you can see a breathtaking sweep that includes the Lapa, the Estrêla, the Lousa and Buçaco ranges, and the Serras da Gralheira and do Montemura, as well as the coastal plain. To reach the best viewing place on the 3,500-foot-high peak, take Avenida Abel de Lacerda from Caramulo west to the N230-3 road and then go about half a mile on foot.

Another panoramic vista spreads out from the summit of **Cabeço da Neve,** off the same road taken to go to Caramulinho.

Museu de Arte do Caramulo, 3475 Caramulo (tel. 032/86-12-70), houses at least 60 veteran and vintage cars, including a 1905 four-cylinder Dedion-Bouton, a 1909 Fiat, an 1899 Peugeot, a 1902 Oldsmobile, a 1911 Rolls-Royce, and a 1902 Darracq. These antique cars are restored to perfect condition. A few early bicycles, one dating back to 1865, and motorcycles are also exhibited. In addition to the ground-floor car display area, workshop, and library, there is an upper gallery where more vehicles are exhibited. Access to this is gained by a wide staircase at one end of the balustrade formed of crankshafts and camshafts from vintage engines. The museum also contains Portuguese and foreign paintings, sculpture, designs, engravings, the art of the goldsmith, ceramics, antique furniture, and tapestries. Admission is 500$ ($3.35) and hours are daily from 10am to 6pm.

These attractions are 50 miles north of Coimbra, midway between Aveiro and Viseu. Caramulo is 174 miles north of Lisbon. Its **tourist office** is at Estrada Principal do Caramulo (tel. 032/864-37).

There is no train service to Caramulo. If you're coming by bus from Lisbon, you have to go first to Tondela, from which you can make bus connections into Caramulo. You can also go from Lisbon to Viseu (see below), then make a connection by bus to Caramulo, although you'll have to allow at least 5 hours for this trip. One connection is by train from Lisbon to Coimbra (see above), then a connecting bus to Tondela, and another connecting bus to Caramulo.

For accommodations Caramulo has an inn.

WHERE TO STAY & DINE

High as an eagle's nest, **Pousada de S. Jerónimo,** 3475 Caramulo (tel. 032/86-12-91), is near the crest of a mountain ridge. Its panoramic view is comparable to sights encountered in Switzerland and Austria. The inn is like a spread-out chalet, with an esthetically pleasing design. You ascend to the reception, living, and dining rooms, with one salon flowing into another. In winter guests sit by the copper-hooded fireplace. Beyond the wooden grille is a pleasant dining room, the window wall providing views of the hills. Dinner is candlelit, and guests sit on hand-carved provincial chairs sampling the country-style cooking. If you're just dropping in, a table d'hôte luncheon or dinner goes for 2,470$ ($16.55) to 3,250$ ($21.75). Food is served from 12:30 to 3pm and 7:30 to 10pm daily.

The six double rooms are small but attractive, all with private bath and phone. Portuguese antiques and reproductions are used—ornate iron headboards, a slab of wood as a console. Wide windows open onto private balconies where you can take in the vista. The cost for a double is 11,500$ ($77.05) daily, and a single goes for 10,000$ ($67), including breakfast. The pousada has a private park, a swimming pool, and a playground. If you enjoy fishing, the Rivers Agueda and Criz provide trout and *achigas,* a local barbel. From here, you can follow the Besteiros valley and from its Varandahs, 48 miles along, you can see the impressive Estrêla mountains. Parking is free. AE, DC, MC, V.

Nearby Places to Stay & Dine

On a well-traveled road, the Coimbra-Guarda highway, the best place to stop for food and lodging is **Pousada de Santa Bárbara,** Póvoa das Quartas, 3400 Oliveira do Hospital (tel. 038/522-52). Not luxurious, it is suitable for those seeking a mountain spot. There are only 16 double rooms, but each comes equipped with a bath and phone. One person is charged 14,300$ ($95.80) daily for a room with a breakfast, and two people pay 16,200$ ($108.55). Don't be put off by the unimpressive facade. No bedroom in the pousada faces the road. It is very well designed, with a fantastic view of the valley from all the units, lounges, and restaurant.

If you're driving and would like to stop by for lunch or dinner, a set meal in the provincial dining room costs 2,750$ ($18.45) to 3,650$ ($24.45). Food is served daily from 12:30 to 3pm and 7:30 to 10pm. The pousada has one of the best chefs in Portugal. Even the set menu offers a large choice of dishes. My American-style chicken would never have been recognized by an American, but it was superb nonetheless. The trout, however, is the pièce de résistance. Grilled with mushrooms, it's served with the backbone removed and a slice of cured ham. The sweet regional tart evokes a Sintra cheesecake, but with "lashings" of honey and almonds. The pousada has an outdoor swimming pool and tennis courts. Laundry service is available, and room service is offered until midnight. AE, DC, MC, V.

Oliveira do Hospital belonged to the 12th-century Hospitaler religious Order of St. John of Jerusalem. You can visit **Ferreira Chapel,** part of the mother church, and there are traces of an ancient **Roman village** less than 2 miles away. Farther south you come across **Lourosa,** whose parish church dates back to 912. It is the only one in the country in the Mozarab style. About 12 miles from Póvoa das Quartas, in the village of **Avo,** is the mother church, a pillory, and the ruins of a castle whose handsome facade is almost intact.

The River Alva has a plentiful supply of fish and eels.

Hotel Urgeirica, Urgeirica, Canas de Senhorim, 3500 Viseu (tel. 032/67-12-67; fax 032/67-13-28), is set amid the forested countryside near Canas de Senhorim, and is connected with all the major cities of Portugal by fine highways. The hotel lies about 25 miles from the Estrêla mountains, popular with winter sports enthusiasts, and is 186 miles north of Lisbon, 102 miles southwest of Porto, just 50 miles northeast of Coimbra, and 16 miles south of the country town of Viseu. Its baronial granite walls, worthy of a grandee, were erected in 1939 by an English entrepreneur who had just made a fortune mining uranium in the nearby hills. Six years later, realizing the site's potential, he transformed his house into a hotel. It quickly became known as a stylish place to visit, and in time it lured such luminaries as Queen Elizabeth and Sir Anthony Eden. Nowadays, you'll find a less stylish version of its glamorous era, where bartenders still wear uniforms and bow ties, and bowls of flowers are picked hours before in the sprawling gardens.

Even if it's only for a meal, you should consider it for a stopover. The bread is baked on the premises, some of the wine comes from nearby vineyards, and formal service is the norm in a vast and impressive dining room lined with five palace-size portraits of British kings. Meals cost from 1,800$ ($12.05) per person and are served daily from 12:30 to 2:30pm and 7:30 to 9:30pm. A bar whose leather decor and carved oak would be suitable for a private club in London allows guests the pleasure of relaxing before fireplaces of chiseled granite, watching pine roots slowly dissolve into ash. More athletic guests are drawn to the tennis court and the outdoor swimming pool.

One of the most amazing aspects of this hotel is the large number of Georgian antiques filling each of the 50 bedrooms. Their sheer quantities, coupled with high ceilings and English accessories, create the feeling of a wealthy private house where someone is just about to ring the bell to announce supper. The hotel charges 9,200$ ($61.65) daily in a double room, 8,000$ ($53.60) in a single, including breakfast. Rooms contain private baths and phones. Three suites cost 10,500$ ($70.35). Parking is free. AE, DC, MC, V.

---

12. Viseu

The capital of Beira Alta province, Viseu is a quiet country town lying 181 miles north of Lisbon, 60 miles east of Aveiro, and 57 miles northeast of Coimbra. But it is also a city of art treasures, palaces, and churches. Its local hero is an ancient

Lusitanian rebel leader, Viriatus. At the entrance of Viseu is the **Cova de Viriato,** where the rebel, a combination Spartacus and Robin Hood, made his camp and plotted the moves that turned back the Roman tide.

Some of the country's most gifted artisans ply their timeless trade in and around Viseu. Where racks creak and looms hum, the busy weaver women create the unique quilts and carpets of Vil de Moinhos. Local artisans of Molelos produce the region's provincial pottery, and women with nimble fingers embroider feather-fine, light bone lace.

WHAT TO SEE & DO

There is much to see and explore at random in Viseu: the cubistic network of tiled overlapping rooftops and entwining narrow alleyways and the encroaching macadam streets. However, if your time is limited, head at once to the **Ardo da Sé,** one of the most harmonious squares in Portugal, often referred to as the showplace of Viseu. There you'll find the town's three leading buildings: a cathedral, a museum, and a church.

The severe Renaissance facade of the **Viseu Cathedral (Sé)** evokes a fortress. Two lofty bell towers, unadorned stone up to the balustraded summit with crowning cupolas, can be seen from almost any point in or approaching the town. The second-story windows in the facade, two rectangular and one oval, are latticed and symmetrically surrounded by niches containing religious statuary.

On your right, you will first find the two-story Renaissance cloister adorned with classic pillars and arcades faced with azulejos. The interior of the sé is basically Gothic, but is infused with Manueline and baroque decorations. Plain, slender Romanesque columns line the nave, supporting the vaulted Manueline ceiling with its nautically roped groining. The basic color scheme inside plays brilliant gilding against muted gold stone. However, the full emphasis is centered on the Roman arched chancel, climaxed by an elegantly carved retable above the main altar. The chancel makes ingenious use of color counterpoint, with copper, green gold, and brownish-yellow complementing the gilt work. The ceiling is continued in the sacristy.

Next door to the cathedral is the **Museu de Grão Vasco** (tel. 032/262-49), named after the 16th-century painter, also known as Vasco Fernandes. The major works of this Portuguese master are displayed here, especially *La Pontecôte,* with the lancelike tongues of fire hurtling toward the saints, some devout, others apathetic.

Besides the works of this fine Portuguese primitive and his followers, the museum has a moving and tender *St. Raphael* by the outstanding 18th-century sculptor Machado de Castro. Enameled reliquaries, Byzantine artifacts, liturgical apparel, a Manueline monstrance dating from 1533, and a chalice with vermeil pendants from 1626 are a few of the items on view. The museum is open from 10am to 12:30pm and 2 to 5pm Monday to Saturday. Admission is 200$ ($1.35); children 10 and under are admitted free.

Across the square from the cathedral is the palatial **Misericórdia Church** from the 18th century. Its pristine facade contrasts with the cathedral's baroque granite decorations, spirals, large windows and portal frames, balustrades, and matching towers.

WHERE TO STAY

In the heart of town, **Grão Vasco,** Rua Gaspar Barreiros, 3500 Viseu (tel. 032/42-35-11; fax 032/270-47), surrounded by gardens and parks, is built motel fashion, with the bedroom balconies overlooking the swimming pool. After days of driving in the hotel-lean environs, it's a pleasure to check into this establishment. Popular with businesspeople, it also attracts tourists, especially in the summer months. The decor is colorful and contemporary. The 110 bedrooms are usually large, utilizing Portuguese traditional furnishings, each with private bath, phone, TV, and air conditioning. The price for a double room starts at 12,000$ ($80.40) daily; for a single, the rate is 10,000$ ($67), including breakfast. The dining room has a baronial stone fireplace, plus good cuisine, with many international dishes. If you're just dropping in you can sample an à la carte luncheon or dinner for 2,500$ ($16.75) to 3,200$ ($21.45). Parking is free. AE, DC, MC, V.

Hotel Avenida, Avenida Alberto Sandaio 1, 3500 Viseu (tel. 032/42-34-32; fax 032/256-43), is a personalized small hotel right off the Rossio, the main plaza of town. Inside, it is the domain of the personable Mário Abrantes da Motto Veiga, who has combined his collection of antiques from Africa and China with pieces of fine old Portuguese furniture. He's created an inviting aura, bound to attract admirers of his eclectic taste. Each of the bedrooms varies in size, character, and price, and 30 of the 40 rooms have private shower or bath. Each room has a phone. Singles or doubles without bath cost 5,250$ ($35.20), rising to 5,750$ ($38.55) with bath. There's a nice room (210B) with a high coved bed and an old refectory table and chair, which includes an adjoining chamber with a wooden spindle bed and a marble-topped chest that is like a nun's retreat. Meals in the plain, family-style dining room are well prepared and generous. They cost from 2,200$ ($14.75). Parking is free. AE, DC, MC, V.

WHERE TO DINE

Outside of the hotels, **Cortiço,** Rua Agusto Hilário 47 (tel. 42-38-53), is usually the first name mentioned when you ask a discerning local for a good independent eatery. This is the type of place the Portuguese call *típico,* meaning it is decorated in a typical local style and serves good regional cookery. You can dine in one of several rooms any day from noon to 2:30pm and 7 to 11pm. Meals are reasonable in price, costing from 2,800$ ($18.75) à la carte or 1,400$ ($9.40) for a tourist menu. Specialties include bacalhau (cod), cabrito assado (roast kid), and steak Cortiço. Reservations are necessary. AE, DC, MC, V.

You might also try **Trave Negra,** Rua do Loureiros 40 (tel. 261-38), which features the local cookery of the region, and does so daily from noon to 3pm and 7 to 10pm. The cost is from 2,800$ ($18.75) for a well-prepared meal if ordered à la carte. A tourist menu costs 1,400$ ($9.40). The regional wines are good, too. Before dinner you might drop into the bar for an apéritif. Reservations are recommended. AE, DC, MC, V.

---

13. Serra da Estrêla

From January to May, the great granite Serra da Estrêla is the winter-sports center of Portugal. In summer, campers, trout fishermen, and mountain climbers dominate. Once almost completely isolated from the rest of the country, the major points of interest in the Serra da Estrêla are now linked by roads.

The land is also the home of the Cão de Sena, or "dog of the mountain." The area is a major sheep-raising district as well and is infested with wild animals, especially packs of wolves. Reader A. Wayne Magnitzky writes: "The throats of the sheep dogs are protected from the teeth of wolves by an iron collar with long sharp spikes. Imagine the wolf's surprise when he attempts to throttle the dog and ends up with a long spike through his mouth!" The dogs survive by sucking ewes' milk.

One major auto route is from Covilha to Seia via **Torre,** the latter the highest point in Portugal, at an altitude of 6,500 feet. From its summit, a panoramic view unfolds.

Covilhã is on the southern flank of the Serra, near the Zêzere Valley. A town of steep and narrow streets, it is known for its Monument to Our Lady of the Conception, a 25-foot statue of the Virgin Mary carved out of granite. Steps also carved out of granite lead to the statue. The sculptor was killed near this spot in a car accident, shortly after completing his work. The town is at its liveliest from June 22 to 25 when people from the neighboring hills come in for the Fair of Sãotiago, and sell handcrafts.

Covilhã used to be known as the "dormitory" for the **Penhas da Saúde** sports area, at 4,500 feet above sea level.

WHERE TO STAY & DINE AT MANTEIGAS

Instead of continuing to Seia, an alternate route is to go along the Rio Zêzere to **Manteigas,** a little town with several balconied 17th-century houses. It lies between mountain ranges. The town of Manteigas is known to have been the last refuge of the primitive fighting groups of the Herminíos Mountains. King Sancho I gave the town a charter in 1178, ratified by King Emanuel I in 1514. From there you can take an excursion to the **Poço do Inferno,** or Hell's Mouth. This is a gorge with waterfalls. The distance from Manteigas along an unsurfaced and narrow road is about 4 miles.

Manteigas lies 220 miles northeast of Lisbon and 30 miles west of Guarda. The **tourist office** is at Rua 1° de Maio (tel. 075/472-29).

Hotel Manteigas, Caldas de Manteigas, 6260 Manteigas (tel. 075/985-14), about 1¼ miles from the town of Manteigas, is in the Estrêla mountains. Its 26 well-furnished rooms have been restored and redecorated, and there is a lounge for the guests. Singles rent for 7,800$ ($52.25) daily, and doubles go for 9,500$ ($63.65). Meals in the large, pleasant dining room consist of wholesome food, including the famous Serra da Estrêla mountain cheese, and cost from 2,200$ ($14.75). Parking is free. AE, DC, MC, V.

About 8½ miles from Manteigas, the government runs the **Pousdada de São Lourenço,** Penhas Douradas, Estrada de Gouveia, 6260 Manteigas (tel. 075/981-50), which stands at a height of 4,900 feet above sea level on a mountainside and offers a panoramic view. Twenty-one rooms with bath are available, renting for 15,500$ ($103.85) daily in a single, 17,900$ ($119.95) in a double, including breakfast. One suite costs 23,800$ ($159.45). The comfort at this rustic pousada, surrounded by pine-studded mountains and a serene valley, is outstanding, and the country food is good. You have a selection of regional dishes, including the delectable Serra cheese and Zimbro brandy. A complete meal costs from 2,750$ ($18.40) to 3,650$ ($24.45). The pousada lies about 56 miles from the Spanish border, 2 miles from Penhas Douradas.

From the pousada, you can visit such places as Penhas de Saúde, Torre, Piornos, Covão, Pedras da Marreca, and Portas dos Herminíos, as well as the beautiful mountain lakes. Parking is free. AE, DC, MC, V.

---

14. Castelo Branco

The capital of Beira Baixa, beautiful Castelo Branco lies near the Spanish frontier, 157 miles northeast of Lisbon and 95 miles southeast of Coimbra. The city is often filled with flowers. Shoppers may want to acquire some of the multicolored embroidery done by the women of the town. Some of the designs haven't been changed since the 17th century. Today the economy of Castelo Branco is based on production of cork, cheese, olive oil, and honey.

The **gardens of the former Bishop's Palace** (Jardim do Antigo Paço Episcopal), established in the 17th century, are well kept and formal, with banks of flowers, clipped box hedges, a statue-bedecked staircase, and numerous pools and fountains. The baroque statues in the garden are mostly life-size, depicting signs of the zodiac, the Apostles, and Portuguese royalty. You can visit the gardens daily from dawn to dusk, except that there is no entrance from noon to 1pm.

Museu Francisco Tavares Proença, Rua de Frei Bartolomeu da Costa, in the old Bishop's Palace (tel. 072/242-77), has displays of coins, earthenware, archeological discoveries, arms and armor, and Roman artifacts on the ground floor. As you ascend the staircase, look at the 16th-century Flemish tapestry depicting the biblical story of Lot. Upstairs are more tapestries, as well as paintings by 16th-century Portuguese artists, a 17th-century cupboard carved by skilled Portuguese craftsmen and other old furniture of the country, plus traditional embroidered bedspreads of the town. A room on this floor is devoted to modern art, and you can see a weaver's loom.

The museum is open Tuesday from 10am to noon and 2:30 to 5pm; Wednesday, Thursday, and Friday from 2 to 5:30pm, and Saturday and Sunday from 10am to noon and 2:30 to 5:30pm. It is closed Monday. Admission is 200$ ($13.40) except on Sunday morning when it is free. Children 10 and under are also admitted free.

From the gardens of the old Bishop's Palace, you can go under an arcaded staircase along Rua de Frei Bartolomeu da Costa to see the carved **Cross of St. John,** standing over a crown of seaweed on a twisted base from the 16th century.

The ruins of a Moorish **castle,** rebuilt in the time of King Dinis, are reached by going to the Church of St. Mary of the Castle. From here you can take the stairs up to Miradouro de São Gens, a landscaped lookout that provides a view of the countryside dotted with olive trees and of the town.

The town takes about an hour to explore. Most motorists seem to stop just for a look at the gardens.

The **Castelo Branco Tourist Office** is at Alameda da Liberdade (tel. 072/210-02).

From Guarda (see below) four trains per day arrive in Castelo Branco. There is bus service from Coimbra (see above) to Castelo Branco. Three buses make the 5-hour journey every day. From Guarda, two buses arrive at Castelo Branco, taking 4 hours to make the trip.

WHERE TO STAY

One of the best places to stay—out of an admittedly modest lot—is **Residencial Arraiana,** Avenida 1 de Maio 18, 6000 Castelo Branco (tel. 072/216-34; fax 072/31-884), which rents out 31 simply furnished but comfortable bedrooms, charging from 6,500$ ($43.55) daily in a double and from 4,500$ ($30.15) in a single. The hotel doesn't have a restaurant, but breakfast is included in the tariff. Rooms contain private bath, phone, and TV. Parking is free. MC, V.

Another possibility for an overnight stopover is **Caravela,** Rua do Saibreiro 24, 6000 Castelo Branco (tel. 072/239-39), which is modesty itself but clean and neat. The hotel rents 26 comfortable rooms, 14 with private bath. Singles cost 1,800$ ($12.05) without bath or 2,800$ ($18.75) with bath. Doubles are 2,800$ ($18.75) without bath or 3,200$ ($21.45) with bath. All tariffs include breakfast, the only meal served. Parking is free. No credit cards.

WHERE TO DINE

Restaurants are not outstanding, but most of them offer good value. All of them are inexpensive.

Try **Arcádia,** Avenida Sidónio Pais 13 (tel. 219-33), for a good and filling meal of regional cookery. Everything tastes better when washed down with one of the regional wines. Specialties include bacalhau (codfish) à moda da casa, cabrito assado (roast kid) and lombo de porco assado (roast pork loin). An à la carte menu costs 2,500$ ($16.75), whereas a tourist menu is modestly priced at 1,350$ ($9.05). The cuisine is typically Portuguese, and reservations are recommended. Hours are from noon to 3:30pm and 7 to 11:30pm. Closed Thursday. AE, DC, MC, V.

Another possibility is **Ti Lourdes,** Estrada Montalvão (tel. 210-06), which has many regional Portuguese specialties, along with good and inexpensively priced wines. Seating 100 patrons, it also features fresh shellfish, broiled or grilled. Other specialties include steak Ti Lourdes. It serves from 11:30am to midnight Sunday to Friday. The restaurant closes in December. Meals cost 2,800$ ($18.75) à la carte or else 1,200$ ($8.05) from a tourist menu. In winter a fireplace provides a warming glow. Reservations aren't needed. No credit cards.

---

15. Guarda

Between Porto and Salamanca, a university city in Spain, Guarda is the highest town in Portugal. Built at an altitude of some 3,400 feet, it is some two-thirds of a mile above sea level, in the eastern foothills of the Serra da Estrela. In the Beira Alta, it stands 28 miles west of Vilar Formoso on the Spanish border, 136 miles southeast of Porto, and 212 miles northeast of Lisbon.

Because of its commanding position, the site of Guarda has been occupied since prehistoric days and is thought to have been an outpost of the Roman legions under Julius Caesar. The Visigoths used it as a fortress, which fell to the Moors. They were in turn ousted by the Christians, and Guarda was a stronghold of the Portuguese even up to the early 19th-century French invasion, when it lost its role as guardian of the Beira Alta. Today it is a pleasant summer resort.

Founded in the latter part of the 14th century, its **Sé (cathedral)** deserves some of your time. Originally the architects planned to build it in the Gothic style. However, by its completion in the mid-16th century, Renaissance, even Manueline, stylistic changes appeared in the plans. Two different styles can be seen in the facade facing north. Inside you'll find a Renaissance altarpiece, a fine Gothic tomb, a "Last Supper" altarpiece, and even more interesting is to take the stairs at the corner of the south transept. These will lead you to the rooftop of the cathedral where you'll have an excellent view of not only Guarda but the Serra da Estrêla.

Other sights include the **Ferreiros Tower,** an 18th-century **Misericórdia Church,** and from many vista points **views** of the Mondego and Zêzere valleys below. There are also many ancient churches and old houses, some dating from the 16th century. You'll see many of these around Praça Luís de Camões (Cathedral Square).

The Beira Baixa rail line services the area. Trains arrive from Lisbon to Guarda daily, the trip taking 8 hours. The Beira Alta rail line also services Guarda. This line from Lisbon takes only 6 hours and 30 minutes. Daily trains from Coimbra also run to Guarda, taking 3 hours. Trains also connect Guarda to the Spanish border town at Vilar Formoso in 1 hour, where onward connections can be made to Salamanca in Spain (trip time: 2½ hours). Two buses a day connect Guarda and Coimbra, taking 1½ hours. There are also international buses from Lisbon to Paris, passing through Guarda.

The **Guarda Tourist Office** is at Praça Luís de Camões (tel. 071/222-51).

WHERE TO STAY

A first-class choice, **Hotel de Turismo,** Avenida Coronel Orlindo de Carvalho, 6301 Guarda (tel. 071/21-22-05; fax 071/21-22-04), is centrally located in a traditional building. The 105 rooms are well furnished and comfortable. Singles rent for 11,600$ ($77.70) daily, going up to 13,900$ ($93.15) in a double, including breakfast. Rooms are air conditioned, with private bath. Children traveling with their parents can be housed in the same room at reduced rates. Good Portuguese and international cuisine is featured, with meals costing 3,200$ ($21.45). Parking is free. AE, DC, MC, V.

Residência Filipe, Rua Vasco da Gama 9, 6300 Guarda (tel. 071/21-26-58; fax 071/21-64-02), is the second-best hotel in Guarda, standing in the heart of town a block from the central square and the cathedral, almost opposite the Ferreiros Tower. The 42 rooms are simply furnished but adequate, and you'll be served by an accommodating staff. A double costs 9,000$ ($60.30) daily, and singles go for 5,250$ ($35.20), including breakfast. Rooms are air conditioned, with private baths and phones. There is a dining room, serving good meals for 2,500$ ($16.75) and up. Parking is free. AE, DC, MC, V.

WHERE TO DINE

O Telheiro, Estrada Nacional (tel. 21-24-93), is the best restaurant in the city. Seating some 115 diners who don't need a reservation, the restaurant is air conditioned and opens onto a panoramic vista. Good regional Portuguese cookery and robust wines are the characteristics of the kitchen here. Prices of à la carte meals range from 1,800$ ($12.05) to 2,500$ ($16.75). Service is daily from noon to 3pm and 7:30 to 10:30pm. The location is 1 mile east of the city along highway 16. Motorists will find ample parking. AE, DC, MC, V.

Try also the more central **Fragata,** Rua 31 de Janeiro 17 (tel. 21-24-92), which has fine Portuguese cookery and inexpensively priced wines. Meals begin at a modest 1,900$ ($12.75) à la carte and go up from there. A tourist menu costs 1,100$ ($8.10). Specialties include roast kid, bacalhau Fragata (codfish), and roast pork loin. The waiters are polite and helpful. Go daily from 11am to 3pm and 6 to 10pm. There is also a bar. Reservations aren't needed. AE, DC, MC, V.

THE FORTRESS TOWNS OF THE EAST

Near the Spanish border in the Beira Alta, a string of small towns were fortified throughout the centuries, with Guarda as the main fortress. These medieval guardians of the border area still stand, the remains of their castles and walls still visible. Starting at the farthest northeastern point of the fortifications from Guarda and proceeding clockwise around the leading fortress, they are:

Castelo Melhor, 45 miles northeast of Guarda, is near the confluence of the Douro and Coa rivers. The little village, built onto a rocky promontory, has a well-preserved medieval wall with round towers. Olive trees surround the village.

Castelo Rodrigo, 35½ miles to Guarda's northeast, was a place of importance in the Middle Ages but has become just a pleasant, once-fortified hamlet.

Almeida stands on a hill 37 miles northeast of Guarda, about 6 miles from the Spanish border. Worth seeing are the double fortifications and other protective devices, including arched gateways and bridges leading into the town. The town has some tile-covered mansions.

It is here that the government decided to open one of its "frontier" pousadas, the **Pousada Senhora das Neves,** 6350 Almeida (tel. 071/542-90). An attractive, handsomely decorated place, it offers a total of 21 well-furnished bedrooms.

A single rents for 13,700$ ($91.80) daily and a double for 15,300$ ($102.50), including breakfast. Rooms contain private baths and are air conditioned. The pousada also has a good restaurant and bar serving some of the finest meals in the area, with luncheons or dinners priced from 2,800$ ($18.75). Parking is free. AE, DC, MC, V.

About 30½ miles east of the main guardian town is **Castelo Bom,** dating from the time of King Dinis I. There isn't much left of the early Middle Ages fortress, but the village still clusters around the hill which was once a stronghold. One ruined tower and a Gothic gate still stand. The Coa River runs past.

Quite near Castelo Bom is **Castelo Mendo,** 32 miles almost due east from Guarda on a craggy little hill. An interesting pillory is here, in front of a 17th-century church. The loftiest punishment cage in the province (23 feet up), it stands atop an octagon-shaped pillar. Fragments of a Gothic wall and some Renaissance structures still stand. Little remains of the castle but portions of a keep and a chapel. From the top of the hill on which the castle stood, you can look out over the Coa River valley.

The little town of **Sabugal,** 21 miles southeast of Guarda, is on a hill where the town grew up around the castle. The town belonged to Spain until the late 13th century. It was a part of the dowry of Isabella of Aragón when she became the bride of King Dinis I of Portugal. The castle can be visited by asking for the key at the town hall (Câmara Municipal).

Sortelha, 27 miles south of Guarda, was a 12th-century fortress with a village within the fortified wall. It stands on a promontory that overlooks the valley of the Upper Zêzere River. You enter the old town by one of the big Gothic gates in the fortified wall. The houses climbing up the rise to the headland are built of granite.

Belmonte is a little town 17 miles south of Guarda standing on a spur of a foothill of the Serra da Estrêla, still proudly showing the square towers of the keep of its ancient fortress a long way off. The castle was built by King Dinis I. You can walk around the perimeter. The castle is open daily from 8am to noon and 1 to 5pm.

The man who discovered Brazil, navigator Pedro Alvares Cabral, was born in Belmonte and is honored by a statue standing on the main street. The town also has a parish church, Igreja de São Tiago, which can be visited from 8am to 6pm. It contains the tombs of Cabral and his mother, as well as a 13th-century pietà, carved out of one block of stone. Some mementos of the Roman days are in the church, and there is a Roman tower, **Centum Cellas,** about 2½ miles north of Belmonte.

About 30 miles due west of Guarda is **Linhares,** on a road that ends with a winding rough stretch. Built on a high bluff in the reign of King Dinis I, the outer walls of the castle and two towers still stand. The castle site overlooks the upper valley of the Mondego River.

Celerico da Beira, which lies 17½ miles to the northwest of the main guardian city, is on a hilly outcrop at the end of the Serra da Estrêla, where the castle ruins stand at the top.

On a plateau of the Serra da Estrêla, 30 miles north of Guarda, is **Trancoso,** with the ramparts of its fortress still standing. There is a 9th-century wall that was rebuilt and its fortifications strengthened over the centuries. This is where King Dinis and Isabella of Aragón (the Queen Saint) were married in 1282. An old pillory stands in the middle of the town.

Marialva, 40 miles north of Guarda, has remains of a castle built in 1200. You can see a keep and a tower still standing in the ruined walls, with remnants of the old village here and there.

Last of the fortified towns that can be visited today is **Penedona,** 44 miles directly north of Guarda, on a craggy hill. The castle fortress beside which the town grew up can be visited by going up a set of steps and through the ramparts. Ask at the house on the left at the bottom of the steps. From the parapets of the castle, you can see the rugged plain leading to Trás-os-Montes.

PORTO & ITS ENVIRONS

Portugal's second city, Porto, is the home of port wine, traditionally drunk in tulip-shaped glasses. The grapes that produce the wine come from the vineyards along the arid slopes of the Douro River Valley, many miles inland. At harvest time in autumn, the hills echo with the trilling of flutes, the cadence of drums.

The wine is brought to lodges at **Vila Nora de Gaia,** across the river from Porto, where it is blended, aged, and processed. In the past it was transported on flat-bottomed boats called *barcos rabelos*. With their long trailing rudders and sails flapping in the breeze, these boats with tails skirted down the Douro like swallows. Nowadays they have virtually given way to the train or even the unglamorous truck.

PORTO

Porto not only gave its name to the port wine, but to the whole country, the name deriving from the old settlement of Portus Cale. The Douro, from Rio do Ouro, or river of gold, has always been the source of Porto's life blood. It enjoys many sunny days, yet at times Porto has been called a gray city of mist and rain.

It's set on a rocky gorge that the Douro cut out of a great stone mass. Ann Bridge wrote, "The whole thing looks like a singularly dangerous spider's web flung across space." Porto's most interesting quarter is the **Alfândega**. Here the steep narrow streets, hardly big enough for a car to pass through, and the balconied houses evoke Lisbon's Alfama, although the quarter has its own distinctive character. The

Alfândega preserves the timeless color of many of the old buildings and cobbled ruas lining the riverbank.

Many write off Porto as an industrial city with some spectacular bridges, but that assessment is unfair. The provincial capital and university seat has its own artistic treasures, as we will see.

Porto lies 195 miles north of Lisbon, 189 miles south of La Coruña (Spain), and 366 miles west of Madrid.

1. Orientation

Porto (Oporto in English) stretches along the last 3 miles of the River Douro on its right bank and is the hub of a communication network in north Portugal. The quickest and easiest method of getting there is by airplane. TAP, the Portuguese airline, provides quick connection between the two cities, and there are daily flights all year.

Flights arrive at **Aeroporto das Pedras Rubras** (tel. 02/948-21-41). A taxi, the most convenient transport, from the airport into the center of Porto costs from 2,500$ ($16.75) to 3,000$ ($20.10). There is also good bus service into the center of the city from the airport. The no. 56 bus runs from Praça de Lisboa, a ticket costing 135$ (90¢). For information about TAP at the airport, call 02/948-19-38. The main office of TAP is at Praça Mouzinho de Albuquerque 105 (tel. 02/600-11-11) in Porto.

There are three main **railway stations** in Porto. They include São Bento Station in the center of the city, lying only a block from the Praça da Liberdade. This station has trains serving the Douro Valley, along with destinations in the north, including Viana de Castelo and Braga. West of the center, but connected to São Bento by rail service, Campanhã Station is one of the most important. It serves the south of Portugal, including Lisbon, as well as international routes. For information, phone 01/56-41-41. Less important, Trindade Station handles traffic in the immediate environs of Porto, including to the beach resort of Póvoa do Varzim and to the historic old city of Guimarães (see Chapter 17). Only the Campanhã station can be called for information.

Five trains arrive per day from Lisbon, taking 4½ hours and costing 1,310$ ($8.80) for a one-way ticket. Porto also enjoys 13 trains per day from Viana do Castelo, taking 2 hours and costing 575$ ($3.85) for a one-way ticket. Twelve trains per day arrive from Coimbra, taking 2½ hours and costing 630$ ($4.20) for a one-way ticket. International travelers can take one of two daily trains from Madrid to Porto, going via Entroncamento. Trip time is 12 hours, and the cost of a one-way ticket is 4,600$ ($30.80). One train per day arrives from Paris, taking 27 hours, a one-way ticket costing 16,300$ ($109.20).

It is also possible to come from Lisbon by bus (there are at least eight departures from Lisbon). The trip takes 5 hours and costs 1,400$ ($9.40) for a one-way ticket. Arriving passengers are deposited at the bus depot at Rua Alexandre Herculano 366 (tel. 02/200-69-54). Service is provided by the national bus company, Rodoviária Nacional. There are also 11 trains per day from Coimbra, taking 1½ hours and costing 750$ ($5.05) for a one-way ticket.

Regardless of your method of transport, you will need to acquaint yourself with the geography of this rather complicated city. Its bridges, as mentioned, are famous. Connecting the right bank to the port wine center of Vila Nova de Gaia and the lands south is the **Maria Pía Bridge,** an architectural feat of Eiffel (yes, the same man who designed the Eiffel Tower in Paris). Another much-needed bridge spanning the Douro is the **Dom Luís I Bridge.** An iron bridge of two roadways, it was completed in 1886 by Seyrig, the Belgian engineer inspired by Eiffel. Another bridge, **Arrábida Bridge,** which opened in 1963, is bright and contemporary. Totally Portuguese in concept and execution, it is one of the largest single-span reinforced-concrete arches in Europe, representing the work of Edgar Cardoso.

PORTO

Church ✝︎■ Post Office ⊠ Information ⓘ

0 — 420 m / 460y

PORTUGAL
LISBON ★
● Porto

Rio Douro

Dom. Luis I Bridge

Maria Pia Bridge

Rua da Constituição
Rua de Santa Catarina
Rua de Bonfim
Rua da Alegria
Rua de Santos Posada
Av. F. Magalhães
Rua de Fernandes Tomás
Rua Formosa
Rua de Santo Ildefonso
Rua A. Herculano
Av. Rodrigues de Freitas
Avenida da Paiva Conceiro
Rua de Comoes
Rua Antero Quental
R. Gonçalo Cristóvão
Trindade Station
Praça da República
Praça da Liberdade
Town Hall
Av. dos Aliados
São Bento Station
Rua das Flores
Rua da Boavista
Rua A. Cabral
Rua d. Bragas
Rua de Cedofeita
Rua da Torrinha
Jardim de Cordoaria
Rua Nova da Alfândega
Rua de M. Bombarda
Rua Rosario
Rua Manuel II
Rua da Restauração
Rua de Julio Dinis
Rua do Campo Alegre
Praça Mousinho Albuquerque Av. Boavista
Rua N.S. Fátima
Boavista Station

Archbishop's Palace ❹
Basilica of St. Francis
(Igreja de São Francisco) ❼
Casa Museu de Guerra Junqueiro ❷
Church of Santa Clara
(Igreja de Santa Clara) ❶
Igreja dos Grilos ❺
Museu de São Francisco ❽
Museu Nacional de Soares dos Reis ❾
Pavilhão dos Desportos ❿
Sé ❸
Stock Exchange (Palacio da Bolsa)

The heart of Porto is **Avenida dos Aliados,** a wide paseo with a parklike center where families used to go for a stroll. It is bounded on the south by the **Praça General Humberto Delgado.** Two major shopping streets of Porto lie on either side of the Praça da Liberdade: **Rua Clérigos** and **Rua 31 de Janeiro.** Rua Clérigos leads to the landmark Torre dos Clérigos, which to some is the symbol of Porto.

FAST FACTS: PORTO

AMERICAN EXPRESS: The representative in Porto is Star Travel Service, Avenida dos Aliados 202 (tel. 02/236-37), which is open Monday to Friday from 9am to 12:30pm and 2 to 6pm.

BANKS: In general, banks and currency-exchange offices are open Monday to Friday from 8:30 to 11:45am and 1 to 2:45pm. Two central ones include Banco Espírito Santo & Comercial de Lisboa, Avenida dos Aliados 45 (tel. 02/32-00-31), and Banco Pinto & Sotto Mayor, Praça da Liberdade 26 (tel. 02/32-15-56).

CONSULATES: In Porto, you will reach the **American Consulate** at Rua Julio Dinis 826 (tel. 02/69-00-08). Go to the third floor. There is also a **British Consulate** at Avenida da Boavista 3072 (tel. 02/68-47-89).

DRUGSTORES: Porto is well served by a network of pharmacies. A most central one is the Farmácia Central do Porto, 31 de Janeiro 203 (tel. 02/216-84).

EMERGENCIES: Emergency telephone numbers include **police** (tel. 02/268-21), **fire** (tel. 02/48-41-21), **Red Cross** (tel. 02/66-68-72), and **Santo António Hospital** (tel. 02/273-54).

LAUNDRY: A Laundromat is available at the Shopping Center Brasilia on the third floor. It's the Penguin (tel. 02/69-50-32), open from 10am to midnight Monday to Saturday.

POST OFFICE: If you want to mail a letter, the main post office is at Praça General Humberto Delgado, near the tourist office. It sells stamps Monday to Friday from 9am to 7pm. However, if you had your mail sent general delivery (poste restante), it can be picked up daily from 8am to 10pm at Largo 1 de Dezembro. It is also possible to send telegrams and faxes during those hours.

TELEPHONE: It is possible to place long-distance calls at the post office (see above). Otherwise, you can go to the phone office at Praça da Liberdade 62, which is open daily from 8am to 11:30pm. By placing your calls at these public institutions you avoid hotel surcharges, which can be steep.

TOURIST INFORMATION: One of the most helpful tourist offices in Portugal is the **Porto Tourist Board,** Rua Clube Fenianos 25 (tel. 02/31-27-40). The office is open July through September from 9am to 7pm Monday through Friday, from 9am to 4pm Saturday, and from 10am to 1pm Sunday. Off-season hours are Monday through Friday from 9am to 5:30pm and Saturday from 9am to 4pm. Here you can acquaint yourself with the city by watching a film, *Letter from Oporto,* during office hours without making previous arrangements.

TRANSPORTATION: Porto is well serviced by a network of **buses, trolley buses,** and **trams,** with tickets costing from 135$ (90¢). However, it is cheaper to purchase a Turístico Pass, entitling you to 4 days of transportation, if you plan to do extensive touring in the Porto area. The cost is 980$ ($6.55). It can be bought at various tobacco shops and kiosks around town. Taxis are available 24 hours a day. Call 02/48-80-61 for radio taxis or hail one on the street or at a taxi stand.

---

2. Where to Stay

There had long been a lack of top-rated accommodations in this capital of the north. Some so-called first-class hotels could be recommended only in the direst of emergencies. However, in the 1980s the outlook brightened considerably. With the addition of several new first-class hotels, and the restoration of some interesting older properties, Porto now provides the most interesting selection of superior accommodations north of Lisbon.

VERY EXPENSIVE

The most traditional, and usually the first, choice of visitors to Porto is the plushly furnished **Hotel Infante de Sagres,** Praça de Lencastre 42, 4000 Porto (tel. 02/200-81-01; fax 02/31-49-37). Its rich handcrafted ornamentation convinces most visitors that it dates from the 19th century. Actually it was constructed in 1951 by a wealthy textile manufacturer. Its imposing mass of carved paneling, stained glass, and wrought iron was assembled solely to house the businessman's powerful clients during their trips to Porto. The most beautiful mantelpiece found in any hotel sits beneath the circular balcony ventilating the upstairs music room. The fireplace was designed and carved by one of the hotel's former night porters in his spare time over a period of years.

Its rosters are filled with the names of rich and famous clients who once settled themselves into one of the upholstered armchairs in the antique-laden lobbies. They include Princess Anne and Prince Philip, the president of Portugal, along with many of his cabinet ministers, the governor of São Paulo, and everybody from the president of Zaire to delegations from the People's Republic of China. The 84-room air-conditioned hotel maintains one of the highest ratios of employees to guests (1.3 employees per room) of any hotel in Porto and offers excellent service.

The management has created a parasol- and plant-dotted sun terrace within a central courtyard for warm-weather enjoyment. Bedrooms contain large marble-covered baths, phones, color TVs, minibars, and elegant, conservative furniture. Year-round rates for the standard rooms are 25,000$ ($167.50) to 27,500$ ($184.25) double. Three suites cost from 80,000$ ($536). The hotel's high-ceilinged dining room, D. Filipa, serves formal breakfasts, lunches, and dinners in an old-world setting. In addition, room service is available 24 hours a day.

Parking costs 700$ ($4.70). The hotel sits immediately to the side of a monumental square flanked by the town hall and Porto's showplace, Avenida dos Aliados. Bus: 35, 37, or 38. AE, DC, MC, V.

Le Meridien Porto, Avenida da Boavista 1466, 4100 Porto (tel. 02/600-19-13; fax 02/600-20-31). One of the most dramatically modern hotels in town is fronted with three vertical rows of bay windows stretching to the top of its skyscraping concrete shell. You'll pass beneath a jutting five-sided entrance portico before finding yourself inside this hotel, owned by Air France and designed especially to make both business travelers and vacationers feel at home. Dozens of plants are reflected in the mirrors, which seem to enlarge the marble- and chrome-covered lobby. The musician performing in the modern lobby-level bar might be accompanied by a synthesizer, making the ambience there smooth and mellow. There's a health club on the third floor, plus a terrace restaurant (covered separately in my dining recommendations). A basement-level disco is open Monday to Saturday night from 10:30pm to 4am.

Opened in 1984, the hotel provides 232 well-furnished bedrooms, each with TV, air conditioning, a minibar, in-house video movies, private bath, and phone. Singles cost from 35,000$ ($234.50) daily, and doubles go for 38,000$ ($254.60), including breakfast. The hotel stands about 2 miles from the heart of the city. Bus: Boavista 78. Tram: 2. Parking is free. AE, DC, MC, V.

Porto Sheraton, Avenida da Boavista 1269, 4100 Porto (tel. 02/69-91-41; fax 02/69-14-67). Opened with a flourish in 1986, this is now considered the most stylish and desirable modern hotel in Porto. It rises across the street from its most noteworthy competitor, the Meridien, above the apartments and private villas of the Boavista section, a short distance from the commercial center of the city. Set back from a busy street and ringed with free parking, it was designed with bands of differently hued stone and rows of bronze-colored glass to reflect the sunlight. Inside, leather chairs are clustered within earshot. The hotel contains a heated swimming pool, a squash court, a health club, and 253 air-conditioned bedrooms. Each of these offers a hairdryer, a minibar, radio, TV with video movies, and phone. Singles range from 24,000$ ($160.80) daily, and doubles from 30,000$ ($201), including breakfast. Seventeen suites cost from 80,000$ ($536). The premier restaurant of the hotel, Madruga, provides both an international and regional cuisine, with meals costing from 3,800$ ($25.45) to 5,200$ ($34.85). A businessperson's buffet lunch is provided from 12:30 to 3pm Monday to Friday. In the evening, the chef recommends his gourmet menu, served until 11pm. The Nautilus Bar in the lobby is open daily from 9am to 2am. Famous piano tunes are played nightly, as guests sample the finest port from the hotel's port wine cellars. Room service is 24 hours a day. Other services include laundry/valet/dry cleaning, baby-sitting, and a beauty parlor and hairdresser. Bus: Boavista 78. Tram: 2. AE, DC, MC, V.

EXPENSIVE

Hotel Ipanema, Rua Campo Alegre 156, 4100 Porto (tel. 02/66-80-61; fax 02/633-39), is one of the best four-star hotels in Portugal, having opened its doors in 1984. A sleek modern structure, it has become a feature of the city's skyline. Its elongated rows of smoked glass are visible from the highway stretching toward Lisbon. In fact, one of the establishment's best points is that it's easy to find. Just exit the highway from Lisbon at the signs indicating the direction of Porto, and you'll find it on a cobblestone-covered road leading to the center of town, about a mile away. Inside, an attractive and dimly lit bar looks over a plant-filled atrium. The marble-walled lobby contains an unusual collection of Brazilian sculpture, perhaps to honor the namesake of the hotel. Meals in the Restaurant Rios are especially popular on Sunday, when a buffet is served. Each of the 150 handsomely furnished bedrooms is accented with cedar and has views over Porto, along with a radio, a tile bath, air conditioning, and TV. Singles range from 23,000$ ($154.10) daily and doubles from 28,000$ ($187.60), including breakfast. Free car parking is available on the premises. AE, DC, MC, V.

Tivoli Porto-Atlântico, Rua Afonso Lopes Vieira 61, 4100 Porto (tel. 02/69-49-41; fax 02/633-39), is the residential facility of a complex built on the outskirts of Porto, containing a cinema, gymnasium, inside/outside swimming pool, and a sauna, among other amenities. The hotel has 58 carpeted bedrooms, with balconies and all the conveniences of a five-star hostelry, including private bath, air conditioning, minibar, TV, and phone. Singles range in price from 24,000$ ($160.80) daily, and doubles go for 26,000$ ($174.20), including breakfast. On the premises is a fine restaurant, Foco (see my dining recommendations), with efficient and polite service. The warmly paneled bar has comfortable low-slung leather chairs, and there's an outdoor terrace. Parking is free. AE, DC, MC, V.

MODERATE

Albergaria de São José, Rua da Alegria 172, 4000 Porto (tel. 02/38-02-61; fax 02/38-02-65), is a modern, corner, first-class inn, with all the facilities you'll need for a pleasant stay in Porto. While the lobby, the lounge, and the bar are decorated in a contemporary idiom, the 43 bedrooms have antique furnishings that connect you with regional Portugal. The carved mahogany beds are old world in their elegance. Each room has air conditioning, radio, phones, and a tile bath. A single costs 7,400$ ($49.60) daily, a double 9,500$ ($63.65), including breakfast, the only meal served. There's a private hotel garage costing 700$ ($4.70) a night. AE, DC, MC, V.

Albergaria Miradouro, Rua da Alegria 598, 4000 Porto (tel. 02/57-07-17;

fax 02/57-08-49), is like an eagle's nest, a slim 13-floor baby skyscraper built atop a hill outside the main part of the city. The Miradouro offers vista-scanning rooms (you can watch ships laden with port making their way to the open sea). The small-scale public rooms are tasteful. The lower bar is decorated with wall tiles from Japan and Portugal. Two plush elevators whisk you to an upper bar, with walls opening onto a view. The corner rooms are preferred, of course. In these, two walls have built-in wardrobes and chests (with a built-in pair of beds); the walls are all glass. In all the rooms you'll find a vestibule, luggage storage, a valet stand, desks, and sitting room. There are 30 rooms, all with private bath, TV, and phone. One person pays from 9,500$ ($63.65) daily, and two persons are charged 12,000$ ($80.40). Breakfast is included. The facilities include an underground garage, where parking costs 700$ ($4.70). AE, DC, MC, V.

Even though it was conceived for commercial travelers, **Dom Henrique,** Rua Guedes de Azevedo 179, 4000 Porto (tel. 02/200-57-55; fax 02/201-94-51), is equally accommodating to tourists. In the city center, this hotel, which was recently restored, rises 18 floors and offers 112 rooms, of which 22 are executive suites. Each well-furnished accommodation is equipped with color TV, video, air conditioning, radio, minibar, direct-dial phone, and hairdryer. The charges are 18,400$ ($123.30) daily in a single, rising to 19,500$ ($130.65) in a double. Suites begin at 50,000$ ($335). Breakfast is included. Spectacular views can be seen from the hotel's 17th-floor bar, Anrrique, and 18th-floor restaurant and grill, O Navegador. Food is served daily from 12:30 to 2pm and 7:30 to 10pm with meals costing from 2,500$ ($16.75). On the ground floor, clients can order light meals at the coffee shop, Tabula, which is open daily from 7am to 2am. Bus: 53, 59, 82, or 84. Parking is free. Laundry, baby-sitting, and room service are available. AE, DC, MC, V.

Grande Hotel de Batalha, Praça da Batalha 116, 4000 Porto (tel. 02/200-05-71; fax 02/200-24-68), is highly favored by international buyers of port wine. A substantial businessperson's hotel, it has comfortable rooms and an excellent restaurant where one can order Portuguese specialties. Each of the 142 bedrooms has a radio, air conditioning, TV, phone, and tile bath. A single rents for 11,000$ ($73.70) daily and a double for 12,700$ ($85.10). The bedrooms have a lighter decorative treatment than the public rooms, yet the lounge, the bar, and the restaurant are quite adequate. The hotel is in the center of the city. Parking is 700$ ($4.70). AE, DC, V.

Hotel Castor, Rua da Alegria 685, 4000 Porto (tel. 02/57-00-14; fax 02/56-60-76). Built in the late 1960s, this white-walled hotel lies within a relatively quiet neighborhood in a section of town rarely visited by tourists. Known for its pleasant staff and its scattering of antiques, the hotel boasts a comfortably contemporary interior where two stylish restaurants do a respectable business in their own right, including an Italian-style trattoria, offering pizzas on its bill of fare along with other specialties. A favorite corner of the hotel is Beaver's Disco, where a large-screen TV shows transmissions from throughout Europe. The format is that of a stylish pub (music is played only on weekends). Each of the 58 conservatively decorated and air-conditioned bedrooms contains a private bath, TV, radio, phone, and minibar. With breakfast included, singles cost 12,500$ ($83.75) daily, doubles 14,500$ ($97.15). Three suites cost 19,000$ ($127.30). Laundry service and baby-sitting are provided, and room service is available to 2am. Parking is free. AE, DC, MC, V.

Hotel do Império, Praça da Batalha 130, 4000 Porto (tel. 02/200-68-61; fax 02/200-68-61), is a modern 97-room hotel, close to the railway station in the heart of the city. It's rather well designed and attractive for a railway-station hotel, with a streamlined interior decor. Bedrooms are well thought out, tasteful, with color-harmonized schemes. Units come with wall globe lights, bedside tables, phones, central heating, and private tile baths. The cost of a single is 10,000$ ($67) daily, and a double runs 12,700$ ($85.10), including breakfast. Children up to 8 years are granted a 50% reduction. There is no garage for parking. Laundry service and baby-sitting can be arranged, and room service is available until midnight. AE, DC, MC, V.

Hotel São João, Rua do Bonjardim 120, 4000 Porto (tel. 02/200-16-62; fax 02/31-61-14), is in a class by itself: the only hotel-residênciá of its type to be rated deluxe by the government. Such a designation shows what deep imprint human warmth can make upon a limited framework, especially when the owners have good taste, a certain flair, plus a concern for the welfare of their guests. Accomplishing this is the Baldaque family, who own the top floor of a modern building right in the heart of Porto.

The living room is inviting with its fireplace nook, deep sofa, and antiques, such as a grandfather clock. The main corridor leading to the bedrooms is like an art gallery, with old tapestries, high-back 18th-century chairs, engravings, and large copper bowls of flowers. The bedrooms—only 14 in all, each a double—combine modern with traditional furnishings, reserving a section for a sitting area. Every room contains its own pink-and-white marble bath, TV, and phone. One person pays 10,500$ ($70.35) daily, and two are charged 13,000$ ($87.10), including breakfast. There is no parking available, except in a nearby commercial garage. AE, DC, MC, V.

INEXPENSIVE
Albergaria Girassol, Rua Sá da Bandeira 133, 4000 Porto (tel. 02/20-01-89), is a modest little upper-floor inn. The hotel offers 18 nicely designed and furnished rooms with private bath, phone, and TV. Each bed has a built-in headboard. Rooms at the rear are quieter. Including breakfast, a single rents for 6,000$ ($40.20) daily and a double for 8,000$ ($53.60). There's a small TV lounge with soft leather chairs, all tasteful and cozy. You can have your morning meal in a little breakfast room. Laundry service is provided, and room service is available until 10pm. No credit cards.

You can have a pleasant stay at the **Castelo de Santa Catarina,** Rua de Santa Catarina 1347, 4000 Porto (tel. 02/49-55-99). In the 1920s a Brazilian military officer returned to his native Porto determined to create the most flamboyant residence in town. Drawing upon the resources of his influential family, who manufactured ceramic tiles, he created a sprawling compound of greenhouses, terraced gardens, a chapel, and a sumptuous main house. To encircle them, he added a semicircular crescent of servants' quarters. Today the tile-covered exterior walls almost give an encapsulated history of Portugal. What used to be one of the residential showplaces of Porto is behind a high wall in a commercial neighborhood about a mile from the center where the owner has arranged 24 bedrooms for rent.

After ringing the bell, you'll be ushered down a labyrinthine series of halls and narrow stairways. To get to your room, you'll pass through opulent but disorganized sitting rooms and ballrooms, illuminated with crystal chandeliers. Each of the small bedrooms contains a set of carved antique furniture, often of rosewood. The plumbing fixtures are designed with a florid, appealing art nouveau flair. Doubles rent for 7,500$ ($50.25) daily, and singles cost 5,250$ ($35.20), with breakfast included. The hotel also rents one suite for 9,500$ ($63.65). Laundry and baby-sitting can be arranged, and room service is available 24 hours. Parking is free. Bus: 49 or 53. No credit cards.

Hotel Peninsular, Rua Sá da Bandeira 21, 4000 Porto (tel. 02/200-30-12; fax 02/38-49-84). The only reminder of this building's original purpose as an outbuilding to a nearby church is a lobby mural crafted from blue-and-white tiles, showing a coronation. Today the building is an unpretentiously pleasant hotel, outfitted with 50 simple and low-cost bedrooms. It stands near the train station of St. Bento in the heart of the city. There's a restaurant one floor above the street, which is accessible via a darkly stained stairway near the reception desk. The belle époque facade is marked with an incongruous neon sign. The hotel rents 45 bedrooms, each with private bath or shower, phone, and TV. Singles cost from 3,500$ ($23.45) to 4,500$ ($30.15) daily, with doubles renting for 5,000$ ($33.50) to 6,000$ ($40.20), including breakfast. Laundry service is available, and baby-sitting can be arranged. Room service is available 24 hours, but there is no parking. AE, DC, MC, V.

Pensão Residencial Rex, Praça da República 117, 4000 Porto (tel. 02/200-45-48). The facade of this establishment fits in gracefully with its location on one of the most beautiful squares of Porto. Its design is a classicized derivation of art nouveau, replete with sea-green tiles, cast-iron embellishments, and Roman-style window treatments. The semimajestic marble staircase leading into the reception area from the street is lined with richly colored paneling that looks as if it had just been oiled. The lobby and each of the 21 bedrooms is crowned with an ornately molded plaster ceiling embellished with painted highlights, and much of the furniture is antique. The bathrooms, however, have been modernized. With breakfast included, a double or a single rents for 9,200$ ($61.65) daily. There's a tiny bar in the TV lounge at the back of the ground floor, but no restaurant. The iron gates enclosing an adjacent driveway swing open on request to allow you to park a car free. No credit cards.

3. Where to Dine

When Prince Henry the Navigator was rounding up the cattle in the Douro Valley for his men aboard the legendary caravels, he shipped out the juicy steaks and left the tripe behind. Faced with the tripe, the denizens of Porto responded bravely and began inventing recipes for it. To this day they carry the appellation of tripe eaters, and it has become their favorite local dish. To sample the most characteristic specialty of Porto, you can order *tripas à moda do Porto* (tripe stewed with spicy sausage and string beans). Of course, the city offers other viands, and quite good ones at that.

EXPENSIVE

Foco, Hotel Tivoli Porto-Atlântico, Rua Afonso Lopes Vieira 86 (tel. 66-72-48). The entrance to this attractive restaurant outside town is adjacent to the already-recommended hotel that houses it. It's worth the excursion by taxi from the center, partially because of its unobtrusive and polite but very thorough service. You'll find the establishment within a quadrangle created by a complex of residential apartment buildings, a few minutes' drive past Le Meridien Hotel. Before dinner, you can enjoy a drink in one of the low-slung leather chairs in a tiny corner of the restaurant. You'll then be ushered past a screen of plants to a chair in the luxuriously modern dining room. From the windows you'll have a view of the swimming pool. Portuguese meals are priced from 6,000$ ($40.20) à la carte and might include trout Transmontana style, grilled squid on a skewer, pork chunks Minho style, roasted kid, smoked salmon, and a daily specialty of the chef. A tourist menu costs 2,500$ ($16.75). Food is served daily from 12:30 to 3pm and 7 to 11pm. Reservations are recommended. Closed in May. Bus: 3 or 78. AE, DC, MC, V.

Garrafão, Rua António Nobre 53, Leça da Palmeira (tel. 995-17-35), a traditional restaurant in the suburbs, overlooks the Praia Boa Nova. Attractively situated, with a pleasant decor, it seats about 100 and serves mainly seafood. The prices of the seafood specialties vary according to the season. The Garrafão is known also for its wine cellar, containing a large selection of the best Portuguese wines. À la carte Portuguese specialties feature a shrimp omelet, shellfish soup, grilled sole, veal dishes, and caramel custard. The tab is likely to run 4,500$ ($30.15) for a complete meal. A tourist menu costs 3,500$ ($23.45). The restaurant has a pleasant dining room with windows over the beach. It is open from noon to 5pm and 7pm to midnight Monday to Saturday. Reservations aren't needed. Closed: August 15 to 31. AE, DC, MC, V.

Les Terrasses, Le Meridien, Avenida da Boavista 1466 (tel. 02/600-19-13), advertises itself as a restaurant and brasserie, but its uniformed maître d'hôtel and its plush gardenlike decor give it the aura of a formal dining room. Off the lobby of this hotel owned by Air France, it lies nearly 3 miles from the city center reached by Boavista bus no. 78 or tram no. 2. A wooden terrace, covered with lacy cast-iron garden furniture, offers the option of dining under the trees outside. Most guests, however, prefer the air-conditioned interior because of the noise of passing traffic. Tables are separated into semiprivate alcoves. Menu specialties reflect a strong French influence, with the addition of many Portuguese regional dishes as well. The wine steward will be pleased to suggest a reasonably priced vintage of Portuguese wine to accompany your meal, which might cost as much as 6,000$ ($40.20). Reservations are necessary. Hours are daily from 12:30 to 3pm and 7:30 to 11pm. AE, DC, MC, V.

Portucale Restaurante, Rua da Alegria 598 (tel. 57-07-17), perches on the rooftop of the Albergaria Miradouro. Seemingly the highest point in town, outside the heart of the city, it offers wide views of the river, the boats, and rooftops. Two elevators zip you to the 13th floor, from which you ascend to the dining room via a spiral staircase, crossing a tiny lily and fish pond. Despite the infinity of the panoramic sweep, the restaurant is fairly intimate, with tables set with fine silver, china, and flowers. There's an appetizing pastry cart.

The hand-woven hanging is by Camarinha, the artist who designed the à la carte menu. The cuisine is Portuguese. Specialties of the house include *bacalhau* (dried codfish) a marinheiro, *cabrito a serrana* (kid in wine sauce), smoked swordfish, lomos do pescado, steak flambé, rice, and mushrooms, and homemade cakes. For a complete dinner the costs range from 5,500$ ($36.85) to 7,000$ ($46.90). Open daily from 12:30 to 3pm and 7:30 to 10pm. Reservations are needed. AE, DC, MC, V.

MODERATE

Aquário Marisqueiro, Rua Rodrigues Sampaio 179 (tel. 200-22-31), is one of the finest seafood restaurants in Porto—actually two, connected by a central kitchen. Its location is within sight of the City Hall, and close to either of two leading hotels: the Infante de Sagres and the Hotel São João. Marine fare reigns supreme at this "aquarium." Soup made by boiling the shells of mariscos is a good beginner. Main fish orders include cod, of course. An excellent fish dish is clams in the Spanish style, but the house specialty is an açorda (a type of bread panada) of shellfish. The prices of these two dishes vary according to the season. Sole is your safest bet, and trout with ham is even more interesting. A typical dinner here will cost 3,800$ ($25.45) à la carte or 2,200$ ($14.75) on a tourist menu. Hours are 11:30am to 11pm Monday to Saturday. Reservations are necessary. Bus: 6 or 78. AE, DC, MC, V.

Restaurante Escondidinho, Rua Passos Manuel 144 (tel. 200-10-79), is a regional tavern, popular with the leading port wine merchants and the English. The name means "hidden" or "masked." The entrance alone is a clue, a facade in burnt-orange tile framing an arch leading to the L-shaped dining room. Inside is a world of time-blackened beams and timbers, a corner baronial stone fireplace, and carved wooden shelf brackets holding a collection of antique Portuguese ceramics. The chairs, with their intricate carving and brass studs, are just right for a cardinal, or at least a friar. The waiters are old world, yet proud of the prevailing informality. They feel free to speak their minds, candidly telling you the day's best dishes. Take their word.

The cuisine is Portuguese. The shellfish soup and the charcoaled sardines are always reliable. The chef's special dishes include hake in Madeira sauce and a chateaubriand for two. Desserts include a kirsch omelet or an orange pudding. An average meal will cost from 2,800$ ($18.75) to 3,800$ ($25.45), served from noon to 3pm and 7 to 10pm. Telephone for reservations. Closed Sunday. AE, DC, MC, V.

Restaurante Orfeu, Rua de Julio Dinis 928 (tel. 643-22). Don't confuse this completely competent restaurant with the shabby café and snack bar that occupies its street level. Descend stone stairs to reach the basement-level restaurant, which is especially popular with Porto's business community. Once seated at one of the roomy tables, a battalion of polite waiters will take your order. You can select from such Portuguese and continental dishes as leg of lamb, chateaubriand, perhaps partridge or hare. Calves' kidneys are prepared with a Madeira sauce and, for dessert, you might like the bananas with cognac. Meals cost from 2,800$ ($18.75) to 4,200$ ($28.15). Hours are from 8am to midnight daily. The restaurant is air conditioned, and reservations aren't necessary. AE, DC, MC, V.

INEXPENSIVE

Abadia, Rua do Ateneu Comercial do Porto 22 (tel. 200-87-57), stands on a short street with a patio entrance. It has an open dining mezzanine. The cook specializes in fresh fish dishes, such as codfish Abadia and codfish Gomes de Sá. He also offers other dishes such as tripe stew Porto and fried pork. Soups are hearty and full of flavor. The cuisine is Portuguese. Count on spending 2,500$ ($16.75) à la carte or 1,500$ ($10.05) on a tourist menu. Large and clean, the restaurant serves daily from noon to 10pm. It is closed Sunday from June through September. Reservations aren't accepted. No credit cards.

A Brasileira, Rua do Bonjardim 116 (tel. 200-71-46), is an art deco coffeehouse, the virtual social center of Porto, plus a first-class restaurant and a bustling snack bar. In the restaurant part of the complex you can order cream of shellfish soup followed by such main dishes as roast chicken, grilled trout, or veal liver, topped off by chocolate mousse. The cuisine is Portuguese, as reflected by such specialties as bolinhos de bacalhau (codfish). A tourist menu goes for 2,000$ ($13.40), and most à la carte meals average 2,500$ ($16.75). Hours are Monday to Saturday from noon to 11pm. Reservations aren't needed. AE, DC, MC, V.

Mesa Antiga, Rua de Santo Ildefonso 28 (tel. 200-64-32). Its impeccably crafted blue-and-white tiles combine with its gnarled ceiling beams for a hint of the dignified severity of old Portugal. Above well-ordered rows of dining tables, brass trumpets rise from the curves of brass chandeliers. The Portuguese food served here, all homemade, is among the best regional cuisine in Porto. Conjured from a tiny kitchen by members of the owner's family, platters emerge steaming hot. Full meals cost from 1,800$ ($12.05) to 3,200$ ($21.45) and are served from noon to midnight; closed Saturday. Specialties include a delectable version of grilled sole served with a fresh and aromatic green sauce, squid on a spit, and an array of daily specials. The most typical dish is tripe prepared in the old-fashioned method of Porto. The restaurant is on a crowded and narrow street in the commercial center. Reservations are recommended. MC, V.

Restaurante Chinês, Avenida Vimara Peres 38 (tel. 200-89-15), is Porto's leading Chinese restaurant. Housed in a modern building at the entrance to Dom Luís I Bridge, it is an incongruous combination of the new and the old. Setting the mood are traditional Chinese lanterns and a dragon mural. It is a spacious two-level dining room. For your appetizer you might select egg flower soup, fried wonton, or even fried almonds. Main courses include prawns with curry, sweet-and-sour fish, and breast of chicken with pineapple. For dessert, there are many appetizing selections, including bananas with honey. A dinner begins at 2,500$ ($16.75) à la carte or 1,800$ ($21.70) on a tourist menu. Food is served daily from 12:30 to 2:30pm and 7:30 to 10:30pm. Reservations aren't necessary. AE, DC, MC, V.

Restaurant Tripeiro, Rua Passos Manuel 195 (tel. 200-58-86). This restaurant's textured stucco walls and elaborately crafted wooden ceiling offer a cool, dark retreat from the glaring sunlight outside. A group of efficient waiters serves full meals priced from 1,800$ ($12.05) to 3,400$ ($22.80) apiece. You can enjoy vinho verde (green wine), which is ideal with the specialty of the chef, *tripas* (tripe) à moda do Porto, in honor of the namesake of the restaurant. In addition, you might order several different preparations of codfish or any of several beef or shellfish dishes (the latter priced by the kilo). The cuisine is Portuguese and reservations aren't necessary. Meals are served from noon to 3pm and 7 to 10:30pm. Closed Sunday. AE, DC, MC, V.

Taverna do Bebobos, Cais de Ribeira 21–25 (tel. 31-35-65), is perhaps the oldest (founded 1876) and smallest restaurant in Porto, directly on the riverside dock. Women sell fish on the quay, and overhead, fluttering from wrought-iron balconies, are lines of laundry. Inside, the ground floor has a service bar with every sort of knickknack on its little tables. A narrow open staircase leads to an intimate dining room upstairs with a corner stone fireplace, a coved ceiling, an iron scale filled with sprouting onions, a 5-foot-high coffee mill, brass and copper pans, ships' lanterns, and a flamboyantly painted pottery crèche. On the tables are hunks of dark, crusty bread, and the portions are large enough to be shared. To begin your typically Portuguese meal, you might order a hearty bowl of caldo verde or a plate of grilled sardines. For a main course, I'd suggest either trout with ham, regional codfish, or pork prepared in the Alentejana style (that is, with a savory clam sauce). A fruit salad finishes the meal nicely. Count on spending 1,800$ ($12.05) to 3,000$ ($20.10) for a complete meal, plus the cost of your wine. Because of the small number of tables, it's necessary to have your hotel call and make a reservation for you. The place is open from noon to 2:30pm and 7 to 9:30pm Monday to Saturday. No credit cards.

---

4. What to See & Do

Exploring the sights of Porto requires some probing. But your discoveries will compensate for the effort. The tourist office suggests that one needs at least 3 days to explore Porto, but most foreign visitors don't spend that much time here. For those on a rushed schedule, the most famous sightseeing attractions include a visit to a wine lodge at Vila Nova de Gaia; the panoramic view from the Torre dos Clérigos, with its view of the Douro; a visit to the Sé (cathedral); a stroll through the most important museum, Soares dos Reis National; a walk through Ribeira, the old quarter, with its little alleyways leading to the harbor (best seen on market days); and if time remains, a visit to the Gothic church of St. Francis, with its stunning baroque interior.

THE CATHEDRAL DISTRICT

At the Terreiro de Sé, the **Sé (cathedral)** has grown and changed with the city —that is, until about the 18th century. Originally founded by a medieval queen and designed in a foreboding, basically Romanesque style, it is now a monument to changing architectural tastes. Part of the twin towers, the rose window, the naves, and the vestry are all elements of the original 13th-century structure. However, the austere Gothic cloister was added at the end of the 14th century and was later decorated with azulejos depicting events from the Song of Solomon. Opening off the cloister is the Chapel of St. Vincent, built in the closing years of the 16th century.

The main chapel was erected in the 17th century, and in 1736 the baroque architect Niccolò Nasoni of Italy added the north facade and its attractive loggia. The monumental altar is flanked by twisted columns, the nave by fading frescoes. In the small baroque Chapel of the Holy Sacrament (to the left of the main altar) is an altarpiece fashioned entirely of silver, the work so elaborate that the whole piece gives the illusion of constant movement.

Outside on the Cathedral Square is a Manueline-style pillory and a statue of Vimara Peres, the warrior of Afonso III of León, who captured ancient Portucale in 868. To the side, also on the same square, is the 18th-century **Archbishop's Palace,** sequestered for municipal offices. Noted for its granite-cased doors and windows, it also contains an exceptional stairway inside.

In back of the cathedral is one of the most charming típico streets of Porto: **Rua da Dom Hugo.** Along its route, you'll pass the **Chapel of Our Lady of Truths.** It's invariably closed, but you can peek through the grillework at the gilded rococo altar, with a statue of the Virgin at the center.

Down the same street, you'll reach **Casa Museu de Guerra Junqueiro,** Rua D. Hugo 32 (tel. 02/31-36-44). This famous Portuguese poet lived between 1850 and 1923. The house was built by the Italian architect Niccolò Nasoni (1691–1773). Each room is arranged to preserve the private art collection and memorabilia of Guerra Junqueiro.

The collection includes Georgian and Portuguese silver, Flemish chests, Italian, oriental, Spanish, and Portuguese ceramics, and ecclesiastical wood and stone carvings. Joining the many examples of religious sculpture are an Italian Renaissance desk, metal plates said to have been made in Nürnberg, a 16th-century Brussels tapestry, as well as interesting Portuguese furniture. It is open Tuesday through Thursday from 10am to 12:30pm and 2 to 5pm, Friday and Saturday from 10am to 12:30pm and 2 to 5:30pm, and Sunday from 2 to 5:30pm. Closed Monday. Children under 10 years of age are admitted free. Admission is 96$ (65¢), except on Saturday and Sunday when it is free.

In the same district, you can cross the busy artery, Avenida Dom Afonso

Henriques, and head down Rua Saraiva de Carvalho until you reach Largo de 1 de Dezembro and the **Church of Santa Clara.** First completed in 1416, the interior was transformed by the impassioned artists of the 17th century, masters of woodwork and gilding. The number of man-hours invested is staggering to contemplate. There is hardly a square inch that isn't covered with angels, saints, cherubs, patterned designs, and great knobbed bosses in an architectural scramble of rococo and baroque, one of the most exceptional examples in Portugal. The clerestory windows permit the sunlight to flood in, making a golden crown of the upper regions. The facade is squat and plain, however.

If the keeper of the keys takes a liking to you, he'll take you on a behind-the-scenes tour of the precincts. In the Tribute Room, for example, you'll see a devil carved on the choir stalls. Throughout the tour you will see a hodgepodge of many bad, fading paintings, some not even hung—just propped casually in the corner. But it's intriguing to see what lies beyond all the glitter and glamour out front.

Sights Near the Cathedral

Passing alongside the water, you can look for a front row of buildings on **Rua Nova da Alfândega.** Underneath these structures is an arcade that is a continuous row of Romanesque arches. Perhaps they faced the waterfront until the street was built at a high level like a dike.

Up from this major artery is one of the most colorful sectors of Porto. If time allows, wander through some of the stepped back streets. In other places, the area might be called a slum or ghetto, but in Porto, the district has such style—vegetable-and meat-stuffed arcaded markets, churches, museums, monuments, even such elegant buildings as the Stock Exchange and the British Factory—that it retains a certain punch.

A good point to begin your exploration is on the main **Praça do Infante Dom Henriques,** named after the Porto-born Henry the Navigator, who launched Portugal on its Age of Discovery. At this square you can visit the big covered food market, where tripe is sold in great quantities.

Facing the square is the **Stock Exchange,** entered on Rua da Bolsa (tel. 02/38-45-66), housed in the imposing 19th-century Palácio da Bolsa. It is known for its Moorish Hall, a much-modified pastiche resembling a room in the Alhambra at Granada. The walls, ceiling, and balcony are a gilded mass of patterns and geometrical configurations.

The pastel-blue column bases glow in sunlight filtered through intricately latticed octagonal skylights and floral side windows. It is open June through September Monday through Friday from 9am to 6pm and Saturday and Sunday from 10am to noon and 2 to 5pm. In the off-season, it is open only Monday through Friday from 9am to noon and 2 to 5:30pm. Admission is 200$ ($1.35). Children 12 and under are admitted free. Take bus no. 15 or tram no. 1 to reach it.

Basilica of St. Francis, reached by steps up from the waterfront and opening onto Rua da São Francisco, was built in the Gothic style between 1383 and 1410. But in the 17th and 18th centuries it underwent extensive rococo dressing. The vault pillars and columns are lined with gilded woodwork: cherubs, garlands of roses, cornucopia of fruit, and frenzied animals, entwined and dripping with gold. Many of the wide-ribbed Gothic arches are made of marble resembling the Italian forest-green serpentine variety. The marble almost seems to fade and blend with the gray granite columns and floors.

The Romanesque rosette dominates the facade, whose square portal is flanked by double twisted columns. Above the columns, a profusely ornamented niche contains a simple white statue of the patron saint. In the rose window, 12 mullions emanate from the central circle in apostolic symbolism, ending in a swaglike stone fringe. The steps seem to spill out into the square fanlike along the base of the curved walls.

Next door you can visit the **Museu de S. Francisco,** Rua da Bolsa 44 (tel. 02/200-64-93). The sacristan estimates that 30,000 human skulls have been interred in the cellars. Even though he may be exaggerating, this dank building was once the burial ground for rich or poor. Nowadays it is a catacomb unique in Portugal.

A section of it looks like an antiques shop. There are paintings too, one of St. Francis of Assisi worshiping Christ on the Cross. Oddities include some of the first paper money printed in Portugal and an 18th-century ambulance that was really a sedan chair. The Sala de Sessões adds a note of unexpected elegance. Built in the rich baroque style, it is now a meeting hall with a Louis XIV table and João V chairs. Wherever you go in the room, the painted eyes of framed bishops follow you, watching like Big Brother. It is open from June through September from 9am to 5pm, and in the off-season from 9am to noon and 2 to 7pm. It is closed on Sunday. Take either bus no. 15 or tram no. 1 to reach it. Admission is 100$ (65¢).

Also reached by steps up from the water is one of the city's leading museums, sheltered on a típico square and rarely visited. Culture seekers are usually beset with escudo-hungry children who live in the jumble of dwellings nearby.

Museu de Etnografia e História do Douro Litoral, Palácio de S. João Novo, Largo S. João Novo (tel. 02/200-20-10), celebrates the arts, handcrafts, and culture of the Douro River Valley. It's a rustic potpourri of spinning wheels, looms, and animal and fish traps nostalgically evoking the simple life-style of the peasant. Roman coins and other artifacts remind one that legions from far afield once marched in and settled on the banks of the river.

Earthenware jugs from Vita-da-Feira, gold filigree work, a bas-relief of a provincial cottage, and a three-faced Christ are among the exhibits, along with primitive puppets, provincial bedrooms, ceramics, dolls in regional costume, ship models, decorative ox yokes, weathervanes, cannonballs, spears, antique sarcophagi, even a wine press. Any or all of the above may be viewed from 10am to noon and 2 to 5pm Tuesday to Saturday. Admission is free.

Created in 1833, by order of the king, Dom Pedro IV, **Soares dos Reis National Museum,** Rua de Dom Manuel II (tel. 02/200-71-10), was called the Museu Portuguêse when it was opened to the public in 1840. One hundred years later it was declared a National Museum and was dedicated to Soares dos Reis (1847 –89), the noted sculptor from Porto, and the name was changed. *Desterrado* and *Flor Agreste* are remarkable sculptures by this artist, but good portraits and allegorical figures can also be seen in the same gallery.

In the foreign painters collection, you'll find Dutch, Flemish, Italian, and French works, including two François Clouets (1522–72) portraits and landscapes by Jean Pillement (1727–1808). The most representative and unified display is that of the Portuguese 19th-century painters, particularly from the Porto School. Henrique Pousão (1859–87) and Silva Porto (1850–93) are represented by fine naturalistic work.

Also displayed in the museum are decorative arts, including ceramics, glassware, gold and silver work, furniture, and other objects.

Admission is 200$ ($1.35) except on Sunday morning, when it is free. Children 10 years of age and under are admitted free. Hours are Tuesday through Sunday from 10am to 1pm and 2 to 5pm. Bus: 3, 6, 20, 35, 37, or 41.

PORT WINE LODGES

Across the river from Porto, at **Vila Nova de Gaia,** are the port wine lodges. Like the sherry makers at Jerez de la Frontera, Spain, these establishments are hospitable, inviting guests to tour their precincts. Take bus no. 57 or 91 to reach these lodges.

The largest of these lodges, **Real Vinícola,** Avenida Diogo Leite (tel. 02/30-54-62), is a prime example of the art of wine making. It is here that the blending, aging, and selection processes take place. Dating from 1889, the warehouses contain specially treated oaken vats. The wine is bolstered with brandies and vintage wines to maintain its character. The vast cellars, dark, cool, and moist, are the resting place for port that ranges in age from 5 to 70 years. However, the oldest bottle in the company's museum is dated 1765. In one tunnel section alone there are four million bottles of Portuguese sparkling wines.

If you wish to learn the intricacies of production and development of port wine, from tasting to decanting, arrive and announce yourself. You'll be guided through the cask- and vat-lined cellars and tunnels. At the company tavern, you can purchase fine wine packed in wicker baskets. Hours are 9am to noon and 2 to 5pm Monday to Friday.

You can also visit many other port wine centers. One of the most famous is **Porto Sandeman,** Largo Miguel Bombarda 3 (tel. 02/30-40-81). Hours are from 9:30am to 12:30pm and 2 to 5pm Monday to Friday from October through March, and from 9:30am to 5pm daily from April through September. The House of Sandeman also operates a museum, tracing the history of port wine and of Sandeman. Many artifacts displayed date from centuries ago. The museum is unique. Visitors can also purchase Sandeman products on the premises, not only wines but promotional items such as T-shirts, umbrellas, and posters.

There are many other monuments and sights worth exploring in Porto, especially the 18th-century **Torre dos Clérigos** (tel. 217-29), the landmark tower of the city, rising to a height of nearly 250 feet. The tallest tower in Portugal, it was designed by an Italian named Niccolò Nasoni. From its summit there's a view of the Douro River, the valley gorge, and the far reaches of the city. The tower can be visited from 10:30am to noon and 3:30 (3pm on Sunday) to 5pm Thursday to Tuesday. Entrance is 40$ (25¢).

SHOPPING

The capital of the north boasts some of the finest gold- and silversmiths in Portugal. You'll find dozens of shops, especially along **Rua das Flores,** offering displays in their window cases. The most outstanding one is **Pedro A. Baptista,** Rua das Flores 235 (tel. 200-51-42), which offers an unusual collection of antique as well as new jewelry (often based on traditional designs), plus several upper floors of decorator items. In the ground-floor jewelry section you'll find intricate and delicate lacelike filigree pins, brooches, pillboxes, and bracelets, in both solid gold (19¼ karats) or gold-plated silver, plus an exquisite silver collection, including elaborately decorated tea services.

The owner buys rare and beautiful antique jewelry which he "offers first to my wife." The decorative bric-a-brac collection upstairs features many ornate gilt pieces, such as a 3-foot-high carved-wood church candelabrum and a trestle dining table.

Fábrica de Loíca de Sacavem, Rua das Carmelitas 40 (tel. 200-20-33), across from the Clérigos Church, is Porto's leading outlet for ceramics and china. Long established, it is important enough to have wares made especially for it. Generally the china selections are sophisticated, but regional motifs are offered as well. Worth considering are some of its decorative vases, based on old designs, along with a wide assortment of mugs, tureens, platters, cups, saucers, and glasses. Of course, pastel-colored china comes in many different arrangements at widely varying prices. Take tram no. 3, 18, or 19.

Shopping Center Brasilia, Praça Mouzinho de Albuquerque 113 (tel. 69-74-25). Its bustle, its multilevel attractions, and its omnipresent marble floors evoke an upscale shopping complex in South America. But the merchandise and patrons are pure Portuguese. Its main entrance faces the snarling lion and bloodied eagle atop the column of the Praça Mouzinho de Albuquerque, one of the city's busiest commercial centers. This is the most important shopping complex in Porto, laden with all kinds of goods and services such as shoes, casual wear, sportswear, haute couture, furs, jewelry, electronic gadgets, libraries, toys, ceramics, furniture, supermarket, exchange, and unusual bars and restaurants. In fact, spread before you will be the flashiest array of merchandise in the north of Portugal. It's open until midnight. Take bus no. 82 or 84.

There's a place for everybody's taste, including **Gôgô,** Galeria 51, Loja 51-E3 (tel. 69-85-12), which sells upscale gift items, many of them organic, from around the world. You'll also see sophisticated silver or ivory baubles from Zaire, China, and the Philippines. If you've ever yearned for a basket of preserved ostrich eggs, or perhaps a stuffed viper in attack position, this is the place. Bus: 82 or 84.

EVENING ENTERTAINMENT

There's no better way to begin your evening in Porto than by paying a visit to the **Solar do Vinho do Porto,** housed in the building of the Romantic Museum of

Quinta da Maceirinha at Rua de Entre Quintas 220 (tel. 69-77-93). This is maintained by the Port Wine Institute, a government body that controls the quality of the wine and authorizes its export. At the address given, visitors can taste the different types of port from 10am to 11:30pm Monday to Friday and from 11am to 10:30pm Saturday. Closed Sunday. In this old building, you will also have a view of the Douro. Take bus no. 2, 35, 37, 52, or 56.

The real fado is in Lisbon, but Porto does offer a club or two where you can hear these typical songs and listen to guitar music. **Mal Cozinhado,** near the river at Rua do Outeirinho 13 (tel. 38-13-19), a "casa de fado," is the best. It's a safe bet, as the music is excellent. The so-called Bad Kitchen also serves food, but in case its name frightens you away you can visit for drinks only. A minimum of 3,000$ ($20.10) is imposed, but it can be spent on drinks. A tourist menu costs 3,250$ ($21.80), although it costs 7,000$ ($46.90) to dine à la carte. Hours are Monday to Saturday from 8:30pm to 3am.

While in Porto, you shouldn't miss having coffee in one of the old-time "Brazilian" cafés. The local favorite is the **Majestic Café,** Rua de Santa Catarina 112 (tel. 200-38-87), one of those ornate places where burghers and poets congregated. The wood-and-mirror decor, jasper pillars, and sculpted cherubs over pilasters evoke the craftsmanship of another era. Rows of leather-backed banquettes line both sides of the oblong room, in front of which two rows of round-top tables stand. In the rear is a small garden and a counter where coffee is prepared in the old way. A coffee with milk is served in a large glass placed within a bronze holder, so you won't burn your fingers. The café was opened in 1922 and is still going strong. You can enjoy the best port wine and also order beefsteak and light meals, costing from 1,400$ ($9.40). A beer costs 80$ (55¢) to 120$ (80¢). It is open Monday to Saturday from 8am to 11pm.

Member's Restaurant and Twin's Disco, Rua do Passeio Alegre 1000 (tel. 68-57-40), are found in one of the most fashionable parts of Porto, the Foz. The restaurant is chic and sophisticated, perhaps more so than any other spot in town. After a satisfying meal, you can enjoy action in the disco club, contained in the same three-story building near the beach at the mouth of the Douro. Reservations are recommended for dinner on the top floor, which serves Monday to Saturday nights from 8pm to 3:30am, full meals costing from 6,000$ ($40.20) à la carte or 4,200$ ($28.15) on the tourist menu. Specialties include crabmeat crêpes, fresh fish, and an array of grilled meats prepared in both classic and modern ways. One floor above the restaurant is a pub where an open fireplace and a piano player compete for attention. Alluring and sedate, the pub is open daily from 8pm to 4am. On the street level, the disco is open nightly from 11pm to 4am. Entrance to its black-and-white precincts costs 5,000$ ($33.50) for nonmembers. Once inside you can spend that amount on drinks which costs 900$ ($6.05) each. The restaurant section closes in August.

Drinks (Chequers) Pub, fifth floor, Shopping Center Brasilia, Praça Mouzinho de Albuquerque 113 (tel. 69-73-25), is a watering spot within this massive shopping center. It opens at 1pm but isn't dependent on the whims of shoppers, as it remains open until 2am, long after the last shopper has retreated. The decor is warmly upholstered and modern, and the place is popular with young people, who order beer at 200$ ($1.35) or mixed drinks at 500$ ($3.35). A small band plays on Friday and Saturday nights.

NEARBY BEACHES

A long, busy beach at **Matosinhos,** 5 miles north of Porto, draws large crowds in good weather. The bustling little fishing town lies at the mouth of the River Leça. It is reached by following Avenida da Boavista out of the city. Separated by rocky crags are the beaches of Matosinhos, Leça (which also has swimming pools), Cabo do Mundo, Paraíso, and Angeiras.

In the town, you can visit the **Church of Bom Jesus of Matosinhos,** whose major treasure is an ancient wooden statue of Christ at the end of the high altar. The statue has made the church a place of annual pilgrimages. The 18th-century church has coats-of-arms, pinnacles, and torches on the exterior. Note the wood carvings in the chancel and the coffered ceiling.

5. Espinho

A popular place on the Costa Verde is Espinho, 12 miles south of Porto. This modern beach resort offers many activities and is drawing larger crowds of vacationers each year. The town has a range of shops and restaurants, hotels and campsites in the pinewoods near the sandy beach. Sports enthusiasts will find tennis courts, a bullfighting ring, and an 18-hole golf course.

The big gray **casino** at Espinho (tel. 02/72-02-38), open all year, has a restaurant and nightclub in addition to the gaming tables. Here you can play roulette, French banque, baccarat, and slot machines. International cabaret is offered in the nightclub.

Water sports available here include sailing and rowing on the Paramos Lagoon and surfing in the Atlantic. Cabanas line part of the beach, and there are swimming pools in the Solar Atlântico recreation complex overlooking the ocean.

The **tourist office** is at Angulo das Ruas 6 (tel. 02/72-20-08).

WHERE TO STAY & DINE

The best place to stay in Espinho is the **Hotel Praiagolfe,** Rua 6, 4500 Espinho (tel. 02/72-06-30; fax 02/72-08-88), a totally renovated accommodation offering many modern comforts. It overlooks the sea, and the railway station is about 165 feet away. Each of its 139 bedrooms has a private bath, TV, air conditioning, and direct-dial phone. Doubles rent for 15,500$ ($103.85) daily, and singles go for 12,600$ ($84.40) with breakfast included. A fixed-price lunch or dinner costs from 2,200$ ($14.75). The hotel offers an indoor swimming pool, a squash court, and a health club, as well as a disco. Tennis courts and golf courses are nearby. In summer, the establishment is almost continuously booked, so making advance reservations is imperative. Parking is free. AE, DC, MC, V.

A Nearby Place to Stay & Dine

Hotel Solverde/Granja, Estrada N109, Praia da Granja, 4000 4400 Vila Nova de Gaia (tel. 02/72-66-66; fax 02/72-62-36), is one of the most luxurious hotels in the north of Portugal. Opened in 1989, it stands on the beach of Granja, about 10 miles north of Porto and less than a mile south of Espinho. It is about 20 miles from the Porto airport. There are 177 well-furnished bedrooms, each with air conditioning, TV, and phone. The tariffs are among the lowest in Portugal for a five-star hotel. Singles range from 18,000$ ($120.60) daily, with doubles costing 20,500$ ($137.35), including breakfast. Facilities include a grill and a restaurant, a coffee shop, several bars, a disco, a health club, and three swimming pools with salt water (one of them indoors), four tennis courts, and a heliport.

EXPLORING THE COAST

An underrated stretch of coastal resorts and fishing villages lies between Porto and the southern reaches of the Minho district. The Atlantic waters, however, are likely to be on the chilly side, even in July and August. The communities along this northern highway of the sun are patronized mainly by the Portuguese. In recent years, these resorts have grown tremendously. They are, however, known more to European vacationers than to Americans (the latter still prefer the Algarve).

6. Vila do Conde

Lying at the mouth of the River Ave, the little town of Vila do Conde—with its fortress-guarded sandy beaches, rocky reefs, and charm—has been discovered by summer vacationers. Along the wharfs you may still see piles of rough, hand-hewn timbers used in the building of the sardine fleet, for shipbuilding is a traditional industry of the town, and a few wooden-hulled vessels are still made, some for the local fishing fleet and others for use on the cod banks of Newfoundland.

The women of the town have long engaged in the making of lace using a shuttle, a craft handed down from generation to generation. So revered is this activity that a festival, the Feast of St. John, from June 14 to 24, celebrates it with processions by the lacemakers, called *rendilheiras,* together with the *mordomas,* the women who manage the cottage-industry homes, the latter wearing magnificent chains and other ornaments of gold. Lacemakers parade through the narrow, 16th-century streets of the town. Visitors are welcomed at the lacemaking school on Rua do Lidador, **Escola de Rendas.**

The famous hand-knit and embroidered fishermen's sweaters are also made here. The making of sweets (there is a famous confectionery from convent recipes) is another occupation in the town, providing part of the rich local cuisine.

The **Convent of St. Clare** (Mosteiro de Santa Clara), a large, squat structure sitting fortresslike on a hill, was founded in the 14th century. In the upper rooms you can see relics and paintings garnered through the centuries by the Poor Clares. The building is now a charity home. Simplicity and opulence play against each other in a combination of Gothic and Romanesque styles in the structure. The plain altar of its church offers contrast to the gilded stalls behind the communion grilles and the ornately decorated ceilings. A side chapel contains 14th-century sarcophagi. One is the elaborately carved tomb of Dom Afonso Sanche, founder of the convent, the feet of his effigy resting on a lion. The tomb of his wife, Dona Teresa Martins, topped by a figure dressed in the habit of a Franciscan Tertiary nun, and those of two of their children are also here.

The present monastery was built in the 1700s, accompanied by construction of a 999-arch aqueduct bringing water from Póvoa do Varzim, close by. Part of the water conduit is still visible.

The **Parish Church** (Igreja Matriz), dating from the 16th century, and a pillory can also be seen.

Just 17 miles north of Porto, Vila do Conde is served by a modern highway. The **tourist office** is at Rua 25 de Abril 103 (tel. 02/63-14-72).

WHERE TO STAY
Estalagem do Brasão, Avenida Dr. João Canavarro, 4480 Vila do Conde (tel. 052/63-20-16; fax 052/63-20-28), is styled like a gracious pousada. Located in the center of the village, it's worth considering if only for its lofty dining room. The 30 bedrooms are compact, of contemporary design, with tile baths, phone, TV, minibar, and air conditioning. Rooms have built-in headboards, and comfortable stylish armchairs. The cost, including breakfast, is 5,000$ ($33.50) daily in a single, 7,000$ ($46.90) in a double. A set lunch or dinner goes for 2,400$ ($16.10). The chef turns out three specialties on the à la carte menu—codfish Brasão, beef Brasão, and omelet Brasão. There's a combination bar and disco, plus a private parking lot. Parking is free. AE, DC, MC, V.

WHERE TO DINE
There are a number of beachfront restaurants, of which **Pioneiro,** Avenida Manuel Barros (tel. 63-29-12), is not only one of the best, but one of the largest.

PORTO & ITS ENVIRONS

0 —— 8 mi
N —— 12.7 km

Braga
Rio Ave
Ofir ⑧ ⑨ Fão
N14
Guimaraes
Fate
N13
N206
N101
Póvoa do Varzim ⑦
Vila Nova
Famalicao
⑥
Santo Tirso
Vila do Conde
N105
Lousada
E50
Paredes
Matosinhos ⑤
Valongo
N15
Penafiel
PORTO ④
N106
Rio Tamega
Vila Nova de Gaia ③
Gondomar
D O U R O
N108
Praia da Granja ②
Carvalhos
N222
Sobrado de Paiva
Espinho ①
Raiva
Atlantic Ocean
N1
N321
N109
L I T O R A L
Arouca
S. João de Maeira
Praia do Furadouro
E50

Porto &
Environs

PORTUGAL

LISBON

Espinho ①
Fão ⑨
Matosinhos ⑤
Ofir ⑧
Porto ④
Póvoa do Varzim ⑦
Praia da Granja ②
Vila do Conde ⑥
Vila Nova de Gaia ③

Offering a panoramic view of the water, it can seat up to 265 patrons. Along the esplanade, it specializes in the cookery of the region and fresh shellfish. The chef also prepares roast kid and tripe in the style of Porto. Meals cost 3,000$ ($20.10) to 5,000$ ($33.50), and hours are noon to 3pm and 7 to 10pm. It is closed on Monday and from September 15 to 30. Reservations are necessary. AE, DC, MC, V.

---

7. Póvoa do Varzim

In the big bustling cafés of this town, beneath ornate roofs and gables, skimpily clad tourists idyllically take their afternoon glass of port wine (some have several). Seemingly unaware of them, the *pescadores* (fishermen) of the town go on with their work. Franz Villier wrote: "Here the boat-owners are kings, and morality reigns. Drunkards and debauchees may not aspire to the honour of fishing, unless it happens that the owner is one himself."

The southern part of the town is occupied by the fishing industry, which has remained the major economic support of the town, despite its emergence as a seaside resort. On weekdays (except holidays), the auction of the fishermen's catch is fascinating to watch, the women selling what their men have brought in. Along the beach in the fishermen's quarter, huge piles of seaweed, drying for use as fertilizer, look like little round thatched huts.

Póvoa de Varzim has developed into a leading resort on the Costa Verde. Its broad, sandy north beaches are dotted with white canvas tents known as *toldo*, suspended on two poles. Other entertainment amenities include an Olympic swimming pool, tennis courts, a roller-skating rink, and a gambling casino.

The **casino,** which has a restaurant offering international cuisine, is open all year from 3pm to 3am. The games people play are roulette, French banque, and slot machines. Nightly cabaret with a floor show is presented.

Of interest in the immediate countryside are the "sunken gardens" that farmers have established among the sand dunes. They dug deep into the sand to find moisture for their crops, planting grape vines in the sand heaps above to keep them from sliding down. From these vines, they get a good crop of wine grapes each year, and in the gardens at the bottom they produce many types of vegetables growing right out of the unfriendly sand.

The **tourist office** is at Avenida Mouzinho de Albuquerque 166 (tel. 052/61-46-09). The resort lies 216 miles north of Lisbon and 39 miles north of Porto.

WHERE TO STAY

The most desirable accommodation in town is **Vermar Hotel,** Avenida dos Banhos, 4490 Póvoa do Varzim (tel. 052/61-55-66; fax 052/68-35-77), a highrise with 208 well-furnished bedrooms, each with private bath, air conditioning, and TV. In fact, this is among the leading hotels of Portugal. The service, for example, is among the finest I've encountered in the north. Once you're inside, the heat, noise, and the traffic of this bustling resort seem far away. The hotel is about half a mile from the town center, standing back from a road flanking the shoreline.

A stylish and spacious series of ground-floor public rooms contain unusual ceramic murals, several pieces of sculpture ringed with plants, a bar, and a modern dining room. The comfortably low-slung chairs of one of the reading areas looks out over the hotel's pair of curved swimming pools and the nearby tennis courts. There's even an occasional Portuguese antique scattered amid the greenery and the brown marble of the interior. Facilities include a sauna, a disco, and a children's playground. Each of the bedrooms contains a sun terrace and radio. Singles cost 13,500$ ($90.45) daily, and doubles go for 15,300$ ($102.50), including breakfast. Laundry and room service are available. Parking is free. AE, DC, MC, V.

In the Environs

Estalagem Santo Andre, A-Ver-o-Mar, 4490 Póvoa de Varzim (tel. 052/61-56-66; fax 052/61-58-66). Set at the edge of the sea, amid a flat alluvial landscape that evokes Holland, this angular hacienda-style beach hotel draws a largely Portuguese clientele, especially in summer. Many visitors prefer its isolation and its position among the dunes to the more congested neighborhood of Varzim, whose high-rise buildings are visible across the landscape.

The inn's public rooms are the kind of airy places where open hearths blend well with modern paintings. The elegant restaurant sports a formally dressed staff, windows on three sides, and a view of the sand and the Atlantic. Built in the mid-1970s, the hotel contains 46 bedrooms, each with private bath, color TV, phone, and piped-in music. Each also overlooks the sea and has a private balcony. Suitable for one or two occupants, rooms range from 12,200$ ($81.75) with breakfast included. Three suites rent for 13,800$ ($92.45). If you just want to stop in for a well-prepared meal, averaging 2,800$ ($18.75), you can do so daily from 12:30 to 2:30pm and 7:30 to 9:30pm throughout the year. Laundry service is available, and room service is offered until midnight. Parking is free. AE, DC, MC, V.

WHERE TO DINE

Everybody's favorite restaurant seems to be **Casa dos Frangos II,** Estrada Nacional 13 (tel. 68-18-80), in spite of its location just north of Póvoa de Varzim on the route to Viana do Castelo. Often a very, very busy establishment, it is known for its fish stew, a savory kettle of Neptune's delights. Other regional specialties are served as well, and you can enjoy them in air conditioning from noon to 11pm Tuesday to Sunday. Most people gravitate to the frango no churrasco (barbecued chicken). You can also order shellfish rice. À la carte meals cost 1,800$ ($12.05), and a tourist menu goes for 1,345$ ($9). Reservations are not needed. Closed in October. No credit cards.

SHOPPING

In the tourist office, Avenida Mouzinho de Albuquerque 166 (tel. 61-46-09), you can see a display of local costumes, including the famous fishermen's sweaters, made locally, as well as rag cloaks and rugs. These items are available at shops in the town.

Ourivesaria Gomes, Rua da Junqueira 68 (tel. 62-46-38), is sought out by Portuguese people from all over the country. A 100-foot-long counter gleams with a display of silverware, and you can watch the smiths at work at their benches.

Lindomar, Rua dos Cafés 24 (tel. 62-06-06), sells pottery, fishermen's sweaters, and filigree work, as well as souvenir items.

To perhaps take home something from one of the country's largest collections of wines, liquors, and liqueurs, go to **Garrafeira do Alberto,** Estrada Nacional 13 (tel. 68-26-66), which is open Monday through Saturday from 10am to noon and 2:30 to 8pm.

---

8. Ofir & Fão

Once through the pine forests of **Ofir,** 29 miles north of Porto, you gaze down on a long white sandy spit dotted with windswept dunes and suffused with the sharp cries of sea gulls. The beach is dramatic any time of the year, but exceptional during the summer months. Ofir is considered by many as the best beach resort between Porto and Viana do Castelo. The White Horse Rocks, according to legend, were formed when fiery steeds from the royal stock of King Solomon were wrecked upon the beach.

While the hotels of Ofir offer guests every convenience in a secluded setting, the nearest shops and more local color are found one to 2 miles inland on an estuary of the Cávado River at **Fão,** which dates back to Roman times. Framed by mountain ridges in the background and a river valley, the village is the sleepy destination of all visitors to Ofir. The *sargaceiros* (literally, gatherers of sargasso), with their stout fustian tunics, rake the offshore breakers for the seaweed used in making fertilizer. On the quays you can lunch on sardines off the smoking braziers. At the end of the day you can soothe your overdose of sunshine with a mellow glass of port wine.

The accommodations in these two towns are among the best along the coast north of Porto.

The nearest **tourist office** is at Esposende, Rua 1 de Dezembro (tel. 053/96-13-54).

WHERE TO STAY IN OFIR

Hotel De Ofir, Avenida Raúl de Sousa Martins, Praia de Ofir, 4740 Fão (tel. 053/96-13-83; fax 053/98-18-71), competes with the resort developments on the Algarve. It's a resort unto itself, with a vast playground terrace, two swimming pools (one for children), two tennis courts, and a flagstone terrace bordering soft green lawns. The hotel has a disco and a bowling alley as well.

The hotel is divided into three sections, containing 194 bedrooms. The older central core contains bedrooms furnished in the traditional Portuguese fashion, with reproductions of regional furniture; the adjoining wings are modern. One section is quite luxurious, built motel style right along the dunes, with a row of white tents and a pure sandy beach in full view of the second-floor bedroom balconies. There are rather well-styled public rooms for the evening's activities, but the principal focus is on the wide oceanfront terrace, where guests sunbathe and order refreshments under umbrellas. A dining room with comfortable armchairs opens onto the sea. The bedrooms have a well-conceived sense of style with substantial pieces of furniture placed against pleasantly colored backgrounds. Each room has a private bath and phone, and 50% of them offer TV, minibar, and air conditioning. Singles peak at 12,500$ ($83.75) daily and doubles at 15,500$ ($103.85). Eight suites cost from 18,000$ ($120.60) to 24,000$ ($160.80). Laundry service and baby-sitting are available, and room service is offered 24 hours. Parking is free. AE, DC, MC, V.

Estalagem Parque do Rio, Ofir, 4740 Esposende (tel. 053/96-15-21) is a modern first-class inn on the Cávado River in a pine-covered garden, 5 minutes from the main beach. It has two excellent garden swimming pools with surrounding lawns. The resort, planned for those who stay for more than 1 day, offers a full social life. The amenities include a natural stone fireplace. In the beamed dining room, a snug wood-paneled bar is set against a stone wall, and you'll find several lounges for get-togethers. Each of the 36 bedrooms is well conceived, having a tile bath, a private balcony, a telephone, and central heating. The rate ranges from 7,080$ ($47.45) daily in a single to 10,760$ ($72.10) in a double, including breakfast. Parking is free. AE, DC, MC, V.

THE MINHO DISTRICT

The Minho occupies the northwestern corner of Portugal, and is almost a land unto itself. The district begins some 25 miles north of Porto, stretching to the frontier of Galicia in northwestern Spain. In fact, the Minhotons and the Galicians share many common characteristics.

Granite plateaus undulate across the countryside, broken by the green valleys of the Minho, Ave, Cávado, and Lima rivers. Bountiful granite quarries stand agape amid the hills. From the great church facades in Braga and Guimarães to the humblest of village cottages, this material has been employed for centuries. Green pasturelands contrast sharply with forests filled with cedars and chestnuts.

The small size of the district and the proximity of one town to another makes hamlet-hopping easy. Even the biggest towns—**Viana do Castelo, Guimarães, and Braga**—are provincial. You can sometimes see wooden carts in the streets drawn by pairs of dappled and chocolate-brown oxen. These noble beasts have become subjects for the regional pottery and ceramics for which the Minho, and especially Viana do Castelo, are known.

Religious *festas* are excuses for bringing the hardworking people out into the streets for days of merrymaking and celebrations including folk songs, dances, and, of course, displays of traditional costumes. The young girls and women often wear woolen skirts and gaily decorated aprons in floral or geometric designs. Their bodices are pinned with golden filigree and draped with layers of heart- or cross-shaped pendants.

Historically, the Minho was the spawning ground of Portuguese independence. It was from here that Afonso Henriques, the first king, made his plans to capture the south from the Moors. Battlemented castles along the frontier attest to the former hostilities with Spain, and fortresses, ruined sentinels that once protected the river accesses to the heartland, still stand above the coastal villages.

1. Guimarães

The cradle of Portugal, Guimarães suffers from a benign malady which the French call "embarras de richesses." At the foot of a range of serras, this first capital of Portugal has successfully preserved a medieval atmosphere in its core.

Guimarães is easily reached from Braga (see below), with frequent bus service during the day taking an hour. For bus information for the area call 053/41-12-29. A one-way bus ticket between Braga and Guimarães costs 265$ ($1.80). Trains also run between Braga and Guimarães at the rate of eight per day, taking 1¾ hours and costing 305$ ($2.05) for a one-way ticket.

WHAT TO SEE & DO

Dominating the skyline is the 10th-century **Castle of Guimarães,** where Afonso Henriques, Portugal's first king, was born sometime between 1094 and 1111 (historians disagree). The castle dates from 996. High-pitched crenels top the strategically placed square towers and the looming keep, said to have been the birthplace of Afonso. The view is magnificent. With the church bells ringing in the distance, and roosters crowing early in the morning, the setting seems straight out of the Middle Ages.

Almost in the shadow of the castle is the 12th-century **St. Michael of the Castle,** a squat, rectangular Romanesque church where the liberator was baptized. Nearby is a heroic statue of the mustachioed Afonso, his head helmeted, his figure clad in a suit of armor, sword and shield in hand.

From the keep of the castle you can see the four-winged **Paço dos Duques de Bragança,** Avenida Conde D. Henrique (tel. 053/41-22-73). Constructed in the 15th century, it has been heavily restored. Many critics have dismissed the rebuilt structure with contempt. However, if you're not a purist, you may find a guided tour interesting. Perched on the slope of a hill, the palace possesses a varied assortment of treasures, including a number of portraits such as Catherine of Bragança, who married Charles II of England, the merrie monarch and lover of Nell Gwyn. There are copies of the large Pastrana tapestries depicting scenes from the Portuguese wars in North Africa, scabbards and helmets in the armor room, antiques, Persian hangings, Indian urns, ceramics, and Chinese porcelains. The chapel opens onto the throne chairs of the duke and duchess. Nearby are the double-tiered cloisters. Hours are daily from 10am to 5:30pm. The admission is 300$ ($2); children 10 and under enter free.

By far the most dramatic interior of any church in town belongs to **São Francisco,** on Largo de São Francisco. Entered through a Gothic portal, the spacious interior is faced with Delft-blue and white azulejos. Some of the color tones seem to bathe the whole interior in moonlight. In the transept to the right of the main altar is a miniature re-creation of the living room of a church prelate. With meticulous detail, from the burgundy-colored cardinal's chapeau resting on a wall sconce, to the miniature dog and cat. On the second altar on the right is a polychrome tree of life, representing 12 crowned kings and the Virgin, her hands clasped, her feet resting upon the heads of three cherubs. The palace next door, with its embellished tile facade, may be visited by appointment only (tel. 053/41-22-28).

If you'd like to step into the Middle Ages for an hour or two, take a stroll down **Rua de Santa Maria,** which has remained essentially unchanged, except nowadays you're likely to hear some blaring music, in English no less. Proud town houses, once the residence of the nobility, stand beside humble dwellings. The hand-carved balconies, aged by the years, are most often garnished with iron lanterns, not to mention laundry.

At the end you'll come upon a charming square in the heart of the old town, **Largo da Oliveira** (Olive Tree Square). Seek out an odd chapelette in front of a church. Composed of four ogival arches, it is said to mark the spot where in the 6th

century Wamba was asked to give up the simple toil of working his fields to become the king of the Goths. Thrusting his olive stick into the tilled soil, he declared he would accept only if his stick sprouted leaves. So it did, and he did—or that was the tale told.

The church, called the **Collegiate Church of the Olive Tree** (Igreja Nossa Senhora da Oliveira), was originally a 10th-century temple erected by Mumadona, a Galician countess. It has changed with the centuries: Romanesque giving way to Gothic, and then to more sterile neoclassicism.

In the Romanesque cloister, and in the buildings of the old monastery of the church is the **Museu de Alberto Sampaio,** Largo de Oliveira (no phone). Besides a large silver collection, it displays the tunic worn by João I at the battle of Aljubarrota that decided Portugal's fate. In addition, there are priestly garments, paintings, ceramics, and medieval sculpture. A fresco illustrates a gloating Salome, rapturous over the severed head of John the Baptist. In one of the rooms, there are pieces from a baroque chapel with enormous wood-carved angels bearing torches. The museum is open from 10am to 12:30pm and 2 to 5:30pm; closed Monday and holidays. Admission is 200$ ($1.35); free for children 10 and under.

Museu Martins Sarmento, Rua de Paiva Galvão (tel. 053/41-59-69), situated partially in the Church of St. Dominic (São Domingos) Gothic cloister, has on display artifacts from the prehistoric (Bronze Age to Iron Age) settlements at Sabroso and Briteiros, excavated by the archeologist for whom the museum was named. Hours are 10am to noon and 2 to 5pm; closed Monday. Admission is 200$ ($1.35). Children 12 and under are admitted free.

Guimarães lies 226 miles north of Lisbon, 30 miles northeast of Porto, and 43 miles southwest of Viana do Castelo. The **Guimarães Tourist Office** is at Avenida de Resistência ao Fascismo 83 (tel. 053/41-24-50).

WHERE TO STAY

Its foundations date from the 12th century, but **Pousada de Santa Marinha da Costa,** Estrada de Penha, 4800 Guimarães (tel. 053/51-44-53; fax 053/51-44-59), in its restored version, is arguably the most impressive pousada in Portugal. It was originally built in 1154 as an Augustinian convent by the mother of Afonso Henriques. The baroque facade was added in the 18th century when the soaring interior hallways and sporting fountains were installed as crowning touches. The ornate Manueline church that occupies part of the building still offers mass on Sunday, but the sprawling ex-convent was never outfitted as stylishly as you'll see it today. The property lies at the end of a winding road about 1¼ miles north of the center of town. Signs indicate the direction. You park free in the hilltop courtyard outside the main entrance.

You'd be well advised to explore both the upper hallways and gardens. One of the favorite rooms is a large, beautifully furnished salon. A sunken bar, ringed with blue-and-yellow tiles, serves drinks near the anteroom of the vaulted dining room. At the end of one of the soaring hallways, a fountain bubbles beneath an intricate wooden ceiling, surrounded by an open arcade that encompasses a view of the faraway mountains.

Bedrooms are a pleasing blend of old stonework, modern plasterwork, plush accessories, efficient baths, and a scattering of Portuguese lithographs. Each has a private phone and air conditioning. With breakfast included, the 51 rooms rent for 19,700$ ($132) daily in a single, going up to 22,500$ ($150.75) in a double. Four suites range from 28,700$ ($192.30) to 43,400$ ($290.80). Meals, costing 3,300$ ($22.10) to 4,000$ ($26.80), are served in the dining room daily from 12:30 to 2:30pm and 7:30 to 9:30pm. Laundry service is provided, and room service is available until midnight. AE, DC, MC, V.

Pousada de Santa Maria de Oliveira, Largo de Oliveira, 4800 Guimarães (tel. 053/51-41-57), is now the second pousada in town, quite different in ambience from the previously recommended hotel. It was created when a handful of very old town houses were combined into a single rambling hotel. Many of their original features have been preserved. The street that contains the pousada is so narrow that you'll have to park free somewhere within a well-marked lot about 100 feet from the front entrance. It still has a loyal clientele who value its location on one of the most beautiful medieval squares of Portugal, as well as its distinctive country-inn flavor. This establishment exudes a cozy kind of intimate warmth. The feeling is heightened by the wooden ceilings, tavern bar, and the fireplace inside the warmly decorated restaurant, whose windows look out over the square.

The views from the 13 comfortably efficient bedrooms usually look out past spindle-turned balustrades over the stone-trimmed city around it. Bedrooms contain private bath, TV, and phone. With breakfast included, singles cost 14,300$ ($95.80) daily, while doubles go for 16,200$ ($108.55). Three suites cost from 21,300$ ($142.70). Fixed-price meals in the dining room, served from 12:30 to 2:30pm and 7:30 to 9:30pm, cost 2,750$ ($18.45) to 3,650$ ($24.35). Specialties include a special beef à la pousada, fondue for two persons, and flambé versions of beef and veal. Laundry and baby-sitting can be arranged, and room service is available until 10pm. Parking is free. AE, DC, MC, V.

Fundador Dom Pedro Hotel, Avenida Dom Afonso Henriques 740, 4800 Guimarães (tel. 053/51-37-81; fax 053/51-37-86), stands in the center of the city, offering 63 comfortable rooms, each equipped with phone, private bar, TV, air conditioning, piped-in music, and a minibar. The Dom Pedro, along with the previous recommendations, makes a night in Guimarães a lot more palatable than in days of yore. The hotel isn't necessarily great on style, but it's modern, functional, well kept, and, as a further compensation, offers fine service. Two elevators take you to the rooms, which cost from 13,000$ ($87.10) daily in a double, from 11,500$ ($77.05) in a single, including breakfast. The hotel, inaugurated in 1980, has a penthouse bar with snacks, and there's free private parking. AE, DC, MC, V.

WHERE TO DINE

Many people think **Virabar,** Alameda 25 (tel. 41-41-16), is the best restaurant outside the pousadas. It is certainly one of the most pleasant in town, seating 70 diners in air-conditioned comfort. Alternatively, it warms them with a fireplace in winter. A good local cuisine is served, costing from 3,000$ ($30.10) to 5,200$ ($34.85). Regional wines accompany most menus. Hours are daily from noon to 3pm and 7 to 10pm. Reservations are advised. AE, DC, MC, V.

Nicolino, Largo Toural 106 (tel. 41-20-83), is patronized heavily by locals who enjoy its good fish and meat dishes. Specialties include filetes de pescada (hake filets) and bife a cortador (the house steak). Service is efficient, and meals cost 2,500$ ($16.75) à la carte. A tourist menu goes for 1,600$ ($10.70). Food is dispensed from noon to 3pm and 7 to 11pm daily. Reservations aren't needed. AE, DC, MC, V.

Mirapenha, Estrada de Fafe (tel. 51-65-32), is a typical restaurant just outside the town, a reasonably priced taxi ride's distance. Fine local food is served, an average meal costing from 2,300$ ($15.40) à la carte or 1,600$ ($10.70) on the tourist menu. Specialties include bacalhau (codfish) a Mirapenha, bife a Mirapenha (steak), and other regional dishes. Hours are daily from 12:30 to 2:30pm and 8 to 10pm. Reservations aren't necessary, and the restaurant closes in August. No credit cards.

QUINTAS IN THE ENVIRONS

If you plan to spend a few days exploring the Minho, you may want to anchor in at one of the following quintas, which are among the best accommodations in the area. In restored manors, you can live with Portuguese aristocracy in a style far more luxurious than the usual hotels.

Casa do Ribeiro, S. Cristóvão do Selho, 4800 Guimarães (tel. 053/53-28-81), lies on the road to Pevidem in the village of São Cristóvão do Selho. It is a noble house, whose ancient walls contain valuable details and traces of the elegant and grand style of life that prevailed there. That alone justifies a visit. D. Maria do Carmo Ferraz Pinto rents three rooms which share sitting rooms and a dining room. Each unit has a private bath. Singles cost 8,600$ ($57.60) daily, with doubles costing 9,200$ ($61.65), including breakfast. Guests are welcomed from March to November, and pleasant gardens and a farm surrounded by woods are part of the property. Parking is free. No credit cards.

Paço de São Cipriano, Taboadelo, 4800 Guimarães (tel. 053/48-13-37), is tucked away on the outskirts of Guimarães and can be reached by taxi or private car. It is known for its dignified aristocratic architecture and its beautiful gardens. João Santiago de Sottomayor has five handsomely furnished double rooms with private bath for rent. The charge for a single occupant is 10,500$ ($70.35) daily, with two persons paying 13,400$ ($89.80), including breakfast. The guesthouse has a garden, game room, reading room, and chapel. Parking is free. AE, DC, MC, V.

2. Braga

Nearly everywhere you look in Braga there's a church, a palace, a garden, or a fountain. Known to the Romans as Bracara Augusta, it also resounded to the footsteps of other conquerors—the Suevi, the Visigoths, and the Moors. For centuries it has been an archepiscopal see and a pilgrimage site (the Visigoths are said to have renounced their heresies here).

Braga is 31 miles north of Porto and 228 miles north of Lisbon. The Braga train station is on Largo Estação (tel. 053/22-166). Fourteen trains per day arrive from Porto, taking 1½ hours and costing 370$ ($2.50) for a one-way ticket. Twelve trains per day arrive from Coimbra, taking 4 hours and costing 755$ ($5.05) for a one-way ticket. If you're in the north you can take one of 13 trains from Viana do Castelo, arriving in Braga in 2 hours and costing 520$ ($3.50) for a one-way ticket.

There are also good bus connections. The bus station is at Central de Camionagem (tel. 053/23-433), a few blocks north of the heart of town. Buses arrive every 30 minutes throughout the day from Porto, taking 30 minutes and costing 450$ ($3) for a one-way ticket. From Guimarães there are 11 buses per day, taking 1 hour and costing 300$ ($2). From Lisbon, four buses head north to Braga daily, taking 8 hours and costing 1,200$ ($8.05) for a one-way ticket.

The **Braga Tourist Office** is at Avenida da Liberdade (tel. 053/225-50).

WHAT TO SEE & DO

Inside the town, interest focuses on the **Sé,** the **Cathedral of Braga,** Sé Primaz (tel. 053/233-17). It was built in the 12th century by Count Henry of Burgundy and Dona Teresa. Following his demise, she was chased out of town because of an illicit love affair; but in death Henry and Teresa were reunited in their tombs in the Chapel of Kings.

The Sé didn't escape subsequent decorative and architectural styles. The north triple-arched facade is austere and dominating, with a large stone-laced Roman arch flanked by two smaller Gothic ones. What appear to be the skeletons of cupolas top the facade's dual bell towers, which flank a lofty rooftop niche containing a larger-than-life statue of the Virgin and Child. Under a carved baldachin in the apse is a statue of "Our Lady of the Milk"—that is, the Virgin breast-feeding the infant Jesus Christ. The statue is in the Manueline style—but somehow pious, restrained.

Once inside the structure, you'll believe you've entered one of the darkest citadels of Christendom. However, if you can see them, the interior decorations are profuse, particularly a pair of huge 18th-century organs gilded with baroque decorations. In the 1330 Capela da Glória is the sarcophagus of Archbishop Dom Gonçalo Pereira, with an unctuous expression on his face, carved by order of the prelate himself.

You can visit the **Treasury of the Cathedral** and the **Museum of Sacred Art,** an upstairs repository of Braga's most precious works of art. Included are elaborately carved choir stalls from the 18th century, embroidered vestments from the 16th through the 18th centuries, a 14th-century statue of the Virgin and a Gothic chalice from the same period, plus the custódia of Dom Gaspar de Bragança. This treasury house may be visited daily from 8:30am to 6:30pm from June through September, from 8:30am to 12:30pm and 1:30 to 5:30pm from October through May. In the cloister is a *pietà,* reflecting human grief. Admission is 200$ ($1.35); free for children 10 and under.

Museu dos Biscainhos, Rua dos Biscainhos (tel. 053/276-45), is in Biscainhos Palace, a building from the 17th and 18th centuries that for about 300 years has been the house of a noble family. The original gardens, including the baroque ornamental garden, an orchard, and a kitchen garden are still there. The museum, whose interior has painted and ornamented ceilings and walls with panels of figurative and neoclassic tiles, offers an example of an 18th-century Portuguese aristocratic home. Its exhibition rooms contain collections of Portuguese furniture and pottery, glassware, silverware, textiles and Portuguese, Oriental, and Dutch Delft porcelain. The museum is open from 10am to 12:30pm and 2 to 5:30pm; closed Monday and holidays. Admission is 200$ ($1.35), except on Sunday morning, when it's free. Children 10 and under enter free.

Three miles southeast of Braga is the nationally renowned **Bom Jesus do Monte.** The hilltop pilgrimage site is reached via foot, funicular, or a tree-lined roadway. A double baroque granite staircase dating from the 18th century may look exhausting; but if it's any consolation, pilgrims often climb it on their knees.

Less elaborate than the stairway of Remédios at Lamego (see Chapter 18), the stairs at Bom Jesus (Good Jesus) are nevertheless equally impressive. On the numerous landings are gardens, grottoes, small chapels, sculptures, and allegorical stone figures set in fountains.

Designed by Carlos Amarante in 1811, the hilltop **Chapel of the Miracles** contains many reminders, even anatomical re-creations, of the diseased and sick who have claimed cures. In foggy weather the mountain is enshrouded in mist, but on most days you can walk along the mosaic sidewalks and belvederes, past white-and-black swans, and view the provincial capital at every turn.

WHERE TO STAY

The best hotel in town, **Hotel Turismo Dom Pedro,** Praceta João XXI, Avenida da Liberdade, 4700 Braga (tel. 053/61-22-00; fax 053/61-22-11), is in a 1950s-era 11-story building fronted with flowering gardens and a parking lot. As you face the sprawling building, you'll find its entrance beneath an arcade that also shelters some cafés. Inside, all is air-conditioned calm and comfort. The two-story lobby is set below a spacious lounge bar and restaurant, where you can enjoy a drink and a meal in a warmly burnished wood-paneled ambience. Each of the 32 comfortable bedrooms contain a spacious balcony, whose walls are covered with blue-and-white tiles. There's a rooftop swimming pool and a snack bar on the eighth floor for residents. The bedrooms rent for 9,000$ ($60.30) daily in a single, rising to 13,000$ ($87.10) in a double, including breakfast. Rooms are air conditioned and contain private bath.

The hotel stands on a busy corner of traffic arteries, just outside the most densely populated section of Braga. Parking is free. AE, DC, MC, V.

Hotel João XXI, Avenida João XXI 849, 4700 Braga (tel. 053/221-46; fax 053/61-22-11), is a good stopover hotel in its bracket (second class). On a tree-shaded avenue leading to Bom Jesus do Monte, it stands opposite the leading first-class hotel of Braga. The entry to this modern little six-floor hotel is a salute to the 19th century. The tiny street-floor reception room is decorated à la Louis XVI. The social center of the hotel is the living room–lounge with well-selected furnishings featuring an open fireplace for the nippy months. At the restaurant on the sixth floor you can order breakfast or an evening meal. The latter costs from 3,500$ ($23.45) per person. The bedrooms are in a warm modern decor, furnished with semitraditional pieces, with the accent on neatness and efficiency. Each of the 28 rooms has its own private bath; the singles have double beds, and you get either a shower or tub as you require. Rooms also have phones. The price, including breakfast, for a single is 6,000$ ($40.20) daily, and a double costs 6,200$ ($41.55). Parking is free. AE, DC, MC, V.

The **Hotel Francfort,** Avenida Central 7, 4700 Braga (tel. 053/226-48) is the kind of hotel where you might share the hallway, and possibly the bathroom at the end of the corridor, with a research group from England. The hotel is characterized by its century-old landmark facade, covered with scarlet tiles. It sits across a busy street from one of the flowering gardens of Braga. None of the staff is likely to speak

English. The simply furnished bedrooms are one of the bargains of the town. The hotel rents 18 rooms, of which 15 are without bath. Singles range from 2,500$ ($16.75) without bath nightly, with doubles going for 3,500$ ($23.45) without bath or 5,000$ ($33.50) with bath, including breakfast. There's a simple restaurant in a room adjacent to the ground-floor lobby. Room service is available until midnight. Parking is free. No credit cards.

Nearby Places to Stay at Bom Jesus Do Monte

Many visitors to Braga prefer to stay high on the hill overlooking the city at the sanctuary of Bom Jesus do Monte. If you're interested in views and don't mind mingling with a lot of pilgrims, then you might want to do the same. The views at night are among the most exciting in the north of Portugal.

Hotel do Elevador, Bom Jesus do Monte, 4700 Braga (tel. 053/67-66-11; fax 053/67-66-79), is not unlike a private hillside villa—furnished in a plush manner with antiques, paintings, and objets d'art—except for the 25 bedrooms, which have contemporary appointments. Every unit has a private bath, air conditioning, and phone. The price for one person is 9,900$ ($66.35) daily, 11,300$ ($75.70) in a double, including breakfast. At your table, with a view, the price of a complete luncheon or dinner is around 2,500$ ($16.75). AE, DC, MC, V.

Hotel do Parque, Bom Jesus do Monte, 4700 Braga (tel. 053/67-65-48), is a turn-of-the-century villa that reopened in 1987 as one of the best hotels in the Braga area. Furnished in a high standard traditional style, it offers 49 bedrooms. Each is well-furnished and equipped with all the modern amenities, including a private bath, TV, and radio, as well as air conditioning. Singles rent for 9,900$ ($66.35) daily, with doubles costing 11,300$ ($75.70), including breakfast. Set on elegantly maintained grounds, the hotel serves only breakfast, but lunch or dinner can be ordered at the previously recommended Hotel do Elevador, which is under the same ownership. Guests enjoy drinks in the hotel bar or else relax in a spacious sitting room with an open fireplace. Parking is free. AE, DC, MC, V.

A Nearby Place to Stay East of Braga

The most romantic accommodation is in the environs. At Frades, near Póvoa de Lanhoso, to the east of Braga, the **Casa de Requeixo,** Frades 4830, Póvoa de Lanhoso (tel. 053/63-11-13), is an elegant and massive stone mansion of the 16th and 17th centuries. From a base here, you can explore the area by taking one of several itineraries in either the Minho or the National Park of Peneda-Gêres. Dr. Manuel Artur Norton has four beautifully furnished rooms each with a private bath, large living room, a dining room, and a kitchen. Charges are 10,000$ ($67) daily in a double, 12,000$ ($80.40) in a single, including breakfast. The quinta combines the best qualities of the past with modern-day comfort, and offers both in a bucolic setting. It's also possible to dine here, with typically Portuguese meals costing from 1,500$ ($10.05) to 2,000$ ($13.40), including wine from local vineyards. No credit cards.

WHERE TO DINE

An old stone structure, **O Inácio,** Campo das Hortas 4 (tel. 61-32-25), has rugged walls and hand-hewn beams. In the colder months a fire burns in an open hearth. The decor is rustic, with regional pottery and oxen yokes. Your host will often advise about his Portuguese specialties of the day. Usually these are bacalhau (codfish) a Inácio, papas de sarrabulho (a regional stew), and bife na caçarola. Roast kid is also featured occasionally. Most fish dishes (and they're fresh) are good alternative choices. The dessert surprise is a rum omelet soufflé. Count on spending 2,600$ ($17.40) to 3,500$ ($23.45). The owner has a well-stocked wine cellar, and in my opinion, serves the best cuisine in Braga. Hours are noon to 3pm and 7:30 to 10pm; closed Monday and the first week in October. Reservations are recommended. AE, DC, MC, V.

Helvética, Quinta do Casal-Penoucos (tel. 61-45-65), on the outskirts, is another good bet for change-of-pace fare. It offers not only Portuguese regional dishes, but French cuisine as well. Seating some three dozen diners in air-conditioned comfort, it serves Thursday to Tuesday from noon to 3pm and 7 to 10pm. Regional wines accompany most meals here. À la carte dinners cost 3,000$ ($20.10), although a tourist menu is offered for 2,000$ ($13.40). The restaurant closes in August. No credit cards.

Marisqueira, Rua Castelo 1 (tel. 221-52), as its name suggests, serves some of the best shellfish dishes. A local favorite, it charges from 2,800$ ($18.75) for a fish dinner, unless you order lobster or shrimp. A tourist menu costs 1,600$ ($10.70). The chef also recommends roast kid cooked in the oven and grilled sole. The restaurant is open daily from noon to 3pm and 7 to 10pm. Reservations are not necessary. No credit cards.

---

3. Barcelos

Fourteen miles west of Braga, and 227 miles north of Lisbon, Barcelos is a sprawling river town, resting on a plateau ringed by green hills. Wrought-iron street lanterns glimmer late in the evening long after the market in the open square of **Campo da República** has closed down. Barcelos does not feature any single major attraction, only itself, taken as a whole, with its ensemble of sights and curiosities, and that is more than enough.

Market day, on Thursday, in the fountain-centered Campo da República, almost 450 yards square, is a major event. You can purchase such local handcrafted items as rugs, dyed pillows stuffed with chicken feathers, Portuguese chandeliers, crochet work, local pottery, and, of course, the Barcelos cockerels. These hand-painted earthenware cocks are the most characteristic souvenirs of Portugal and often seem a symbol of the country. The worship of the Barcelos Rooster derives from a legend concerning a Gallego sentenced to hang, despite his protestations of innocence. In a last-hour appeal to the judge (who was having dinner at the time), the condemned man made a bold statement: If his manifestation of innocence were true, the roasted rooster resting on the magistrate's plate would get up and crow. Suddenly, a gloriously scarlet-plumed cockerel rose from the plate, crowing loud and long. The man was acquitted, of course.

The Barcelos bus station is on Avenida Dr. Sidónio Pais. Ten buses a day come here from Braga, taking 30 minutes and costing 315$ ($2.10) for a one-way trip. The train station is on Avenida Alcaides de Faria. Train connections are possible from Braga, at the rate of 13 per day, taking 1¼ hours and costing 250$ ($1.70). Fifteen buses a day come here from Viana do Castelo, taking 1 hour and costing 270$ ($1.80) for a one-way ticket.

The **Barcelos Tourist Office** is at Largo da Porta Nova (tel. 053/81-18-82).

WHAT TO SEE & DO

Opening onto the tree-studded main square are some of the finest buildings in Barcelos. The **Igreja do Terço** from the 18th century resembles a palace more than a church, with a central niche facade topped by finials and a cross. The interior tilework around the baroque altar depicts scenes of monks at labor and a moving rendition of the Last Supper. Also fronting the campo, with its fountain, is the **Hospital da Misericórdia,** a long formal building of the 17th century, behind a spiked fence, taking up almost half a side of the square.

Of more interest, however, is the small octagonal **Temple of Senhor da Cruz,** with a cupola faced with tiles. An upper balustrade, punctuated by large stone finials and a latticed round window about the square portal, provide contrast to the austerity of the walls. The interior is more sumptuous, with crystal, marble, and gilt.

Overlooking the swirling Cávado River are the ruins of the **Palace of the Braganças,** dating from 1786. The original palace site, as well as the town of Barcelos itself, was bestowed on Nuño Álvares by João I as a gift in gratitude for his bravery in the 1385 battle at Aljubarrota.

On the facade is a representation of the palace, re-created in splendor. You can wander through the ruins, which have been turned into an archeological museum, left relatively unguarded and filled with sarcophagi, heralded shields, and an 18th-century tile fountain. A museum of ceramics underneath the palace encapsulates the evolution of that handcraft (look for the blood-red ceramic oxen, with their lyre-shaped horns).

The shadow from the high palace chimney stretches across the old pillory in the courtyard below. The structure even exceeds in height the bell tower of the adjoining **Igreja Matriz.** Fronting the river, this Gothic church contains a baroque altar and an interior whose sides are faced with multicolored tiles. The altar is an array of cherubs, grapes, gold leaf, and birds.

WHERE TO STAY

Not only is the **Albergaria Condes de Barcelos,** Avenida Alcaides de Faria, 4750 Barcelos (tel. 053/81-10-61), the one really good hotel in Barcelos, but it has a delightful pousada style with furnishings made by local artisans. Beds are intricately carved. The 30-bedroom inn, a part of a three-story complex, stands mostly on thick pillars, in the Corbusier manner, and has an inner courtyard. The hotel is just a little way from the center of town, within walking distance of the artisan sales museum. Natural wood paneling is used generously in the dining room, the main lounge, and the bar-lounge. The cost for a double is 8,500$ ($56.95) daily, and singles run 5,500$ ($36.85), including breakfast. Two suites are also rented for 9,000$ ($60.30). Laundry service is available, and room service is offered until midnight. Parking is free. AE, DC, MC, V.

Pensão Residencial Arantes, Avenida da Liberdade 35, 4750 Barcelos (tel. 053/81-13-26), is one of the largest boardinghouses in town. It offers 12 comfortable rooms for 2,800$ ($18.75) to 3,800$ ($25.45) daily in a single, 3,600$ ($24.10) to 4,800$ ($32.15) in a double, with breakfast included. All rooms contain private bath and shower. There is no garage, but free street parking is usually available. No credit cards.

Pensão Residencial Dom Nuno, Avenida Dom Nuno Alvares Pereira 76, 4750 Barcelos (tel. 053/81-50-84; fax 053/81-63-36), is preferred by many visitors over the Albergaria Condes de Barcelos. The Dom Nuno is on a quieter street, about half-way between the tourist zone of the village and the Condes de Barcelos. The rooms are attractively furnished, and everything has a bright, modern look. Each room has a private bath or shower. The rate, with breakfast included, is 5,800$ ($38.85) daily in a double and from 4,000$ ($26.80) in the one single. This is one of the friendliest little inns you are likely to find in this part of Portugal. The hotel has a bar and room service is available until midnight. Parking is free. No credit cards.

WHERE TO DINE

One of the local favorites has long been **Dom António,** Rua Dom António Barroso 87 (tel. 81-22-85). On a pedestrian street in the heart of town, it occupies the ground floor of a town house. Regional food and wine are dispensed here throughout the day from 11:30am to 11pm. Meals cost from 2,500$ ($16.75) à la carte or 1,800$ ($12.05) on a tourist menu. The chef's specialties include frog fish on the spit and grilled veal. Reservations are not necessary. AE, DC, MC, V.

Arantes Restaurant, Avenida da Liberdade 35 (tel. 81-16-45), is one of the largest restaurants in town. It too offers Portuguese cookery, with many regional dishes, serving complete meals for 2,200$ ($14.75). Hours are daily from noon to 3pm and 7 to 10pm. No credit cards.

SHOPPING

Centro do Artesanato de Barcelos, Torre da Porta Nova (tel. 831-35), is a unique shopping center tucked away in a provincial town. But it displays some of the best regional handcrafts at the most compelling prices of any shop I've encountered in the north. It's in an age-old stone tower, opposite the Church of S. da Cruz. On its street level and upper floor is found a wide display of goods.

Outstanding (and worth the trip to Barcelos) is the collection of witty and sophisticated ceramics from the heirs of Rosa Ramalho, who was known as the Grand-ma Moses of Portuguese ceramics. Some of these figures were influenced by Picasso. Ms. Ramalho created figures depicting eerie people, some looking as if they stepped out of a painting by Hieronymus Bosch. She put the heads of wolves on nuns, gave goats six legs, and so forth, all in her muted forest green or butterscotch brown.

In addition, there is a good selection of the ceramic red-combed Barcelos cock-erels, with many variations on the traditional motif in red and black. Local wares include black ceramic candlesticks, earthenware bowls traditionally used for caldo verde, hand-knitted pillows, handmade rugs in bold stripes, and hand-loomed bed-spreads. As a novelty, the rugs and pillows made from flamboyantly dyed chicken feathers may attract you.

---

4. Esposende

Esposende is a beach-resort town between Viana do Castelo, 12½ miles to the north, and Porto, 30 miles to the south. (Esposende lies 228 miles north of Lisbon.) The pines and sand dunes are swept by the Atlantic breezes, and cows graze in near-by pastures. The surrounding countryside is no longer as unspoiled as it used to be, although you'll still see an occasional ox cart in the street. The area has been exten-sively developed, and there's a wide new road running along the seafront. Men and women in fustian clothes and broad-brimmed hats work the vineyards in the foot-hills. The beach is large and fine, lining both sides of the Cávado estuary. Small fishing vessels plod up the river carrying anglers to the bass upstream. Recent arche-ological diggings have revealed the remains of a Roman city and necropolis, but that doesn't seem to have disturbed Esposende in the least.

From Porto, daily buses run to Fão and Esposende, heading for Viana do Caste-lo. The trip from Porto to Esposende takes 1 hour.

The **Esposende Tourist Office** is at Rua 1 de Dezembro (tel. 053/96-13-54).

WHERE TO STAY

A semimodern hotel on the river, **Hotel Sauve Mar,** Avenida Eng. Arantes e Oliveira, 4740 Esposende (tel. 053/96-14-45; fax 053/96-22-49), attracts budgeters who don't want to pay for the superior first-class accommodations at neighboring Ofir and Fão. The lodgings are pleasant and comfortable, and the place has 68 bedrooms, each with private bath, phone, and air conditioning. Singles or doubles rent for 10,500$ ($70.35). It's also possible to visit just for a meal, costing from 2,200$ ($14.75). One reader found the barbecued chicken "the best I've tasted in Portugal." The Sauve Mar is open all year, although you may have the place to yourself off-season. Parking is free. AE, DC, MC, V.

Nélia Hotel, Avenida Valentin Ribeiro, 4740 Esposende (tel. 053/96-12-44), is an inn in the center of the resort. The interior has a regional style. The 42 bed-rooms have wall dressing tables and mirrors, plus hand-carved wooden beds with interwoven leather headboards. Each has a private bath, air conditioning, and phone. Doubles cost 9,650$ ($64.65) daily, and singles go for 9,000$ ($60.30), including breakfast. Parking is free. AE, DC, MC, V.

Estalagem Zende, Estrada Nacional 13, 4740 Esposende (tel. 053/96-18-85; fax 053/96-856), is rated by the government as a luxury inn. It lies on the main road to Viana do Castelo, right outside Esposende. Twenty-five well-maintained bedrooms are rented, each with private bath, TV, phone, and air conditioning. Thir-ty percent of the rooms have minibar. The charge is from 11,000$ ($73.70) daily in a double room, 9,000$ ($60.30) in a single, including breakfast. One suite costs 13,500$ ($90.45). The inn has a good restaurant and cocktail bar, and it serves some of the best food in Esposende. A meal costs from 2,200$ ($14.75) and up. In win-ter, a fire blazes on the hearth. Food is served daily from 12:30 to 3pm and 7:30 to

10pm. The hotel offers a solarium and private free parking. Laundry service is provided, and room service is available until 2am. AE, DC, MC, V.

WHERE TO DINE

Martins dos Frangos, Rua de São, Januário (tel. 96-18-65), is among the best of the independents, and it's reasonable in price, charging from 2,000$ ($13.40) for a complete à la carte meal. A tourist menu costs 1,350$ ($9.05). It's one of the biggest restaurants in the area, seating some 375 diners. It also keeps long hours from 11am to 11pm. Try the barbecued chicken or the grilled meat and fish. The location is on the road between Porto and Viana do Castelo. You'll spot it after the bridge over the Cávado River. Reservations aren't needed. AE, DC, MC, V.

---

5. Viana do Castelo

Viana do Castelo sits between an estuary of the Lima River and a base of rolling hills. This is northern Portugal's city of folklore. The setting is enhanced by an occasional ox cart with wooden wheels clacking along the stone streets. Some of the boatmen of the city, their faces weather-beaten, can be seen near the waterfront, offering to sell visitors a slow cruise along the riverbanks.

But for the best view, scale the **Monte de Santa Luzia,** reached by a funicular ride or, if you have a car, along a twisting road. From the Hotel de Santa Luzia at the summit, a great view unfolds, including Eiffel's bridge spanning the Lima.

Viana do Castelo is noted for its pottery and regional handcrafts (many can be purchased in the Friday market). It is even better known for its regional dress, best seen at the annual festa (the Friday, Saturday, and Sunday nearest to August 20) of Nossa Senhora de Agonia (Our Lady of Agony) when the women wear bright, strident colors of oranges, scarlets, and Prussian blue, with their layers of golden necklaces with heart- and cross-shaped pendants.

WHAT TO SEE & DO

The center of town is **Praça da República,** one of the handsomest squares in Portugal. At its heart is the much-photographed **Chafariz Fountain,** constructed in the 16th century, with water spewing from the mouths of its figures. The most impressive building on the square is the **Misericórdia,** a dour, squat, three-story structure, unique in the country. The lower level is an arcade composed of five austere Roman arches, whereas the two upper levels are ponderous Renaissance balconies. All are crowned by a rooftop crucifix. The four supporting pillars of each level are primitive caryatidlike figures between which are interspersed bright red geraniums in flower boxes. Adjoining the Charity Hospital is a church fronting Rua da Bandeira. Inside is a combination of pictorial tiles made in 1714, ornate baroque altars, a painted ceiling, and wood carvings.

The other building dominating the square in the old **Town Hall,** constructed over an arcade made up of three wide and low Gothic arches. The crenel-topped facade displays a royal coat-of-arms and wrought-iron balcony windows above each arch. Originally the Paços do Concelho, it was constructed during the reign of Manuel I and completed under João III. From the small sidewalk tables and chairs, you can observe the square's activities and sample pastries such as torta de Viana.

Igreja Matriz, down Rua Cabral at Largo do Instituto Histórico do Minho, was begun by João I in 1285 and completed in 1433. Dominated by a large Gothic arched portal, the facade is flanked by two battlemented towers. The interior archway is carved with granite figures, acanthus leaves, and simplistic statuary with moon-shaped faces. The inside is cold but with an excellent trompe l'oeil ceiling.

Viana do Castelo, 44 miles north of Porto and 241 miles north of Lisbon, offers large, sandy beaches, guarded by an age-old fortress standing at the river's mouth.

The Viana do Castelo train station is along Avenida Combatentes (tel. 058/222-94 for information). Here 12 trains per day arrive from Porto, taking 2½ hours and costing 480$ ($32.15) for a one-way ticket. The bus station, Central de

Camionagem, is at the eastern edge of the city (tel. 058/222-94 for information, the same number as for the train station). Nine buses per day arrive from Porto, taking 2 hours and costing 450$ ($3) for a one-way ticket.

The **Viana do Castelo Tourist Office** is at Rua de Hospital Velho (tel. 058226-20).

WHERE TO STAY

Some 3½ miles from the center, **Hotel Santa Luzia,** Monte de Santa Luzia, 4900 Viana do Castelo (tel. 058/221-92), sits on a wooded hillside high above the most congested part of the city. It stands just behind the illuminated dome of the Basilica de Santa Luzia, which was constructed in the neo-Byzantine style. Built in 1895, the hotel has neoclassical details and granite balconies, giving it the appearance of a royal palace, especially when it is floodlit at night. To reach it, you have to negotiate winding cobblestone roads, which, because of their curves, take motorists through a forest. Once at the summit, the view over the city and the river is the best in the region.

In 1986 the hotel was completely renovated, an art deco sheen added to the high-ceilinged public rooms. It has long expanses of glistening marble, stylish accessories from the Jazz Age, a comfortable bar and restaurant, and 55 spacious and comfortably furnished bedrooms arranged along both sides of enormous and echoing hallways. Each room contains a private bath and phone. Singles rent for 15,000$ ($100.50) daily, and doubles go for 16,700$ ($111.90), with breakfast included. The hotel rents three suites for 24,000$ ($160.80). Fixed-price meals in the dining room begin at 3,000$ ($20.10) and are served daily from 12:30 to 3pm and 7:30 to 10pm. There's an outdoor swimming pool sunk into one of the hotel's gardens. Parking is free. AE, DC, MC, V.

Hotel Afonso III, Avenida Dom Afonso III 494, 4900 Viana do Castelo (tel. 058/82-90-01; fax 058/266-38), is a first-class hotel, which opened in 1971. Offering eight floors of comfort, it contains 89 accommodations, each with its own bath and private phone. More than half are graced with a private balcony as well. The attractively furnished rooms rent for 12,000$ ($80.40) daily for one person, increasing to 13,500$ ($90.45) for two, including breakfast. One suite costs 17,500$ ($117.25). The contemporary decor consists mainly of black-and-white marble, with a lobby sheathed with nautically inspired designs crafted from richly grained hardwood. The overall tone is both simple and sophisticated. A restaurant on the seventh floor provides a panoramic view over the Lima River. Meals cost 2,500$ ($16.75). Other facilities include a convention hall, a boîte, and swimming pools. Bar facilities are available. Laundry service is available, as is room service 24 hours a day. Parking is free. AE, DC, MC, V.

Hotel do Parque, Praça da Galiza, 4900 Viana do Castelo (tel. 058/82-86-05; fax 058/82-86-12), is a 124-bedroom four-star hotel at the base of the bridge crossing the Lima River on the edge of town. It has a motel/mini-resort flavor, its lounges overlooking two swimming pools. On its rooftop is a panoramic restaurant, serving regional and international dishes, and adjoining it is a solarium with a refreshment area. Intermixed with the main-floor lounge is an interior winter garden. The lounges have soft leather armchairs. For evening entertainment there is a disco-boîte. Bedrooms are quite contemporary, with plenty of built-in furnishings, tile baths, heating, phone, piped-in music, and balconies. Singles cost 13,900$ ($93.15) daily, and doubles go for 16,900$ ($113.25), with breakfast included. Parking is free. AE, DC, MC, V.

Hotel Viana Sol, Largo Vasco da Gama, 4900 Viana do Castelo (tel. 058/82-89-95). Set behind a dignified granite-and-stucco facade, near a commemorative column and fountain in the center of town, this well-designed hotel opened in 1986. In contrast to its elegantly severe exterior, its spacious public rooms are sheathed with layers of white marble, capped with a mirrored ceiling, and illuminated with a three-tiered atrium lit with a skylight and filled with plants. A lobby bar lies within earshot of a pagoda-shaped fountain. Each of the well-furnished and air-conditioned bedrooms, 65 in all, contains a private bath, TV, and phone. Singles cost 10,000$ ($67) daily, and doubles go for 12,000$ ($80.40). Breakfast is included. There's a restaurant on the premises, plus a swimming pool, health club, tennis courts, and squash courts. Parking is free. AE, DC, MC, V.

Hotel Aliança, Avenida dos Combatentes da Grande Guerra, 4900 Viana do Castelo (tel. 058/82-94-98), was originally built in the 18th century, but its facade was restored in 1962, leaving a streamlined stucco sheathing with granite window trim. It sits on the corner of the town's main street at the edge of the river, within sight of the loading derricks and cranes. This is by no means a stylish or upscale hotel, but its slightly dowdy charm and the sincere concern of the Portuguese family who run it more than compensate. Each of the 26 rooms is likely to have a high ceiling, slightly frayed furniture, and a blandly old-fashioned color scheme, along with accessories from the 1930s. Fifteen of the rooms contain private baths. Singles without bath cost 4,000$ ($26.80); doubles without bath 6,000$ ($40.20), and doubles with bath 8,000$ ($53.60), including breakfast. Laundry service is available, as is room service until midnight. Parking is free. No credit cards.

Residencial Viana Mar, Avenida dos Combatentes da Grande Guerra 215, 4900 Viana do Castelo (tel. 058/82-89-62), is on the main commercial thoroughfare of town behind a granite facade whose severity is relieved by colorful awnings. Inside, near the nondescript reception area, lies a sunken bar. Sixteen of the 36 simple bedrooms contain private baths, and each is filled with basic furnishings. Singles without bath costs 5,000$ ($33.50) daily, and doubles with bath rent for 8,000$ ($53.60), with breakfast included. A few of the hotel's rooms are contained in two nearby annexes. Parking is free. AE, DC, MC, V.

WHERE TO DINE

Like a country house in the center of town, **Os 3 Potes,** Beco dos Fornos 7–9, (tel. 234-32), off Praça da República, was an old bakery before its conversion into one of the best regional restaurants in Viana do Castelo. From Praça da República, head down Rua de Sacadura Cabral (the restaurant is somewhat hard to find, but worth the search). The atmosphere is rustic, and on Friday and Saturday from June to September folk dancing is offered. The Portuguese and international food is good too, but you should have your hotel call in advance to make a reservation. I'd suggest caldo verde to begin, followed by such good-tasting main dishes as codfish 3 Potes, lampreys (eels), or fondue bourguignonne. I always skip dessert, settling for the Irish coffee instead. Expect to spend 2,800$ ($18.75), plus the cost of your wine. The restaurant serves food from noon to 3:30pm and 7pm to midnight Tuesday to Sunday; closed Monday. MC, V.

Hotel do Parque Restaurant, Parque da Galiza (tel. 82-86-05). In addition to offering a good selection of well-prepared Portuguese and international food, this panoramic restaurant in a previously recommended hotel offers a sweeping view of the River Lima and the famous bridge designed by Gustave Eiffel. The restaurant sits on the topmost floor of this hotel, reached via an elevator from the lobby. Amid a modern decor of turquoise and white, you can enjoy full meals costing from 3,200$ ($21.45) and served daily from 12:30 to 2:30pm and 7:30 to 9:30pm. The bill of fare includes cream soups, pork piri-piri, peppersteak, and grilled turbot. Reservations aren't needed. AE, DC, MC, V.

Alambique, Rua Manuel Espregueira 86 (tel. 82-38-94). You enter this typical Portuguese restaurant through a large wine vat. Inside you'll find many of the specialties for which the cooks of northern Portugal are known, including codfish Antiga Viana, *churrasco de porco* (pork), *cabrito* (goat), tripe Porto style, and lampreys bordelaise. One of the chef's most memorable dishes is *feijoada a transmontana,* a bean-and-meat stew. For a beginning, you can order either sopa a alentejana or sopa do mar. A complete meal costs from 4,000$ ($26.80) and is served from noon to 3pm and 7 to 10pm. Reservations aren't needed. AE, DC, MC, V.

Dolce Vita, Rua do Poço 44 (tel. 248-60), as its name suggests, is an Italian eatery and pizzeria. The food is good here, and reasonable in price: meals cost from 2,600$ ($17.40) à la carte or 2,000$ ($13.40) on the tourist menu. Service is from noon to 3pm and 7 to 10pm Tuesday to Sunday. The pizzas are considered the best in town, and you might try some concoctions unfamiliar to you, including one made with bacalhau (codfish). You can also order some good pastas, such as lasagne Dolce Vita. Among more familiar Italian specialties are beef pizzaiola, veal cutlet bolognese, and risotto piemontese. Reservations aren't needed. AE, DC, MC, V.

Túnel, Rua dos Manjovos 3 (tel. 82-21-88), has an excellent regional cuisine. It lies right off Avenida dos Combatantes da Grande Guerra. At certain times you can order quail or roast kid. The fish dishes are usually the best, however. You might begin with a rich-tasting vegetable soup, made with fresh vegetables from the field. Count on spending 1,800$ ($12.05) or more. A five-course tourist menu costs 1,600$ ($10.70). The dining room is on the second floor. You pass through a simple snack bar at ground level. Hours are Sunday to Friday from 11:30am to 2pm and 7 to 10pm. Reservations aren't necessary. AE, DC, MC, V.

SHOPPING

This old city of the Minho district should also be considered if you're on a shopping tour of northern Portugal. Its regional costumes, for example, are the most intricate and colorful in the country. The women are known for their embroidery, and many of their items, such as tablecloths, make ideal gifts. The region also turns out an array of colorful rugs, ceramics, and filigree work.

In Viana do Castelo, the handcrafts of the local artisans can best be viewed by walking along **Avenida dos Combatentes da Grande Guerra** near the water. Here handcraft shops line the street, and you can walk along inspecting the merchandise both inside and out of doors.

A specific shop that merits inspection if you're an antique collector is **O Coche,** Largo Vasco da Gama (tel. 058/82-37-17). Owned by members of the Coelho family, this jumbled and dusty shop attracts professional antiques dealers from as far away as Lisbon and Porto. It stands near the Hotel Viana Sol, and it's considered the most interesting antique store in town. The trio of showrooms usually contains several good-quality reproductions, but most of the pieces are 19th-century originals. The rustic farmhouse implements, such as intricately carved ox yokes, are rapidly becoming collector's items.

QUINTAS IN THE ENVIRONS

The most romantic way to stay in and around Viana do Castelo is not at one of the hotels recommended above, but at one of the antique quintas in the environs. In restored manor houses you can stay with the Portuguese aristocracy. You can make reservations through **Delegação de Turismo de Ponte de Lima,** TURIHAB—Associação Turismo de Habitação, Praça da República, 4990 Ponte de Lima (tel. 058/94-23-35). Payment is made by check sent directly to the owners, with 50% prepayment required when your reservation is made. A minimum stay of 3 nights is required, and bookings must be made at least 3 days before your planned arrival. The environs of Viana do Castelo have some of the most elaborate and stylized quintas and manor houses in all of Portugal. A random sampling of the best ones include the following:

Solar de Cortegaça, Subportela, 4900 Viana do Castelo (tel. 058/97-16-39), lies in the parish of Subportela on the left bank of the Lima River near the road connection (EN203) between Viana do Castelo and Ponte de Lima. Recently restored, it has much modern comfort, but its architectural characteristics have been preserved. The house dates back four centuries. D. Maria Filomena de Abreu Coutinho rents three double rooms with private bath, charging 8,000$ ($53.60) daily for a single, 9,500$ ($63.65) for a double, including breakfast. There are several sitting and dining rooms, as well as a garden. Parking is free. The establishment can only be reached by private car or taxi. No credit cards.

Casa de Requeijo, Lugar de Requeijo, 4970 Arcos de Valdevez (tel. 058/652-72), is a 17th-century house standing behind a crenellated wall typical of the 18th century. It overlooks the River Vez, where you can go boating or canoeing. Catherine and Alberto Alves Pereira rent out three apartments and five double rooms with private baths. A single costs 8,250$ ($55.30) daily, a double 11,000$ ($73.70), including breakfast. Apartments for two are rented for 13,300$ ($89.10). In the main building, guests can use the sitting room with TV, video bar, and piano, or play cards in the living room. Ping-Pong and tennis can be played in the garden, and there's a terrace with a barbecue. Parking is free. AE, DC, MC, V.

At Meadela, just outside Viana do Castelo on the road to Ponte de Lima, **Casa do Ameal,** Rua do Ameal 119, 4900 Viana do Castelo (tel. 058/82-24-03), is the domain of Mrs. Maria Elisa Vilhena. The property has a long aristocratic heritage, and is almost a small museum of valuable costumes collected by the family over the generations. The casa offers two double rooms and four apartments. Doubles are without bath, but the apartments contain facilities. Rates are 8,800$ ($58.95) daily in a double, and 13,500$ ($90.45) in an apartment for four guests. Guests are free to enjoy the gardens and grounds and the swimming pool. Parking is free. No credit cards.

Paço d'Anha, Anha, 4900 Viana do Castelo (tel. 058/32-24-59), has centuries of tradition. A fine example of Portuguese aristocratic architecture, it is in a beautiful setting near the Atlantic coast, with pinewoods, lawns, and vineyards where the fine and fruity Paço d'Anha Vinho Verde white wine is produced. In the annexes next to the main building there are four apartments, each with two double beds, a bath, a sitting room with a fireplace, and a kitchen. The price of one of the apartments is 15,740$ ($105.45) daily for four persons, including breakfast. Each unit has a private bath, phone, TV, and air conditioning. Guests can use the facilities available at the farm, including a tennis court. They can take walks in the surrounding gardens and woods and visit the manor and cellars that date from the 17th century. There's always a supply of wood available for the fireplaces. Parking is free. AE, DC, MC, V.

---

6. Ponte de Lima

Upriver 12 miles from Viana do Castelo is Ponte de Lima, which is exactly what one hopes a Portuguese village will be like. The drive along the north side of the river takes you through grape arbors, pastoral villages, and forests of cedar, pine, and chestnut. Red-cheeked peasants stand silhouetted against moss-green stone walls or cease their toil in the cabbage fields to watch you pass. A modern bridge and motorway lead into the town from upriver, although the original bridge here was built by the Romans.

The town, founded on the site of a Celtic settlement, was developed by the Romans, who named it Forum Limicorum. It was important to them for both river trade and river defense, and the town was enclosed with thick stone walls, guarding the bridge across the Lima. Part of the Roman bridge is still in use, together with its buttressed extension, made under King Dom Pedro in 1355 because of changes in the river's course. Sometimes you'll see women wringing out their clothes along the banks of the river. At certain times of the year the Lima is likely to be dry, but when it is full, anglers often catch trout in its waters.

The Roman wall has been partially destroyed to make room for roads, but you can walk along the top of what's left. An 18th-century fountain graces the town's main square, and houses of that era are still occupied. Ruins of ramparts from the Middle Ages and a solitary keep can be seen, opposite the old bridge.

Go up the stone steps of the keep to visit the **Biblioteca Public Municipal,** founded in the early 18th century. Here archives are rich in historic documents of the town.

Two churches at right angles to one another, **São Francisco** and **Santo António,** have been secularized and now contain museum treasures and artwork, especially handsome wood carving. Of particular interest in São Francisco is a strange image of St. George astride a saddle on a wooden trestle. The museum is open Wednesday to Monday from 10am to noon and 2 to 5:30pm.

The fame of the Ponte de Lima **market** is known throughout Portugal. In a riverside setting, it takes place on alternate Mondays. The sellers show up in regional costumes. On the north side of the bridge is the cattle market where oxen and steers are sold. A little bag nestling between the horns of the animals contains a "magic potion" said to ward off the evil eye. Below the bridge is a place reserved for eating such al fresco delights as roast sardines accompanied by glasses of vinho verde. Taking the riverside walk, you can survey the stalls of various craftspeople, including cobblers, carpenters, and goldsmiths.

The **tourist office** is at Praça da República (tel. 058/94-27-29).

STAYING AT QUINTAS, FARMS & MANORS

In recent years Ponte de Lima has opened a collection of beautiful properties, including manor houses and farms, that makes staying in this northern area reason enough to visit. For information on properties in and around Ponte de Lima, get in touch with **Delegação de Turismo de Ponte de Lima** at the address given above, under "Quintas in the Environs."

Casa de Sabadão, Arcozelo, 4990 Ponte de Lima (tel. 058/94-19-63), lies in the hamlet of Sabadão, in the suburbs of Ponte de Lima. The area is known for its gentle landscape and peaceful atmosphere. This special quinta offers three well-furnished double rooms, each with a private bath. Everything is in good taste, and tourists enjoy the comfort and hospitality. They also share use of the living room and dining room. Rates for two persons range from 8,800$ ($58.95) daily, including breakfast. One apartment for two persons costs 10,000$ ($67). Baby-sitting can be arranged. Facilities include a TV room, garden, and reading room. Parking is free. No credit cards.

Casa de Outeiro, Lugar do Outeiro, Arcozelo, 4990 Ponte de Lima (tel. 058/94-12-06), is a large farm, an 18th-century quinta that provides one of the coziest and most comfortable country homes in the area. Dr. João Gomes de Abreu Lima rents two double with bath and one apartment with kitchen, sitting room, and private bath. The rate for two persons is 8,800$ ($58.95) nightly, including breakfast. An apartment for two rents for 9,500$ ($63.65). Sitting rooms, a dining room, and a large kitchen are provided for guests' use. The location is on the outskirts of Ponte de Lima. Open April through October. Parking is free. No credit cards.

A lovely farm near Ponte de Lima, the **Casa de Antepaco,** Lugar de Antepaco, 4990 Ponte de Lima (tel. 058/94-17-02), is owned by Dr. Francisco de Abreu Lima. It is a beautifully restored stone house that has been modernized with all up-to-date conveniences. The hospitable doctor rents out four double rooms, each with private bath, charging 8,800$ ($58.95) nightly for two persons, including breakfast. Guests have use of a living room with a fireplace, a library, and a kitchen. There is an attractive terrace and a garden opening onto a view of the Lima River. Parking is free. AE, DC, MC, V.

Casa de Abades, São Martinho da Gandara, 4990 Ponte de Lima (tel. 058/94-16-27), is a lovely manor house in a thickly wooded area, most suitable for an idyllic retreat. Mrs. Maria Madalena Graça rents a private apartment with a sitting room and a small kitchenette. Four persons can stay here at a cost of 13,500$ ($90.45) per night. The casa operates only from July through September. Parking is free. No credit cards.

Casa das Torres, Lugar de Arribão, Facha, 4990 Ponte de Lima (tel. 058/94-13-69), run by Manuel Correia Malheiros, is a majestic house, an example of the aristocratic architecture that existed at the time of Dom João V. It overlooks the countryside, and is an ideal location for the gentle life. There is a double room with private bath in the main building, priced at 8,800$ ($58.95) per night, and an annex has an apartment with two double rooms and a private bath, as well as a sitting room and kitchenette, costing four persons 13,500$ ($90.45) daily. Breakfast is included. The estate also has lovely gardens and, as another lure, a swimming pool. It is open May through October. Parking is free. No credit cards.

Casa do Barreiro, Gemieira, 4990 Ponte de Lima (tel. 058/94-81-37). Gaspar Malheir has adopted this 17th-century manor house to accommodate paying guests in luxurious style. The casa offers seven double rooms (five with bath and two without). The charge is 7,700$ ($51.60) daily for two without bath or 8,800$ ($58.95) for two with bath. The place is lavishly decorated with antiques and set in a farming area. On the grounds is a small swimming pool and tennis court. Parking is free. No credit cards.

WHERE TO DINE

A good local independent eatery is **Encanada,** Praça Municipal (tel. 94-11-89). Opening onto an esplanade, it offers some 140 diners a panoramic view of this beautiful countryside. Meals are served daily from noon to 3pm and 7 to 10pm; closed Thursday night. Good regional fare and wines are featured. If you don't like the two chef's specialties—rice cooked in pig's blood and eels with rice, try the special fried pork. An à la carte meal averages 2,500$ ($16.75), with a tourist menu going for 1,800$ ($12.05). Reservations aren't necessary. The restaurant is closed from September 15 to 30. AE, DC, MC, V.

Gaio, Rua Agostinho J. Taveira (tel. 94-12-51), also has its devotees. Even larger, it serves a bountiful Portuguese cuisine, much of it coming from the garden-rich district of the Minho. Meals, costing only 2,000$ ($13.40), are served from noon to 3pm and 7 to 10pm. A tourist menu costs 1,250$ ($8.40). It is closed on Wednesday. Specialties include rice cooked with pig's blood, special fried pork, and bacalhau (codfish) a Gaio. Reservations aren't necessary. Closed in October. AE, DC, MC, V.

---

7. Valença do Minho

The walled battlements of Valença do Minho, 33 miles northeast of Viana do Castelo, stand today as a reminder of ancient hostilities between Portugal and Spain. In fact, when Afonso III ruled Portugal, the forces of Castile and León besieged and destroyed much of Valença do Minho.

A narrow covered gateway across a moat takes you into the center of this walled village of cobblestone streets, ancient stone houses, pots of geraniums, wrought-iron balconies, and old street lanterns. Incorporated into the 13th-century fortress, a government-owned pousada opens onto a belvedere, from which you can enjoy one of the finest views in the Minho. The old cannons are still mounted, no longer seriously, looking down on the **International Bridge** across the Minho to Spain.

On the other side of the river is the Spanish town of **Túy,** once a blood enemy, and now a friendly neighbor town to Valença do Minho. Túy is noted for its narrow, steep streets and walls erected on top of ancient Roman fortifications. The battlemented turrets and towers of the cathedral-fortress have stood guard on the frontier since 1170.

While in Valença do Minho, you may get hooked on the local specialty, lampreys (eels). Order them fresh from the river, served in a spicy pepper sauce.

From Porto, daily trains run to Valença, taking 2½ hours. Buses also run between Porto and Valença, heading for Vigo, across the border in Spain.

The **tourist office** is along Estrada Nacional 13 (tel. 051/233-74).

WHERE TO STAY

An attractive, comfortable place to stay is the **Pousada de São Teotónio,** 4930 Valença do Minho (tel. 051/82-40-20). The Portuguese government tried to outshine its rival counterpart across the border, a Spanish parador. Although lodged among some of Portugal's most unspoiled antiquities, the pousada is contemporary in concept. It's built villa-fashion on several levels, with an entrance portico connecting the main building with an annex. Most of the lounges and 15 bedrooms not only have a view of the river and Túy, but also open onto a courtyard with a lawn and reflecting pool.

The public rooms are spacious, flowing one into another, containing wooden ceilings, tile floors, and various retreat nooks. The lounge has a wide stone fireplace, a 15-foot plank coffee table, and hand-loomed rugs. Many of the bedrooms have balconies and all of them are equipped with private baths. Single rooms cost 15,500$ ($103.85) daily; doubles, 17,900$ ($119.95), including breakfast. If you stop only for a meal (and many do), the cost ranges from 2,750$ ($18.45) to 3,650$ ($24.45) for a five-course table d'hôte luncheon or dinner. The helpings are bountiful and the dishes good, if you like regional cooking. The wooden-ceiling dining rooms takes full advantage of the view of the river and Spain. Laundry service is provided, and room service is available until 10pm. Parking is free. AE, DC, MC, V.

WHERE TO DINE

Outside of the pousada, your best bet for a good meal is **Arcádia,** Estrada Nacional 13, Tuído (tel. 233-46), which does good grills—both fish and meat—along with many regional Portuguese specialties. It also has a good wine cellar. Meals cost from 1,600$ ($10.70), and service is Friday to Wednesday from noon to 3pm and 7 to 10pm. You can enjoy an apéritif in the bar before being shown to your table. In winter the place is warmed by a fireplace. Reservations aren't needed. AE, DC, MC, V.

---

8. Pousadas of the Minho

Many visitors consider pousada-hopping the most rewarding way of exploring Portugal. Every government-owned inn lies in a characteristic region, as well as a special scenic spot. (The first *pousada,* a place to rest, was founded in the 12th century, offering pilgrims a roof, a bed, and a candle. That hospitality today includes all the amenities of modern comfort.)

Pousada de São Bento, Caniçada do Minho, 4850 Vieira do Minho (tel. 053/64-71-90), overlooks the winding road that runs between Caldeirinhas and Pontes do Rio Caldo. The pousada was originally built as the opulent private villa of an engineer who supervised the construction of a nearby dam. It was later enlarged. Undeniably romantic, it has stone walls and smallish windows that remind some guests of an alpine chalet, except for the masses of vines trailing across its facade. Inside, a cathedral ceiling is supported by decoratively massive wooden trusses, creating a kind of canopy over a pair of granite fireplaces.

This pousada has 30 bedrooms, each with bath. Singles rent for 15,500$ ($103.85) daily, and doubles go for 17,900$ ($119.95), including breakfast. Meals, served from 12:30 to 2:30pm and 7:30 to 9:30pm, cost 2,750$ ($18.45) to 3,650$ ($24.45). A magnet with guests is the swimming pool. The landscape is so beautiful, however, that you may prefer to make the pousada a base from which to explore. This area abounds in luxuriant vegetation and rippling waterfalls, and there's lots of game in the wooded areas. The park of Peneda-Gerês and the ancient stone cloisters of Santa Maria do Bouro and Our Lady of Abadia are easy sightseeing targets. The pousada, on the Braga-Gerês highway, is 16 miles from Vieria do Minho at Caniçada do Minho and about 18½ miles east of Braga. Laundry service is provided, and room service is available until 10pm. Parking is free. AE, DC, MC, V.

Pousada de Dom Diniz, Praça da Liberdade, 4920 Vila Nova de Cerveira (tel. 051/79-56-01), lies within the remains of an ancient fortress, in the northwestern town of Vila Nova de Cerveira, close to the Minho River and the Spanish border. The history of this government-run hotel goes back to 1321 when Dom Diniz granted the castle its charter. Parts of the original interior of the castle have been incorporated into the pousada, whose rooms are in seven buildings, all within crenellated ramparts entered through a massive arched gate reached by going up the hill from the main square of the village, site of the reception area. It contains 26 rooms and 3 suites; 11 of the units have private patios. Each room has a private bath, TV, phone, and air conditioning. Some of the rooms look out over the cobblestone streets of the village. The accommodations are pleasantly decorated with reproductions of old Minho furniture. You can take your apéritif on the stone terrace with a view of the countryside. The rates range from 22,500$ ($150.75) daily for a double with breakfast, from 19,700$ ($132) for a single. Suites range from 28,700$ ($192.30) to 43,300$ ($290.10). Food is served daily from 12:30 to 3pm and 7:30 to 9:30pm. The pousada has a bar and a disco. Laundry service is provided, and room service is available until midnight. Parking is free. AE, DC, MC, V.

TRÁS-OS-MONTES

The far northeastern province of Portugal is a wild, rugged land—Trás-os-Montes, a name meaning "beyond the mountains." Extending from south of the Upper Douro at Lamego, the province stretches north to Spain. Vila Real is its capital. The high plateau, lying between the mountain ranges of Marão and Gerês, is broken up by rocky crests as well as deep valleys where most of the population lives, usually in houses constructed from shale or granite. Much of the plateau is arid land, but swift rivers and their tributaries supply ample water for the use of the people, and some of the valleys have fertile farmland. The Tâmega River Valley is known for the thermal springs found there as far back as Roman days.

This land is rich in history and tradition, offering the visitor a new world to discover, from pre-Roman castles to prehistoric dolmens and cromlechs to pillories and interesting old churches. The inhabitants of this region are of Celtic descent, and most speak a dialect of Galician.

You can reach Trás-os-Montes by train from Porto to Régua, not far from Lamego, which serves as a gateway into the province in the Pais do Vinho, where grapes from vineyards on the terraced hills provide the wines that are credited to Porto. Lamego is actually in the province of Beira Alta. You can drive through this land of splendid savagery, but don't expect superhighways.

1. Amarante

The little town of Amarante is not actually in Trás-os-Montes, but lies along the border of that province. It serves as a good gateway to this little-known and underexplored region. The town lies north of the Upper Douro Valley on the Tâmega River as it flows southward to join the Douro east of Porto, which is 40 miles from Amarante. Amarante is 30 miles west of Vila Real, the capital of Trás-os-Montes, and 231 miles northeast of Lisbon.

From the Ponte de Amarante, built over the Tâmega in 1790, you can see wooden balconies that extend out over the river, with willow trees drooping on the banks—a lovely and romantic setting. At the entrance to the bridge sits the former **Convent of St. Gonçalo** with a tile-faced dome.

Inside is a theatrical welter of baroque decoration. The altarpiece is a cherubic romp, with silver-haired cherubs frolicking all over the columns and ceiling. The pillars on each side of the altar are festooned with wreaths and bouquets of flowers, and the supporting columns have bizarre hermaphroditic figures costumed in black, gold, and scarlet. Notable is the baroque organ, held up by a gilded merman.

The convent contains the tomb of St. Gonçalo, the patron saint of marriages and unmarried women. His feast day is on the first weekend of June, and it is the custom for unmarried women and bachelors to exchange cakes baked in the shape of phalluses on that day. It seems that the vestige of a pagan fertility rite has survived, or else St. Gonçalo himself is having a final chuckle.

In the town of Livração, an hour east of Porto by train, you can make connections on the narrow-gauge Tâmega rail line which will take you up to Amarante in 30 minutes or so. This antiquated line follows the course of the Rio Tâmega north, climbing into the Serra do Marão. It is possible to make nine rail connections from Livração to Amarante along this old line. There are also four daily bus connections from Livração to Amarante.

The **Amarante Tourist Office** is at Rua Cañdido dos Reis (tel. 055/42-29-80).

WHERE TO STAY

If you'd prefer to stay in Amarante, the best choice is the **Hotel Navarras,** Rua António Carneiro, 4600 Amarante (tel. 055/42-40-36; fax 055/42-58-91). Rooms are usually available here throughout the year, except during the feast of St. Gonçalo. The hotel rents 61 comfortably furnished rooms, which for the most part are large, well kept, and furnished in a contemporary style. Each has a private bath, TV, phone, and air conditioning. The single rate is 7,000$ ($46.90) daily, rising to 8,350$ ($55.95) in a double, including breakfast. Many of the bedrooms also open onto a terrace. There is also a most welcome swimming pool. The hotel has a restaurant and bar, specializing in regional Portuguese cuisine, with meals costing from 2,200$ ($14.75). Parking is free. AE, DC, MC, V.

On a remote mountain pass, **Pousada de São Gonçalo,** Ansiães Serra do Marão, 4600 Amarante (tel. 055/46-11-23), 16 miles from Amarante along Route N15, is almost snowbound in winter, but a sun trap in summer. A modern version of a roadside inn, it is a retreat. The approach, between Amarante and Vila Real, is forlorn, with no signs of life. The place is called Bela Vista, near the Alto de Espinho. Pinewoods grow for miles around in every direction.

The pousada is furnished in the regional style, more like a hilltop home than an inn. Antique console tables, high wooden chests, tile floors, country-style armchairs, an open fireplace, and statuary add to that effect. Only 15 rooms with bath are available, so it's wise to make reservations. The rooms are furnished with a few antiques interspersed with passable reproductions. A single rents for 9,600$ ($64.30) daily and a double for 10,000$ ($67), including breakfast.

Meals are hearty and filling. A complete table d'hôte lunch or dinner costs from 2,740$ ($18.35) to 3,250$ ($21.80) and includes homemade bread and a ceramic pitcher of wine. You may want to try cabbage soup, trout stuffed with smoked ham, or kid stew serrana style, or roasted until it's brown and crispy. Desserts are the special pride of the cook: perhaps you'll receive a creamy layer cake studded with almonds that looks just like a porcupine. Food is served daily from 12:30 to 3pm and 7:30 to 9:30pm. Laundry service and baby-sitting are provided, and room service is available until 10pm. Parking is free. AE, DC, MC, V.

WHERE TO DINE

Within the town, the best food is served at **Zé da Calçada,** Rua 31 de Janeiro (tel. 42-20-23). In fact, many discerning local patrons prefer this 60-seat place to the cookery at the pousada. A four-star restaurant, Zé da Calçada offers good home-cooking and specialties from various regions of Portugal. Naturally, it has a superb collection of the best wines of this vineyard-rich part of Portugal. Meals cost from

5,500$ ($36.85) and are served daily from noon to 3:30pm and 5 to 10pm. The decoration is in the regional style, and there is a pleasant terrace in summer, a fireplace in winter. Reservations are recommended. No credit cards.

---

2. Lamego

This old bishopric on the wooded slopes of Mount Penude is a good example of baroque harmony. Many of its public and private buildings (even the town cinema) show this unifying style, an example of community planning rarely achieved. The main square has a public garden and adjoins a leisurely, tree-lined esplanade, where the denizens of Lamego promenade in the evenings. Behind the statue of Bishop Dom Miguel is his former palace, converted into a museum displaying sculpture and French tapestries.

Lamego lies 229 miles northeast of Lisbon, 25 miles south of Vila Real, and 44 miles north of Viseu.

Lamego can be reached by bus. A RN (national express bus) leaves Viseu daily at 8:10am, and there is also bus service from Guarda on Monday through Friday, leaving Guarda for Lamego at 6:10am and 1:35pm.

The **Lamego Tourist Office** is at Avenida Visconde Guedes Teixeira (tel. 054/620-05).

WHAT TO SEE & DO

The **Cathedral of Lamego (Sé)** was originally built in the Romanesque style, then overlaid with Gothic and baroque ornamentation. The ceilings are frescoed, but in dire need of repair. Adjoining is a Renaissance cloister, with a chapel containing a large baroque altar. A second chapel contains pictorial tiles illustrating a touching scene of children bathing in a tub.

Crowning a forested serra, overlooking Lamego, is the well-known 18th-century mecca of **Nossa Senhora dos Remédios** (Our Lady of the Cures). Leading to it is an elegant baroque stairway, the Spanish Steps of Lamego, broken by nine fountain-centered and profusely decorated landings. The faithful scale the steps on their knees, as they do on Rome's Scala Santa (Holy Steps).

The granite balustrade is topped with various resplendent finials and statues in Roman battle dress, vases and urns, spheres and niches, plus some saccharine pictorial tiles. The fountains are interesting; one is decorated with four grotesques, each spouting water from its mouth.

The ruins of a 12th-century fortified castle stand on a hill opposite the one occupied by the sanctuary.

Museu de Lamego, Largo de Camões (tel. 054/62-008), fills more than 30 rooms of the old Bishop's Palace. Of special note are five paintings on wood from the early 16th century, from the altarpiece of the cathedral, and the Brussels tapestries, also from the 16th century. You'll see lots of reminders of the baroque period in the museum, including two chapels of gilded, carved wood upstairs and examples of ecclesiastical sculpture from the Middle Ages to the 17th century, plus a baroque chapel, on the ground floor. Chinese porcelains and paintings on silk, azulejos, pottery, furniture, paintings, sculpture, and gold and silver religious objects are also displayed. The museum has guided tours from 10am to 12:30pm and 2 to 5pm Tuesday to Sunday. Admission is 200$ ($1.35); free on Sunday. Children 10 and under are admitted free.

You can visit the **Chapel of the Exile** (Igreja do Desterro) by asking for the key at Rua Cardoso Avelino 126, right across the street. The 1640 chapel has 17th-century azulejos and 18th-century carved, gilded wood. The ceiling, with paintings of the life of Christ, is particularly noteworthy.

WHERE TO STAY

Near the commercial outskirts of the town, **Albergaria do Cerrado,** Lugar do Cerrado, Lamego, 5100 Viseu (tel. 054/631-64), lies behind a yellow balconied

facade. By almost anyone's standards, this is considered the most up-to-date and comfortable hotel in town. It is certainly the most convenient and the best accessorized, but not necessarily the most charming. Popular with business travelers, it contains 30 bedrooms, each outfitted with a predictable international style, including a private bath, phone, balcony, and piped-in music. With breakfast included, singles cost 9,500$ ($63.65) daily; doubles 11,500$ ($77.05). Parking is free. AE, DC, MC, V.

Hotel Parque, Santuário de Nossa Senhora dos Remédios, 5100 Lamego (tel. 054/621-05). Its severe dignity and pristine facade hint at its origins early in the 20th century as the monastery connected to the Church of Nossa Senhora dos Remédios, a few steps away. In the late 1960s it was converted into a 38-room hotel, with all units renovated in 1984. No other hotel in Lamego affords visitors such a desirable location, next to one of the finest baroque ensembles in north Portugal. If you select this hotel, allow enough time for a leisurely promenade down the lushly ornate stairs leading to the center of town, 15 pedestrian minutes away. The experience is well worth the effort.

Each room at the hotel contains a private bath and phone, and comes with breakfast included in the price. Singles cost 6,100$ ($40.85) daily, and doubles go for 7,500$ ($50.25). Don't overlook the Parque's dining room as a luncheon or dinner possibility. Meals, costing from 2,500$ ($16.75), are served daily from 12:30 to 2pm and 7:30 to 9:30pm. Parking is free. AE, DC, MC, V.

WHERE TO DINE

Outside the hotels, Lamego has several places at which you can eat. One of the most convenient, because of its hours, is **Welwitschia,** Rua da Columela 24 (tel. 632-53). Good regional cookery is the feature here, and the chef is rightly proud of his fresh shellfish, which he prepares in many different ways. Specialties include Valencia rice and beef with mushrooms. You can patronize either the restaurant, ordering full-course meals, or use Welwitschia as a snack bar. Charging from 2,200$ ($14.75) for a meal, it serves from 10am to 10pm daily except Sunday in winter. Reservations are necessary. No credit cards.

Turisêrra, Serra de Meadas (tel. 633-80), is the choice of if you want not only more elaborate cooking but a panoramic view. Local food and regional specialties from throughout Portugal are served here Tuesday to Sunday from noon to 3pm and 7 to 10pm. Meals cost from 2,000$ ($13.40) à la carte, or 1,300$ ($8.70) from the tourist menu. Specialties include bacalhau (codfish) Turisêrra and cabrito assado (roast kid). Reservations aren't needed. AE, DC, MC, V.

---

3. Vila Real

The capital of Trás-os-Montes is a lively little town 70 miles east of Porto, built on a hilly plateau in the foothills of the Serra do Marão. Some parts of the town are linked with others by bridges across the ravines. Gorges cut by the Corgo and Cabril rivers, which flow together here, can be seen from a terrace high above, where a castle once stood. The lookout is reached in a direct line from the cemetery. From this vicinity, you can also see houses overhanging the ravine of the Corgo.

The **Cathedral (Sé) of São Domingos** is in the main square. The Gothic building has a high altar with gold reredos.

St. Peter's Church (Igreja São Pedro), just off the main street of the town, Avenida Carvalho Araujo, has a handsome ceiling of high relief, carved, gilded paneling, plus a chancel lined with colorful azulejos.

The **House of Diogo Cão,** Avenida Carvalho Araujo 19, is reputedly the birthplace of the navigator who discovered the Congo River in Africa in 1482. The exterior of the house was altered and is now in the 16th-century Italian Renaissance style.

The **Town Hall** (Câmera Municipal; tel. 059/228-19), also on the main street, has an Italian Renaissance–style stone staircase. In front stands a lantern pillory.

If you happen to be in the area toward the end of June, you may get to purchase some of the fine black pottery of the region, which is sold at St. Peter's Fair.

Five trains per day connect Porto with Vila Real, going via Régua. Trip time is 3 hours, and a one-way ticket costs 655$ ($4.40). The train station lies at the end of Avenida 5 de Outubro (tel. 059/221-93 for information). The bus station is along Rua Dom Pedro de Castro (tel. 059/222-47). Here three buses per day make the 3½ hour trip from Porto, costing 615$ ($4.10) for a one-way ticket. There are two buses which make the 7-hour trip from Lisbon, a one-way ticket costing 1,750$ ($11.75).

For information about Vila Real and the surrounding country, stop at the **Tourist Center (Turismo)**, Avenida Carvalho Araujo 69 (tel. 059/228-19), which is in an interesting old building.

WHERE TO STAY

The best place to stay is a four-star hotel, **Albergaria Cabanelas**, Rua Dom Pedro de Castro, 5000 Vila Real (tel. 059/231-53; fax 059/741-18). It is a modern hotel, with a desirable "heart of town" location, and it has an elevator as well as a polite staff. The 24 rooms of the inn are simply furnished but comfortable, all well maintained. Each has a private bath, minibar, and phone. Singles cost 5,600$ ($37.50) daily and doubles 8,500$ ($56.95), including breakfast. You can also enjoy a meal based on regional cuisine (see below). Laundry service and baby-sitting are available, and room service is offered 24 hours. Parking is free. AE, DC, MC, V.

Its chief competitor is the even more modern **Hotel Miracorgo**, Avenida 1° de Maio 76, 5000 Vila Real (tel. 059/250-01), in a commercial section of the city. A tall, somewhat impersonal structure, this hotel offers a total of 56 single and double bedrooms that contain private bath, phone, and TV. Singles rent for 6,600$ ($44.20) daily, and doubles cost 8,700$ ($58.30), including breakfast. Rooms are color coordinated and simply furnished in a modern idiom. On the premises are an indoor swimming pool and a health club. Many of the upper rooms open onto panoramic views. Other facilities include a sauna and a solarium. Laundry service is available, and room service is 24 hours. Parking is free. AE, DC, MC, V.

WHERE TO DINE

Restaurante O Espadeiro, Avenida Almeida Lucena (tel. 223-02), is the finest independent restaurant in town. In business since 1969, it adopted the trade name O Espadeiro (the swordsman) after a brave transmontano warrior, Lourenço Viegas. You climb a flight of stairs to this modern, well-decorated restaurant, which has a large sunny terrace and a bar, opening onto a good view. Its chefs are proud of their region and its foodstuffs. They feature such fare as bundles of stewed tripe, roast kid from the oven, and a delectable grilled trout stuffed with a Parma-style ham. However, many diners come here just to sample that local version of a great Brazilian dish, *feijoada à transmontana*, a savory, well-seasoned and spiced stew with beans and various types of meats. Meals cost from 2,500$ ($16.75) à la carte or else 2,000$ ($13.40) on the tourist menu. Hours are daily from noon to 3pm and 7 to 11pm. Reservations aren't needed. AE, DC, MC, V.

An alternative choice in a previously recommended hotel is **Cabanelas**, Rua Dom Pedro de Castro (tel. 231-53), which has good food and wine, and dispenses both with good service. Meals costing from 2,500$ ($16.75), are served daily from noon to 3pm and 7:30 to 10pm. Provincial cookery is the style here, and you get a good selection of meat and fresh fish. You can sample such dishes as grilled pork, grilled shrimp, or a well-flavored fish stew, perhaps beginning with a caldo verde. The dining room lies one floor above street level. Parking is available. Reservations aren't needed. AE, DC, MC, V.

MATEUS

About 2 miles east of Vila Real, on the road to Sabrosa, is the village of Mateus where the quinta of the Conde de Vila Real is centered. The grapes of the original Mateus rosé wine were grown in the vineyards here.

Fundação da Casa de Mateus, Solar de Mateus (tel. 059/23-121), dates from the early 18th century. Although the facade looks like the picture on the Mateus rosé bottles, the house, a creation of the architect Niccolò Nasoni, is better than the picture. The solar now belongs to a cultural organization, the Foundation of the Casa de Mateus, internationally known for its activity in the fields of music and plastic arts, plus international seminars. In summer, hours are from 9am to 1pm and 2 to 6pm Monday to Saturday. In winter tours are given Monday to Saturday from 9am to noon and 1 to 4pm. The gardens are among the most beautiful of Europe. Seven buses a day go from Vila Real to Mateus and return, costing 130$ (85¢) for a one-way ticket. To visit the palace and gardens costs 600$ ($4) per person. The gardens only can be visited for 500$ ($3.35). Everybody pays the same except children 5 and under.

4. Alijó

The village dates back to the year 1226, and those who it seek out, 27 miles east of Vila Real and 97 miles east of Porto, will be rewarded. It has a heritage rich in pre-Roman fortifications and antiquities. In its midst is a giant plane tree, planted in 1856, whose trunk measures almost 20 feet in circumference.

In the heart of the Douro wine-producing region of Portugal, Alijó is a pleasant stop for the visitor in search of rural charm and a delightful sampling of regional Portuguese food and wine.

A daily bus runs between Alijó and Vila Real (see above). The nearest tourist office is in Vila Real.

WHERE TO STAY & DINE

Within the town, **Pousada do Barão de Forrester,** Rua José Rufino, 5070 Alijó (tel. 059/954-67), will give you a taste of Trasmontanian hospitality. It's a very pleasant pousada with only 11 bedrooms, all with bath and phone, along with comfortable lounges and a wood-beamed restaurant with two terraces (one closed in, the other open). There are two bars, and if you're here on a cold wintry day, the cozy fireplace is a welcome sight. The inn is decorated in regional style, and in keeping with the character of the area there is a vineyard as well as a garden, a swimming pool (one of the bars is beside it), and a tennis court. The rates at the pousada run from 12,000$ ($80.40) daily in a double, from 10,500$ ($70.35) in a single, with breakfast included. A three-course country dinner can be enjoyed for 2,470$ ($16.55) to 3,250$ ($21.80). Food is served daily from noon to 3pm and 7:30 to 9:30pm.

The pousada is dedicated to a Scotsman, Joseph James Forrester, who first opened the Douro River to navigation, and was given the title of "Barão," or baron, by Fernando II in recognition of his contribution to the wine trade. Laundry service is available, as is room service until 10pm. Parking is free. AE, DC, MC, V.

5. Vidago & Pedras Salgadas

In the heart of the northwest section of Trás-os-Montes are two little spa towns —Vidago, 27 miles north of Vila Real, and Pedras Salgadas, 19 miles north of Vila Real. The valley in which they are situated, 1,000 to 2,000 feet above sea level, is a favorite vacation spot for the Portuguese that became popular in the country's days of empire. Today the spa region has a mild climate with many sunny days, and many recreational facilities are offered in both places.

Vidago, as a hot-spring resort, offers a modern swimming pool with a bar, two clay tennis courts, a mountain golf course with nine holes and pro golf instruction, horseback riding, gambling, discos, boating on a large lake, a children's playground, and a beach about 3 miles away on the Tâmega River, where food and drink are available. There is a large park where visitors can stroll along paths shaded by tall trees.

It's a short drive from Vidago to Pedras Salgadas. Along the way you might like to turn off to see a Roman road and bridge and the tiny mill for grinding corn.

At Pedras Salgadas, you can take the waters of the spa at the springhouses or just go to look at these ornate facilities with their doors and windows of intricate wrought iron. The little spa town has discos, a casino, and swimming, plus tennis courts, mini-golf, horseback riding, boating, and amusements for children. Many of the Portuguese who come here for holidays like to camp out. Hiking in the surrounding country is a popular pursuit, and you can even head for the Minheu Mountain, a high day's climb, if you wish.

Restoration is being carried out on turn-of-the-century hotels in the spa region, which is gaining in popularity with many European tourists in addition to the Portuguese.

You can catch a daily bus from Vila Real to Vidago. Ask in Vila Real at the tourist office (see above) for any information they have.

WHERE TO STAY

Palace Hotel, Vidago, 5455 Pedras Salgadas (tel. 076/973-56; fax 076/97-359), stands in the heart of this little spa village. Built in the grand manner in 1910, this sprawling pink-and-white hotel is one of Portugal's most vivid architectural symbols of the belle époque. Set within acres of gardens and forest, it opens all its soaring public rooms in summer, when Iberian breezes carry scents of flowers past one of the most elegant horseshoe-shaped staircases in the north. In winter, only the modern granite-sided annex, known as the Estalagem, is open, with a bar and Wolf's Restaurant, considered the best in the area, serving daily in both summer and winter from 12:30 to 2pm and 7:30 to 9pm, and offering meals costing from 2,800$ ($18.75). In summer, the main hotel is open, as well as all the annexes and the Edwardian-era main dining room. Singles cost 11,100$ ($74.35) to 13,500$ ($90.45) daily, and doubles go for 14,000$ ($93.80) to 17,000$ ($113.90), including breakfast. The rooms in the modern inn are more expensive and considered more desirable, but tradition-minded guests may prefer the more vintage accommodations. All 68 rooms have private bath, phone, and minibar. As in any turn-of-the-century hotel, the quality, size, and exposure of the bedrooms will vary greatly. Some are outfitted in a very grand manner, with lots of room, whereas others are smaller and simpler in amenities. Around the hotel are tennis courts, swimming, golf, lakeside volleyball courts, a disco, and spa baths. Laundry service and baby-sitting are provided, and room service is 24 hours. Parking is free. AE, DC, MC, V.

WHERE TO DINE

Besides the major hotel, you can find simple food and good regional wines at **Bringelas,** Estrada Nacional 2 (tel. 972-31), in Vidago. This no-frills place is patronized by locals who come here for the home-cooking, and features such traditional dishes as codfish, roast veal, and tripe in port wine. Charging from 1,800$ ($12.05) for a complete meal, it serves daily from noon to 3pm and 7:30 to 11pm. Outside of town, the restaurant lies on the road to Pedras Salgadas. In summer, tables are placed outside, offering a view over the valley. Reservations aren't necessary. No credit cards.

In Pedras Salgadas, the best place to dine is a large restaurant, **São Martinho** (tel. 442-78), which is capable of seating as many as 400 diners. Charging from 1,800$ ($12.05) for a simple meal, it serves daily from noon to 3:30pm and 7 to 9:30pm. A tourist menu costs only 1,100$ ($7.35). Good provincial cookery is featured, along with plenty of wine. Specialties include loin of veal on the spit, bacalhau (cod) a Zé do Pipo, and cabrito assado no forno (roast kid in the oven). Parking is available, and in winter a fireplace burns brightly. Reservations aren't needed. No credit cards.

6. Chaves

A quiet spa town today, Chaves, on the banks of the Tâmega River, was known to the Romans as Aquae Flaviae. The thermal springs brought the place to prominence, and it became an important stop on the route from Astorga in what is now Spain to Braga in Portugal. Trajan fortified the town and had a handsome 16-arch bridge built across the river. Chaves takes its name from the fact that it was the key (*chave*) or gateway to northern Portugal, lying only about 7 miles south of the Spanish border and 40 miles northeast of Vila Real. It is 295 miles northeast of Lisbon.

The **Chaves Tourist Office** is at Terreiro de Cavalaria (tel. 076/210-29). Chaves has two daily bus links to Bragança (see below) taking 3 hours.

WHAT TO SEE & DO

The town was under Moorish control for a few centuries and was refortified after being liberated by the Christian forces. The new defenses were set up to discourage inroads by the Spanish. The castle, built by King Dinis, was the home of the first duke of Bragança, an illegitimate son of King João I. All that remains is the keep and the outer wall, with towers. **A Military Museum,** occupying four stories of the keep, displays ancient arms and armor, guns and uniforms from World War I, and mementos of Portuguese wars. If you are hardy enough to climb the 120 steps to the top, you can look out over the town and the farms of the fertile valley below. Guided tours of the Military Museum may be taken on a combination ticket with admission to the **Flaviense Region Museum** (Museu de Regão Flaviense; tel. 076/219-65), in the palace of the Dukes of Bragança, next to the Castle of Muralha on Praça de Camões. The castle keep is a military section, with displays dating from the time of King João I to the present. The duke's palace includes archeology, epigraphy, heraldry, numismatics, painting, ethnography, and other sciences. The museum is open from 10am to noon and 2 to 6pm Tuesday to Sunday. Admission is 50$ (35¢).

The **Church of the Misericord,** at right angles to the parish church on Praça de Camões, is a baroque building with balconies and salomonic (twisted) columns. Inside are huge panels of blue-and-white azulejos showing New Testament scenes, a gilded altarpiece of wood, and 18th-century ceiling paintings. In front of the parish church is a Manueline-type pillory.

From the ancient bridge, gardens run down to the river. The bridge no longer has all its arches and parapets, but at its south end are milestones with Roman carvings.

WHERE TO STAY

Accommodations tend to be limited and simple here. The best of the lot is **Hotel Trajano,** Travessa Cândido dos Reis, 5400 Chaves (tel. 076/224-15). Clean, contemporary, and accented with such accessories as Roman breastplates and wall-mounted chariots pulled by griffons, this pleasant hotel is on a narrow cul-de-sac in the commercial center of town. The comfortably high-ceilinged public rooms are filled with exposed bricks and clusters of sofas. Its basement contains a separately recommended restaurant (described below). Each of its 39 bedrooms has high Iberian headboards, a private bath, and a phone. Singles cost 5,700$ ($38.20) daily, and doubles go for 6,800$ ($45.55), with breakfast included. Parking is free. MC, V.

Hotel de Chaves, Rua 25 de Abril 25, 5400 Chaves (tel. 076/211-18). Its antiquated interior and its lack of dining facilities earn it only one star from the Portuguese government. But anyone yearning for a taste of old-fashioned life might find this an ideal stopover. It lies in the center behind a solid stone facade that looks vaguely fortified. Inside, a high series of ceilings, a creaky wrought-iron elevator, wide upper hallways, and vintage furniture might qualify it as a movie set. The hotel was built around 1920 by members of the Alves family, and neither the owners nor the furnishings have changed much since. You'll be greeted by a staff who speak very little English, then shown to one of the 40 bedrooms, half of which contain private baths. Singles without bath cost 2,500$ ($16.75) daily, going up to 4,200$ ($28.15) with bath. Doubles without bath rent for 3,600$ ($24.10), rising to 5,400$ ($36.20) with bath. Shared bathroom facilities are found in each of the hallways, and breakfast is included in the price.

WHERE TO DINE

The independent restaurants within the town center are a lackluster lot. The best food is obtained at the previously recommended **Hotel Trajano,** Travessa Cândido dos Reis (tel. 224-15). In the basement of this hotel, the restaurant offers attentive service, a fine Portuguese regional cuisine, and a high-ceilinged decor of decorative arches and thick brick stucco. Lunch is daily from 12:30 to 3pm and dinner from 7:30 to 10pm. Full meals cost from 1,800$ ($12.05). Offerings include the predictable range of specialties, as well as stewed codfish, filet of veal, and shrimp omelets. Reservations aren't needed. MC, V.

Arado, Ribeira do Pinheiro (tel. 219-96), seems to be heavily preferred by discerning locals. However, it is suitable only for motorists, as it lies about 5 miles outside of Chaves on the road to Mirandelo. It's a former private villa transformed into a small-scale restaurant, and is known for its regional cookery and wines. Specialties include codfish gratinée and veal on the spit. The staff is helpful, and they serve daily from noon to 3pm and 7 to 10pm. Meals cost from 2,700$ ($18.10) à la carte or 2,000$ ($13.40) on the tourist menu. While dining, guests enjoy a panoramic vista. In winter a fireplace adds an extra glow. Reservations aren't needed. No credit cards.

---

7. Bragança

The medieval town of Bragança (Braganza, in English), which became a duchy in the middle of the 14th century, was under the aegis of the House of Bragança, ruling house of Portugal from 1640 until its overthrow early in this century. During those years the heir to the throne of Portugal bore the title of Duke of Bragança. The old town on a hilltop is surrounded by a long, fortified wall. It overlooks the modern town in the northeastern reaches of the country on a rise of ground in the Serra da Nogueira, some 2,000 feet above sea level. Bragança lies about 86 miles northeast of Vila Real and 323 miles northeast of Lisbon.

Bragança is an 8-hour bus ride from Porto. Three buses a day also run between Chaves and Bragança, taking 3 hours. The **Bragança Tourist Office** is at Avenida Cidade de Zamora (tel. 073/222-73).

WHAT TO SEE & DO

In the lower town, the **cathedral (Sé),** originally the Church of São João da Baptista, is not up to the standard of many of the cathedrals of Portugal, but there are nine churches in Bragança, so you may find one you like. For instance, the **Church of Santa Maria do Castelo,** beside the Town Hall in the old town, is outstanding for its painted ceiling, depicting the Assumption of the Virgin in many colors. Salomonic (twisted) columns frame the front door.

The oldest **Town Hall** (Domus Municipalis) in Portugal is beside St. Mary's Church. Ask for the key at Rua Dom Fernão o Bravo da Cidadela-Bragança 40 to enter this massive pentagonal structure built over a cistern. The interior is a cavernous room lit by little round arches.

In a small public garden in the citadel stands a Gothic **pillory.** The medieval shaft has been driven through the stone effigy of a boar, which has a depression carved in its snout. The boar is believed to date from the Iron Age, and it is possible that it was used in some ancient pagan rituals.

The **Church of Santa Clara,** renovated in 1764, can be visited, as well as the ancient **Bishop's Palace** (now Baçal's rustic museum) and the 13th-century **Church of St. Vincent.**

To visit the **citadel,** you go through the St. Vincent Square and climb upward. Cars must be left outside the ramparts.

WHERE TO STAY

A government-owned inn to the southeast of the town, **Pousada da São Bartolomeu,** Estrada de Turismo, 5300 Bragança (tel. 073/224-93), is about a half-hour drive from the Spanish frontier town of Quintanilha. The pousada is on the slope of the hill of São Bartolomeu. The 16 rooms have balconies, phones, and private baths, and are furnished in attractive, comfortable style. The room rate for two persons is 12,000$ ($80.40) daily; for a single 10,500$ ($70.35), including breakfast. The one suite costs 17,700$ ($118.60). Built in 1959, the pousada is attractively decorated in part with regional artifacts. The view from its premises at night is the most spectacular in Bragança, taking in the crenellated fortifications of the old city. Drinks are served in a large, masculine lounge ringed with hewn stone and richly textured paneling, within sight of a fireplace alcove dotted with bronze pots. The food served here is the best in Bragança; both regional and international dishes are offered. Meals cost from 2,740$ ($18.35) to 3,250$ ($21.80) and are served daily from 12:30 to 3pm and 7:30 to 10pm. Laundry service is provided, and room service is available until 10pm. Parking is free. AE, DC, MC, V.

Hotel Bragança, Avenida Doutor Francisco de Sá Carneiro, 5300 Bragança (tel. 073/225-78), is the leading modern hotel in the town. A boxy, concrete structure, it stands in a commercial center and is popular with traveling businesspeople. However, it comes in handy in summer when the pousada is full. Boldly designed with big windows and loggias, it offers 42 reasonably comfortable rooms. The rate in a single is 10,000$ ($67) daily, rising to 12,000$ ($80.40) in a double, including breakfast. The hotel also has a suitable restaurant, serving meals, either lunch or dinner, for 2,200$ ($14.75). Other facilities include a solarium. Laundry service is available, as is room service until midnight. Parking is free. AE, DC, MC, V.

The best choice for economy is **Albergaria Santa Isabel,** Rua Alexandre Herculano 67, 5300 Bragança (tel. 073/224-27; fax 073/269-37). It's a small-scale hotel set among a handful of stores and businesses in the center of town. The 14 well-scrubbed but simple bedrooms lie behind the modern blue-and-white tile facade. Each unit contains a private bath and phone, renting for 5,000$ ($33.50) daily in a single, 6,000$ ($40.20) in a double, with breakfast included. In the basement is a breakfast room and bar. Guests who want to watch TV head for one of the leather-upholstered couches in a room near the street-level reception desk. Laundry service is available, and room service is offered until midnight. Parking is free. No credit cards.

WHERE TO DINE

Outside the hotel dining rooms, the best restaurant is **Plantório,** Estrada Cantarias (tel. 224-26). Offering some 150 diners a panoramic view, it dispenses regional cookery with politeness from noon to 2:30pm and 7 to 9:30pm daily. The wine list is extensive and reasonable in price. Try either the meat or fish dishes, which are well prepared. Meals cost 2,200$ ($14.75) and up. Reservations aren't needed. MC, V.

Another interesting choice is **Arca de Noé,** Avenida do Savor (tel. 227-59), the best-known wine cellar in Bragança. It has a varied menu of good regional dishes, and of course, the stock of wine is superb. Meals, costing from 2,200$ ($14.75), are served Saturday to Thursday from noon to 3pm and 7 to 11pm. The restaurant has a bar and a fireplace. Reservations aren't needed. No credit cards.

---

8. Miranda do Douro

The town, 63 miles southeast of Bragança and 325 miles northeast of Lisbon, is perched on a high upland above the Valley of the Douro, which separates Portugal from Spain at this point. A medieval castle once stood guard over the entrance to the town, but only the ruins of the once-proud fortress remain. The people of this old town speak their own dialect, called *Mirandes,* which sounds like a form of Low Latin.

Old customs are still followed here, one of the most interesting being the Pauliteiros Dance, performed on most holidays and always on Santa Bárbara's feast day, the third Sunday in August. The men of the area, wearing white flannel kilts, colorfully embroidered black shirts, and flower-bedecked black hats with red ribbons, perform a dance that consists of striking the *paulitos* (sticks) to a rhythmic beat. This dance is similar to the pyrrhic dance of the ancient Greeks, which was brought to Rome by Julius Caesar.

The former **cathedral (Sé),** a granite Renaissance building, contains some fine gilded wood-carved altarpieces. The choir stalls, also of gilded wood, have backdrops of landscape paintings. Don't miss the little statue of the baby Jesus wearing a top hat; it stands in a glass case in the south transept. From the cathedral terrace you can see the ruins of the cloister of the Bishop's Palace and the Douro flowing far below. You can visit the old cathedral from 8am to 12:30pm and 2 to 6pm Tuesday to Sunday.

An interesting excursion from the town is to the **Miranda do Douro dam,** 2 miles away along a narrow highway. This is the first of a series of five dams on the section of the river between Spain and Portugal providing electrical power. The power station can be visited. Even if you don't want to go inside the station, the sight of this multibuttressed dam in a rocky ravine is stunning.

WHERE TO STAY

If you'd like to stay in the area, **Pousada da Santa Catarina,** 5210 Miranda do Douro (tel. 073/422-55), overlooks the great dam. In this scenic spot, the government-owned inn rents out 12 pleasantly furnished double rooms, all with private bath and phone. A party of two is charged from 15,300$ ($102.50) daily, with singles renting for 13,700$ ($91.80), including breakfast. The restaurant at the hotel serves a typically regional Portuguese cuisine, with meals costing from 2,750$ ($18.45) to 3,650$ ($24.45). Laundry service is available, and room service is offered until 10pm. Parking is free. AE, DC, MC, V.

WHERE TO DINE

Most guests dine at the pousada. But if you'd like to seek out independent eateries, give **Boteco,** Largo Dom João III (tel. 421-50), a try. It has good food and is most reasonable in price, charging from 2,000$ ($13.40) for an à la carte menu. A tourist menu costs 1,650$ ($11.05). Food is served daily from noon to 3pm and 7 to 10pm. Private parking is available. From the typically Portuguese menu, you can order bacalhau (cod) a Boteco, or posta Mirandesa, the famous grilled steak dish of Miranda do Douro. No reservations are needed. The restaurant closes in January. AE, DC, MC, V.

MADEIRA

The island of Madeira, 530 miles southwest of Portugal, is the mountain peak of a volcanic mass. Its craggy spires and seacoast precipices of umber-dark basalt end with a sheer drop into the blue water. The surrounding sea is so deep that large sperm whales often come near the shore.

The summit of the undersea mountain is found at Madeira's center where the **Pico Ruivo,** often snowcapped, rises to an altitude of 6,105 feet above sea level. From that point project the rocky ribs and ravines of the island, running to the coast. If you stand upon the sea-swept balcony of **Cabo Girão,** one of the world's highest ocean cliffs (1,933 feet above the sea), you'll understand the Eden-like quality of Madeira. Camões called it "at the end of the world."

Madeira, now an autonomous archipelago, is only 35 miles in length, about 13 in breadth at its widest point. It contains nearly 100 miles of coastline, but no beaches. In its volcanic soil, plants and flowers blaze like the Tahitian palette of Gauguin. From jacaranda and masses of bougainvilea, to orchids and geraniums, whortleberry to prickly pear, poinsettias, cannas, frangipani, birds of paradise, and wisteria, the land is a botanical garden. Custard apples, avocados, mangoes, and bananas grow profusely. Fragrances such as vanilla and wild fennel intermingle with sea breezes and pervade the ravines, sweeping down the rocky headlands.

Claimed by the British as a sentimental dominion, Madeira has been popular with them ever since. The post-Victorians arrived, the women in wide-brimmed hats to protect them from the sun. Now that has changed: They make their way here specifically to enjoy the sun. Legend has it that two English lovers discovered the island about half a century before its known date of exploration. Supposedly Robert Machim and Anna d'Arfet, fleeing England, were swept off their course by a tempest and deposited on the eastern coast.

In 1419, João Gonçalves Zarco and Tristão Vaz Teixeira, captains under Henry the Navigator, discovered Madeira while exploring the African coastline, some 350 miles to the east. As it was densely covered with impenetrable virgin forests, they named it Madeira, meaning wood. Soon it was set afire to clear it for habitation. The holocaust is said to have lasted 7 years until all but a small northern section was reduced to ashes.

The hillsides are so richly cultivated today one would never know there had ever been a fire. Many of the groves and vineyards, protected by buffers of sugarcane, grow on stone-wall ledges, which almost spill into the sea. The farmers plant so close to the cliff's edge that they must have at least a dash of goat's blood in them. The terraced mountain slopes are irrigated by a complex network of *levadas* (water channels). It is estimated that there are some 1,330 miles of these levadas, and that includes about 25 miles of tunnels. These levadas were originally constructed by slaves and convicts. Built of stone, they are most often 1 to 2 feet wide and deep. Water from mountain springs is carried in them.

About 25 miles to the northeast, **Porto Santo** is the only other inhabited island in the Madeira archipelago. *Réalités* called it "another world, arid, desolate and waterless." Unlike Madeira, Porto Santo contains beaches, but is not yet developed for mass tourism. It is previewed at the end of this chapter.

GETTING THERE FROM LISBON

The quickest and most convenient way to reach Madeira from Lisbon is on a TAP flight (the trip takes 1 hour and 30 minutes). The plane stops at the Madeira Airport, then goes on to Porto Santo. However, if you're booking a TAP flight from, say, New York to Lisbon, you can have the side trip to Madeira included at no extra cost, providing you have a regular—that is, not an excursion—ticket.

In addition, TAP has a weekly direct flight between Faro in the Algarve and Funchal, an extension of its Frankfurt-Faro service.

---

1. Orientation

The capital of Madeira, Funchal, is the focal point of the entire island and the gateway to outlying villages. When Zarco landed in 1419, the sweet odor of fennel led him to name it after the aromatic herb, called *funcho* in Portuguese. Today the southern coast city of hillside-shelved villas and narrow winding streets is the garden spot of the island. Its numerous estates, including the former residence of the discoverer Zarco, the Quinta das Cruzes, are among the most exotic in Europe.

With a population of 100,000, Funchal has a long street running along the waterfront called **Avenida do Mar.** This often traffic-clogged artery runs in an east-west direction. North of this wide boulevard is **Avenida Arriaga,** which is considered the "main street" of Funchal. At the eastern end of this thoroughfare is the cathedral (sé), and at the western end is a large traffic circle whose center is graced with a fountain. As the Avenida Arriaga heads west, site of most of the major hotels, it changes its name to **Avenida do Infante.** However, as it moves east it becomes known as **Rua do Aljube.** Running in a north-south direction, the other most important street of Funchal, **Avenida Zarco,** links the waterfront area with the heart of the old city.

Chances are you won't be staying directly in the heart of Funchal, but in one of the hotels on the outskirts. However, for those who want to be right in the heart of

Madiera: Mean Temperatures Year Round (in °Fahrenheit)	
January/March	66.9°
April/June	71.2°
July/September	76.8°
October/December	70.3°

the action (and not dependent on transportation), I will have a few suggestions, all of which are reasonable in price. The most expensive hotels—that is, those with swimming pools and resort amenities—are on the outskirts. The center of Funchal is filled with heavy traffic most of the day, which means that hotels in the center often tend to be noisy. Nevertheless, for shopping and the widest selection of restaurants Funchal is a magnet for the visitor.

Unless you're a skilled driver, used to narrow roads, reckless drivers, and hairpin turns, I don't recommend renting a car on the island, although there are several local companies that will be only too happy to furnish you a car for a price. Most hotels can make arrangements for **car rentals.**

GETTING AROUND

Chances are, you'll have winged your way in on **TAP.** In that case, you may want to reconfirm your ongoing ticket at the main office in Funchal at Avenida do Mar 10 (tel. 091/301-51), along the waterfront. Hours are daily from 9am to noon and 2 to 5:30pm. Buses run frequently between the center of Funchal and the airport.

The less adventurous tourist will rely on hiring a **taxi.** The going rate is about 10,000$ ($67) to 12,000$ ($80.40) a day, although this should always be negotiated and agreed upon in advance. When the cost is divided among three or four passengers, it isn't so steep. Most taxis are often Peugeots or Mercedes, so you'll ride in relative safety and not have to cope with the nightmarish roads. If you're in Funchal and want a taxi to take you back to your hotel in the environs, you'll usually find a line of them waiting across from the tourist office along Avenida Arriaga. Many of the taxi drivers speak English.

Of course, the cheapest way of getting around Madeira—providing you're not rushed for time—is by **bus.** Local buses go all over the island, and they're a most economical means of transport. A typical fare in town is 130$ (85¢), but rides in the countryside can cost up to 500$ ($3.35). A helpful reader, Herman Marcuse, of Arlington, Virginia, wrote: "One of the best-kept secrets on Madeira is that you can make excursions on local buses at a fraction of the cost charged by the tour companies."

Most buses depart from the large park at the eastern part of the waterfront-bordering Avenida do Mar. If you're going to Camacha or Camiço, you'll find buses leaving from a little square at the eastern sector of Rua da Alfândega, which runs parallel to Avenida do Mar near the marketplace.

Buses leave for the **airport** at Santa Cruz (phone 091/522-73 for information) from Avenida do Mar daily from around 7 in the morning until 11pm.

Remember that distances are short on Madeira, but regardless of where you're going, allow plenty of time to get there because of the road conditions.

FAST FACTS: MADEIRA

AMERICAN EXPRESS: The local representative is **Star Travel Office,** Avenida Arriaga 23 (tel. 091/320-01), which is open Monday through Friday from 8:30am to 12:30pm and from 2 to 6pm.

BOOKSTORES: A good English bookstore is **Livraria Inglesa,** Rua Carreira 43 (tel. 091/244-90), open Monday through Friday from 10am to 7pm and Saturday from 10am to 1pm.

CONSULATES: The **U.S. Consulate** is at Avenida Luís de Camões, Apt B (tel. 091/474-29), off Avenida do Infante. The **British Consulate** is at Rua Sé 14 (tel. 091/212-21).

DRUGSTORE: Drugstores are open from 9am to 1pm and 3 to 7pm Monday to Saturday. There is a rotation emergency and night service schedule posted on the door of all chemists. Sunday has a special schedule, too. A centrally located and reliable local chemist is **Farmácia Honorato,** Rua da Carreira 62 (tel. 091/232-97).

EMERGENCIES: Emergency numbers to keep in mind include 115 for, well, an emergency; 091/220-22 for the police; 091/200-00 for the Red Cross; 091/421-11 for a hospital emergency.

LAUNDRY: A good Laundromat in Funchal is **Lavandaria Donini,** Rua das Pretas (tel. 091/244-06). Any clothing can be laundered or dry cleaned here within 1 or 2 days. It is open Monday to Friday from 9am to 7pm.

POST OFFICE: If you've had your mail sent *posta restante* (general delivery), you can pick it up at the Zarco Post Office, Avenida Zarco, 9000 Funchal (tel. 091/321-31), near the tourist office, but you should bring your passport to identify yourself. You can also place long-distance phone calls here, which will help avoid steep hotel surcharges. It's also possible to send telegrams, faxes, and telex. The office is open Monday to Friday from 8:30am to 8pm and Saturday from 9am to 12:30pm. Other post offices offering the same service include Calouste Gulbenkian, Avenida Calouste Gulbenkian (open 9am to 12:30pm and from 2:30 to 6:30pm Monday to Friday), near Monument of the Infante D. Henrique; Monumental, Estrada Monumental, near Lido swimming pool (open 9am to 7pm Monday to Friday); Mercado, Rua do Arcipreste, near Municipal Market (open 9am to 6:30pm Monday to Friday).

Many CORREIOS signs can be found in the center pointing out the way to the nearest post office.

SHOPS AND OFFICIAL BUILDINGS: Most shops are open from 9am to 1pm and 3 to 7pm Monday to Friday, and from 9am to 1pm Saturday; usually closed Sunday. Municipal buildings are open from 9am to 12:30pm and 2 to 5:30pm Monday to Friday.

TOURIST INFORMATION: An English-speaking staff runs the desk at the Madeira tourist office, Avenida Arriaga 18 (tel. 091/256-68). Hours are Monday to Saturday from 9am to 7pm and Sunday from 9am to 1pm. Here you'll be given a map of the island, and the staff will also, if asked, make suggestions about the best ways to explore their beautiful island. You can also inquire about ferry connections to the neighboring island of Porto Santo.

WEATHER: Call 091/331-61 24 hours a day for information.

---

2. Where to Stay

In summer, when every other European resort on the seafront socks you with its highest tariffs, Madeira used to experience its "low season." And not because of bad weather, although August is still not the most desirable month to visit because of the *capacete,* a shroud of mist that often envelops the island.

Summer was traditionally considered the low season because the early British visitors, the first tourists really, set a pattern of mass descent in winter, thereby crowding the hotels and inflating its tariffs.

That long-ago pattern, however, seems to have broken, and Madeira now experiences more of an all-year-round popularity. In fact it's become hard to get an airplane seat there in the peak summer months without reservations made way in advance.

The hotels of Madeira, among the best in all of Portugal, range from some of the finest deluxe citadels in Europe to attractively priced and old-fashioned "quintas" for budgeteers. Many of the best hotels, as mentioned, are on the outskirts of Funchal.

VERY EXPENSIVE

The legendary place to stay in Funchal is **Reid's Hotel,** Estrada Monumental 139, 9000 Funchal, Madeira (tel. 091/230-01; fax 091/304-99), which was founded by William Reid, a young Scotsman, in 1891. Its position is smashing, along the coastal road at the edge of Funchal, on its own 2 acres of multiterraced gardens all the way down the hillside to the rocky shores. Midway down are two saltwater swimming pools thrust out onto a cliff edge, the pair joined by a bridge and fountain. On a still-lower terrace is yet another pool (reached by an elevator) built onto a ledge of rocks. You feel you're swimming in the ocean. The English who frequent the hotel in large numbers (famous guest of the past: Sir Winston Churchill) spend their days strolling along the scented walks lined with blue and pink hydrangeas, hedges of geraniums, gardenias, banana trees, ferns, and white yuccas.

The public rooms and a wing added in 1968 are all tastefully and successfully combined. The main drawing rooms are refreshingly decorated in the colors of the sea with country estate furnishings in either tropical prints or soft solid colors. Afternoon tea is served at the Tea Terrace with a magnificent view of the gardens and Funchal Bay. Lunch is offered in the Garden Restaurant overlooking the pools or at the poolside buffet. The two-level main dining room is classically dignified with pink-and-white marble and Murano crystal lamps, plus the inevitable and very English silver trolley holding roast beef. Reid's gourmet restaurant, Les Faunes, on the sixth floor in the garden wing, is recommended separately in the restaurant section. Less formal is Villa Cliff, serving a typically Portuguese cuisine.

Of the 173 air-conditioned rooms with private bath, phone, and radio, all but 15 face the ocean. The spacious rooms are conservative in the finest sense, with well-chosen pieces, plenty of storage space, sitting areas, and desks. The baths have marble or tile walls and floors. In winter, singles range from 26,200$ ($175.55) daily, with doubles going for 37,300$ ($249.90) to 40,800$ ($273.35). In summer and fall, prices are 22,500$ ($150.75) daily in a single, 32,200$ ($215.75) to 35,200$ ($235.85) in a double. Twenty-one suites begin at 57,000$ ($381.90). Tariffs include breakfast.

It's hard to be lured away from Reid's garden park, but tennis courts are at your disposal. The hotel is owned by the Blandy family of wine and shipping fame. Shoe shining, laundry service, and a children's playroom are provided. Room service is 24 hours, and a hairdresser is on the premises. Parking is free. AE, DC, MC, V.

EXPENSIVE

The latest addition to the luxury hotels of Funchal is the **Casino Park Hotel,** Avenida do Infante, 9000 Funchal, Madeira (tel. 091/331-11; fax 091/298-75). Just a 7-minute walk from the center of town, the hotel is nestled in a subtropical garden overlooking the harbor. Designed by architect Oscar Niemeyer, the creator of Brasilia, the main building is low (only five stories) and undulating, as if poised for flight from its position on the cliff above the deep waters. The complex is made up of the hotel and conference center and a separate casino. Every conceivable convenience and luxury is available within the Casino Park, including shopping facilities, tennis courts, swimming pools, saunas, billiards, and a health club. Special facilities, including a shallow swimming pool, are provided for the children. You can even arrange fishing, sailing, and golf excursions through the hotel. Variety in dining is also thoughtfully provided, from the luxurious and spacious dining room overlooking the port and town of Funchal, or the international Grill Room with its extensive wine cellar, to the simpler coffee shop adjacent to the swimming pool for a refreshing snack after a swim.

The 400 fully air-conditioned rooms each have their own balconies offering superb views of the harbor and town. Each room also has its own private bath, TV, minibar, phone, and radio. The rooms are tastefully coordinated with bright, sunny colors that seem to bring the radiance of the island and the sea indoors. A single costs from 19,000$ ($127.30) daily, and a double 24,000$ ($160.80), both with a buffet breakfast included. Thirty-six suites begin at 55,000$ ($368.50). There are two comfortable lounge areas on each floor. Parking is free. AE, DC, MC, V.

Hotel Savoy, Avenida do Infante, 9006 Funchal, Madeira (tel. 091/220-31; fax 091/231-03), is one of the leading five-star hotels not only of Madeira but of Portugal. Long known for style and elegance, it stands at the edge of Funchal. Its origins go back to the turn of the century when it was started by a Swiss-trained hotelier, and over the years, like Topsy, it just grew and grew. Today it has a total of 370 rooms, including 12 suites, with private baths, phone, minibar, TV, air conditioning, and balconies. Faced with escalating popularity, each generation of management has brought enlargements and improvements. In a double, the cost ranges from 29,600$ ($198.30) to 34,600$ ($231.80) daily, and singles go for 21,800$ ($146.05) to 25,300$ ($169.50), including breakfast. Suites begin at 42,200$ ($282.75).

The hotel is superbly situated, opening onto the ocean and the Bay of Funchal. With its vast public facilities, it captures a peculiar kind of Madeira dolce vita. For your before-dinner libations you have a choice of two bars. There are several restaurants from which to choose, or you can have lunch by the pools. Restaurants include the Bellevue, the Bakkhos Wine/Snack Bar, the Alameda coffee shop, and the Neptunus by the pool. For more deluxe dining, there is the elegantly decorated Fleur-de-Lys, a grill room with belle époque trappings. This room, closed Sunday, has a panoramic view.

During the day, you can reach two seawater swimming pools (one heated) by elevator. There are also tennis courts, plus a host of other facilities, including a health center, mini-golf, a shopping arcade, hairdressers for both men and women, and the Galaxia nightclub on the top floor, with a panoramic sweep. Baby-sitting, room service, and laundry service are provided. Parking is free. AE, DC, MC, V.

Madeira Carlton, Largo António Nobre, 9007 Funchal, Madeira (tel. 091/310-31; fax 091/233-77), is a luxurious, 17-story, high-rise structure near the casino with direct access to the sea. The 375-room hotel offers three swimming pools, a restaurant for 500 persons, Os Arcos, plus an English pub, O Farol, and a disco. The hotel has some amusing eccentricities of design—two trapezium-shaped elevators that transport guests down to their rooms from the reception area. All the accommodations, many furnished in a provincial style, are air-conditioned, with private balconies, baths, radios, direct-dial phones, and TV sets in the suites. A single ranges from 18,500$ ($123.95) to 22,500$ ($150.75) daily, and doubles go for 28,000$ ($187.60) to 35,000$ ($234.50). The least expensive rates are for the standard mountain view, the more expensive for deluxe rooms with a sea view. The rates quoted include breakfast. Suites begin at 49,000$ ($328.30). The hotel lies on a promontory overlooking Funchal Bay in the fashionable Vale-Verde Garden district, next to the century-old landmark, Reid's. Its oceanfront exposure to the south offers dawn-to-dusk sunlight on all pool terraces and seaside guest room balconies and patios. Room service (24 hours), laundry, and baby-sitting are provided. AE, DC, MC, V.

Madeira Palácio, Estrada Monumental 265, 9000 Funchal, Madeira (tel. 091/300-01; fax 091/254-02), is a luxurious hotel of 260 well-appointed and air-conditioned rooms and 18 suites on the seaside route to Câmara de Lobos, about 2 miles from the center of Funchal. The hotel is perched on a cliff over the sea. From here, Madeira's famous high cliff, Cabo Girão, can be seen looming in the distance. Each room is complete with private bath, minibar, direct-dial phone, radio, color TV with video systems, and a balcony. Rooms opening onto the mountains are less desirable than those facing the sea. Rates in a double range from 15,000$ ($100.50) to 33,000$ ($221.10) daily, from 12,000$ ($80.40) to 23,000$ ($154.10) in a single. Suites begin at 35,000$ ($234.50). Tariffs include breakfast.

The star-shaped hotel is most contemporary, with three wings. The public salons and guest rooms are colorfully coordinated, and local woods, native construction materials, and Madeiran fabrics have been used judiciously. During the day guests enjoy a heated swimming pool, an outdoor snack bar, tennis courts in the gardens, and a shopping arcade complete with a hairdresser and a sauna, even table tennis. Visitors may select the hotel's main restaurant, Cristovão Colombo, with its menu of local and international dishes, or they may prefer the regional dishes of Le Terrace. International cuisine is served in the hotel's gourmet restaurant, Vicerei. Later, entertainment is provided in the nightclub. Occasional folk dances are staged here as well. Room service, laundry, and baby-sitting are provided, and parking is free. AE, DC, MC, V.

MODERATE

Girassol, Estrada Monumental 256, 9000 Funchal, Madeira (tel. 091/310-51; fax 091/254-41), is a 133-room hotel offering immaculate accommodations at reasonable tariffs. It's on the outskirts of Funchal, overlooking the Tourist Club, where guests are allowed access to the sea at a small charge. Every one of its accommodations has a sunny balcony, half overlooking the mountains, the rest viewing the sea. Each chamber also comes complete with private bath, including a shower, plus a radio, air conditioning, and a phone. Most double rooms are, in fact, suites, consisting of bedroom, bathroom, small sitting room, and veranda. The room decor is bright and cheerful. Two people can stay here at a cost of 11,000$ ($73.70) daily. Singles go for 8,200$ ($54.95), and all tariffs include breakfast. Two swimming pools are available, one for children. Guests can also catch the sun on the 12th-floor solarium. On the street level is a bar and social lounge; even a hairdressing salon. Ballroom dancing and floor shows are offered in the disco, and there's a tea lounge on the second floor. Two other special features are an entrance courtyard with a series of interconnected angular reflecting pools and a dining room with sea views. Parking is free. AE, DC, MC, V.

Hotel Alto Lido, Estrada Monumental 316, 9000 Funchal, Madeira (tel. 091/291-97), on the road at the western end of the environs of Funchal, has staggered concrete balconies and a riot of lushly planted vines, aloe plants, and bougainvillea. Its verdant screening helps to create one of the most appealing facades in Madeira. Built in 1983, the hotel has a swimming pool, a restaurant, two bars, a sauna, and a much-needed free parking garage, along with 118 comfortably furnished bedrooms. Each of these units has a TV, private bath, phone, minibar, and balcony. Prices quoted to you in the marble-sheathed lobby, including breakfast, are 15,220$ ($101.95) daily in a single, 16,800$ ($112.55) in a double. Portuguese cuisine is served in the dining room. Laundry service is available, as is room service until 10pm. AE, DC, MC, V.

Hotel Raga, Estrada Monumental 302, 9000 Funchal, Madeira (tel. 091/330-01; fax 091/208-87). Only its windows face onto the sea and the traffic artery of the Estrada Monumental, about a half mile west of the center of town. Its lobby is reached via a winding and hilly road stretching through a neighborhood of multistoried modern buildings. It was originally designed as an apartment building, which explains its large rooms, big closets, and kitchenettes (however, you can use only the refrigerators, not the stoves). Each of the 159 bedrooms has a tile bath, a wedge-shaped balcony, a phone, and in most cases, a sofa that can be converted into an extra bed. Singles cost 9,000$ ($60.30) daily, and doubles go for 15,000$ ($100.50) with breakfast included. The hotel contains a pair of restaurants, a snack bar, a basement nightclub with a three-piece band, a TV lounge, and a many-sided swimming pool sunk into the slope of the terraces overlooking the ocean. Parking is free. AE, DC, MC, V.

Hotel Santa Isabel, Avenida do Infante, 9006 Funchal, Madeira (tel. 091/231-11; fax 091/231-03), is adjacent to Hotel Savoy and under the same management. It is an excellent small hotel with a homelike feeling and a well-deserved reputation for service and comfort. In the center of the deluxe hotel belt, it has a rooftop terrace, with a small swimming pool and solarium, snack bar, cocktail bar, well-appointed lounge overlooking the gardens, solarium, and use of the numerous facilities of the Hotel Savoy. The 69 bedrooms all have tile baths, phones, TVs, minibars, and radios. There are two grades of accommodations, ranging from the more expensive ones facing the sea to the cheaper units opening onto a garden and a mountain view. Bed-and-breakfast in a double costs from 12,900$ ($86.45) to 22,300$ ($149.40) daily, and a single rents for 9,600$ ($64.30) to 14,900$ ($99.85). Meals are taken in the Savoy dining room. Parking is free. AE, DC, MC, V.

Hotel Vila Ramos, Azinhaga da Casa Branca 7, 9000 Funchal, Madeira (tel. 091/641-81), built in the mid-1970s and surrounded by sloping banana groves, lies on the western outskirts of Funchal. Rated four stars, it is known for its attractive swimming pool and its conservative decor. It contains such amenities as an English-style reading room, a duet of restaurants, an outdoor gazebo-shaped bar, an attentive staff, and a balconied facade composed of brown tile and pink-painted concrete. Each of the 116 rooms has a private bath, phone, balcony, air conditioning, and radio. Singles range from 9,000$ ($60.30) daily and doubles from 12,000$ ($80.40), including breakfast. AE, DC, MC, V.

Standing on a hillside above the town, **Hotel São João,** Rua das Maravilhas 74, 9000 Funchal, Madeira (tel. 091/461-11; fax 091/416-25), is a modern four-star hotel with a total of 192 well-furnished bedrooms and 15 suites. Each of the rooms is equipped with private bath, air conditioning, phone, and a private terrace. The hotel charges from 10,200$ ($68.35) daily in a single, 13,200$ ($88.45) in a double, including breakfast. Suites begin at 22,000$ ($147.40). You can quench your thirst at one of the three well-decorated bars or assuage your hunger at either the self-service snack bar at poolside or the restaurant, both of which serve good Portuguese food and wine. During the day, guests have the use of three swimming pools (one for children), and the hotel also has several planned activities, bringing in folkloric shows and bands for dancing. A courtesy bus makes frequent runs into Funchal. The hotel has three bars, offers laundry service and baby-sitting, and provides room service until midnight. Parking is free. AE, DC, MC, V.

A gracious old manor house, **Quinta da Penha de França,** Rua da Penha de França 2, 9000 Funchal, Madeira (tel. 091/290-87; fax 091/292-61), has been turned into a guesthouse. Like a family home, the quinta is chock full of antiques, paintings, and silver. Near the Savoy, it stands in its own garden right on a ledge almost hanging over the harbor. It's a short walk to the center of the bazaars and is opposite an ancient chapel. The four-story antiga casa is bone white with dark-green shutters, plus small-panel windows overlooking the ocean. Across the front terrace is a good-sized swimming pool with white iron garden chairs arranged for lazy lounging. Set on the hillside in the midst of poinsettias, bamboo, sugarcane, and coffee plants is a wine lodge and stone washhouse now converted into guest rooms. Twin-bedded rooms, 39 in all, with bath and phone go for 16,000$ ($107.20), including breakfast. Parking is free. AE, DC, MC, V.

Quinta do Sol, Rua Dr. Pita 6, 9000 Funchal, Madeira (tel. 091/76-41-51; fax 091/76-62-87), a four-star hotel, is among the best in its category in Madeira. Occupying an attractive setting, it offers a total of 120 well-furnished bedrooms, plus about six suites. Each comes with a private bath, phone, TV, and air conditioning, and some have their own balconies. The charge is 13,000$ ($87.10) in a single, 18,000$ ($120.60) in a double, with a buffet breakfast included. Suites begin at 35,000$ ($234.50). The hotel has a number of public facilities that make it resort worthy, including a swimming pool, well-decorated lounges, a rooftop solarium, and a bar and restaurant offering good food and wine. MC, V.

INEXPENSIVE

Hotel do Carmo, Travessa do Rego 10, 9000 Funchal, Madeira (tel. 091/290-01; fax 091/239-19), provides modern accommodations right in the center of Funchal. It is erected in a cellular honeycomb fashion, each bedroom opening onto its own private balcony. While there is no surrounding garden, guests gather during the day for dips in the L-shaped rooftop swimming pool from which there is a good view of the harbor. Created by the Fernandes family, it was designed for guests who have limited purses and want to be near the bazaars in the heart of the city's life. The 80 bedrooms are simple, with contemporary furnishings, TVs, phones, and tile bathrooms. For a room and breakfast, one person pays 6,800$ ($45.55) daily; two people, 8,000$ ($53.60). Meals are served in a spacious dining room, decorated with a green harlequin tile floor. A little lounge opens onto an inner patio. Facilities include a sauna and solarium, and laundry service and baby-sitting can be arranged. Room service is 24 hours. Parking is free. AE, DC, MC, V.

Hotel Madeira, Rua Ivens 21, 9009 Funchal Codex, Madeira (tel. 091/300-

71), is in the center of Funchal behind the park and in the quietest part of the town. The rooms are clean and comfortable, and there is a rooftop swimming pool with a solarium area, where the bar and snack services never give you a chance to be thirsty. It has the most extraordinary panoramic view of the town, mountains, and sea. The hotel rents a total of 30 bedrooms, each with a private bath, costing 7,500$ ($50.25) daily in a double, 6,500$ ($43.55) in a single, including breakfast. Rooms are arranged around a plant-filled atrium. One of the nicest aspects of this hotel, built in 1971, is the sheltered sun windows attached to each of the accommodations. Parking is free. AE, DC, MC, V.

Hotel Orquidea, Rua dos Netos 71, 9000 Funchal, Madeira (tel. 091/260-91). "The Orchid" blooms right in Funchal. A first-class hotel, it offers 70 small but comfortable bedrooms, each with private bath and phone. Most of the accommodations open onto their own terraces. Inside, the atmosphere is sleek modern, with polished marble surfaces. For a room with a buffet breakfast, one person pays 7,000$ ($46.90) daily, that fee increasing to 8,750$ ($58.65) for two. The best feature of the hotel is its rooftop terrace, with a panoramic view of the town and port. Parking is free. AE, DC, MC, V.

Hotel Windsor, Rua das Hortas 4C, 9000 Funchal, Madeira (tel. 091/33-081), opened with fanfare in 1987, is one of the most stylish hotels in Funchal. Rated four stars, it has a marble-sheathed lobby laden with plants, wicker chairs, and art deco accessories. The hotel was constructed in two separate buildings, connected by an aerial passageway stretching above a sun-flooded enclosed courtyard. There is also a café and bar designed like a Jazz Age nightclub a few paces from the reception desk. The free parking garage is almost a necessity in this crowded commercial neighborhood. Also popular is a cramped but convivial rooftop swimming pool with an outdoor bar. Because of its enclosure by the buildings in the town center, few of the 67 bedrooms have any kind of view. But each is nicely decorated, with wall-to-wall carpeting, phone, and private bath. With breakfast included, singles cost from 7,000$ ($46.90) daily, and doubles rent for 9,400$ ($63). No credit cards.

Residencial Santa Clara, Calçada do Pico 16B, 9000 Funchal, Madeira (tel. 091/241-94; fax 091/382-37), in the upper reaches of Funchal, is a breakfast-only hotel reached via the narrow winding streets of an old-fashioned residential section. Behind an iron gate, at the end of a narrow driveway bordered with fragrant vines and hibiscus, lies the kind of villa many visitors dream of owning for themselves. Prefaced with a gracefully curved double staircase, the villa was built in 1926 by a wealthy Portuguese family in an orange art nouveau style. Inside, floors crafted from Brazilian hardwoods compete for attention with trompe l'oeil ceilings and a scattering of antiques. The hotel contains 22 rooms, each with bath and phone. Singles cost from 5,500$ ($36.85) daily and doubles from 6,500$ ($43.55). Its only drawback is its popularity, which might make getting a room difficult without an advance reservation. Laundry service is provided, and room service is available until midnight. No credit cards.

BUDGET

Albergaria Catedral, Rua do Aljube 13, 9000 Funchal, Madeira (tel. 091/300-91; fax 091/351-80), for its price bracket, is a good choice if you want to be in the center of town. Don't judge it by its dark and narrow entrance, lying across the street from the cathedral. Climb a flight of stairs to a slickly "moderno" reception area, where you'll be assigned one of the establishment's 25 comfortable bedrooms. They occupy four floors of a five-story building, and the quieter ones in the rear, unfortunately, don't have much of a view. In front, many of the units have balconies open to the street noise. Each room has a phone and private bath. With breakfast included, doubles cost 5,500$ ($36.85) daily, and singles rent for 5,000$ ($33.50). The sunniest and most pleasant rooms lie on the two uppermost floors. Parking is free on the street if you can find a place. AE, DC, MC, V.

Pensão Santos, Estrada Monumental 200, 9000 Funchal, Madeira (tel. 091/618-82), standing a few inches from the edge of a busy street, a half mile west of the center of Funchal and a few paces from Reid's Hotel, rises proudly in faded but aristocratic neoclassical splendor. It was built in 1925 as a private house, but was converted into a budget-conscious pension 11 years later. Its proprietors are the sprightly and kind-hearted Ricardo Santos and his wife. The place contains seven rooms to rent, each of which has a labyrinthine floor plan, with doors and passageways that may be opened or closed depending on the space a client requests. The rooms are furnished with an eclectic mix. Only three contain private baths. The atmospheric dowdiness merely adds to the charm, and a slightly overgrown garden beckons to any visitor. With breakfast included, a single without bath costs 2,000$ ($13.40) or 2,500$ ($16.75) with bath. A double without bath costs 3,500$ ($23.45) or 4,500$ ($30.15) with bath. Free parking is on the street. No credit cards.

Residencial Greco, Rua do Carmo 16, 9000 Funchal, Madeira (tel. 091/300-81; fax 091/330-80), in one of Funchal's concrete towers, offers 28 slightly frayed but comfortable bedrooms, scattered over four floors of the building. Prices quoted in the narrow reception vestibule, with breakfast included, range from 3,500$ ($23.45) to 3,900$ ($26.15) daily in a single, 4,800$ ($32.15) to 5,600$ ($37.50) in a double. Each accommodation has a balcony, private bath, phone, and relatively large dimensions. The best units are quiet because of their exposure to the sprawl of Funchal's residential sections and the faraway sea. Parking is free. No credit cards.

MACHICO

At Machico, on the east coast where the Portuguese first landed, you'll find more hotels. This part of land-scarce Madeira is being rapidly developed. Scores of tiny vacation villas climb the hillside. In the complex is a yacht club, plus an elegant bridge club. Machico is about 5 minutes from the airport, but a good 30-minute run along a twisting road 18 miles west of Funchal.

The best hotel here is **Hotel Dom Pedro Baia,** Estrada de São Roque, 9200 Machico, Madeira (tel. 091/96-57-51; fax 091/96-68-89), a modern structure that boasts sea views, private baths, and phones for every room. The 218 comfortably furnished rooms are well kept and tastefully appointed. On the bed-and-breakfast plan, the single rate is 12,000$ ($80.40) daily, that tariff rising to 17,500$ ($117.25) for two. An extra meal is 2,600$ ($17.40). Good food is served in the Panoramic Restaurant. A bar, a heated saltwater swimming pool, sun terraces, a beach, even a disco, make this a nice choice. Parking is free. AE, DC, MC, V.

---

3. Where to Dine

Many of the major hotels require full or halfboard in high season; but perhaps you'll be able to sneak away for a regional meal at one of the recommendations listed below. The list begins, however, with the pick of the hotel restaurants, which are all in the grill rooms, the specialty restaurants, of the three leading five-star hotels of Madeira.

EXPENSIVE

Fleur-de-Lys, Hotel Savoy, Avenida do Infante (tel. 220-31). Its most devoted admirers claim that this restaurant serves the finest food in Madeira. It is certainly one of the most panoramic spots for dining, opening onto the twinkling lights of Funchal. Decorated vaguely in a belle époque style, it has an eclectic decor with antique reproductions and Oriental carpets. Guests can observe the activity in an open-grill kitchen covered with pewter facsimiles of the establishment's namesake. Only dinner is served, and it's offered nightly from 7 to 11:30pm. Reservations are important, and even with one you sometimes have to wait a long time. Meals cost from 7,000$ ($46.90) and are likely to include an array of well-prepared international dishes such as grilled salmon steak, lobster Mornay, spring lamb cutlets, beef Stroganoff, and duckling in orange sauce. AE, DC, MC, V.

Try to dine at least once at **Les Faunes,** Reid's Hotel, Estrada Montumental 139, (tel. 230-01), generally conceded to be the island's finest restaurant. On the sixth floor of the hotel's garden wing, diners have musical entertainment by a pianist. Both guests and the local gentry consider it the perfect place to celebrate a new amour or console oneself after the loss of an old love. True to English tradition, clients in winter often still dress for dinner, the women perhaps in silk, the men sedate in black tie.

The chef offers a wide variety of French specialties and also some typical Portuguese dishes. For your palatable preliminaries, you can try everything from Portuguese soup to the chef's own smoked fish. Particular favorites are the caldeirada, a fish stew, and lobster (grilled or poached). To top your repast, you can select from the dessert trolley or ask for a hot soufflé, preferably made of passion fruit or strawberries. A meal here will cost you an average of 7,500$ ($50.25). Dinner, the only meal served, is offered daily from 7:30 to 11pm. Reservations are needed. AE, DC, MC, V.

Another elegant choice for dining, the **Vigia Grill Room** of the Casino Park Hotel, Avenida do Infante (tel. 331-11), is superb. The grill is housed in a large, modern dark-bronze room, opening onto an outdoor terrace. Pin lighting and candles, along with an impeccably polite staff, add to this glamorous ambience. Not only do you receive well-prepared international food and immaculate service, but the view of Funchal at night is enthralling. For 7,000$ ($46.90), a diner can enjoy a cocktail before dinner, then perhaps the shrimp flambé, prepared right in front of you. This is one of the chef's many specialties, including not only the shrimps, but mushrooms, onions, brandy, wine, and a tomato sauce. It comes with a fresh vegetable such as peas and carrots. Main courses include chateaubriand (for two), piccata of pork and shellfish is a saffron-flavored sauce. If you're not flambéed out, you can order for dessert a crêpe Suzette flamed in brandy. Go only for dinner, from 7:30 to 11pm Monday to Saturday. Reservations are needed. AE, DC, MC, V.

MODERATE

Casa da Carochinha (Lady Bird), Rua de São Francisco 2A (tel. 236-95), is a favorite local retreat, known especially to the British visitors and expatriates who are so fond of Madeira. The restaurant faces the Centenary Gardens, near the tourist office. The casa abounds in Edwardian English charm and serves a refined continental cuisine. This is perhaps the only place in Madeira where the chef does not use garlic. Specialties include coq au vin, beef Stroganoff, roast beef with Yorkshire pudding, and duck with orange sauce. Meals begin at 3,000$ ($20.10), and each guest enjoys a complimentary glass of Madeira with the food. A flag of his or her country is also placed on the spotless white Nottingham lace tablecloth. The casa is open Monday to Saturday for lunch, served from noon to 2pm, and for dinner, 7 to 10pm. It is also possible to visit for afternoon tea from 3:30 to 5:30pm. Reservations aren't needed. Closing times are July 1 to 15 and September 1 to 15. AE, DC, MC, V.

Casa dos Reis, Rua Imperatriz D. Amélia 103 (tel. 251-82), in an appealing neighborhood just downhill from the Madeira Carlton, is elegant and tranquil, with polished mahogany armchairs, brass chandeliers, and the aura of an aristocratic private club. The establishment serves French meals daily from 7 to 10:30pm. Avoid the snack bar one flight above street level and head for a table in the more formal dining room. Full meals cost from 2,900$ ($19.45) and include the chef's special fish soup, grilled scabbard fish, chateaubriand, chicken curry, shellfish stew, and fried squid in garlic. Reservations are necessary. AE, DC, MC, V.

Golfinho, Largo do Corpo Santo 21 (tel. 267-74), lies in the eastern section of town, near the waterfront, in the midst of the largest cluster of restaurants in Funchal. Even without a reservation, you can always manage to get a table at one of these establishments because there are so many of them.

The rich and warm-textured decor of the Golfinho cost its owners a fortune. Virtually every corner of its compact but well-decorated interior is covered with an eye-catching array of burnished pieces that make for a visual feast. After the waiter seats you on one of the scallop-backed Portuguese chairs, you order some of the best fresh fish and shellfish served in Madeira. You might, for example, begin with smoked swordfish and then follow with either grilled steak or lobster. However, fresh lobster should be ordered in advance; likewise, that savory kettle of fish, caldeirada, as preparation takes about 3 hours. A more typical fish, and one famous in Madeira for its taste, is espada. The bulbous eyes and fearsome teeth of this fish belie its tasty flesh. Sometimes espada is served with a fresh banana. Meals cost from 3,200$ ($21.45) at the Golfinho, which is open from noon to 3pm and 7 to 11pm Monday to Saturday. AE, DC, MC, V.

Kon-Tiki, Rua do Favila 9 (tel. 647-37), offers some of the best food on the island in a location near the Hotel Sheraton. The building is part of an old-fashioned quinta. You will be shown to a table either in their intimate restaurant, or on a glassed-in terrace overlooking a well-tended garden. From noon to 11pm Tuesday to Sunday you can enjoy such international dishes as warm home-smoked fresh mackerel, chicken with curry, or goulash soup. You can cook your own filet steak on a sizzling hot beefstone imported from Finland, or order a peppersteak, perhaps espada flambé with prawns. Everything seems to be good, especially the fresh fruit flambés to finish off a meal. Meals cost from 5,000$ ($33.50). Reservations are necessary. AE, DC, MC, V.

Right on the waterfront is **Restaurant Caravela,** Avenida do Mar 15–17 (tel. 284-64), a modern dining spot. You can dine on a glass-enclosed terrace with an open fireplace or else in the inner room where you sit in wicker chairs. Reached by elevator, the top-floor restaurant gives guests a view of the cruise ships arriving and departing. You can order both lunch and dinner, as well as afternoon tea with open-faced Danish smørrebröd sandwiches. Perhaps the finest regional dish is *espetada,* skewered meat flavored with garlic and bay leaves, and served only on special request. Unpretentious and proud of the native Portuguese dishes, the restaurant features Caravela fish, but also turns out international dishes, such as chateaubriand flambé. Meals begin at 2,500$ ($16.75), to which you must add the cost of your wine. The restaurant is open 7 days a week, with lunch served from noon to 3pm; dinner from 6:30 to 11pm. Reservations aren't necessary. AE, DC, MC, V.

Restaurant Romana, Largo do Corpo Santo 15 (tel. 289-56), under French management, is one of the leading restaurants of Madeira. The service is excellent. Customers have included the king and queen of Sweden, the queen mother of Denmark, the great fadista, Amália Rodrigues, and the Prince of Monaco. Comfortable and decorated in a rustic style, the Romana is considered a top rendezvous spot in town for both residents and visitors. The owner oversees a kitchen that is based on fresh fish and top-quality meats, served in both Madeira and international style. You can eat a full-course lunch for 1,200$ ($8.05) or an à la carte dinner for about 2,500$ ($16.75). Open all year, daily from 11am to 10:30pm. Reservations for dinner are recommended. The Romana will send a free minibus to pick you up. AE, DC, MC, V.

INEXPENSIVE

The popular **Bakkhos Wine Bar,** Rua Imperatriz D. Amélia (tel. 220-31), owned and operated by the Hotel Savoy, lies at the rear entrance to that hotel. You'll dine amid Moroccan lattices at smallish tables serviced by English-speaking waiters in red coats. The place is open daily from 11am to 11pm, serving Portuguese meals from 2,300$ ($15.40). The menu lists "typical dishes of the islands," including tuna steaks, stewed octopus, Portuguese-style liver, and wine by the carafe. Another offering is pasta, such as lasagne, spaghetti, or fettuccine, as well as salads or sandwiches, if you're dining light. Reservations aren't needed. AE, DC, MC, V.

Dos Combatentes, Rua Ivens 1 (tel. 213-88), is a good choice for regional food, a favorite of Funchal's colony of doctors and lawyers. At the top of the Municipal Gardens, this simple Portuguese restaurant serves well-prepared dishes, including rabbit stew, roast chicken, stewed squid, and codfish. The Portuguese eat a lot, so the portions are ample, and two vegetables and a green salad come with the main dish if required. Desserts are likely to be simple, including caramel custard and chocolate mousse or fresh fruit, and most dinners begin with a bowl of the soup of the day. A dinner is likely to cost from 2,000$ ($13.40). The waiters are efficient, and hours are daily from noon to 3pm and 7:30 to 10pm. Reservations aren't needed. AE, DC, MC, V.

Gavinas, Rua do Gorgulho (tel. 629-18), is reached by heading out the Estrada

Monumental to the Lido. Once this was only a little garagelike cottage, drawing the "slumming" chic of Madeira. But its popularity grew until its owners tore down the old shack and reconstructed a modern restaurant. The fish is as fresh as one can imagine. No fancy sauces, no elaborate service—just hearty sea fare, Portuguese style, is still the rule of the kitchen. Perhaps you'll be there the day when a savory caldeirada (fish stew) has just been prepared. Most guests, however, gravitate to one of the fresh grilled fish platters. The price of a meal (including a salad and bread) begins at 2,000$ ($13.40), plus the cost of your beer or wine. Gavinas is open daily from noon to midnight. Reservations aren't needed. AE, DC, MC, V.

O Espadarte, Estrada da Boa Nova 5 (tel. 280-65), is an uncluttered and unpretentious restaurant in a low-slung concrete building perched between a steep road and the mountains, about a mile east of Funchal on the road to the airport. It's owned and operated by a team of Portuguese entrepreneurs who have spent time in many other parts of the world. Guests dine at long trestle tables. Portuguese specialties include grilled trout, peppersteak, beef on a skewer, grilled pork cutlets, and fresh sardines. In honor of its namesake, which means swordfish, the restaurant does its own smoked swordfish, which is the most delectable appetizer you can order. Some nights are devoted to folklore and fado. Open Tuesday to Sunday from noon to 3pm and 7 to 11pm, the establishment serves full meals, priced from 2,000$ ($13.40). Reservations are recommended for dinner. No credit cards.

In the center of town, **O Pátio Jardim Tropicale,** Avenida Zarco 21 (tel. 273-76), is totally concealed within the inner courtyard of a complex of commercial buildings. Its entrance near a newspaper kiosk is easy to overlook because of its narrow width and insufficient lighting. Once inside, however, you'll enter a welcome refuge from the noise and traffic outside. You can sip coffee at one of the iron tables in the atrium, but many of the local shopkeepers head every day for the pleasant restaurant. One of the best lunchtime bargains in Funchal is a heaping platter of the dish of the day, usually roast chicken or stewed codfish with onions. Full Portuguese meals cost from 2,000$ ($13.40) à la carte, and might include house-style beef or squid, followed by pineapple flambé. The well-scrubbed wooden tables fill up from noon to 3pm and 7 to 10pm Monday to Saturday. Reservations aren't needed. AE, DC, MC, V.

Pensão Restaurante Universal, Rua de João Tavira 4 (tel. 206-18), stands in the center of town, 1 minute from the cathedral. Three restaurants are in an old house, said to be the first hotel in Madeira. Various steaks are charcoal-grilled for you and you can also order such international fare as scabbard fish prepared five different ways and roast chicken Mexican style. The cook also prepares a filet espada. Expect to spend from 1,500$ ($10.05) for a complete meal. One of the restaurants is open daily from 8am to 10pm, serving meals and snacks all day. The other two operate only from noon to 3pm and 6 to 10pm. The same menu is served in all three restaurants. Reservations aren't needed. MC, V.

A good place to have lunch, **Escola de Hotelaria e Turismo da Madeira** (Madeira Hotel and Tourism School), Quinta Magnolia, Rua Dr. Pita 10 (tel. 76-40-13), is in a charming old estate overlooking the bay. The daily Portuguese menu offers a good choice of specially prepared dishes for each course. The bar opens at 12:30pm, with cocktails made by advanced students, who are attentive to the desires of the patrons. Lunch is served promptly at 1pm, Monday to Friday, accompanied by wine and coffee. A four-course lunch costs from 2,000$ ($13.40). It is necessary to reserve a table by telephoning in advance. No credit cards.

AFTERNOON TEA

An old-fashioned tea and pastry shop as well as a restaurant, **Casa Minas Gerais** (The Corner Shop), Avenida do Infante (tel. 233-81), has been around for some 50 years. At its central serving bar, waiters make pots of tea and coffee or else pour Madeira wine. Before sitting at one of the little tables, clients pick out a pastry. A pot of tea for two costs 250$ ($1.70). One section of the establishment is a restaurant, serving meals for 2,000$ ($13.40), including such fare as spaghetti bolognese, mixed grill, grilled chicken, and fish soup. The cuisine is international, and reservations aren't necessary. Hours are 9am to 11pm daily. The tall ceiling is supported by painted columns capped with vine motifs. The Corner Shop opens onto a circular fountain and the busy boulevard. AE, DC, MC, V.

NEARBY PLACES TO DINE

While exploring Madeira, you may want to arrange dining stopover at one of the following recommendations:

The government-owned **Pousada dos Vinháticos,** Serra de Agua, 9350 Ribeira Brava (tel. 091/95-23-44), is near the top of a pass on the winding road to São Vicente. Guests can visit just for a meal or else spend the night. The pousada, a tavern-style building with a brick terrace, is built of solid stone. Visitors can absorb the unmarred mountain views from the terrace. The cooking is regional, and complete meals, served daily from noon to 3pm and 7 to 9:30pm, cost 2,470$ ($16.55) to 3,250$ ($21.80). Most of the 12 bedrooms are in Portuguese modern, although a few accommodations contain antiques. All have private baths and good views and are kept immaculate. The price of a double room is 11,000$ ($73.70) daily, and a single is 9,500$ ($63.65), including breakfast. Parking is free. Reservations aren't needed. AE, DC, MC, V.

Aquário, Seixal S. Vicente (tel. 85-23-26), is a waterfront fish restaurant too often ignored by visitors who flock to the dining spots of Porto Moniz, where they have to fight for a seat. Clients at Aquário enjoy some of the tastiest Portuguese cooking on the island. The kitchen turns out simple fare, but its cooking often outdistances the table d'hôte menus served in the deluxe hotels. Everything is prepared fresh. The proprietor oversees every serving by the waitresses. To begin with, one gets a heaping basket of homemade bread and a carafe of the local wine. I recommend the grilled fish of the day, served with three vegetables. Soups are hearty, the helpings generous. The price of a meal ranges from 2,500$ ($16.75). The decor is nautical, the walls decorated with objects rescued from the sea. On sale are handmade straw and reed baskets. Lunch is offered, and you can arrive daily from noon to 3:30pm. Dinner is daily from 7 to 10pm. Reservations aren't necessary. AE, DC, MC, V.

A Seta, Estrada do Livramento 80, Monte (tel. 476-43), is for regional cuisine supreme. The mountainside restaurant is a tavern where you can order inexpensive and tasty Portuguese meals. The decor is rustic, with a burnt-wood trim, walls covered with pinecones, and crude natural pine tables. An inner dining room adjoins an open kitchen, with a charcoal spit and oven, ideal for those who want to watch the action.

First of all, a plate of coarse brown homemade bread still warm from the oven is put at your place. Above each table is a hook to which is attached a long skewer of charcoal-broiled meat. You slip off chunks while mopping up the juices with your crusty bread. There are three specialties: beef, chicken, and grilled dry codfish. Seasoned with olive oil, herbs, garlic, and bay leaves, these concoctions are called *espetadas*. Fried potatoes are always done well here (ask for some hot sauce). For a fine repast, count on spending 2,700$ ($18.10). Hours are noon to 3pm and 6 to 11pm Thursday to Tuesday. Reservations aren't needed. A Seta closes every year in either May or June (so call first). AE, DC, MC, V

---

4. What to See & Do

Funchal is the center of Madeira's wine industry. Grapes have grown in the region since the early 15th century when Henry the Navigator introduced vines and sugarcane to the slopes. In Funchal, the must (fresh wine) from the black and white grapes is used to make Bual, Sercial, and Malmsey. It's cultivated for its bittersweet tang (women used to scent their handkerchiefs with it). The wine growers still transport the foot-pressed must in goatskin bottles over the rough terrain by *borracheiros*. Naturally, it undergoes extensive pasteurization in its refinement and blending.

Madeira Wine Company, Avenida Arriaga 28 (tel. 201-21), next to the tourist office, offers samples from its diverse stock. Inside this former convent, dating from

1790, are murals depicting the wine pressing (by foot) and harvesting processes, which proceed according to traditions established hundreds of years ago. You can savor the slightly burnt sweetness in a setting of old barrels, wine kegs, and time-mellowed chairs and tables made from aged wine kegs. Incidentally, Napoléon passed this way on his journey into exile on St. Helena in 1815. Bottles from a vintage year were given to him, but death came before the former emperor could sample them.

Of the churches of Funchal, the most intriguing is the rustic 15th-century **Sé (cathedral),** with its Moorish carved cedar ceiling, stone floors, Gothic arches, stained-glass windows, and baroque altars.

Just down the street from the Cruzes Museum is the baroque **Convent of Santa Clara,** Calçada de Santa Clara, with walled tiles, a painted wooden ceiling, and the tomb of Zarco, the discoverer of Madeira. The church is said to have been built by the granddaughter of Zarco the year Columbus discovered America.

Museu da Quinta das Cruzes, Calçada do Pico 1 (tel. 223-82), is the ancient residence of Madeira's discoverer, João Gonçalves Zarco. The surrounding park is of botanical interest and contains an orchid collection of note. The museum houses many fine examples of English furniture and China trade porcelains brought to Madeira by expatriate Englishmen during the 18th century, rare Indo-Portuguese cabinets, and the unique chests, native to Madeira, fashioned from *caixas de açúcar* (sugar boxes, which date from the 17th century). Also worth noting is a superb collection of antique Portuguese silver. The museum is open Tuesday to Sunday from 10am to noon and 2:30 to 6pm and charges 100$ (65¢).

The land and aquatic animal life of the archipelago is represented at the **Museu Municipal do Funchal,** Rua da Mouraria 31 (tel. 297-61). Moray eels, eagle rays, scorpion fish, sea cucumbers, sea zephyrs, sharp-nosed puffers, and loggerhead turtles, as well as many of the beautifully plumed birds seen around Madeira, are represented here. Tuesday to Friday, the museum and aquarium are open from 10am to 8pm. On Saturday and Sunday hours are noon to 6pm. Closed Monday. Admission is 65$ (45¢); free to children under 12. Access is either by private car or taxi (no buses).

The **Municipal Square** is a study in light and dark, its plaza paved with hundreds of black-and-white lava half moons. The whitewashed buildings surrounding it have black stone trim and ocher-colored tile roofs. In all, it's an atmosphere of stately beauty.

You can also visit a **lota** (fish auction) and many bazaars selling local handcrafts. At the lota, seafood is auctioned off to housewives and restaurant owners. Horse mackerel, grouper, mullet, tunny (sometimes weighing hundreds of pounds), freshwater eels, even a slab of barracuda, will find its way to the stalls.

In the bazaars you can purchase needlepoint tapestries, Madeira wines, laces, embroidery on Swiss organdy or Irish linen, plus all sorts of local crafts such as goatskin boots or Camacha basketry of water willows. The **City Market,** at the Praça do Comércio on Saturday, is a study in color, offering everything from yams to pawpaws.

Jardim Botânico lies about 2½ miles from Funchal on the road to Camacha. It is said to be one of the best botanical gardens in Iberia, with faraway views of the bay. It is open daily from 9am to 6pm, charging an admission of 250$ ($1.70). For more information, phone 360-37. Take bus no. 30.

The most exciting (and most crowded) time to visit Funchal is during the **End of the Year Festival,** December 30 to January 1. Fireworks light up the Bay of Funchal, the mountains in the background forming an amphitheater. Floodlit cruise ships anchor in the harbor to the delight of passengers who revel until dawn.

---

5. Sports & Recreation

The pleasant climate of Madeira invites visitors to enjoy outdoor activities, even if they consist mainly of strolling through the city of Funchal and along park pathways and country lanes. Time was when the visiting Victorians (some of the men looking like Mr. Pickwick) were carried around the islands in hammocks slung on poles and supported by two husky bearers. Nowadays this form of transport is a nostalgic memory. As one official put it: "The Communists objected to it. They consider it a form of slavery." A more popular means of transport in Funchal is to hire a bullock-pulled, wheel-less sledge on the Avenida do Mar, near the pier.

By far the most famous rides, however, are . . .

THE TOBOGGAN RIDES

Descents are made by toboggan from Terreiro da Luta. You ascend by taxi, about a 20-minute trip costing 1,300$ ($8.70) one-way. Before you begin your descent, you can visit the **Church of Nossa Senhora do Monte,** which contains the iron tomb of the last of the Hapsburgs, the Emperor Charles who died in Madeira in 1922 of pneumonia. From a belvedere nearby, you can look down on the whole of Funchal: the narrow streets, the plazas, and especially the *cais,* that long docking pier set in deep-blue mirrorlike water.

The toboggan is a wide wicker basket with wooden runners. The baskets were the main means of transport in Monte from 1849 to 1942. The nearly 2-mile ride takes 10 minutes. As it rushes down the slippery smooth cobblestones, it is directed and sometimes propelled by two expert, straw-hatted guides who yaw the ropes like nimble-footed seamen. You may need to fortify yourself with a glass or two of Madeira wine before taking the plunge. From Terreiro da Luta to Funchal the ride costs 1,800$ ($12.05) per person. At Terreiro da Luta, at a height of 2,875 feet, you'll enjoy a splendid view of Funchal. Here also are monuments to Zarco and Our Lady of Peace.

SWIMMING

Since Madeira doesn't have beaches, guests use one of the swimming pools, most often provided by a hotel. However, if your hotel doesn't have one, you can use the facilities of the **Lido Swimming Pool Complex** (Complexo Balnear do Lido), Rua do Gorgulho (tel. 76-22-17), which has an Olympic-size pool, plus a spacious pool for children as well. It is open in summer daily from 8:30am to 7pm (in the off-season from 9am to 6pm). Adults pay 170$ ($1.15) and children 80$ (55¢) to use the pool. A special ticket, costing 40$ (25¢), is sold to visitors who want to use the upper deck only. You can rent sunbeds and umbrellas for 160$ ($1.05).

The complex is equipped with several facilities, including a café, a restaurant, an ice-cream parlor, bars, and a water-sports headquarters. To reach it, head out the Estrada Monumental from Funchal, turning onto the Rua do Gorgulho (the turnoff is marked). Take bus no. 6.

GOLF

In the northeastern part of Madeira, in the hamlet of Santo da Serra, is the **Madeira Golf Course** (tel. 55-21-39). The golf course, at more than 2,000 feet above sea level, enjoys an attractive setting in a forested area with mimosa and eucalyptus. It opened as a six-hole course, but there was an almost immediate demand to extend it to 27 holes. There is a clubhouse room, as well as a lounge area and bar. Clubs can be rented, and local caddies are available. Greens fees cost from 3,000$ ($20.10).

TENNIS

Most of the first-class and deluxe establishments have their own courts. If you're in a hotel without a court, you can often obtain permission to play at a major hotel if you make a reservation (you'll be charged a small fee, of course). Naturally, guests of the hotel get priority.

HORSEBACK RIDING

For equestrians, the **Centro de Hispismo da Madeira,** Caminho dos Pretos (tel. 79-25-82), arranges this increasingly popular activity. Vacationers go riding Tuesday to Sunday from 9am to 5pm. The cost is 2,500$ ($16.75) per hour.

WATER SPORTS

The activities desks of several of the major hotels, including the Savoy and Reid's, will arrange these activities for you, even if you're not a guest of the establishment. Naturally, you must pay for whatever services you book. Waterskiing can be arranged, as can windsurfing and boat rentals. Sailing dinghies can also be rented. If you want to go snorkeling or scuba diving, check with the Inter Atlas Hotel, Garajau-Caniço (tel. 93-24-21).

DEEP-SEA FISHING

This is a popular sport in Madeira. The catch is mainly longtail tuna, blue marlin, swordfish, and several varieties of shark, along with other denizens of the deep. Boats can generally be rented for moderate costs. The tourist office will supply you with up-to-date information about boat rentals and the latest rates.

---

6. Where to Shop

Casa do Turista, Rua do Conselheiro José Silvestre Ribeiro 2 (tel. 249-07), near the waterfront, Funchal, is one of the best places on the island at which to purchase handcrafts of Madeira. Privately managed, it has a policy of clearly labeled and "firm" prices, unlike many of the bazaars which pick up added business by paying to have cruise-ship passengers directed to their establishments, or else having employees chase you down the street quoting lower tariffs after you've nixed their higher tabs. The setting of the Tourist House is beguiling, in an old quinta, once inhabited by a distinguished local family. Its elegant rooms are a natural setting to show off the beautiful handmade items. You're treated as a guest in a private home.

In the patio, with a fountain and semitropical greenery, is a miniature village, with small-scale typical rooms furnished in the local style. Among the merchandise offered are handmade embroideries in linen or cotton (the fabric is often imported from Switzerland and Ireland), tapestries, wickerwork, Portuguese pottery and ceramics, Madeira wines, fruit, and flowers. You'll find all types of embroidery and appliqué, as well as "shadow work," the tariffs determined by the number of stitches.

Specific merchandise includes embroidered Irish linen handkerchiefs for men (some with monograms); handbags made of banana skins, in different sizes; the characteristic goatskin boots; 12-string guitars; 15-piece embroidered placemat and napkin sets; appliquéd tray cloths in shadow work; old Madeira-style tablecloths; and embroidered bridge cloths with four napkins.

In one of the rooms is a display of old wines, with ceramic jugs. Old wines (*velho*) are sold in their original bottles, some costing very little. In addition, a half pint of sugarcane brandy is for sale in souvenir packages of five miniature varieties.

Other shops include the following:

Casa Oliveira, Rua da Alfândega 1B (tel. 293-40), which has an embroidery factory right on the premises.

Likewise, **Jabara,** Rua Dr. Fernão Ornelas 59 (tel. 295-00), has its own embroidery factory, and specializes in regional articles.

Madeira Gobelins, Rua da Carreira 194 (tel. 220-73), is a specialist in art needlework, and you can visit its showroom and factory. In addition to needlework, it specializes in the production of Portuguese rugs, hand-stitched, as well as monogrammed linens and other items. It also has a second outlet in Funchal, the Savoy Boutique No. 2 on the Avenida do Infante.

Madeira Superbia, Rua do Carmo 27 (tel. 240-23), is known for its fine embroidery (of excellent quality) and is a specialist in tapestries.

Lino and Araujo Ltd., Rua Dos Murcas 15 (tel. 207-36), specializes in hand-embroideries and knitted goods. This shop is frequented by many non-Portuguese residents of Madeira.

Cayres Department Store, Rua Dr. Fernão Ornelas 56A–56B (tel. 261-04), is a good tourist shopping center, where you can find a variety of items personally selected by the store owner, who is also an art specialist. Regional art includes embroidery, tapestry, glass, crystal, pewter, porcelain, ceramics, and the famous Arraiolos carpets. Women's fashions are in the Boutique, and there are sections of the store dealing in antiques, paintings, furniture, and Chinese porcelain.

7. Evening Entertainment

Casino Park Complex, Avenida do Infante (tel. 311-21), open daily from 8pm to 3am, is the glittering target for most visitors to the island. On its own grounds in the center of town, it is just minutes from most of the big hotels. "Indoor sports" include roulette, French banque, craps, blackjack, and slot machines for the "Dixie cup" crowd. Designed by Oscar Niemeyer, the architect of Brasilia, the complex features a 400-room, five-star deluxe hotel (the Casino Park), plus a dance club, Bacara, which charges a cover of 1,000$ ($6.70). Guests can dine in Chez Oscar Monday to Saturday from 7:30 to 10:30pm and at the Panoramic Restaurant Monday to Saturday from 7:30 to 9:15pm.

Admission to the casino is easy for tourists, who take along their passports or some other identification card. The entrance fee to the game room is 350$ ($2.35) but only 100$ (65¢) for hotel clients.

The Prince Albert, Rua da Imperatriz D. Amélia (tel. 35-793), is a Victorian pub in Madeira, complete with plush cut-velvet walls, tufted banquettes, and English pub memorabilia. You're greeted with a "Good evening, sir (or madam)." Next to the Savoy, the pub serves oversize mugs of beer and a cross sampling of all the accents of England. Drinks are offered at the curved bar or at one of the tables under Edwardian fringed lamps. Beer costs from 220$ ($1.45); mixed drinks 300$ ($2). The establishment is open daily from noon to 2am.

O Farol Disco Club, Madeira Carlton, Largo António Nobre (tel. 310-31), considered the best, most interesting, and safest disco on the island, lies in a circular outbuilding near the lagoon-shaped swimming pool of this five-star hotel already recommended. To reach it, most visitors pass through the hotel lobby, descending open-toed flights of stairs and passing through the hotel gardens. The disco offers current music, rows of curved windows overlooking the sea, and several tiers of curved platforms whose visual focus is the dance floor. Visitors pay 1,000$ ($6.70) at the door, which builds up a drink credit. Scotch and soda costs 650$ ($4.35). The music lasts Monday to Saturday night from 10pm to 3am.

Joe's Bar, Quinta da Penha de França, Rua da Penha de França (tel. 290-87), stands on the grounds of the previously recommended hotel. It is decorated in a turn-of-the-century style. Beer costs 190$ ($1.25); mixed drinks 400$ ($2.70). Piano music is featured. Hours are daily from 12:30pm to 2am.

8. Touring the Island

To explore and savor Madeira, the adventurous visitor with endless time will go on foot across some of the trails. Hand-hewn stones and gravel-sided embankments lead one (but definitely not the queasy) along precipitous ledges, down into lush ravines, across flowering meadows. These dizzying paths are found everywhere from the hillsides of the wine-rich region of Estreito de Câmara de Lobos to the wickerwork center of Camacha. A much easier way to go, of course, is on an organized tour, or to use the local buses, although you may prefer to risk the hazardous driving on hairpin curves.

Heading west from Funchal, you'll pass banana groves almost spilling into the sea, women doing their laundry on rocks, and homes so tiny they're almost like dollhouses. Less than 6 miles away lies the coastal village of **Câmara de Lobos** (Room of the Wolves), the subject of several paintings by Sir Winston Churchill. A sheltered and tranquil shell-shaped cove, it is set amid rocks and towering cliffs, with hill-climbing cottages, terraces, and date palms. In the late afternoon naked youngsters loll and play in the cove, alongside the bobbing fishing boats in such colors as sunflower gold, kelly green, and marine blue.

The road north from the village through the vineyards leads to **Estreito de Câmara de Lobos,** the heart of the wine-growing region that produces Madeira. The men who cultivate the ribbonlike terraces can be seen laboring in the fields, wearing brown stocking caps with tasseled tops. Along the way you'll spot women sitting on mossy stone steps, doing Madeira embroidery. At times clouds move in over the mountaintops obscuring the view, then pass off toward the sea or tumble down a hillside.

Scaling a hill studded with pine and eucalyptus, you'll reach **Cabo Girão,** the oceanside cliff mentioned in the introduction. Considered the second-loftiest promontory in Europe, a belvedere overlooks the sea and the saffron-colored rocks below. Close by, you can see how the land is cultivated in Madeira, one terrace seemingly no larger than a small throw rug. (Incidentally, the blondes you see in and around here aren't peroxided. Rather, the straw-colored hair was inherited from early Flemish settlers sent to the island.)

Try to return to Funchal by veering off the coastal road, past São Martinho to the belvedere at **Pico dos Barcelos.** In one of the most idyllic spots on the island, you can see the ocean, the mountains, orange and banana groves, bougainvillea, poinsettias, and the capital. Whether it's roosters crowing, babies crying in faraway huts, or goats bleating, the sound carries for miles.

By heading north from Funchal, you can visit some of the most outstanding spots in the heart of the island. Going first through Santo António, you'll eventually reach **Curral das Freiras,** a petite village huddled around an old monastery at the bottom of an extinct volcanic crater. The site, whose name means Corral of the Nuns, was originally a secluded convent that protected the good sisters from seaweary, woman-hungry mariners and pirates.

If you go north in a different direction, one of the goals is **Santana.** Many visitors have described it as something out of Disney's *Fantasia.* Picture an alpine setting, complete with waterfalls, cobblestone streets, green meadows sprinkled with multicolored blossoms, thatched cottages, swarms of roses, and plunging ravines. Of it, novelist Paul Bowles once wrote: "It is as if a 19th-century painter with a taste for the baroque had invented a countryside to suit his own personal fantasy. It is the sort of picture that used to adorn the grocer's calendar."

Southwest of the village is **Queimadas,** the site of a 3,000-foot-high rest house. From here, many people make the 3-hour trek to the apex of **Pico Ruivo** (Purple Peak), referred to earlier as the highest point on the island, 6,105 feet above sea level.

In the east, about 18 miles from Funchal (a short drive from the airport) is historic **Machico,** with its much-visited **Church of Senhor dos Milagres,** dating from the mid-15th century. According to legend, the church was built over the tombs of the two star-crossed English lovers, Robert Machim and Anna d'Arfet. Try to view the village from the belvedere of **Camöe Pequeno.** In the vicinity is a grotto 300 feet long, said to be the deepest in Madeira.

On the way back from Machico, you can detour inland to **Camacha,** perched in a setting of flowers and orchards. It's the island center of the wickerwork industry. You can buy here (although the stores in Funchal are heavily supplied), or just watch chairs and other items being made by the local craftspeople.

ORGANIZED TOURS

Those who stay only in Funchal miss what the island is about. If you don't care to venture into the mountains in your own automobile, then take one of the many excursions to different sections of the island. The tours reach virtually every accessible point in Madeira from Porto Moniz to Câmara de Lobos, and many of the excursions are terminated in Terreiro da Luta where you can finish with a toboggan ride into Funchal. Various tours leave every day; the major jaunt to Porto Moniz and Cabo Girão costs 6,000$ ($40.20), including lunch. A half-day volcano-and-toboggan tour costs 2,500$ ($16.75). One of the more interesting tours is a visit to the wickerworks at Camacha, among other attractions, costing 2,300$ ($15.55).

Madeira possesses a number of travel agencies, including Wagons-Lits Cook. If you go to any of them, you can receive detailed information about the island tours available. Not all are by motorcoach; some are by boat. You can also pick up information at the **Official Tourist Bureau,** Avenida Arriaga 18 (tel. 256-68).

9. Porto Santo

Another island of the little Madeira group is Porto Santo, some 24 miles northeast of the main land mass and very different from that island. It is only 9 miles long and three miles wide, yet it boasts a 4-mile strip of fine, sandy beach along the southern shore. The island is not as hilly as Madeira: Its highest elevation is about 1,670 feet above sea level, at **Pico do Facho.**

This island was the first on which the discoverers of Madeira, João Gonçalves Zarco and Tristão Vaz Teixiera, landed in 1418. These captains, serving Prince Henry the Navigator, took refuge here when a storm blew them off course, and named it Porto Santo (Holy Port) to express gratitude for their survival. It was not until 1419 that they were in condition to sail on and make the landfall at Madeira. Henry gave Teixiera and Zarco authority to run Madeira, but he placed Porto Santo in the hands of Bartolomeu Perestrello, who made his mark on the island. At least, he is reported to have brought in rabbits as a future food source, but instead, it is said, they ate everything in sight, laying waste to the vegetation already there and not helping future crops much.

Christopher Columbus slept here. He married Isobel Moniz, the daughter of Perestrello, before going on to Funchal to prepare for his planned sea exploration. The house in which he is claimed to have lived is in an alley back of the little white church in the town of **Villa Baleira,** which is also called Porto Santo.

The island gets very dry in summer, which makes it popular with beach-goers but not very good for crops. Produced in winter, the foodstuffs grown on Porto Santo include grain, tomatoes, figs, and melons, as well as grapes from which a sweet white wine is made. Islanders who don't farm go fishing. The low hills are crowned here with a few remaining unusual windmills.

The water of Porto Santo is supposed to have therapeutic values, which have made it a popular drink not only on the island but also in Madeira and Portugal. The water-bottling plants, fish canneries, and a lime kiln are industries of Porto Santo.

The little town with two names lies beneath **Pico do Castelo,** a height on which stands a ruined 16th-century castle built for defense. For a long time Madeira let Porto Santo shift for itself in this regard, and it fell prey to pirates now and then.

Try to go to the **Fountain in the Sands** (Fonte da Areia), near cliffs above a rocky coast. Here local women wash their clothes in the water flowing out.

Good points from which to get views of the island and its surroundings are **Portela** and **Castelo Peak** (Pico do Castelo). **Ponta da Calheta** is another sight provided by nature, on the south of the island. This point looks to Baixo Islet across a reef-strewn channel constantly pounded by the sea. Black basalt rocks dot the beach.

Independência, a hydrofoil, sails from Funchal to Porto Santo daily, if the weather is good. The trip takes 1½ hours each way and costs 5,900$ ($39.55) round-trip. Call 252-81 for reservations. Some hotels or quintas will pack a picnic lunch, which guests can enjoy on the beach. The boat leaves Madeira at 8am Wednesday through Monday, returning at 6pm and giving passengers plenty of time on the Porto Santo beach. The ride is often rough, and many passengers get sick from motion sickness, so be duly warned. For 6,900$ ($46.25), you can fly over in the morning on a **TAP** flight, catching a Funchal-bound plane in Porto Santo in the early evening. In summer, at least six flights are operated daily. Call TAP at 98-23-79 for reservations.

WHERE TO STAY

The four-star, first-class **Hotel Porto Santo,** Campo de Baixo, 9400 Porto Santo (tel. 091/98-23-81; fax 091/98-26-11), has only two floors. It was constructed a little more than a mile from Vila Baleira at Suloeste, in a garden setting bordering directly on the large (4-mile-long) beach of gold-colored sand. The Porto Santo offers 89 well-furnished rooms, including four suites, each with private bath, phone, and a terrace overlooking the bay. For your room and breakfast, rates are 10,900$ ($73.05) daily in a single, 13,300$ ($89.10) in a double. Suites begin at 18,000$ ($120.60).

The hotel also has a large restaurant serving a bountiful lunch or dinner for 2,500$ ($16.75). The main lounge has been attractively furnished, and mercifully, air conditioned. It leads to the main terrace and garden, where there is an open bar. After the hot sun retires a bit, the tennis courts are popular. A swimming pool has been built for guests, and windsurfing is also available. Laundry and baby-sitting are available, and room service is offered until 10pm. Parking is free. AE, DC, MC, V.

Hotel Praia Dourada, Rue Dr. Pedro Lomelino, 9400 Porto Santo (tel. 091/ 98-23-15; fax 091/98-24-87), is the leading hotel at Vila Baleira (not that there's much competition). Rooms, each with private bath and phone, are simply furnished but clean. The 110 accommodations are rented to both tourists and persons who have business on the island. Charges range from 7,200$ ($48.25) daily in a single to 9,900$ ($66.35) in a double, including breakfast. Laundry service is available. The hotel has an outdoor swimming pool. Parking is free. AE, DC, MC, V.

Pensão Central, Rua Abel Magna Vasconcelos, 9400 Porto Santo (tel. 091/ 98-22-26), is modesty itself, but clean and immaculate. Also in the capital, Vila Baleira, the pension is among the least expensive places to stay on the island. It rents 12 bedrooms, each with private bath. Charges range from 4,300$ ($28.80) daily in a single, and from 5,500$ ($36.85) in a double, including breakfast. The little inn is homelike, its owners welcoming. They offer guests the use of a bar, sun terrace, and restaurant. Parking is free. No credit cards.

WHERE TO DINE

Arsénios, Avenida Dr. Manuel Pestana Júnior (tel. 98-43-48), is perhaps *número uno* in Porto Santo. It was patterned after a restaurant owned by the same entrepreneur in Funchal, and its Madeira success formula was imported to nearby Porto Santo. It is said to produce the best paella in town. Full Portuguese meals, including many fresh fish dishes (which depend on the catch of the day), cost from 3,000$ ($20.10). Hours are daily from 11am to 3pm and 6 to 11pm. The restaurant is located in town on the main road opposite the sea. It is housed in a modern building with large panoramic windows. Reservations aren't needed. AE, DC, MC, V.

Marqués, Rua Maximiliano de Sousa Maxç (tel. 98-23-19), is another good restaurant, lying in a modern building near the center of town. It serves many varieties of grilled fish and seems to take pride in the offerings of its Portuguese kitchen. Try several kinds of grilled or fried fish or espetada (steak on a spit). Hours are from 9:30am to midnight daily, and meals cost from 2,500$ ($16.75). Reservations aren't needed. AE, DC, MC, V.

Por-do-Sol, Sítio da Calheta (tel. 98-23-80), lies on the western tip of the island. Installed in a brick-walled house, it is simply decorated and stays open without interruption daily from noon to midnight. Three Portuguese food specialties include espetada (steak on a spit), caldeirada (fish stew made with several kinds of fish), and grilled fish (whatever the catch turned up that day). A meal costs from 2,000$ ($13.40). Reservations aren't needed. No credit cards.

THE AZORES

Those seeking an offbeat holiday in Europe can strike out for the remote Azores. It is an archipelago where the winds of the ocean meet, where the cyclones call on each other. Robin Bryans called the islands a "muted mood, a pianissimo untouched by the strident dissonance of industrial Europe."

When the first explorers directed their ships' prows into the Atlantic, the volcanic slopes of the Azores were the westernmost known points of land. Whether the Vikings, the Genoese, the Phoenicians, or whoever, first put into these lands remains unknown. There are those who believe that the Azores are all that remain of the lost continent of Atlantis.

The autonomous archipelago spans a distance of more than 500 miles from the southeastern tip of Santa Maria to the northwestern extremity at Corvo. The main island of **São Miguel** lies about 760 miles west of Portugal (2,110 miles east of New York), making the Azores the most isolated islands in the entire Atlantic.

Completely uninhabited when discovered, the Azores were named by Diogo de Silves (a captain of Henry the Navigator) after the hook-beaked *açor* (compared to both a hawk and an eagle), which sailed on the air currents over the coast. The date: 1427 (give or take a year or two). It wasn't long before settlements sprang up. Besides the Portuguese settlers, many from the north, Flemish immigrants came to the central Azores, where place and family names today show this influence.

Eventually it was learned that the entire island group was actually composed of three distinct archipelagos: the eastern section of **Santa Maria** and **São Miguel;** the central with **Terceira** (scene of bullfighting in the streets), **Graciosa** (about 11 miles in length, known for its Sulfur Cave), cigar-shaped **São Jorge** (Raúl Brandão's ethereal island of dust and dream), **Pico** (with a cloud-capped mountain), and **Faial** (vulnerable to earthquakes and known for the eerie crater of the extinct volcano, Caldeira); and the western group made up of **Flores** (Flowers) where vegetation runs riot in a setting of lakes, waterfalls, and valleys, and **Corvo** (the smallest member—everybody knows everybody else—and a visit by a foreigner is an occasion).

The Azores are a study in color. The writer who once made the much-publicized characterization, the "Gray Azores," must have been color-blind. Much of the color of the archipelago comes from the flowers that grow rampantly in its volcanic soil: azaleas, camellias, heather, agapanthus, rhododendrons. Although occasionally lashed by violent storms, the enchanted islands enjoy a mild climate: The temperature averages around 58° Fahrenheit in winter, only 75° Fahrenheit in summer.

Its rugged people who daily contend with the elements of nature are hospitable to strangers, even though one might have expected such isolated islanders to be insular. Coming back from a walk in the São Miguel hills, two American visitors were stopped by a boy riding a mule. Under a straw hat with a hoe slung over his shoulder, the boy smiled as he bid them *boa tarde*. The word YALE was written across his sweatshirt. Learning that he spoke a bit of English, the visitors inquired about the letters. It seemed that his uncle had attended Yale. "Do you know him?" the boy asked. "He now lives in Boston."

Every man, woman, and child in the island chain seemingly has relatives living in the United States. Many settled in New Bedford, Massachusetts (of *Moby-Dick* fame), during the whaling heyday of that port, taking jobs as sailors, fishermen, whalers, and caulkers. Many of the immigrants returned to the Azores, however, after earning their fortunes across the sea.

GETTING THERE

At any **TAP** office or at your local travel agent, you can learn the times and frequency of flights to the Azores. If you hold a round-trip ticket from New York to Lisbon, you are allowed to stop free in the Azores, if you make arrangements when you purchase your ticket. The free stopover, however, may not be valid on special excursion tickets.

TAP flies a scheduled service between Logan Airport in Boston and Lisbon, going via Terceira. In winter there is one flight a week in each direction, increasing to two flights per week in each direction after March 30.

Most flights leaving the Azores for Lisbon depart from San Miguel's airport near Ponta Delgada. This creates confusion for some North American travelers who, coming from Boston, have the intention of exploring one or two of the islands before continuing their trip to the mainland of Portugal. The plane from Boston lands on Terceira, but because of airline schedules, the only convenient departure for Lisbon is from a neighboring island, San Miguel.

You can travel by boat between the two islands, but even the local residents find this both inconvenient and uncomfortable. Far more practical would be to fly.

Service within the Azores is operated by **SATA (Serviço Açoreano de Transportes Aéreos).** Reservations and information about SATA can be made from anywhere in North America by calling the nearest TAP office (or their toll-free number, 800/221-7370). All but the tiny island of Corvo have airports, but planes will sometimes choose not to fly during the worst of Atlantic storms.

SATA, however, is generally efficient and punctual. In fact, since 1984 when SATA upgraded its equipment and increased the number of its flights among the islands, boat transportation has been slowly phased out, except for transport among the islands of the Azorean middle group. Boat schedules vary with the seasons, and the local tourist offices will keep you abreast of last-minute schedules.

Because of their geographical situation, the Azores are a favorite port of call for cruises crossing the Atlantic, including, on occasion, the *QE 2.* However, stopovers are short. Yachts crossing the Atlantic also stop off here frequently. A favorite yachting event among British sailors is the Azab (Azores and back), and the Dutch also hold a similar race.

---

1. São Miguel & Ponta Delgada

The eastern group of the Azores archipelago, consisting of Santa Maria and São Miguel, was the first to be discovered by the Portuguese and claimed for their crown.

São Miguel, the second discovery, is the largest of all the islands, measuring about 37 miles long by 9½ miles wide, occupying 290 square miles of land far from mainland Portugal. Also called Ilha Verde (Green Island) because of the color of its pastures and forests, São Miguel glories in vegetation—masses of hydrangeas, azaleas, and cannas, as well as money crops such as tobacco, tea, and pineapple, grown under glass. Development and stock-breeding have made São Miguel one of the most prosperous islands in the Azores.

Ponta Delgada became the capital and principal town of the island in 1546, having become well populated in the less than 100 years of settlement. Ponta Delgada is also the seat of the regional government of the Azores. It is a flat, rectangular town about 2 miles long, lying along the west bank of a lovely bay and conforming to the indentations of the natural coastline. A promenade along the waterfront still lures strollers along its length at night, when the twinkling lights from vessels in the bay add a festive note. The zebra-striped **Avenida Infante Dom Henrique,** circling the waterfront, is the venue for the traditional *passeio,* the leisurely stroll indulged in by parents and their marriageable daughters, by young gallants, visitors, and sailors from ships in the harbor. The promenade area was constructed in the 1860s by the building of a 2,800-foot-long breakwater, making the wide boulevard possible.

In early days, artistic expression in the Azores mainly went into the decoration of churches and chapels and Ponta Delgada has its share of places of worship with magnificent interior decoration.

The **Convent and Chapel of Nossa Senhora da Esperança** dates from the cult of the image of Senhor Santo Cristo, given by Pope Paul III in 1530. The chapel in which the image is kept is completely lined with azulejos. The image is accompanied by a reliquary and jewels that have been accumulating since the 17th century and now completely cover the statue.

The walls of the **Church of São José** are lined with blue-and-white 18th-century glazed tiles alternating with haut-relief carving. A baroque pietà stands in the baptismal chapel.

The **Parish Church of São Sebastião** has a choir in carved cedar and such exotic woods as palisander. Built in the 16th century, its facade shows traces of the Manueline style with Renaissance influence in later renovation.

The **Convent of Santo André** houses the **Carlos Machado Museum,** known for historical archives, a library, an art collection, natural history exhibits, ethnological artifacts, and a collection of toys.

On the outskirts of Ponta Delgada, you can arrange to visit one of the pineapple factories, actually greenhouses, where the fruit is grown under sloping glass roofs that have been whitewashed. The plants are smoked several times during their growth, as this *fumo* method is said to make all of them flower at the same time. For information, check with **Pineapple Plantation,** Rua Dr. Augusto Arruda (tel. 091/241-26).

The local **tourist office** is at Avenida Infante Dom Henrique (tel. 096/25-743), in Ponta Delgada.

TRANSPORTATION

Both **SATA** and **TAP** airlines fly to the Ponta Delgada Airport (tel. 096/262-61).

SATA's offices on São Miguel are in Ponta Delgada on the Avenida Infante Dom Henrique (tel. 096/272-21), and at the airport (Nordela) (tel. 096/232-61). At Ribeira Grande, the office is at Largo Jardim 7 (tel. 096/721-47).

TAP's booking office in Ponta Delgada is on the Avenida Infante Dom Henrique (tel. 096/262-06). At the airport, call TAP at 096/246-72.

If you prefer to be an oceangoing visitor to or from the island, get in touch with **Junta Autónoma do Porto de Ponta Delgada,** Rua Teófilo Braga 1, in Ponta Delgada (tel. 096/252-21), for information.

Rent-a-car and taxi service are provided by: **Ilha Verde Rent-a-Car,** Praça 5 de Outubro 19 (tel. 096/252-00); and **Micauto Rent-a-Car,** Avenida Infante Dom Henrique 109 (tel. 096/243-82). Outside the capital, Micauto has branches at the

airport (tel. 096/243-82), at Ribeira Grande (tel. 096/721-21), and at Furnas (tel. 096/542-54).

WHERE TO STAY IN PONTA DELGADA

You can savor the ambience of past centuries at the **Hotel de São Pedro,** Largo Almirante Dunn, 9500 Ponta Delgada, São Miguel, Açores (tel. 096/222-23; fax 096/62-93-19), while you enjoy the comforts of the 20th. The building was the work of the island's most colorful and legendary figure, Thomas Hickling, who came from Boston on a schooner in 1769. He and his descendants profited from a thriving business growing and exporting oranges to London and St. Petersburg (Leningrad). From their wealth, they built a family homestead with the help of imported craftsmen, and shipped in loads of fine antiques from the continent to furnish it. Their town house, with its Georgian colonial interior, is on the sea, with a high garden wall to provide privacy from the street. Throughout its history it has known many vicissitudes (it was used in World War I as a headquarters for the American navy).

Nowadays one can stay here in comparative luxury for moderate tariffs. Modernization has been carried out effectively.

Because of the noncommercial atmosphere, guests are likely to intermingle freely, and the staff is considerate. The drawing room is formal, with two bronze-and-crystal chandeliers, a pair of fine 18th-century fruitwood chests, velvet chairs, and a sofa set in front of an Adam-style fireplace. Fresh flowers are everywhere, as important to the character of São Pedro as changing the linen sheets. The drinking lounge seems right from Old Salem, Massachusetts, with its hand-hewn beams and spoke chairs. Drinks are also served on the tiled loggia where you can enjoy the view of the lawn, the water, the stone urns, and the century-old trees. The 20 bedrooms are equipped with traditional pieces, and 6 suites are furnished in the grand manner —one with a huge Napoleonic sleigh bed, another with spindle twin beds. The dining room, scene of many bountiful meals, is recommended separately. Singles range from 10,000$ ($67) daily, with doubles costing 14,000$ ($93.80). Suites for two persons cost from 22,000$ ($147.40). Parking is free. Laundry service is available, and room service is provided until midnight. AE, DC, MC, V.

Hotel Canadiano, Rua do Contado 24A, 9500 Ponta Delgada, São Miguel, Açores (tel. 096/274-21; fax 096/62-94-36). Built as a hybrid between a hotel and a motel in 1982, it lies on a hillock beside a busy and narrow cobblestone street a brisk walk from the harbor. The hotel has a comfortable and streamlined lobby, a cozy bar (called The Canuck), and a snack bar. Its 48 bedrooms lie around a courtyard in back, as well as within a multistory block facing the street. Each unit contains a phone, an intercom, a private bath, and a veranda. With breakfast included, singles cost 7,500$ ($50.25) daily, and doubles go for 9,800$ ($65.65). There's a TV lounge, plus a tennis court on the premises. Laundry service is provided, and room service is available until midnight. AE, DC, MC, V.

Hotel Gaivota Apartamentos, Avenida Marginal 103, 9500 Ponta Delgada, São Miguel, Açores (tel. 096/232-86; fax 096/272-09). Set on the main seaside promenade, this is one of the few hotels in town offering rooms with private kitchens. Built in the early 1980s, it has a nautically inspired lobby of panels accented with driftwood, an elevator, and a largely European clientele. Each of its 35 units has a phone, TV, air conditioning, minibar, and a pleasant and tasteful collection of Iberian-inspired furnishings. The best accommodations also have a private balcony. Doubles range from 10,000$ ($67) to 15,000$ ($100.50), plus another 750$ ($5.05) for breakfast. Parking is free on the street. AE, DC, MC, V.

Hotel Avenida, Rua Dr. José B. T. Carreiro, 9500 Ponta Delgada, São Miguel, Açores (tel. 096/62-76-98; fax 096/62-76-98). The distinctive facade of this six-story hotel has a series of angled windows. It is one of the most modern and up-to-date hotels on the island, rated four stars. In the center of town, it is but a short walk from the beach. Each of its well-decorated and cozy bedrooms, 80 in all, comes with private bath, color TV with in-house video, phone, radio, and air conditioning. With breakfast included, singles rent for 9,500$ ($63.65) daily, and doubles cost from 10,900$ ($73.05). The comfortable lounges and the attractive bar, with its adjacent restaurant, are fully air conditioned. Laundry service and baby-sitting can be arranged, and room service is until midnight. Parking is free. AE, DC, MC, V.

Casa das Palmeiras, Rua Diário dos Açores 26, 9500 Ponta Delgado, São Miguel, Açores (tel. 096/226-21). The street outside is crowded, noisy, and commercial, but once you step into its walled semitropical garden, all the hubbub will be forgotten. Ringed with gnarled olive trees, this neoclassical villa was once the most prominent building in the neighborhood. Today its high ceilings and slightly tatty walls envelop nine comfortably coordinated bedrooms. Each of these has a refrigerator, phone, and private bath, and several contain some antiques. With breakfast included, singles cost 4,500$ ($30.15) daily, and doubles rent for 5,800$ ($38.85). The building's multicolored central spire, an unusual amalgam of turn-of-the-century styles, can be seen for many blocks. Parking is free. No credit cards.

Residencial América, Rua Manuel Inácio Correia 53, 9500 Ponta Delgada, São Miguel, Açores (tel. 096/243-51; fax 096/251-86), is one of the best buys for the money on the island. A simple inn, it offers 23 plain but comfortable bedrooms, each well maintained with private bath and phone. Some of them also have TVs. With breakfast included, singles cost 5,200$ ($34.85) daily, doubles go for 6,500$ ($43.55), and triples for 7,800$ ($52.25). The owners of the inn also have a rent-a-car service. Parking is free. AE, DC, MC, V.

WHERE TO DINE IN PONTA DELGADA

The best restaurant on the island is in the previously recommended **Hotel de São Pedro,** Largo Almirante Dunn (tel. 222-23). Admiring the architecture and the detailing of this elegant hotel is as much a part of its experience as the Portuguese cuisine. The dining room, on the second floor, is without equal in charm on the island. A battalion of uniformed waiters give impeccable service. The setting is one of Empire-era chairs, soaring ceilings, and paneling crafted from tropical hardwoods. Naturally, there's a view of the water, along with Sheraton-style cupboards. You can order a full lunch of dinner for 2,200$ ($14.75) to 3,000$ ($20.10), depending on whether you prefer one or two courses. Fish and meat, prepared in traditional Portuguese recipes, are the usual fare. Meals are served from 12:30 to 2:30pm and 7 to 9pm daily. Reservations are advised. AE, DC, MC, V.

Outside the hotels, one of the best restaurants is incongruously named **London,** Rua Ernesto do Canto 21 (tel. 225-00). Its chef presents a Portuguese menu with daily specialties that are well prepared and attractively served. The bill of fare is likely to include grilled creatures of the sea, such as swordfish, whitefish, or octopus. You might also order fried pork chops with bacon, perhaps saltimbocca, having begun with a fish soup. Meals cost from 2,500$ ($16.75) à la carte or 1,800$ ($12.05) on a tourist menu, and are offered Monday to Saturday from noon to 2:30pm and 7 to 10pm. The cozy restaurant, seating more than two dozen patrons, also has a darkly elegant bar. To reach the restaurant, you climb a flight of stone steps from the street below. Reservations aren't needed. AE, DC, MC, V.

Arturu's, Rua João Francisco Cabral 49F (tel. 249-90), is the most elegant and stylish restaurant on the island. It is located in a modern building at the edge of the center of town. In its air-conditioned interior, you can order an array of international dishes and local specialties. Fresh fish and shellfish dishes are favored. Service is polite and efficient. Full meals cost 2,500$ ($16.75) and are served from noon to 3pm and 7 to 11pm daily.

Coliseu, Avenida Roberto Ivens (tel. 271-20), has some of the best Portuguese regional cooking on the island. It has a large, airy, and white-walled interior, with paper table coverings. In all, it's clean, respectable, and a neighborhood institution. Waiters are helpful, and the kitchen is "on exhibit." The fresh fish is invariably recommended. Try the grilled squid or baked octopus. Meals, costing from 2,200$ ($14.75), are served from noon to 3pm and 6 to 9pm. The restaurant, seating 85 patrons, is closed on Tuesday. Reservations aren't needed. AE, DC, MC, V.

Boavista, Rua Ilha do São Miguel 12 (tel. 242-72), is known for having the best shellfish in town, along with a fine selection of Portuguese country cooking. You can sample a selection of fresh fish dishes costing from 2,200$ ($14.75) for a complete meal. Regional dishes include mixed blood sausage, broiled fish with shrimp, and various seafood dishes. Service is from noon to 3pm and 6:30 to 10:30pm except on Sunday. The restaurant is just outside the center of town, and is most often reached by taxi. Reservations aren't needed. AE, DC, MC, V.

O Corisco, Rua Manuel da Ponte 28 (tel. 244-44), is one of the best-respected restaurants in the center of Ponta Delgada. It is both a restaurant and a pub, offering regional as well as international cuisine. The chef specializes in shellfish dishes. From noon to 3pm and 6:30 to 11pm daily good-tasting meals are served for just 2,000$ ($13.40). No lunch is offered on Monday or Tuesday. For a lunch, especially if it's a hot day, you might settle for the tuna salad. However, you can also order more substantial fare, including grilled swordfish, grilled veal, and grilled pork cutlets, followed by coconut pudding or perhaps some Cheddar cheese from the Azores. Reservations aren't needed. DC, MC, V.

TOURING THE ISLAND

There are several points of interest on São Miguel, most of them bestowed by nature on the island.

Furnas

Following in the footsteps of rheumatic Victorians who shunned the sea cocktail at Brighton to take the baths at Furnas, you'll arrive at one of the richest spas in Europe. The thermal spa season lasts from July 1 to September 30, but a visit is interesting at any time of the year. The geysers and springs make the valley steamy in the district where sulphur fumes pour forth from craters.

The New Yorker described the springs as a place of "bare black rock, blasted by geysers, hot oozing clay, and sulphur-scented smoke. In a grim-looking cave, water boils furiously, now and then leaping up and spilling over in a smoking stream that runs steeply downhill between lava banks." David Dodge called the waters at the baths "cold, warm, boiling, carbonated, uncarbonated, radioactive, tasty, clear, muddy and as you like it, twenty-two kinds to choose from."

The major attraction is **Terra Nostra Park,** founded in 1770, according to an inscribed boulder, by Thomas Hickling, the American vice-consul discussed earlier in the description of São Pedro in Ponta Delgada. Where Hickling left off, the Marquês da Praia eventually took up. However, the latter's grandson at one point was about to destroy the park; but it was rescued by Vasco Bensuade in 1937. A pavilion was built that same year at Furnas Lake, and 2 years later a nine-hole championship golf course was opened.

It is a botanical garden, filled with azaleas, ferns, camellias, hydrangeas, pines, japonica, and jacaranda. Plants were brought from China, Japan, South America, Mexico, New Zealand, Asia, even the southern United States. White swans float majestically in the ponds studded with red and white lilies, and in the park is an egg-shaped swimming pool filled with muddy thermal waters. Changing cabins are nearby.

Before you go, you may want to take a trip to **Lake Furnas** for a volcano-cooked luncheon. This type of cuisine can be arranged through the Hotel Terra Nostra at Furnas. The cooking is known as à la caldeira. Everything from pullet to horse mackerel is covered with paper or some other wrapping after being well spiced with aromatic herbs. It then is buried in the hot earth, the way the Haitians roast kid. Sometimes whole chickens and yams are dropped into the simmering pools. On Sunday especially, you see families coming to the lakeside for picnics, washing down their meals with *cheiro,* a regional wine.

For dining or accommodations try:

Hotel Terra Nostra, 9675 Furnas, São Miguel, Açores (tel. 096/543-04; fax 096/543-04), is difficult to find, and the village's labyrinth of one-way streets makes reaching it a bit of an ordeal. Even when you arrive, the restrained detailing of its art deco facade might easily be overlooked if not for its position opposite a rose garden, the largest botanical garden in the Azores. Within its valleys, you'll find lush planting, along with a large oval basin designed like a giant reflecting pool, and a stone-sided villa like one of the imperial palaces of Brazil.

The 74-room hotel was recently expanded. Spacious rooms are rented, each with private bath, phone, and such art deco touches as curved walls and windows made from glass blocks. Forty rooms contain TVs. Singles rent for 7,500$ ($50.25) daily, and doubles go for 11,500$ ($77.05), including breakfast. Fixed-price meals in the dining room cost from 2,200$ ($14.75) and are served daily from 12:30 to 3pm and 7 to 9:30pm. AE, DC, MC, V.

Sete Cidades

The Seven Cities, an hourglass-shaped lake, was named after a legend; in fact, it is the subject of many myths. The lake, about 8 or 9 miles in circumference, the upper part blue, the lower emerald green, was supposedly formed by tears shed over a broken love affair: one by a blue-eyed princess, the other by the shepherd boy she loved who was green-eyed. The appellation of Sete Cidades stems from a legend that claims that this site was actually the center of a powerful empire on the lost continent of Atlantis. You can visit a park near the blue lake, called **Jardim Pitoresco,** and enjoy the wafting aroma of the pittosporum flower. The vegetation on the slopes makes this a lush setting.

Cavalo Branco, Rua do Meio Moio 23, Santa Bárbara, near Capelas (tel. 983-65). While exploring Sete Cidades, this restaurant provides the most appealing dining choice. The lunch hour is long, stretching from noon to 4pm daily, so it easily fits into a sightseeing agenda. The food is good too, with an array of Portuguese cookery and regional specialties. Care and attention go into the menu planning and the selection of food items. For example, they make their own sausage. The oven is fired by wood, which gives added flavor to the grills. Meals cost from 2,500$ ($16.75), and the restaurant is closed on Monday. If you're there for dinner, hours are 6:30 to 10pm. Reservations aren't needed. MC, V.

Pinhal Da Paz Recreational Reserve

Known also as **Mata das Criações,** Pinhal da Paz, comprising more than 120 acres, provides an unforgettable spectacle of color when the flowers are in bloom. Azaleas form a border along the roads through the reserve. Some of the colorful hedges run for nearly 10 miles.

Lagoa do Fogo

"Fire Lake" occupies the enormous crater of an extinct volcano in the center of the island. It is surrounded by dense vegetation, some of flowering plants. A nature reserve has been created here to protect the area, which includes the Lombades gorge, covered with luxuriant greenery.

Ilheu de Vila França

This islet, just off Vila França do Campo on the south coast, is one of the great local attractions. It forms a perfectly circular natural swimming pool in which numerous water sports are pursued. The rocks, worn into strange shapes by sea and wind, include a formation that looks like an ancient man-made column.

Where to Stay at Lagoa

Caloura Hotel Resort Jubileu, Agua de Pau, 9560 Lagoa, São Miguel, Açores (tel. 096/932-40; fax 096/932-06). The stone buttresses that lean against the balconied sides of this whitewashed hotel give it the look of a Mayan or Aztec temple. It's on the southern coast of the island, about 11 miles from the airport at Ponta Delgada. The establishment is as close to a full resort as anything you'll find on the island. It's set against a windbreak of grass and shrub-dotted hills, within view of the rocky coastline whose waters lap against tormented rocks. Swimming is possible from a natural swimming pool, a variety of sheltered coves, and the nearby beach at Baixa da Areia.

The 50 comfortably contemporary rooms offer spacious seaview terraces, phones, good beds, and private baths, costing from 10,000$ ($67) daily in a single and from 11,500$ ($77.05) in a double, including breakfast. The hotel also offers car-rental facilities, an 80-seat panoramic restaurant with a view over the sea, and a bar. Menu specialties in the dining room include both international specialties and regional cookery. Meals cost from 2,500$ ($16.75). Parking is free. No credit cards.

ISLAND CHURCHES

At Vila Franca do Campo, capital of the island until 1546, the 15th-century **Parish Church of São Miguel** has a carved and gilded chancel and fine stoups in carved basalt. The campanile on the south side has a large decorated bell, the oldest on the island.

The **Chapel of Nossa Senhora da Paz** stands on a hill of the same name, to the north of Vila França. The steps up to this sanctuary of the Virgin Mary are built in an unusual design.

The town of Ribeira Grande has some interesting architecture in buildings of basalt with original windows and decorations. Its **Church of Nossa Senhora da Estrêla,** consecrated in 1517, contains a chapel decorated with pictures, and a Flemish triptych painted on wood. In the upper choir, see the glass case full of little rice flour and gum arabic figures depicting scenes from the Bible.

FESTIVALS

Religious celebrations play an important part in the lives of Açoreans.

The yearly festival honoring the image of **Senhor Santo Cristo,** the possession of the Church and Convent of Esperança in Ponta Delgada, takes place on the fifth Sunday after Easter with a procession through the streets of the capital, which have been carpeted with flowers, particularly azaleas. Lights in the buildings and trees, and carried by participants, make this a sparkling occasion, expressing the religious devotion of the people.

From April to June, the **Festival of the Holy Ghost,** one of the most traditional in the whole archipelago, is held. The celebrations at the village of Rabo de Peixe, on the north coast, are arguably the most colorful, with decorated carts and oxen.

An event on the first Sunday after Easter is the procession of **Senhor dos Enfermos** (Our Lord of the Sick). This is held at many places on São Miguel and other islands, but one of the most impressive observances is the one at Furnas.

As Cavalhadas is a colorful folk event taking place annually at Ribeira Seca (Ribeira Grande) in the north. On June 29, observed as a municipal holiday, the people go on pilgrimage honoring St. Peter, patron saint of the town.

Two other religious celebrations of importance take place on varying dates, which you can check when you arrive on the island. The **procession of St. Michael,** at Vila França do Campo on the south coast, is a curious relic of medieval society, with representations of the various categories of workers around their patron saints. Another celebration is that of **Os Romeiros** (The Pilgrims). Dating back to the 16th century, this event takes place during Lent. A vow is made by men, who go on foot around the island for 8 days, praying at all the churches that have an altar to the Blessed Virgin.

SHOPPING

You should make at least one shopping expedition in Ponta Delgada, where you're likely to find bargains galore. You may want to browse through a basket bazaar, with not only a wide selection of baskets, but also wicker and willow chairs, handbags, even some articles made from the pith of a fig tree. Handcrafts produced on São Miguel are simple, made from the material at hand on the island. You'll see flowers fashioned from fish scales, feathers, paper, and cloth; hand-painted pottery; mats made of cornhusks; embroidered linen; hand-woven rugs and bedspreads.

Shops are open Monday to Friday from 9am to 12:30pm and 2 to 6:30pm.

Casa Regional da Ilha Verde (Regional House of the Green Island), Rua do Aljube 6 (tel. 237-00), is one of the island's better-stocked stores, specializing in embroidered goods. The lacy tablecloths, lace gloves, and bed linens are made in private homes by women throughout the Azores. Other types of goods are pottery, wood carvings, and wickerware.

Capote e Capelo (named for the traditional form of dress from the 18th century), Rua Dr. Gil Mont'alverne Sequeira 20 (tel. 255-25), has a good selection of souvenir items, regional articles, embroidery, pottery, wickerwork, regional wines and liqueurs, and tobacco products, some from the island's own tobaccos.

Radiante has a variety of products in a number of shops, ranging from jewelry to ceramics to items of decorative arts. Ourivesaria Radiante, Rua Machado Santos 46–48 (tel. 238-97), offers gold, silver, jewelry, watches, and filigree work. The other four Radiante ships offer decorative-arts items and artistic and regional ceramics. They are at Rua Machado Santos 51 (tel. 247-74), Rua Manuel Inácio Correia 27 (tel. 251-97), Rua Bruno Tavares Carreiro 3 (tel. 238-97), and Rua São João 13 (tel. 246-06).

Miranda & Ca., Lda., Rua Machado Santos 57 (tel. 263-98), has a good selection of gold, crystal, silver, watches, and other jewelry.

---

2. Santa Maria

Historians consider this little easternmost island of the Azores to be the first of the archipelago discovered by the Portuguese, sometime between 1427 and 1432. Santa Maria's settlement rapidly followed discovery, and the first municipality of the Azores was created here by 1472. In 1493, on the way home from the discovery of America, Columbus moored the *Niña* off Santa Maria to let some of his men go ashore near the village of Anjos to fulfill a vow made on the high seas that they would hear mass on the first land reached where there was a church dedicated to the Virgin Mary.

Santa Maria is unique in the archipelago in having fossils and other formations of sedimentary origin in its soil. Its countryside is varied, from a hilly section in the northeast to the flat portion in the south. The island is only 6 miles wide and 11 miles long, but it is fairly heavily populated. In the settlement period, people came mainly from the provinces of Alentejo and Beira in Portugal, and many of the customs of those regions persist, although time and distance have brought alterations.

Handcrafts of the island consist of articles made to fill everyday needs, including woolen and patchwork quilts and coverlets; linen cloth; work done in wood, leather, straw, and wicker; iron tools; and various kinds of decorative work. Interesting items of homespun clothing are sweaters of coarse wool, embroidered linen shirts, embroidered women's jackets, and suits of estamin. Folk music heard here had its origins on the mainland, although permutations are evident in the songs, dances, and musical instruments. The small, island-made guitars (*violas*) are prevalent.

The principal town of the island is **Vila do Porto,** which has two churches of interest. The **Parish Church,** built in the 19th century over a 15th-century ruin, has the Chapel of Santa Catarina, with a Manueline ceiling, as the sole remaining portion of the original structure. The **Convent of São Francisco** was founded in 1607 and destroyed by pirates 9 years later. It was rebuilt in the 18th century and enlarged in the 19th. Of special interest are the chapels with fine reredos in carved work and valuable glazed tiles.

Anjos Chapel, on the north coast, is probably the oldest house of worship in the archipelago. It has work in precious whitewood, fine glazed tiles, and a remarkable 15th-century triptych.

In the village is the **Parish Church of Nossa Senhora da Purificação,** a 16th-century building with a baroque facade of island stone, added in the 18th century. Tradition says the church stands on the spot where mass was first celebrated in the Azores.

Other churches of interest are found throughout the little island, especially at Pedras de São Pedro, not far from Vila do Porto.

The highest point on the island, **Pico Alto,** about 1,950 feet above sea level, is a fine spot for a panoramic view of the island and the sea. The coastline is indented all around, with headlands and inlets providing sites for water sports.

Air transport to Santa Maria is provided by SATA (tel. 096/824-97). The huge, little-used airport near Vila do Porto (tel. 096/821-37) was built by the U.S. Air Force in 1944 and later accommodated international flights. These, however, have mostly been transferred to Terceira and São Miguel.

For information regarding boat travel to and from the island, contact the tourist office, **Junta Autónoma do Porto de Ponta Delgada,** in Vila do Porto (tel. 096/822-47).

WHERE TO STAY & DINE

Aeroporto Hotel, Estrada do Aeroporto, 9580 Vila do Porto, Santa Maria, Açores (tel. 096/86-211), is barely adequate as a hotel, but on this island you take what's available. In the closing months of World War II, this site was an Officers Club for the American Air Base of Santa Maria. With the opening of the airport to international jet travel, it was remade into a hotel, rated second class by the government, to provide stopover accommodations, bungalow style.

The living room has fireplaces, a high beamed ceiling, and groups of furniture set for conversation and beverages. There's a bar and a spacious dining room in the Terminal Building providing a hearty and very simple Azorean cuisine. Geared to passengers making the transition between the Old and New Worlds, the Aeroporto Hotel contains 71 rooms with private bath and phone. A double goes from 6,500$ ($43.55) to 7,100$ ($47.55) daily, and singles cost 5,800$ ($38.85) to 6,200$ ($41.55), including breakfast. Laundry service is provided, and parking is free. AE, DC, MC, V.

---

3. Terceira

The third-largest island in the Azores archipelago, and the third to be discovered in the 15th century, is fittingly named Terceira (pronounced Ter-*say*-ra), the Portuguese word for—you guessed it—third. Some 18 miles long and 11 miles wide, the island is the largest of the central group of the Azores, with development leading to a constantly increasing population. The presence here of an international airport, at Lajes, has contributed to the island's becoming more and more engaged in tourism as a major economic factor. An 18-hole golf course, bathing installations on beaches or at natural swimming pools, sea fishing and other water-oriented sports, football fields, cinemas, nightclubs, and "rope" and arena bullfights draw people to Terceira.

For information, go to **Delegação de Turismo da Terceira,** Rua Rio de Janeiro 47A (tel. 2-33-93), at Angra de Heroísmo.

WHAT TO SEE & DO

Behind the indented coastline is an area dotted with villages and divided into walled fields called *cerrados*. A few miles from the ocean, green pastures contrast with barren lava zones called *mistérios,* and peaks, lakes, and extinct craters attest to the volcanic origin of the Azores. Blossoming shrubs, including the ubiquitous hydrangea, soften the vistas, even in the lava regions of Pico da Bagacina and Pico do Cabrito, where wild cattle are bred. At Boscoitos, on the north coast, you can see unusual volcanic formations together with the noted vineyards in enclosures called *curraletas.*

The principal town of Terceira, **Angra** (now **Angra do Heroísmo**), was the first place in the Azores raised to the status of town, in 1534, the same year it was declared a bishopric by Pope Paul III. (The words "do Heroísmo" were added to honor the bravery of the people in an 1829 struggle that was won by the Royalists of Portugal.) The town was planned in the 16th century, but the outstanding houses were built in the 17th and 18th centuries. The oldest part of the town is considered a regional monument.

Built on the bay (*angra*), the town rises from its center up gentle hills. Damaged by an earthquake in 1980, it has since recovered. From the harbor, if you walk along

Rua de Lisboa, which runs to Praça da Restauração, you'll see the imposing **Town Hall**. The old white houses, in a style that is typical of Portuguese rural architecture, are distinguished from those on the mainland by the fact that they are required to have sash windows.

The **Castle of São João Baptista**, built by King Philip II of Spain at the time he was also King of Portugal, dominates the town at the foot of Monte Brasil. The main doorway with the royal arms above, an arched bridge, turrets, and a rich interior make this worth seeing. It served at one time as a prison for the notorious sadist, King Afonso VI, and other famous persons have also been incarcerated in it.

Museu de Angra do Heroísmo, Rua João Deus, is housed in the former Convento de São Francisco. It contains collections of weapons, coins and medals, furniture, paintings, musical instruments, ceramics, porcelain, and an interesting ethnology section. It is open Monday to Friday from 9 to 11:30am and 2 to 5:30pm.

Palácio Bettencourt, a 17th-century mansion, is now the home of the District Archives and the Public Library.

Churches of interest in Angra do Heroísmo are the cathedral from the 16th century, with a rich treasury; the Colégio Church (16th and 17th centuries), with its collection of Dutch glazed tiles; the Church of São Francisco where Vasco da Gama buried his brother, Paulo, who had died on a voyage to India; and the Church of São Gonçalo, with its gilt-edged triptych.

Festivals of Terceira are mainly religious, and of special note here is that those dedicated to the Holy Spirit, the most important, continue from Whitsuntide until the end of summer. During this time the residents of the villages contribute offerings that are placed in small, simple structures with elaborate facades, known as *impérios,* looking like little chapels by the roadside. The contributions are then handed out to needy passersby. The festivities end, especially in outlying areas, with rope bullfights in which the bull, held on a rope maneuvered by strong men, is challenged in a run down the village streets.

The largest caldeira in the Azores is on Terceira, **Caldeira de Guilherme Moniz,** with a 9-mile perimeter. In the interior of the island, **Algar do Carvão,** a number of underground grottoes, some more than 300 feet deep, contain striking stalagmites and stalactites.

TRANSPORTATION

Airlines serving Terceira at the international airport in Lajes, about a 20-minute drive from Angra do Heroísmo, all have offices in the capital. **SATA** has facilities on Rua da Esperança 2 (tel. 220-13), in Angra do Heroísmo and at the Lajes airport (tel. 095/520-11).

TAP offices are at Rua Rio de Janeiro 25 (tel. 095/244-89) in Angra do Heroísmo, and at the Lajes airport (tel. 095/521-11).

Information regarding ships taking passengers to and from Terceira is available at Junta **Autónoma do Porto de Angra do Heroísmo,** Rua Direita 115 (tel. 095/22-181), in Angra do Heroísmo.

Buses take visitors on excursions around the island, where sights at Vila Praia de Vitória, Biscoitos (mentioned above), and Santa Barbara can be visited. **Empresa de Viacõo Terceirense, Lda.,** Rua Dr. Sousa Meneses 15, in Angra do Heroísmo (tel. 095/241-01), arranges these trips.

Car-rental/taxi agencies servicing the island include **AçorAuto Rent-a-Car,** Rua Gervasio Lima 27B, Praia da Vitória (tel. 095/523-73), where you can arrange to be picked up and delivered back to the Lajes airport.

Ilha 3, Rua Direita 22 (tel. 095/231-15), is another well-known car-rental concern. It requires a minimum rental of 1 day.

WHERE TO STAY

In Angra Do Heroísmo

A modern hotel in the center of town, **Hotel de Angra,** Praça da Restauração, 9700 Angra do Heroísmo, Terceira, Açores (tel. 095/240-41), built in 1970, is a substantial establishment, set back from a pie-shaped plaza studded with trees. The hotel overlooks a semitropical garden, lying just minutes from the water and the Monte Brasil Park. Not overwhelming in any way, it still has its own dignity and style. The service is good. In all, it sleeps some 172 people in 86 rooms, each of which is well equipped with private bath, phone, and balcony. Singles rent for 10,000$ ($67) daily, and doubles cost 12,000$ ($80.40). The hotel also has a good restaurant with a regional menu, plus other specialties. Meals cost from 2,500$ ($16.75) and are served from noon to 2pm and 7 to 9:30pm. The dining room has a panoramic view. In summer, you can overlook the action in the plaza below from an outdoor terrace. Parking is free. MC.

Albergaria Cruzeiro, Praça Dr. Sousa Júnior, 9700 Angra do Heroísmo, Terceira, Açores (tel. 095/240-71; fax 095/240-75), in the heart of town, is a most recommendable place to stay if you appreciate up-to-date facilities. All 47 rooms come with private bath, phone, minibar, TV, and air conditioning. Singles cost from 7,500$ ($50.25) daily, doubles from 8,500$ ($56.95). Five suites are rented, costing from 10,800$ ($72.35). Breakfast is included. The hall contains wrought-iron furniture and green plants. In addition, there's a restaurant and bar serving meals for 2,800$ ($18.75). Parking is free. AE, DC, MC, V.

Residencial Beira Mar, Esplanada (Rua de São João), 9700 Angra do Heroísmo, Terceira, Açores (tel. 095/251-88; fax 095/259-99). This establishment is best known as a restaurant, previewed below. But the staff will also rent you one of its 15 simple but cozy bedrooms upstairs. Each unit contains a private bath, minibar, TV, and phone. Singles rent for 3,500$ ($23.45) daily, doubles 4,900$ ($32.85), with breakfast included. The location, at the edge of the harbor in the center of the most atmospheric section of town, is ideal. Parking is free. AE, V.

Outside of Town

In a setting of natural beauty, **Motel das Nove Ilhas,** Estrada Regional, Cabo da Praia, 9760 Praia da Vitória, Terceira, Açores (tel. 095/531-25), is a holiday house for those seeking a tranquil retreat. A member of the staff of the hotel meets guests at Lajes Airport and provides free transportation to the facilities of Nove Ilhas, about 3½ miles away.

In one of the nine apartments, clients are near the largest Azorean beach and only 2 miles from the historic town of Praia da Vitória. The Terceira Island Golf Course is 8½ miles away, and the city of Angra do Heroísmo is 11½ miles away. Each apartment has two bedrooms and a full bath, with tub and shower. A combined living and dining room comes with the apartment, as does an equipped kitchenette, with cutlery, silverware, and dishes. Linens are also provided. One person is charged 3,850$ ($25.80); two persons pay 5,500$ ($36.85); and three persons share a room for 6,300$ ($42.20). Breakfast is not served.

On the precincts are a restaurant, a small market, plus facilities for dry cleaning and laundry. Baby-sitting can be arranged for parents wanting to be free to tour Terceira.

WHERE TO DINE

Most of the restaurants are concentrated at Angra do Heroísmo. However, if you have a car, you can drive along the water and discover other choices.

In Angra do Heroísmo

The best choice is **Marcelino's,** Rue São João 47 (tel. 258-28), an air-conditioned steak house with good food and wine. It is widely acclaimed for its Azores beer. Meals, costing 2,800$ ($18.75) and up, are served Friday to Wednesday from 12:30 to 3:30pm and 5:30pm to midnight. The chef is adept at preparing meat in almost any style, ranging from peppersteak to Stroganoff. The filet mignon is exceptional, but the chateaubriand (served for two) is perhaps the finest I've had in Portugal. It's especially popular with Americans living on the island. You can also order fish and shellfish dishes from the Portuguese cuisine repertoire. The restaurant is in a second-floor room with a beamed ceiling and heavy pine furniture. There's a bar on the ground level. No reservations are required. AE, DC, MC, V.

Adega Lusitânia, Rua de São Pedro 63 (tel. 223-01), is the place to go if you're seeking some of the best of the regional cuisine of the island. The restaurant is housed in a two-story island villa, with a wrought-iron balcony. It lies about a 10-minute walk from the center. If you're there in hot weather, you can also enjoy some of the best shellfish served on the island or try such dishes as veal chops or filet of hake. The service is willing and informal. Meals, costing from 2,000$ ($13.40), are served Monday to Saturday from noon to 3pm and 6 to 10pm. No reservations are needed. AE, DC, MC, V.

Restaurante Beira Mar, Esplanada (Rua de São João; tel. 251-88), is a lovely restaurant set within a severely dignified villa near the water's edge in the center of town. Large and airy, and staffed with a uniformed battalion of polite waiters, it is ringed with blue-and-yellow tiles and patronized by colonies of Portuguese families. It's open Tuesday to Sunday from noon to 3pm and 6:30 to 10pm. Full meals cost from 2,500$ ($16.75) and include a solid array of regional dishes such as hunter's steak and local octopus, along with fresh spider crab and grilled squid. Fresh fish is also available, and international favorites include American-style fried chicken and chateaubriand. Reservations are needed. MC, V.

Outside Town

Some other good restaurants are found at Praia da Vitória south of the airport, if you like dining with a view of the water and the beach.

Locals tell me that **Churrasqueira Praiense,** Rua Alfândega (tel. 521-59), is the best for fresh shellfish in the summer months. It's popular with U.S. service personnel. Out in the middle of the ocean you expect good fish, and you are served it here. The chef prepares it well, and the portions are large. Meals, costing from 2,000$ ($13.40), are served Thursday to Tuesday from 11am to 3pm and 5 to 8:30pm. The restaurant closes for 2 weeks in April and 2 weeks in September (dates vary). No credit cards.

There's another good restaurant in the area, **Girassol,** Cabo da Praia, Praia da Vitória (tel. 533-56), which offers a good Portuguese menu and some fine wine. It's best enjoyed in the summer months because of its esplanade. Meals cost from 2,500$ ($16.75) and are served daily from noon to 3pm and 5:30 to 11pm. Stick to the simplest items, such as fish, and you should find everything pleasing. Alcatra (steak) is a specialty, as is fresh fried fish. Service is casual. Reservations aren't needed. No credit cards.

---

4. Graciosa

The island acclaimed by its name as "gracious," Graciosa is also known as Ilha Branca (White Island) because of some of its place-names—Pedras Brancas, Serra Branca, and Barro Branco. With its low elevation (highest point is Pico Timão at 1,320 feet), this may also be seen as a white island because of surging sea foam and white sandy beaches, which are the backdrop for the white houses that prevail.

The least humid of the Azores, Graciosa occupies a 10- by 4-mile chunk of land, northernmost in the central group of the archipelago. The landscape differs from that of most of the other islands, with waving fields of wheat, vineyards, and an occasional windmill flapping in the breezes, but there are also volcanic formations worth seeing.

Furna do Enxofre, also called Furna da Caldeira, in the southwest is a lake of warm sulfur water reached by a tunnel between steep rocks. The lake is best seen between 11am and 2pm when the sun penetrates the narrow mouth at the surface so that you can view the tunnel interior and the lake 330 feet below.

A few miles farther southwest is **Termas do Carapacho,** a spa known for its medicinal waters.

The island's main town is **Santa Cruz da Graciosa,** where you can visit the **Parish Church,** built in the 16th century, with three fine rose windows. See the five 16th-century paintings on wood depicting scenes from the Gospels.

An **Ethnological Museum** displays material on local life, especially the tradition of wine-growing.

Pottery, including bowls, teapots, and mugs, is produced on the island, as are musical instruments. The regional *violas* (small guitars) of Praia, Santa Cruz, and Farol da Ponta da Barca are among island specialties.

SATA provides air service to Graciosa from Santa Maria. Offices are at Largo Cons, Jacinto Cândido (tel. 095/724-56), and at the airport (tel. 095/724-58).

WHERE TO STAY

The place to stay on the island is the unassuming three-story hostelry, **Residencial Santa Cruz,** Largo Barão Guadalupe, 9880 Santa Cruz, Graciosa, Açores (tel. 095/723-45; fax 095/728-28). You get good rooms that are clean and well kept, as well as a pleasant reception. Each of the 20 simple rooms contains a bath and a phone. A single costs 3,300$ ($22.10) daily, and a double goes for 4,100$ ($27.45), with breakfast included. You get a strong dose of local flavor here. The hotel stands in the northeastern corner of the island, the arrival point for most visitors. Parking is free. No credit cards.

---

5. São Jorge

The long, skinny island of São Jorge—32 miles long by less than 5 miles wide —lies some 40 miles south of Graciosa in the central group of the Azores. Along its length is a range of minor mountains, the highest peak of which is Pico da Esperança, about 3,500 feet above sea level. The plateau of the uplands is used for pastures, and the lower levels are planted in vegetables, vineyards, and orchards. São Jorge is noted for its dairy products; its cheese is internationally known.

The first settlement on the island was at Topo, on the far-southeastern tip, but today the main town is **Vila das Velas,** which is graced by a Parish Church built in 1460, under terms of the will of Prince Henry the Navigator. Its architecture is interesting, as is the fine carved work of its chapels. The Town Hall in Velas was built in the 17th century.

Besides its cheese, São Jorge is known also for the regional coverlets produced as a cottage industry by many of the women of the island, as well as multicolored rugs woven on primitive looms.

Transportation to and from São Jorge is possible by both boat and plane. For information on seagoing service, get in touch with the **Junta Autónoma dos Portos** in Velas (tel. 092/423-60) and in Calheta (tel. 092/461-42). In summer, ferryboat service is possible daily, although transportation is curtailed in winter.

Air service is provided by **SATA,** Rua de Santo André, in Velas. Call either the office (tel. 092/221-45) or the airport (tel. 092/224-35).

For information, contact **Posto de Turismo de São Jorge,** Rua da Capela, 9880 Velas (tel. 092/422-14).

WHERE TO STAY

In the town of Velas, a suitable bet is **Residencial Neto,** Rua Dr. José Pereira 14, 9800 Velhas, São Jorge, Açores (tel. 092/424-03; fax 092/423-33). One of the main attractions of this well-maintained inn is its swimming pool, reserved for the use of guests. Each of its 16 spacious and comfortable rooms contains a private bath, as well as a phone, radio, and TV with video. Doubles rent for 5,000$ ($33.50) daily, and singles cost 4,400$ ($29.50), with breakfast and transportation to and from the airport included. The owners can direct visitors to producers of the world-famous cheese of the island. Parking is free. No credit cards.

WHERE TO DINE

Restaurants tend to be very simple on the island, and also very cheap.

One of the best is **Restaurant Velense,** Rua Dr. José Pereira (tel. 421-60), in Velas. You get hearty, well-flavored dishes here, including roast octopus, "kid stew," and fresh clams. Portions are generous, and meals cost from 2,200$ ($14.75). Open daily from 11am to 10pm. No reservations are needed and credit cards aren't accepted.

---

6. Pico

No island of the Azores shows more clearly the volcanic origin of the archipelago than Pico, the Portuguese word for peak, given to the island because of the impressive mountain rising from it to 7,750 feet above sea level. The cloud-shrouded peak, Pico Grande, often snowcapped in winter, can be climbed, but the journey is arduous and only to be made by the stout-hearted and strong-limbed, and with a guide.

The island, today measuring about 29 miles in length and 9 miles in width, and lying 4½ miles from Faial and 11 miles from São Jorge, was rocked by volcanic eruptions in the 18th century. These gave rise to strange stretches of black lava formations, which are known locally as *mistérios*. They provide interesting sights today. Villages are built of the lava material, and the soil with volcanic ash is excellent for the vineyards from which comes much good Azores wine.

Also growing on the island are fruit trees, local cedar, local laurel, and a wealth of flowers. Development of more rugged zones for pastureland bordered by trees has created a delightful countryside with a variety of fauna. Preservation of the natural resources of the island is undertaken through establishment of the Nature Reserve of Pico Island.

Many churches and chapels are scattered throughout the island, ranging from the simple to the grand, and there are also old manor houses, dating from the 17th and 18th centuries, made of basalt with noteworthy ashlar work. A number of religious festivals are held, one of the most interesting being the **Festa dos Baleeiros** (Whalers' Festival), which takes place on the last Sunday in August and is attended by large crowds of islanders and visitors.

Pico produces some of the finest sailors of Portugal. The capital, **Lajes do Pico,** was known as a whaling capital, and the town commemorates it in a **Whalers' Museum** (Museu dos Baleeiros), in the former Casa dos Botes, Rua Capitao-mor Garcia Gonçalves Madruga. Here a unique collection of whalebone and cachalot ivory has been gathered together, along with the various utensils and equipment used in whaling, a whaling boat, and the first motorboat used in this activity. Logbooks of past whaling expeditions have been acquired for the museum.

Near the capital is one of the most interesting of the island's natural formations, the **Furna da Malha,** a 1½-mile natural tunnel formed by sea and volcano action.

In the western coast not far from the little town of Madalena is **Furna de Frei Matias,** one of the most famous caves on the island.

Madalena is the most progressive town on the island, from the modern point of view. Here you can rent a car or take a taxi to explore the surroundings.

SATA provides air service to Madalena. It has offices at Rua Doctor Maria da Glória Duarte (tel. 092/924-11) and at the airport (tel. 092/924-13).

For information, contact **Posto de Turismo da Lajes** (tel. 092/974-05), at Lajes.

WHERE TO STAY

In Madalena

A helpful staff welcomes you to **Residencial Pico,** Rua dos Biscoitos, 9950 Madalena, Pico, Açores (tel. 092/922-92). The hotel has 31 simple rooms, each with private bath, TV with video, and phone. Singles staying at this three-star establishment pay 5,500$ ($36.85) daily, with doubles going for 7,000$ ($46.90). Breakfast is included in the rates.

The hotel also operates one of the best restaurants on Pico, serving regional specialties. In summer fresh shellfish is abundantly featured, with meals costing 2,500$ ($16.75) and up. Hours are daily from noon to 2pm and 7 to 9pm. It is closed on Sunday in winter. Parking is free. MC, V.

WHERE TO STAY & DINE

In Lajes do Pico

At the Azores Whaling Center, **Residencial Açor**, Rua D. João Paulino 5, 9930 Lajes, Pico, Açores (tel. 092/974-38), with views of both sea and mountains from its 13 rooms, offers peace and proximity to the island's nostalgia-laden neighborhoods. The rooms, each with private bath, balcony, and direct-dial phone, are comfortably furnished and reasonably priced: from 5,000$ ($33.50) daily in a single, rising to 6,000$ ($40.20) in a double, with breakfast included. Parking is free. DC, V.

Restaurante Lagoa, Lajes, Pico (tel. 97-272), is one of the best places to eat on the island especially in hot weather when you can enjoy the esplanade and the chef's prize collection of shellfish dishes, which he often prepares with savory sauces. You can also order grilled steaks. Meals cost from 2,300$ ($15.40) and are served daily from noon to 3pm and 6 to 10pm. The restaurant is closed on Saturday in winter. All year round good regional cookery, backed up by Portuguese wines, is served to as many as 90 diners. No reservations are needed. AE, DC, MC, V.

---

7. Faial

Shaped roughly like a pentagon, Faial is the most westerly of the central group of islands in the archipelago, and because of its active port, Horta, perhaps the most visited in its group. Faial has had a place in the history of the Azores since its discovery in the middle of the 15th century and its colonization, principally by Flemish people, soon after. Its capital, Horta, was named for the Flemish nobleman, Josse de Hurtere (or Huerta), who led the settlement of the island.

Faial is a place of restful valleys, verdant fields, hydrangea-hedged hillsides; camellias are found in the Flemish Valley. Faial and Pico are the chief tourist islands of Horta. Many water sports are offered here, including big-game fishing, sailing, rowing, scuba diving, and windsurfing, as well as swimming. There are also tennis and hiking, in case you're not sea oriented. The island measures about 9 miles across and 13 miles long, so that most of its attractions can be reached easily by walking or short drives. Because of the many hydrangea hedges, Faial is sometimes called the Blue Island.

Horta is attractive, with graceful buildings and a port that draws ships and yachts of many nations, even though it has lost some of its prestige as a naval base attained during World War I and World War II. It was also the center for transatlantic air transport in earlier days when planes crossing the ocean had to have a refueling site.

The port, besides its hustle and bustle as a safe harbor, marina, and fishing scene, has a curious show of fascinating graffiti—the wall of the dock carries hundreds of signatures, dedications, and paintings inscribed here by sailors who have passed through over the years.

Horta has many monuments and churches of interest, as well as museums, which include **Museu da Horta** (Horta Museum), Palácio do Colégio, Largo Duque d'Avila e Bolamo (tel. 092/233-48), and **Museu de Arte Sacra** (Museum of Sacred Art), at the Church of São Francisco, Rua Conselheiro Medeiros, remarkable for its collection of religious art as well as work in figwood.

Fort of Santa Cruz dates from the 16th century and has seen history in the making, from attacks by Spanish and British troops to involvement in the Portuguese civil war.

Interesting religious houses include the 17th-century **Parish Church of São**

Salvador, with its chapel of São Paulo, known for its two panels of tiles. The **Convent of São Francisco,** built in 1696 on the site of an older structure, has gilt carved work and paintings, but it is probably known for the walls of the chancel lined with azulejos.

In 1958 major volcanic eruptions rocked the northwest coast of the island. **Ponta dos Capelinhos** draws many visitors who come to see the effects of that eruption from the island's westernmost point. The volcano is now classed as dormant. You can also make an excursion to the **center of the island,** where a volcanic crater is covered inside with vegetation and contains a lake, Cabeço Gordo. This is the highest spot on the island, providing views of Pico and the neighboring islands.

Handcrafts of Faial include embroidery, lace, work in tulle embroidered with straw, wickerwork, and work in figwood.

A major event of the island is **Sea Week,** which starts on the first Sunday in August. It includes all activities connected with the sea as well as cultural events, and is becoming of international importance.

For car rentals and taxi service at Horta, get in touch with **Auto Turística Faialense,** Rua Conselheiro Medeiros 14, Horta (tel. 092/311-50).

Both **SATA** and **TAP** (Air Portugal) provide air service. The **airport** at Castelo Branco, west of Horta, Aeroportos e Navegação Aérea-ANA E.P., can be reached by phoning 092/230-81. SATA has offices at Rua Serpa Pinto in Horta (tel. 239-13), and at the airport (tel. 221-11). TAP's office is at Rua Vasco da Gama 28 (tel. 092/226-65) in Horta.

Information on ships is available from **Junta Autónoma do Porto da Horta,** at the Horta dock (tel. 092/234-53).

WHERE TO STAY

A 5-minute walk from the port, the **Hotel Faial,** Rua Consul Dabney, Angustias, 9900 Horta, Faial, Açores (tel. 092/221-81; fax 092/221-89), is a four-star, first-class hotel, consisting of six buildings like a village in a park. It was originally built as headquarters by Western Union, housing crews working on the laying of the transatlantic cable. The situation is tranquil, as the Faial is surrounded by gardens offering views onto the sea. The establishment is the major social center for Horta.

The 123 bedrooms are simple but well styled, with modern furnishings. All the units have private bath, TV, and direct-dial phone, and many open onto views of the bay and the inner harbor. Doubles cost 11,500$ ($77.05) daily, and singles rent for 10,500$ ($70.35), with breakfast included in all tariffs. The food, served in a panoramic restaurant overlooking the port, is typical of the region but also has a selection of international dishes. The menu changes daily, with meals costing from 2,750$ ($18.45) if you order the set dinner. Food is served daily from 12:30 to 2pm and 7:30 to 10pm. The hotel has a swimming pool, two tennis courts, a disco, a beauty center, and a gift shop. Parking is free. AE, DC, MC, V.

Estalagem de Santa Cruz, Castelo do Santa Cruz, Rua Vasco da Gama, 9900 Horta, Faial, Açores (tel. 092/230-21; fax 092/822-55). Rated four stars, this inn was built into the foundation of a 16th-century fort at the edge of the harbor overlooking the marina. Most of what a visitor will see, except for the stone crenellations separating the newest section from the salt-sprayed rocks, is a comfortably contemporary 25-room hotel. The bedrooms usually open through sliding glass doors onto spacious verandas, often shaded from the sun with awnings. Each unit has a well-upholstered set of furniture, with a few wicker pieces thrown in and contains a private bath as well. Other amenities include phone, TV, minibar, and air conditioning. Singles cost from 8,400$ ($56.30) daily, and doubles go for 10,200$ ($68.35), with breakfast included. There's a small but well-maintained garden on the premises, as well as a bar, a dining room, and a fireplace. Meals, costing from 2,500$ ($16.75), are served daily from 12:30 to 2:30pm and 7:30 to 9:30pm. The dining room is severely dignified in the Iberian tradition, with straight-back chairs, white walls, and a big-windowed view of the "fortified" terrace and the sea. Laundry is provided, and room service is offered until midnight. AE, DC, MC, V.

One of the least expensive places to stay on the island is **Pensão-Residencial**

São Francisco, Rua Conselheiro Medeiros 13, Matriz, 9900 Faial, Açores (tel. 092/229-51), a three-star hotel, offering 35 bedrooms in unpretentiously simple comfort. Rooms have private baths and phones. The management is helpful, and will often give you suggestions about what to see on their island. Singles cost from 3,800$ ($25.45) to 5,200$ ($34.85) daily, while doubles go for 4,600$ ($30.80) to 6,000$ ($40.20), including breakfast. Parking is free. No credit cards.

WHERE TO DINE

Restaurante O Lima, Rua Serpa Pinto 9 (tel. 223-87). Its focus of attention might be on the blaring TV set, but the decor is utterly simple and clean. Still, a drink or a meal here will give you a chance not only to order regional food but to look at local life. The stand-up bar is open Monday to Saturday from 7am to midnight, and you can eat during those hours. Full meals cost from 1,800$ ($12.05) and might include roast chicken, regional preparations of beef, roast veal, and generous chunks of the deliciously salty island Cheddar cheese. Reservations aren't needed. No credit cards.

Peter's Café Sport, Rua Tenente Valadim 9 (tel. 223-27). On rainy weekends, it seems as if half the population of the island jams itself between the paneled walls of this watering spot. It's without parallel as the place on the island for yacht owners to mingle with local residents. Scrimshaw is sold from display cases in the walls, and an official-looking exchange office operates out of one of the corners. Naturally, the bar does a brisk business in liquor, snack food, and sandwiches. Famous in yachting circles on either side of the Atlantic, this raffishly unpretentious rendezvous is the domain of José (Peter) Azevedo, a Portuguese-born mariner who worked for many years in the British navy. Unfailingly polite and gentlemanly, Senhor Azevedo has created a legend for himself because of his efforts at keeping visiting sailors and their entourages afloat.

The café opens daily in the early morning, for coffee, eggs, and bacon, but closes its doors from 1 to 4pm. The place then reopens, doing a thriving business until at least midnight. Sandwiches cost 150$ ($1), and drinks begin at 114$ (75¢). Upstairs is a scrimshaw museum. Senhor Azevedo has been collecting the intricately carved pieces of whalebone and walrus tusk for more than 50 years. Today the extraordinary collection comprises more than 2,500 pieces, making it the largest museum of its kind in the world. Pieces range from the religious (you'll see lots of crucifixes) to the profane, but each reflects the hours of isolated tedium of 19th- and 20th-century sailors far from home with time and a penknife in their hands. The entrance cost is 100$ (65¢), and hours are daily from 9am to 6pm except for a 3-hour break at 1pm. Look for the intricately detailed view of the island of Pico as seen from the shoreline of 19th-century Faial, carved into a 5-foot section of whale jawbone. No credit cards.

---

8. Flores

The westernmost island of the Azores, and of Europe, is Ilha das Flores, or Island of Flowers, the most beautiful of the archipelago. It has been described as a garden floating on the foam of the sea. Flores and its neighbor island, Corvo, were the last of the Azores to be discovered by the Portuguese, being claimed for the country in 1452. Early colonization efforts failed, and it was not until 1528 that permanent settlers moved in, many from provinces in the north of Portugal. Fishing is the economic mainstay here.

The island has great natural beauty, with long, dense clumps of hydrangeas climbing over the hills and deep valleys and surrounding the lakes, rocks with grottoes, peaks, and caldeiras, the remains of former volcanoes.

The **grotto at Enxaréus,** between Santa Cruz das Flores, the main village of the island, and **Caveira,** a short distance south along the coast road, is one of the major attractions of Flores. The coast is indented, and the cliffs are spectacular. Waterfalls cascade into the sea at Vale da Fajãzinha, and stone formations, produced by erosion, dot the land. There are seven lakes in the center of the island. The most beautiful, **Lagoa Funda,** is surrounded by sand and sheltered by mountains, with clumps of hydrangeas burgeoning everywhere.

There are a number of churches on Flores, some containing interesting carved work. At **Santa Cruz,** an ethnological museum displays collections of local handcrafts, particularly in ivory objects and lacework. The crafts also include items made of wicker, raffia, seashells, and wood, as well as weaving and work in rushes, based on patterns from the west coast of Africa.

The **Church of São Pedro** in Santa Cruz, built in the 16th century and renovated in the 18th, has a notable high altar in carved, gilded, and painted work.

In the parish of Fajãzinha, on the western coast of the island, **Nossa Senhora dos Remédios** is a large house of worship with three naves and an interesting chancel. It was built in the late 18th century.

Transportation by air and by boat to and from Flores is possible. The airport at Santa Cruz, **Aeroportos e Navegação Aérea-ANA E.P.** (tel. 092/521-51), accommodates small planes. The airline servicing the island is **SATA,** Rua Senador André Freitas 5 (tel. 092/524-25).

WHERE TO STAY

If you're heading for Flores, you can stay at **Residência Vila Flores,** Rua Senador André Freitas, 9970 Santa Cruz, Flores, Açores (tel. 092/521-90; fax 092/526-21). It is modern, cozy, and unpretentious. There are 38 beds in 18 reasonably comfortable rooms. Each room has a phone, but only 13 have TV. Three rooms are without bath. A single without bath costs 2,000$ ($13.40), or 3,250$ ($21.80) with bath. A double without bath rents for 2,750$ ($18.45), but only 4,150$ ($27.80) with bath. Breakfast is included. There is a good restaurant one flight above street level. Parking is free. No credit cards.

AN EXCURSION TO CORVO

The little neighbor of Flores, lying about 15 miles to the northeast of the larger of the westernmost part of the archipelago, is Corvo. It got its name from the writings of a Spanish friar who called it "Isla de los Cuervos Marinos," or Island of the Sea Crows. This tiny spot of land, about 8 square miles, in the vastness of the Atlantic, is rugged, with volcanic peaks and rocks serving as reminders of its origins.

The one village on the island, **Vila Nova do Corvo,** consists of cottages all built in the same style, with whitewashed walls and red-tile roofs, laid out in little streets known as *canadas.* From the town, you can see Flores in the distance. Its facilities are very basic and not necessarily recommendable. Hence, it is visited by only the most adventurous of tourists who reach it by boat.

APPENDIX

1. MENU TRANSLATIONS
2. A CAPSULE VOCABULARY

French is still traditionally spoken by guides in provincial museums, but English is increasing in popularity, and is now taught in most schools.

Usually in Lisbon, Estoril, Cascais, Madeira, and on the major coastal resorts of the Algarve, you'll have no problem if you speak only English. However, if you venture inland—to towns of the Alentejo, for example—you may find a few words in the "Capsule Vocabulary" helpful.

Likewise, menus tend to be bewildering, especially when a chef has named a bean and tripe dish after his favorite aunt. Nevertheless, a basic knowledge of the main dishes in the Portuguese cuisine is essential, especially if you're planning to stay at second-class hotels or eat at local taverns where there's nobody around to translate for you.

1. Menu Translations

SOUPS (SOPAS)

caldo verde potato and cabbage
canja de galinha chicken soup
creme de camarão cream of shrimp
creme de legumes cream of vegetable

sopa a alentejana Alentejo soup
sopa de cebola onion
sopa de mariscos shellfish
sopa de queijo cheese
sopa de tomate tomato

EGGS (OVOS)

com presunto with ham
cozidos hard boiled
escalfados poached
estrelados fried

mexicos scrambled
omeleta omelet
quentes soft boiled
tortilha Spanish omelet

FISH (PEIXE)

ameijoas clams
atum tuna
bacalhau salted codfish
cherne turbot
camarãos shrimps
eiró eel
lagosta lobster
linguado sole
lulas squid

ostras oysters
peixe espada swordfish
percebes barnacles
pescada hake
robalo bass
salmonete red mullet
santola crab
sardinhas sardines

SPECIALTIES (ESPECIALIDADES)

bife na frigideira steak with mustard sauce
caldeirada fishermen's stew
cozido à portuguêsa Portuguese stew

porco alentejano pork in a sauce of tomatoes and clams

MEAT (CARNE)

bife steak
borrego lamb
cabrito kid
carneiro mutton
coelho rabbit
costeletas chops
dobrada tripe
iscas liver

lingua tongue
porco pork
presunto ham
rim kidney
salchichas sausages
vaca beef
vitela veal

POULTRY (AVES)

borracho pigeon
frango chicken
galinha fowl
ganso goose

pato duck
perdiz partidge
peru turkey

VEGETABLES (LEGUMES)

aipo celery
alcachôfra artichoke
arroz rice
azeitonas olives
batatas potatoes
berinjela eggplant
beterrabas beets
cebola onion
feijão bean
nabo turnip

cenouras carrots
cogumelo mushroom
couve-flor cauliflower
couve cabbage
ervilhas peas
espargos asparagus
espinafres spinach
favas broad beans
pepino cucumber
tomate tomato

SALAD (SALADA)

agriãos watercress
alface lettuce
salada mista mixed salad

salada verde green salad
Russa Russian salad

DESSERTS (SOBREMESA)

arroz doce rice pudding
bolo cake
gelados diversos mixed ice creams
maçã assada baked apple
pastelaria pastry
pêssego Melba peach Melba

pudim flan egg custard
pudim de pão bread pudding
salada de frutas fruit salad
sorvetes sherbets
queijo cheese

FRUITS (FRUTAS)

abacate avocado
alperches apricots
ameixa plum
ananas pineapple
cerajas cherries

figos figs
framboesa raspberry
laranjas oranges
limão lemon
maçãs apples

melancia watermelon
melão melon
morangos strawberries
pêras pears
pêssegos peaches

roma pomegranate
tâmara date
toronja grapefruit
uvas grapes

BEVERAGES (BEBIDAS)

água water
água mineral mineral water
café coffee
chá tea
cerveja beer
com gelo with ice
laranjada orangeade

leite milk
sumo de fruta fruit juice
sumo de laranja orange juice
sumo de tomate tomato juice
vinho branco white wine
vinho tinto red wine

CONDIMENTS (CONDIMENTOS)

açúcar sugar
alho garlic
azeite olive oil
caril curry
manteiga butter

mostarda mustard
compota jam
pimenta pepper
sal salt
vinagre vinegar

MISCELLANEOUS

chocolate chocolate
biscoito cracker
gelo ice

gelado ice cream
pão bread
pão torrado toast

COOKING TERMS

assado no forno baked
cozido boiled
estufada braised

frito fried
mal passado rare
bem passado well done

---

2. A Capsule Vocabulary

		Pronounced
Hello	**olá**	oh-lah
How are you?	**como está?**	como esh-tah
Very well	**muito bem**	muy-toh bym
Thank you	**muito obrigado**	muy-toh obree-gah-do
Good-bye	**adeus**	adeush
Please	**faça favor**	fassa fah-vohr
Yes	**sim**	seem
No	**não**	naion
Excuse me	**desculpe-me**	dash-culpa-meh
Give me	**dê-me**	deh-meh
Where is?	**onde fica?**	ondeh feecah
the station	**a estação**	o aish-tassaion
a hotel	**um hotel**	oom hotel
a restaurant	**um restaurante**	om rash-tauranteh
the toilet	**a casa de banho**	ah cahzah de bahnhoo
To the right	**à direita**	aah deeraitah
To the left	**à esquerda**	aah ash-kerdah
Straight ahead	**em frente**	ym fraintah

I would like—	gostaria de	goosh-tareeah de
to eat	comer	coh-mere
a room	um quarto	oom quarr-toh
How much is it?	quanto custa	quahnto coosh-tah
The check, please	a conta se faz, favor	ah cohnta sa fahsh, fah-vohr
When	quando	quandoh
Yesterday	ontem	ohntym
Today	hoje	hoyhje
Tomorrow	amanha	ahmain-hayh
Breakfast	pequeno almoço	paikainoh aahlmohssoh
Lunch	almoço	aahlmohssoh
Dinner	jantar	jain-taah

1	**um** (oom)	**14**	**catorze** (cahtohrzeh)	**40**	**quarenta** (quaraintah)
2	**dois** (doysh)	**15**	**quinze** (keenzeh)	**50**	**cinquenta** (sseenquaintah)
3	**três** (traishe)	**16**	**dezasseis** (dehzaissaish)	**60**	**sessenta** (ssaissaihntah)
4	**quatro** (quaahtroh)	**17**	**dezassete** (dehrzassaihteh)	**70**	**setenta** (ssaitaintah)
5	**cinco** (sseencoh)	**18**	**dezóito** (dehzoytoh)	**80**	**oitenta** (oyhtaintah)
6	**seis** (ssaish)	**19**	**dezanove** (dehzanohveh)	**90**	**noventa** (nohvaintah)
7	**sete** (ssaiteh)	**20**	**vinte** (veenteh)	**100**	**cem** (sym)
8	**oito** (oytoh)	**30**	**trinta** (treehntah)		
9	**nove** (nohveh)				
10	**dez** (daish)				
11	**onze** (onzeh)				
12	**doze** (doze)				
13	**treze** (traihzeh)				

INDEX

GENERAL INFORMATION

DESTINATIONS

KEY TO ABBREVIATIONS: *I* = Inexpensive; *M* = Moderate; *E* = Expensive; *VE* = Very Expensive

NOW, SAVE MONEY ON ALL YOUR TRAVELS!
Join Frommer's™ Dollarwise® Travel Club

Saving money while traveling is never easy, which is why the **Dollarwise Travel Club** was formed 32 years ago to provide cost-cutting travel strategies, up-to-date travel information, and a sense of community for value-conscious travelers from all over the world.

In keeping with the money-saving concept, the annual membership fee is low—$25 for U.S. residents and $35 for residents of Canada, Mexico, and other countries—and is immediately exceeded by the value of your benefits, which include:

1. Any TWO books listed on the following pages;
2. Plus any ONE Frommer's City Guide;
3. A subscription to our quarterly newspaper, *The Dollarwise Traveler;*
4. A membership card that entitles you to purchase through the Club all Frommer's publications for 33% to 40% off their retail price.

The eight-page **Dollarwise Traveler** tells you about the latest developments in good-value travel worldwide and includes the following columns: **Hospitality Exchange** (for those offering and seeking hospitality in cities all over the world); and **Share-a-Trip** (for those looking for travel companions to share costs).

Aside from the various Frommer's Guides, the Gault Millau Guides, and the Real Guides you can also choose from our Special Editions, which include such titles as *Caribbean Hideaways* (the 100 most romantic places to stay in the Islands); and *Marilyn Wood's Wonderful Weekends* (a selection of the best mini-vacations within a 200-mile radius of New York City).

To join this Club, send the appropriate membership fee with your name and address to: Frommer's Dollarwise Travel Club, 15 Columbus Circle, New York, NY 10023. Remember to specify which single city guide and which two other guides you wish to receive in your initial package of member's benefits. Or tear out the pages, check off your choices, and send them to us with your membership fee.

FROMMER BOOKS
PRENTICE HALL TRAVEL　　　　　　**Date**_____
15 COLUMBUS CIRCLE
NEW YORK, NY 10023

Friends: Please send me the books checked below.

FROMMER'S™ COMPREHENSIVE GUIDES
(Guides listing facilities from budget to deluxe, with emphasis on the medium-priced)

☐ Alaska	$14.95	☐ Italy	$19.00
☐ Australia	$14.95	☐ Japan & Hong Kong	$17.00
☐ Austria & Hungary	$14.95	☐ Morocco	$18.00
☐ Belgium, Holland & Luxembourg	$14.95	☐ Nepal	$18.00
☐ Bermuda & The Bahamas	$17.00	☐ New England	$17.00
☐ Brazil	$14.95	☐ New Mexico	$13.95
☐ California	$18.00	☐ New York State	$19.00
☐ Canada	$16.00	☐ Northwest	$16.95
☐ Caribbean	$17.00	☐ Puerta Vallarta (avail. Feb. '92)	$14.00
☐ Carolinas & Georgia	$17.00	☐ Portugal, Madeira & the Azores	$14.95
☐ Colorado (avail. Jan '92)	$14.00	☐ Scandinavia	$18.95
☐ Cruises (incl. Alaska, Carib, Mex, Hawaii, Panama, Canada & US)	$16.00	☐ Scotland (avail. Feb. '92)	$17.00
		☐ South Pacific	$20.00
☐ Delaware, Maryland, Pennsylvania & the New Jersey Shore (avail. Jan. '92)	$19.00	☐ Southeast Asia	$14.95
		☐ Switzerland & Liechtenstein	$19.00
☐ Egypt	$14.95	☐ Thailand	$20.00
☐ England	$17.00	☐ Virginia (avail. Feb. '92)	$14.00
☐ Florida	$17.00	☐ Virgin Islands	$13.00
☐ France	$15.95	☐ USA	$16.95
☐ Germany	$18.00		

0891492

FROMMER'S CITY GUIDES

(Pocket-size guides to sightseeing and tourist accommodations and facilities in all price ranges)

☐ Amsterdam/Holland	$8.95	☐ Minneapolis/St. Paul	$8.95
☐ Athens	$8.95	☐ Montréal/Québec City	$8.95
☐ Atlanta	$8.95	☐ New Orleans	$8.95
☐ Atlantic City/Cape May	$8.95	☐ New York	$12.00
☐ Bangkok	$12.00	☐ Orlando	$12.00
☐ Barcelona	$12.00	☐ Paris	$8.95
☐ Belgium	$7.95	☐ Philadelphia	$11.00
☐ Berlin	$10.00	☐ Rio	$8.95
☐ Boston	$8.95	☐ Rome	$8.95
☐ Cancún/Cozumel/Yucatán	$8.95	☐ Salt Lake City	$8.95
☐ Chicago	$9.95	☐ San Diego	$8.95
☐ Denver/Boulder/Colorado Springs	$8.95	☐ San Francisco	$12.00
☐ Dublin/Ireland	$10.00	☐ Santa Fe/Taos/Albuquerque	$10.95
☐ Hawaii	$12.00	☐ Seattle/Portland	$12.00
☐ Hong Kong	$7.95	☐ St. Louis/Kansas City	$9.95
☐ Las Vegas	$8.95	☐ Sydney	$8.95
☐ Lisbon/Madrid/Costa del Sol	$8.95	☐ Tampa/St. Petersburg	$8.95
☐ London	$12.00	☐ Tokyo	$8.95
☐ Los Angeles	$8.95	☐ Toronto	$8.95
☐ Mexico City/Acapulco	$8.95	☐ Vancouver/Victoria	$7.95
☐ Miami	$8.95	☐ Washington, D.C.	$12.00

FROMMER'S $-A-DAY® GUIDES

(Guides to low-cost tourist accommodations and facilities)

☐ Australia on $40 a Day	$13.95	☐ Israel on $40 a Day	$13.95
☐ Costa Rica, Guatemala & Belize on $35 a Day	$15.95	☐ Mexico on $45 a Day	$18.00
		☐ New York on $65 a Day	$15.00
☐ Eastern Europe on $25 a Day	$16.95	☐ New Zealand on $45 a Day	$16.00
☐ England on $50 a Day	$17.00	☐ Scotland & Wales on $40 a Day	$18.00
☐ Europe on $45 a Day	$19.00	☐ South America on $40 a Day	$15.95
☐ Greece on $35 a Day	$14.95	☐ Spain on $50 a Day	$15.95
☐ Hawaii on $70 a Day	$18.00	☐ Turkey on $40 a Day	$22.00
☐ India on $40 a Day	$20.00	☐ Washington, D.C., on $45 a Day	$17.00
☐ Ireland on $40 a Day	$17.00		

FROMMER'S CITY $-A-DAY GUIDES

☐ Berlin on $40 a Day	$12.00	☐ Madrid on $50 a Day (avail. Jan '92)	$13.00
☐ Copenhagen on $50 a Day	$12.00	☐ Paris on $45 a Day	$12.00
☐ London on $45 a Day	$12.00	☐ Stockholm on $50 a Day (avail. Dec. '91)	$13.00

FROMMER'S FAMILY GUIDES

☐ California with Kids	$16.95	☐ San Francisco with Kids	$17.00
☐ Los Angeles with Kids	$17.00	☐ Washington, D.C., with Kids (avail. Jan '92)	$17.00
☐ New York City with Kids (avail. Jan '92)	$18.00		

SPECIAL EDITIONS

☐ Beat the High Cost of Travel	$6.95	☐ Marilyn Wood's Wonderful Weekends (CT, DE, MA, NH, NJ, NY, PA, RI, VT)	$11.95
☐ Bed & Breakfast—N. America	$14.95		
☐ Caribbean Hideaways	$16.00	☐ Motorist's Phrase Book (Fr/Ger/Sp)	$4.95
☐ Honeymoon Destinations (US, Mex & Carib)	$14.95	☐ The New World of Travel (annual by Arthur Frommer for savvy travelers)	$16.95

(TURN PAGE FOR ADDITONAL BOOKS AND ORDER FORM)

0891492

☐ Paris Rendez-Vous $10.95
☐ Swap and Go (Home Exchanging). $10.95
☐ Travel Diary and Record Book. $5.95
☐ Where to Stay USA (from $3 to $30 a
night). $13.95

FROMMER'S TOURING GUIDES

(Color illustrated guides that include walking tours, cultural and historic sites, and practical information)

☐ Amsterdam. $10.95
☐ Australia $12.95
☐ Brazil. $10.95
☐ Egypt. $8.95
☐ Florence. $8.95
☐ Hong Kong $10.95
☐ London $12.95
☐ New York $10.95
☐ Paris $8.95
☐ Rome. $10.95
☐ Scotland. $9.95
☐ Thailand. $12.95
☐ Turkey $10.95
☐ Venice $8.95

GAULT MILLAU

(The only guides that distinguish the truly superlative from the merely overrated)

☐ The Best of Chicago $15.95
☐ The Best of Florida $17.00
☐ The Best of France $16.95
☐ The Best of Germany $18.00
☐ The Best of Hawaii $16.95
☐ The Best of Hong Kong $16.95
☐ The Best of Italy. $16.95
☐ The Best of London $16.95
☐ The Best of Los Angeles $16.95
☐ The Best of New England $15.95
☐ The Best of New Orleans $16.95
☐ The Best of New York $16.95
☐ The Best of Paris $16.95
☐ The Best of San Francisco $16.95
☐ The Best of Thailand. $17.95
☐ The Best of Toronto $17.00
☐ The Best of Washington, D.C. $16.95

THE REAL GUIDES

(Opinionated, politically aware guides for youthful budget-minded travelers)

☐ Amsterdam $9.95
☐ Berlin. $11.95
☐ Brazil. $13.95
☐ California & the West Coast $11.95
☐ Czechoslovakia $13.95
☐ France $12.95
☐ Germany $13.95
☐ Greece. $13.95
☐ Guatemala $13.95
☐ Hong Kong $11.95
☐ Hungary $12.95
☐ Ireland $12.95
☐ Italy. $13.95
☐ Kenya. $12.95
☐ Mexico. $11.95
☐ Morocco $12.95
☐ New York $9.95
☐ Paris $9.95
☐ Peru. $12.95
☐ Poland $13.95
☐ Portugal. $10.95
☐ San Francisco $11.95
☐ Scandinavia $14.95
☐ Spain $12.95
☐ Turkey $12.95
☐ Venice $11.95
☐ Women Travel $12.95
☐ Yugoslavia $12.95

ORDER NOW!

In U.S. include $2 shipping UPS for 1st book; $1 ea. add'l book. Outside U.S. $3 and $1, respectively.

Allow four to six weeks for delivery in U.S., longer outside U.S. We discourage rush order service, but orders arriving with shipping fees plus a $15 surcharge will be handled as rush orders.

Enclosed is my check or money order for $_____

NAME _____

ADDRESS _____

CITY _____ STATE _____ ZIP _____

0891492